Brian Heap

14th edition

Choosing Your
Degree
Course &
University

trotman t

M|P|W

Mander Portman Woodward

Choosing Your Degree Course & University

This fourteenth edition published in 2014 by Trotman Publishing, an imprint of Crimson Publishing Ltd, The Tramshed, Walcot Street, Bath BA1 5BB

© Brian Heap 2014

Editions 11, 12 and 13 published by Trotman Publishing in 2008, 2010 and 2012

Editions 1–10 published by Trotman and Co Ltd

Author: Brian Heap

British Library Cataloguing in Publication Data
A catalogue record for this book is available from the British Library

ISBN 978 1 84455 602 1

Typeset by IDSUK (DataConnection) Ltd

Printed and bound in Malta by Gutenberg Press Ltd

M|P|W

Mander Portman Woodward

Founded in 1973, **Mander Portman Woodward (MPW)** is one of the UK's best known groups of independent sixth-form colleges with centres in London, Birmingham and Cambridge. It offers over 40 subjects at AS and A2 with no restrictions on subject combinations and a maximum class size of eight.

MPW has one of the highest numbers of university placements each year of any independent school in the country. It has developed considerable expertise over the years in the field of applications strategy and is frequently consulted by students facing some of the more daunting challenges that may arise in areas such as getting into Oxbridge, Medicine or Law. This expertise is available to a wider audience in the form of **Getting Into** guides on higher education and the seminars that are run for sixth-formers at its London centre. We are grateful to Trotman for publishing the Guides and hope that this latest edition of **Choosing Your Degree Course & University** will prove as popular and useful as ever.

If you would like to know more about MPW Courses or Getting Into guides, please telephone us on 020 7835 1355 or visit our website, www.mpw.co.uk.

CONTENTS

INTRODUCTION

Universities and degree courses have made the headlines in the past year, not least because of the introduction of higher fees. Such media attention can only add greatly to the confusion of students who need to decide what course to choose and where to go. The purpose of this new edition of *Choosing Your Degree Course & University*, however, is not to suggest that a university education is the only choice or indeed the best one. Some students will fit naturally into a new environment and a demanding method of continuous study for the next three or four years, while others will not; and this must be something students, parents and advisers should seriously consider. 'University for all' is not an appropriate target.

This book aims to offer a menu of the types of courses available in higher education and how they are presented. But it is an ever-changing field – new courses are constantly being introduced every year, other courses withdrawn and the structure of individual courses amended depending on the demand and the availability of staff. It is therefore important to regularly check university websites for up-to-date information.

In the preparation of this book, my thanks must go to the team at Trotman Publishing for their research and continued advice throughout, and also to the University of Surrey and the Higher Education Statistics Agency for additional information on graduate employment.

Brian Heap
BA (Da Manc) ATD

ABOUT THIS BOOK

Students: read this book if you're just beginning to think about applying for university ... it's essential reading.

Parents: read this book if you want to know about higher education and you want to help your sons or daughters.

Careers staff and sixth-form tutors: read this book if you want to impress your sixth form with your extensive knowledge of universities and their courses! (A must if you have to take group career sessions.) (You could use Chapters 1 and 2 as your syllabus!)

THE DECISION
* A university course can last three, four or more years and can include tuition fees of up to £9,000 a year, plus living costs and personal spending money.
* There are over 43,000 courses, covering over 1,200 subjects, offered by over 300 universities and colleges.

If you are in Year 13 your application will probably have to be submitted in January. (Many schools demand early applications in September each year, even when students haven't had enough time to decide. No wonder over 20,000 university students drop out of courses each year!)

Choosing Your Degree Course & University is in two parts. Part 1 explains:

* how to make your first decision, listing ideas from A level examination subjects or career interests to vocational, partly vocational and academic interests
* how to make a first choice of degree subjects from the eight main subject areas – Business courses; Social Studies and Law; Medicine and Health; the Sciences; Engineering, Mathematics and Computing; learning a language; creative subjects and the Arts and Humanities. Each 'option' lists examples of all the alternative subjects available
* how to choose your university and course, university characteristics to consider, questions to ask about that university's course and when you go to an open day or an interview.

Part 2 provides:

* a list of over 100 main degree subject tables in detail. Each university that offers that course is included, and there is a short profile of the features of the course
* a look at final career destinations – types of jobs you could enter from your degree.

Good luck!

Brian Heap

Part 1

1 | THE CHOICE

For many students the idea of going to university has become a way of life – the obvious next step from school and college. Some do consider going into full-time employment but many probably feel that a simple office or lab job with fairly repetitive work lacks the excitement of university life or a gap year abroad (although a gap year in full-time employment could be even more challenging and 'educational' than tramping around Peru!). On the other hand, many hope that going to university will lead to 'management' careers and certainly many university courses seem to wish to convey this impression. But even new graduates will still probably find themselves doing similar office jobs as the school leavers, the difference being that employers hopefully will consider that after three years at university they should have management potential!

Many parents, however, will certainly see the benefits of and regard a university education as essential, although this is where their advice and influence might fall down because many only seem to consider a small number of degree subjects (and certain universities) as the best preparation for the best jobs, which is often quite misleading.

Make sure you choose the right course for you – but be prepared for some difficult questions at home!

You might have decided to apply for an English degree, but be ready for the obvious question – 'What can you do with English?' Well you could say that you had thought about becoming the Director of MI5, which is what Stella Rimington (one-time director) did after her English degree at Edinburgh! What about a degree in Classics and French? One graduate went into teaching and then became a millionaire ... when she wrote about Harry Potter! But then of course Sir Richard Branson didn't go to university at all. So take your pick, but remember that what you choose to study at university can often bear little relation to your future career.

For a few surprises, a survey of graduate employment destinations at York University revealed that apart from those graduates who went into subject-related careers, others went into a wide range of other occupations, for example:

* from Archaeology to – Care Assistant, Advertising, Youth Work (USA) and Retail Management
* from Biological Sciences to – Pensions Administrator, Insurance, Share Dealing and Catering Management
* from Chemistry to – Electricity Board Administration, Market Research, Music Promotion and Accountancy
* from Electronics to – Banking, Network Rail, News Assistant (TV) and Soccer Coach (USA)
* from English to – Publishing, Law, Ministry of Defence and Hospital Administration
* from Philosophy to – Building Society Work, Local Government, Voluntary Youth Work and Data Processing
* from Politics to – Accountancy, an Army Commission, Journalism and the NHS.

For more information on career destinations turn to Chapter 6.

Many parents – and students – still believe that a degree is meant to be a type of training for a future job, which in fact only applies in a very few cases (Medicine, Dentistry, Architecture and Physiotherapy etc.). **A degree is meant to teach you how to learn.** On a university course you will be given a wide range of topics to study. In each case you will have to research the problem yourself, test your conclusions and present your decisions, which is what every manager has to do every day, no matter what the job. So, as the saying goes, **'learn how to learn and you can learn to do anything'**.

No matter which subject you choose you will find that at university you will have to work on your own for most of the time, just as you will once you're in a job – the moral being: don't go to university if you are not prepared to be a self-starter.

Remember that in today's society, people don't necessarily have the same job for life; many change their career direction at least once or even twice before they retire, so it's important to be able to know how to adapt to new careers and how to adjust to new systems.

But at present you still have at least four or five years to go before you start your first career and have plenty of time to think about what you really want to do, so choosing a career at this stage isn't absolutely necessary. However, choosing a course and a university is, so browse through the next few chapters and the important decisions you need to make might become clearer.

MAKING THE FIRST DECISION

There are over 1,200 degree subjects from which to choose and making the right choice has its problems! Much depends on the type of person you are, which means that you need to do a bit of self-analysis.

To begin with, all university and college courses fall into one of three categories. Which one fits you?

Vocational courses
* Vocational courses are really 'training courses' for entry to specific careers, e.g. Medicine, Dentistry, Pharmacy, Architecture, Occupational Therapy, Radiography, Optometry, Podiatry and several others.
* These are professional courses monitored by professional bodies, and on graduation you will be qualified to practise from day one.
* In addition, some of these courses are planned so that you spend some time working with an employer (sandwich courses), in some cases for up to a year, often on full pay. In many cases students are offered jobs with these firms on graduation.
* Some of these courses are very competitive; for example at one university there are 16 applicants for each place for Dentistry, at another, there are 11 Pharmacy applicants per place and at yet another, 22 applicants for every Physiotherapy place.
* Admissions tutors will expect you not only to have a good knowledge of the career, but also to have engaged in some work experience before applying and above all to know the disadvantages of the work as well as the attractions.

Partly vocational
* These courses aim to provide you with a clear picture of the type of work done in certain careers.
* Courses include such subjects as Business Studies, Environmental Science, Biological Sciences, Chemistry, Physics and Media Studies. (Many of these also arrange work placements with firms.)
* Within each of these careers are many specialist fields so the degree itself isn't a specialist qualification in its own right, but only an introduction to the types of work you might be asked to do once you are employed. Once in your first job you will go on to specialise in a particular field, probably taking additional professional qualifications.
* For example, depending on their choice of career and firm, Business Studies graduates may go on to complete the examinations of the Institutes of Marketing and Public Relations or the Chartered Insurance Institute or the Institutes of Purchasing and Supply or Logistics and Transport.

Exam subjects or interests
* The third way is to consider the academic or non-vocational subjects you are taking at school or college, with the possibility of continuing the same subject at university.
* If so, consider: which are your best subjects? Which are your favourite subjects? Would you like to study one or even two of them on a joint or combined course for the next three years?

✳ Alternatively you could take a subject which is new to you but which you find interesting such as American Studies, Philosophy, Anthropology, International Relations or a new foreign language such as Chinese, Japanese or Scandinavian Studies ... but more about these options later.

If you do choose an examination subject it's really quite important to choose the one which you also enjoy the most ... after all, you've got to study it for the next three or four years! Every year over 20,000 students drop out of their courses, not because the work is too difficult, simply because they found the course too boring and not what they expected.

If you are thinking about choosing a subject you studied at school take a look at the lists in Chapter 3. You might find a new subject interesting or intriguing.

CHOOSING DEGREE SUBJECTS

Students are different in many ways, not least in their attitudes to life and their interests (some enjoy sport or prefer music, the arts, the environment, politics or law, for example) and as a result you might feel that your personality and study interests are suited to certain types of jobs more than others.

Have a look at these main career groups and try some self-analysis.

1. **Science careers.** Are you taking chemistry, biology or other science subjects? If so, do you enjoy them? If not move on ...
2. **Technical careers.** These occupations often focus on maths and physics and are very appropriate for those with a practical outlook and aptitude. Interested? If not move on ...
3. **Artistic careers.** Do you enjoy art, music, dance, drama, creative writing or designing things? In short are you a creative person? If not move on ...
4. **Outdoor/active careers.** Are you energetic? Do you enjoy the open air? If not move on ...
5. **Communication careers.** Do you enjoy meeting people, are you a leader, do you enjoy debating the problems and issues of the day? Or are you one of those quiet retiring types who likes to keep out of the limelight? If so move on ...
6. **Social careers.** Do you enjoy helping people? Do your friends always come to you first when they have problems? If you'd prefer they didn't ... then move on!
7. **Business careers.** Are you an 'organiser'? If so, these courses are well worth considering. Business Studies graduates join a range of industrial and commercial organisations and whether you are working in an office, a laboratory or on a building site, business skills apply. Over 200,000 students applied for Business programmes last year, but not to worry, there are plenty to choose from. So begin your degree subject journey in Option 1 in the next chapter ... the answer to your problems could be there or further on!

2 | THE OPTIONS

OPTION 1: BUSINESS COURSES

There was a time not so long ago when some students – and quite a lot of parents – seemed to think that employers took a poor view of students with a Business Studies degree. Certainly, many years ago, when the new universities introduced these new degree courses, many people were sceptical about their value. But now these courses are very well established and widely accepted. One university careers adviser said that many employers always gave first priority to good Business Studies graduates since they are well prepared in all those essential **transferable skills**. These skills cannot be overlooked, no matter what your course at university. The world of employment is looking for graduates with verbal, written and time management skills, information technology know-how and the ability to work in a team.

Unfortunately many sixth formers interested in business simply look for degrees called **Business Studies** or **Business Administration** and seem to forget that there are many other courses covering aspects of the business field such as **Hospitality Management**, **Environmental Management**, **Marketing** and **Property Development** and over a hundred more at the end of this section!

Sandwich courses
Business courses tend to fall into two main categories: the traditional three-year full-time course and the four-year **sandwich programme** which would mean that you will usually spend one year or two six-month periods working full time in industry or commerce, often with full pay. One advantage of the sandwich option is that if you impress your employer then you could be offered a sponsorship or even a permanent job with the firm when you graduate. This often happens and sandwich course students usually come out top in the graduate employment stakes.

It isn't unusual for sandwich students on placement in industry or commerce to earn £11,000 to £12,000 during their year which helps a lot when you are faced with a student loan, top-up fee or an overdraft!

Sandwich courses were introduced many years ago and now many institutions offer a wide range of such courses. Among several well-established universities offering sandwich courses are Aston, Bath, Bradford, Brunel, City, Kent, Kingston, Loughborough, Oxford Brookes, Portsmouth, Salford and Surrey. In fact, most universities have now introduced various types of work placement schemes.

Programme information
In addition to choosing between full-time and sandwich courses, applicants should also check the range of topics offered in the many Business courses. Some programmes will offer an **academic bias** with a focus on the economic, mathematical and statistical elements of the subject, whilst other courses are more **practical** and 'hands-on'. Business courses provide a general grounding in all the main aspects of management, such as marketing, sales, operations, human resources management (personnel management), industrial relations and finance. All courses will naturally involve IT and most universities will expect at least a GCSE grade C in Mathematics, with the more academic courses expecting a grade B or even an A, and some may even require A level Mathematics.

If you are considering the possibility of working abroad, there are also **International Business** courses, some with a year in the US. In the case of **European Business Studies** degrees, students can use their language skills with placements in one of many European countries. Bradford is one of many universities that offered such a course; one of their students went into the Diplomatic Corps when she graduated, which simply proves that you don't have to go into business when you've done a business course, although part of her work was dealing with exports from Canada to the UK. But it doesn't end there. You could consider a course in one of the business specialisms such as **Marketing**, which is not just public relations and advertising but also product development, distribution of products, pricing and promotion. **Human Resources Management** is another popular option and covers such topics as industrial relations, employee development and the economic, financial, legal and human issues when dealing with people at work.

Alternatively other business options include **Hospitality Management** (a new title for hotel management) offered at a number of universities, or you could consider **Public Relations** or **Advertising** at Bournemouth, for example, or **Tourism** at Derby or Aberystwyth, in addition to many other universities and colleges.

Other options include **Sport Management** offered at institutes including London Metropolitan, and **Fashion Buying** at universities such as Westminster and Manchester. There are also business courses dealing with property, such as **Planning and Property Development** offered at a range of universities including Bristol UWE and Kingston and **Estate Management** (not a course in agriculture) at Reading. Most of these courses lead to qualification as a surveyor. In the field of transport it's possible to study **Logistics** at Aston and **Transport Management** at Loughborough, for example, where there is also a degree specialising in **Air Transport Management**.

Then there is the huge area covered by courses in **Finance**. These involve degrees in **Accountancy**, **Banking**, **International Finance**, **Investment Banking**, **Risk Management**, **International Securities** and **Actuarial Studies** and in the broader field of **Financial Services**.

Finally, it's worth remembering that a very large proportion of graduates from other subjects – History, Geography, Geology, Languages and Law, etc. – still go into business, being trained by firms to fit their own style of management operations. Employers are, after all, entitled to assume that if you are bright enough to get a degree then you should be able to adapt to their system!

Preparation

One other point to remember is that you don't always need to have done Business Studies at A level to do a degree in the subject, but you do need to be able to show an understanding of the subject on the dreaded UCAS application! But how? Not simply by saying that 'I'm interested in it' but by getting some first-hand work experience and describing the work you have done and explaining what you have gained by it. **Talk to people in business.** Even if you are only stacking shelves in a supermarket you should find out about the problems of running the store. Talk to the manager. What is the turnover of the store? What are the best-selling lines? Are there any staffing problems and how are they overcome? What problems are caused by customers? By discussing these topics on your personal statement you are demonstrating some awareness of the problems of business which is what admissions tutors will expect.

Manchester Metropolitan University state that they insist on such experience before recommending students to employers, whilst Cardiff Metropolitan University looks for sociable, ambitious, team players. Another university reported that students who are not interested in widening their horizons or who do not demonstrate leadership skills are likely to be rejected.

Putting information about your experiences on the UCAS application will demonstrate that you have given some serious thought to making your decision and the admissions tutor will take your application more seriously.

Course options

General courses

Administration, Business Administration, Business Decision Analysis, Business Finance, Business Information Management, Business Information Systems, Business Studies, combined degrees with Business, Commerce, Decision Studies, Management, Management Science, Operational Research, Operations Management, Organisation Studies and Quality Management.

Specialised courses

Accountancy, Accountancy and Finance, Actuarial Studies, Agricultural Management, American Business Studies, Animal Management, Antiques and Collections Management, Arts Management, Attraction

Park Management, Banking, Beauty Therapy Management, Building Management, Business Computer Systems, Business Economics, Business Finance, Careers Management, Catering Management, Civil Engineering Management, Community Management, Conservation Management, Construction Management, Countryside Management, Countryside Recreation Management, Design Management, Distribution Management, Earth Resources Management, Engineering Management, Entertainment Management, Environmental Management, Equine Management, Estate Management, European Business Administration, Events Management, Exercise and Health Management, Facilities Management, Farm Management, Financial Services Management, Fisheries Management, Food Manufacturing Management, Food Marketing, Forestry Management, Garden Design Management, Golf Course Management, Golf Management, Health and Safety Management, Healthcare Management, Heritage Management, Horticultural Management, Hospital Management, Hospitality Management, Hotel Management, Housing Management, Human Resources Management, Information Management, Institutional Management, Insurance, International Hotel Management, International Marketing Management, International Tourism Management, International Transport Management, Investment Management, Land Management, Land Use Management, Landscape Management, Legal Practice Management, Leisure Management, Libraries Management, Licensed Retail Management, Livestock Management, Marketing Management, Music Industry Management, Optical Management, Pharmaceutical Management, Poultry Management, Print Management, Property Management, Public Administration, Quality Management, Real Estate Management, Recreation Management, Retail Management, Rural Resources Management, Social Administration, Sports Management, Stage Management, Supply Chain Management, Technical Management, Textile Management, Tour Management, Travel and Tourism Management, Urban Estate Management, Veterinary Management, Waste Management, Water Management, Wildlife Management.

OPTION 2: SOCIAL STUDIES AND LAW

Many applicants imagine that the **Social Sciences** are only appropriate if you are aiming to be a social worker which is certainly not the case. These degree courses cover a wide range of subjects. Take for example the combined honours degree programme at Durham on which students are able to design their own degree course and make a choice of subjects from **Anthropology, Archaeology, Economics, Education, Geography, History, Management Studies, Politics, Psychology, Sociology, Social Policy** and **Sport**. At Bristol a degree in **Accountancy and Finance** is included in the subjects offered in the Faculty of Social Sciences and at King's College, London, degree programmes include **War Studies** (a study of the impact of war on society, from ancient to modern times, and the moral and ethical dilemmas it raises). Also there is a course at Heriot Watt in **Geography, Society and Environment** which combines study of human and physical geography, environmental planning and social policy. **Town and Country Planning** courses are closely related to human geography since they explore the man-made environment and all the aspects in which towns and cities affect our lives, including urban design, transport issues, industrial and tourist sites and conservation areas. Finally there is also **Human, Social and Political Sciences** at Cambridge (HSPS).

Working with people

Would you like to work with people? And more importantly not only work with them but provide care and other forms of support? Medical and health occupations cover many of the caring careers and some of these jobs come quite close to or even overlap into social work. Although it is possible to go into social work from any degree or diploma course, students especially interested in this type of work could focus their attention on degrees in **Social Work, Social Policy, Social Sciences** or **Social Administration**. These subjects cover topics relating to sociology, politics, social history and economics and will include such issues as the family, unemployment, poverty, health, equal opportunities, housing and education.

Social work is a challenging and demanding career and degree courses will cover a range of problems which could involve race and ethnic identity, family problems, old age, drug addiction, health and illness, mental health, deviance, disability, housing and the penal system. Despite the challenging nature of the work, however, statistics show a 90% increase in applications in recent years. It's obviously a career for which motivation is very important and many mature students are accepted on courses without the benefit of higher education or even A levels, simply because they have the right qualities and usually some experience. An interest in social work will also extend to working in the community and several universities offer degrees in **Community Development**, **Youth and Community Studies**, **Community Arts** and **Education**.

Other programmes
One of the most popular courses in this huge field is that of **Psychology** with 20 applications for each place at Bath and similar ratios at many other universities. On many courses it is possible to specialise in certain aspects; for those interested in a medical emphasis there are studies in the field of clinical, abnormal and health psychology whilst other courses will cover occupational, consumer and educational psychology and child development. Those wishing to qualify as psychologists (about 20% of all applicants eventually do so) need to be sure that their chosen degree is validated by the British Psychological Society. Not all degree courses provide such validation and, in particular, students should check the status of joint courses before applying. Some other courses worth considering in this sector include **Neuroscience** (a study of the nervous system), **Cognitive Science** (investigating human mental processes and the relationship between natural and artificial intelligence), **Developmental Psychology** (which focuses on how we become the people we are) and **Counselling**, in which interpersonal skills are developed and which, at Chester, can be combined with **Criminology**, **Psychology** and **Sociology**.

Degrees in **Education** are immediately associated with teacher-training courses. This is not necessarily the case since the subject can be studied on a much wider base than that which is normally undertaken by trainee teachers. Courses in Education focus not only on schools and children but on the history, sociology and philosophy of education. By comparison, **teacher-training** courses cater for a variety of student needs whether they wish to work with the very young or pupils in the secondary age range. Some courses offer specialisms in subjects such as English, Design Technology, Mathematics, Physical Education, Religious Studies and Science.

Those students interested in the idea of a career in the teaching profession but who have not followed a teacher-training course can choose to follow a degree course, for example in English, Geography, History or languages, and then take an extra year leading to a Postgraduate Certificate in Education.

The **Social Sciences** also include **Sociology**, another popular course, which presents a broad view of social problems. Courses explore the structure of the society in which we live: the nature of crime and punishment, poverty, social protest and exclusion, social movements and social divisions of class, gender and ethnicity. Some courses go into much greater depth, covering human rights, criminology and criminal justice, women's studies, gender studies, race and ethnic studies and psychosocial studies. Courses in **Criminology** have become extremely popular in recent years and it should be noted that these degrees are not law courses as such, being more concerned with understanding major social problems and the means of dealing with them. **Criminal Justice** courses examine the causes of crime and the operation of the criminal justice system and will prepare graduates to work in the Probation and Prison Services as well as Social Services. However, for those aiming for careers in law, some Criminal Justice courses can lead on to the Common Professional Examination or the Postgraduate Diploma in Law. Alternatively, direct entry might be possible to the graduate training programme for those interested in the police. Check with your university of choice for further information.

Anthropology is a study of the human species from a totally different perspective: from a biological or social emphasis. Scientific aspects could cover human evolution, genetics, nutrition and human disease whilst social studies could include political systems, religion and kinship studies focusing on countries throughout the world.

Other social issues are taken up in degree programmes in **Politics and Government**; these have attracted increasing numbers of students in the past two years. Politics courses explore the main philosophies through history and also cover parliamentary and presidential systems, party politics, conflict and social attitudes. Political systems abroad will also be included, with specialisms arising from the research fields of university staff. When choosing universities it is also worthwhile considering some four-year courses in which placements abroad are included. Another related course worth considering is a degree in **International Relations** which will include the diplomatic, economic and military relations between states, international agencies and multinational companies and the factors which lead to and determine the course of war and peace. A more detailed study of some of these factors is also developed in courses in **Peace Studies**, **War Studies**, **Conflict Resolution** and **War and Security Studies**.

In all societies, however, legal issues arise, and these are covered in the most comprehensive way in **Law** degrees. It is, however, not necessary to have a degree in Law to become a solicitor or barrister, entry being open to graduates in many subjects providing they have a good class of degree.

Law is one of the most popular degree courses and involves a wide spectrum of subjects. Students are well advised to read *Learning the Law* by Glanville Williams before embarking on a course. Only about half of those who follow Law degrees will enter the career. In 1972 there were approximately 26,000 practising solicitors in the UK and by February 2014 the total had risen to just over 127,000. Women account for almost half of all working solicitors, and 12.6% are from ethnic minority groups. Be warned, however: there is a high failure rate in law examinations at this level.

Economics is a subject which is primarily concerned with monetary issues such as exchange and interest rates, price increases and movements in the stock market; there are also specialist areas covering business, labour, environmental and public-sector economics. Some universities will require Mathematics at A level; this will be dictated by the content of the course. However, it isn't widely known that an A level in Economics is not a necessary requirement for many courses, although a background knowledge and an interest in the subject obviously helps students to make a decision to choose such courses.

Course options

Anthropology, Applied Social Studies, Behavioural Science, British Sign Language, Business Law, Childhood Studies, Citizenship, Cognitive Science, Communication, Community Studies, Conductive Education, Conflict Resolution, Consumer Studies, Counselling, Criminal Justice, Criminal Law, Criminal Psychology, Criminology, Deaf Studies, Development Studies, Early Childhood Studies, Economics, Environmental Studies, Ethics, Philosophy and Religion, Gender Studies, Housing Management, Human Communication, Human Resources Management, Human Rights, Industrial Relations, International Development Studies, International Relations, Marketing, Peace and Security, Peace Studies, Philosophy, Philosophy, Logic and Scientific Method, Police and Criminal Investigation, Policing, Politics, Politics, Philosophy and Economics, Population Science, Psychology, Psychosocial Studies, Public Administration, Race and Culture, Religious Studies, Security Studies, Social Administration, Social Research, Social Work, Society and Cities, Society, Culture and the Media, Sociology, Teaching, Town and Country Planning, Trade Union Studies, War Studies, Women's Studies, Youth Studies.

OPTION 3: MEDICINE AND HEALTH

Medicine

Forty-five GCSEs at the same time that's how one medical school admissions officer described a course in **Medicine**! This might appear to be a slight exaggeration but the fact remains that the workload should never be underestimated, which is why medical schools are looking for a good spread of grade As at GCSE, AS and A levels. Consequently expect the normal offers to be high – often in the A*AA–ABB range, although some medical schools might be prepared to make slightly lower offers depending on their policies, the school or college references, the results of BMAT or UKCAT tests and the personal statement.

Bearing in mind then that all applicants are equally strong academically and will receive good references from their tutors, the only opportunity to make a personal bid for an offer comes in the personal statement. However, before putting pen to paper it's important to answer a few questions – not least: why do you want to be a doctor? The hours are long, the work is arduous, the responsibilities are enormous and mistakes could be dire!

It's not enough just to want to be a doctor simply because you want to **'help people'**. The real question is **'are you a scientist?'** From the moment you become a medical student and throughout your career, you will be making scientific decisions every day of your working life. You will need to update your knowledge continuously, since new scientific developments in medicine, surgery and pharmacology are taking place on a very regular basis.

So, how interested are you in science? You need to consider the scientific world around you, not just your A level subjects. You should be interested enough to follow articles in the news on topics such as pollution, public health and the spread of diseases. Do you read scientific journals, medical journals, magazine articles on health and developments in medicine? You might not understand all the medical terms but you should have a good general knowledge of current medical issues and personal opinions to support them.

At interview you could be asked such questions as: do you agree with the principle of private medicine? Would you refuse to treat a patient with lung cancer who refused to give up smoking? What has been the most important advance in medicine in the past 50 years? Should we pay for blood donations or for donor organs?

Work experience, too, is essential. It might be in a hospital, but it could also be in an old people's home, learning about geriatric conditions, homes for the mentally handicapped or the blind or even in a hospice for the terminally ill.

Talk to doctors, matrons and nurses, as well as health workers in the community. What problems do they face and how do they overcome them?

When you realise that all the other medical applicants have the same academic levels of achievement, these extra experiences are important. Special interests you might have in science and medicine and other activities which you can discuss on the UCAS statement could get you to the interview and, ultimately, a place in medical school. The advice from Imperial London is standard for most medical schools:

We look for resourceful men and women with wide interests and accomplishments and a practical concern for others. Academic ability, motivation, character and depth of interests are all assessed.

For most medical applicants the next problem is where to study. London medical schools traditionally have had a good reputation and they attract a lot of applicants. But your first aim will be to get a good basic medical education and all medical schools will provide an excellent start for any doctor. After completing the course you can then go on to specialise, if that's your aim.

Other health programmes

The popularity of any degree course or career will always raise the stakes. Applications for entry to Medicine quite recently were up by 22% and for **Dentistry** by 14%. Expect high offers too for **Veterinary Medicine**, for which girls represent the majority of applicants. **Optometry** is also popular, with about nine applicants per place at some universities, mainly because of the small number of institutions offering the course. In recent years **Pharmacy** has also become very popular, but be aware that there's a difference between Pharmacy and **Pharmaceutical Sciences**, the latter being a study of chemistry and biochemistry and medical issues pertaining to drugs. **Pharmacology** focuses on the study of and uses of drugs and **Toxicology** is a study of the science of poisons.

Other courses allied to medicine include: **Nursing** and **Midwifery** (applications up by 18% and 27% respectively). **Physiotherapy** is another scientific career which also attracts a lot of applicants with 20 to 30 applicants per place not uncommon. **Speech Therapy** involves assessing and treating speech and language disorders and **Audiology** is the treatment of hearing disorders. Students of **Nutrition and Dietetics** study food intake, health and individual needs and **Radiography (Diagnostic** and **Therapeutic)** involves using healthcare technology to diagnose conditions and administer treatments, e.g. radiotherapy for cancer patients. **Occupational Therapy** covers the treatment and management of physical and psychological conditions by the use of various activities and **Orthoptics** is the speciality for those interested in the investigation, diagnosis and management of visual defects and abnormalities of eye movement. Courses in **Podiatry** are focused on the management of disease and disability in the lower limbs and treatments involving feet. **Prosthetics and Orthotics** is the provision of artificial body limbs – prostheses – and the provision of supports for conditions of the limbs and spine. There are also other more specialist courses such as **Chiropractic** for the diagnosis and treatment of the disorders of the neuro-musculoskeletal system, whilst **Osteopaths** use manual and manipulative methods of treatment for conditions affecting the musculoskeletal system. **Paramedic Practice** is available at degree level at Plymouth and Hertfordshire with diploma and foundation courses available elsewhere.

Finally, in addition to the vocational courses above, there has been an increase in the number of Health Studies/Sciences degrees on offer in recent years. These include courses in **Health Psychology**, **Health Promotion**, **Health and Safety**, and **Herbal Medicine**.

For those students seeking a more scientific base for their studies, and in some cases those hoping to proceed to a degree in Medicine after graduation, there are also courses in **Biological Sciences** covering **Anatomy and Physiology**, **Microbiology** and **Genetics**.

Course options
Aromatherapy, Arts Therapy, Audiology, Beauty Therapy, Care Practice, Caring Services, Childhood Studies, Chiropractic, Clinical Science, Community Health, Complementary Medicine, Deaf Studies, Dental Technician, Dentistry, Dietetics, Dispensing Optician, Environmental Health, Health and Fitness Studies, Health Education, Health Psychology, Health Science, Herbal Medicine, Medicine, Midwifery, Naturopathic Medicine, Neuroscience, Nursing, Nutrition, Occupational Health and Safety, Occupational Therapy, Optometry, Orthoptics, Orthotics, Osteopathic Medicine, Paramedic Practice, Pharmaceutical Science, Pharmacology, Pharmacy, Physiotherapy, Podiatry, Psychology, Public Health, Radiography (Diagnostic or Therapeutic), Rehabilitation, Sign Language, Speech Therapy, Sport and Health, Toxicology, Veterinary Medicine, Veterinary Nursing.

OPTION 4: THE SCIENCES
This group of courses covers a huge field and if you are studying the sciences then you will be familiar with many of them. Even so, check through all the options at the end of this section and see the range of possibilities ... which is, after all, what research scientists are doing all the time!

Biochemistry, **Biological Sciences**, **Biology**, **Chemistry** and **Physics** are the obvious starting points when choosing science courses. In fact, these are the safe, broad science courses which can lead to many of the specialised studies which follow because they form the foundation of science careers. In many universities these are the subject areas with a shortage of students.

Specialisations in Biology, Biochemistry and Biological Sciences
Students taking courses in Biological Sciences can usually specialise in their chosen field in the second or third year of the course in such areas as **biomedical sciences**, **microbiology**, **physiology**, **immunology**, **genetics** or **botany**. At Lancaster, for example, 10 modules are taken in Year 1: five in biological subjects and a further five subjects related to biology or in 'stand-alone' subjects reflecting the student's particular interests. Specialisation then begins in Year 2. Warwick has a similar 'deferred choice' arrangement where further specialist subjects cover molecular genetics, cell biology, microbiology, virology or environmental resources.

Other more specialised courses include: **Medical Engineering** (the application of engineering principles to medicine including rehabilitation and orthopaedic engineering and medical physics), **Biotechnology** (the application of biology to industry, e.g. agriculture, food or medicine), **Bioarchaeology** (links between archaeology and biology involving human skeletons, ecology and fossils) and **Biogeography** (ecology, the environment and earth sciences). However, the more highly specialised your subject choice then the narrower the range of subject-related job opportunities available in that field.

Biosciences degrees will also include areas related to health and medicine such as pharmacy, and the paramedical professions which are covered in Option 3.

Agriculture and **Agricultural Sciences**, **Forestry**, **Animal and Equine Science** and **Aquaculture** (not just fish farming but the culture of aquatic species from prawns and shrimps to turtles and crocodiles) are other options with a biological emphasis. Many courses are multidisciplinary and have a strong scientific bias and can include biotechnology, fisheries management and food production, in addition to business aspects such as countryside management, marketing and rural tourism. It's also a short step from a course in agriculture to **Crop Science** and **Horticulture**, courses concerned with growth on a commercial scale, compared with the more scientific application of a degree in **Botany**, now more commonly referred to as **Plant Sciences**. It is not uncommon to study Plant Sciences after the first year of a course in Biological Sciences.

Specialisations in Chemistry
Chemistry, for which there is a great shortage of applicants, is the broadest of the traditional physical sciences and provides a considerable foundation for specialisation leading for example to **Forensic**

Science. Unfortunately Forensic Science, like Media Studies, is currently attracting large numbers of applicants, due to certain TV programmes, and many students are often disappointed when they graduate and realise the limited job opportunities open to them. A **Chemistry** degree, however, is the passport to many careers, including in pharmaceuticals, the food science industry, environmental issues, the petroleum industry, cosmetics, plastics and ceramics to mention but a few. However, applicants should not overlook the fact that for a number of these courses an A level, or at least an AS level, in Mathematics is important. Four-year master's degrees leading to an MChem are common and in many cases these courses include a year in industry.

Specialist areas in Chemistry which might be considered include **Medicinal Chemistry**, **Pharmaceutical Chemistry**, **Environmental Chemistry**, **Colour and Polymer Chemistry**, **Cosmetic Science**, **Materials Chemistry**, **Forensic Chemistry**, or **Nanoscience** or **Nanotechnology** (defined as the study of organic or inorganic materials with dimensions on the nanometre scale – a nanometre being one-millionth of a millimetre) offered at institutions including Hull and Leeds. **Chemical Engineering** and **Polymer Science** also come into the chemistry and technology field. Furthermore at some universities you can combine all science courses with almost any other science or non-science subject, such as Education, Computing, Languages, Business Management, Geography, History, Music or Politics.

Specialisations in Physics

The skills picked up in a Physics degree are not only mathematical and experimental but involve problem-solving, the analysis of information and team management, hence the reason why so many careers are open to the Physics graduate. As in the case of Chemistry, MPhys and MSc courses are also popular among about a third of Physics undergraduates. Those applying for Physics can also choose a range of specialisms which include for example **Medical Physics** at King's College and University College, London, **Nuclear Physics** at Liverpool, **Astrophysics** at Kent, or **Physics and Environmental Studies** at Keele. Physics is also involved in many other courses and is an essential A level for most **Engineering** courses.

Other science courses

Some changes have taken place in recent years in the overall structure of degrees in **Geography**. Students will explore the natural environment in what is now a multidisciplinary subject. Courses will cover **Human Geography** and **Economic and Social Geography** whilst **Physical Geography** will include modules in climate change, river catchments, glacial processes and environmental management. In addition, most courses will also focus on geographical issues worldwide, and field courses and placements abroad are not uncommon. As such it is not a world away from **Environmental Science/Studies**, another broad subject which could include population biology, environmental chemistry and ecology as well as sociology, law and conservation. Along a similar theme, courses in **Geology** and **Earth and Marine Sciences** link closely with physical geography and a study of planet earth, its land forms, surface features, volcanoes, earthquakes, oceans and the changes in its structure over billions of years. **Marine Studies** can also include **Oceanography** (a study of wave formations, ocean currents, water density and tides), **Marine Chemistry** (seawater and pollutants), **Marine Biology** (marine plants and animals) and **Coastal Environmental Management**.

Environmental Science courses, some of which are interdisciplinary (meaning that they cover a range of subjects leading to one degree), could also suit students looking for breadth in a science degree. Some courses may have a bias, however, towards biology, as at Plymouth and Hull, or **Marine Conservation** at Anglia Ruskin, **Environmental Management** with an agricultural bias at Harper Adams University College, or **Environmental Hazards** at Kingston. Alternatively, courses may be tailored to the student's preference between chemistry, geology, ecology or management as at East Anglia. Then of course there is the geographical emphasis in courses in **Urban Studies** or **Town and Country Planning**. However, courses in Environmental Science or Environmental Studies shouldn't be confused with **Environmental Health** since this is a specialised career training leading to work as an environmental health officer.

Requirements

As one would expect, at least one A level in science is usually a requirement for all courses, except for foundation courses which allow students to embark on the first year of a four-year course without the necessary science subjects.

Don't confuse foundation courses with foundation degrees, which are quite different. Foundation degrees are offered to those who are in employment and who wish to add to their qualifications by aiming for a degree.

Whilst you can take a single honours degree in any science subject, there are several additional routes. Many universities will offer a whole batch of similar science degrees with all students taking the same course in the first year; these are called **modular courses**. Thereafter in the second and third years students choose their specialist option. In most cases science subjects can be taken at some universities with industrial placement or with a year abroad, thus extending the course to four years. You will usually be paid by the firm during your year away from university ... and often offered a job when you graduate.

As in the case of other degree courses, admissions tutors expect your interests to go beyond your studies at school. Information on the UCAS application should therefore include evidence of your interests culled from sources other than your A level syllabus, such as scientific journals, the internet, newspapers and popular magazines. You're not expected to know everything about your chosen subject but you would be expected to have made an effort to focus on one or two areas of special interest if only to demonstrate a depth of interest.

Course options

Agricultural Biochemistry/Biology/Biotechnology/Zoology, Agriculture, Agroforestry, Anatomy, Animal Biology/Nutrition, Applied Biology, Applied Chemistry, Aquaculture, Astronomy, Astrophysics, Bacteriology, Biochemistry, Biological Sciences, Biology, Biomaterials Science, Biomedical Science, Biophysics, Bioscience, Biotechnology, Brewing and Distilling, Cell Biology, Ceramic Sciences, Colour Chemistry, Consumer Science, Cosmetic Science, Countryside Management, Crop Science, Earth Science, Ecology, Environmental Biology/Chemistry/Science, Fisheries Science, Food Science, Forensic Science, Genetics, Geochemistry, Geology, Geophysics, Horticulture, Human Biology/Nutrition/Physiology, Immunology, Maritime Studies, Materials Science, Medical Microbiology, Molecular Biology, Ocean Science, Paper Science, Parasitology, Pharmaceutical Chemistry/Science, Physics, Physiology, Plant Sciences, Polymer Science, Rural Resources Management, Soil Science, Toxicology, Underwater Science, Urban Land Economics, Urban Studies, Virology, Water Science, Zoology.

OPTION 5: ENGINEERING, MATHEMATICS AND COMPUTING

Engineering

A few years ago, a sixth former applied for university sponsorship with a large engineering firm. He was called for an interview and on arrival he was sent to a waiting room. In the centre of the room there was a table and on it something rather bulky was covered with a cloth. The first question he was asked when he was interviewed was: 'What was underneath the cloth?' The model of a jet aircraft under the cloth was not quite as important as the fact that the student was inquisitive enough to have a look, the interviewer's reasoning being that all good engineers are inquisitive!

Wanting to know how things work, wanting to make things work, or wanting to invent new ways to make things work therefore would seem to be a fairly good indication of a technically minded student. If you are one of these then you might have already thought about a career in engineering, although you might not be familiar with the very wide range of engineering specialisms available.

Most universities offer **Bachelor of Engineering (BEng)** and **Master of Engineering (MEng)** programmes, the latter with a higher entry requirement, although it is possible to move upwards from a BEng degree. Sandwich courses should also be considered since they include a year of paid work experience and often good contacts are made for future employment opportunities.

Some applicants might simply wish to do a broad course in Engineering which will involve different aspects of the work; if so, you could aim for a **General** or **Integrated Engineering** degree in which all first-year students follow the same course, choosing their preferred specialism in Year 2. Several universities including Bath, Cardiff, Durham, Leicester and Liverpool offer these courses. The work of an engineer covers maintenance, research and development, irrespective of the branch of engineering you decide to follow – and there are up to 30 different specialisms from which to choose.

Electrical and Electronic Engineering is a major field in this industry concerned with electricity generation, supply and distribution and includes **Software Engineering, Audio Engineering, Computer and Control**

Engineering and **Communications Engineering**. **Aeronautical and Aerospace Engineering** covers both civil and military aircraft and at some universities a study of space exploration is included. In addition, **pilot training** is offered by Brunel, Liverpool, Salford and Sheffield. It is also worth noting that many similarities exist between the design of aircraft and sea-going craft. Consequently the courses offered in **Naval Architecture** by four universities (Southampton, Newcastle, Plymouth and Strathclyde) could be worth more than a cursory glance, whilst **Boat and Yacht Design** can be studied at Southampton Solent.

Mechanical Engineering is probably the most diverse field and is specifically concerned with the design, development, installation, operation and maintenance of just about anything which has movable parts, and it also includes **Automobile**, **Acoustical**, **Marine** and **Agricultural Engineering**. Often linked to Mechanical Engineering is **Manufacturing Engineering** (at one time referred to as Production Engineering). These engineers cover the entire production process, designing manufacturing systems closely linked to the final product, in the right quantities, at the right price, for the right delivery date.

Engineering is not always concerned with 'engines', however, as in the case of **Civil Engineering** which focuses on the building structures and stresses and strains involved in high-rise buildings, railways, dams, airports, bridges, motorways, harbours and tunnels. Other specialisms in this category include **Structural**, **Highway**, **Transport**, **Mining**, **Environmental** and **Water Engineering**, as well as **Offshore Engineering** which includes the construction of drilling platforms used in North Sea oil exploration.

In considering the built environment, it's a short step from Civil Engineering to **Building and Construction Management**. Specialist areas in these careers cover **Building**, **Land**, **Hydrographic** and **Quantity Surveying** and also **Building Services Engineering** (heating and ventilation, refrigeration, lighting, air conditioning, water supply and elevators).

The field of **Chemical Engineering** involves several areas from the pharmaceutical, food, brewing and cosmetics industries, to the exploration of offshore gas and oil which in turn links with **Petroleum Engineering**. Courses in **Fire and Explosion** and **Nuclear Engineering** are other branches of this industrial field.

But probably the best-kept secret in the careers library is **Materials Science and Engineering**, a great field for research and a mix of chemistry, physics and engineering. The simple fact is that sixth formers don't know what it is and never get round to reading about it, hence the shortfall of applicants! Materials Science is the study of a range of materials; originally developed from metallurgy, a study of metals and their properties, it now also involves product manufacturing in plastics, glass and ceramics.

The testing of materials is constantly taking place. Go into an aircraft establishment and you are likely to see a jet fighter on the rig being shaken continuously for days and weeks until something cracks! At one university they were testing an aero engine for bird strike and had reached the limit of a 12lb bird hitting the engine at a speed of 700mph, without too many ill effects for the plane!

Whilst Mathematics and Physics are the subjects most appropriate for engineering courses, graduates in both these subjects also enter careers in engineering, specialising in their own subject fields, in addition to a wide range of other occupations.

Mathematics
Mathematics is fundamental to every sphere of life, hence the vast range of careers open to graduates. Mathematics at university, however, is much broader than that experienced by the average student and prospectus information should be scanned carefully before choosing courses which can vary considerably with pathways leading into **Pure** and **Applied Mathematics**, **Statistics**, **Computing and Operational Research**. In addition, joint courses with Mathematics include related subjects such as Physics, Statistics, Computer Science, Electronics, Astronomy, Accountancy and Finance. Currently, the largest percentage of Mathematics graduates go into financial activities with many also going into other areas of business, education and manufacturing.

Computing
Finally in this group of subjects it is impossible to ignore the impact which **Computer Science** has had on the work of engineers, technologists and mathematicians. However, bearing in mind some of the

misconceptions, students should recognise the range of openings in this area with opportunities existing for business analysts, systems analysts and designers, programmers and software developers.

Most courses have a strong practical focus and many students are attracted to them because of their interests in information technology and various computer packages. Yet Computer Science degrees offer far more. Many embrace hardware and software network systems and database design, and some can involve electronic engineering and mathematics.

When choosing courses it is important to step carefully and to be aware of the range of optional subjects and degree courses in Information Systems and Information Management, Artificial Intelligence, Cybernetics and Multimedia.

Course options
Acoustics, Aerospace Engineering, Applied Mathematics, Applied Statistics, Architecture, Astronomy, Astrophysics, Automotive Engineering, Avionics, Civil Engineering, Communications Engineering, Computer Science, Computer Systems Engineering, Cybernetics, Electrical Engineering, Electronics Engineering, Ergonomics, Integrated Engineering, Marine Engineering, Mathematics, Mathematics Teaching, Mechanical Engineering, Meteorology, Mining Engineering, Naval Architecture, Offshore Engineering, Operational Research, Opto-electronics, Physics, Probability and Statistics, Quantity Surveying, Robotics, Statistics, Surveying, Systems Analysis, Systems Modelling, Teaching.

OPTION 6: LEARNING A LANGUAGE
There is a true story of a man who spent a week with a tribe of American Indians. He couldn't speak their language but he listened to the sounds they were making and at the end of the week he could put some of the sounds together and make himself understood. If you come to think about it, that's the way you learned your language – by listening. Learning a vocabulary and putting the words in the right order comes much later.

Unfortunately, however, one problem is that the British are too complacent when it comes to learning languages. We take it for granted that foreigners will be able to speak or at least understand English. Another problem seems to be that language students, who presumably enjoy studying and have a special ability for learning their chosen foreign language at school, seem to be unenthusiastic about extending this gift to learning new ones.

Many language students go on to study a foreign language at university, but quite often they choose the same language, **French**, **German** or **Spanish**, which they have studied at school for four or five years. That's fine, but are they making such choices merely as a means to an end, just to spend three or four years at university to get a degree? One language applicant admitted at interview that she wasn't really interested in going abroad!

If you have this gift for languages why not set a target to see how many other languages you can learn in the next five or six years? Why not in fact take a **two-language degree**? Having a second language is an advantage when it comes to applying for a job – although if you are going to work abroad, having a knowledge of dialects is also important. One German from Munich spoke of the difficulties he sometimes faced with visitors from Hamburg and Frankfurt because of the differences in dialects.

Studying a new language
In choosing a course it's important to establish the type of degree which you prefer and whether you want a literature option or a course which emphasises the written and the spoken word. Whilst A levels in the target language are required for courses in **French**, **German**, **Spanish** and **Hispanic Studies**, other languages can be started from scratch (ab initio), although universities will expect applicants to have good grades in one or two modern languages, just to show that they have some flair for language study. So, why not choose **Chinese**, **Czech**, **Italian**, **Japanese**, **Modern Greek**, **Portuguese**, **Russian** or **Scandinavian Studies**? (For other languages see 'Course options' below.) In some respects there's probably a better chance of a subject-related job choosing an unusual language rather than French, German or Spanish from which several thousand students graduate each year and with competition coming from many Europeans who are able to speak perfect English. **Welsh**, **Irish** and **Gaelic** also offer

a stimulating challenge for linguists although such interests are more likely to stem from an attraction to the historical, social and cultural aspects of these areas.

Broader language courses

In addition and linked to European languages, it is also possible to follow a broader course by way of a degree in **European Studies**, **European Business Studies**, **European Social and Political Studies**, **Contemporary Europe** or **European Union Studies**. For those particularly interested in Spanish studies, a degree in **Portuguese** or **Latin American Studies** might be considered. Latin America has 400 million inhabitants and in many ways represents a new world with considerable potential and opportunities, and there are degree courses covering political, social and cultural aspects.

In addition, French, German and Spanish, which are offered by most universities, may be combined with a host of other subjects, for example French at Leeds can be taken with over 30 subjects. One very popular option at a number of universities is **Business Studies**, in which it is often possible to spend a year with a firm abroad. Aston, Canterbury Christ Church, Oxford Brookes and Sunderland are popular universities offering these combinations.

Finally, for something quite different, there are also courses in **Translating and Interpreting** at universities including Aston, East Anglia and Heriot-Watt.

When it comes to choosing a new language don't do it just for the novelty; you should obviously have some interest in the country or region concerned!

Course options

Amharic, Anglo-Saxon, Norse and Celtic, Applied Languages, Arabic, Asia-Pacific Studies, Bengali, Brazilian, Bulgarian, Burmese, Cambodian, Chinese, Czech/Slovak, Danish, Dutch, East European Studies, European Studies, European Union Studies, Finnish, French, Gaelic, Georgian, German, Greek, Hausa, Hebrew, Hindi, Hispanic Studies, Hungarian, Icelandic, Indonesian, International Business Studies, Iranian, Irish, Italian, Japanese, Korean, Latin, Latin American Studies, Linguistics, Malay, Modern Greek, Modern Languages, Nepali, Norwegian, Persian, Polish, Portuguese, Punjabi, Romanian, Russian, Sanskrit, Serbian/Croatian, Sinhalese, Somali, Spanish, Swahili, Swedish, Tamil, Thai, Tibetan, Translating and Interpreting, Turkish, Ukrainian, Urdu, Vietnamese, Welsh, Yoruba, Zulu.

OPTION 7: CREATIVE SUBJECTS

One could argue that creative people are the lucky ones, since artists, musicians, actors and actresses seem to have energy and enthusiasm to maintain their interests in their work throughout their lives without really thinking about retiring. They are often described as being 'gifted', almost as though painting pictures or playing musical instruments comes without trying, which is far from the truth. Equally of course some people find mathematics, the sciences or languages easier than others, but as in the case of art and music, achievement doesn't come without a lot of effort.

Creative courses such as **Art and Design**, **Music** and **Drama** are specialist subjects which can, and often do, lead to specific careers. One exception, however, is the field of **Fine Art**, with painting and sculpture being very difficult areas in which to get established. Many students will choose a degree subject with the intention of following it into a similar career, but in the case of creative subjects it's well worth realising that, unlike business courses and computer studies, job opportunities can be limited. It's also important to realise that universities and colleges do not accept the responsibility of finding jobs for students when they graduate. So from the student's point of view, the best institutions will be those with good facilities for the chosen course and good contacts with the industry for job placements. If you are concerned about the latter, check the destinations of graduates on open day visits or at interview.

Art and Design

Art and Design covers a vast area which probably accounts for the fact that it attracts more applicants than any other degree subject. **Fashion and Textile Design** is a particularly large and popular field which extends into contemporary fashion, knitwear design, clothing design, fashion marketing and promotion, textile surface decoration (carpets, tiles etc.) and textile management.

Students choosing **Graphic Design** can follow specialisms in advertising, illustration and animation and job opportunities can be reasonably good. **Industrial Design** is more specialised still and covers furniture design, interior design, theatre and stage design and car and transport design, and finally there is **Three-dimensional Design** which can involve glassware, ceramics, silverware, metal and jewellery.

Architecture should also be regarded as a creative subject and whilst A level Art is not a requirement for most courses, evidence of the ability to express ideas visually is extremely important and is often seen as a requirement for entry to most schools of architecture. Most applicants will finally aim to work as architects and when applying for courses it's important to check that the degree offered by the university or college is validated by the Royal Institute of British Architects. One specialised field of architecture is that of **Landscape Architecture** which focuses on the design of the environment surrounding buildings.

Don't confuse Landscape Architecture with garden design, although landscaping building environs will include trees and other vegetation as well as the design of water features and paving.

Finally in the art field and for those more interested in the theory than the practice there are courses in the **History of Art and Design**, the principal areas of study being painting, sculpture and architecture, often referred to as 'high art'. Courses can be chosen which offer specialised studies in various historical periods of art and architecture or aspects of applied art such as furniture and textiles or modern design. Many courses have now also expanded into other areas such as design, photography and film history.

Music
Students applying for **Music** face similar problems and decisions with some aiming to be performers and some seeking other outlets at the end of their degree. Music courses can be quite broad in their approach. Some are exclusively performance courses and some are not, and still others provide a range of topics such as that offered by Leeds University which covers analysis, research skills, history and culture, with second-year students choosing to specialise in performance, notation, composition or history and criticism. Separate courses are offered in **Popular** and **World Music**, **Multimedia and Electronics** and **Music Theatre**. Southampton also offers a wide range of music subjects, covering everything from madrigals to jazz as well as joint courses with acoustics, languages and management. In addition, several universities offer courses in **Music Technology** and **Music and Sound Recording**, notably Surrey.

Performance arts and further creative courses
Students interested in **Drama** or **Dance** can choose specialist courses in these areas or aim for **Performing Arts**, which could include some acting, dancing and music, whilst other courses give a greater focus to drama and include stage management. Specialist fields on several drama courses include directing and the aspects of drama related to films, video, radio or live theatre. It's worthwhile remembering that not all drama courses are acting courses, although many have acting modules; some may also offer theoretical and practical studies in radio, TV, film and theatre techniques.

However, creativity is not restricted to art, music and drama. The ability to produce new ideas is basic in many jobs but none more so than careers in the media. This is a very wide field which can include courses in **Journalism**, **Radio and TV Production**, **Film and Video**, **Photography**, **Public Relations**, **Publishing**, **Creative Writing** and **Scriptwriting**. There are also broader courses, for example **Communication and Media Studies** at Loughborough University, which examines the social, political and economic impact of communication and the media. Needless to say you should also choose your media studies courses with care.

Course options
Art and Design
Animation, Art and Design, Art Education, Blacksmithing, Book Arts and Crafts, Calligraphy and Heraldry, Ceramics, Community Arts, Design Crafts, Embroidery, Fashion, Film and Television, Fine Art, Furniture Restoration, Furniture Studies, Graphic Design, Industrial Design, Interior Design, Jewellery, Leather Studies, Lettering, Metalwork, Modelmaking, Moving Image, Painting, Photography, Plastics, Printed Textiles, Product Design, Public Art, Sports Equipment Design, Surface Pattern, Textile Crafts, Textile Design, Three-dimensional Design, Virtual Reality Design, Wildlife Photography, Wood.

Dance
Art and Teaching of Ballet, Choreography, Community Dance, Costume for Stage and Screen, Dance and Movement Studies, Dance Education (distance learning), Dance with Related Subjects, Performing Arts.

Drama
Acting Studies, Actor Musician, Alternative Theatre, Circus, Community Theatre, Contemporary Theatre, Directing, Drama, Drama Education, European Theatre Arts.

Music
Actor Musician, Applied Music, Audio and Music Technology, Commercial Music, Jazz, Music, Music Education, Music Industry Management, Music Production, Music Systems Engineering, Music Technology, Musical Theatre, New Music and Media, Performing Arts, Popular Music, Puppetry, Recording Arts, Technical Theatre, Theatre Sound.

Other creative courses
Architecture, Art Galleries and Heritage Management, Arts Management, Communication Studies, Creative Studies, Creative Writing, Floristry, History of Art and Design, Media and Special Effects, Media Studies, Screenwriting Studies, Television and Radio.

OPTION 8: OTHER ARTS AND HUMANITIES SUBJECTS

Arts degrees cover a wide field, and apart from those subjects chosen as a preparation to enter the teaching profession they are non-vocational but (hopefully) studied for pleasure and scholarship. One of the most popular courses in terms of the numbers of applicants is **English**.

English

In the personal statement, in her UCAS application, one applicant wrote: 'I've just read *Birdsong* and *Charlotte Gray* by Faulks and couldn't put them down. I keep reading *The Famished Road*, which in the world of the bizarre is in a different realm to other works I have read. Locked away in book after book over the years, I enjoy literature because it opens windows into many worlds unreachable in any other way. That's ... "Why English?"'

Such enthusiasm speaks for itself and such is the scope offered to applicants in a wide-ranging study of literature through poetry, fiction and drama that the extent of the subject seems limitless. In addition to Shakespeare, Chaucer, Donne, Milton, Swift and others, students are able to engage with children's literature, science fiction and film literature and in recent years **Creative Writing** has appeared as a degree subject or as an option at a number of universities including East Anglia, Hull, Liverpool John Moores, London (Royal Holloway) and Warwick.

When choosing courses check the prospectuses carefully because a course listed as English might simply mean English Literature or English Language or both.

There are also courses in **Literature and Modern Languages** which cross international boundaries, **American Studies** which covers the literature and history of North America and **Linguistics** focusing on a study of language itself, which may include topics such as children's language, dialect and slang, language handicap, and advertising language.

Humanities

Degree courses in **History** vary enormously, exploring different ages in different countries and cultures and applicants should tread carefully to select those universities offering the course best suited to their interests. **Economic and Social History** is another branch of the subject whilst **Ancient History** leads on to **Classical Studies**, **Classics** and on towards **Archaeology**, which can be studied from a scientific as well as an historical base.

Courses in **Theology** and **Religious Studies** explore religious beliefs and how individuals practise their beliefs (a BBC poll stated that 70% of people in the UK believe in a 'higher being' or a spiritual force). These beliefs strongly affect the world in which we live and, whilst the subject is non-vocational in one sense, an awareness of these beliefs and an understanding of the major faiths and the standards and values of others in a multicultural society are now an essential part of our working lives. However, an examination of beliefs, the differences between knowledge and opinion, the nature of good and evil and ethical issues can also take us into **Philosophy**, a subject close to the heart of anyone who enjoys an argument, balancing one issue against another, whether the topic be free will or predestination or the existence of God. **Social** and **Cultural Anthropology** also explore religions, as well as kinship, ritual systems, art and politics within the organisation of society, whilst **Biological Anthropology** looks at the evolutionary processes, genetics and physical differences.

Sport

For something completely different, those interested in **Physical Education** can choose from a number of degrees offered in sporting subjects such as **Sport Science** and **Sport Studies**. Courses are now offered in abundance, and can include **Leisure and Recreation Management**, **Coaching**, **Sport Therapy** and **Exercise Science**, **Fitness Management** and **Sport Psychology**.

Teaching

Those students interested in the idea of a career in the teaching profession but who have not followed a teacher-training course can follow a degree course, for example in English, Geography, History or languages, and then take an extra year leading to a Postgraduate Certificate in Education.

Course options

Advertising, African Studies, American Studies, Ancient Civilisation, Ancient Greek, Ancient History, Ancient Mediterranean Studies, Anglo-Saxon, Anthropology, Archaeology, Arts Management, Asia-Pacific Studies, Australian Studies, Biblical Studies, Bioarchaeology, Broadcasting Studies, Byzantine Studies, Canadian Studies, Celtic Studies, Church History, Classical Archaeology, Classical Civilisation, Classical Studies, Communication Studies, Conservation, Creative Writing, Cultural Studies, Development Studies, Divinity, Earth Sciences, East Mediterranean History, Economic History, Economics, Egyptology, English, English Language, English Literature, European History, Film History, Film Studies, Fine Art Valuation, Furniture Restoration, Greek, Greek and Roman Studies, Heritage Management, History, History of Architecture, History of Art, Information Management, International Relations, Jewish History, Journalism, Land Management, Latin, Law, Linguistics, Literary Studies, Literature, Maritime History, Media Studies, Medieval Studies, Middle Eastern Studies, Peace Studies, Politics, Publishing, Religious Studies, Scottish Literature, Scottish Studies, Sports Science, Sports Studies, Theatre Studies, Theology, TV Studies, Victorian Studies, Welsh History.

3 | CHOOSING A DEGREE BY WAY OF SCHOOL SUBJECTS

Below are lists of A level examination subjects, followed by a list of related degree course subjects. If you particularly enjoyed a subject at school, sixth form or college, use these lists to view the wide range of programmes available to you. You may then want to look into some course details in Part 2.

Accounting/Applied Business
Accountancy
Actuarial Science/Studies
Agricultural Economics
Banking
Business Administration
Business Economics
Business Studies
Economics
Estate Management
Finance
Financial Services
Hospitality Management
Industrial Economics
Insurance
Land Economics
Management Sciences
Marketing
Quantity Surveying
Retail Management

Ancient History
Ancient Civilisation
Ancient Greek
Anglo-Saxon
Anthropology
Archaeology
Art and Archaeology of the Ancient World
Biblical Studies
Byzantine Studies
Celtic Studies
Classical Archaeology
Classical Civilisation
Classical Studies
East Mediterranean History
Egyptian Ecology
Greek (Ancient)
Greek and Roman Studies
Greek Archaeology
Heritage Management
History

History of Architecture
History of Art
Jewish History
Middle Eastern Civilisation/Cultures
Religious Studies

Archaeology
Anthropology
Archaeological Sciences
Art and Design
Bioarchaeology
Byzantine Studies
Celtic Studies
Classical Civilisation
Classical Studies
Combined Studies
Conservation (Restoration)
Conservation of Buildings
East Mediterranean History
Environmental Archaeology
Geoarchaeology
Geology
Greek and Roman Studies
Greek Archaeology
History of Architecture
History of Art
History of Design
Maritime History
Middle Eastern Studies

Art and Design/Applied Art and Design
Advertising
  Copywriting
  Design
  Management
  Photography
Animation
Applied Arts
Archaeology
Architecture
Art (Teaching)

Bookbinding
Ceramic Design
Combined Studies
Communication Studies
Conservation
  Archaeological
  Building
  Restoration
Costume Design
Creative Arts
Design Crafts
Designs for Media
Digital Modelling
Embroidery
Fashion Design
Fashion Promotions
Film Studies
Fine Arts
Fine Arts Restoration
Floral Design
Furniture Design
Garden Design
Glass Design
Graphic Arts
Heritage Management
History of Architecture
History of Art
History of Design
History of Film
Illustration
Industrial Design
Interior Design
Landscape Architecture
Media Studies
Modelmaking
Moving Image (Design)
Photography
Print Design
Product Design
Sculpture
Silversmithing, Goldsmithing and Jewellery
Textile Design
Theatre Design
TV Studies
Typography
Valuation (Fine Arts)
Virtual Reality Design
Visual Arts
Visual Communications
Visual Studies

Biology/Applied Science
Agricultural Biochemistry
Agricultural Biology
Agricultural Biotechnology
Agricultural Botany
Agricultural Zoology

Agriculture
Agroforestry
Agronomy
Anatomy
Animal Behaviour
Animal Biology
Animal Management
Animal Nutrition
Animal Science
Animal Welfare
Anthropology
Applied Biology
Aquaculture
Aquatic Bioscience
Arboriculture
Bacteriology
Behavioural Studies
Biochemical Engineering
Biochemistry
Biological Chemistry
Biological Sciences
Biology (Teaching)
Biomaterials Science
Biomedical Sciences
Biomolecular Chemistry
Biophysics
Bioprocess Engineering
Biosciences
Biosciences (Medical)
Biotechnology
Brewing and Distilling
Cell Biology
Childhood Studies
Conservation Biology
Consumer Sciences/Studies
Cosmetic Sciences
Countryside Management/Recreation
Crop Protection
Crop Science
Dental Technology
Dentistry
Developmental Psychology
Dietetics
Earth Resources
Earth Science Studies
Ecology
Environmental Biochemistry
Environmental Biology
Environmental Health
Environmental Management
Environmental Protection
Environmental Science/Studies
Environmental Toxicology
Equine Science/Studies
Exercise and Health
Farm Business Management
Floriculture

Food and Consumer Studies
Food Economics
Food Management
Food Manufacturing
Food Marketing
Food Production
Food Quality
Food Science
Food Technology
Forensic Science
Forest and Woodland Management
Forest Products (Wood) Technology
Forestry
Garden Design
General Science
Genetics
Golf Course Management
Health and Community Studies
Health and Exercise Psychology
Health and Fitness
Health Promotion
Health Sciences Studies
Healthcare
Horticulture
Human Biology
Human Communication
Human Ecology
Human Geography
Human Life Sciences
Human Nutrition
Human Physiology
Human Psychology
Human Sciences
Immunology
Land Management
Land Use Studies
Landscape Architecture
Landscape Design
Learning Disabilities
Life Sciences
Marine Biology
Marine Biotechnology
Marine Environment
Marine/Maritime Studies
Marine Resources
Medical Biochemistry
Medical Biosciences
Medical Electronics
Medical Genetics
Medical Microbiology
Medical Physics
Medicinal Chemistry
Medicine
Microbiology
Midwifery
Molecular Biology
Molecular Sciences

Natural Resources
Natural Sciences
Neuroscience
Nursing
Nutrition
Nutritional Biochemistry
Occupational Health
Occupational Therapy
Ocean Science
Oceanography
Optometry
Orthoptics
Osteopathy
Palaeobiology and Evolution
Paramedic Science
Parasitology
Pathobiology
Pharmaceutical Chemistry
Pharmacology
Pharmacy
Physical Education (Teaching)
Physical Geography
Physiology
Physiotherapy
Plant Sciences
Podiatry
Polymer Science
Population Biology
Prosthetics and Orthotics
Psychology
Public Health
Radiography
Recreation Management
Rural Environment Management
Rural Resource Development
Social Anthropology
Social Care
Social Psychology
Social Work
Soil Science
Speech Sciences Therapy
Sports Science
Toxicology
Turf Science/Technology
Underwater Studies
Veterinary Nursing
Veterinary Science
Wildlife Management
Zoology

Business Studies/Applied Business
Accountancy
Administration
Advertising
American Business Studies
Arts Management
Banking

Building Management
Business
  Administration
  Analysis
  Computing
  Decision Analysis
  Economics
  Information Systems
  Information Technology
  Law
  Mathematics Studies
  Psychology
  Studies (Welsh)
Consumer Studies
Countryside Management
E-Business
E-Commerce
Economics
Estate Management
European Accountancy and Finance
European Business/Management
European Economics
European Logistics Management
European Management Science
European Tourism
Events Management
Farm Management
Financial Services
Food Marketing
Health Administration
Heritage Management
Hospitality Management
Hotel Management
Industrial Relations
Institutional Management
International Business Hospitality
International Management
International Marketing
International Tourism Management
Land Economy
Land Management
Leisure Management
Management Science/Studies
Marketing
Operational Research
Organisational Studies
Property Management
Public Administration
Publishing
Purchasing
Quality Management
Retail Management
Risk Management
Rural Business Management
Rural Economics
Social Administration
Stage Management

Surveying
Tourism Management
Transport Management

Chemistry/Applied Science
Agricultural Biochemistry
Agricultural Biology
Agricultural Chemistry
Agriculture
Analytical Chemistry
Animal Nutrition
Animal Sciences
Applied Chemistry
Bacteriology
Biochemical Engineering
Biochemistry
Biological Chemistry
Biological Sciences
Biomedical Sciences
Biotechnology
Brewing and Distilling
Cell Biology
Ceramic Science
Chemical Physics
Chemical Product Technology
Chemistry (Teaching)
Chemistry of Materials
Colour Chemistry
Cosmetic Science
Dental Materials
Dentistry
Engineering
  Chemical
  Fire
  Food
  Fuel and Energy
  Nuclear Process
  Petroleum
Environmental Biochemistry
Environmental Biology
Environmental Chemistry
Environmental Geoscience
Environmental Toxicology
Food Science
Forensic Science
Fuel Science
General Science
Genetics
Geochemistry
Health Sciences
Horticulture
Human Biology
Human Nutrition
Human Physiology
Human Sciences
Immunology
Life Sciences

Marine Chemistry
Materials Science
Medical Biosciences
Medical Microbiology
Medicinal Chemistry
Medicine
Minerals Engineering
Minerals Surveying
Molecular Biology
Molecular Genetics
Molecular Pathology
Molecular Sciences
Natural Sciences
Neurosciences
Nursing
Nutrition
Ocean Science
Parasitology
Petroleum Geology
Pharmaceutical Chemistry
Pharmacology
Pharmacy
Plant Science
Polymer Science
Soil Science
Sports Science
Toxicology
Zoology

Classics and Classical Civilisation
Ancient Civilisations
Ancient Greek
Ancient History
Ancient Mediterranean Studies
Archaeology
Biblical Studies
Classical Studies
Greek
History (Greek and Roman Studies)
History of Architecture
History of Art
Latin
Roman Civilisation

Computing/Applied ICT
Artificial Intelligence
Business Computing
Business Information Systems
Business Information Technology
Cognitive Science
Computational and Experimental Mathematics
Computational Chemistry
Computational Linguistics
Computational Physics
Computational Science
Computer-Aided Design
Computer-Aided Engineering

Computer Animation
Computer Studies
Decision Systems
Engineering
   Control and Systems
   Information Systems
   Software
Information Science
Information Systems
Intelligent Systems
Robotics

Dance
(See under **Theatre Studies**)

Design and Technology/
   Applied Art and Design
Architecture
Art and Design
Building
Ceramic Design
Dental Technology
Design and Technology (Teaching)
Design Crafts
Design History
Furniture Design
Industrial Design
Interior Design
Jewellery
Landscape Architecture
Product Design
Prosthetics and Orthotics
Silversmithing, Goldsmithing and Jewellery
Technical Illustration

Drama
(See under **Theatre Studies**)

Economics/Applied Business
Accountancy
Actuarial Science/Studies
Agricultural Economics
Applied Economics
Applied Mathematics
Applied Statistics
Banking
Business Administration
Business Analysis
Business Decision Management
Business Decision Mathematics
Business Economics
Business Information Systems
Business Studies
City and Regional Planning
Development Studies
Economic and Social History
Economics (Teaching)

Environment Economics and Ecology
European Business Administration
European Economics
European Logistics Management
European Marketing
European Politics
European Studies
Farm Management
Finance
Financial Economics
Financial Services
Food Marketing
Geography
Government
Human Resource Management
Industrial Economics
Information and Library Studies
International Business Economics
Land Economics
Management Science
Mathematical Economics
Mathematical Statistics
Mathematics
Money, Banking and Finance
Operational Research
Planning
Politics
Quantity Surveying
Social History
Social Sciences
Social Studies
Sociology
Statistics
Technological Economics
Tourism and Leisure Economics

Electronics/Engineering/Applied ICT

Astrophysics
Audio and Music Technology
Audiotechnology
Avionic Systems
Broadcasting
Communications Engineering
Computer Science/Systems
Control Systems
Digital Systems
Electro-acoustics
Electronic Design
Electronic Media
Electronic Music
Electronic Systems
Engineering
  Aeronautical
  Aerospace Systems
  Computer Systems
  Electronic
  Information

Mechatronic
Physics
Software
Systems
Telecommunications
Intelligent Systems
Internet Technology
Laser Systems
Media Systems
Medical Electronics
Microelectronics
Music Technology
Opto-electronic Engineering
Planetary Physics
Power Systems
Signal Processing
Telecommunications

English

Advertising (Copywriting)
American Studies
Anglo-Saxon
Arts
  Combined
  General
Broadcast Media
Broadcasting Studies
Communications Studies
Contemporary Writing
Creative Writing
Cultural Studies
Drama
English (Teaching)
English as a Foreign Language
English Literature
Information and Library Studies
Information Science
Journalism
Linguistics
Literary Studies
Literature
Media Studies
Publishing
Scottish Literature
Theatre Studies
TV Studies

Environmental Science/Applied Science

Agriculture
Agroforestry
Animal Science
Architecture
Biology
Botany
Chemistry
City and Regional Planning
Combined Studies

Conservation
Countryside Management
Crop Science
Development Studies
Earth Resources and Management
Ecology
Economics
Environmental Chemistry
Environmental Planning
Estate Surveying
Forestry
Garden Design
Geography
Geology
Heritage Management
Horticulture
Land Management
Landscape Architecture
Leisure Management
Marine Environment
Oceanography
Population Studies
Recreational Land Management
Rural Resources
Surveying
Topographic Science
Town and Country Planning
Underwater Studies
Urban Estate Management
Urban Studies

Film Studies
(See under **Media Studies**)

Geography/Applied Science
African Studies
Afro-Asian Studies
Agriculture
Agroforestry
Anthropology
Applied Ecology
Applied Geology
Archaeology
Canadian Studies
Caribbean Studies
City and Regional Planning
Countryside Management
Development Studies
Earth Sciences
East Asian Studies
Ecology
Economics
Environmental Planning
Environmental Studies
Estate Management
Estate Surveying
European Land Management

Food Marketing
Geochemistry
Geographical Information Systems
Geography (Teaching)
Geology
Geophysics
Geoscience
Government
Human Geography
Land Economy
Land Management
Land Surveying
Landscape Architecture
Marine Resources and Management
Maritime Studies
Meteorology
Mineral Surveying
Mining Geology
Nautical Studies
Oceanography
Planning
Politics
Population Studies
Recreational Land Management
Rural Resources Management
Strategic Studies
Surveying
   Estate
   Minerals
   Valuation
Surveying and Mapping
Topographic Science
Town and Country Planning
Transport
Travel and Tourism
Underwater Studies
Urban Estate Management
Urban Studies

Geology/Applied Science
Agriculture
Applied Ecology
Archaeology
Astronomy
Chemistry
Earth Science
Ecology
Environmental Science
Geochemistry
Geographical Information Systems
Geography
Geological Engineering
Geomorphology
Geophysical Science
Geotechnics
Human Geography
Hydrography

Meteorology
Mineral Surveying
Mining Engineering
Mining Geology
Natural Resources
Ocean Science
Offshore Engineering
Petroleum Geology
Physics
Rural Resources
Soil Science
Surveying
Topographic Science

Government and Politics

African Studies
Afro-Asian Studies
Agricultural Economics
American Studies
Anthropology
Applied Social Sciences/Studies
Asian Studies
Banking
Broadcasting Studies
Business Economics
Business Law
Business Studies
Canadian Studies
Chinese Studies
City and Regional Planning
Commerce
Communication Studies
Community Sciences/Studies
Defence and Security Studies
Development Studies
Earth Resources and Management
Economics
Education (not Teaching)
Environmental Policy
Environmental Protection
Environmental Studies
European Business Economics
European Community Studies
European Politics
European Social Policy
European Studies
Financial Economics
French Law
French Studies
German Law
German Studies
Government
Health Administration
History
Housing Management
Human Organisation

Industrial Relations
International Agriculture
International Business Economics
International Finance
International History
International Marketing
International Politics
International Relations
International Studies
Investment
Italian Studies
Japanese Studies
Law
Natural Resources
Peace and War Studies
Peace Studies
Philosophy
Political Economy
Politics
Public Policy and Administration
Public Sector Economics
Race Studies
Scandinavian Studies
Social Administration
Social Anthropology
Social Care
Social Ethics
Social History
Social Policy
Social Research
Social Work
Sociology
Strategic Planning
Town Planning
Urban Studies
Welfare and Social Policy
Youth and Community Work

History

African Studies
American Studies
Ancient Civilisations
Ancient History
Anglo-Saxon
Anthropology
Archaeology
Biblical Studies
Byzantine Studies
Canadian Studies
Chinese History
Church History
Classical Civilisation
Classical Studies
Classics
Conservation
    Building

Restoration
Criminal Justice
Cultural Studies
Divinity
East Mediterranean History
Economic History
European History
Film History
History (Teaching)
History of Architecture
History of Art
History of Design
History of Ideas
History of Science
International History
International Relations
Irish Studies
Islamic Art and Archaeology
Italian Studies
Jewish History
Latin American Studies
Law
Medieval Studies
Near and Middle Eastern Studies
Peace Studies
Politics
Religious Studies
Scottish History
Social History
Social Sciences
Social Studies
Sociology
Strategic Studies
Victorian Studies
War Studies
Welsh History

History of Art/Applied Art and Design

Advertising
Anthropology
Archaeology
Architecture History
Art and Design
Art History
Arts Management
Church History
Conservation
  Archaeological
  Buildings
  Restoration
Costume Design
Crafts (Printmaking)
Film History
Fine Art Valuation
Furniture Restoration

Heritage Management
History
Victorian Studies

Home Economics/Applied Science/ Health and Social Care

This subject area also involves courses concerned with food and drink and the consumer.
Administration
Advertising
Animal Nutrition
Applied Consumer Studies
Behavioural Science
Biological Sciences
Biology
Brewing and Distilling
Business Studies
Chemistry
Chemistry of Food
Communications Studies
Community Studies
Consumer Product Design
Consumer Sciences
Consumer Studies
Culinary Arts
Dietetics
Environmental Studies
Fashion
Food
  Bioprocessing
  Economics
  Manufacturing
  Marketing and Management
  Production
  Quality
  Technology
Health and Community Studies
Health and Safety
Health Services
Healthcare
Home Economics (Teaching)
Hospitality (Hotel) Management
Housing Studies
Human Biology
Human Nutrition
Human Psychology
Human Sciences
Industrial Design
International Hospitality Management
Leisure Studies
Marketing
Media Studies
Nursing
Nutrition
Psychology
Retail Management

Social Administration
Social Policy
Social Studies
Sociology
Textile Arts
Women's Studies
Youth and Community Work

Languages

Students of modern (or ancient) languages frequently choose the same languages to study at degree level. It should be noted, however, that the ability to speak and write in a range of foreign languages can be an important asset when applying for jobs. It is therefore suggested that those students with an interest and ability in languages should look beyond their A level skills into new languages.

African Languages
Akkadian
Ancient Greek
Anglo-Saxon
Asian Languages
Assyriology
Bantu
Bengali Studies
Breton
Bulgarian
Burmese Studies
Celtic
Chinese
Communication Studies
Czech and Slovak
Danish
Dutch
East European Studies
Egyptian
European Studies
   French
   German
   Italian
   Russian
   Spanish
European Tourism
Finnish
French
French (Teaching)
French Law
Gaelic
German
German (Teaching)
German Law
Greek (Modern)
Hausa
Hebrew
Hindi
Hispanic Studies
Hungarian

Indonesian
International Hospitality
   Management
International Studies
Interpreting and Translating
Iranian
Irish
Italian
Italian (Teaching)
Italian Law
Japanese
Korean
Languages for Business
Latin
Latin American Studies
Linguistics
Literature
Marathi
Modern Languages
Nepali Studies
Norse
Norwegian
Oriental Languages
Pakistan Studies
Persian
Polish
Portuguese
Romanian
Russian
Russian (Teaching)
Sanskrit
Scandinavian Studies
Serbo-Croat
Sinhalese
Slavonic Studies
South Asian Studies
Spanish
Spanish (Teaching)
Spanish Law
Swedish
Tamil
Tourism
Travel
Turkish
Urdu
Vietnamese Studies
Welsh

Law

American Legal Systems
Business Law
European Community Studies
European Law
Government
History
International History
International Relations
Legal Studies

Legislative Studies
Police Studies
Politics
Property Management
Public Administration
Social Administration
Social Policy
Strategic Studies
Urban Studies

Mathematics/Statistics
Accountancy
Acoustical Engineering
Actuarial Science
Applied Mathematics
Applied Statistics
Architecture
Astrophysics
Automotive Engineering
Banking
Building
Business Computing
Business Economics
Business Information Systems
Business Studies
Cognitive Science
Commerce
Computer Science
Decision Systems
Economics
Engineering
  Aeronautical
  Aerospace Systems
  Avionics
  Civil
  Communications
  Computer Systems
  Control Systems
  Electrical
  Electronic
  Marine
  Mathematical
  Mechanical
  Mining
  Physics
  Software
  Systems
Environmental Engineering
Ergonomics
European Business Economics
Financial Analysis
Financial Services
Industrial Mathematics
Information Science
Insurance
Integrated Engineering
Intelligent Systems
Investment

Management Science
Mathematics (Pure and Applied)
Mathematics (Teaching)
Mathematics and Statistics
Naval Architecture
Offshore Engineering
Operational Research
Opto-electronics
Probability and Statistics
Quantity Surveying
Risk Management (Financial)
Robotics and Cybernetics
Ship Science
Surveying
Systems Analysis
Systems Modelling

Media Studies
Advertising
Art
Art and Design
Arts Management
Audio-visual Production
Band Studies
Broadcasting
Communication Studies
Design (Advertising)
Drama
Electronic Music
Ethnic Studies
Film Studies
Human Organisation
Human Psychology
Jazz Studies
Journalism
Leisure Studies
Marketing
Media and Theatre Studies
Music
Music Technology
Photography
Politics
TV Studies
Visual Arts
Visual Performance

Music/Music Technology/ Performing Arts
Acoustics
Band Musicianship
Book Publishing
Broadcasting
Creative Music Technology
Dance
Drama
Electronic Music
Ethnomusicology
Jazz Studies

Media Production
Media Studies
Music (Teaching)
Performance Arts
Stage Management
Theatre Studies

Performance Arts/Studies
(See under **Theatre Studies**)

Philosophy
Ancient Civilisation
Cognitive Science
Conflict Resolution
Divinity
Economics
Educational Studies (not Teaching)
European Philosophy
Government
History
History and Philosophy of Science
History of Ideas
History of Religions
Law
Peace Studies
Philosophy of Science
Politics
Psychology
Religious Studies
Social Ethics
Theology
Women's Studies

Photography
(See under **Art and Design**)

Physical Education/Health and Social Care
Chiropractic
Coaching Science
Dance Studies
Exercise and Health
Exercise Science
Golf Studies
Health Education
Health Psychology
Health Science
Healthcare
Human Life Science
Nursing
Occupational Health and Safety
Occupational Therapy
Osteopathy
Outdoor Pursuits
Physical Education (Teaching)
   Primary, Secondary (Teaching)
Physiotherapy

Sport and Exercise Science
Sport and Health
Sport Coaching
Sport Equipment Design
Sport Management

Physics/Engineering/Applied Science
Acoustics
Aerodynamics
Air Transport Engineering
Applied Physics
Architecture
Astronautics
Astronomy
Astrophysics
Automotive Engineering
Biophysics
Broadcasting
   Electronics
Building
Ceramic Science
Chemical Physics
Computer Science
Cybernetics
Digital Systems Engineering
Electro-acoustics
Engineering
   Aeronautical
   Aerospace Systems
   Agricultural
   Avionics
   Communications
   Computer Systems
   Electrical
   Electro-mechanical
   Electronic
   Mechanical
   Nuclear Physics
   Software
   Systems
   Telecommunications
Fire Engineering
Fuel and Energy Engineering
Geophysics
Glass Technology
Hydrography
Information Engineering
Laser Systems
Materials Science
Mechatronic Engineering
Metallurgy
Meteorology
Microelectronics
Mineralogy
Mining Engineering
Naval Architecture
Oceanography

Offshore Engineering
Optometry
Physics (Teaching)
Planetary Physics
Prosthetics and Orthotics
Radiography
Robotics
Ship Science
Signal Processing
Solid State Electronics
Technology

Psychology/Health and Social Care
Advertising
Animal Behaviour
Anthropology
Artificial Intelligence
Behavioural Science
Business Studies
Childhood Studies
Clinical Psychology
Cognitive Science
Community Studies
Counselling
Criminal Justice
Criminology
Drama
Education
Educational Psychology
European Social Psychology
Gender Studies
Health Administration
Health and Fitness
Health Psychology
Hospitality Management
Human Biology
Human–Computer Interaction
Human Evolution
Human Geography
Human Life Science
Human Organisations
Human Psychology
Human Resource Management
Industrial Relations
Journalism
Life Sciences
Management
Medicine
Neuroscience
Nursing
Occupational Psychology
Occupational Therapy
Organisational Behaviour
Psycholinguistics
Public Health
Public Policy
Public Relations

Robotics
Social Administration
Social Care
Social Ethics
Social Policy
Social Psychology
Social Work
Sociology
Speech Therapy
Tourism
Town Planning
Urban Studies
Women's Studies
Zoology

Religious Studies
Anthropology
Applied Theological Studies
Behavioural Studies
Biblical Studies
Christian Ministry
Christian Studies
Church History
Comparative Religion
Divinity
Education
Ethnic Studies
Health and Community Studies
Hebrew
History
History of Religion
Jewish Studies
Philosophy
Psychology
Psychosocial Sciences
Religious Studies (Teaching)
Social Administration
Social Anthropology
Social Ethics
Social Policy
Sociology
Theology

Science for Public Understanding
(See under **Science, Technology and Society**)

Science, Technology and Society/ Applied Science/Engineering/ Applied ICT
Agricultural Sciences
Agriculture
Animal Sciences
Astronomy
Biology
Biotechnology
Botany
Building

Chemistry
Computer Science
Conservation
Ecology
Engineering
Environmental Science
Food Studies
Forestry
General Engineering
General Science
Human Science
Marine Resources
Materials Science
Nutrition
Ocean Science
Sports Science
Technology
  Building
  Chemical
  Food
  Geological
  Leather
  Marine
  Polymers

Social Policy/Business/Health and Social Care

Administration
Arts Management
Banking
Business Studies
City and Regional Planning
Community Studies
Education
Estate Surveying
European Planning
European Politics
European Social Policy
Government
Health and Community Studies
Housing
Human Organisations
Human Resource Management
Industrial Relations
International Relations
Land Management
Law
Leisure Management
Marketing
Organisation Studies
Police Studies
Politics
Public Administration
Public Health
Public Policy
Public Relations
Public Sector Economics

Public Services
Social Administration
Social Care
Social Work
Sport and Health
Tourism
Town and Country Planning
Transport
Urban Studies
Women's Health
Youth and Community Work

Sociology/Health and Social Care

Administration
Anthropology
Behavioural Studies
Broadcasting
Business Studies
City and Regional Planning
Communication Studies
Consumer Studies
Development Studies
Economic and Social History
Economics
Environmental History
Environmental Science
Geography
Government
History
Industrial Relations
Management Studies
Organisation Studies
Police Studies
Politics
Psychology
Public Administration
Social Administration
Social Policy
Social Work
Town and Country Planning
Urban Studies

Textiles/Applied Art and Design

Art and Design
Clothing Engineering
Consumer Studies
Costume Design
Fashion Design
Footwear Design
History of Art
History of Design
Home Economics
Industrial Design
Interior Design
Knitwear
Printed Textiles
Textile Design

Textile Economics
Textile Management
Textile Marketing
Textile Technology
Visual Arts

Theatre Studies/Leisure and Recreation/Performing Arts

Acting
Arts Management
Broadcasting
Classical Civilisation
Communication Studies
Dance
Drama
Education
English Literature
Film Studies
Literature
Media Studies
Performance Arts
Stage Management
Theatre Design

Theatre Studies
TV Studies

Welsh

Celtic Civilisation
Celtic Studies
Communication Studies
Drama
Education
History
Irish Studies
Literature
Media Studies
Performance Arts
Welsh
  Drama
  History
  Literature
  Teaching

World Development

(See under **Government and Politics**)

4 | WHICH UNIVERSITY?

Students – and parents – always ask the same question: **Which is the best university?**

Let me answer by asking another question: which is the best restaurant in town? To which you will reply: it depends on what you want – Chinese, Thai, French, Italian?

It's much the same with universities and colleges, since every institution can offer a completely unique experience. They can vary in location and facilities: do you want to study in a town or city, in the country, on the coast or on a campus located out of town? Do you want a sporty university, one that is strong in the arts or one that has a high ranking?

Hand in hand with the university's facilities is the course that is on offer.

Not all universities will necessarily offer the subject or subject combination or the type of course you want. The actual course content can also vary considerably.

For example, the History BA offered at Coventry focuses on events of the 20th century whereas the specialist course in Viking Studies offered at Nottingham looks at the Viking age through the disciplines of English, history and archaeology.

Similarly Aston's Computing Science course places an emphasis on programming languages whereas Derby's Computing degree focuses on maintaining and developing software systems.

Most courses will offer a broad range of topics with the opportunity to specialise through optional modules. Have a look at Part 2 to see how courses differ and think about what you would like to specialise in.

The choice about where to go to university should be a combination of both what the institution can offer and what the course contains. If you focus on only one of these, you may be disappointed and wish you'd done some more research before committing yourself to a university where the course content doesn't interest you, or a place that lacks the facilities you want.

Once you've thought about these factors, you'll also have to consider, rather crucially, **whether your grades are good enough to get you into your preferred university!**

CHOOSING YOUR UNIVERSITY
Going to a 'good' uni
In the minds of many students the reason for getting into a university with a 'good name' means only one thing – you will get a good job when you leave! Far from it: that depends on you, not just the name of the university. The universities won't find you a job – that's your problem, although they all provide a careers advisory service and can suggest firms to which you could apply; after that it's up to you. Even a degree course at a top university won't prepare you to write an application or teach you how to cope with a job interview. Despite this, however, many graduates get good jobs irrespective of where they studied. It's true that some employers might be more impressed if you have been a student at one of the very popular universities since they know that you will have had to achieve good grades to get a place, but they also look at many other factors when choosing employees, not just the university.

But, you may ask, aren't some universities better than others? This is a common-enough question because students naturally become confused when yet another newspaper produces another set of league tables of 'best' universities. In fact, some students don't seem to care where, or even what, they study so long as the university they choose is high up in the list, or is where their friends are headed!

Many applicants and their parents rely too much on the information appearing in league tables, particularly those referring to 'teaching quality'. These tables are also misleading to students since individual members of staff are not 'inspected' as in school inspections. They are not about the ability of the staff to teach their subject; they are tables about the facilities in the department and the overall work of the subject department. As one university professor explained, the quality of the lectures, whether awful or brilliant, has no bearing on teaching quality league table scores ... points on these tables are only awarded for paperwork, systems and procedures, not for the effectiveness, stimulation or brilliance of the lectures!

Think about what your key values are. Are these in line with the league tables' criteria? What constitutes a 'good' university will be different for each individual.

It might be difficult therefore to decide which is the 'best' university, but when it comes to getting a place we are given a fairly good idea which ones are among the most popular at present and set high entry standards for many of their courses. These include **Bath**, **Bristol**, **Cambridge**, **Durham**, **Edinburgh**, **Exeter**, **Imperial London** (no longer part of London University), **Leeds**, **London (King's)**, **(UCL)**, **London LSE**, **Newcastle**, **Nottingham**, **Oxford**, **Oxford Brookes**, **St Andrews**, **Southampton**, **Warwick** and **York**.

All medical and veterinary schools, and law schools in the older universities are also high in the popularity stakes.

Some reasons why students and parents often consider a university to be good are:

* because it's an old, established institution and quite well known, e.g. Oxford, Cambridge, Edinburgh, Bristol, LSE. Have a look at newer institutions and see what they have to offer in comparison; often they are more innovative and 'cutting-edge'
* because it's located near an attractive town or city. (Not always a good reason, although these universities do attract a lot of applicants so they can pick and choose their students and thus set high entry standards, e.g. Bath, Warwick, York.) Whilst location is important, have a look at local transport links; a university that seems distant might actually be closer to that desirable city than you think!
* because your teacher went there and advises you to apply. Not necessarily a good reason because it depends upon when he or she graduated and their advice might be a little out of date. Universities and their courses are constantly changing
* because some students say it's a good place. These students can give you good advice about their own university and the course they are taking, but not about every course, nor are they in a position to compare their university with any others
* because a lot of your friends are applying. The best decision for your friend is not necessarily the best decision for you.

Some reasons why universities might be less popular are:

* because they are small. There might be fewer facilities for students but smaller places are usually more friendly – check out the university; you might be wrong and be missing a good course
* because it seems far away and difficult to reach by public transport. This doesn't seem to affect St Andrews, which is remote enough, but then a Prince went there and since then it's been overwhelmed with applications! So check out Aberystwyth, Bangor, Stirling and Swansea – all first-rate universities with excellent track records
* because it doesn't have a familiar name and it's difficult to identify where it's located, e.g. Anglia Ruskin (Cambridge and Chelmsford) and Brunel (Middlesex), both of which offer a good range of courses. (Make sure you know your geographical locations – one student travelled from London to Bangor, thinking he was going to Bognor!)

Other things to consider when choosing a university

Below are a few things to keep in mind when you are looking at different universities.

The location of the university
* You're likely to be living at or near the university for at least two years so its location is of utmost importance.

* Some universities are ideally located for students who love sports and outdoor activities, with facilities and the countryside nearby.
* Others are located in or near cities for students who prefer a more cosmopolitan lifestyle.

The size of the university
* Larger universities will often offer you a busy, diverse atmosphere and smaller institutions place merit on the friendliness and reassurance of a small campus and student body. Think about the environment you want to be in.
* Campus-based universities have all facilities in one location. Would you enjoy having everything on your doorstep or would you prefer a university spread across a city?

Transport links
* You'll need to consider both local and national transport links.
* How well connected is the local area? You'll need to think about how you'll get to the local shops – can you walk, take a bus or will you need a car?
* It's likely that you will want to visit your home town every now and then. Look into the journey home. How long will it take and how much will it cost?

Accommodation
* Most students live in halls of residence in their first year, moving to rented accommodation with friends in following years.
* Information on the cost of rent in student accommodation will be available through the university. Make sure you know if utilities are included in the price. Some halls require students to use 'top-up' cards.
* Find out how many people you would have to share the kitchen or bathroom with, or if the rooms come with en-suite facilities.
* Most universities will offer catered and non-catered rooms. Some universities will offer inclusive breakfast and dinner but check prices, times and food options!
* After your first year it is likely that you will move out of halls into a rented accommodation. Check local rental prices and ask if the university offers an estate agent or advice service.
* Remember when renting a property outside the university you will often have to set up your own utilities, including TV and internet.
* Have a look at the living costs of the local area. Are they higher or lower than what you are used to? A good indicator is to look up the local takeaways!

Facilities
* Universities can offer a range of facilities; think about which ones are important to you.
* Some universities have 'student villages' with mini-supermarkets and bookshops that stock textbooks; others have smaller shops, stocking the essentials.
* Does the university have a student gym? Often membership prices are lower for students and the location is convenient.
* The library is an important resource at any university. Have a look at the range of books offered and whether they are relevant to your course. Check the library opening times and whether the university provides digital library services such as online journals.
* Although most students have PCs or laptops, computer facilities at the university can be useful. Have a look at how many computer suites are offered and if you don't have a printer check printing charges.
* Care services are usually offered including a campus doctor, counselling services and chaplaincy services.
* The Students' Union bar offers students the chance to relax and socialise after studying. Have a look at the types of nights organised by the SU. These can range from live music to comedy and quiz nights.

Catering
* Most universities will have a cafeteria. Check the opening times, prices and the variety of meals. Some universities even have fast food chains on campus.
* There might even be a coffee bar which will offer you a place to chat with friends or relax between lectures.

Societies
* Student-run societies allow students with similar interests to socialise and enjoy themselves.
* Sports societies and teams give sporty students the opportunity to compete or learn a new sport.
* The range of societies on offer is astounding, from music and games through to interests and activities. If you have a particular interest have a look to see if there is a society where you will find like-minded people – if there isn't, the Students' Union will support you in setting up your own society.

The Students' Union
* It can be a rewarding experience to take an active role within your Students' Union.
* Students' Unions often produce a magazine or newspaper which is run and read by students. If you have an interest in journalism, want to develop your design skills or just want people to hear what you have to say there may be opportunities to get involved.
* There will be opportunities to take on a role within the union. These are usually won through an election and are a great addition to any CV. Check to see how active the Students' Union is – does it have an impact on the university or local community?

Job opportunities
* Some students take on part-time or casual jobs either within the university or in the local area to supplement their maintenance loan.
* Students often staff the bar or shop within the university and some take on roles within the library.
* There may be opportunities for casual work at the university. Many institutions pay students to be ambassadors on open days or events or to man the phones for fundraising campaigns.
* You might be able to get a job in the local town in a shop or café. If you visit have a look around and don't feel scared about asking potential employers about future opportunities.
* Whilst looking for work bear in mind the course you are studying and your career aspirations. Are there any work opportunities which complement your course? If you are taking a Drama course, could you work in the local theatre? If you are studying English would a part-time job in a bookshop boost your CV?

UNIVERSITY RANKINGS

The rankings are calculated from student satisfaction statistics, student to staff ratio, the amount the university spends on each student, entry levels and the percentage of students in employment six months after graduating.

1 Cambridge
2 Oxford
3 London LSE
4 St Andrews
5 UCL
6 Durham
7 Bath
8 Surrey
9 Imperial London
10 Warwick
11 Lancaster
12 Exeter
13 Leicester
14 Loughborough
15 Birmingham
16 York
17 East Anglia
18 Heriot-Watt
19 Edinburgh
20 Kent
21 Glasgow

22 London (SOAS)
23 Bristol
24 Southampton
25 Buckingham

(Source: *The Guardian*'s University Guide 2014: University league table)

FINDING THE RIGHT COURSE FOR YOU

When choosing a university, there is always a great temptation to rush to the university league tables for guidance on the best place to apply. The variety of league tables available online through newspaper, student and university websites are useful for that initial overview as they are formulated based on the average student satisfaction statistics across a range of factors such as student/staff ratios, facilities, quality of teaching and graduate employment prospects. However a university can offer a large number of subjects (by way of BA, BSc, BEng courses etc.) for several thousand students, so 'average' information can be misleading when trying to consider the best university and, most importantly, the best course for you. If possible, make sure you visit the university, the subject department you have chosen and talk to existing students about the course before making your application.

Here, we'll give you the basics you should consider when looking at different courses.

Subjects are presented in a variety of ways.

* **Single honours** degree courses – you will graduate in one subject. Each university offering the same subject will offer different options throughout your years – check the modules on offer.
* **Joint honours** courses – these involve the study of two different subjects. Your choice of subjects might be related, such as Mathematics and Physics, or quite different, such as Computing and Creative Writing.
* **Combined honours** courses – similar to joint courses but some universities such as Durham and Newcastle offer up to three subject choices.
* **Major/minor** courses – students choose two subjects, one being studied over a longer period than the other, e.g. 75%/25%.
* **Sandwich** courses – alternating periods of study and work-related experience (for up to a year), usually on full pay, in commerce and industry. Students are frequently offered full-time employment when they graduate.

Things to consider when looking at the difference in degree courses

Here are some questions to bear in mind whilst researching your course. Check what your chosen courses at your chosen universities can offer.

* **Is the course modular?** Most universities now offer modular courses. This means that your degree course will consist of a study of compulsory and optional units. Compulsory units are essential to achieve a degree in your chosen subject. Optional units allow you to choose other specialised topics appropriate to your degree subject, which suit your special interests. On some courses it may be possible to study some subjects not related to your degree for part of the time. Modular courses are not offered in Medicine, Dentistry or Veterinary Science.
* **What exactly will I study each year?** Courses can differ wildly especially in subjects such as Business, Computing, Drama, English, History and Art and students may find themselves studying areas they have no interest in. Check the range of modules available: are they in line with your interests? Are the core modules interesting and are the optional modules varied?
* **Can I change degree course if it is not what I expected?** Some universities will allow you to transfer to another course in the first year if you are unhappy or if you want to change to or from a single or joint/major/minor programme. If you are unsure of your decision check the university's policies on transferring courses.
* **Does the course contain a sandwich year or placement?** Courses offering a sandwich year (usually between the second and final year) allow students to gain experience whilst at university. Some courses come with compulsory sandwich years and others can be taken as an option. Many courses also involve work experience placements of varying lengths which can be taken locally, nationally or sometimes internationally.

* **Is there an opportunity to study abroad?** Many universities offer exchange programmes enabling students to spend a semester in a foreign country with a partner institution. Check with your chosen course to see if they offer an exchange scheme and if so which countries it is possible to study in.

* **When does the course start?** Most undergraduate degree courses commence in September or October but some institutions offer commencement dates in January, February or July. Check with the university if you are unsure.

* **How long will the course last?** Most undergraduate courses are between three and five years in length but this can depend on: the qualification (some courses offer an integrated master's, adding an extra year); the degree (medical subjects require longer training); the programme structure (sandwich degrees are usually four years in length); and the institution (Buckingham offers two-year degrees).

* **How much flexibility does the course offer?** Many courses can be studied as a combined/ joint/major/minor programme allowing you to choose modules from more than one subject area. Some courses offer a delayed choice of degree subjects, often with students deciding their award pathway after the first or second year of study.

* **How is the course taught?** Most courses are taught through a combination of lectures and seminars with the option of one-on-one tutorials. Check class sizes and delivery methods to see if they suit you.

* **How is the course assessed?** Think about whether you prefer exams or essays and if you want to embrace or avoid group work and presentations. It might be impossible to avoid certain types of assessments but check how the majority of modules are assessed before you commit to a course.

* **Can I intercalate?** An intercalation year is when you take a year out of your normal studies in Medicine, Dentistry or Veterinary Studies to complete the final year of a BA or a BSc. Intercalation is usually offered to students achieving a certain level in the first two years of their degree. Check which courses are on offer at your chosen institution, and remember this will add an extra year on to your degree.

* **Is the university well known for excellence in my chosen subject area?** Some institutions are leading universities in certain subject areas; Imperial London is a leading university in Science and Engineering and London LSE in Social Sciences. Have a look at any news surrounding your chosen department – does it sound like an inspiring or exciting place to be?

* **Is my course supported by good resources?** If your course requires specialist equipment, material or space it is vital that you are happy with what the university provides. If you are studying sciences check that the labs are well equipped. If you study performance make sure there is space for you to rehearse.

* **Does the course look at issues outside the Western world?** Many degrees offer optional modules which look at the degree subject in a non-Western context. Asia, Africa and the Middle East are the focus of all degree programmes offered at London (SOAS).

* **Can I study a foreign language or learn a new language whilst studying?** While many courses offer opportunities to take languages as optional modules, some universities offer Languages for All schemes that can be taken alongside academic studies. Universities including Essex, York and Edinburgh offer a range of languages to all students.

* **Does the university have a specialism?** Some universities offer a more focused range of subjects such as London (Courtauld) which offers the History of Art, the University of London Institute in Paris which offers French Studies, London (School of Pharmacy) which offers Pharmacy, London (Royal Veterinary College) which offers Veterinary Studies and London (Heythrop) which offers courses specialising in Theology, Philosophy and Psychology. If you want to study a specialist course it is worth looking at institutions which are dedicated to the subject area.

* **Will I need to pay for resources or activities on top of the fees?** Most courses will require students to purchase core textbooks – check to see if you can get hold of them second hand or if they are available in the library to save money. If you are studying a design course you will often have to pay for your own materials – make sure you can budget for this expense. Field trips or visits will usually incur extra charges; ask the department if there are many field trips and if so how much they usually charge. Theatre or Drama courses may require students to attend the theatre on a regular basis but many theatres offer discount rates to students and group bookings.

VISITING UNIVERSITIES

There's only so much internet research and prospectuses can tell you. Once you've shortlisted a few universities it's important to visit them to see if they live up to, or fall short of, your expectations. Universities offer open days throughout the year and some even offer taster days where potential students can take part in lectures and student life. It's useful to visit more than one university, even if you are sure of your choice, so that you can compare what's on offer. Make sure you get a chance to look at the facilities and the accommodation.

Bear in mind the points above while looking around the institution and see how the atmosphere suits you.

If you have time, explore the local area – can you imagine yourself living and learning there for the next few years?

Questions to ask students and staff at an open day or interview

It's useful to hear directly about other people's experiences of the course and university you are interested in. Whilst visiting the university feel free to ask questions about the course, the facilities and student life.

You could ask about:

* *New students*
  Are there induction courses for new students?
  Are students advised on study skills and time management?
  What student services are available?
  What advice and help can the Students' Union offer?
  Is it possible to purchase second-hand set books?

* *The facilities in the department*
  In science departments, is the equipment 'state of the art' or just adequate?
  Do students have to pay for materials?
  Are the libraries well stocked? Are they open all hours?
  Are there plenty of places for private study or do rooms and work places become overcrowded?

* *The teaching staff*
  What is the quality of the teaching?
  Do the staff have flair and enthusiasm for their subject?
  What are their research interests?
  Are they approachable?
  Do they mark the work? How often? Is the feedback helpful?

* *The teaching style*
  How will you be taught, e.g. lectures, seminars, tutorials?
  What types of assessments are used?
  Are examinations seen or unseen?
  Are there good computer facilities?
  Are computer-assisted packages used in teaching?
  Are you taught how to use the computer facilities?
  How much will you be expected to work on your own?
  Will you be expected to attend field courses? If so, do you have to pay towards them?

* *Transferable skills*
  Does the department provide training and experience in communication skills, teamwork exercises, time management and information technology? (All these are regarded as important skills by employers irrespective of the subject you are studying.)

* *Accommodation*
  Which types of accommodation does the university offer?
  Which types are the most popular?

What are the costs?
Which are the best halls of residence?
Is transport provided from the halls of residence to the university?

＊ *Finance*
Does the university permit students to take part-time employment?
Are students assisted in finding part-time employment?
Are scholarships or other awards offered by the university or the department?
What are the best ways of saving money?
Do firms sponsor students on the course?

＊ *Sandwich courses*
Will the department organise your work placement or are you expected to find your own firm?
Are the placements good?
Do they count towards your degree assessment?
Can the staff advise on sponsorships?
When you are on a sandwich placement will the staff keep in touch with you to advise you or
   will they visit you?

As you may have noticed there is a lot to consider and the decisions on where to go and what to study
are inextricable. **Part 2** covers the major subject areas and gives you a taster of what each university
offers for that course.

Part 2

5 | COURSE PROFILES

USING THE PROFILES

This chapter aims to give you a 'taster' of what is on offer in a whole range of major subject areas. Each subject table provides a profile of the course or courses available in that subject area at each university, thus enabling you to note the main differences between courses and the range available in that subject area. Information in each subject entry will give you an overview of the range of topics on offer.

You will also notice that in most subject areas many universities cover similar topics in the first year of a course. However, in Years 2 and 3 the range of different topics that you can choose might differ considerably, so watch out for the options.

When reading through the subject tables you should note that the information given under **Subject requirements/preferences** is provided as a general guide only to the GCE A level and GCSE subjects that are normally required or preferred by the universities. However, each admissions tutor makes his or her own value judgement on each applicant and might be prepared to waive the need for preferred subjects or specific grades, depending on individual circumstances. Always check the prospectuses and websites before applying and if you are not sure that you will be able to meet course requirements or preferences, contact the university.

A level applicants should also note that offers for university places may include a preference or requirement for a GCE A level subject, in some cases at a specific grade. Contact the university department and website and also refer to *Heap 2015: University Degree Course Offers* (also published by Trotman Publishing, see the Booklist in Appendix 2), the companion book to *Choosing Your Degree Course & University*.

Many of the vocational courses available (for example, Accountancy, Architecture, Engineering and Surveying) will give exemptions from professional body examinations. These exemptions will vary, depending on the course and modules taken. Contact the university department for details of the professional body requirements and possible exemptions given for successful completion of the course. Also, you could write to the professional bodies themselves (again, see *Heap 2015: University Degree Course Offers* for contact details).

Many hundreds of subjects are offered by universities and, as described in here, these are organised in such a way as to produce many thousands of course combinations. Because of this, it is not possible to include all degree courses in this book, but the course profiles in this chapter give an insight into the range of subject combinations that institutions provide for students.

It is important also to recognise that universities frequently make changes to their courses and course titles each year and some courses are abandoned and new ones introduced. **It is therefore essential that you consult up-to-date prospectuses and websites before making your final decisions of course and university.** Remember, about 20% of students drop out of degree courses in their first year, many in their first term, simply because the course is not what they expected. Therefore you need to find out as much as possible from as many sources of information as you can find, so that you know **exactly** what your chosen courses involve – including any professional body accreditation – and the careers to which they might lead.

ABBREVIATIONS USED IN THE COURSE PROFILES

AAT	Association of Accounting Technicians
CABE	Chartered Association of Building Engineers
ACCA	Association of Chartered Certified Accountants
Am Int Univ	American International University
BPS	British Psychological Society
BusColl	Business College
CA	College of Art(s)
CAD	College of Art and Design
CAFRE	College of Agriculture, Food and Rural Enterprise (Northern Ireland)
CAg	College of Agriculture
CAT	College of Advanced Technology or Arts and Technology
CIAT	Chartered Institute of Architectural Technologists
CITB	Construction Industry Training Board
CII	Chartered Insurance Institute
CIM	Chartered Institute of Marketing
CIMA	Chartered Institute of Management Accountants
CIOB	Chartered Institute of Building
CIOT	Chartered Institute of Taxation
CMI	Chartered Management Institute
CmC	Community College
CMus	College of Music
CMusDr	College of Music and Drama
Coll	College
CT	College of Technology
DAS	Diploma in Area Studies
DIS	Diploma in Industrial Studies
GIS	Geographic information system
ICAEW	Institute of Chartered Accountants in England and Wales
IFHE	Institute of Further and Higher Education
IHE	Institute of Higher Education
Inst	Institute
King's	King's College (London University)
LIPA	Liverpool Institute of Performing Arts
LLB	Bachelor of Laws
LSE	London School of Economics and Political Science
NCH	New College of the Humanities
Nescot	North East Surrey College of Technology
PPE	Philosophy, Politics and Economics
QM	Queen Mary (London University)
QTS	Qualified Teacher Status
RAc Dance	Royal Academy of Dance
RAcMus	Royal Academy of Music
RCMus	Royal College of Music
RConsvS	Royal Conservatoire of Scotland
RegColl	Regional College
RH	Royal Holloway (London University)
RICS	Royal Institution of Chartered Surveyors
RNCM	Royal Northern College of Music
RSC	Royal Society of Chemistry
RVC	Royal Veterinary College (London University)
SA	School of Art
SchSpDr	School of Speech and Drama
SOAS	School of Oriental and African Studies (London University)

SRUC	Scotland's Rural College
TC	Technical College
UC	University College
UCA	University College of the Arts
UCL	University College London
Univ	University

ACCOUNTANCY/ACCOUNTING

(see also **Finance**)

(* indicates universities with entry requirements over 340 UCAS points)

SUBJECT REQUIREMENTS/PREFERENCES

GCE A level: Mathematics preferred at some universities. **GCSE:** Mathematics essential for all courses.

SUBJECT INFORMATION

All courses offer financial management and accountancy training. Accountancy courses are not necessarily intended just for those wishing to become accountants since they provide an excellent training for any career in business. Students should note that a degree in Accountancy or Accounting is not the only method of qualifying as an accountant. Applicants should note that in addition to degree courses many institutions offer foundation courses that provide opportunities to move directly into degree courses.

Most Accountancy courses will give graduates exemptions from the examinations of the various professional accounting bodies. Applicants should check with universities before applying since these examinations are essential for those wishing to qualify as accountants in various specialist fields.

QUESTIONS TO CONSIDER

* Am I looking for a purely vocational course, or do I want to study accountancy in a wider social and theoretical context?
* I want to undertake a professional placement; what does the course offer? Will I need any additional qualifications, such as a foreign language for overseas placements?
* Can I take an alternative to a sandwich-year placement, such as setting up my own entrepreneurial business, or working with local organisations on a weekly basis?
* Areas studied can vary widely, from management and marketing to forensic accounting and government finance – what is it that interests me about accountancy?

Aberdeen Accountancy at Levels 1 to 4 focuses on financial and management accounting and covers the practice of accountancy in modern society, financial reporting, management accountancy and taxation.

Abertay No first year entry, applications are made through the Finance and Business or Business Studies and Finance courses with the Accountancy course commencing in Year 2. This is a broad vocational degree in Accounting. The course includes information technology, industrial studies and the opportunity to continue (or begin) a language (French, German or Spanish). Specialisms follow in Year 3.

Aberystwyth The scheme in Accounting and Finance covers finance, financial accounting, management accounting and information systems. Special interests in such subjects as auditing, financial strategy and taxation are offered in Years 2 and 3. There is also a degree in Business Finance. Several joint Accounting schemes are available with subjects such as Law, Economics, a European language, Computer Science and Mathematics and with major/minor options. A voluntary year in employment is offered between Years 2 and 3.

Anglia Ruskin A degree course in Accounting and Finance is offered with key topics in management accounting and corporate finance. There is also a degree course in International Finance Markets. It is possible to commence this course in February.

Aston* The Accounting for Management course (with exemptions from some examinations of professional bodies) focuses on the crucial role that financial information plays in management decision-making and in the monitoring and planning of a business organisation's activities. A compulsory professional placement year is available.

See *Heap 2015: University Degree Course Offers* (Trotman Publishing) for details of offers

Bangor The ACCA-accredited Accounting and Finance course offers training in accounting skills with an emphasis on financial theory and decision-making techniques, providing integration with marketing, economics and banking disciplines. There is an option to change to any other business degree up to the start of Year 2. There are also courses in Banking and Finance which include management and marketing topics and Management with Accountancy.

Bath* The three- or four-year Accounting and Finance course is a specialist programme for those aiming for a career in the field of accounting and finance. Economics, law, IT and people and organisations are some of the topics included. The course includes a one-year industrial placement with the opportunity to study abroad.

Bedfordshire The Accounting course is a vocational programme specially designed for the training of accountants. It is also offered as part of the modular credit scheme on a major, joint or minor programme. Accounting is also offered with Management. A BSc in Accounting and Finance is also available.

Birmingham* The Accounting and Finance degree emphasises the study of accounting and finance throughout the three years of the course. The course includes business skills, development, computing, economics, industrial relations, law, information technology and marketing. Also check out Money, Banking and Finance. There is a four year 'package' which includes a degree course, a professional accountancy qualification and work experience with KPMG plus all tuition fees and student accommodation costs paid by KPMG.

Birmingham City Students on the Accountancy course take core subjects in each year in addition to project work, with an option to take a 12-month placement after Year 2. Core subjects in the Accountancy course include law, computer studies, financial management and taxation, with options in the second and third years in organisational behaviour, international and management accounting and languages. Courses in Accountancy and Business and Accountancy and Finance are also offered. See also **Finance**.

Bolton The course in Accountancy covers financial and management accountancy and has a strong vocational emphasis and may be taken by way of full or part-time studies. A semester in Europe or Dubai may be available.

Bournemouth Financial and management accounting are covered in each year of the Accounting and Finance course, with options commencing in Year 2 that include taxation, money markets and vocational language studies. Accounting can also be taken with Economics, Law or Taxation. There is also a Finance and Business degree with an optional 40-week placement.

Bradford Accounting and Finance can include a one-year work placement. Students follow the same programme as that of the Business and Management Studies degree in Year 1. Specialisms begin in Year 2.

Brighton Accounting and Finance is a three-year full-time or four-year sandwich course. Year 1 includes financial and management accountancy, law and economics. Years 2 and 3 are divided into two semesters and develop the accountancy and management themes with specialist options such as human resources management, marketing and small business development. There is also a course in Finance and Investment. See also **Finance.**

Bristol* Accounting is offered with Finance and Management, and with opportunities to study in continental Europe.

Bristol UWE Accounting and Finance is a vocational course (three-year or four-year sandwich alternative) and provides a sound basis for careers in other fields of management. The first-year course includes electives from a wide range of subjects, with a range of options available in the third year including business languages.

Brunel Accounting is offered as part of the Business and Management programme with modules in auditing and taxation, with the option of a one-year professional placement. There is also a course in Finance and Accounting.

Buckingham Accounting and Financial Management is a two-year course (starting in January or September). It also provides options in accounting and financial management, economics and insurance. This leads to more advanced studies, granting exemptions from foundation examinations of all the leading accountancy bodies. Tutorial groups are small – not exceeding eight students. Accounting is also available with Economics, Communication Studies, French and Spanish, and there is also a degree in Financial Services.

Bucks New This practical course in Accountancy and Finance provides significant exemptions from the examination requirements of professional accountancy bodies.

Canterbury Christ Church The Accounting and Finance degree provides a general knowledge of management with a specialised knowledge of accounting. Accounting can also be taken with either Business or Marketing.

Cardiff* The Accounting course covers all aspects of accountancy and also provides supporting courses in relevant areas of financial and management accountancy, economics, business studies and law. Also offered with a European language and overseas placement in Year 3. It is possible to have a year in industry with the Accountancy and Finance degree. Accounting is also available in the BSc Economics joint honours course, and there is also a course in Banking and Finance.

Cardiff Met (UWIC) All aspects of Accounting are covered in the BA degrees with a work placement possible in the Accountancy and Finance programme. Options are available in European law, taxation, auditing and investment management.

Central Lancashire The Accounting course focuses on a study of the current practice, problems and developments in accounting and the practical applications of computers. Distinguishing features of the course include an integrated approach to the teaching of computing, an information technology course in Year 2, a case study approach to the teaching of law, with simulated meetings, and a choice of options in Year 3. Accounting is also offered with Economics, Business and Financial Studies.

Chester The Accountancy course attracts partial exemptions from the main professional bodies' exams and is also offered as part of the combined honours degree. A one-year paid work placement is also available.

Chichester There is a practical and vocational focus to the Accountancy degree preparing students for a career in financial management.

City* Several courses are offered with a financial bias, including Economics with Accounting, Accounting and Finance, Actuarial Science, Banking and International Finance, and Investment and Financial Risk Management. Optional placement years are possible on most of the courses.

Coventry Accounting covers several business subjects in Year 1 with specialist subjects following in Years 2 and 3 and an optional year's work experience. Joint courses are also offered including Management and Professional Accounting, Accounting and Finance, and International Finance and Accounting.

De Montfort Accounting and Finance is offered as a vocational or non-vocational subject which can be studied with Business Management and Economics. Finance is also offered as a joint honours course.

Derby Accounting and Finance is offered as a single honours course and with a year in industry. A joint honours programme is also offered.

Dundee Three- and four-year degrees are offered accredited by UK accountancy bodies. Specialisms include business finance, management information systems, languages, management or accountancy. Applied Computing, Management, languages and Mathematics can also be combined with Accountancy. A course in Finance is also available. The BSc course includes two science courses in Years 1 and 2 and three courses in Year 3.

See *Heap 2015: University Degree Course Offers* (Trotman Publishing) for details of offers

Durham* The degrees in Accounting and Finance, Business and Finance and Business share a common first year with the option to transfer at the end of Year 1. The four-year degree in Accounting leads to exemptions from some professional bodies' exams and offers a placement with KPMG in Years 1 to 3. A course in Accountancy and Management is also offered.

East Anglia The Accounting and Finance degree combines the traditional approach to accountancy with a focus on computing and management control. Core subjects are taken in Years 2 and 3; in Year 3 students choose from a wide range of options. There are also courses combining Accounting with Management, and Economics with Accountancy course. There is also a course in Actuarial Science which can include a year in industry.

East London Accounting and Finance is a three-year course that provides a business education covering law, management accountancy, taxation, computing and insurance finance. Information Technology, Law, and Business Studies are offered with Accounting on the combined honours programme. There is also a degree in Finance.

Edinburgh* A very flexible course in which Accountancy can also be taken with Business, Finance, Economics or Law.

Edinburgh Napier The Accounting degree is focused on training students for the profession. Information technology, financial management, taxation and law are important components of the course. There are also joint courses with Economics, Finance, Law and Marketing.

Essex The Accounting course focuses on financial or management accountancy. Optional courses are offered in Year 3.

Exeter* The Accounting and Finance single honours course has a vocational emphasis, and can also be studied as a four-year course with work placement or international study options. Economics and Mathematics are also offered with Accounting. Work experience can be arranged through leading accountants.

Glasgow* The four-year BAcc degrees in Accountancy or Accountancy with Finance or Mathematics and Statistics all lead to professional recognition.

Glasgow Caledonian The Accountancy course has options in Financial or Management Accountancy taken in Year 4. Joint courses are also offered with Economics, Law and Management. There is also a degree in Financial Services covering all aspects of finance operations in the business field.

Gloucestershire The degree in Accounting and Financial Management gives some exemptions from the ACCA and the CIMA professional examinations and offers students an optional one-year paid work placement. Business Management can also be taken with Accountancy.

Glyndŵr A Business Accounting course is offered with the option to choose an alternative degree at the end of Year 1.

Greenwich There are courses in Finance, Accounting and Finance and Accounting and Financial Information Systems. It is possible to transfer between courses at the end of Year 1.

Heriot-Watt A four-year course is offered in Accountancy and Finance. Accountancy is also offered as a joint course with Business Law. There are opportunities to study abroad and take a modern languages unit on both courses.

Hertfordshire The degree in Accounting and Finance can include study abroad or on a work placement. The course can be studied alongside a range of business and language subjects. There is also a separate degree in Finance.

Huddersfield The first-year course in Accountancy and Finance focuses on basic accounting, business law, financial and management accountancy. In the second and third years there is an emphasis on the use of financial information in business planning, control and decision-making, insolvency and employee relations. Courses in Accountancy and/with Financial Services Information Systems and Law are also available.

See *Heap 2015: University Degree Course Offers* (Trotman Publishing) for details of offers

Hull Twelve courses are offered, three with an international bias and one with professional experience. In the first year, students take compulsory courses in academic and professional skills, business economics, managing people, accounting and finance, and marketing, plus a sixth choice selected from a range of options. Financial accounting, management accounting and the principles of economics are taken in the second year. The course emphasis is on finance, accounting and computing. The course in International Accounting involves Year 3 being spent abroad. Accounting can also be studied with Business Economics, Financial Management and Marketing, with each course offering a period of professional experience.

Keele Thirty-one dual honours degree courses in Accountancy are offered and there are dual honours degrees in Finance. A degree in Accounting and Finance with Computing is also offered. A single honours degree in Accounting and Finance with options in banking and economic forecasting is available.

Kent In addition to the single honours degree in Accounting and Finance (with the option of a year in industry) a degree in Accounting and Finance and Economics is also offered. An important feature of the School of Business is the option of a year in industry as part of the course.

Kingston The Accounting and Finance course provides an in-depth study of accounting and financial management including company law, accounting and revenue law and taxation. The core subject in Year 1 is legal and financial strategy. Option choices include marketing, languages, international accountancy and computer systems. An optional year in industry is available.

Lancaster* The BA/BSc course in Accounting and Finance is intended for accounting specialists. Other courses focus on auditing, finance and management. There is also a broad study of finance.

Leeds* The Accounting and Finance course covers the main aspects of financial and management accounting, economics, taxation and business finance. The option of spending a year either in industry or studying abroad is available.

Leeds Beckett The degree in Accounting and Finance is a three-year full-time degree that provides an academic foundation for a career in accounting or finance in either public or private sector organisations.

Leeds Trinity Courses are offered in Accountancy and Accountancy and Business. There are options to focus on accountancy or management.

Lincoln Accountancy is studied as a single subject or can also be studied as a joint degree in combination with Advertising, Management, Marketing, Business, Human Resources Management or Finance.

Liverpool* The Accounting degree is both a theoretical and practical course covering micro- and macro-economics, mathematics, statistics, financial reporting, management accounting and options from accounting, business and economics modules. There is a joint course in Accounting and Computer Science. Options for studying abroad or a year in industry.

Liverpool Hope The course is geared to the professional qualifications of the Association of Certified and Corporate Accountants.

Liverpool John Moores The course in Accounting and Finance, which can include a year's sandwich placement, concentrates on financial and management accountancy. Students choose from a wide range of options in Years 2 and 3.

London (King's) See under **Business**.

London (RH)* Accounting is offered with either Management or Finance and Economics.

London LSE* The Accounting and Finance course covers both managerial and financial accountancy. Other subjects such as anthropology, geography, history and psychology can be taken in Years 1, 2 and 3 in place of an accounting option. There is also a course in Actuarial Science.

See *Heap 2015: University Degree Course Offers* (Trotman Publishing) for details of offers

London Met The Accounting and Finance course is biased towards the qualitative aspects of economic and business analysis and decision-making. There are over 20 joint courses with Accounting. See also **Finance**.

London South Bank The Accounting and Finance course covers financial and management accounting, law, economics, auditing, taxation and financial institutions. The course is accredited by the ACCA.

Loughborough* Accounting and Financial Management is a four-year sandwich course that provides a broad educational base for a career in management. Various aspects of management are studied in depth. Economics and Mathematics are also offered with Accounting and there is a well-established course in Banking, Finance and Management.

Manchester* In the BA (Econ) degree it is possible to specialise in Accounting or in Finance or in both areas. There are also degrees in Accounting and Finance Management, and Economics and Finance.

Manchester Met Accounting and Finance is a three-year full-time or four-year sandwich course with an emphasis on management accountancy and options in banking and insurance. There is also a course in Accounting Information Systems.

Middlesex Full-time and sandwich courses in Accounting and Finance can be taken, whilst Accounting can also be studied with Business Management. There is also a Business Accounting degree.

Newcastle Economics and law are included in the first-year Accounting and Finance course with additional options in the second and third years. Accounting can be studied with Mathematics. There is also a degree course in Business Accounting and Finance with paid work placements.

Northampton In addition to the degree in Accounting and Finance, several joint courses with Accounting are offered, all on a three-year full-time basis.

Northumbria This is a three-year full-time Accounting course with a comprehensive overview of business operations leading to professional accreditation opportunities. There is also a course in Finance and Investment Management.

Nottingham* A degree in Finance, Accounting and Management provides a broad introduction to the world of finance, while a more specialised focus on finance is offered in the Industrial Economics with Insurance degree.

Nottingham Trent Accounting and Finance is offered as a three-year full-time or four-year sandwich course with industrial placement in Year 3. There is also a course in Accounting and Information Systems.

Oxford Brookes Several subjects are offered with Accounting and Finance in the modular programme. There is an optional placement in Year 3. The course is ACCA-accredited.

Plymouth The Accounting and Finance course provides a broad overview of business, a detailed study of the accounting function and an understanding of business information systems. Language studies are offered, and a year-long paid placement or the opportunity to work with local organisations is available.

Portsmouth Courses are available in Accounting with Finance, Business, or Financial Management.

Queen's Belfast* The degree in Accounting is intended to provide an academic education in accounting and an introduction to professional studies. The course includes specialisms in Financial Accounting, Management Accounting and Taxation and Finance. Accounting is also offered with French, German or Spanish and there is a degree in Finance, and in Actuarial Studies.

Reading* Accounting is offered with Economics, Business, Finance or Management. There are also courses in International Securities, Investment and Banking, and Investment and Finance in Property.

See *Heap 2015: University Degree Course Offers* (Trotman Publishing) for details of offers

Robert Gordon The Accounting and Finance degree is a four-year course with a 12-month paid placement. The degree is accredited by professional accountancy bodies.

Salford The degree in Finance and Accounting has a bias towards management and financial accounting with the option of an industrial placement. It sends a good proportion of its graduates into industry in addition to the more usual destination of the chartered profession. There are also degrees in Business Finance and in Property Management and Investment.

Sheffield First-year students following the Accounting and Financial Management course take an introductory course with two other subjects and a course in statistical methods. In the second and third years students take a number of core courses, some of which are options. Managerial analysis is studied in the third year by students working in groups. Accountancy, Finance and Management is also offered with Economics, Informatics and Mathematics.

Sheffield Hallam Accounting and Finance is a vocational course which is offered as a three-year full-time or four-year sandwich course with an optional placement in Year 3. Courses in Forensic Accounting, and International Finance and Banking Investment, or Economics are also available.

South Wales Accounting can be studied as a singe subject or jointly with Business, Economics, Maths and Finance. There are also courses available in Forensic Accounting and Finance. There is the opportunity to spend a year in a commercial or industrial placement. The ACCA Platinum-accredited Accounting programme is part of the Newport Business School, enabling students to transfer to the MSc in Accounting on completion.

Southampton* Accounting is offered with Economics, Finance and Management Sciences. Scholarships are offered for Actuarial Studies.

Southampton Solent Accountancy graduates may claim exemptions from the later stages of professional examinations for management and corporate accountants. There are also degrees in Finance.

Staffordshire Accounting and Business can be chosen in Year 2 after a common first year with other Business courses. In addition, there are courses in Accounting with Information Systems, Business and Economics.

Stirling The BAcc Accountancy course includes units of economics and business law and covers all the relevant aspects, giving exemptions from all the professional accountancy bodies' examinations. Ten Accountancy combined honours degrees are also available including Accountancy with Business Law, Management Science, Languages and Mathematics.

Strathclyde* In the Business with Accounting degree, financial accounting and finance are taken in Years 1 and 2 followed by options in business law, economics, finance, human resource management, law, management science, marketing or tourism. Accounting is also offered jointly with over 10 other subjects including languages and international business.

Sunderland A three-year course in Public Relations and Accountancy is on offer. A one-year top-up degree in Accounting and Financial Management is also available.

Surrey The Accounting and Financial Management degree leads to qualification in Management Accountancy. The degree offers a sandwich placement in industry or commerce.

Sussex Accountancy and Finance is offered with a one-year industrial placement.

Swansea Accounting is offered with Business Studies or Management Science.

Teesside Accounting and Finance is part of the modular Business scheme in which students take eight subjects (common to all Business degrees) and progress to their special degree subject in Years 2 and 3. A degree in Accounting can also be studied with Law, and there is also a unique course in Finance, Accounting and Cybercrime.

See *Heap 2015*: *University Degree Course Offers* (Trotman Publishing) for details of offers

Trinity St David (Swansea) The Accountancy course gives a number of exemptions from the professional chartered accountancy bodies' exams. There is also a course specialising in Business Finance.

Ulster* The Accounting course provides a firm foundation in accounting and other related subjects. It is recognised by the professional accountancy bodies and exemptions are gained from their examinations. Final-year options include auditing and financial management and two from business policy, information systems management, public sector accounting and economics or finance. Combined courses are also offered.

Warwick* The first year of the Accounting and Finance degree is largely common with the Management Sciences course and provides a broad base for the study of accountancy. A choice of four specialist subjects is made in Year 3 from a list of financial options and includes a choice of one non-finance subject. The university has one of the largest business schools in the UK.

West London A course in Accounting and Finance is offered with modules in management accounting and taxation. Courses commence in both September and February.

West Scotland Accounting can be taken as a three-year or four-year course, with the option of a year-long paid placement between Years 2 and 3 of the course. There are also courses in Business Accounting and Business Information Technology with Accounting.

Westminster A course is offered in Accounting with Management with an optional sandwich placement or the chance to study abroad. Business Management courses specialising in accounting and economics are also available.

Wolverhampton Accounting is offered as a specialist route in a combined studies degree and can also be studied as a single honours course. It is also offered with Law, Marketing and Computing. There is also a three-year full-time or a four-year sandwich degree in Accounting and Finance.

Worcester See under **Business**.

York* A course is offered in Accounting, Business Finance and Management with an optional year in industry.

OTHER INSTITUTIONS OFFERING ACCOUNTANCY/ACOUNTING COURSES

Blackburn (Coll), Blackpool and Fylde (Coll), Bradford (Coll Univ Centre), Croydon (Coll), Duchy (Coll), Highbury Portsmouth (Coll), Kaplan Holborn (Coll), Kensington Bus (Coll), Northbrook (Coll), Norwich City (Coll), Somerset (Coll), West Cheshire (Coll), Westminster Kingsway (Coll), Wirral Met (Coll).

ALTERNATIVE COURSES

Actuarial Studies, Applied Mathematics, Banking, Business Studies, Economics, Finance, Mathematics, Statistics.

ACTUARIAL SCIENCE/STUDIES

(* indicates universities with entry requirements over 340 UCAS points)

SUBJECT REQUIREMENTS/PREFERENCES

GCE A level: Mathematics and one other subject. **GCSE:** Most institutions will require grade A or B Mathematics.

SUBJECT INFORMATION

Actuaries are reputed to have one of the highest paid careers in finance, and so naturally Actuarial Science courses attract a large number of applicants! Training as an actuary, however, is extremely demanding and must not be underestimated. An alternative route for actuarial work would be a Mathematics degree course. See also **Accountancy/Accounting** and **Finance**.

Courses usually offer full exemptions from some of the examinations of the Institute and Faculty of Actuaries that lead to professional qualifications.

City* The Actuarial Science course, which includes a foundation year, covers subjects such as actuarial science, mathematics, statistics, economics and accounting. There are study placements in Canada and with firms in the UK.

East Anglia* The three-year programme on Actuarial Science is designed for those wishing to enter the profession and covers computing, mathematics and business.

Heriot-Watt* Actuarial Science covers real-life office procedures, pension funds and risk theory. The course provides a sound grounding in mathematics, probability, statistics and actuarial mathematics. A small number of students study abroad or take an industrial placement for one year.

Kent* A strong mathematical background is required for the Actuarial Science course, which covers economics, computing, probability and inference, mortality, operational research and life contingencies. There is an optional year in industry.

Kingston Courses are offered in Actuarial Science and Actuarial Mathematics and Statistics. Optional industrial and professional placements are available on both courses.

Leeds* The course in Actuarial Mathematics covers significant content of The Actuarial Profession's core technical subjects and graduation from the course offers exemption from some of the Institute of Actuaries examinations.

London LSE* The Actuarial Science course covers statistics, mathematical methods, investigations and life contingencies. Options are offered in statistics, mathematics, economics, sociology, social psychology and population studies.

Manchester* A course is offered in Actuarial Science and Mathematics, and is accredited by the Institute of Actuaries.

Queen's Belfast* The four-year Actuarial Science and Risk Management programme combines courses in actuarial modelling, financial reporting, insurance, pensions, economics and financial mathematics, with a year on an industrial placement.

Southampton* The Actuarial Studies course (with either Economics or Mathematics) provides the opportunity to study French, German or Spanish.

ALTERNATIVE COURSES

Accountancy, Applied Mathematics, Banking, Business Studies, Economics, Financial Services, Insurance, Mathematics, Statistics.

AFRICAN STUDIES

(*indicates universities with entry requirements over 340 UCAS points)

SUBJECT REQUIREMENTS/PREFERENCES
GCE A level: Languages at grade A or B might be required. **GCSE:** English, Mathematics (grades A–C).

SUBJECT INFORMATION
African Studies can involve geography, history, popular culture, political science and sociology.

Birmingham African Studies can be taken as a joint honours degree with seven subjects or as major/minor courses with Anthropology or Development. The course combines perspectives from the history, cultures, environments and societies relating to the African subcontinent. An optional fieldwork trip to Ghana occupies one month during a summer vacation.

London (SOAS)* There are different approaches offered in the African Studies course by way of geographical region or its language and culture – Amharic (Ethiopia), Hausa (Nigeria), Somali (Eastern Horn of African), Swahili (East Africa), Yoruba (Nigeria) and Zulu (South Africa). In each case the language is supported by studies covering social anthropology, history, law, linguistics, art and archaeology. There are also joint courses available with Management, Geography, Law and Politics. A BA in African Language and Culture is also available.

London (UCL)* An African language can be studied with French.

ALTERNATIVE COURSES
Anthropology, International Relations, Politics.

AGRICULTURAL SCIENCES/AGRICULTURE

(including **Landscape Design**)
(* indicates universities with entry requirements over 340 UCAS points)

SUBJECT REQUIREMENTS/PREFERENCES
GCE A level: Science subjects required. **GCSE:** English and Mathematics usually required. Practical experience may be required.

SUBJECT INFORMATION
Agriculture is a wide-ranging subject covering practical farming, animal and crop science, biochemistry, bacteriology, food production and aspects of biology; other aspects include business studies and countryside management.

Aberystwyth A four-year course in Agriculture is offered with work experience in Year 2. From a base of crop science and production, and animal science and production, this modular course introduces farm business, management, marketing and crop and animal production in Years 3 and 4. The Welsh Institute of Rural Studies also offers degrees in Countryside Management, Conservation and Recreation, Animal

Science, Plant Biology and Agriculture with Marketing and with Business and Management. Scholarships are available. A two-year foundation degree in Agriculture is also offered.

Bangor The degree in Agriculture, Conservation and Environment is a broad programme covering ecological and social aspects of land use. The focus is mainly agricultural with modules in soil and plant environments, livestock, grassland and crop production supported by wildlife conservation and environmental planning.

Derby The Countryside Management course covers rural studies, landscape conservation and countryside management.

East Anglia Development Studies is a very broad subject touching on topics such as agricultural production systems, environmental management and planning, resource development and conservation, natural resources, economics, sociology and politics. The focus extends to world problems. Courses in Conservation and Biodiversity and Landscape Design, Conservation and Plant Biology are also available.

Glasgow Courses are offered in conjunction with the Scottish Agricultural College at Auchincruive, Ayrshire. These include a Bachelor of Technology course in Agriculture, Countryside Management, Rural Tourism and Horticulture. See also **Biology**.

Gloucestershire The Garden Design course covers plant sciences and horticulture, the design of formal and informal gardens, and the history of landscapes. There is also a course in Landscape Management and Landscape Architecture.

Greenwich Courses are offered in Garden Design, International Agriculture and Medicinal and Commercial Horticulture.

Harper Adams (UC) Many agricultural courses are offered covering animal science, marketing and crop, farm and environmental management.

Kent A course is offered in Wildlife Conservation.

Kingston A course is offered in Landscape Architecture.

Leeds Beckett A BA in Landscape Architecture and Design can be studied.

Manchester Met Courses are offered in Sustainable Development and Landscape Architecture.

Newcastle* The wide range of Agriculture courses on offer includes Agriculture, Agronomy, Animal Production Science, Countryside Management, Rural Resource Management, Farm Business Management, Rural Studies and Organic Food Production. Many of these subjects are degree options at the end of the Deferred Choice degree (D400).

Northampton Land Management and a two-year FdSc in Horticulture and Garden Design are available.

Nottingham Pre-university practical experience desirable. Courses are offered in Agriculture with Crop Science, Environmental Science or Livestock Science which are either three-year degrees or four-year courses with European Studies involving a European year out between Years 2 and 3. These courses came top in a survey of student satisfaction. Animal Science and Crop Science can also be studied as a three-year degree or as four-year course with European Studies.

Nottingham Trent A course is offered in Conservation and Countryside Management covering rural skills, ecology, planning, leisure and business management. A degree course in Horticulture is also offered.

Plymouth The Applied Bioscience programme has pathways in agriculture and environment, agriculture, food and nutrition, and plant sciences.

Queen's Belfast The new School of Agriculture and Food offers three degree courses: Food Quality, Safety and Nutrition covers diet, health and management; Land Use and Environmental Management includes biology, geography, economics and law; Agricultural Technology focuses on animal husbandry and crop production.

See *Heap 2015: University Degree Course Offers* (Trotman Publishing) for details of offers

Reading The Agriculture course is divided into three parts: Part I (two terms) includes agriculture, crop production, animal production, plant and soil science and agricultural economics; Part II (three terms) includes crop physiology, crop protection, plant breeding and animal breeding; Part III (four terms) offers a choice of one of 12 options. Other courses offered include Agricultural Business Management, Horticulture and Landscape, Rural Resources Management and Botany.

Royal Agricultural Univ Agriculture courses offered with a focus on specialised studies including Livestock, Crops, Farm Management, Agricultural Science, Soil Management or Farm Mechanical Management.

Stirling Courses are available in Conservation Management and Land Resources.

Strathclyde Degree courses are offered in Landscape and Garden Design.

Worcester The Horticulture BSc leads to specialisation in either Amenity and Landscape Management or in Crop Production.

OTHER INSTITUTIONS OFFERING AGRICULTURAL SCIENCES/AGRICULTURE COURSES
Askham Bryan (Coll), CAFRE, Duchy (Coll), Kirklees (Coll), Myerscough (Coll), Sparsholt (Coll), SRUC, UHI, West Anglia (Coll), Writtle (Coll).

ALTERNATIVE COURSES
Animal Sciences, Biochemistry, Biological Sciences, Biology, Botany, Chemistry, Conservation Management, Crop Science, Ecology, Environmental Sciences, Estate Management, Food Science and Technology, Forestry, Geography, Horticulture, Land Surveying, Plant Sciences, Veterinary Science, Zoology.

AMERICAN STUDIES

(including **Latin American Studies**)
(* indicates universities with entry requirements over 340 UCAS points)

SUBJECT REQUIREMENTS/PREFERENCES
GCE A level: English and/or History may be required. **GCSE:** Grades A–C English, a foreign language, Mathematics and science may be required.

SUBJECT INFORMATION
American literature and history represent the core of most courses, with the option of a year spent in the US. Not all courses require a year to be spent in North America.

Aberdeen The course in Hispanic Studies gives equal weight to Spanish and Latin American culture. The third year is spent in a Spanish-speaking country.

Birmingham The three- or four-year American and Canadian Studies course consists of specialist studies in American history, literature and politics, and Canadian Studies. In the four-year course, Year 3 is spent in the US or Canada. The subject can also be taken as a joint honours or major/minor course.

Bristol A four-year BA in Hispanic Studies is available, with a year spent on overseas placement.

Canterbury Christ Church American Studies is offered with a study of either Canada, the US or Latin America, or of all three. There are also courses focusing on American studies in the context of History and Politics, Film and Art, and Geography and Anthropology.

Central Lancashire American Studies is a three-year course with the opportunity to study in the US. Literature, history, film, music, architecture and popular culture are studied.

Derby American Studies is offered as an honours degree or in the Credit Accumulation Modular Scheme, covering film, literature, music and history, with a semester in the US. Joint honours degrees with one or two other subjects are also available.

East Anglia The preliminary programme in American and English Literature (two terms) covers literature, history and philosophy or linguistics plus options. The final honours programme is chosen at the end of the second term from a wide choice of subjects covering English and American literature, history, drama, film studies, linguistics and philosophy. In the American Studies course, emphasis is on modern American cultural studies. Courses are also offered in American and English History, American History with Politics, and American Literature with Creative Writing.

East London Anthropology is offered with North American Studies and includes a year in New Mexico.

Essex The history, literature, culture, social and political structure of the US are covered in the American (United States) Studies four-year course, with the third year spent in the US. Optional courses on American topics are available in the School of Comparative Studies and in the School of Social Studies. The course is also available with Criminology and Film. There is also a degree in Latin American Studies with options in history, politics, sociology, literature and the art of Latin America.

Hertfordshire Joint and combined courses are offered with American Studies.

Hull All students on the American Studies course study American history and literature, film and the arts. Special honours students select one ancillary subject from a wide range on offer. The American Studies course lasts four years (with Year 2 in the US). There are also seven joint courses. The department is very highly rated for its teaching provision.

Keele The American Studies course (three or four years) covers history, geography, literature and politics. Keele is noted for its dual honours courses with American Studies being offered with 28 other subjects.

Kent American Studies is offered as a multidisciplinary course with the option to focus on History, Latin American Studies or Literature. The third year of these four-year courses, is spent in the US. There are also courses in English and American Literature.

Lancaster All American Studies students study English, history and politics in Year 1. The three-year course covers American history and literature with Year 2 being spent in the US.

Leeds A course is offered in Spanish, Portuguese and Latin American Studies.

Leicester The American Studies course focuses on American literature, history and politics, with a supplementary subject taken in Year 1. The subject can also be studied within the Combined Arts programme with other subjects. There is an optional fourth year in the US.

Lincoln A three-year course is offered and also joint honours programmes with English, Drama, Media Studies, Journalism and History.

Liverpool Three-year and four-year courses are offered in Comparative American Studies and Latin American Studies.

London (Goldsmiths) English and American Literature and Spanish and Latin American Studies courses are on offer.

London (King's) American Studies is offered with a bias towards history and literature; and is taken with a year abroad. There is also a joint course with Film Studies and a course in Spanish, Portuguese and Latin American Studies is also available.

London (UCL)* A course is offered in Spanish and Latin American Studies.

See *Heap 2015: University Degree Course Offers* (Trotman Publishing) for details of offers

London Met The American Studies course covers American history, literature, film and politics. Study is possible in the US.

Loughborough* There is a degree course in English with a minor option in North American Film and Literature.

Manchester Three-year courses are offered in American Studies and English and American Literature. There is an option to study in North America. American Studies is also available with History. There is also a four-year course in American and Latin American Studies.

Manchester Met American Studies is offered as part of a joint honours and a Humanities and Social Studies programme. The course is based on the Crewe campus.

Newcastle A course is available in Spanish, Portuguese and Latin American Studies.

Northampton Over 20 joint honours courses are offered with American Studies. Transfer to single honours courses is possible at the end of Year 1. There is also a course in American Literature and Film.

Northumbria A unique course is offered in British and American Cultures examining the similarities and differences between the respective countries. It draws on literature, history and film, with the second year of the course being spent at Georgia State University.

Nottingham The American Studies course covers history, literature, politics, music and the visual arts. Single honours students devote two-thirds of the course to American Studies and the remainder to a subsidiary course outside the department. There are optional modules on Canada and Year 2 can be taken in Canada or the US. There are also joint courses with several subjects including English, Chinese Studies, History or Latin American Studies.

Plymouth American Studies can be taken as part of the Combined Studies programme with English, History, Media Arts or Popular Culture, or as a single honours course.

Portsmouth Courses are offered in Latin American Studies with Spanish and in American Studies with English, History or languages. There is an optional semester in the US, Mexico or Brazil.

Queen's Belfast The American Studies course offers modules in the history, literature, politics and society of the US.

Reading This American Studies course is taught in four departments (English, Film and Drama, Politics and History). Students spend a period of their studies in the US.

Salford A course in English with American Studies is on offer.

Sheffield The American Studies course covers American history from the Revolution to the present day and American literature from the colonial period to the first half of the 19th century. During the first year, students take a third arts or social science subject, for example politics, geography, economics or a language. A course in Hispanic Studies is also available.

Southampton Latin American Studies can be taken with Spanish.

Sunderland American Studies can be taken as a single or joint course offered with over 20 other subjects. Opportunities exist to spend one or two semesters in Year 2 at an American university.

Sussex American Studies may be studied with an emphasis on literature and culture or history and politics. All students take complementary courses within the School of English and American Studies. This is a four-year course with Year 3 spent at a university in the US.

Swansea Both single and joint honours courses offer the opportunity to spend a year at an American university.

Ulster American Studies with a semester in the US covers literature, culture and film and is available as a major or minor option.

Warwick* History, Literature and Cultures of the Americas students take two courses on themes and problems in North America, Latin America and the Caribbean, and a beginners' course in Spanish. Second-year students choose four options of which one must relate to North America and one to Latin America; two should be either historical or literary. Final courses are chosen from a range of options in this multi-disciplinary course that covers politics, history, literature and film studies. The third year is spent at a university in the US, Latin America, Canada or the Caribbean.

Winchester American Literature is offered as a single, main, joint or subsidiary subject. American Studies can also be taken with Film or Literature. There is an optional exchange scheme with several American universities.

Wolverhampton American Studies is taken as part of an extensive Humanities programme with 15 joint options or as a specialist subject with one or two other subjects.

Worcester The American Studies course covers history, literature, film, music, drama and politics with the opportunity to study in the US.

York St John American Studies can be taken with Film Studies and History.

ALTERNATIVE COURSES
English Literature, Government, History, International History, International Relations, Latin American Relations, Spanish American Studies and Politics.

ANIMAL SCIENCES

(* indicates universities with entry requirements over 340 UCAS points)

SUBJECT REQUIREMENTS/PREFERENCES
GCE A level: Biology or Chemistry required or preferred. **GCSE:** Mathematics usually required.

SUBJECT INFORMATION
Animal Sciences is a popular course in its own right and is often an appropriate option for those who fail to obtain a place in Veterinary Science. Courses cover a biological study of animals, reproduction and nutrition. Equine Studies has also become popular in recent years.

Aberystwyth After a common first year for all students one of four pathways can be chosen – Animal Production Science, Animal Biology, Equine Science or Companion Animal Science. A course is also available in Animal Behaviour, studying farmed and domestic animals with opportunities to observe animals, birds and sea life in their natural habitats and also one in Equine Studies.

Anglia Ruskin Animal Behaviour is offered as a three-year full-time degree or with Psychology or Ecology or Wildlife Biology.

Bristol There are courses in Animal Behaviour and Welfare involving problems with the behaviour in domestic animals. See also **Biology**.

Bristol UWE Animal Science focuses on nutrition, anatomy and physiology and has options in aquatic and avian studies. There are also degrees in Animal Management and Equine Science offered with either Business Management or Sport Science.

Bucks New Courses are offered in Animal Behaviour Management including specialist areas in Animal Welfare Law and Training and Learning.

Canterbury Christ Church Full-time or part-time courses are offered in Animal Science, with options in ecology and conservation in Year 3. There is also a focus on animal health and welfare.

Central Lancashire Equine Studies is a validated course at the nearby Myerscough College and focuses on management with optional routes in physiology or behaviour and welfare. There is also a course in Animal Conservation Science at the Penrith campus which includes the study of ecology and wildlife identification.

Chester The course in Animal Behaviour includes theoretical studies and practical modules that are taken at Reaseheath College, Nantwich and Chester Zoo. There are also courses in Animal or Zoo Management and in Wildlife Conservation and Ecology.

Cumbria The course in Animal Conservation Science covers ecology, animal behaviour, habitat, genetics and wildlife.

Exeter* Two degree schemes are offered in Animal Behaviour, one with Biology. This is an interdisciplinary programme covering zoology, ecology, conservation biology, psychology and neuroscience.

Gloucestershire There is a course in Animal Biology covering evolution, physiology, ecology and behaviour.

Glyndŵr There are courses in Animal Studies and Animal Biology covering the ecology, evolution and behaviour of animals.

Greenwich Degrees are offered in Animal Management, Equine Management, Animal Conservation and Biodiversity, and Applied Animal Behavioural Science and Welfare.

Harper Adams Animal Studies degrees include Behaviour and Welfare, Health and Welfare, and Animal and Bioveterinary Science.

Kent There is a course in Wildlife Management.

Lancaster Animal Sciences can be taken as a course option in Biological Sciences.

Lincoln Courses in Equine Science and Sport Science, Animal Behavioural Science and Animal Management and Welfare are offered.

Liverpool John Moores The Animal Behaviour degree covers the welfare, husbandry and conservation of animals. There is also a degree in Wildlife Conservation with extensive fieldwork and opportunities for a sandwich-year work placement.

Manchester Met The course in Animal Behaviour can include study in Europe, North America or Australia.

Newcastle The Animal Production Science course involves physiology, biochemistry, nutrition and reproduction and the health and welfare of livestock. Studies also cover the environmental concerns over the production of meat and other animal products. There is also a course in Animal Science involving dogs, cats, horses and less common pet species.

Northampton There are degree courses in Equine Management including modules in event management. An Applied Animal Studies course is offered including modules in zoo animal management and conservation.

See *Heap 2015: University Degree Course Offers* (Trotman Publishing) for details of offers

Nottingham Specialist topics in the Animal Science course include animal production, physiology and nutrition and environmental science (plants and animals). This is also offered with European Studies on a four-year course with the opportunity for overseas study.

Nottingham Trent There are courses in Equine Sports Science, which also include a specialism in equestrian psychology, and separate courses in Animal Science, Animal and Zoo Biology and Wildlife Conservation.

Oxford Brookes Equine Science can be taken as a three-year full-time course, and covers breeding, anatomy, ethics and event management. There are also courses in Thoroughbred Management and in Animal Biology.

Plymouth Animal Science can be studied with a bias towards equine studies, animal behaviour, management and welfare. There is also a course in Animal Conservation Science.

Reading The Animal Science course has a focus on farm animals with applications in biology, immunology and animal production. Final-year options include captive animal management, equine management and wildlife.

Royal Agricultural Univ The Equine Management course covers scientific aspects, such as genetics and nutrition, as well as the business side.

Staffordshire A course is offered in Animal Biology and Conservation. Topics covered include wildlife, marine and field biology, with optional Year 3 units in advanced DNA profiling and planning for climate change.

Stirling The course in Animal Biology covers conservation management, with ecology and fieldwork in Scotland and Switzerland. There is also a degree in Aquaculture.

Wolverhampton Animal Biology and Behaviour emphasises fieldwork and research skills and offers an optional sandwich placement year or international field courses. Courses are also available in Animal Management and Equine Sport Performance.

Worcester See under **Biological Sciences**.

OTHER INSTITUTIONS OFFERING ANIMAL SCIENCES COURSES
Askham Bryan (Coll), Barony (Coll), Bishop Burton (Coll), CAFRE, Cornwall (Coll), Craven (Coll), Duchy (Coll), Guildford (Coll), Kirklees (Coll), Leeds City (Coll), Myerscough (Coll), Nescot, Northop (Coll), Solihull (Coll), Sparsholt (Coll), SRUC, UHI, Warwickshire (Coll), West Anglia (Coll), Writtle (Coll).

ALTERNATIVE COURSES
Agricultural Sciences, Agriculture, Veterinary Science, Zoology.

ANTHROPOLOGY

(including **Social Anthropology**)
(* indicates universities with entry requirements over 340 UCAS points)

SUBJECT REQUIREMENTS/PREFERENCES
GCSE: Grade A–C in Mathematics may be required.

See *Heap 2015: University Degree Course Offers* (Trotman Publishing) for details of offers

SUBJECT INFORMATION

The study of anthropology will include some biology, some history and a study of the cultures, rituals and beliefs of humankind (ancient and modern) with extensions into art, kinship, family, religion, and political and legal structures.

Aberdeen A new programme in Anthropology with close links with cultural history and sociology. The collections of the University's Marischal Museum and Elphinstone Institute are used as resources. The Anthropology course covers society, nature and cultural differences, the anthropology of religion and the anthropology of the North. Also available as a joint honours with another subject.

Bournemouth There is a strong focus on laboratory and field science in the Archaeology, Anthropology and Forensic Science degree.

Birmingham Anthropology is offered as a joint course with eight other subjects.

Bristol Programmes are offered in Archaeology and Anthropology and Biological Anthropology with topics including early human origins, kinship and marriage and other current debates in anthropology.

Brunel Anthropology is offered as a three-year full-time course or a four-year course with two shorter placements during the first and second years, which usually link to the dissertation. It can also be taken with Sociology or with Psychology.

Cambridge* See under **Social Sciences/Studies**.

Dundee* A degree in Forensic Anthropology introduces the student to anatomical and medical investigations of human remains. Voluntary and paid laboratory summer work placements are usually undertaken between Levels 3 and 4.

Durham* Anthropology teaching and research focuses on social and biological anthropology (no previous knowledge is assumed). The former covers social institutions and cultures, with specialised studies in family, religion, political and legal structures. Biological anthropology involves the evolution of the species and ecology. There are also degrees in Medical Anthropology, Human Sciences and Health and Human Sciences at the Stockton campus and joint courses offered with Anthropology include Archaeology and Sociology. IT is also offered in the combined honours programme and in Natural Sciences. (High research rating.)

East Anglia Anthropology is offered with Archaeology and Art History and can include a year in Australia or North America.

East London The unique degree in Anthropology links biological and social anthropology. A year in New Mexico is part of the degree with Native American Studies.

Edinburgh* Social Anthropology courses focus on ritual, religion, family, marriage and the Third World, or alternatively on current issues such as environment, society and gender. At present there are five joint courses with Social Anthropology.

Exeter Anthropology is offered by way of BA or BSc pathways depending on the applicant's preferences and is also available in the Combined Honours programme.

Glasgow Anthropology is offered as a joint subject with a range of courses. Societies in Melanesia, Africa, Australia, South America and Indonesia can be studied. See also **Social Sciences/Studies**.

Hull The Anthropology course covers world cultures and diversity issues, and is offered as a component of single honours Sociology or as part of Sociology and Anthropology with a joint honours in Gender Studies, Geography, French, Spanish or German.

See *Heap 2015: University Degree Course Offers* (Trotman Publishing) for details of offers

Kent The Anthropology BSc (Hons) focuses on the biological, cultural and social processes that underlie the human experience in non-industrial and industrial societies. Combined courses with European languages are also offered. There is also a BA (Hons) in Social Anthropology, which offers a year abroad or language studies, and courses in Archaeology and Anthropology, Medical Anthropology and Biological Anthropology.

Liverpool A new course is offered in Evolutionary Anthropology developing from the course in Human Evolution. Topics covered include anatomy, psychology, human and animal behaviour and Palaeolithic Art.

Liverpool John Moores A course is offered in Forensic Anthropology focusing on the study of human remains for medico-legal purposes, taught through a combination of lectures, fieldwork and laboratory sessions. An optional placement year between Years 2 and 3 is available.

London (Goldsmiths) Anthropology courses, which can also be studied with History, Media or Sociology, cover a range of specialist studies including anthropological aspects of food, health, complex societies, European integration, art, sex, gender and psychology perspectives.

London (SOAS)* Anthropology and Sociology examines topics including ethnography, philosophy, culture and tourism, and is offered with a range of other subjects including Economics, Geography, History and Languages. Social Anthropology is offered with over 30 subjects including African, Asian and Oriental Languages.

London (UCL)* The Anthropology Department is unusual in covering all three branches of anthropology: biological, social and material culture. Students study all three branches for the first two years, after which they may choose to specialise in one field or to combine courses from two or three branches. Combined honours are offered in Ancient History and Social Anthropology and Anthropology and Geography.

London LSE* In Year 1 of the BA/BSc in Social Anthropology students may take an additional course in economics, geography, government, history, international relations, law, politics or psychology, and core units are studied throughout the three years. The course has a focus on Third World development, industrialisation and globalisation.

London Met A BA in Anthropology is offered covering topics which include human rights, racism, ethnography and globalisation.

Manchester The Social Anthropology course follows a similar pattern and covers the same topics as other courses in this field, with departmental interests covering Africa and the Far East. A degree in Anthropology can be taken with Criminology, Philosophy or Sociology.

Oxford* Anthropology is offered as part of the Human Sciences degree and is also combined with Archaeology (see under **Archaeology**). The course includes a compulsory three-week fieldwork placement in any worldwide location of the student's choosing.

Oxford Brookes Anthropology is offered as a single or combined course with 40 other subjects. Area specialisms include South Asia, Japan and Europe, and there are opportunities to study abroad during the course.

Queen's Belfast Single and joint honours courses are offered in Social Anthropology. A wide range of modules can be studied in Year 3.

Roehampton Courses are offered in Biological and Social Anthropology, allowing students to focus on either topic with a wide variety of optional modules. Human Biosciences examines the central aspects of human biology, such as physiology, behaviour, evolution, disease and ecology. It may be studied as a single honours course or a combined course with Psychology or Sport Science. A three-year course in Anthropology is also provided.

St Andrews* The Social Anthropology degree provides a study of tribal and peasant societies comparing Western and non-Western cultures. Particular attention is given to Africa, India and the Americas. Social Anthropology can also be studied with a number of joint subjects.

Southampton Anthropology is offered as one of four pathways in the Applied Social Science degree programme.

Sussex Anthropology is offered as a single or joint honours degree. Human sciences and joint degrees are offered in which equal amounts of time are spent on each subject; alternatively, a minor subject may be chosen in which three-quarters of the time is spent on anthropology. Opportunities exist for placement overseas through the Erasmus exchange programme.

Trinity St David The Anthropology course offers topics in contemporary human societies with an emphasis on the study of art and material culture including film and museum studies.

ALTERNATIVE COURSES
Archaeology, History, Psychology, Religious Studies and Sociology.

ARCHAEOLOGY

(* indicates universities with entry requirements over 340 UCAS points)

SUBJECT REQUIREMENTS/PREFERENCES
GCE A level: For BSc courses Chemistry may be required. Latin or Greek may be required by some universities. **GCSE:** Mathematics or science usually required for BSc courses.

SUBJECT INFORMATION
It would be unusual for an applicant to pursue this degree course without having been involved in some basic fieldwork. Studies can cover European, Greek, Roman or African archaeology.

Aberdeen The four-year course in Archaeology has a northern focus covering Scottish history and antiques with optional courses in Scandinavian, Northern European, North American and Viking Archaeology.

Aberystwyth The three-year BA in Museums and Gallery Studies allows students to examine how historical cultures and geographical areas are represented in collections and exhibitions. The course in Archaeology and Landscape History focuses on the theory and practice of archaeology and landscape studies.

Bangor Archaeology is offered with History or Welsh History and focuses on British prehistory and archaeology. There is also a course in Heritage, Archaeology and History with opportunities to undertake a placement with a museum or heritage site.

Bournemouth The Archaeology course has an emphasis on practical archaeology. There is a strong vocational focus that includes financial, personnel and management skills. There is the opportunity to undertake overseas work placements on excavations. Archaeology is also offered with Forensic Science and Prehistory and there are also specialist degrees in Archaeology of Shipwrecks and Roman Archaeology

Bradford Six courses are offered. The Archaeological Sciences course has a strong applied science input and Bioarchaeology has a strong element of applied biology focusing on the human environment. The BSc in Archaeology is available as a four-year course with a year in placement. Other courses focus on Forensic Science and Geography.

Bristol The course focuses on the practice, theory and history of archaeology and has a range of options covering European, Aegean and Ancient Mediterranean Studies. Practical units involve site visits, artefacts, environmental archaeology and heritage management. Courses in Archaeology and Anthropology or with Ancient History are also available as are part-time courses.

Cambridge* See **Social Sciences/Studies**.

Cardiff The Archaeology course focuses primarily on British, European and Mediterranean archaeology and involves 'hands-on' experience in various archaeological techniques such as drawing, surveying and excavation. For students with an appropriate science background, particularly in chemistry, there is also a degree course in Conservation of Objects in Museums and Archaeology. There are also combined courses with, for example, Ancient History or Medieval History.

Central Lancashire The Archaeology degree provides a comprehensive study of all aspects of the subject and includes an eight-week compulsory practical excavation and a two-week field course in Kenya in the final year.

Chester The degree is offered as a single, minor, major or joint course. There are regular field units with some modules involving a larger element of practical work. Areas of study include British prehistory, medieval Britain and archaeology and contemporary society. There are also combined courses.

Durham* The first year of the Archaeology and Anthropology course, which is available as a BA or BSc, consists of a general introduction to the history and nature of archaeology for the prehistoric, Roman and early medieval periods. Single honours students in Archaeology also take an ancillary subject in the first year. The second-year course covers both scientific and practical techniques. Archaeology is also offered with Ancient History as a joint course, in the Social Sciences combined honours programme and as a part of the Natural Sciences programme.

East Anglia Archaeology can be studied alongside Anthropology and Art History or alternatively with a year in Australia or North America through the Erasmus scheme.

Edinburgh* The Archaeology degree covers the early civilisations in Europe and the Near East. Joint courses are introduced in Year 3 and include Environmental Archaeology, or Archaeology with History or Social Anthropology. There are opportunities to study abroad through exchange agreements with universities in Greece and Italy.

Exeter After a general introduction in Year 1, Archaeology students have a wide choice of options in Years 2 and 3 with substantial practical and field work. European study is also offered in Year 3 prior to completing the course in Year 4. There are also courses in Archaeology and Anthropology or Forensic Science, or a combined honours with Ancient History. There are opportunities for professional placement and study abroad.

Glasgow* This Archaeology course is offered in the Faculties of Science, Arts or Social Science, the choice being dependent on the other subject students wish to study. The course covers British (and Scottish) archaeology from the earliest times to AD1000 and later, and also examines European and Mediterranean areas. There is an emphasis on the practical and scientific aspects as well as opportunities to study abroad.

Hull Archaeology courses are available with History, Medieval History and Art History and with opportunities to study abroad. The course introduces history, theory and method involving theoretical and practical studies.

Kent Classical and Archaeological Studies covers literature, art, philosophy, history and archaeology. As the course progresses, students specialise in their preferred interest. Students have the opportunity to learn Latin or Ancient Greek. The course can also be taken as a joint honours degree with 11 other subjects.

Leicester The Archaeology course covers Europe, Western Asia, Africa, Australasia and the Americas, and also archaeological methodology. Ancient History, History and Geography are also offered with Archaeology along with other joint degree programmes. See also **Combined Courses**.

Liverpool The BA courses in Archaeology offer a broad programme of fieldwork and analysis. The BSc courses focus on laboratory work covering artefacts and environmental analysis. Archaeology also features in the Combined Arts, Science or Social Science programmes and can be combined with Ancient History, Anthropology and Ancient Civilisations.

London (King's)* The Classical Archaeology course unit structure, covering the art and archaeology of Greece and Rome, allows great flexibility but all students undertake some study of Latin or Greek. (A beginner's level course is an option.)

London (RH) Courses are offered in Classical Archaeology and Environmental Archaeology with Geography.

London (SOAS)* Archaeology is offered under Asian and African specialisms combined with History of Art.

London (UCL)* Core courses in Year 1 of Archaeology (General) lead on to a choice of more than 80 courses covering prehistoric and Western, Asiatic, Greek and Roman and medieval archaeology, Egyptology and conservation. The BA and BSc courses are common for the first two years then divide with the BSc offering a greater element of scientific analysis. The course is now offered as a four-year programme with a year spent studying overseas through one of the university's Erasmus-Socrates agreements.

Manchester The Archaeology course explores the period from Neolithic man to the Middle Ages, covering British prehistory, African and Pacific archaeology and providing a general foundation in the subject. Archaeology is also available with Ancient History, Anthropology and Art History.

Newcastle Archaeology is based around three subject strands: prehistory, historical archaeology and theory and practice. It involves comprehensive practical training, including fieldwork, excavation, museum work, computing etc. Two-week practical fieldwork placements are undertaken during the summer. There is also a joint course in Archaeology and Ancient History, whilst Archaeology is also offered with other subjects in the Combined Studies programme.

Nottingham The first two years of the Archaeology BA and BSc courses cover the methods used by archaeologists and a study of the development of civilisation in Britain and Europe over 11,000 years. The third year follows specialist studies in prehistoric, Roman, medieval or European regional archaeology as well as historical buildings, numismatics and mathematical and computer applications in archaeology. Compulsory excavation placement takes place between terms. Subsidiary language study is possible and six joint honours courses are available. Several joint courses are offered including a unique course in Viking Studies covering language, literature, geography, history and art history.

Oxford* The course in Archaeology and Anthropology covers world archaeology and introduces anthropological theory. Topics include human evolution and ecology, social analysis and interpretation, cultural representations and beliefs and urbanisation. The geographical areas studied cover the Aegean, Middle East, Maritime South East Asia, South America, Africa and the Islamic world. A minimum of three weeks' archaeological work is mandatory. There is also a course in Classical Archaeology and Ancient History.

Queen's Belfast Archaeology (history of past human activities) can be combined with Paleoecology (the study of past environments) and courses in European prehistory and history from the Middle Ages. Special attention is given to the British Isles, Europe and Ireland. Single, joint and major/minor Archaeology courses are available.

Reading Prehistoric, Roman, and medieval archaeology in Britain, Europe and the Mediterranean form the foundations of the BSc/BA Archaeology courses. Four-week training excavations take place during the summer vacation. Archaeology is also available as a joint course with Classical Studies or History.

St Andrews* Archaeology is offered with Ancient or Medieval History, with modules covering the Roman Empire and ancient Greece.

Sheffield The Archaeology course provides opportunities for single honours students to focus on European archaeology at the beginning of the second year. Option courses are offered in the second and third years. Courses are also offered in Classical and Historical Archaeology, Archaeology and Archaeological Science. In addition there are nine joint courses.

Southampton* A flexible thematic Archaeology course is offered ranging from ancient Mediterranean studies to the archaeology of towns and cities. A wide range of options follows in Years 2 and 3, including ancient maritime trade and underwater archaeology.

Swansea Courses are offered in Egyptology and Anthropology, Ancient History and Classical Civilisation. The Classical Civilisation programme includes modules in the study of archaeological material, and visits to sites and museums.

Trinity St David The Archaeology course focuses on societies from Paleolithic to modern. There are particular strengths in landscape, prehistoric, environmental and forensic archaeology. Students participate in an annual excavation at the Cambrian mountains, near the university campus. Archaeology is also offered with joint subjects including Anthropology and with a focus on either environmental or practical or world cultures.

Warwick The Ancient History and Classical Archaeology course focuses on Ancient Greek and Roman cultural and political history, with the opportunity to study Latin or Greek language modules.

Winchester There is a course in Archaeological Practice and a more theoretical degree in Archaeology.

Worcester Several courses are offered combining Archaeology and Heritage Studies (BA or BSc) with one of 11 other subjects including Landscape Studies and Heritage Studies.

York The Archaeology course is concerned with both archaeological method (including a significant practical element) and theory (with special courses on the interpretation of archaeological data). One main course is taken each term on single themes, covering Europe from the Bronze Age onwards. There are opportunities to study a foreign language. The department has particular strengths in medieval history and medieval archaeology. Degree courses are also offered in Bioarchaeology, Historical Archaeology and Heritage Studies.

OTHER INSTITUTIONS OFFERING ARCHAEOLOGY COURSES
Peterborough (Reg Coll), Truro (Coll).

ALTERNATIVE COURSES
Ancient History, Anthropology, Art and Design, Classical Studies, Classics, Geology, History, History of Architecture, Medieval History, Prehistory, Social Anthropology.

ARCHITECTURE

(including **Architectural Technology** and **Landscape Architecture**)
(* indicates universities with entry requirements over 340 UCAS points)

SUBJECT REQUIREMENTS/PREFERENCES
GCE A level: Mathematics or Physics may be required. **GCSE:** English and Mathematics.

SUBJECT INFORMATION
Institutions offering Architecture have very similar courses. An awareness of the relationship between people and the built environment is necessary, plus the ability to create and to express oneself in terms of drawings, paintings etc. Most Architecture schools will expect to see a portfolio of work, particularly drawings of buildings or parts of buildings.

QUESTIONS TO CONSIDER
* Does the course carry professional examination exemptions (Royal Institute of British Architects – RIBA) or industry body accreditations (Chartered Institute of Architectural Technologists – CIAT)?
* Can I move on directly to a BArch or MArch course after completing my undergraduate degree? Will I need to achieve a minimum grade for unconditional entry?
* After I complete my degree, I want to spend a year working in the industry before I continue my studies – will the university help me in finding work? What have previous graduates gone on to do?
* Which areas of architecture inspire me the most – interior design, environmental concerns, management?

Anglia Ruskin BSc courses in Architecture and Architectural Technology share common first-year modules that include design and technology, building construction, project management and urban studies.

Bath* For the BSc in Architectural Studies (Faculty of Engineering), the first year is spent in the University with Semester 2 and the summer terms spent in training. The course gives exemptions from Part 1 of the RIBA final examination. The course leads on to the Master of Architecture degree but admission is not automatic as the minimum requirement is a lower second class honours degree. Bath has a joint School of Architecture and Civil Engineering with architecture and engineering students working together on joint projects. See also **Engineering**.

Birmingham City The School of Architecture is one of the largest in the country and draws strength from its association with the Departments of Planning, Landscape and Construction and Surveying. Following the three-year BArch course, a postgraduate diploma course gives complete exemptions from RIBA examinations. Architecture can also be studied with an emphasis on urban design, conservation or regeneration. A BA course in Landscape Architecture is also offered.

Bolton The degree in Architectural Technology is accredited by the Chartered Institutes of Architectural Technologists and Building.

Bournemouth Arts Courses are offered in Architecture and Interior Architecture and Design.

Brighton The Architecture course provides a balance between environmental needs, technology and creative design. The programme covers basic design and graphic skills, history, and materials and interior design, and there are visits to European cities. The course carries exemption from the RIBA Part 1 examination. The course in Architectural Technology (three-year or four-year sandwich) is a building course with a greater emphasis on design. There is also a three-year degree in Interior Architecture.

Bristol UWE The Architecture BA honours course is followed by the two-year BArch course (the second undergraduate degree) which some students study on a part-time basis. The first part of the latter course is built around work placement and both are validated by the RIBA. There are also courses in Architectural Technology, Architectural and Environmental Engineering and Architecture and Planning.

Cambridge* Architecture Parts IA and IB and II, each lasting a year, provide a basic training in architecture through design and studio exercises covering the history of European architecture. After the degree, students normally take a further two years of supervised office experience with RIBA Parts 2 and 3 examinations leading to registration. Not available at the following colleges: Corpus Christi, Homerton, Hughes Hall and St Catharine's.

Cardiff* The Architectural programme is a two-tier scheme of study, first leading to a BSc in Architectural Studies in three years and then followed by two years of study (including one year of practice) for the MArch degree. Visual communication, interior design, town planning and landscape design are included throughout the BSc course and opportunities exist for a specialist study in the BArch degree. There is a focus on design creativity integrated with technological and environmental concerns of modern architectural practice. The School of Architecture works in close liaison with the Town Planning Department in the fields of urban design, housing and landscape. (High research rating.)

Cardiff Met (UWIC) Architectural Design Technology is offered as a HND and a BSc. Both include a study of building technology, materials and environmental studies, and are accredited by the CIAT. There is also a course in Interior Architecture.

Central Lancashire A three-year full-time course is offered in Architectural Technology covering building design and technology, with sponsorship available on application. There is also a course in Architecture.

City Three-year BEng and four-year MEng sandwich courses combining Civil Engineering and Architecture are offered.

Coventry The Architecture course involves collaboration with courses in Germany and the Netherlands. A course in Architectural Technology is also offered, covering design, construction technology and professional practice, leading to a support career for architects.

Creative Arts Three courses are offered in Architecture, Architectural Technology and Interior Architecture and Design. The BA (Hons) Architecture carries exemption from the RIBA Part 1 examination.

De Montfort The three-year Architecture course focusing on studio-based projects is followed by one year of practical study and a further two years, leading to the graduate diploma. The course carries exemption from the RIBA Part 1 examination.

Derby The School of Technology offers Architectural Technology and Practice (CIAT-accredited), and Architectural Venue Design (accredited by the Chartered Society of Designers), as well as Architectural Design and Property Development as joint honours courses.

Dundee The MArch course is a five-year programme that comprises three years leading to the BArch, which carries exemption from the RIBA Part 1 examination, followed by the March after a further two years, which carries RIBA Part 2 exam exemption. A year of practical experience may be taken between the third and fourth years. Exchange programmes take place with seven European countries.

East London Environmental design, history, construction, conservation, law, the building industry and urban studies are topics covered in this standard Architecture course. The course is suitable for students with an arts-based background. An extended degree in Architecture is also offered, as well as a one-semester course in Architecture: Computing and Design.

Edinburgh* A four-year course is offered in Architectural Design, leading on to an MArch course. The course has Architects Registration Board (ARB) accreditation. There is also a degree in Architectural History.

See *Heap 2015: University Degree Course Offers* (Trotman Publishing) for details of offers

Edinburgh Napier Students of the four-year course in Architectural Technology are eligible for the Best Timber Design project prize. Landscape Architecture is also available.

Glasgow* Architecture is offered by the Mackintosh School of Architecture. The course leads to an ordinary or honours degree after which graduates study for the Diploma in Architecture for professional recognition. BEng and MEng courses in Civil Engineering are also offered with Architecture.

Glyndŵr The course in Architectural Design Technology includes computer-aided design and conservation.

Greenwich Architecture is a three-year design-based course with strong visual studies and computing input. A two-year HND/HNC in Architectural Design is available, as well as courses in Building Studies, Garden Design and Design and Construction Management. Architecture can also be studied with Landscape Architecture.

Huddersfield Design, design technology, communication and context of design are the four main subject areas in the BA Architecture course. The Architecture (International) course is unique in the UK. A course of three years only, it is designed specifically to apply the principles of design on a worldwide basis and examines the architecture of developing countries. The course carries exemption from the RIBA Part 1 examination. Extensive overseas fieldwork is part of the course. The course in Architecture runs parallel for Year 1, after which students decide their course route. There is also a course in Architectural Technology.

Kent* A BA degree (three years, with RIBA Part 1 exemption) followed by an MArch course (two years, with RIBA Part 2 exemption) was introduced in 2006. Both courses provide a thorough grounding in design, technology, law and management aspects for those wishing to enter a career in architecture. Up to a year in industry is usually taken between Years 1 and 2 of the BA. There is also a degree in Interior Architecture and Design.

Kingston The Architecture course has design as its principal core element. A particular feature of the course is the use of continuous assessment. Courses in Landscape Architecture and Landscape Planning and Historic Building Conservation are also available.

Leeds Beckett Architectural design is the main feature of the Architecture course, which is linked with building, design management, urban and landscape design and environmental control. Interior design and a study of Third World housing are also included. A one-year Graduate Certificate course follows the three-year BA course, which carries RIBA Part 1 exemption. There are also courses in Landscape Architecture, Landscape Planning, Garden Art and Design and Architectural Technology.

Lincoln The Architecture course is structured around project-based design teaching covering technical, professional, human and social aspects and historical studies. A course in Interior Architecture and Design is also available.

Liverpool* The Architecture course has a strong emphasis on design and has close links with building, civil engineering and civic design areas. Exemption from RIBA Part 1 is carried. Transfer to the new Design Studies BA is an option at the end of Year 1. Graduates from the Architecture BA who gain a first or upper second class degree are eligible for unconditional entry to the university's MArch programme.

Liverpool John Moores The Architecture course involves design, history, theory, technology and practice and gives exemption from the RIBA Part 1 examination. Studies cover the history of architecture from the 18th century to contemporary. The postgraduate diploma exempts from the RIBA Part 2 examination. There is also a degree in Architectural Technology with an optional sandwich year.

London (UCL)* This three-year Architecture course for a BSc degree is largely based on design projects and provides a very broad academic education for those who are concerned with planning, design and management of the built environment. After completing the degree, most students then undertake a year working in industry in the UK or overseas before proceeding to the two-year diploma programme.

See *Heap 2015: University Degree Course Offers* (Trotman Publishing) for details of offers

London Met A three-year Architecture course with RIBA Part 1 exemption is offered, focusing on design and urbanism. European and international field trips are taken throughout the course. There is also a course in Interior Architecture and Design and a four-year extended degree in Architecture and Interior Design.

London South Bank The Architecture Studies course includes design, information technology and history of architecture, and carries RIBA Part 1 exemption. There are also courses in Architectural Technology and Architectural Engineering.

Manchester* The three-year BA course in Architecture leads on to the two-year study for the Bachelor of Architecture degree. The course is predominantly design-based. Field trips in the UK and abroad are compulsory and exchanges at BArch level take place in France, Germany, Spain and Italy.

Manchester Met* This is a three-year full-time or four-year sandwich course in Architecture with design projects supported by studies in technical and administrative skills. It leads onto the two-year MArch degree. There is also a course in Landscape Architecture. The course is run jointly with the University of Manchester.

Newcastle* This three-year course in Architectural Studies covers the theory and history of architecture, building technology, studio design projects and environmental design. It is followed by a year's practical training leading on to a two-year course of advanced architectural design for the BArch degree. The course presents a realistic view of the environment of architecture and encourages students to develop a personal philosophy of design. It is strongly biased towards project work. There is also a new course in Architecture and Urban Planning.

Northampton The CIAT-accredited BSc (Hons) in Architectural Technology combines computer-aided design (CAD) skills with theoretical ideas and case studies. A two-year HND in Architectural Technology is also available.

Northumbria Technological and managerial skills are included in the Architecture course, which carries RIBA Part 1 exemption. There is also a course in Interior Architecture.

Norwich Arts The three-year BA course in Architecture is an entry to further studies leading to full qualification.

Nottingham* A three-year BA course in Architecture is followed by two years for the BArch degree. A year of practical experience follows the BA course. The course is planned around project work investigating a wide variety of building problems and achieves a balance between art and technology and stresses the integration of technical work with projects but is without a strong scientific bias. BArch students can register on a year out in practice. There are also courses in Architectural and Environmental Engineering and Architecture and Environmental Design.

Nottingham Trent A BArch degree in Architecture with RIBA Part 1 status is offered and also courses in Architectural Technology and Interior Architecture and Design.

Oxford Brookes* The Architecture BA is a three-year project-based course supported by environmental and construction technologies, social sciences, history and philosophy. Exemption from RIBA Part 1 is carried. The course is highly rated by students. The graduate diploma course of two years follows with a year of practical experience. There are also courses in Interior Architecture: Design and Practice and joint programmes in Cities and Environment Design.

Plymouth The Architecture degree is a three-year full-time course followed by practical experience and two further years of study leading to a diploma. The course is ARB-prescribed and carries RIBA Part 1 exemption. There is a possibility of studying abroad. An engineering course in Architectural Technology and the Environment is also available.

Portsmouth The Architecture degree is based on design projects (50% of the course). The first year covers drawing techniques, user studies, planning and circulation, and environmental comfort. The second and third years focus on three themes: the house, urban residential and commercial buildings, and a public building – supported by history, drawing, CAD, computing and construction. There is also a course in Interior Design.

Queen's Belfast Architecture is a three-year course intended as a first degree for those wishing to take postgraduate studies and become professionally qualified architects. This course typically covers design and communication, building technology and professional skills.

Robert Gordon A BSc in Architectural Technology and an MSc in Architecture are offered.

Sheffield* The Architecture degree offers a balanced education, covering theory, design and professional experience. There are several options open to those who take the standard BA degree, which, combined with practical experience, leads to exemptions from RIBA examinations. Work experience advised before application. There are also courses in Architecture and Landscape and Civil or Structural Engineering with Architecture.

Sheffield Hallam The Architecture and Environmental Design degree includes modules in environment and technology and urban design and landscape, and leads to RIBA accreditation. There is also a degree in Architectural Technology.

Southampton* A course is offered in Civil Engineering with Architecture with modules covering architectural principles, acoustics and urban design.

Strathclyde The four-year BSc in Architectural Studies includes the study of historical, design, cultural and legal subjects and can be studied alongside European Studies.

Ulster The BA in Architecture carries RIBA Part 1 exemption, while the BSc in Architectural Technology and Management covers CAD skills and includes a year in professional practice. An MArch course is offered.

West London Full-time and part-time courses are offered in Architectural Technology.

Westminster* The Architecture course is largely based on design project work and covers a study of architectural form and the physical, social and psychological needs of the user. There are also courses in Architecture (Interior Design; Urban Design) and in Architectural Technology.

Wolverhampton Courses are offered in Architectural Technology, Architectural Studies plus another subject and Interior Architectural Design.

OTHER INSTITUTIONS OFFERING ARCHITECTURE COURSES
Blackpool and Fylde (Coll), Bradford (Coll Univ Centre), Dudley (Coll), Edinburgh (CA), Glasgow (SA), Hereford (CA), Kirklees (Coll), Leeds (CA), Menai (Coll), Pembrokeshire (Coll), Ravensbourne, UHI, Wigan and Leigh (Coll), Worcester (CT).

ALTERNATIVE COURSES
Building, Building Surveying, Civil Engineering, Estate Management, Land Surveying, Landscape Architecture, Quantity Surveying, Town and Country Planning.

ART AND DESIGN

(see also **History of Art and Design**)

(* indicates universities with entry requirements over 340 UCAS points)

QUESTIONS TO CONSIDER

✳ I'm not sure which area I'd like to specialise in – can I study a broad range of artistic practices such as painting, photography, sculpture and printmaking, and choose as I progress?

✳ Do I have skills or interest in a specific craft, like silversmithing or glassmaking, which might be offered by fewer courses?

✳ Do I want to study at a dedicated institution for the creative arts? Will their facilities and staff be better suited to the work involved?

✳ Do I want to gain practical skills which might be useful for a range of career opportunities – for example, in IT or graphic design?

Abertay The degree course in Computer Arts (requiring previous studies in art and design) applies traditional art and design concepts to digital media narratives and entertainment, and includes modules in Japanese with opportunities to study in Japan. There is also a course in Visual Communications and Media Design.

Aberystwyth The three-year scheme in Fine Art begins with a broad visual education in Year 1, and in Years 2 and 3 allows the student to specialise in one or more from drawing, painting, printmaking, photography and book illustration. Fine Art can be studied with one of a range of subjects, including Art History, Film and Television Studies, Information and Library Studies, Mathematics, Museum and Gallery Studies, and Welsh History.

Anglia Ruskin BA Art degree courses are offered in Fine Art, which covers film, printmaking and installations, Illustration, Illustration and Animation, Fashion Design, Graphic Design and Photography. There is also a course in Computer-aided Product Design.

Aston The university offers a number of programmes in product design, based in its School of Engineering and Applied Science. These are: Transport Industrial Design, Industrial Product Design and Product Design an Management.

Bath Spa The Creative Arts course allows students to choose two areas of practical creative study, which include art, ceramics, visual design and mixed media textiles. Other options in the programme include drama, dance and music. A Fine Art course covering painting, sculpture, printmaking and photography is also available. There are also courses in Ceramics, Contemporary Arts Practice, Graphic Design, Fashion and Textile Design.

Bedfordshire Courses are offered in Graphic Design, Photography and Video Art, Advertising Design, Art and Design, Illustration, Interior Architecture, Interior Design and Animation.

Birmingham City BA courses are offered in Design, Fine Art, Fashion Design, Textile Design (Embroidery; Constructed Textiles; Printed Textiles; Retail Management), Three-dimensional Digital Design (Digital Product Design; Digital Spatial Design), Jewellery and Silversmithing, Visual Communication and Product Design (Furniture; Industrial; Design in Business). The School of Jewellery also offer a unique degree course in Horology requiring creative and practical competence (and attention to detail!). The course covers the design, maintenance and repair of time pieces both mechanical and electronic.

Bolton Courses are available in Animation and Illustration, Art and Design, Film Production, Fine Arts, Graphic Design, Interior Design, Photography, and Textile/Surface Design. Joint honours degrees are available for some subjects.

Bournemouth Design courses are offered in the School of Design, Engineering and Computing. These include Product Design, Design Business Management and Interior Design. Courses are also offered in Photography, Digital Media Design, Computer-aided Product Design and Fashion and Textiles.

See *Heap 2015: University Degree Course Offers* (Trotman Publishing) for details of offers

Bournemouth Arts Courses are available in Animation Production, Commercial Photography, Costume with Performance Design, Fashion, Film Production, Fine Art, Graphic Design, Illustration, Make-Up for Media and Performance, Modelmaking, Photography, Textiles and Visual Communication.

Bradford There are three courses in Design – Automotive Design Technology, Industrial Design and Product Design – offered in the School of Engineering. Product Design carries the option of a year in an industry placement.

Brighton The Fine Art Critical Practice course places equal emphasis on theory and practice and includes traditional drawing, painting or photography. There are also Fine Art Painting, Printmaking and Sculpture courses, Graphic Design, Illustration, Moving Image Photography, Product Design, Fashion Design (with Business Studies or Textiles) and Three-dimensional Design courses with specialisms in wood, metal, ceramics and plastics.

Bristol UWE Degree courses are offered in Fine Arts and Art and Visual Culture, which share a common first year with the decision on the degree of choice in Year 2. There are also degrees in Drawing and Applied Arts, Illustration, Animation, Fashion/Textiles and Graphic Design. There is also a Creative Product Design course with industrial placements.

Brunel The Department of Design offers Industrial Design and Technology, available as a four-year sandwich course with an industry placement, Industrial Design Engineering and Product Design. Close links with industry exist for student placements.

Bucks New Courses are offered in a broad portfolio of subjects including Fine Art, Graphic Arts and Creative Advertising. Specialised studies are also offered in Ceramics and Glass, Design for Digital Media, Photography, Jewellery, Product Design and Surface Design, and Three-dimensional Design. The university is also a leader in the UK in the field of Furniture Design and Furniture Conservation and Restoration.

Canterbury Christ Church Courses are offered in Fine and Applied Arts including Ceramics, Painting, Printmaking, Sculpture and Studio Media and Drawing Technologies. The Creative Arts BA includes options in arts management and visual art and design.

Cardiff Met (UWIC) Ceramics, Textiles, Fine Arts, Graphics, Illustration and Product Design courses are offered.

Central Lancashire The degree in Fine Art has major areas in painting, printmaking, sculpture and time-based media (film, video, animation). There are also courses in Fashion, Fashion Promotion, Advertising, Graphic Design, Animation, Audio Visual Media, Illustration, Industrial Design, Interior Design, Product Design, Jewellery and Surface Pattern with Crafts. Design Studies can also be taken with Fashion and Brand Promotion or Photography or Journalism. Fashion courses also include Styling, Marketing and Asian Fashion. There is also a new course in Antiques and Design Studies.

Chester The Fine Art degree covers historical and cultural contexts and non-traditional practices, and includes a work experience module. The course is available as a single or combined honours degree. Courses are also available in Photography, which includes a professional work placement, and Graphic Design.

Chichester The Fine Art programme includes textiles, painting, sculpture, media studies and printmaking and offers the option of developing a 'hybrid' practice combining these techniques.

Colchester (Inst) Courses are offered in Fashion and Textiles, Fine Art, Graphic Media, Photography and Three-dimensional Design.

Coventry The School of Art and Design offers courses in Consumer Product Design, Automotive and Transport Design, Fashion Design and Fashion Accessories, Graphic Design, Art and Craft involving textiles, ceramics and metal, and in Fine Art comprising painting, printmaking, sculpture, public art and art history. There is also a course in Contemporary Crafts.

See *Heap 2015: University Degree Course Offers* (Trotman Publishing) for details of offers

Creative Arts The university has five campuses: UCA Canterbury – Fine Art, Interior Architecture; UCA Epsom – Fashion, Graphics; UCA Farnham – Advertising, Animation, Computer Games, Fine Art, Graphics, Interior Architecture, Photography, Product Design, Textiles for Fashion, Three-dimensional (Ceramics; Glass; Metal; Jewellery); UCA Maidstone – Graphics, Photography; UCA Rochester – Fashion, Product Design, Photography, Three-dimensional (Silverware; Goldsmithing; Jewellery).

Cumbria Art and Design courses cover Animation, Applied Arts, Fine Art, Graphic Design, Illustration and Photography.

De Montfort Art and Design courses are offered in Animation Design, Fashion Fabrics and Accessories, Fashion Buying, Fashion Design, Fine Art, Graphic Design, Footwear Design, Furniture Design, Interior Design, Textile Design, and Photography and Video.

Derby Courses are offered in Animation, Fashion Studies, Fine Art, Graphic Design, Illustration, Product Design, Photography and Textile Design.

Dundee (Duncan of Jordanstone Coll) After a general course in art and design, degree specialisations follow in Animation, Graphic Design, Illustration, Jewellery and Metal Design, Textile Design, Interior and Environmental Design, Digital Interaction Design and Time Based Art and Digital Film, and Fine Art with specialisms in Digital Media, Drawing and Painting, Printmaking, Sculpture. There is also a course in Art, Philosophy and Contemporary Practices, with fine art occupying 60% of the teaching programme and including studio projects.

East London Courses are offered in Animation, Fashion Design with Marketing, Fine Art, Graphic Design (Illustration; Photography; Printmaking), Product Design Futures, Photography, Moving Image, Printed Textiles and Surface Decoration, and Visual Theories.

Edge Hill The course in Animation focuses on the theoretical aspects of two- and three-dimensional digital animations and production techniques. A Design for Performance course is also available.

Edinburgh The four-year BA courses in Intermedia Art, which follows Fine Art disciplines, Painting, Photography and Sculpture share a common first year with the General Art degree, allowing students to develop a specialist path. Courses in Animation, Glass, Fashion, Graphic Design, Illustration, Jewellery and Silversmithing, Product Design and Textiles are also available. The MA (Hons) in Fine Art is taught jointly by the University and the Edinburgh College of Art, with equal amounts of practical and academic work.

Edinburgh Napier A four-year BDes in Graphic Design is available, covering aspects of digital media, aesthetics and professional practice. Courses are also offered in Design Futures, Interior Architecture and Consumer Product Design. Photography, Film and Imaging is also available.

Edinburgh Queen Margaret A vocational and highly practical course is offered in Costume Design for stage, film and TV, with three placements throughout the country.

Falmouth Art courses include Three-dimensional Design, Fashion, Fine Art, Graphics, Illustration, Interior Design, Textiles, Theatre Design and Photography.

Glasgow See **Engineering** for Product Design Engineering taught partly by the Glasgow School of Art, which also offers a BA in Design. This is a four-year honours course and has a common first year with the degree in Fine Art. Thereafter Design students go on to specialisms in ceramics, textiles, visual communication, photography, interior design and silversmithing and jewellery. Fine Art students may specialise in environmental art/sculpture, painting/printmaking or photography.

Glasgow Caledonian Courses are offered in Interior Design, Graphic Design for Digital Media and Fashion Business and Marketing.

Gloucestershire A three-year full-time course in Fine Art leads to specialising in Painting, Photography or Video. Courses are also offered in Graphic Design and Animation, and Illustration. The Creative Media course includes Animation.

Glyndŵr Specific degrees are offered in Fine Art, Graphic Design and Illustration with broad courses covering Creative Lens Media, Applied Arts, Animation, Games Art, Computer Arts and Decorative Arts.

Greenwich Courses offered include a BA Fine Arts as a top-up for students who have already completed a Fine Art foundation degree or HND, Graphic Design with Digital Design or Advertising, and Visual Art.

Heriot-Watt The School of Textiles and Design is located in Galashiels and the Scottish Borders. Six courses are offered in Fashion including Design for Industry, Textile and Fashion Design, Technology, Menswear, Womenswear, Marketing and Retailing and Communication. There are opportunities to study abroad.

Hertfordshire The faculty offers degree courses in Applied Arts (ceramics, glass, textiles and jewellery), Fine Art (painting, sculpture, printmaking and photography, with the opportunity to undertake work placements), Model Design, Product Design, Graphics Design and Illustration, Digital Modelling, Digital Animation, Digital and Lens Media, Fashion, Industrial and Interior and Spatial Design.

Huddersfield Courses are offered in Fashion Design and Textiles, Fashion Buying, Promotion, marketing and Production, Advertising and Graphic Design, Illustration, Fine Art, Interior Design, and Product and Transport Design. The Contemporary Arts course includes photography and performance, and Interdisciplinary Art and Design features workshops in ceramics, jewellery and digital imaging.

Hull Courses are offered in Digital Arts, Design for Digital Media, Art History and Archaeology, and Web Design and Development.

Kent The Fine Art course is a theoretical course with practical studio work and options in photography. Visual and Performing Arts covers art history and some drama and film studies. There are also courses in Digital Arts, Interior Design and Interior Architecture. History and Philosophy of Art and Art and Film Studies can also be studied alongside another humanities subject. See also **Film, Radio, Video and TV Studies**.

Kingston The Design Faculty offers five main subject areas – Fine Art (painting, sculpture, printmaking, photography and computing), Graphic Design (communication media, moving image, animation, lettering, typography and packaging), Illustration (including animation and video), Interior Design, Product and Furniture Design, and Fashion and Museums and Gallery Studies. There is also a course in Art, Performance and Digital Media, offering a range of skills including the moving image and music.

Lancaster The three-year BA Fine Art covers painting, drawing, sculpture and digital art and installation. Creative Arts integrates creative work with art history of the 20th century and Art and Art History is largely concerned with art history with options in practical work. There is also a Creative Arts course offering four art forms – art, creative writing, music and theatre studies. Students choose two specialisms starting in Year 2.

Leeds The Art and Design course focuses on studio practice with a study of historic, technological and cultural aspects. The School of the Textile Industries provides a Textile Design programme in addition to Textile and Fashion Management. The Fine Art course offers a 50/50 balance of theory and practice. There is also a course in Design and Colour Technology. A BA History of Art and a degree in Graphic Communication and Design is also available.

Leeds Beckett In addition to the course in Art and Design, which covers most art specialisms, degree courses are also offered in Animation, Fashion, Fine Art, and Graphic Arts and Design. There is also a Garden Art and Design course, involving horticulture and planting design, and a course in Product Design.

Lincoln Single subject degree courses are offered in Advertising, Animation, Contemporary Lens Media, which covers digital photography and moving images, Fashion, Fine Art, Furniture Design, Decorative Crafts, Conservation and Restoration, Graphic Design, Graphic Illustration, Interior Design, Product

Design, Jewellery and Object, and Museum and Exhibition Design. The Conservation and Restoration degree covers a wide field, including decorative and fine arts, historical artefacts and archaeological specimens.

Liverpool Hope The Creative and Performing Arts degree has options in sculpture and painting. There is a Design degree with options in textiles, product design, silversmithing and jewellery, ceramics, wood or metal, and a combined honours option leading to BA/QTS in Fine Art and Design. The BA Combined Honours in Art and Design History provides theoretical and critical perspectives on 19th- and 20th-century work.

Liverpool John Moores The School of Art and Design (founded in 1910) offers courses in Fine Art, Graphic Design and Illustration, Fashion and History of Art.

London (Goldsmiths) Separate courses are offered in Art Practice and in Fine Art, the latter combining studio practice and contemporary critical studies with art history. A four-year Fine Art extension degree is available for students from outside the EU. The Design Studies degree course is studio-based, covering all aspects of the practical and social aspects of design. Fine Art can also be studied with History of Art. In addition, a Design and Technology course offers Qualified Teacher Status at secondary level and there is also a degree course in Textiles.

London (UCL) The Slade School of Fine Art places great emphasis on the creative and intellectual development of individual students. The Fine Art programme is 'taught by artists for the education of artists'. BFA students follow one studio discipline in painting, sculpture, fine art or media (photography, printmaking, film, video and electronic media), while BA students study History and Theory of Art. A course is also offered in Italian and Design.

London Met Three-year courses are offered in Fine Art (with pathways in mixed media, photography, printmaking and painting), Design (furniture and product, graphics), Textiles, Furnishing Design and Manufacture, Interior Design, and Silversmithing and Jewellery. An Art and Media Design extended degree option is available.

London South Bank There are courses in Digital Photography and Product Design, including Sports Products Design, which is a four-year sandwich course.

Loughborough Courses are offered in Textile Design, Fine Art (Painting; Printmaking; Sculpture) New Media and Industrial Design Technology and Three-dimensional Design: New Practice, comprising furniture, ceramics, metalwork, jewellery and silversmithing.

Manchester Art History and Archaeology is offered as a three-year degree course. The three-year BA History of Art examines worldwide visual cultures from antiquity to the present. The Department of Textiles offers a wide range of courses including Design Management for Fashion Retailing, Textile Design and Design Management. Fashion and Textile Retailing, Design Management and Textile Design courses are also offered and include business management with industrial experience and study abroad.

Manchester Met The Faculty of Art and Design offers degree courses in Design and Art Direction (with opportunities to study abroad), Illustration with Animation, Fine Art, Fashion (including embroidery, printed, woven or knitted textiles), Textiles, Interior Design, and Three-dimensional Design (involving wood, metal, ceramics and glass). There are also courses in Clothing Design and Technology, Fashion Buying in Retail, International Fashion Marketing, and Community and Contemporary Arts. The Interactive Arts course includes CGI animation training and has opportunities for overseas university exchanges.

Middlesex Courses are offered in Design and Technology, Fashion, Fine Art, Jewellery and Accessories, Printed Textiles, Product Design (Graphic Design and Illustration), Interior Architecture and Photography.

See *Heap 2015: University Degree Course Offers* (Trotman Publishing) for details of offers

Newcastle A four-year Fine Art degree is offered by way of studio practice underpinned by historical and theoretical studies. European and international student exchanges are available through the Erasmus scheme.

Newman Art and Design covers a wide range of specialist subjects with special facilities for printing, ceramics, textiles, photography and computer imaging. There are also courses in Creative Arts and Primary Teaching (Art).

Northampton Courses are offered in Fine Art (drawing and painting), Graphic Communication, Fashion Illustration, Interior and Product Design and Textile Design.

Northumbria The Faculty of Art and Design offers courses in Fine Art, Animation, Graphic Design, Design for Industry, Fashion, Fashion Marketing, Interior Design, Three-dimensional Design (Furniture and Fine Products), and Product Design Engineering.

Norwich Arts Art courses include Animation, Fashion, Fine Art, Games Art and Graphics.

Nottingham Trent The Faculty of Art and Design offers a very wide range of courses covering Furniture and Product Design, Decorative Arts, Design and Development: Landscape and Interiors, Interior Architecture and Design, Graphic Design, Fashion and Textile Management, Fashion Knitwear Design and Knitted Textiles, Decorative Arts (glass, metal, wood), Fine Art (sculpture, painting, video and photo-print), Photography, Textile Design and Theatre Design.

Oxford* The degree of Fine Art involves drawing and painting, printmaking and sculpture together with the history of art and anatomy. Most students have completed a foundation course prior to application, and entry is very competitive. A three-year History of Art course is also available.

Oxford Brookes A degree course is offered in Fine Art as a single or combined honours degree, introducing the student to a range of practices. Courses are also available in History of Art, Graphic Design and Illustration: Narrative and Sequential.

Plymouth Several Design courses are offered focusing on Illustration, Fashion, Textiles, Photography, Graphic Communication, Fine Art, Applied Arts (ceramics, glass and metals), Silversmithing and Jewellery, Media Arts, TV Arts, and Three-dimensional Design (product, furniture and interiors).

Portsmouth Illustration, Fashion and Textile Design with Enterprise, Photography, Contemporary Fine Art and Photography are among the courses offered. Core studies in studio practice and history are undertaken by all students.

Reading Four-year degrees in Fine Art and Art are offered with studio facilities for painting, wood, metal, plastics and printmaking, photography and video. A unique degree is also offered in Graphic Communication. Art is also offered as a joint course with History of Art, Philosophy, Psychology, and Film and Theatre.

Robert Gordon Gray's School of Art offers courses in Design and Craft (Visual Communication; Textile and Surface Design; Fashion Design; Three-dimensional Design (ceramics, glass or jewellery)), Design for Industry (product design, graphic design or digital media), Fine Art (painting, printmaking, sculpture, or photographic and electronic media) and a one-year course in Commercial Photography.

Salford Courses are offered in Design Studies, Animation, Advertising Design, Design Management, Graphic Design, Product Design and Development, Spatial/Interior Design, Visual Arts, Fashion Design (links with top fashion firms) and Sports Equipment Design.

Sheffield Hallam Degree courses are available in Contemporary Fine Art (painting and printmaking, sculpture and time-based art), Graphic Design, Furniture Design, Interior Product and Transport Design, Packaging Design and Metalwork and Jewellery. There is also a broad course in Visual Arts.

See *Heap 2015: University Degree Course Offers* (Trotman Publishing) for details of offers

South Wales A three-year full-time degree is offered in Art Practice covering courses in ceramics, three-dimensional studies, drawing, painting, fashion design and photography. Degrees are also offered in Advertising, Animation, Games Art and Design, Graphic Design and Communication, Fashion, Interior Design, Photography and the internationally regarded course in Computer Animation. Creative and Therapeutic Arts gives a practical introduction to using creative arts in a therapeutic context.

Southampton Courses are offered in Fine Art Practice and Theory (painting, printmaking and sculpture) Graphic Arts, and in Textiles, Fashion and Fibre (textile art and design). The courses are based at Winchester School of Art.

Southampton Solent Courses are offered in Creative Industries, Design Studies, Interior Design, Design Technology, Fashion, Fine Art, Illustration, Graphic Design and Photography.

Staffordshire Degrees are offered in Fine Art (with options in photography, animation and theory), Design (graphics, animation, electronic graphics, multimedia graphics, media production, photography, product design, surface pattern, crafts, glass and ceramics), Design Management, Design Technology, Modern Art, Design and Visual Media, Product Design and Transport Design.

Strathclyde Product Design and Innovation is offered by way of a four-year course.

Sunderland The Art and Design BA offers 18 subjects. Two of these subjects (minimum) to a maximum of four are chosen in Level 1 and students progress in at least two subjects in Levels 2 and 3. The modules on offer are fine art, photography, ceramics, dance, drama and graphics. Degree courses are also offered in Advertising, Fine Art and Glass. There is also a teaching course in Design and Technology.

Teesside Degree courses are available in Fine Art, Fashion and Textile Design, Graphic Design (including advertising, illustration and computer graphics), Interior Architecture and Design, Contemporary Three-dimensional Design, Product Design, Photography and Design Marketing.

Trinity St David (Swansea) Fine Art, Graphic Design and Illustration, General Illustration, Design for Advertising, Photography in the Arts, and Surface Pattern Design courses are offered.

Ulster Courses are available in Fine Arts (painting, sculpture, performance, printmaking, lens-based media, history and theory). Combined Studies available include graphic design and illustration, textile and fashion design and visual communication. Design, Graphic, Product and Interactive Design, Textiles and Fashion Design, Visual Communication and Technology and Design with the Diploma in Industrial Studies are also offered.

West London Courses are offered in Games Design and Development, Fashion and Textiles, Fine Art, Graphic Design, Interior Architecture, Illustration and Three-dimensional Studies.

West Scotland Design courses are offered covering Computer-aided Design, Product Design, Photography and Design with Manufacturing Systems.

Westminster Courses are offered in Ceramics, Fashion, Graphic Information Design, Animation, Illustration and Visual Communication and Mixed Media Fine Art (photography, video, painting, printmaking, digital and web-based practices, performance art and media theory).

Wolverhampton Degrees are offered in a wide range of courses including Design and Applied Arts, Animation, Ceramics, Design for Interior Textiles, Fashion and Textiles, Glass, Computer-aided Design, Design, Digital Media, Fine Art, Furniture Design, Illustration, Graphic Communication, Figurative Sculpture and Modelling, Three-dimensional Design (wood, metals and plastics). There are also courses in Product Design focusing on innovation and technology.

Worcester The Art and Design course offers modules in drawing, painting, graphic design, fine art, illustration, textiles and ceramics. There is a work placement in Year 3. A three-year BA in Fine Art Practice is also available.

OTHER INSTITUTIONS OFFERING ART AND DESIGN COURSES

Arts London (Wimbledon CA), Barking (Coll), Birmingham Met (Coll), Bishop Grosseteste, Blackburn (Coll), Blackpool and Fylde (Coll), Bradford (Coll Univ Centre), Central Nottingham (Coll), Chichester (Coll), Cleveland (CAD), Cornwall (Coll), Coventry City (Coll), Craven (Coll), Croydon (Coll), Doncaster (Coll Univ Centre), Edinburgh (CA), Exeter (Coll), Farnborough (CT), Glasgow (SA), Gloucestershire (Coll), Grimsby (Univ Centre), Havering (Coll), Hereford (CA), Hopwood Hall (Coll), Hull (Coll), Kirklees (Coll), Leeds (CA), Leeds City (Coll), Liverpool (LIPA), Liverpool City (Coll), Llandrillo Cymru (Coll), London (Royal Central Sch SpDr), Menai (Coll), Neath Port Talbot (Coll), Nescot, NEW (Coll), Newcastle (Coll), North Warwickshire and Hinckley (Coll), Northbrook (Coll), Norwich City (Coll), Nottingham New (Coll), Peterborough (Reg Coll), Ravensbourne, Richmond (Am Int Univ), Rose Bruford (Coll), Rotherham (CAT), St Helens (Coll), Sheffield (Coll), Shrewsbury (CAT), Sir Gâr (Coll), Solihull (Coll), Somerset (Coll), South Tyneside (Coll), Southport (Coll), Stamford New (Coll), Stockport (Coll), Stratford upon Avon (Coll), Suffolk (Univ Campus), Swindon (Coll), Truro (Coll), Tyne Met (Coll), UHI, Uxbridge (Coll), Walsall (Coll), West Anglia (Coll), West Cheshire (Coll), West Thames (Coll), Westminster Kingsway (Coll), Wirral Met (Coll), Worcester (CT), York (Coll), Ystrad Mynach (Coll).

ALTERNATIVE COURSES

All practical Art and Design courses. Archaeology, Architecture, Classical Civilisation, Communication Studies, Film Studies, Landscape Architecture, Media Studies, Performance Studies.

ASTRONOMY/ASTROPHYSICS

(* indicates universities with entry requirements over 340 UCAS points)

SUBJECT REQUIREMENTS/PREFERENCES

GCE A level: Two or three science subjects. Mathematics and Physics important.

SUBJECT INFORMATION

These courses have a mathematics and physics emphasis. Applicants, however, should also realise that subject-related careers on graduation are limited. Astrophysics courses involve both physics and astronomy and are more difficult than single honours; students weak in mathematics and physics should avoid them.

Birmingham* Physics and Astrophysics is taken as a major theme in Year 3 by those with an interest in astronomy and astrophysics who wish to combine this with a training in basic physics. An optional year's course in Computer Science is offered after Year 2. There is the opportunity to study in Europe during the third year through the university's Erasmus exchange programme. All Physics courses have a common Year 1 and 2. There are also programmes which include space research and particle physics with cosmology.

Bristol* A four-year course in Physics with Astrophysics is offered, including cosmology, stellar structure and advanced electromagnetism (also with industrial experience). Options are taken in astrophysics and in particle physics and astronomy alongside units common to the BSc Physics programme.

Cambridge* Astrophysics is offered as a third year (Part II) course in the Natural Science Tripos. Students usually enter on completion of Part IB in either Mathematics or Physics. Part III Astrophysics leads to an MSci.

Cardiff* Physics with Astronomy is a four-year course designed for those aiming at less theoretical work and has an emphasis on laboratory work, astronomy and observational techniques. A four-year course in Astrophysics is also offered.

See *Heap 2015: University Degree Course Offers* (Trotman Publishing) for details of offers

Central Lancashire Astronomy and Astrophysics degrees are offered on three-year BSc and four-year MPhys courses. Practical observations are made with Britain's largest optical telescope. Completion of the course leads to graduate fellowship of the Institute of Physics. Astronomy can also be taken with Mathematics. A part-time distance-learning course in Astronomy is also offered (by way of direct application).

Durham* Three- and four-year courses are offered in Physics and Astronomy, with theoretical studies in physics, stars and galaxies, and materials for sustainable energy supported by laboratory sessions.

Edinburgh* The first two years of the Astrophysics course are largely similar to those for Physics students. In the third and fourth years the work is divided between astronomy and physics.

Exeter* Physics with Astrophysics can be studied over three or four years. Observational work is taught using the undergraduate teaching observatory.

Glasgow* Astronomy covers a study of the universe and the methods used in assessing the distances, motions and nature of celestial objects. Later studies examine modern developments. Astronomy is also offered with Mathematics and Physics. Lectures are complemented by observatory and planetarium work. No previous knowledge of astronomy is required.

Hertfordshire Three-year BSc and four-year MPhys in Astrophysics are offered with an industrial placement option prior to the final year, or alternatively a year in Europe or North America. There is a well-equipped teaching observatory.

Keele Astrophysics can be taken as a dual honours course with over 28 other subjects, including both science and humanities disciplines.

Kent The three themes of Astronomy, Space Science and Astrophysics give this degree its name and it is taught by the Centre for Astrophysics and Space Science, which has a strong international reputation. Students can spend a year studying at a partner university in the US.

Lancaster* Topics covered on the four-year Physics, Astrophysics and Space Science course include atmospheric and aurora physics and solar winds. Courses in Particle Physics and Cosmology are also offered.

Leeds* Physics with Astrophysics runs parallel to the Physics course during Year 1 and enables transfers between the Physics and the Physics with Astrophysics courses to be arranged up to the end of the first year. There is also a joint course with Philosophy.

Leicester Three-year BSc and four-year MPhys courses are offered in Mathematics with Astronomy, Physics with Astrophysics and Physics with Space Science and Technology, or Planetary Sciences which includes solar physics and space flight dynamics.

Liverpool* The course in Astrophysics follows a common core with the Physics programme in Years 1 and 2 with one or two variations. Specialisms follow in Year 3. Astronomy is also offered with Physics. There is a field trip to an observatory in Tenerife at the end of Year 2.

Liverpool John Moores The four-year course in Astrophysics is a collaborative venture between John Moores and Liverpool University. The course covers physics, mathematics and computing. Some observational work is carried out at Jodrell Bank and at La Laguma University in Tenerife. There is also a course in Physics with astronomy.

London (King's)* A three-year BSc and a four-year MSci are offered in Physics or Mathematics and Physics, with astrophysics as an option in Year 2.

London (QM) The degree in Astrophysics offers a physics programme accompanied by specialised topics such as stellar and galactic structure and cosmology.

London (RH)* BSc and MSc courses are offered in Astrophysics. The former covering physics and quantum physics with an emphasis on astrophysics and cosmology.

See *Heap 2015: University Degree Course Offers* (Trotman Publishing) for details of offers

London (UCL)* BSc and MSc courses are offered in Astrophysics, both with common structures in Years 1 and 2. A visit to the Observatoire de Haute Provence in France is available in the third year.

Manchester* Physics and Astrophysics, available as a three-year BSc or a four-year MPhys, is primarily a Physics course with specialist studies in astrophysics. There is also a course in Geology with Planetary Science.

Nottingham* Three- and four-year courses are offered in Physics with Astronomy, the latter leading to an MSc. A three-year BSc in Physics with Theoretical Astrophysics is also available, with a reduced practical component and fewer module options to provide a broad overview of physics and theoretical astrophysics.

Nottingham Trent A three-year degree is offered in Physics with Astrophysics or Astronomy. A year-long paid industry placement is optional on the Physics with Astrophysics programme.

St Andrews Astrophysics is offered as a five-year or a four-year degree course. The university has its own observatory.

Salford Four-year degrees in Space Technology and Physics are offered. Industrial placements are offered.

Sheffield* Physics and Astrophysics is available as a three-year BSc and a four-year MPhys. One or two students per year are selected to work during their final year at the Isaac Newton Group of Telescopes on La Palma. Astronomy is offered with Physics and Mathematics.

South Wales* A three-year BSc in Observational Astronomy is available. Students have regular access to two-metre Faulkes Telescopes in Australia and Hawaii.

Southampton* A course is offered in Physics with Astronomy either by way of one degree in both subjects (single honours) or two degrees in each subject (double honours). Physics with Astrophysics is also available as a BSc or MPhys. Mathematics with Astronomy is also available.

Surrey* Nuclear Astrophysics is available with Physics. There are also courses in Satellite Technology. All programmes are accredited by the UK's Institute of Physics.

Sussex Students taking the Astrophysics option spend about a quarter of their time on this subject and the rest on physics and undertake a fourth year project in Astrophysics.

York* Physics with Astrophysics covers courses on planetary science. Stellar physics is taken in Year 2 and observational astronomy in Year 3, with core mathematics modules in Years 1 and 2.

ALTERNATIVE COURSES
Applied Physics or Physics, Computer Science, Electronics, Geology, Geophysics, Materials Science, Mathematics, Meteorology, Mineral Sciences, Oceanography, Optometry.

BIOCHEMISTRY

(* indicates universities with entry requirements over 340 UCAS points)

SUBJECT REQUIREMENTS/PREFERENCES
GCE A level: Chemistry, usually supported by another science subject; Physics, Mathematics or Biology often preferred.

SUBJECT INFORMATION

Biochemistry is the study of life processes at the molecular level, involving animals and plants. There are also applications in human and veterinary medicine, biotechnology, environmental science, agriculture and forestry.

Aberdeen After introductory studies in Chemistry and Medical Sciences, the Biochemistry and Biochemistry (Immunology) courses cover molecular aspects of biotechnology and genetics. Industrial placements are available for some courses and there are exchanges in Europe and North America.

Aston Biological Chemistry (with a bias towards chemistry) is available as a three-year full-time or four-year sandwich degree. The course covers a range of topics including health, safety and the environment, polymer chemistry, human disease and biotechnology.

Bath* Biochemistry is a three-year full-time or four-year sandwich course. Biochemistry is taken with chemistry, genetics and cell biology in the first year, together with plant and animal physiology and microbiology. Professional placement takes place in the third term in Years 2 and 3. The Department of Biology and Biochemistry has a range of training placements in Europe and the US, although these cannot be guaranteed. Students can switch courses to Biology or Molecular and Cellular Biology up to the end of Year 1.

Birmingham Biochemistry is offered with Biotechnology, Molecular and Cell Biology or Genetics. Years 1 and 2 are common, leading to specialist studies in Year 3 in areas including genetics, biotechnology and molecular cell biology. An additional year can be spent in industrial research or study in France, Spain or Germany. There is also a course in Medical Biochemistry. See also **Combined Courses**.

Bristol* A study of biochemistry and chemistry is the focus of Year 1 of the Biochemistry course, plus an optional unit that can bias the programme towards molecular biology, medical biochemistry or general biochemistry. In Year 2 other units include genetics, pathology, pharmacology, and physiology and specialist options follow in Year 3. Degrees are available in Biochemistry with Medical Biochemistry and Biochemistry with Molecular Biology and Biotechnology. Transfer to Biochemistry with Study in Industry may be possible at the end of Year 1. Students are assigned a personal tutor to support learning throughout the programme.

Brunel See under **Biological Sciences**.

Cambridge* See also **Combined Courses**.

Cardiff Biochemistry is taught as a modular course in the School of Biosciences. There is a common first-year course after which students make a choice to specialise. Separate degree courses are offered in Anatomy, Neuroscience, Physiology and Pharmacology. A four-year course including a year in industry is available.

Coventry Biochemistry is a three-year full-time or four-year sandwich course, the latter with Year 3 in professional training or industry. A range of options is available in the final year. There is also a European option with concurrent language study in all years from French, German, Italian or Spanish ab initio. Biochemistry is also offered with Chemistry or Pharmaceutical Chemistry, and courses are available in Biomedical Science and Applied Biomedical Science.

Dundee* The Biochemistry course covers chemistry and biology in Year 1 and life sciences with other modules in Year 2 prior to embarking on a specialised biochemistry programme in Years 3 and 4. Students are encouraged to undertake summer work placements. Biochemistry can also be taken with Pharmacology or Physiology. See also **Biological Sciences**.

East Anglia There is an introduction to biochemistry, cell and molecular biology and genetics in the first year of the Biochemistry courses, allowing students, if they wish, to transfer to degree courses in Biological or Chemical Sciences. In the second year, biochemistry and molecular biology are taken with a selection from microbiology, physiology, protein engineering and biotechnology. In the third year, students make a selection from a range of subjects. Biochemistry can also be taken with a year in Australia, New Zealand, Europe, Canada or the US. The degree has official recognition from the Royal Society of Chemistry, allowing graduates to qualify as an associate member.

East London Biochemistry is a modular degree involving cell and molecular biology, genetics, medical and plant biotechnology. There is the opportunity to switch between courses in life sciences (students' specialist course on entry is not binding). A four-year sandwich option is available.

Edinburgh* There is a common first year for all Biochemistry students entering courses in the School of Biology, covering cell formation, components and interaction. Students can specialise in one of 12 programmes. See also **Biological Sciences**.

Essex Biochemistry students take a course in biosciences in Year 1 that leads to a degree course in Biochemistry in Years 2 and 3. At the end of the first year it is possible to take Biomedical Sciences including biochemistry with cell biology. Students obtaining good marks in Year 2 and a satisfactory UKCAT test are guaranteed interviews for graduate entry to a medical school place at Queen Mary Medical School. An optional year in industry placement is available.

Exeter A course is offered in Biological and Medicinal Chemistry designed for those graduates who wish to take advantage of new opportunities in the rapidly expanding field of biotechnology. Options for a year in industrial placement or studying abroad are available.

Glasgow* In the Biochemistry course an optional one-year placement is offered between Levels 3 and 4. There is a strong emphasis on practical laboratory work. Courses in Medical Biochemistry and in Environmental Biogeochemistry are offered. See also **Biological Sciences**.

Greenwich See under **Biological Sciences**.

Heriot-Watt A four-year full-time course in Biochemistry is offered, covering organic, inorganic and physical chemistry and molecular and cell biology. There is also a course in Chemistry with Biochemistry.

Hertfordshire See under **Biological Sciences**.

Huddersfield A modular course in Biochemistry is offered, of three or four years (which includes Year 3 in employment) and the final year with research into a major study of selected specialisms including immunology, biotechnology, genetic engineering and medical biochemistry. An optional year in industrial placement is available.

Imperial London* Biochemistry is taught on a course unit system with specialisms in Year 3. Seven courses can also be taken including a year in industry or abroad. Biochemistry with Management (three-year or four-year courses) and Biotechnology programmes are also available. New courses in Biochemistry with French for Science or German for Science are also available.

Keele Biochemistry is taken as a dual honours subject with a second subject and carries an emphasis on human biochemistry and disease. A sandwich placement of a year in industry is offered at the end of Year 2. Biochemistry can be taken in combination with a choice from over 17 other subjects.

Kent Biochemistry can be studied as a three- or four-year (sandwich) degree, with a bias towards biotechnology, cell or molecular biology, medical biosciences, microbiology or physiology.

Kingston The Biochemistry course covers chemistry, physiology and computing with other modules in the biology of disease, microbiology, pharmacology, immunology and medical biochemistry, which is also available as a degree course. Options include pharmacology, haematology and toxicology.

Lancaster Biological sciences, chemistry and one other subject are taken in the first year of the Biochemistry course. Specialisation then follows in Year 2. Courses include a Year 2 option to study abroad. Biochemistry with Genetics, Biomedicines and Cell Biology are also offered.

See *Heap 2015: University Degree Course Offers* (Trotman Publishing) for details of offers

Leeds* Biochemistry, a modular programme within the School of Biological Sciences, gives great flexibility of choice. Specialisms at Level 3 include plant and medical options, and an original research project is undertaken in the final year. Biochemistry can also be taken with Chemistry.

Leicester Biochemistry is offered as part of the Biological Sciences programme. Modules from medical school courses are taken in the first and second years of the course in Medical Biochemistry. A year in industry placement is available. See also **Biological Sciences**.

Lincoln A new course from 2013 covering aspects of pharmaceuticals, agricultural sciences and biotechnology.

Liverpool Courses in Biochemistry and Biochemistry (Year in Industry) are offered; the latter includes work placement following Year 2. The course includes computer skills and options in biotechnology, immunology and studies relating to cancer. An individual research project covers two modules in the third year. See also **Biological Sciences**.

Liverpool John Moores The School of Biomolecular Sciences offers full-time or sandwich courses in Biochemistry or Forensic Science, and also Medical Biochemistry and Applied Medical Biochemistry. All programmes have an optional industrial sandwich year or a year of study abroad.

London (King's)* Biochemistry has a common first year with other subjects in the life sciences field. A course is also offered in Biomedical Science and can be taken by way of a sandwich course. A year spent in industry placement or research in the UK or overseas may be offered.

London (QM) The course overs organic and inorganic chemistry and biology in the first year, leading to a range of specialties offered in years two and three.

London (RH) Students following degree courses in Biochemistry and Molecular Biology share a common first-year programme and have the option to change courses at the end of the year. The Biomedical Science course includes physiology and a hospital experience course in the summer vacation of the second year. Specialist courses include nutrition, birth control, disease and pollution.

London (UCL)* Biochemistry is offered with Biotechnology, the latter covering molecular biology, biological engineering and experimental biochemistry hence the combination course.

London Met A three-year full-time course in Biochemistry is offered, with options in pharmacology, immunology and pathology. Summer school courses are available, with subjects including Behavioural Science, Embryology and Patient, Doctor and Community.

London South Bank Biochemistry is offered as a part of the Bioscience programme and covers modules including nutrition, social aspects of science and genomes. A four-year sandwich course is available. A course in Biochemistry (Clinical) is also offered.

Manchester* Biochemistry is offered as a three-year degree course, or as a four-year course if studied with a modern language, or with industrial experience. Medical Biochemistry can also be taken with industrial experience. There is a modular course structure within the Faculty of Life Sciences that allows for early transfer. Students choose second- and final-year modules in keeping with their career aspirations.

Newcastle* The Biochemistry degree shares a common first year with Genetics and covers DNA synthesis and repair, immunology, virus and plant biology. Students may then change courses after Stage 1.

Nottingham In the first year of the Biochemistry and Biological Chemistry course students take biochemistry, chemistry and a third subject, usually physiology and pharmacology, languages or maths. In the second and third years the teaching is shared equally between the Departments of Biochemistry and Chemistry, leading to specialisms in pharmaceutical and agrochemical science, enzyme technology or toxicology. The final year includes an in-depth research project with a range of options. BSc courses in Nutritional Biochemistry and Biochemistry and Genetics are also offered.

Nottingham Trent See under **Biological Sciences**.

See *Heap 2015: University Degree Course Offers* (Trotman Publishing) for details of offers

Oxford* There is a four-year course in Molecular and Cellular Biochemistry. The fourth year involves a research project which may extend to other areas such as clinical biochemistry, pathology and pharmacology for some students in one of several European universities. A course in Biomedical Sciences is also available, with the choice of specialism in either cells and systems biology or neuroscience.

Portsmouth All students taking Biological Sciences follow a common course for the first three semesters. Specialisation in Biochemistry starts in the fourth semester. Biochemistry is also offered with Forensic Biology, Microbiology or Genome Science.

Queen's Belfast In the first year the Biochemistry course focuses on chemistry and includes a 16-week work placement period. After Level 1 the flexible modular system enables students to decide which special degree programme they wish to follow and includes Enzymology, Genetics and Physiology. The degree with Professional Studies includes a 40-week placement period. A course in Microbiology is also available.

Reading There is a focus on biology and chemistry in the first year of the Biochemistry course followed by a specialised subject choice. A range of option modules can be studied in each year, including cancer, clinical trials and mammalian reproduction. See also **Biology**.

St Andrews* Biochemistry is offered as part of the Biology programme, the final choice of degree being made at the end of Year 2. Subjects covered include cell structure, comparative physiology and ecology.

Salford The Biochemistry course is offered in the School of Biological Sciences with modules available in biological chemistry and genetics. There is also a chance to study in the US for a year.

Sheffield* Biochemistry students take core units in the main subject and biology modules in Year 1. Further studies lead to medical and industrial applications. Biochemistry can also be studied with Physiology, Genetics and Microbiology and there are also degrees in Biological Chemistry and Medical Biochemistry.

Southampton* Biochemistry includes molecular biology, pharmacology and physiology. The structure of courses in the School of Biological Sciences is extremely flexible and allows students to transfer between various single and combined degrees in the second and third years, with optional modules including neuroscience, pharmacology and toxicity.

Staffordshire A three-year full-time course is offered in Biochemistry and Microbiology, involving biomedicine and medical microbiology. Degrees in Biomedical Science and Biology are also offered.

Strathclyde Five joint honours degrees are offered in Biochemistry, Biological and Biomedical Sciences allowing students to combine two subject options – Biochemistry and Immunology, Microbiology or Pharmacology – or more specialist degrees and enabling a choice of career paths in industry or the public sector.

Surrey Five degree courses are available: Biochemistry, Biochemistry (Medical; Toxicology; Neuroscience; Pharmacology). All are common for the first two years, allowing interchange up to the end of the second year. These are four-year courses, with the third year consisting of professional training away from the university. In the fourth year, Biochemistry students select three options from a wide range of modules.

Sussex Biochemistry is taught in the School of Biological Sciences and provides the opportunity to pursue different specialisms in the subject, including endocrinology, cell signalling and genomics. It is offered as a three-year or four-year sandwich course. There is an optional sandwich year in industry.

Swansea The degree scheme is made up of modules covering a broad spectrum of topics covering the biochemistry of medicine and pharmacology, and environmental and physiological aspects. Courses are also offered in Biochemistry with Genetics or Zoology. There are also degrees in Medical Biochemistry, Genetics and Medical Genetics.

See *Heap 2015: University Degree Course Offers* (Trotman Publishing) for details of offers

Warwick A common first year in the Department of Biological Sciences allows entrants to Biochemistry the option to transfer to degree courses in Microbiology and Virology, Microbiology and Biological Sciences at the end of the year. Options in the final year include industrial biology and oncology as well as other subjects, for example business, music and languages. Students are given tuition in the use of computers for data analysis.

West Scotland Biochemistry is offered only in a joint course with Applied Bioscience. A 12-week work placement is optional.

Westminster Biochemistry can be taken as a single honours course or with free choice modules in each year. Subjects covered include protein biochemistry and enzymes.

Wolverhampton Biochemistry is a three-year full-time or four-year sandwich course taught on the flexible modular system with one or two other subjects, including Food Science and Molecular Biology. The course covers biology, microbiology and pharmacology. Biochemistry can also be taken with Biomedical Science, Food Science or Pharmacology.

York* Biochemistry, Chemistry and Biology students are taught together for the first part of the course. In the remaining two parts, Biochemistry specialisms include major practical courses in microbiology and biophysical techniques and biology as well as a range of selected optional subjects. Placements in industry or at a European university are optional in Year 3. Weekly tutorials for all students, in groups of four, are a distinctive and effective feature.

OTHER INSTITUTIONS OFFERING BIOCHEMISTRY COURSES
See under **Biology**.

ALTERNATIVE COURSES
Agricultural Sciences, Agriculture, Biological Sciences, Botany, Brewing, Chemistry, Food Science, Geochemistry, Medicine, Microbiology, Nutrition, Pharmacology, Pharmacy.

BIOLOGICAL SCIENCES

(including **Biomedical Sciences**)
(see also **Biochemistry, Biology** and **Biotechnology**)
(* indicates universities with entry requirements over 340 UCAS points)

SUBJECT REQUIREMENTS/PREFERENCES
GCE A level: Two or three subjects from Mathematics/sciences; Chemistry usually essential.

SUBJECT INFORMATION
In many universities the Department or School of Biological Sciences will offer a modular programme covering subjects such as biochemistry, botany, biotechnology, genetics, physiology and zoology. This type of programme usually offers a common first year for all students, allowing them to make a final choice of single or joint degree course in Year 2. In other universities Biological Sciences is offered as a single named subject.

Aberdeen Courses offered include Biology, Biomedical Sciences, Conservation Biology, Ecology, Wildlife Management and Zoology.

Abertay Flexible programmes are offered in Biomedical Sciences (bursaries available to eligible students) and Medical Biotechnology. A clinical placement is included in the second semester of Year 2. There are also degree courses in Forensic Sciences (professionally accredited) and Forensic Psychobiology.

Aberystwyth The Institute of Biological, Environmental and Rural Sciences offers courses including Animal Behaviour, Biochemistry, Biology, Bioinformatics, Genetics, Life Sciences, Marine Biology and Zoology. The Life Sciences honours degree scheme includes a foundation year and is recommended for students with a non-traditional background or who do not have adequate A levels in a relevant science subject for other courses.

Anglia Ruskin The Biomedical Science course aims to provide a focus on the human body in health and disease. Special studies are offered in Years 2 and 3. It is possible to transfer to Applied Biomedical Science in Year 2 to gain specialised knowledge of laboratory skills.

Aston See under **Biology**.

Bangor The School of Ocean Sciences, one of the largest in Europe, also offers degree courses in Oceanography, Ocean Science and Marine Biology, Chemistry, Coastal Water Resources and Ocean Informatics. A BSc (Hons) in Biomedical Science is also available, with the option of paid clinical laboratory placements in Year 2. See also **Biology**.

Bedfordshire There is a broad course in Biological Sciences and a course in Biomedical Sciences which focuses on the function of the human body and consists of specialist areas covering genetics, microbiology, nutrition, pathology, pharmacology and physiology. There is also a degree in Forensic Science.

Birmingham Over 20 specialisms in Biological Sciences follow a common first and second year taken by all students. These cover animal biology, biotechnology, environmental biology, genetics, plant biology, zoology or conservation biology. There is also an option to study in Continental Europe or in industry, and field project modules are offered in Brazil and Florida. See also **Combined Courses**.

Bournemouth The Biological Sciences course covers a wide range of topics including biology, chemistry, ecology, toxicology, evolution and anthropology. The course offers a mixture of laboratory and fieldwork. Courses in Biological Anthropology and Ecology and Wildlife Conservation are also available.

Bradford Cellular pathology, medical biochemistry or microbiology can be taken as specialised options in Year 3 of the Biomedical Sciences course. A year in industrial placement is available. There is also a Clinical Sciences degree that offers entry for some students to Medicine at Leeds.

Brighton The Biological Sciences course offers modules in cell biology, biochemistry, ecology, environmental biology and human physiology. Two or three of these are chosen in the final year. Students may combine the course with study of a language. There are also degree courses in Applied Biomedical Sciences and Human Ecology; students on the former are employed by the Regional NHS Laboratory during their course.

Bristol* The largest department in the UK offers three subjects in Year 1 alongside a subsidiary subject. Flexibility continues in Years 2 and 3 when the subjects offered include biology, botany, zoology, biology and geology or geography and psychology and zoology. Biology is available as a joint honours course with Geology. There are separate degree courses in Biology, Cellular and Molecular Medicine, Neuroscience, Pathology and Microbiology, Physiological Science and Zoology.

Bristol UWE Courses can be followed in Applied Biomedical Sciences (covering conservation biology, biological sciences, human biology, microbiology, forensic science and genetics). There are sandwich courses with some abroad placements.

Brunel The Bioscience field offers six courses in Biomedical Sciences, and with specialisms in Biochemistry, Forensic Science, Genetics, Human Health and Immunology. All courses have a sandwich placement, with overseas options including the US, Switzerland and Malaysia.

Cambridge* See under **Combined Courses**.

Canterbury Christ Church The Biosciences degree offers specialisations in general biological sciences, environmental science or physical science. Studies cover animal health and welfare, anatomy, physiology, ecology and conservation and an individual study in Year 3. The course is also available as a joint or combined honours degree. There is a course in Forensic Investigation with modules in policing, jurisprudence and a subject module from another department.

Cardiff In the Biomedical Sciences course, specialisations are offered in applied biology, anatomical science, biology, biotechnology, ecology, genetics, microbiology or zoology in the second and third years. Anatomy Sciences, Neuroscience, Physiology are also offered.

Cardiff Met (UWIC) Biomedical Science can be taken focusing on biology, forensic toxicology or sport. An HND in Biomedical Science is available for international students.

Central Lancashire The Biological Sciences degree is modular offering studies in biology, genetics, biochemistry, physiology and pharmacology. A work placement module is offered in Year 2. There are also degree courses in Biomedical Science, Neuroscience, Applied Biomolecular Sciences, with specialisms in Biotechnology, Clinical Sciences, Molecular Chemistry and Pharmaceutics, and Microbiology, which is also offered jointly with seven other subjects.

Chester Single and combined honours courses are offered in Biomedical Sciences. In the final year, students have the option of undertaking a research dissertation or another mode of independent learning. Courses are vocational leading to careers in industry and the health services.

Coventry Biological Sciences degrees are offered, including a study placement year in the UK or in Europe and an opportunity to specialise in several subjects in Year 3, including biotechnology, genetics and biomedical sciences. Biological Sciences can also be studied with Forensic Sciences.

Cumbria A degree in Forensic Science has modules in evidence, criminal law, drugs and genetics. A course in Biochemistry of Toxic Chemicals is also available.

De Montfort The Medical Science degree covers laboratory and clinical approaches to investigating the human body. There is an option to spend a year out on a sandwich placement in industry.

Derby The BSc (Hons) Biology is recognised by the Society of Biology; graduates of the course will qualify for associate membership. Courses are also offered in Forensic Science and Zoology.

Dundee* The BSc in Biological Sciences covers Biology, Biomedical Sciences, Microbiology, Pharmacology and Zoology. The programmes emphasise laboratory teaching and practical field work. Degrees in Anatomical Sciences, Biomedical Science, Pharmacology and Physiological Sciences are also offered, as well as a course in Sports Medicine.

Durham* All Biological programmes have a common first year leading on to specialisms in 10 subjects including Biology, Cell Biology, Ecology, Plant Sciences and Zoology, all with or without industrial placement. Additional subjects, such as modern languages, can be studied in Year 1. This is also available as part of the programme in Natural Sciences and with Education Studies. Biomedical Sciences is also offered.

East Anglia The BSc programme commences with a common first year for all students after which a choice of final degree is made from Cell Biology, Microbiology, Molecular Genetics or Ecology. A wide range of courses can be selected in Ecology and Climate Change, most of which offer a year in industry or in Europe, North America or Australasia.

East London* A course is offered in Biomedical Sciences, with an optional sandwich placement. The course is accredited by the Institute of Biomedical Sciences (IBMS). There are also degrees in Chemical Sciences, Immunology, Medical Biotechnology, Forensic Science and Clinical Science.

Edinburgh The School of Biology offers degrees in Biochemistry, Biological Sciences, Developmental Biology, Biotechnology, Ecology, Genetics, Immunology, Infectious Diseases, Medical Microbiology,

Molecular Biology, Neuroscience, Pharmacology, Physiology, Plant Science, Virology and Zoology. Students cover a broad curriculum in Year 1, taking up to six courses with options available in other academic areas such as languages or management. Several combinations are possible, the final choice of subject being made at the end of Year 3.

Edinburgh Napier The three-year or four-year sandwich course in Biological Sciences allows specialisation in microbiology, biomedical science, toxicology, animal biology and human biology.

Essex In the first year students follow a pathway covering a range of subjects thus enabling a choice of degree to be made at a later stage. Degrees are offered in Biological Sciences, which provides a broad overview of modern biology including ethical issues, Genetics, Ecology, Marine and Freshwater Biology and Biodiversity and Conservation.

Exeter Single honours Biological Sciences students take core modules from cell structure and physiology, genetics, microbiology, biochemistry, animal physiology, plant physiology, animal biology, plant biology, biological investigation, and human impact on the biosphere. Non-core biological options, such as geography, psychology and chemistry, can then be taken. Courses are offered in Biological Sciences with pathways in Animal Biology, Microbiology and Molecular Cell Biology, Biological and Medicinal Chemistry, Human Biosciences and, in Cornwall, Conservation, Biology and Ecology.

Glasgow The three-year Biological Sciences programme offers five degree pathways: Animal Biology, Biomolecular Sciences, Human Biology, Infection Biology and Sports Science. The opportunity to study abroad through the Erasmus scheme is available. In addition, degrees are offered in Genetics, Parasitology, Pharmacology, Physiology, Virology and Zoology.

Glasgow Caledonian Human Biosciences offers specialisation in biomolecular sciences, microbiology or physiological sciences. There are degree courses in Biomedical Sciences (with some work placements available in Scottish hospitals, allowing graduates to apply for registration as a biomedical scientist with the HPC), Food Bioscience, Microbiology and Pharmacology.

Gloucestershire Biological Sciences and Animal Biology are offered as single and joint honours courses with work placement opportunities. A Biology degree is also available.

Glyndŵr Degrees are offered in Forensic Science, with modules including cell biology and forensic genetics, and/with Criminal Justice. Part-time study is also available.

Greenwich Biosciences is a broad-based course offering specialisms in medical physiology, biological sciences, medical biochemistry, biochemistry or molecular biology. At the end of Year 2 it is possible to change to other life science degrees. It can be taken on a sandwich basis and combined with European study. Degrees in Biomedical Science and Forensic Science are also offered.

Heriot-Watt All courses in Biological Sciences follow a common core of subjects in Years 1 and 2. In addition, Biological Sciences courses focus on cell biology, food science, human health or microbiology. Courses in Applied Marine Biology, Biochemistry, Life Sciences and Brewing and Distilling are also offered.

Hertfordshire The School of Biosciences offers degrees in Applied Biology, Biochemistry, Biotechnology, Biological Sciences, Biomedical Sciences, Forensic Science, Microbiology, Molecular Biology and Physiology. Most Science courses offer a year studying at a partner university in Europe or North America. Human physiology and pharmacology are offered within the Applied Biology course.

Huddersfield Courses are offered in Forensic and Analytical Science, Food/Nutritional Science, Microbiology, Medical Genetics and Applied Science.

Hull Courses are offered in Aquatic Zoology, Biology, Human Biology and Marine and Freshwater Biology with optional diving training, and Biomedical Science. The BSc in Biomedical Science is currently accredited by the Institute for Biomedical Science.

Imperial London* There is a very large Faculty of Life Sciences covering a range of courses in Biochemistry, Biotechnology, Biology, Biomedical Science, Microbiology, Ecology and Zoology. New courses in Biology or Biochemistry with French, German or Spanish for Science are also available.

See Heap 2015: University Degree Course Offers (Trotman Publishing) for details of offers

Keele Biomedical Science is offered as a single honours course. After the first year, students may apply for selection onto the IBMS-approved Applied Biomedical Science route. An optional one-year sandwich placement in an approved hospital or laboratory is offered. Forensic Science can be taken with other subjects. Single and joint honours are offered in Neuroscience. See also **Biology**.

Kent The School of Biosciences offers programmes of study in Biology, Biochemistry and Biomedical Science. In all cases a sandwich degree or a year in Europe is an option, adding an extra year to the three-year degree. Foundation years are available, and there is also a course in Forensic Science.

Kingston Courses are offered in Biomedical Sciences, which is available as a four-year sandwich course, and Forensic Science. The Biological Sciences programme offers specialisms in Environmental Biology, Genetics, Human Biology or Medical Biology.

Lancaster Biological Sciences is a very flexible modular course giving students a chance to tailor their own course. There is also an option to study abroad. Biological Sciences is also offered with Biomedicine. Courses in Biomedicine, Cell Biology and two Ecology courses are also offered, one with a year abroad.

Leeds* Degrees in Ecology, Genetics and Human Genetics form part of the Biology programme, a broad first year followed by a flexible choice of subjects from Year 2. There are also degrees in Anatomy, Microbiology, Nanotechnology and Neuroscience, Physiology and Zoology. There is also a course in Medical Sciences for students interested in focusing on health careers including a course in Biomedical Ethics (also for dental and veterinary students). The Biological Sciences degree does not assume a strong background in chemistry.

Leeds Beckett Biomedical Sciences can be taken with Microbiology, Human Biology, Physiology and Pharmacology.

Leicester The School of Biological Sciences offers eight courses of three- and four-year duration, all with a common first year; the latter may involve a sandwich placement abroad. Courses focus on Biochemistry, Genetics, Microbiology, Physiology with Pharmacology or Zoology. There are also courses in Medical Biochemistry and Medical Genetics. See also **Combined Courses**.

Lincoln Courses are offered in Biomedical Science and Forensic Science. The former covers microbiology, pathology, biochemistry and immunology and is available as a four-year sandwich course, with a year spent in industrial placement enabling graduates to work in the NHS as qualified biomedical scientists. There is a separate degree course in Zoology.

Liverpool A large number of subjects are offered, with specialist studies being chosen in Year 3. Current specialisms in the Biological Sciences course include Biochemistry, Biology, Marine Biology, Biotechnology, Environmental Biology, Genetics, Microbiology, Tropical Disease Biology and Zoology. Three-year courses in Biological and Medical Sciences and Genetics are also available.

Liverpool John Moores The IBMS-accredited and Health Professions Council-approved Biomedical Science course has an optional sandwich year in employment. There is also a degree in Forensic Science.

London (King's)* The School of Biomedical and Health Sciences offers a flexible programme with a common first year, leading to a choice of specialist subjects in Years 2 and 3. These include Anatomy, Biochemistry, Biomedical Sciences, Human Sciences, Genetics, Medical Physiology, Neuroscience, Pharmacology and Physiology. A BEng in Biomedical Engineering is also available.

London (QM) Several Biomedical Science students go on to study Dentistry and Medicine as the course covers anatomy, physiology, microbiology and pharmaceutical science subjects. A degree course in Zoology is also available.

London (RH) The degree in Biomedical Sciences covers the study of disease, clinical diagnosis, immunology, neuroscience and the physiology of sport and exercise. Some special Year 3 options are taught at St George's. Courses in Biochemistry and Medical Biochemistry are also offered.

London (St George's) A study of a range of biological science subjects including physiology and pharmacology are studied in the Biomedical Science course, which is designed as a first degree in the sciences underpinning modern medicine.

London (UCL)* The BSc and MSc Biological Sciences degrees offer options in generalist, whole organism or cells studies. There are also courses in Biomedical Science, Human Genetics and Neuroscience. All Biological Sciences courses share a common first year.

London Met Biological Sciences can be taken with Chemistry, Sports Science or Consumer Studies. Degrees are also offered in Biomedical Sciences, Forensic Sciences Medical Biosciences, Biotechnology and Microbiology.

London South Bank The degree in Biosciences offers specialist studies in biochemistry, microbiology and nutrition. The Applied Science course focuses on the biological sciences. Both are available as a four-year sandwich course. There is also a degree in Forensic Science.

Manchester* The Faculty of Life Sciences offers a wide range of courses coupled with considerable flexibility to change direction as career plans develop. Subjects offered cover Anatomical Sciences, Biochemistry, Biology, Biomedical Sciences, Biotechnology, Cell Biology, Genetics, Life Sciences, Medical Biochemistry, Microbiology, Molecular Biology, Neuroscience, Pharmacology, Physiology, Plant Science and Zoology. Most degrees are available as a four-year sandwich course, and can be studied with a modern language.

Manchester Met Degrees available include Biomedical Science, Forensic Science, Physiology, Microbiology and Molecular Biology, and Ecology and Conservation. See also **Biology**.

Middlesex A Biosciences course is offered which includes microbiology and immunology. An IBMS-accredited Biomedical Science degree and a Sports Biomedicine course are also available.

Newcastle* Courses are offered in Biomedical Sciences, Biomedical Genetics or Medical Microbiology, Marine Biology and Marine Zoology. Options include Genetics, Management, Medical Microbiology and Pharmacology. An industrial placement year option is available with the Biomedical Sciences course, which can also be studied with Business. New degrees in Biology (Cellular and Molecular; Ecology and Environmental) are also available. See also **Biology**.

Northumbria Biomedical Sciences is a three-year full-time or four-year sandwich course available as a single honours (including an optional year abroad) or combined with Chemistry. There are also degrees in Applied Sciences, Forensic Science, Biotechnology and Human Biosciences.

Nottingham* A three-year course is offered in Biotechnology, and in addition there are courses in Biomedical Sciences, Biology with Forensic Biology, Genetics, Human Biosciences, Plant Science, Food Microbiology, and Neuroscience.

Nottingham Trent The Biological Sciences degree has pathways in biomedical science, biochemistry, microbiology, ecology and pharmacology. Three Forensic Science degrees are also offered. Paid year-long placements are available.

Oxford* The Honours School of Biological Sciences covers biochemistry, biology and physiological science. The essence of this course is flexibility and the choice exists of specialising in plant studies, animal studies, environmental biology or cell biology. A degree is offered in Human Sciences covering the biology of organisms, genetics and evolution, sociology and social anthropology and populations. In Years 2 and 3 there are several optional papers including psychology and languages. There are also degrees in Biological Sciences (Molecular and Cellular) and Physiological Sciences.

Oxford Brookes Single and combined honours courses are offered in Biomedical Sciences, Biomedical Sciences, Medical Sciences and Molecular Biology, each with opportunities for laboratory placement and study abroad.

See *Heap 2015: University Degree Course Offers* (Trotman Publishing) for details of offers

Plymouth Biological Sciences is a modular course covering ecology, plant science, microbial and cellular biology, human and marine biology. Specialisation can be delayed. Each area may be studied as a specialist degree or combined with other subjects. There are also courses in Human Biosciences and Biomedical Science, as well as Applied Biosciences with pathways in agriculture and environment, aquaculture and food and nutrition, and an extensive range of marine subjects.

Portsmouth Subjects taken in the first three semesters are common to all students. These are followed by a choice of pathways in Biology, Biochemistry, Environmental Biology, Genome Science and Forensic Biology. Students have the opportunity to study at a European university under the Socrates and Erasmus schemes, as well as to assist with international conservation projects.

Queen's Belfast The Biological Sciences course provides an in-depth study of biochemistry, biological diversity, environmental biology, genetics and molecular biology and micro-organisms. In the final honours year, projects are offered in biochemistry, environmental biology, plant science, marine biology, genetics, microbiology and zoology. Degrees are also offered in Genetics, Microbiology and Biomedical Science, Physiology, Anatomy, Biomedical Sciences and Zoology.

Reading The Biological Sciences degree covers a range of modules including botany, biomedical science, biotechnology and microbiology. A four-year sandwich option with industry placement is available. Specialisation takes place in Year 3. See also **Biology**.

Robert Gordon Four-year full-time degrees are offered in Biomedical Science, which is IBMS-accredited and HPC-approved, and Forensic Science, with placements in Years 2 and 3.

Roehampton All areas of biology are covered in Year 1 of the Biological Sciences course. In Years 2 and 3, the main topics focus on human biology, organisms and ecology, and molecular biology and physiology. Biomedical Sciences is offered as a single honours subject, as is Zoology and Conservation Biology. Combined honours are offered in Biological Sciences, Biological Anthropology and Human Biosciences.

St Andrews See under **Biology**.

Salford The Biological Sciences course has an applied biology emphasis and a common first year with Biochemical Science (which has a biochemistry emphasis). The final choice of course is made at the end of Year 1. Year 3 can be spent in industry or in the US. There are also courses in Human Biology with Infectious Diseases and Biomedical Sciences, which offers the opportunity to study at a European university.

Sheffield* A wide range of courses is offered, including Biomedical Science, Microbiology and Genetics. All students follow the same course in Years 1 and 2, and specialise in Year 3. There is also a course in Biomedical Science.

Sheffield Hallam There is a course in Biological Sciences for Business and courses in Human and Forensic Biosciences. The Biomedical Sciences degree, which is IBMS-accredited, is available as a four-year sandwich course.

Southampton* Biomedical Sciences has a common first year with other subjects in the School of Biological Sciences. Options can be taken in other subjects outside the field. See also **Biochemistry**.

Staffordshire Biomedical Sciences, Biochemistry and Forensic Science courses are offered by way of a flexible modular system allowing for a change of degree at the end of Year 1. Biomedical Sciences graduates can apply to register as a biomedical scientist in the NHS.

Stirling Aquaculture, Ecology and Freshwater Science are offered as four-year degrees, Aquatic Science as a three-year course. See also **Biology**.

Strathclyde See under **Biochemistry**.

Sunderland The Biomedical Sciences degree focuses on human health and biology. Accreditation from the Department of Health professional bodies is currently under review.

Surrey The course in Biomedical Science includes biochemistry, physiology and pharmacology, with practical training in clinically relevant techniques. Optional subjects such as microbiology, nutrition and food science can also be studied. Courses involving Microbiology are offered with specialisms in medicine, food science and genetics. There are also Food Science and Biotechnology degrees.

Sussex A course is offered in Biomedical Sciences covering genetics, neuroscience and cell biology. Options including a foundation year or sandwich year are also available. See also **Biology**.

Swansea The deferred choice allows Biological Sciences students to delay their choice of degree specialisation until the end of the first year, while the alternative course allows students to specialise in two areas of biological sciences, e.g. biochemistry, genetics or zoology. Fieldwork options in Year 3 include terrestrial ecology, animal ecology, and activities in the Indian Himalayas. There is also a degree in Medical Sciences which enables students to apply for graduate entry to medical schools. Courses are also offered in Clinical Physiology and Zoology.

Ulster Graduates of the Biomedical Science degree are eligible for licentiate IBMS membership or associate membership of the Society of Biology, depending on degree classification. The course includes the option to study abroad in Marine Sciences. See also **Biology**.

Warwick Biological Sciences is a flexible course. Students opt for Biochemistry, Cell Biology, Biological Sciences, Environmental Biology, Biomedical Science, Biomedical Chemistry, Chemical Biology, Microbiology, or Virology. Opportunities exist for late decisions and transfers between courses. A good first class or upper second degree in Biological Sciences may admit students to the four-year Medical degree at the Leicester Warwick Medical School.

West Scotland The degree in Applied Bioscience features an optional 12-week placement in Year 3, and can be studied with Biochemistry, Environmental Science, Forensic Investigation, Immunology, Microbiology, Multimedia, Psychology and Zoology. Graduates with industrial experience may obtain the status of membership of the Institute of Biology. There is also a course in Biomedical Science.

Westminster Biological Sciences subjects share common modules, with specialism possible in biomedical science, biotechnology, biochemistry, or microbiology. There is also a course in Biomedical Science and a BEng in Biochemical Engineering.

Wolverhampton The Biological Sciences course, with an optional third year in industry, enables students to specialise in specific areas of biotechnology, animal biology, microbiology, biochemistry, physiology, genetics, plant science and food science. These subjects can be taken as specialist subjects or as combined studies. Sandwich-year options are available. There are also courses in Biomedical Science, Forensic Science, Genetics, Microbiology and Physiology.

Worcester After a common first year students choose a specialist pathway from Animal Biology, Biology, Ecology, Human Biology, Human Nutrition or Plant Science.

OTHER INSTITUTIONS OFFERING BIOLOGICAL SCIENCES COURSES
See under **Biology**.

ALTERNATIVE COURSES
Agriculture, Bacteriology, Biochemistry, Biology, Botany, Dentistry, Ecology, Environmental Sciences, Forestry, Medicine, Pharmacology, Pharmacy, Speech Science.

BIOLOGY

(see also **Biological Sciences**)
(* indicates universities with entry requirements over 340 UCAS points)

SUBJECT REQUIREMENTS/PREFERENCES

GCE A level: Chemistry and another science, usually Biology. **GCSE:** Mathematics and English stipulated in some cases.

SUBJECT INFORMATION

Biology courses usually are more specialised than Biological Sciences, with such options as aquatic biology, human biology, animal and plant biology. Many of these options are also offered on Applied Biology courses. (For research ratings see also **Biological Sciences**.)

Aberdeen The broad four-year BSc course in Biology has options in biomedical sciences, molecular and cell biology, plant and soil science and zoology and places a strong emphasis on field-based teaching.

Aberystwyth The Biology course will be of interest to those wishing to study molecular biology, cellular and physiological aspects of biology, with modules offered in genetics, plant physiology, microbiology and immunology. Field courses in Europe and the UK are available. There are also degree courses in Marine and Freshwater Biology, Environmental Biology, Genetics, Microbiology, Life Sciences, Plant Biology and Zoology.

Anglia Ruskin There is a comprehensive course in Marine Biology Biodiversity and Conservation focusing on ecology and conservation in the UK and overseas.

Aston In addition to the course in Biomedical Science there are four biology programmes focusing on the application of biology to human health and disease. There are common first and second years in each case prior to the choice of specialised subject and named degree in the third year. Placement years are also offered.

Bangor The Biology degree offers a range of options including biotechnology, wildlife conservation and freshwater biology. There is also a laboratory placement option in Year 2. Optional modules, including languages, form part of the first-year courses in the degrees in Biology (which offers a Tenerife field course in Year 3), Molecular Biology, Cancer Biology (currently only four other courses in the UK), Ecology and Zoology with Animal Behaviour, Animal Ecology, Conservation or Marine Zoology.

Bath* A flexible programme is offered covering Biology and Molecular and Cellular Biology, and Biochemistry, with three-year or four-year courses and possible placements or overseas study in industry in the UK or Europe and at universities in the US. (High research rating.) See also **Biochemistry** and **Combined Courses**.

Bath Spa A very broad study of biology, covering a range of biological subjects including human biology, nutrition, wildlife conservation, marine biology, environmental management and ecology. Residential UK field trips are offered.

Bedfordshire See under **Biological Sciences**.

Birmingham Core subjects are offered in Year 1 of this Human Biology degree. The course is very flexible and students choose from a wide range of options in Year 3, including bacterial and viral diseases, genetics and neurobiology, taught through both seminar work and practical laboratory sessions.

An optional year in professional placement is also possible. There are also courses in Medical Sciences, Biomedical Materials, Science and Bioinformatics.

Bolton The Biology degree offers pathways in animal biology and molecular sciences. A placement is offered in Year 3, with the opportunity to study at an exchange university in the US.

Bournemouth See under **Biological Sciences**.

Bradford See under **Biological Sciences**.

Brighton A three-year Biological Sciences programme is available, which offers a broad range of options and includes opportunities for language study and a field course (currently in South Africa). Courses are offered in Biogeography and Human Ecology. There is also a Joint Science programme in which Biology can be combined with Geography.

Bristol* Biology is offered as a single honours course and with Geology. There is also a Cancer Biology course combined with Immunology with the option to study in industry as part of the courses. (High research rating.) There is a degree in Anatomy with optional units in biomedical sciences and human and veterinary anatomy.

Bristol UWE A degree is offered in Biology and IT in Science, developing theoretical and practical skills with the effective use of IT in science, data collection, interpretation and storage. There are also courses in Human, Sports and Conservation Biology, with opportunities to undertake an overseas placement.

Brunel See under **Biological Sciences**.

Cambridge* See under **Combined Courses**.

Canterbury Christ Church The three-year Biosciences degree covers a wide overview of microbiology, molecular biology, physiology and optional modules including animal care and radiobiology. The course is also available as a joint or combined honours programme. A broad study of the sciences leads to the degree in Environmental Biology.

Cardiff There is a common first year for Biology and Applied Biology which covers cells, microbes, physiology, evolution, ecology, biological chemistry, maths, statistics and computing. Students then choose their special study in Year 2 leading to a degree in Applied Biology, Biology, Biotechnology, Ecology and Environmental Management, Genetics, Microbiology or Zoology. Field trips in the UK and Europe are available. This is a three-year full-time or four-year sandwich course.

Central Lancashire The three-year degree in Biological Sciences covers areas including molecular and cellular biology, human physiology and microbiology, with a research project in Year 3 contributing towards the final assessment. A work placement module forms part of Year 2. A degree is also offered in Biomedical Science with core units in human physiology, genetics, microbiology and nutrition. Specialist areas include pharmacology, physiology, immunology and food microbiology.

Chester Biology is available as a three-year combined degree and focuses on animal behaviour, environmental, nutrition, ecology, human and biomedical aspects of the subject. There is also a degree course in Forensic Biology, which can be combined with such subjects as Psychology, Law, Biology or Criminology.

Cumbria The Conservation Biology degree allows specialisation in areas such as aquatic conservation and conservation genetics, with an optional sandwich year studying or working abroad. A course in Forensic Science is also offered.

Derby The three-year Biology course offers study abroad and is recognised by the Society of Biology, enabling graduates to qualify for associate membership. Courses are also available in Conservation and Chemical Biology. There is also a joint course with Zoology.

Dundee Students following the Biology course take a range of subjects in the first- and second-year science courses. They then proceed to an honours course in Biology, with modules available in botany, ecology, microbiology and zoology in the Department of Biological Sciences. A course in Mathematical Biology is also available.

Durham* All departments in the Faculty of Science offer main, double main, main and subsidiary or subsidiary units that lead to single or joint honours degrees in Natural Science. The first-year course in Biology includes genetics, biochemistry, animal and plant biology, physiology, ecology and behaviour. Further core subjects are taken in Year 2, and in Year 3 a modular scheme allows for considerable specialisation.

East Anglia The School of Biology offers a wide range of courses covering Plant Biology, Cell Biology, Molecular Biology and Genetics and Microbiology. There is considerable flexibility in these programmes, allowing students to specialise as their subject interests develop. The Biological Sciences programme is also available as a sandwich course, with a year spent in industry or studying in Europe, North America or Australia.

East London Applied Biology has modules in genetics, microbiology, medical biochemistry and pharmacology. Students are encouraged to take the four-year sandwich degree option.

Edge Hill The Biology degree has a strong practical base and covers plant and animal studies and marine communities. Residential field courses are free of charge. There are also degrees in Environmental Science and Human Biology.

Edinburgh See under **Biological Sciences**.

Edinburgh Napier The four-year Biological Sciences degree includes the study of microbiology, toxicology and immunology. Animal, Environmental, Forensic and Marine and Freshwater Biology are also offered as three-year or four-year full-time courses or as five-year sandwich courses.

Edinburgh Queen Margaret Human Biology is a four-year multidisciplinary course covering aspects of biochemistry, microbiology, health biology, nutrition, health psychology and sociology. Years 1 and 2 are shared with Applied Pharmacology and Nutrition, giving students the option of changing courses up until the end of Year 2. The degree leads to a variety of scientific and health-related careers.

Exeter Conservation Biology and Ecology can be studied at the Cornwall campus witth an option to study abroad.

Glasgow* A flexible course structure allows for late decisions on all specialist subjects. All students take three subjects from a wide choice in Year 1. Named degree subjects include Anatomy, Biochemistry, Biomedical Engineering, Immunology, Marine and Freshwater Biology, Microbiology, Molecular and Cellular Biology, Neuroscience, Physiology, Parasitology, Virology and Zoology. Some courses offer the opportunity to work on overseas research expeditions.

Glasgow Caledonian Human Biology is a multidisciplinary course with sociology and psychology. Courses are also available in Cell and Molecular Biology, Human Biosciences, Forensic Investigation and Human Biology with Sociology and Psychology. All are four-year sandwich courses.

Gloucestershire The degrees in Animal Biology and Biology are both available as a joint or single honours degree and offer one-year placements and field courses in the UK and overseas. See also **Animal Sciences**.

Heriot-Watt See under **Biological Sciences**.

Hertfordshire See under **Biological Sciences**.

Huddersfield The Biology course has optional work placements in Year 3. Final-year options include immunology, medical biology and DNA technology. There are also courses in Human, Medical and Sport Biology, as well as separate degrees in Human and Medical Biology, and Medical Genetics and Microbial Sciences which offer optional placements.

Hull After taking Biology in Year 1 it is possible to transfer to degrees in Marine and Freshwater Biology, Aquatic Zoology with a Fisheries option, Biomedical Sciences and Biomolecular and Biomedical Science. There is also a course in Coastal Marine Biology. A Biology course is also combined with Ornithology

Imperial London* The Biology department offers three-year courses in Biology, Biology with Management, Microbiology, Ecology and Zoology, and four-year courses in Biology with a year in Europe, management or research. The Management course includes one year in the Business School. Degrees are also available in Biology with an additional language course in French, Spanish or German for Science. All courses lead to the award of the BSc degree.

Keele The Biology dual honours course offers modules in cell biology and biochemistry, behaviour and ecology, genetics, plant and animal physiology, with the option of studying abroad and vocational placement work. There are also courses in Biomedical Sciences, Forensic Science and Neuroscience. There are also 29 subject combinations in the dual honours programme including Human Biology.

Kent The Biology degree includes a new enterprise start-up as a final-year option, and may be taken with a placement in industry or study abroad. There is also a course in Forensic Science with an optional year in industry.

Kingston The Biology degree enables students to follow a broad-based course in the biological sciences or to focus on environmental biology or biotechnology at Levels 2 and 3, and can also be studied as a half or major field with an additional subject such as Business, Sports Science or Psychology. There are also courses in Forensic and Human Biology.

Lancaster As well as a general course in Biological Sciences, which covers a broad range of topics and is available with a year abroad, other courses include Cell Biology, Conservation Biology and Environmental Biology, the latter with possible placements in North America or Australia. Biology can also be taken with Geography and Psychology. Biochemistry and Biomedicine Science are also available.

Leeds* The three-year Biology degree is a popular course giving either breadth of study or the opportunity to specialise and change to Zoology or Ecology in Year 3. See also **Biological Sciences**.

Leeds Beckett The Biomedical Sciences programme has pathways in microbiology, physiology and human biology. The option to study abroad as part of the university's exchange programme is offered.

Liverpool The Life Sciences Unit scheme provides flexibility by enabling students to select a range of units related to the choice of degree including courses applicable to Medicine. Applied Biology is also available on a four-year sandwich course – students specialising in one of plant science, environmental biology, genetics, marine biology, zoology and molecular biology. There are also degrees in Tropical Disease Biology and Zoology. See also **Biological Sciences**.

Liverpool Hope Biology and Human Biology are available as single honours courses or combined honours leading to a BA/QTS. Other popular combinations include Health and Psychology.

Liverpool John Moores Biology can be taken with an optional sandwich year.

London (King's)* Courses are offered covering Cell Biology (Biomolecular Sciences), which covers pharmacology and molecular genetics, and Human Biology (Human Sciences), which offers study options in cancer, drug dependence and the biology of ageing. A modern language can be studied in Year 2.

London (QM) Courses include Biology, Biology with Psychology and Aquatic Biology. Field courses form part of the study. (High research rating.) See also **Biological Sciences**.

See *Heap 2015: University Degree Course Offers* (Trotman Publishing) for details of offers

London (RH) A very flexible course focusing on a study of aspects of plant and animal life.

London (UCL)* The course provides a broad and flexible Biology programme and also acts as an entry route for those who decide to transfer to more specialised degrees including Cellular and Molecular Biology, Environmental Biology and the Biology of Fertility and Embryo Development. A course in Biomedical Sciences is also available.

Loughborough Degree courses are offered in Human Biology, with modules in genetics, psychology and nutrition, and Ergonomics (Human Factors Design) which includes Psychology, Anatomy and Physiology.

Manchester* Biology is offered with industrial experience, a modern language or Science and Society, or as a single honours course. Biology is also part of the Life Sciences programme. Courses are also available in Anatomical Sciences and Developmental Biology.

Manchester Met Biology is offered by way of a large number of joint courses, with an option to study in North America. Human or Lifestyle Biology can also be taken as single honours degree courses, and degrees are also available in Animal Biology, Microbiology and Molecular Biology, and Biomedical Science.

Newcastle Biology is available as a three-year single honours degree, with the option to specialise in Cellular and Molecular or Ecology and Environmental after the first year. Also available are Animal Science (with options in companion animal studies or livestock technology), Applied Biology (with options involving biochemistry, microbiology and biotechnology), Marine Biology and Zoology. Under a Biological Sciences deferred choice scheme, students can choose their final degree at the end of the first year.

Northampton Biology can be taken as a single honours subject and in addition there are over 20 joint courses in Biological Conservation. The Human Biosciences course covers genomics, neuroscience and health topics.

Northumbria Applied Biology (which can be taken jointly with Forensic Biology) is offered as a three-year full-time or four-year sandwich course with an emphasis on laboratory and analytical methods. There are also courses in Biology and Forensic Biology, Applied Conservation Biology and Human Biosciences.

Nottingham A comprehensive Biology course is offered covering microbiology, plant, animal and human biology plus a wide range of specialisms. The course is available as an MSci, recommended for students hoping to continue their research training at master's level, and as a BSc, suggested for students seeking a background in biological sciences to support a range of career options. Courses are also offered in Applied Biology, Biotechnology and Environmental Biology.

Nottingham Trent The course in Biology offers themes in living systems, clinical biochemistry, genetics, human systems and immunology. There are also courses in Animal Science, Biomedical Sciences, Microbiology and Biotechnology.

Oxford* Biology is taken as part of the three-year single honours degree in Biological Sciences. The Human Sciences course open to science and arts applicants covers animal behaviour, ecology, populations and society and social geography.

Oxford Brookes Degree courses are offered in Biology, Environmental Biology, Human Biology (with the opportunity to undertake a work placement or study abroad through the Erasmus exchange scheme) and Conservation Biology as a pathway in Environmental Sciences. All are offered as single or joint courses.

Plymouth The Biological Sciences course provides an overview of biological topics and includes options in biochemistry, microbiology, plant science and health and disease. A foreign language can be studied in Year 2. There are also courses in Biomedical Sciences, Environmental and Marine Biology and Coastal Ecology, Toxicology, and Human Sciences.

Portsmouth After a common first three semesters, Biology students choose one of the elective streams leading to a range of named degrees including Environmental and Forensic Biology. A course in Marine Biology is also offered. See also **Biological Sciences**.

Queen's Belfast A broad modular course in Environmental Biology is offered covering natural and human environments and providing pathways in environmental biology, biological sciences, marine biology and paleobiology. Several modules feature a field-course unit.

Reading The Biological Sciences programme provides a wide range of modules allowing students to specialise in chosen fields covering biological subjects, and is available with a year of industrial experience. Alternatively it is possible to change degrees to Biomedical Sciences, Biochemistry, Botany, Medical Microbiology or Zoology. See also **Biochemistry** and **Biological Sciences**.

Roehampton See under **Biological Sciences**.

St Andrews* After a broad first year, Biology students can specialise in one of 11 specialist areas, including biochemistry, human, animal and plant biology, cell biology ecology and genetics. Another subject can also be studied alongside Biology, such as Geography, Psychology or Maths.

Sheffield* Several biology courses are offered with a modular format which enables the student to select from several subject specialisms with opportunities to study abroad. There are also degrees combining Conservation, Languages and Archaeology. (High research rating.)

Sheffield Hallam A degree in Human Biology is offered with a paid industrial placement in Year 3. The main focus lies in a study of human physiology leading to careers in healthcare and medical applications.

South Wales Biology is a three-year full-time course studying living organisms, their structure and survival mechanisms. Core modules include zoology, physiology, genetics, plant and animal diversity, and physiological ecology. Biology can be studied as part of a combined honours programme and there are degrees in Forensic Biology, Human Biology and International Wildlife Biology. All Biology degrees are recognised by the Society of Biology.

Southampton Courses offered by the department are based on a unit structure with a common first year (units in cell biology, ecology, genetics and biochemistry) after which students can specialise. Courses are also offered in Marine Biology, Pharmacology, Oceanography and Zoology.

Staffordshire All Biology students take core modules at Level 1 with transfers possible at the end of this stage. Courses offered include Biology, Human Biology, and Biology with Sport and Health or Forensic Science.

Stirling After an introductory course, students can proceed to specialist areas including animal physiology, plant physiology, ecology, marine and freshwater biology and aquatic science. A degree in Animal Biology is also available.

Strathclyde See under **Biochemistry**.

Sussex A broad range of biology courses are taken in Years 1 and 2 followed by specialist options in Year 3, including a research or communication project as part of the final assessment.

Swansea First-year Biology students take two other subjects in the biological sciences as well as biology, or they may take botany, zoology and one other subject from geography, psychology or mathematics methods. In the second year, course work covers genetics, biochemistry, cell and molecular biology, plant and animal biology. There is also a research project. The final year is devoted to a specialised area. Courses are also offered in Marine Biology, Environmental Biology and Zoology.

Teesside Biological Sciences, which is recognised by the Society of Biology, and Forensic Biology are offered as full-time or sandwich courses.

See *Heap 2015: University Degree Course Offers* (Trotman Publishing) for details of offers

Ulster The first year of the course in Biology is taken in common with degrees in Biomedical Sciences, Molecular Bioscience, Human Nutrition, and Food and Nutrition, thus allowing transfers in Year 2. Biology is offered with an optional DIS or DAS.

Warwick* See under **Biological Sciences**.

West Scotland Environmental Biology is available with specialist studies in a wide range of subjects in Years 3 and 4. A course in Applied Bioscience is also available, and can be taken with Psychology, Zoology or Forensic Investigation.

Westminster The Biological Sciences course covers human physiology and anatomy and laboratory research; or can be taken with a focus on specialist areas including microbiology, biotechnology, and molecular biology and genetics. Courses are also offered in Human and Medical Science and Forensic Biology.

Wolverhampton Animal Biology and Ecology and Applied Biology courses are on offer. An optional sandwich year is available. Biology joint courses are also available with Computing, Psychology, Environmental Science, Geography and Business.

Worcester The course in Forensic and Applied Biology offers extensive practical training. Validation by the Forensic Science Society is being sought. A course in Animal Biology is also available. See also **Biological Sciences**.

York* Five courses are offered: Biology, Molecular Cell Biology, Genetics, Biotechnology and Ecology, with the option for a year in Europe or industry. First-year modules include genetics, evolution and ecology, leading on to a choice of nine programmes. Students may also elect to transfer to the Biology with Education course at the end of Year 1.

OTHER INSTITUTIONS OFFERING BIOLOGY COURSES
Bishop Burton (Coll), Blackpool and Fylde (Coll), Cornwall (Coll), Loughborough (Coll), Riverside Halton (Coll), St Mary's, South Devon (Coll), Southport (Coll), SRUC, Suffolk (Univ Campus), Truro (Coll), Warwickshire (Coll), Writtle (Coll).

ALTERNATIVE COURSES
Agriculture, Bacteriology, Biochemistry, Botany, Dentistry, Ecology, Environmental Health, Environmental Science, Forestry, Medicine, Microbiology, Pharmacology, Pharmacy, Speech Science.

BIOTECHNOLOGY

(* indicates universities with entry requirements over 340 UCAS points)

SUBJECT REQUIREMENTS/PREFERENCES
GCE A level: Chemistry usually required with two or three mathematics/science subjects. **GCSE:** Mathematics grade A–C.

SUBJECT INFORMATION
Biotechnology is an interdisciplinary subject that can cover specialisms in agriculture, biochemistry, microbiology, genetics, chemical engineering, biophysics etc. (Courses in these named subjects should also be explored.)

Birmingham Biotechnology is offered as a specialisation of the degree course in Biological Sciences or jointly with Biochemistry. Field courses are offered, including one in Norway.

Bradford An optional placement year in industry is offered in Year 3 to those choosing the degree course in Applied Biotechnology. Third-year specialisms are linked to careers in the industry.

Cardiff The Biotechnology course covers most areas of biological science with a practical emphasis, and also aspects of medicine and agriculture. There are seven biological degrees, all served by the same broadly based first year, with the specialism in Biotechnology following in Years 2 and 3.

City A course is offered in Biomedical Engineering with Applied Physics. Biomedical subjects covered include medical ultrasound and biomedical optics. A professional placement is available.

East London The Biotechnology and Biochemistry course has a one-year industrial placement and involves a study of genetics and biology.

Edinburgh* A course in Biotechnology is offered as part of the Biological Sciences programme. Study abroad is available in Year 3.

Glasgow* The Molecular and Cellular Biology (with Biotechnology) course covers the molecular sciences underpinning practices and debates in biotechnology. A multidisciplinary Biotechnology course covers micro-organisms, animals, plants and industrial and agricultural processes.

Hertfordshire Biotechnology is available as a four-year sandwich course. Final-year modules cover biochemistry, microbiology and molecular biology plus applied aspects such as industrial enzymology, fermentation and process technology.

Kingston Biotechnology is an option in the Biological Sciences degree.

Leeds The Biotechnology course offers advanced studies in the biotechnology of medicine, chemical engineering, genetics and industrial and environmental microbiology, science, medical aspects of biotechnology and computer modelling, protein structure and drug design. A BSc in Genetics is also available.

Liverpool In the Microbial Biotechnology course, which covers modules including molecular biology and virology, 12 weeks are spent in industry. See also **Biological Sciences**.

Liverpool John Moores The three-year full-time or four-year Biochemistry sandwich course covers aspects of manufacturing techniques in agriculture and medicine, placing emphasis on the manipulation of micro-organisms and plants. The MPharm Pharmacy degree includes a module in Applied Biotechnology.

Manchester* The course in Biotechnology provides a preparation for the commercial application of biological systems and can include a year of industrial experience.

Newcastle* The Biotechnology degree has a strong basis in biomolecular sciences including molecular biology, biochemistry, genetics and microbiology. Courses in Biomedical Sciences are also available.

Northumbria The Biotechnology degree provides comprehensive coverage of scientific industrial applications.

Nottingham The Biotechnology degree places emphasis on food production aspects of biotechnology. The degree can also be taken with a European placement following Year 2.

Surrey* Biotechnology is offered by way of three- and four-year programmes. The Biochemistry and Microbiology degrees also feature modules in Biotechnology.

See *Heap 2015: University Degree Course Offers* (Trotman Publishing) for details of offers

Swansea Students on the four-year course in Clinical Technology spend 50% of the time on paid hospital placements (salary currently £17,000). No fees are paid for this course.

Ulster There is a course in Biomedical Engineering, which is accredited by the Institute of Engineering and Technology (IET).

Westminster The Biotechnology course draws on biochemistry, microbiology, genetics and biochemical engineering.

Wolverhampton Biotechnology is offered as a single subject degree, with an optional year in industry, or as part of the Applied Sciences and modular degree scheme programmes with Microbiology or Pharmacology. There is a bias towards microbial and plant biotechnology.

ALTERNATIVE COURSES
Agriculture, Biological Sciences, Genetics, Microbiology.

BUILDING

(see also **Architecture** and **Property Management and Surveying**)
(* indicates universities with entry requirements over 340 UCAS points)

SUBJECT REQUIREMENTS/PREFERENCES
GCE A level: Mathematics may be required. **GCSE:** English, Mathematics and science usually required.

SUBJECT INFORMATION
These courses involve the techniques and management methods employed in the building industry. This subject also covers civil and structural engineering and architecture.

Anglia Ruskin Several courses are offered including Building Surveying, which is accredited by the RICS, Construction and Design, Construction Management, and Quantity Surveying.

Aston A common first year leads to a choice of degrees in Construction Management and Construction Project Management. Courses are RICS-accredited and industrial sandwich placements are available.

Bedfordshire A course in Building Technology covers structures, new materials and techniques.

Birmingham City The Building Surveying course, which is accredited by RICS and the Chartered Institute of Building (CIOB), is a vocational degree featuring field trips to construction projects. The Construction Management and Economics course comprises a strong emphasis on building technology, construction management and cost control with supporting legal, social and economic subjects. There are also courses in Building and Quantity Surveying and Building Services Engineering which covers heating, ventilation and air conditioning. See also **Property Management and Surveying**.

Bolton Several full-time and sandwich degree courses are offered, including Building Surveying and Property Management, Construction, Construction Management and Quantity Surveying and Commercial Management, with the latter leading to qualification as a surveyor.

See *Heap 2015: University Degree Course Offers* (Trotman Publishing) for details of offers

Brighton The Building Studies course covers building technology, construction and management, conservation technology and business management. There are also degree courses in Building Surveying, which is RICS-accredited and offers a placement which may contribute towards graduates' Association of Building Engineers (ABE) Probationers' Diary of Experience, and Project Management for Construction and Construction Engineering and Management. See also **Architecture**.

Bristol UWE There are courses in Construction Management, Building Services Engineering, which is accredited by the Chartered Institution of Building Services Engineers (CIBSE), allowing graduates to attain Incorporated Engineer registration, and a modular degree in Building and Natural Environmental Studies in which there is an optional placement year in industry. There is also a course in Building Surveying. See also **Property Management and Surveying**.

Central Lancashire The Department of the Built Environment offers courses in Construction Project Management, Facilities Management, Building Surveying (RICS- and CIB-accredited), Commercial Management and Quantity Surveying, and Building Services Engineering. See also **Property Management and Surveying**.

Colchester (Inst) The CIB-accredited Construction Management degree is available in commercial and site specialisations.

Coventry Courses are available in Building Surveying (RICS- and CIB-accredited), Quantity Surveying and Construction Management, which can include industrial placement.

Derby There are three Built Environment courses with separate pathways in Architecture, Civil Engineering and Construction. Students have the opportunity to work on briefs issued by companies. The FdEng Civil Engineering course is accredited by the Institution of Civil Engineering Surveyors (ICFS) and the Institution of Civil Engineers (ICE).

Edinburgh Napier Architectural Technology, Building Surveying and Construction and Quantity Surveying are offered. RICS and CIAT accreditation is carried. There is also a course in Property Development and Valuation.

Glasgow Caledonian The Building Services Engineering course covers electrical and computer technology, building law practice, lighting and air-conditioning engineering. There are also degrees in Construction Management, Fire Risk Engineering, Property Management, Project Management (Construction) – which carries CIB, RICS and ABE examination exemption – Building and Quantity Surveying and Building Control. See also **Property Management and Surveying**.

Glyndŵr A Building Studies degree has optional routes in Year 2 leading to Construction Management, Building Maintenance Management or Building Studies. All programmes are accredited by the CIOB.

Greenwich The Building Engineering course has a strong focus on construction technology and building engineering design. A sandwich course option is available. Building Surveying, Construction Business Management, Estate Management, Property Development and Quantity Surveying are also offered.

Heriot-Watt Construction Management, Building Surveying, Building Economics, and Quantity Surveying and Architectural Engineering are offered. International Studies can be taken alongside Civil Engineering and Structural Engineering. There is also a course in Urban Studies allowing transfer to other courses at the end of the year.

Huddersfield There is an optional sandwich course in Construction and Project Management, featuring modules in regeneration, building pathology and regeneration, and a course in Property Development which includes economics and marketing.

Kingston Courses offered associated with Building in the School of Surveying include Building and Quantity Surveying, which is RICS- and CIOB-accredited and is available as a four-year sandwich course, Construction Management and Property Planning and Development.

Leeds Beckett The Construction Management course covers technological management, law, historic building and building conservation. Graduates are exempt from ABE examinations. Special studies include environmental science. Students spend Year 3 in industry; optional placements take place in the UK. Courses in Facilities Management, Building Control Engineering, Building Surveying and Quantity Surveying are also available.

Liverpool John Moores The Construction Management degree is a unique learning programme covering design and construction materials and management. There are also courses in Building Design, Building Surveying (RICS-accredited), Technology and Management. See also **Property Management and Surveying**.

London (UCL) A degree is offered in Project Management for Construction covering building technology and business aspects. The CIOB- and RICS-accredited programme has a strong vocational focus and is available as a four-year sandwich course. Courses in Urban Planning and Urban Studies are also available.

London South Bank The CIOB-accredited Construction Management degree offers an opportunity to study by way of subsidised four-day visits to a European city (previously Amsterdam, Barcelona and Berlin). After a common first year, decisions are made between Construction or Surveying courses. Architectural Technology, Building Services Engineering and Quantity Surveying are also offered.

Loughborough Degree courses are offered in Construction Engineering Management, Architectural Engineering and Design Management, MEng/BEng Civil Engineering (the MEng course satisfies the educational base for a chartered engineer), and Commercial Management and Quantity Surveying. All students are given the opportunity to be sponsored by a consortium of companies.

Northumbria Architectural Technology, Building Design Management, Building Project Management, Building Services Engineering, Building Surveying, Construction Management and Quantity Surveying courses involve a third year spent in work placement. There is also a course in Estate Management.

Nottingham A course is offered in Sustainable Built Environment focusing on the design of energy-efficient buildings and covering renewable energy, ventilation, lighting, acoustics, electricity and control. BEng/MEng courses are also offered in Architectural and Environment Engineering.

Nottingham Trent Courses are offered in Construction Management, Planning and Property Development, Quantity Surveying, Building Surveying and Financial and Project Management in Construction. All courses offer professional placements and carry industry body accreditations.

Oxford Brookes The Construction Project Management degree covers technology, management, design, construction and the maintenance of buildings in this four-year sandwich course. Courses in Quantity Surveying and Real Estate Management are also available.

Plymouth Degrees in Construction Management and the Environment (CIOB- and ABE-accredited), Architectural Technology and the Environment (CIAT-accredited) and Surveying are offered as three-year full-time or four-year sandwich courses.

Portsmouth Construction Engineering Management, Property Development (available with Quantity Surveying) and Building Studies are also offered. See also **Property Management and Surveying**.

Reading The first and second years of the Building Construction and Management course are common with the courses in Quantity Surveying, Building Surveying and Construction Management, Engineering and Surveying. The course will appeal to students interested in building and civil engineering but who do not wish to undertake a highly mathematical and theoretical course and want to concentrate mainly on design. All programmes are RICS- and CIOB-accredited.

Robert Gordon Courses are offered in Construction Design and Management, Architectural Technology and Surveying (Building or Quantity), each course with work placements and industrial body accreditation.

Salford Construction Management is a four-year scheme with two six-month placements in industry covering management studies and technology, which form the core of the programme. There are also courses focusing on facilities, production and process management. Building Surveying and Construction Project Management are also available. See also **Property Management and Surveying**. (High research rating.)

Sheffield Hallam The Built Environment foundation programme offers courses with a common first year. Final decisions are taken in Year 2, and lead to degrees in Architectural Technology, Construction Management, Construction Project Management, Building or Quantity Surveying and Construction Commercial Management.

Southampton Solent Courses are offered in Architectural Technology (CIAT- and ABE-accredited), Construction and Project Management with options in Business, Computing, Engineering, Environmental Management and Health Studies.

Trinity St David (Swansea) Courses are offered in Civil Engineering and Environmental Management, Building Conservation Management and Construction Management. Two-year HNC/HND courses in Quantity Surveying are also available.

Ulster The RICS-accredited Building Surveying course includes a compulsory 12-month placement. There are also degrees in Building Engineering and Materials, Construction Engineering Management, Quantity Surveying, Housing Management and Planning and Property Development.

West London Degrees are offered in Quantity Surveying, Architectural Technology and Construction Management.

Westminster Full-time and part-time degree courses are offered in Building Engineering, Construction Management, Quantity Surveying and Commercial Management, Construction and Surveying, Real Estate and Architectural Technology.

Wolverhampton Construction Management is a broad-based course covering all the major topics required by a building engineer, with law, computing, management and language options. Industrial placement is optional. There are also courses in Building Surveying, Architectural Design Technology, Commercial Management and Quantity Surveying (RICS-accredited) and Computer-aided Design in Construction.

OTHER INSTITUTIONS OFFERING BUILDING COURSES
Bath City (Coll), Blackburn (Coll), Blackpool and Fylde (Coll), Bradford (Coll Univ Centre), Cornwall (Coll), Dudley (Coll), Gower Swansea (Coll), Menai (Coll), SRUC, UHI, Wigan and Leigh (Coll), Worcester (CT), Writtle (Coll).

ALTERNATIVE COURSES
Architecture, Building Services Engineering, Building Surveying, Civil Engineering, Estate Management, Land Economics, Quantity Surveying, Valuation Surveying.

BUSINESS

(including **Human Resources Management Marketing** and **Tourism and Travel**)
(* indicates universities with entry requirements over 340 UCAS points)

SUBJECT REQUIREMENTS/PREFERENCES
GCE A level: Mathematics (or AS level) required or preferred by some universities. Foreign language(s) required for some European or international courses. **GCSE:** English and Mathematics required.

SUBJECT INFORMATION
This is a very large subject area that may consist of courses in general topics (Business Studies or Business Administration), Management Science courses, which tend to have a mathematics emphasis, and more specialised fields that are covered by courses in Advertising, Consumer Science, Company and Public Administration, Financial Services (see also **Finance**), Industrial Relations, Organisation Studies, Retail Management and Travel and Tourism.

At HND level many institutions offer Business Studies courses with specialist streams as follows: accountancy, advertising, broadcasting/media, business administration, company secretaryship, computer studies, distribution, European business and marketing, fashion, food, health, horticulture, journalism, languages, law, leisure, marketing, media, personnel, printing, publicity, purchasing and tourism.

QUESTIONS TO CONSIDER
* Do I already know which area of business I'd like to specialise in, or will I have the option to choose my route as the course progresses?
* I want to improve my foreign language skills for my career – does the course offer language studies with an up-to-date business angle? Which 'business languages' (such as Japanese, Spanish or Mandarin) are available?
* I want to work for a leading firm, and hope to gain contacts and experience as I study – should I consider one of the new corporate sponsored degrees, which involve working for a salary throughout the course?

Aberdeen A degree in Management Studies includes marketing, international business, public sector management, small business management and human resources management as electives at the honours level. Joint honours courses are available with a range of subjects including Accountancy, Economics, Politics and language courses. In addition to a European Management Studies degree, a unique course in Entrepreneurship and Marketing focuses on business development. Marine Resources Management covering fisheries and coastal planning is also offered.

Abertay The four-year Business portfolio has a common first year followed by specialisations in Years 2 and 3 in Finance or Marketing. There are also management courses in Business Administration, International Business, Human Resources, Tourism and Marketing.

Aberystwyth The Business and Management degree scheme of three years has core modules in marketing, business law, management accounting and human resources management in Years 2 and 3. There are also Welsh medium electives focusing on the Welsh economy. A course in Marketing can be taken as a single honours scheme, or as a joint course or minor/major scheme with options including Languages, Politics or Mathematics. In addition there is a course in Tourism Management with the opportunity to study a modern language.

Anglia Ruskin Courses are offered in Business (with over 40 specialist options), Business Studies (with a 48-week placement in Year 3), Business Management Economics and International Business with language modules in French, German and Spanish, each with European programmes in Clermont-Ferrand,

Berlin and Maastricht respectively, and elsewhere in the Netherlands. There is also a course in Human Resources Management and in Modern Business Applications, with modules drawn from business studies, information systems and law, and also Tourism and Marketing degrees.

Aston* The large Business School offers (compulsory placements) sandwich courses on a modular basis. Single honours courses include Business and Management, Business Computing and IT, Managerial and Administrative Studies, Human Resource Management, Marketing, Logistics and Transport Management, International Business and Economics and Management, joint courses in International Business with French, German or Spanish or with two languages, and major/minor courses.

Bangor Business courses are offered jointly with Economics, Computing, Law and Marketing. Other courses include Management, Social Administration, Finance, Banking, Accountancy, Leisure and Tourism.

Bath* The popular Business Administration course is a blend of practical experience and academic study in a four-year sandwich course. First-year core subjects include business economics, behaviour in organisations, accounting and some computing, statistics and law. The course continues with specialisms in finance, employee relations and marketing being selected in Year 2. See also **Combined Courses**.

Bath Spa The Business and Management degree is available as a three- or four-year course, presents a diverse range of topics and includes an optional 10-month work assignment. Business specialisms also include human resource management, marketing and tourism.

Bedfordshire Full-time and sandwich courses are offered in Business Studies with specialist options in management, marketing, accounting and finance, international business, law, psychology and organisation behaviour. There are also courses in Human Resources Management and Tourism. In addition there are also degrees in Accounting, Advertising, Marketing and Public Relations.

Birmingham* Courses are offered with a year in industry, in European Business and with Communications. The three-year specialist programme in Business Administration leads to a BCom degree and provides a window on the modern world of business. French, German, Italian, Japanese, Portuguese and Spanish and 12 engineering subjects are also offered with Business Studies. Courses are also available in International Business, Accounting and Finance and Economics.

Birmingham (UC) A wide range of courses can be followed. These cover Adventure Tourism Management, Arts Enterprise Management, Business Enterprise, Marketing Management and International Tourism. There is also Salon Business Management which includes beauty therapy and prepares students for work in the leisure industry, fitness clubs and health spas. In addition the Spa Management course covers spa treatment and massage therapy.

Birmingham City Courses in the business field cover Advertising, Business Administration, Business Information Technology, Human Resource Management, Tourism Management, Hospitality Management, Retail Marketing and International Marketing and Public Relations.

Bolton Full-time courses with some overseas placements are offered in Business Studies and Human Resources Management, with specialisations in languages, marketing and tourism. There is also a degree in Marketing with options in communications strategy, management and buying behaviour and a course in International Tourism Management.

Bournemouth The Business Studies degree with pathways in Economics, Finance, Human Resources Management, International Business, Law and Marketing includes a 40-week paid placement in industry or commerce in the third year. There are 10 named Business programmes combined with a range of subjects including Languages, Human Resource Management and Law, and in addition an International Business degree, Public Relations and Retail Management courses are also offered, as well as Accounting and Finance degrees and several Marketing and Tourism courses.

Bradford The Management Centre offers a degree programme in Business and Management Studies which provides a broad education with opportunities for later specialisation in accounting, human resource management, international business or marketing. There is also a course in Business and Law giving partial exemption from Law Society examinations as well as courses in Business, Business Computing, Business Finance and Buriness Law. See also **Accountancy/Accounting**.

Brighton Twelve business courses are offered, covering economics, business law, marketing, finance and international business. There is also a specialist course in Wine Business which includes a work placement during Year 2.

Bristol Management is offered as a stand-alone BSc degree or can be taken with Accountancy or Economics.

Bristol UWE A large number of courses are offered in Business. These include Business Studies linked with Financial Management, Accountancy, Marketing, Tourism Management, Human Resources Management and Property. Also offered are International Business and Languages with placements in France, Germany or Spain and Business Mathematics combining business topics and mathematics. Modern language options support some of these courses.

Brunel Courses are offered in Business and Management, with an optional placement year and pathways in Accountancy, Business Administration and Marketing. Business Studies is also offered with Sports Sciences. There are also three-year and four-year (sandwich) courses in International Business, without a language requirement.

Buckingham Courses are offered in Business Enterprise or Management commencing in January for the former or September (a two-year course) with streams in information systems. Language study options are available. Courses are also offered in Accounting, Marketing with Media Communications, Computing, French, Spanish or Psychology.

Bucks New In addition to the Business Management degree there are also specialised courses in Air Travel Management, Air Transport with Pilot Training, Airline and Airport Management, Advertising, Events and Festival Management, Human Resources Management, International Management, Marketing and Music Industry Management and Public Relations Management. Accounting and Finance courses are also available.

Cambridge* A one-year Management course is offered to students who have taken two or three years of another Tripos.

Canterbury Christ Church Courses are offered in Business Studies as a joint or combined honours degree, leading to pathways in accounting, advertising management, computing, human resource management and marketing. Courses are also available in Advertising Management and Entrepreneurship.

Cardiff* A specialist degree scheme is offered in Business Management covering all the main areas relevant to business in Year 1 followed by modules of selected specialist areas in Years 2 and 3. These pathways include general business, human resources, marketing, logistics and international management. Courses are also available with French, Spanish and Japanese with Year 3 spent abroad. (See also **Accountancy/Accounting**, **Finance** and **Economics**.) Transport Management can be studied with Business Administration and there is also a course in Industrial Relations with Sociology.

Cardiff Met (UWIC) Business degrees have pathways in Finance, Human Resources, Law, Information Systems. Students have the opportunity to participate in work placement programmes.

Central Lancashire Over 15 courses are offered covering Advertising, Business Administration and Management, Business Law, International Business, Business Information Technology, Public Relations and Marketing. Business is also offered as part of the combined honours degree course and there are also courses in E-Business, Human Resource Management, Retail Management and Chinese and Business. Several courses are also offered in Ecotourism, focusing on environmental development. There are two overseas placements in the Business Management China programme and a two-week visit to Beijing in Year 1.

Chester The single honours Business degree offers the opportunity for a year in paid placement. Courses are also offered in Business Management, Advertising, Public Relations, Business Information Systems, Marketing Tourism and International Business.

Chichester The Business Studies course covers finance, marketing, human resources management and business law. Business Studies can also be taken with Information Technology. Courses are also available in Accounting and Finance, Human Resource Management, and International Business.

City* The Business School offers courses in Business Studies and Management in which optional placements in the UK and abroad are offered in Year 3. The Management course is interdisciplinary and covers organisational behaviour, management of technology, international relations and marketing. A course in Air Transport Operations is also offered with pilot training. See also **Finance** and **Actuarial Science Studies**.

Colchester (Inst) Four vocational management courses are available covering Hospitality, Sport and General Management.

Coventry There are courses in Business Studies and Business Administration with optional work placement. There are also courses in Advertising, Marketing, Tourism Management, Human Resource Management, Logistics, Events Management, International Business, Disaster Management, Air Transport Operations and Aviation Management.

Creative Arts Marketing and Management courses cover Advertising and Brand Communication, Fashion Management and Marketing, and Fashion Promotion.

Cumbria The Business Studies programme includes Management Studies, Logistics, Marketing and Travel and Tourism.

De Montfort Courses are offered in Business, Business Studies (full-time joint honours), Business Enterprise, Human Resource Management, Arts Management, Retailing, Digital Economy, Advertising, Marketing and International Business.

Derby The Business School offers three-year and four-year (sandwich) courses in Business Management (which are accredited by the CMI and carry exemption from Level 5 Diploma exams), Business Studies, Marketing, International Spa Management, Tourism and International Business. Several Business courses also offer pathways in finance, mathematics, human resources and psychology.

Dundee The Business Management course focuses on accounting and financial management in Years 1 and 2 with a wide range of options in Years 3 and 4, including languages, human resource management and accounting. Management forms part of courses in Engineering (Civil and Electronic), Environmental Studies and Accountancy. There are also courses that focus on Business Economics, Business Computing and International Business (BSc), which is now available with studies including modern languages.

Durham* After a broad first year, Business students spend Years 2 and 3 choosing from a number of course modules including organisations, the Pacific Rim, strategy and international business. Courses are also offered in Management Studies with Chinese or Japanese or as part of the combined honours programme. Business Finance and Accountancy share a common first year with Business, with options to change at the end of Year 1. Industrial placements and overseas exchange programmes are offered.

East Anglia The Business Management degree programme carries accreditation from the CIM and the CII and provides a broad base with the opportunity to specialise, while the Business Finance and Economics course provides a focus for those aiming for careers in accountancy and finance. Management can also be combined with Accounting, Languages, Biology and Mathematics. There are also courses in Business Information Systems, Marketing, International Business Management and Statistics.

East London Business Studies courses are offered with a range of subjects covering business finance, human resource management, marketing, supply chain management, entrepreneurship and corporate social responsibility. There is also a course in International Business with placements abroad and courses in Advertising, Events Management and Tourism, Human Resources Management, Marketing, and Retailing.

Edge Hill All students take a common first year after which it is possible to specialise in Accounting, Advertising, Human Resource Management, Leisure and Tourism, International Business or Marketing. Business is also available with Chinese Studies.

Edinburgh The Business Studies course focuses on the management of organisations and covers strategic planning, employment relations, finance, marketing and technology. Languages, Accounting, Geography and Law are also offered with Business. Overseas study through the Erasmus exchange scheme is offered, and students of International Business can spend their third year abroad.

Edinburgh Napier Business Management programmes are modular, giving considerable flexibility, and also combined with Economics, Finance, Human Resource Management and Marketing. There is also an International Business course with a placement abroad.

Edinburgh Queen Margaret Business Management, Consumer Studies, Marketing, Events Management, Tourism, Public Relations and Retail Business are all offered as single honours courses. Short placements are offered in Year 2 of some programmes. Combinations of some of these subjects can be taken in the fourth year of the course.

Essex The Business Management course offers an in-depth study of the various aspects of the management of commercial and industrial organisations. Financial management subjects are taken in each year of the three-year course. Business Management can also be taken with French, German, Italian and Portuguese, and with Latin American Studies. There are also courses in Accounting and Management and Entrepreneurship and Business.

Exeter* The School of Business and Economics offers courses in Business and Management with Leadership that can also be taken with European Study, in which students spend a year abroad. Management is also available with Marketing or Tourism. Three-year and four-year courses are also offered in Accounting or Economics and Finance, and a course in Leadership and Politics is also available.

Falmouth A comprehensive Public Relations degree is offered covering key aspects of the media. Advertising can also be studied.

Glasgow* Business and Management focuses on the practical and theoretical aspects of business, and has options in small business management, applied managerial psychology and the art of influencing. There is also a course in Business Economics.

Glasgow Caledonian Courses in Business Studies and International Business Studies with placements in Year 3 are offered, with a wide range of specialisations in the final year. Business Economics, Information Management, Marketing, People Management, Consumer and Trading Standards, Public Management, Retailing, Tourism Management, Adventure Recreation Management, Finance and Accounting and Entertainment and Events Management are also available. There is also a separate Marketing degree. Public Relations and Event Management can also be studied as part of the Media and Communications degree.

Gloucestershire The Business Management degree has pathways in human resource management, business management and strategy, and international business. There are also courses in Business Information Technology, Advertising, Tourism and Marketing. A placement year is available. Other degree courses include Public Relations and Publishing.

Glyndŵr Degrees are offered in Business Management, which covers all the main aspects of business including human resource management, business accounting and business marketing.

See *Heap 2015: University Degree Course Offers* (Trotman Publishing) for details of offers

Greenwich Business is offered in a range of programmes. It can be taken on a full-time or sandwich basis, with French, German, Italian or Spanish. It can also be taken as a combined degree with subjects including Maths and Law. There are also courses in Advertising, Marketing (also with languages), International Business, Human Resources Management and Events Management. Some programmes commence in January.

Harper Adams Courses focus on Marketing activities involved with agriculture, and food and business.

Heriot-Watt The School of Management courses include Management with Marketing, Human Resource Management, Operations Management and Business Law. Business and Finance and Business and Economics are also offered. Summer placements are offered. There is also an International Management course with languages and study placements in France, Germany, Austria or Spain. Joint degrees in Business and Economics or Finance are also available.

Hertfordshire Courses are offered in Business Studies (including four-year sandwich courses), Airport Operations, Human Resource Management, Event Management, Tourism Management, Marketing, International Business and Management Science. Joint honours Business courses are also offered. Business Studies can be studied with Languages or Finance. Courses in Accounting and Economics are also available.

Huddersfield Business Studies is offered as a three-year full-time course with an optional placement year in addition to Business Management. Business is also offered with Finance, Psychology, Journalism, Design, Law, Computing and International Business. A year of industry placement or studying abroad is offered. There are also courses in Advertising and Marketing Communications, Enterprise Development, Entrepreneurship and Business, Marketing, International Business, Human Resource Management, Tourism and Leisure Management, and Logistics Management.

Hull From a broad base of economics, accounting and business information technology, the Business degree focuses on marketing, business law, international business and financial management. Other courses include International Business, Business Economics, Management, Public Relations, Marketing, Tourism, and Financial Management. All courses share a common first year followed by specialisation.

Keele Management is offered as a single honours course whilst Business Management is a dual honours course with over 20 combinations in an interdisciplinary Social Science degree with a wide variety of specialist options. Twenty-eight dual honours courses are offered with Marketing, Tourism, Human Resources Management and Management Science. Students have the opportunity to study abroad at a partner university.

Kent Business Administration can be studied with a year in industry. Courses are also offered in Accounting and Management, Industrial Relations and Human Resource Management and in Marketing or with languages.

Kingston The Business Studies course covers all the main business areas, including a foreign language and IT skills, and has links with American and European universities. Other courses include Business with Economics, Information Technology, Law, French, Spanish, Leadership and Human Resource Management, International Business, and Marketing Communications or Management. Several joint honours are also possible. Business can also be studied with Accountancy or Law.

Lancaster* Business Studies (also offered with study abroad) is a three-year degree programme providing a grounding in theoretical and practical aspects of business. Options include accounting and finance, business law, purchasing and international business. There is also a Management course including a human resources option and a Marketing course with design, both including study abroad options. There are also degrees in Advertising, Business Analysis, Marketing Organisation Studies, Management Science and Operations Management, Operations Management and Entrepreneurship, and European Management with Languages. See also **Economics**.

Leeds* The Business School offers courses in Management (economics, operations management, marketing, international marketing and business) and other courses covering Accounting and Finance,

See *Heap 2015: University Degree Course Offers* (Trotman Publishing) for details of offers

and Business Economics, with a wide range of joint courses. Courses are also offered in Human Resource Management, and Fashion Marketing.

Leeds Beckett A wide range of full-time courses and sandwich courses are offered including Business, Business Studies with Languages, Retailing, Human Resources Management, Public Relations, Events Management, Marketing, Advertising and International Business courses.

Leeds Trinity There are business courses available which include management or marketing and a separate Management degree which focuses on HR and people management.

Leicester The Management degree focuses on a wide range of management issues including business ethics, finance and economics, with third-year modules in retailing and marketing. It can also be taken with Economics, Politics, Mathematics or Computer Science, a course which can include a year in industry or a year abroad.

Lincoln Five business courses are offered focusing on management, finance, marketing, international business and advertising. Joint courses are also offered with options for a year in industry or a year abroad.

Liverpool* The Management School offers Business programmes in Accounting and Finance, International Business, Marketing and E-Business.

Liverpool Hope Business can be studied as a single or combined honours course with a range of subjects relating to business including Marketing, Information Technology and Tourism. There is a separate course in marketing management.

Liverpool John Moores Business Management, Maritime Business and Management and courses in Business and Business Studies are offered. The latter includes a full-time option with a choice of specialist route (marketing, purchasing, human resource management, finance or general management) being made in Year 2. The International Business Management course (Year 3 abroad) can be taken with French, Japanese, Chinese or Spanish. Other courses include Business Communications, Business and Public Relations, Human Resources Management, Retail Estate Management and Business, Management Transport and Logistics, Marketing, Tourism and Leisure.

London (King's)* The Business Management programme covers all aspects of business including a foreign language option in Years 1 and 2. Some students take the opportunity to study in Canada, at the University of Toronto, in Year 2. Management is also available with French. There are also specialist fields of study in Acountancy and Finance, Marketing and Human Resource Management.

London (QM) The Business Management course covers accountancy and finance, human resource management and marketing.

London (RH) Management is offered with several subjects as a major subject including Accounting, Economics, Marketing, Mathematics, International Business and European Languages. Core courses in Management focus on the main functional areas of business and cover finance, information systems and management skills in Europe and abroad. An Economics course is also offered.

London (SOAS) A range of International Management courses offer specialist studies focusing on China, Japan, the Middle and Far East and Africa.

London LSE* A course is offered in Management (described as 'an intellectually broad preparation for management drawing on economics, psychology and sociology'). There is also a course in Management Sciences with elements of accountancy, IT and operational research. The degree in Employment Relations includes psychology, sociology and anthropology.

See *Heap 2015: University Degree Course Offers* (Trotman Publishing) for details of offers

London Met Courses offered include single and joint honours degrees in Advertising and Marketing, Arts Management, Aviation Management, Business Enterprise, Business Information Technology, International Business, Logistics and Supply Chain Management, Human Resource Management, Events Management and Public Relations.

London South Bank The Business Studies or Business Administration courses cover advertising, consumer behaviour, international business, finance, industrial relations and marketing. There is also a course in Arts Management covering technology, performance and visual arts, with a placement and project involving setting up an arts company, theatre and events organisations. There are also courses in Business Information Systems, Human Resources Management, International Management, Marketing and Tourism.

Loughborough Business courses cover a range of undergraduate degree programmes: Air Transport Management, Business Studies, Management, Sciences, Retail Management, Transport Management, Leisure Management and International Business. These courses came top in a survey of student satisfaction. There is also a degree in Publishing and English.

Manchester* There is a comprehensive programme of Business, International Business and Management courses with specialisms in Accountancy, Decision Science, Human Resources, Retailing and Marketing. There are also Management Science and Management and Leisure courses. Business is also available with Economics, Politics and Sociology. See also **Art and Design**.

Manchester Met A very wide range of courses lead to degrees in Business including Business Information Technology, Business Management, Marketing, Retailing, Enterprise, Human Resource Management, International Business, Business and Sport and Advertising. Sandwich courses with a year on a placement are available.

Middlesex Business Studies and Business Administration can be studied as full- or part-time courses. Business degrees are also offered with Marketing, Human Resource Management and International Management. International Business can be studied with Mandarin.

Newcastle* Degree programmes in Marketing cover specialist areas such as accounting, marketing and production as well as general, theoretical fields such as economics and organisational behaviour. Degrees in Business Management and Marketing share a common first year, after which students can choose their degree. Business Studies can also be taken with languages and there are several joint courses with Management. Economics, Accounting and Finance courses are also available. A year's placement is offered with several courses.

Newman Management Studies can be taken as a major, joint or minor course with another subject. A course in Business (Sustainability Ethics) is available as a single or combined honours degree.

Northampton A very large number of single and joint courses are offered including Human Resource Management, Advertising, Business Management, Events Management, Travel and Tourism Management, Retailing and Logistics. There is also a unique course in Waste Management. Industrial work placements and overseas study are available with many courses.

Northumbria A wide range of degrees is offered in Business and both full-time and sandwich options are available. Specialisms are offered in Accounting, Advertising, Economics, Finance, Logistics and Supply Chain Management, Human Resource Management, Marketing, Tourism and International Business Management. There is also a course in Corporate Management.

Nottingham* The Management Studies degree offers core modules in management and organisations, strategic management and marketing, finance and accounting and economics for management. There are also courses in Finance and Accounting Management, Business Economics of Contemporary China and in Industrial Economics. Joint courses can also be taken with Languages and Engineering.

See *Heap 2015: University Degree Course Offers* (Trotman Publishing) for details of offers

Nottingham Trent The Business School offers courses in Management Studies, Financial Services, Business Studies (three years with supervised work experience), Business Management with pathways in economics, accountancy, human resources and marketing, and International Business (with optional placements in Germany, France or Spain). Corporate sponsored degrees in Management and Leadership and Management Finance are also available, which carry no fees for Years 2 and 3 and involve salaried work which assignments are based on.

Oxford* The degree in Economics and Management offers an intellectual approach to both subjects and includes an accounting course and the roles of managers in the process of decision-making.

Oxford Brookes A very large number of course combinations are offered in Business subjects, including Business and Management, Business and Marketing, Information Technology for Business, Business of Real Estate, and Economics, Finance, International Business and Tourism. Most courses have work placements or international exchanges.

Plymouth Business Administration (three years) and Business Studies (four-year sandwich) are the main courses focusing on the UK, while International Business and European Business include modern languages (French, German, Italian and Spanish). There are also courses specialising in Business and Tourism, Marketing, Sports Management, International Business with Languages, Human Resources Management, Maritime Business, Rural Business Management and Shipping and Logistics. A course in International Supply Chain and Shipping Management is taught in Hong Kong.

Portsmouth Business Administration/Studies courses provide a very wide range of modules in Year 2 including employee relations, company law, European business and marketing. There are also full-time and sandwich courses in Business Enterprise Development, International Business Studies and European Business, in Human Resource Management (also with Psychology) and Marketing.

Queen's Belfast The degree in Business Management is a three-year course with final-year specialisms in human resource and operations management, marketing, international business, technology or public sector management. An optional placement Year is available between Years 2 and 3. The Business Management course with a modern language offers French or German (post A level) or Spanish or Italian ab initio. There are also courses in Business Information Technology and Consumer Behaviour and Marketing.

Reading A range of Business and Management courses is offered including Accounting and Management, Agricultural Business Management, Business Statistics and Business Analysis. International Management is also offered with French, German and Italian with a year in placement or studying abroad and a course in Behaviour and Marketing.

Robert Gordon A range of Management courses is offered including Management with Finance, Marketing, Economics and Human Resource Management. There are also courses in Fashion Management, Retail Management, and International Business and Tourism Management.

Roehampton International Business, Retail Management and Marketing and Human Resource Management are offered as single honours courses. Business Management is offered as both a single and combined course with a range of other subjects including Computing Studies, Modern Languages, Sociology and Sport Science, and with specialisms in Human Resources and Retail. There are also degree courses in Business Information Systems and Marketing and Multimedia.

Royal Agricultural Univ Two main courses include Business Management with work placements and a second course focusing on International Food and Agribusiness.

St Andrews* Management is offered as a single or joint honours course with a range of humanities and language courses. Topics covered include organisations and societies, management and society, public sector and human resource management, corporate finance and global business.

St Mark and St John Business courses focus on leadership and, for international students, business communication.

See *Heap 2015: University Degree Course Offers* (Trotman Publishing) for details of offers

St Mary's Management Studies can be taken as a single or combined course. There are also degrees in Tourism Management and Business Law.

Salford Business Studies students follow a common core in Years 1 and 2 and then choose specialised pathways in financial, marketing, human resource or quantitative business management, law or international business. There is also a European Business degree that includes a European language and Year 3 spent in Europe and degree programmes in Business with Economics, Human Resources Management, Marketing, Financial Management and Leisure and Tourism Management.

Sheffield The joint degrees in Business Management include consumer behaviour, human resources management, leisure management and information systems organisation. Business Studies can also be taken with a large number of engineering and technological subjects.

Sheffield Hallam Business Studies is offered as a three-year full-time or four-year sandwich course. Other sandwich courses include Business and Marketing, International Business Studies (also with languages), Business Economics, Marketing and Retailing, and courses involving Business and Human Resource Management and Operations Management are also offered.

South Wales Business courses have a broadly common first year enabling students to change pathways at the end of Year 1. Courses offered include Human Resources Management, Marketing, Logistics and Supply Chain Management, Retail Management, and Fashion Marketing and Retail Design. Business is also offered as a joint honours degree with Law, Accounting and Economics.

Southampton* The Management degrees offer modules in accounting, marketing, information systems and languages. The International Marketing course includes a year abroad.

Southampton Solent Business is available as a four-year sandwich course and can be studied with a range of options including Psychology. Courses are also offered in Adventure Tourism, Advertising, Human Resource Management, Marketing and business aspects relating to Maritime Studies and the music and arts industries.

Staffordshire A wide range of degrees can be taken including Business Studies, Business Management, Advertising, Human Resource Management, Marketing, International Business and Travel and Tourism. The business degrees share a common first year, allowing students to decide on a specialisation at the end. Joint courses can also be taken with Electronic Commerce.

Stirling The Business Studies degree includes the study of a foreign language. Optional courses include Personnel Management, Industrial Relations, Employee Training, European Business and Venture Management. Opportunities to study abroad are available. There are also degrees in Human Resource Management, Marketing, Management Science, International Management Studies, Retail Marketing and Business Computing.

Strathclyde For the BA Business course, students choose two principal subjects from accounting, business law, economics, finance, management science, mathematics and statistics, marketing, human resource management, modern languages and tourism. There are also courses in International Business, Business Enterprise, Business Technology, Business Law and Modern Languages.

Sunderland A wide range of courses associated with business is offered. These include Business Administration, Business Studies, Public Relations, Marketing, Human Resource Management, Business, Retail, Enterprise and Management joint courses. Human Resources Management can be taken as a combined course. Courses in Tourism and Hospitality are also offered.

Surrey* Several Business degrees are offered with sandwich placements. The degree in Retail Management covers accounting and business law, human resources and supply chain management and marketing, and includes a year in professional training. Final-year options include fashion or food retail management, food and nutritional management, small business management and optional language modules. Business Management with either French or Spanish is offered as three-year full-time

See *Heap 2015: University Degree Course Offers* (Trotman Publishing) for details of offers

or four-year sandwich course. Chemistry with Industrial Management and Language and Business Culture is also available.

Sussex Business and Management Studies offers core subjects plus pathways in finance, human resources management, marketing and international business. Courses in International Business and Marketing and Management include a sandwich placement year.

Swansea BA or BSc courses are offered in Business Management Studies (or with Accounting). The modular courses provide maximum flexibility, cover all management schemes, and include International Business, European schemes, or American or Australian year abroad schemes.

Teesside Courses are offered in Business Management and Business Studies (CMI-accredited), with the latter enabling students to spend one semester in a range of institutions in the US or across Europe. Foreign languages, retail, marketing and public relations are specialist subject areas. Other courses cover International Business, Sport Management, Marketing and Retailing.

Trinity St David A broad course in Business Management is offered with exchange opportunities in Europe and the US. There is also a degree in sustainable Management.

Trinity St David (Swansea) A vocational course in Business Studies enables students to specialise in Years 2 and 3. A broad course in Management is also offered. Human Resources Management and Marketing can also be taken. The Marketing Management course is CIM-accredited, allowing graduates to progress to the CIM Chartered Postgraduate Diploma.

Ulster Courses are available in Business Studies (and with specialisms in accounting, American business, business law, design, enterprise development, human resource management, management information systems, marketing and operations management). Business Studies can be taken as a major programme with subjects including Drama, Irish History and Languages. There are also modular Business degrees with Advertising and Retail, Languages, Marketing, Human Resources Management, Psychology, and a course in Consumer Studies.

Warwick* The Business School offers courses in Management (with engineering options), International Business or Business Studies and Accounting and Finance. Students taking Management may take a general programme or specialise in marketing operations management, personnel management, information systems or accounting. Business Studies is also available as a minor with German or Law.

West London Degree courses are offered in Business Studies (available with a sandwich internship option), Business Management, Advertising with Marketing, Human Resources Management, Retailing, Event Management, Public Relations, Airline and Airport Management, and Tourism Management.

West Scotland Several Business courses are available including Business (including placement opportunities), Marketing, Human Resources, Enterprise Studies, Information Management and Events Management.

Westminster The Business Studies degree programme comprises a general course or specialisms in finance, human resource management, information management, marketing and service industries. Business Management courses include entrepreneurship, financial services, retailing, law, human resources management or travel and tourism. There is also a degree in International Business with a study year abroad.

Winchester The Business Management programme has several specialisms including E-Commerce, Finance and Economics, Human Resource Management, Information Technology, Marketing and Public Service Management. There are also degrees in Tourism and Leisure Management. See also **Hospitality Management**.

Wolverhampton There are several joint combinations with Business Studies or Business Management, including E-Commerce, Marketing, Human Resource Management, Retailing, Entrepreneurship and Event Management available on three-year and, in some cases, four-year sandwich courses. Marketing courses include specialisms in enterprise and human resource management.

See *Heap 2015: University Degree Course Offers* (Trotman Publishing) for details of offers

Worcester The Business Management course has an optional sandwich year with options in advertising, accounting, human resources management and marketing. A Business Information Technology degree is also available.

York* Courses are offered in Accounting, Business Finance and Management or in Management. Both have optional years in industry. Business Management is also available as a minor subject with programmes including Physics.

OTHER INSTITUTIONS OFFERING BUSINESS COURSES
Askham Bryan (Coll), Barking (Coll), Bath City (Coll), Birmingham Met (Coll), Bishop Burton (Coll), Blackburn (Coll), Blackpool and Fylde (Coll), Bradford (Coll Univ Centre), Bridgwater (Coll), Bristol City (Coll), Chesterfield (Coll), Chichester (Coll), Cornwall (Coll), Coventry City (Coll), Craven (Coll), Croydon (Coll), Dearne Valley (Coll), Duchy (Coll), Durham New (Coll), Ealing, Hammersmith and West London (Coll), East Riding (Coll), Euro Bus Sch London, Farnborough (CT), Filton (Coll), Gloucestershire (Coll), Grimsby (Univ Centre), Guildford (Coll), Havering (Coll), Highbury Portsmouth (Coll), Hopwood Hall (Coll), Kaplan Holborn (Coll), Lakes (Coll), Leeds City (Coll), Llandrillo Cymru (Coll), London Regent's, Manchester (Coll), Mid-Cheshire (Coll), Myerscough (Coll), Neath Port Talbot (Coll), Nescot, NEW (Coll), North Lindsey (Coll), Northbrook (Coll), Norwich City (Coll), Nottingham New (Coll), Peterborough (Reg Coll), Richmond (Am Int Univ), Riverside Halton (Coll), St Helens (Coll), Sandwell (Coll), Sheffield (Coll), Sir Gâr (Coll), Solihull (Coll), South Essex (Coll), SRUC, Suffolk (Univ Campus), Sunderland City (Coll), Tameside (Coll), Totton (Coll), Truro (Coll), UHI, Uxbridge (Coll), Wakefield (Coll), Walsall (Coll), Warrington (Coll), Warwickshire (Coll), West Anglia (Coll), West Thames (Coll), Wigan and Leigh (Coll), Wiltshire (Coll), Worcester (CT), Writtle (Coll), York (Coll).

ALTERNATIVE COURSES
Accountancy, Banking, Economics, Insurance, in addition to the courses listed under **Subject Information** at the beginning of this table.

CHEMISTRY

(* indicates universities with entry requirements over 340 UCAS points)

SUBJECT REQUIREMENTS/PREFERENCES
GCE A level: Chemistry and another science usually required.

SUBJECT INFORMATION
There is a considerable shortage of applicants for Chemistry, which has very many career applications. These include oceanography (marine chemistry), agriculture and environmental work, colour chemistry, medical chemistry, pharmacy, pharmacology and polymer science. Refer to entries covering these subjects.

Aberdeen A broad course covering all aspects of chemistry is offered as an MChem (five years full time) or BSc (four years), leading to degrees in Biochemistry, Oil and Gas Chemistry, Environmental Chemistry and joint courses with Archaeology, Mathematics or Physics.

Arts London A degree course in Cosmetic Science in now offered.

Aston The Chemistry and Applied Chemistry programme emphasises industrial applications with placements and sponsorships. Applied Chemistry is available with Chemical Engineering.

Bangor The broad modular Chemistry course can include industrial placement or a year in Europe in Year 3. A four-year MChem course is also offered (five years with industrial experience). Chemistry can also be taken with Biomolecular Science. There are also courses in Environmental Chemistry and Marine Chemistry in which students spend half of their time in the School of Ocean Sciences.

Bath* Courses are offered in Chemistry and Chemistry and Drug Recovery Education or Management. In all courses there is a common first year with the option to change degree programmes, including the opportunity to progress directly to an MChem degree, and placements which take place in industry, either in the UK or abroad. The final year provides the opportunity to choose from a range of options. See also **Combined Courses**.

Birmingham Core modules are taken in Chemistry with specialisations in several areas, including Analytical Science, Biorganic Chemistry, Business Management and Psychology; major/minor combinations are possible. Industry experience or study abraod is offered. See also **Combined Courses**.

Bradford Chemistry4 provides a choice of four employment pathways (pharmaceuticals, forensic, biotechnology and quality control/analytical) in Year 3 of this three- or four-year course. There is also a course in Chemical and Forensic Science which can also include a sandwich placement, as well as specialist MChem degrees in Chemistry for Drug Discovery, Medicines Development, and Pharmaceutical and Forensic Sciences, all of which include a sandwich placement year.

Brighton Pharmaceutical and Chemical Sciences carries accreditation from the RSC for associate membership, and can be studied either as a three-year full-time or four-year sandwich course. The Chemistry course includes biology, biochemistry, chemistry and microbiology. The course in Analytical Chemistry with Business also has an optional placement year. There is also a Secondary Education Chemistry course which gives qualified teacher status.

Bristol* Seven programmes are offered, both MSci and BSc, all having a common first year and allowing transfer between courses during the first two years. Chemistry is taken in Year 1 with two other subjects from biochemistry, pharmacology, physics, geology and computer methods. In Year 2, chemistry is taken with one other. The third year involves a research project from a range of options. Courses are offered involving study in Continental Europe and North America. There is also a degree in Chemical Physics.

Bristol UWE The RSC-recognised degree in Forensic Chemistry covers biology, organic, inorganic and physical chemistry and genetics. DNA analysis and the interpretation of forensic evidence are compulsory modules.

Cambridge* See **Combined Courses**.

Cardiff Degrees in Chemistry, Chemistry and Physics, and Chemistry with Bioscience or Chemistry with Industrial Experience (BSc and MChem; Year 3 in industry or a year abroad (MChem only)) are available. Optional modules in Year 1 of the Chemistry course include biochemistry, biology, geology, physics and languages. The MChem scheme follows the same syllabus in Years 1 and 2.

Central Lancashire BSc and MChem courses are offered as well as Forensic Chemistry which consists of investigating and analysing information gathered at crime scenes.

Dundee* BSc degrees are offered in Biological Chemistry and Drug Discovery, covering drug design, synthetic chemistry and screening techniques. A year on a placement is available.

Durham* The first year of the Chemistry honours course may be accompanied by a wide range of subsidiary courses (sciences, humanities or languages). Common first-year courses provide maximum flexibility with opportunities for industrial placement and study abroad. Joint honours courses are also offered with a number of subjects including Physics, Mathematics and Earth Sciences.

East Anglia The School of Chemistry offers a number of Chemistry programmes, including three-year BSc and four-year MChem courses, and the flexibility in the choice of units enables a range of scientific areas to be studied. Therefore the overall content of the degree programme depends to a large extent on the interests and strengths of the individual student. The Chemistry with a year in North America course extends over three years. For the Chemistry with a year in Europe course, students study at a university in Denmark, France, Germany or the Netherlands during the third year of their course. Environmental Chemistry and Pharmaceutical Chemistry are also available.

Edinburgh* Thirteen degrees in Chemistry are offered with the options of a year abroad or a year of industrial experience. Specialist options include Environmental and Sustainable Chemistry, Materials Chemistry and Biological Chemistry.

Glasgow* Chemistry is a broad course that provides a basis of the principles of chemical science in the early years and leads to special topics at honours level in the fourth year. The BSc course is RSC-recognised and the MSci is accredited. Chemistry with Medicinal Chemistry, Chemical Studies and Mathematics and Environmental Chemistry are also offered.

Glasgow Caledonian A course is offered in Chemistry with Information Technology and with instrumental specialisation in either environmental analysis or food analysis.

Greenwich Specialist courses within the Chemistry degree structure, either MSc or BSc, include Biochemistry, Microbiology, Biotechnology, Materials Science, and Chemistry in Medicine and Agriculture. Year 3 is spent on an industrial placement, or in work and study in another EU country. A five-year sandwich MChem course is also available. There are also sandwich courses in Pharmaceutical Chemistry and Analytical Chemistry, and a range of joint courses.

Heriot-Watt Fifteen Chemistry courses are offered including BSc and MChem options, with the choice of degree being deferred up to the end of Year 3. There are options in Biochemistry, Computer Science, Materials, Environmental Economics, Forensic Science, Industrial Experience, Management, Pharmaceutical Chemistry and Education. There are study opportunities in Europe, Australia and North America

Huddersfield A modular Chemistry course is offered, with options in Year 2 in chemical technology, forensic science or biology. Similar options follow in Year 4 after work placement throughout Year 3. A sandwich placement year is available.

Hull A range of BSc Chemistry courses (with paid industrial experience possible) follow a similar path in Years 1 and 2 allowing for transfer between degrees. Other honours programmes allow for combinations with, for example, French, German, Nanotechnology, Analytical Chemistry, Applied Chemistry, Molecular Medicine, Toxicology and Forensic Science.

Imperial London* The Department offers 15 Chemistry courses including a three-year course in Chemistry and Management, four-year courses in Chemistry, Chemistry with Management with a year in industry or abroad (with language study), a four-year course offering both a year in industry and a year abroad and Chemistry with either Medicinal Chemistry or with French, Spanish or German for Science.

Keele Chemistry and Medicinal Chemistry are offered as dual honours courses with a large number of combinations from science, social science and humanities subjects. A semester abroad and sandwich placement year are offered.

Kent Chemistry and Forensic Chemistry are both offered with or without a year in industry.

Kingston The Chemistry programme includes industrial placement throughout Year 3. Courses in Medicinal and Forensic Chemistry, and Chemistry with Business Management are also available.

Lancaster Two courses in Environmental Chemistry are offered, one of which includes study abroad; this option is available as a BSc (Hons) and MChem (Hons). The Environmental Science course combines aspects of geography, geology, chemistry and physics.

Leeds Chemistry and Medicinal Chemistry are single-subject courses that have the same academic standing and a common first year; they are offered at BSc and MChem level and may be coupled with a year abroad or in industry. A wide range of joint courses are also offered.

Leicester BSc (three-year) and MChem (four-year) Chemistry courses are offered. In Years 1 and 2 optional modules can be taken that include computing, environmental chemistry, industrial and polymer Chemistry and management. In addition to the sandwich course, it is possible to spend a year in the US or Europe or study Chemistry with Management, or Forensic Science. Specialisms include Polymer Science, Analytical Chemistry and Medicinal Chemistry. There is also a course in Biological Chemistry with the option to take a year in industry or the US, Canada, Europe or Australia.

Liverpool In the first year, Chemistry can be taken with two non-chemistry courses. This is a very flexible Chemistry programme with additional options in the second year including materials science, oceanography, archaeology, computer science, biochemistry or pharmacology. There are also degree courses in Chemistry with Nanotechnology, Medicinal Chemistry with Pharmacology, Oceanography, or Business Studies. A year in industry is also an option.

Liverpool John Moores The School of Chemistry offers courses focusing on Medicinal and Analytical Chemistry. The opportunity for placements is available. There is also a course in Applied Chemical and Pharmaceutical Sciences.

London (QM) The Chemistry course covers organic, inorganic and physical chemistry with modules in spectroscopy and analytical chemistry. Opportunities exist to spend a year in industry. A course is also offered in Pharmaceutical Chemistry.

London (UCL)* For the degree in Chemistry, BSc and MSc students follow the same course for two years with the decision to choose the degree in Year 3. The MSc option is available as an international programme. The course in Medicinal Chemistry includes biology, pharmacology, physiology and biochemistry. Chemistry can also be studied with Mathematics, Management Studies or a European language, with 75% of the course Chemistry and 25% the elected option. All courses may be taken as a three-year BSc or a four-year MSc.

London Met Chemistry is available as a single honours BSc course, which carries RSC accreditation, allowing graduates to register for associate membership. Biological and Medicinal Chemistry, and Chemistry with Forensic Science, Human Nutrition and Sport Science are all offered as three-year full-time degrees. There is also a degree course in Cosmetic Science.

Loughborough Courses offered include Chemistry, Medicinal and Pharmaceutical Chemistry, Chemistry with Analytical Chemistry, and Chemistry and Sports Science, Business or Patent Law or Information Technology. All have three-year or four-year options with sandwich placements.

Manchester A range of Chemistry courses is offered, including Chemistry with Forensic Science, Geochemistry, Medicinal Chemistry or Business Management. There are opportunities to study for a year in industry, Europe or North America. Three-year BSc and four-year MChem full-time courses are offered.

Manchester Met A large and flexible programme is offered with Chemistry as a BA, BSc or MChem with Study in Industry or in Europe (modern languages option in Year 1). Forensic, Pharmaceutical or Analytical Chemistry and over 20 joint courses are available. The Chemical Science course allows transfers to other Chemistry degrees after Year 1.

Newcastle BSc and MChem courses in Chemistry are taken with modules in specific fields. Chemistry can also be taken with Medicinal Chemistry or with study in North America or Europe. A Natural Sciences degree is also offered.

Newman This course is taken in collaboration with Aston University, with Years 1 and 2 taken at Aston.

See *Heap 2015: University Degree Course Offers* (Trotman Publishing) for details of offers

Northumbria Applied Chemistry is a three-year full-time or four-year sandwich course with the industrial training period in Year 3 focusing on industrial applications. The MChem Applied Chemistry course is designed for students interested in pursuing further research in the subject. Chemistry is also offered with Biomedical Sciences and Forensic Chemistry and there is a degree in Pharmaceutical Chemistry.

Nottingham* BSc and MSc Chemistry are modular courses with options in a wide range of subjects (scientific and non-scientific) in all years and the opportunity to transfer to the MSc (four-year) course at the end of the second year. There are also degrees in Chemistry and Molecular Physics, and Chemistry and Management Studies, and a range of Biochemistry degrees. There are also options to spend a research year in industry or an international study year.

Nottingham Trent BSc and MChem Chemistry courses with placements are offered. Chemical Sciences and Pharmaceutical and Medicinal Chemistry courses are offered along with the option to have a paid year in industry or abroad. See also **Pharmacology**.

Oxford* A four-year Chemistry course is offered, covering inorganic, physical and organic chemistry, with the fourth year spent in a full-time research programme. All undergraduates attend a course in computing and their time is divided equally between chemistry lectures, practical work and preparation for tutorials and classes. Some opportunities exist for fourth year students to study in European or American universities.

Plymouth RSC-accredited courses are offered in Analytical and Applied Chemistry, with these specialisms being chosen in Year 3. Forensic and Medicinal Chemistry and Pharmaceutical Science are also available.

Queen's Belfast The course is designed to provide a basic understanding of all the major aspects of chemistry, allowing some degree of choice in the final year of study. It is also possible to follow courses in Medicinal Chemistry, Chemistry with study in Europe (France, Germany or Spain) and Medicinal Chemistry, and Forensic Analysis including a year in industry. BSc and MSci honours options are available.

Reading In Part I of the Chemistry course, students take three units of Chemistry and three from a wide selection of other units. In Terms 3, 4 and 5, Chemistry students spend two-thirds of their time on Chemistry and one-third on a subsidiary subject. Thereafter, their whole time is spent on Chemistry, with equal emphasis on inorganic, organic and physical chemistry throughout most of the course, but with some specialisation in the third year. Chemistry can also be taken with Forensic Analysis or Medical Chemistry or with industrial placements in the UK or Europe.

St Andrews* Basic studies in Chemistry occupy the first and second years, with certain subjects being obligatory. Modules are offered in chemistry and society, organic and biological chemistry and materials science. Placement years in industry are offered. Chemistry can be combined with a large number of other subjects including French, German or Spanish, which can include a year abroad.

Sheffield During the first year of the Chemistry degree, three unrestricted modules are offered (in other subject areas). Most students enrol for the four-year MChem course. There are also degrees in Biological Chemistry, Chemical Physics, Chemistry and Enterprise Management, Mathematics and Informatics. There are opportunities to study in industry, in Europe, Australia and the US. All degrees are accredited or recognised by the RSC. Scholarships available.

South Wales The RSC-accredited Chemistry course includes physical, inorganic, organic and analytical chemistry with specialisms in Years 3 and 4 in pharmaceutical, agrochemistry and food chemistry. The study of a foreign language can be continued throughout the course. Several joint courses are offered along with Combined Science and Combined Studies programmes. There are also degrees in Forensic Science and Forensic Chemistry.

See *Heap 2015: University Degree Course Offers* (Trotman Publishing) for details of offers

Southampton* The Chemistry degree is an extremely flexible course and serves as a basis for the study of physical, organic and inorganic chemistry. Other courses include Chemistry with Medicinal Sciences and with six-month and one-year placements.

Strathclyde Chemistry and Applied Chemistry students take the same course in the first three years, after which there is an industrial placement of five or 12 months. The choice between degrees in Pure Chemistry and Applied Chemistry is then made. There are also courses in Forensic and Analytical Chemistry, Chemistry with Drug Discovery and Teaching and Natural Sciences programmes. An MSci course in Applied Chemistry and Chemical Engineering is also offered.

Sunderland The Chemical and Pharmaceutical Sciences course provides a comprehensive understanding of pharmaceutical and chemical science, developed through extensive study of chemical and biological analysis. Emphasis is placed on the scrutiny of pharmaceuticals, together with drug design and formulation. Final-year specialisms include drug development, medical chemistry, forensic analysis, environmental analysis and food analysis. An optional sandwich year is available. Chemistry is also offered with a large number of other subjects in the joint honours programme.

Surrey Chemistry is a modular course with special options such as forensic chemistry and computing. Here, 90% of entrants take the four-year course with one year of industrial training, mostly in Europe, Canada, Australia and New Zealand. Courses in Medicinal and Computer-aided Chemistry are also offered, as well as a programme in Chemistry with Forensic Investigation. The BSc programmes are recognised by the RSC.

Sussex A four-year MChem and three-year BSc course are offered, which share the first two years and allow students to choose a route at the end of Year 2, with an optional sandwich year in the UK or Europe.

Teesside The BSc Chemistry programme provides specialisms in environmental, forensic chemistry and biomedical science, with an optional industrial placement in Year 3. There is also a degree in Forensic Chemistry.

Warwick Considerable flexibility exists for first-year students to transfer between the courses in Chemistry (MChem and BSc) and Chemistry with Medicinal Chemistry. There are also courses in Chemistry with Management or Mathematics and in Biomedical Chemistry.

West Scotland The Chemistry course offers a broad study of organic, inorganic and physical chemistry, and is available as a three-year BSc or four-year honours course. Optional industrial placement takes place in Year 3. There is also a course in Medicinal Chemistry with an optional placement in industry.

York* All Chemistry students, irrespective of their choice of degree course, follow the same first year (Part I) course that includes some maths, computing, biochemistry and physics. Part II includes more advanced chemistry studies and a choice of modules that lead to a degree in mainstream Chemistry, or Biological and Medicinal Chemistry, Chemistry Resources and the Environment, or Chemistry, Management and Industry. Students on the MChem course can spend their fourth year at York, in industry or in Europe, and industrial sponsorship schemes are available. See also **Combined Courses**.

OTHER INSTITUTIONS OFFERING CHEMISTRY COURSES
Riverside Halton (Coll), South Devon (Coll), Staffordshire Reg Fed (SURF).

ALTERNATIVE COURSES
Agriculture, Biochemistry, Botany, Ceramics, Chemical Engineering, Environmental Science, Pharmacology, Pharmacy.

See *Heap 2015: University Degree Course Offers* (Trotman Publishing) for details of offers

CLASSICAL STUDIES/CLASSICAL CIVILISATION

(*indicates universities with entry requirements over 340 UCAS points)

SUBJECT REQUIREMENTS/PREFERENCES

GCE A level: Relevant subjects include classical civilisation, English literature, archaeology, Latin and Greek. **GCSE:** English and a foreign language often required.

SUBJECT INFORMATION

Classical Studies and Classical Civilisation courses cover the literature, history, politics and culture of Ancient Greece and Rome. Knowledge of Latin or Greek is not necessary for many courses, but check subject requirements carefully.

Birmingham There is a course in Classical Literature and Civilisation with options in art, religion, philosophy and archaeology. It is also available as a joint honours course with a range of humanities subjects. Classical languages are not required for this course but there are optional language courses in Greek or Latin. In Year 2 study tours take place in Greece or Italy.

Bristol* Classical Studies is offered with study in continental Europe for those proficient in a modern language. A joint honours programme in English and Classical Studies is also offered. (This is a leading Classics Department in the UK.) A part-time course is available.

Exeter* Courses in Classical Studies and Ancient History are available without any previous knowledge of Latin or Greek. English, French, Italian or Theology are also offered with Classical Studies. The option to study abroad is offered on all courses.

London (RH) The Classical Studies degree is suitable for those students who wish to give more time to archaeological, philosophical or other less language-oriented topics.

Manchester In the Classical Studies course a wide range of options is offered in Years 2 and 3, giving the opportunity to study Greek and Latin in all years. Joint courses with both subjects are offered. Degrees in Classics, Ancient History, and Latin with English, Italian, French, Spanish and Linguistics are offered with the option of studying abroad.

Newcastle The Classical Studies course is varied and flexible and allows students to concentrate on areas and topics of particular interest to them such as art, archaeology, history and philosophy. No previous knowledge of Greek or Latin is required for entry. The department is noted for its expertise in teaching the languages to beginners.

Newman Classical Civilisation can be studied as a minor subject from 2014.

OTHER INSTITUTIONS OFFERING CLASSICAL STUDIES/CLASSICAL CIVILISATION COURSES

Edinburgh*, Kent, Leeds, Liverpool, London (Birk), London (King's)*, London (UCL)*, Nottingham, Oxford*, Reading, St Andrews*, Trinity St David (Swansea), Warwick*.

ALTERNATIVE COURSES

Ancient History, Archaeology, Classics, Greek, Latin.

CLASSICS

(* indicates universities with entry requirements over 340 UCAS points)

SUBJECT REQUIREMENTS/PREFERENCES
GCE A level: Check courses for Latin/Greek requirements.

SUBJECT INFORMATION
Classics courses focus on a study of Greek and Latin but may include topics related to ancient history and culture.

Bristol* The single honours course in Classics focuses on the Greco-Roman world, specialising in traditional language skills and developing historical knowledge of the ancient world. Reading from the original Latin and Greek is an integral part of the course. (This is the leading Classics department in the UK.) A part-time course is available.

Cambridge* The course encompasses the historical, cultural, architectural, artistic and philosophical aspects of the classical era.

Durham* There are three single honours courses, all with a common first year. The core of the Classics course is language, catering for students with A levels in Greek and/or Latin, but also open to beginners. Language is optional in the Classical Past and Ancient History courses, the core being the cultural and intellectual history of Greece and Rome. Classics and Ancient History is also offered in the combined honours in Arts programme. A joint honours course in Ancient, Medieval and Modern History is also available.

Edinburgh* The Classics course combines the study of Roman and Greek civilisations with linguistic and philological work. Knowledge of Greek or Latin languages is not required but will be taught as part of the course and features heavily in the four-year degree.

Glasgow The Classics course comprises classical civilisation. Knowledge of Greek or Latin languages is not required. Years 3 and 4 are available as a single or joint honours programme. See also **Combined Courses**.

Liverpool The Classics course focuses on the study of ancient languages, Latin or Greek. Study abroad is offered. Classics is also available on the Arts combined and the BA combined honours courses.

London (King's)* The Classics programme covers classics for those wishing to study aspects of the classical world through reading texts in Greek or Latin and, alternatively, a study of culture and thought for those without a classical language. Classics, Latin and Greek are offered as joint courses.

London (UCL)* In the first year of the Classics course, Latin and Greek (prominent in all years) are provided at three levels – beginners, intermediate and advanced. Topics for detailed study include Greek philosophy, sculpture, drama and history, Roman Britain, law and history and Latin satire, elegy, late and medieval Latin, art and architecture. It is possible to take a degree in Greek with Latin or Latin with Greek, and Greek can be taken with Philosophy.

Nottingham* The Classics (Latin and Greek) courses have an emphasis on language and literature. The focus of the honours Latin course is the world of Rome.

Oxford* The largest Classics department in the world offers two main Classics degrees (courses I and II), the former requiring Latin and/or Greek, while no experience of Latin or Greek is required for the latter. Courses are also offered with English, Modern Languages and Oriental Studies.

See *Heap 2015: University Degree Course Offers* (Trotman Publishing) for details of offers

Reading Courses are offered in Classics (in which a fluent reading of Greek or Latin is required), Classical Studies and Ancient History. The main core of these courses lies in a series of options chosen from epic, drama, poetry, satire, the novel, history, art and philosophy. Ample opportunity exists for students to specialise or diversify in their chosen field. Joint courses are also available with Classical Studies, including History of Art and Medieval Studies.

St Andrews* Students studying Classics may specialise in Greek or Latin (language and literature) and, in addition, study ancient history, ancient philosophy or some other aspect of classical studies. Options to study abroad are available. There are also courses in Greek, Latin and Ancient History.

Swansea The department offers a wide range of courses in Classics, Classical Civilisation, Latin and Greek or Roman Studies, Ancient History and Medieval Studies and Egyptology.

Trinity St David The main emphasis of the Classics course lies in the study of languages and classical texts. Courses in Latin, Greek and Classical Studies are also offered, and summer workshops in Greek and Latin skills are held. See also **History**.

OTHER INSTITUTIONS OFFERING CLASSICS COURSES
Exeter, London (Birk), London (RH), Manchester, Newcastle, Warwick.

ALTERNATIVE COURSES
Ancient History, Archaeology, Classical Studies/Classical Civilisation, Philosophy.

COMBINED COURSES

(including **Humanities**)
(* indicates universities with entry requirements over 340 UCAS points)

SUBJECT REQUIREMENTS/PREFERENCES
Varies depending on the course choice.

SUBJECT INFORMATION
In addition to providing single subject degree courses, many universities or their individual faculties now provide students with the opportunity to take two or three subjects throughout their studies. Specific examples of combined-subject courses are listed below.

Bath* The course in Natural Sciences offers a broad first year with a choice of subjects from Biology, Chemistry, Education, Environmental Science, Languages, Management, Mathematics, Pharmacology and Physics. This enables students to sample subjects prior to making a final choice later in the course. Similarly the Social Science programme also offers an initial range of subjects in Year 1 from Economics, Languages, Sociology, Social Policy and Psychology.

Birmingham The Natural Science programme is designed for those with a general interest in science. It offers nine science subjects (Biochemistry, Biology, Chemistry, Earth Sciences, Geography, Mathematics, Physics, Psychology and Sport and Exercise Science) which gives students the chance to sample two major topics and minor topics prior to specialisation later.

Bradford A three-year course in Combined Studies offers a choice of modules from 22 subject fields, with a negotiated route offering one-third core modules and two-thirds selected with the guidance of the course leader.

See *Heap 2015: University Degree Course Offers* (Trotman Publishing) for details of offers

Cambridge* The course in Human, Social and Political Sciences enables students to explore a range of subjects. In Year 1 (Part 1), four subjects are chosen from Politics, International Relations, Sociology, Social or Biological Anthropology, Psychology, Archaeology, Cultures of Egypt or Mesopotamia, Egyptian Language, or Akkadian Language. In Years 2 and 3 (Part 2) a single track subject or a combination of two subjects are chosen. The course in Natural Sciences similarly offers a wide range of subjects covering Astrophysics, Biochemistry, Biological and Biomedical Sciences, Chemistry, Genetics, Geological Sciences, History and Philosophy of Science, Materials Science, Neuroscience, Pathology, Physical Science, Physiology, Plant Sciences, Psychology, Systems Biology and Zoology. In Year 1, three subjects are chosen from a list of eight. A further choice is made in Year 2 and in Years 3 and 4 a single subject is chosen.

Canterbury Christ Church A very large number of subject combinations are offered in the joint honours scheme.

Cardiff In the BA degree scheme three subjects are studied in Year 1, followed in Years 2 and 3 by a study of one or two of these subjects. The BSc Econ degree allows students to choose up to six from 18 subjects in Year 1, followed in Years 2 and 3 by one of the subjects selected. Natural Science subjects are offered in the preliminary year.

Chester A BA combined honours programme offers a choice of two subjects taken from 48 options.

Coventry Up to three subjects can be selected from nine options, including languages with a year abroad. There is also a Humanities degree.

De Montfort In the joint honours programme two subjects are taken from 30 options. Each subject is studied equally.

Derby Combined Studies is a modular scheme in which 50 subjects are available, two or three being chosen on a major, joint or minor basis. All students on the Combined Studies programme are allocated a personal tutor for academic counselling. There is also a very flexible degree in Applied Studies.

Durham* Students may choose two to four familiar subjects or start new subjects. In Combined Studies in Arts the combinations allow for a study of a mixture of arts subjects from Arabic, Art History, British Sign Language, Classics and Ancient History, English, French, German, Greek, Latin, History, Italian, Mathematics, Music, Philosophy, Russian, Spanish and Theology. Combined Studies in Social Sciences is a modular course enabling the student to choose subjects from Anthropology, Archaeology, Business Accountancy and Finance, Criminology, Economics, Education, Geography, Government, International Affairs, Management, Middle Eastern and Islamic Studies, Politics, Sociology and Sport. Natural Science is a flexible modular course with a choice from Astronomy, Biology, Chemistry, Computer Science, Earth Sciences (Geology; Geophysics), Mathematics, Physics, Psychology and Statistics.

East Anglia The very flexible Natural Science course provides the opportunity to combine science subjects from Biology, Chemistry, Computing, Environmental Science, Mathematics and Physics.

East London There is a large number of combined honours degrees covering both joint and major/ minor courses.

Edge Hill A large number of BA and BSc major/minor combinations and joint honours courses is available.

Edinburgh Napier The university offers a customised programme with a wide range of vocational and academic subjects in which students plan their own course.

Edinburgh Queen Margaret Twelve vocational subjects are offered in which applicants choose any two.

Essex The Humanities degree scheme offers a wide range of options, following a foundation year, in Years 2 and 3. The main areas cover sociology, history, philosophy, linguistics, literature, art history and theory, film studies, government, history of art and modern languages. There is also a Politics, Philosophy and Economics course.

Exeter Combined and joint honours programmes are offered, in addition to which there is a Flexible Combined Honours scheme offering modules from a number of different fields. A year of studying or working abroad is offered with the combined honours programme. There is also a Liberal Arts programme with the option to choose between 14 subjects.

Glasgow The General Humanities programme covers options in ancient, creative, historical, literary, linguistic and Scottish studies. A Liberal Arts programme is also offered at the Dumfries campus. See also **Social Science/Studies**.

Gloucestershire The Modular Scheme offers a very wide range of joint honours courses.

Greenwich The Humanities programme enables students to study a range of subjects rather than specialising in one. Three options are chosen from over 30 courses. The International Studies programme allows joint and combined honours study in a range of subject options. There is also an extensive list of combined honours degrees.

Heriot-Watt The Combined Studies course is available as a BSc or BEng and covers sciences, engineering and management, comprising more than 21 subjects offered as modules and awarded by credits. Students obtain the degree by way of achieving the required number of credits over three years.

Hertfordshire In the Humanities scheme four subjects can be chosen (from 16 subjects). All four can be studied for three years (one being English, History or Philosophy) or specialist studies can be selected in one or more of the four. Joint and combined honours programmes are offered in 23 subjects with over 300 study combinations.

Huddersfield A flexible course offering the choice of two or three subjects from an extensive list. In Year 2 decisions are made to choose between a two subject degree (with each subject equally weighted) or a major/minor subject degree. A major subject is chosen from the choice of three.

Keele Three-year dual honours courses are offered with each subject taught in equal amounts. A foundation year is available for applicants without the necessary A levels in eight health subjects, 10 humanities subjects and 20 science subjects. Some single honours courses are offered.

Kingston A very wide range of courses includes 'classic' degrees in Computer Science and Information Systems along with those offering specialist modules such as digital imaging and network communications. There are single and joint honours degrees and opportunities for professional placements in industry.

Lancaster* There is a Combined Science course (22 subjects offered) in which students choose two science subjects plus one non-science, or three science subjects and Natural Sciences with a choice of five subjects. A study abroad option in North America is included. Courses in Combined Linguistics and Combined English Language are also available, with units chosen from other courses in the Department of Linguistics and English Language.

Leeds Students taking joint honours degrees study two named subjects and one or more electives. A personal tutor provides academic support. The Cultural Studies course covers film, literature, music and the visual arts.

Leicester The Interdisciplinary Science degree is Leicester's Natural Science course and covers a mix of biological sciences, chemistry, physics and earth sciences allowing the student to focus on their particular interests.

Lincoln There is a large number of study combinations at the Hull and Lincoln campuses.

Liverpool Three subjects are chosen in the combined honours (BA) course, two being taken for three years. Over 30 subjects are offered (17 subject options) with some limitations on choice. On the combined honours BSc (Hons) programme, students can choose either two science subjects, or one from another department. Modules in a third subject can be taken. For Combined Social and Environmental Sciences, three subjects are taken in Year 1 with an introductory course in Social Sciences. In Years 2 and 3, two subjects are taken or alternatively one of several 'packaged' programmes designed in multidisciplinary pathways. There are 25 subjects offered.

Liverpool Hope An extensive combined honours programme is offered with over 30 subject options.

Liverpool John Moores The Integrated Credit Scheme offers a modular course structure in which students take a main subject plus electives from a very long list of subject topics.

London (Goldsmiths) The Social and Cultural Studies degree enables students to focus on a range of subjects covering anthropology, creative writing, history, journalism, literature, media and communications, politics, psychology and sociology.

London (King's) The very flexible Liberal Arts course offers 20 options in Year 1, 19 options in Year 2 from which a major course is chosen and a final choice of a major subject in year three.

London (QM) A Science and Engineering programme is offered as a BEng or MEng with specialist options in eight subjects.

London (UCL)* Seven subjects are offered in the Statistics, Computing, Operational Research and Economics programme and 20 alternative courses in the Modern Language group. Several interdisciplinary degrees are also available which cover a range of disciplines, including an Arts and Sciences BASc, and BSc courses in Human, Natural or Biomedical Sciences.

London Met Over 100 joint degrees are offered.

Manchester Met In Combined Honours, two subjects are chosen from over 15 options and are taught on a course unit system. Subjects include Business Studies, Drama, Science, Music, Sport and PE, Visual Arts and Writing. They can be taken as major, joint or in some cases minor combinations (English and TESOL may only be taken as a minor or joint option). There is also a joint honours programme. In the Humanities/Social Studies programme up to three subjects are chosen leading to a single honours or major/minor degree. Subjects offered include Economics, English, History, Modern Languages (French, German, Spanish), Philosophy, Politics, Social and Economic History and Sociology. There is also a varied course in Cultural Studies.

Newcastle* Combined Arts is a flexible and varied programme in which three subjects are chosen in Year 1 followed by two or three in Years 2 and 3. Twenty-seven subjects are offered covering such areas as accounting, ancient history, archaeology, Chinese, classical studies, economics, film studies, geography, history of art, Japanese, English, modern languages, politics music and science. Combined Studies in Science offers modules from all science departments (and elsewhere). Science subjects available include Astronomy, Biological Sciences, Chemistry, Computer Science, Software Engineering, Mathematics, Psychology and Surveying.

Northumbria Three subjects are taken from a choice of nine groups. Specialisation in two follows in Years 2 and 3. Nine joint honours Society courses are available.

Nottingham The BA degree in Combined Studies offers a range of flexible study options including archaeology, art history, business, creative writing, English, history, modern languages and music. A part-time course is also available. The BSc (Hons) in Health Studies offers a combined studies pathway or a number of specialist studies pathways.

Nottingham Trent In the Humanities course two main subjects are chosen from English, French, Geography, History, International Relations, Languages, Media and TESOL. Students also take a third main subject or a programme of special studies. Combined Studies in Science provides options in two subjects chosen from 10 options that include Sports Science.

Oxford Brookes Combined Studies offers students who have already completed at least one year of full-time study the opportunity to follow a course designed by themselves: the course is of one or two years' duration. It is possible to spread the programme of study over two or more subjects from a wide choice of options.

Plymouth The Combined Arts scheme offers the choice of the following subjects: Art History, Contemporary History, English, Heritage and Landscape, Media Arts, Theatre Arts and Performance Studies, Visual Arts, Politics, Business Studies or Law. A BSc (Hons) in Combined Social Science is delivered at the university's Cornwall campus.

Queen's Belfast The BA joint course provides for the study of two equal subjects from Economics, Geography, History, Geography, Linguistics, English, Philosophy, Social Policy and Theology.

St Mark and St John Students take two subjects equally as a joint honours degree or as major and minor subjects.

St Mary's Students can choose from a long list of equal and major/minor joint honours combinations giving maximum flexibility to the choice of course. Some single honours courses allow a second subject in Year 1.

South Wales In the BA Combined Studies programme, between three and five subjects may be chosen from a list of over 20, including Business, Computer Science, Criminology, English, Geology, Law, Maths, Physical Sciences and Sport Science. The choice can be reduced during Years 2 and 3. See also **Social Sciences/Studies**.

Southampton The BSc Social Sciences course offers degrees in one subject or two subjects studied equally (combined or joint course). The academic year is divided into two semesters with students taking four courses in each semester. Part 1 provides a background in basic skills. Other units are chosen from a range of subjects including Accountancy, Biology, Economics, Geography, Law, Philosophy, Politics, Psychology and Sociology.

Strathclyde Three subjects are taken in Year 1, specialising later in two in Arts and Social Sciences. There is also a Science programme.

Sunderland Thirty subjects are offered to make up the Combined Subjects programme, with major/minor subjects (with an emphasis on one) or dual (two subjects, equal emphasis) programmes.

Teesside The course structure consists of major and minor subjects. Thirty-nine major subjects and 46 minor subjects are offered. In addition, there is a large number of specialist subjects.

Warwick The MORSE course offers Mathematics, Operational Research, Statistics and Economics with a choice of five subjects. The PPE course offers seven subject combinations. A Combined Technology course is also available, with the opportunity to study a modern language.

West Scotland Over 30 subjects are offered on a combined degree scheme in which students select modules to suit their interests or career aspirations.

Westminster The combined honours programme has a choice of 15 subjects, which can be studied equally or as a major/minor combination.

Wolverhampton Eighteen subjects are offered on the Applied Sciences programme and 65 subjects on the combined degree course.

York All students irrespective of their degree subject, are offered the opportunity to study a foreign language in the Languages for All scheme. First-year students take this course free of charge. The languages on offer include French, German, Spanish, Italian, Dutch, Russian, Japanese, Chinese (Mandarin) and possibly Arabic and Portuguese if there is a demand. A course is also offered in Philosophy, Politics and Economics, and a combined History of Art degree is available.

OTHER INSTITUTIONS OFFERING COMBINED COURSES
Bradford (Coll Univ Centre).

COMPUTER COURSES

(including **Information Technology**)
(see also **Engineering**)
(* indicates universities with entry requirements over 340 UCAS points)

SUBJECT REQUIREMENTS/PREFERENCES
GCE A level: Mathematics required in some cases.

SUBJECT INFORMATION
Programming languages, data processing, systems analysis, artificial intelligence, graphics, software and hardware are all aspects of these courses. Several institutions offer courses with languages and placements.

QUESTIONS TO CONSIDER
　＊ Does the course carry accreditation or recognition from any professional computing bodies?
　＊ How do the various types of degree qualification (BA, BSc, BEng, MEng) differ, and which is best suited to my areas of interest and career aspirations?
　＊ Am I looking to further an interest in a specific area, such as computer animation or artificial intelligence, or gain a broad range of transferable skills?

Aberdeen Single BSc honours courses are available in Computing Science and Computing covering all aspects of programming. Topics include internet information systems, artificial intelligence, robotics, business computing, microprocessors and systems analysis. Computing Science can be taken with French or Spanish. There are also degrees in Information Systems and Artificial Intelligence. There are overseas exchanges and degrees with industrial placements.

Abertay Courses are offered in Computing and Networks, Computer Games Technology and Computing (Games Development) with strong contacts with the games industry. In addition there are courses in Information Systems and a degree in Computer Arts (internationally acclaimed) for those with an artistic interest in the new media industries. There are also degrees in Ethical Hacking and Counter-measures and Digital Forensics.

Aberystwyth A very flexible course is offered in Computer Science, with options to study another subject as a joint honours or major/minor programme. Courses are also offered in Software Engineering, Internet Engineering, Internet Computing and Artificial Intelligence, Computer Games, Information Management and Computer Graphics. All students are encouraged to spend a year working in the computing industry between Years 2 and 3.

Anglia Ruskin Modules in the Computer Science degree include systems modelling, artificial intelligence, programming, graphics, animation and visualisation, format languages and management. There are also four Internet Technology courses and several other specialised courses including Software Development, Computing and Gaming Systems, Computing with a Foreign Language, Multimedia Studies,

Business Information Systems, Internet Security and Forensic Computing and Media Internet Technology. Anglia Ruskin is a designated Cisco Regional Networking Academy.

Aston The Computing Science course has an emphasis on practice in programming languages and applications, data processing and systems analysis (no prior knowledge of computing is required). Artificial intelligence, graphics and software engineering are also part of the course. A placement year is offered. There are also degrees in Computing for Business and combined honours programmes.

Bangor The Computer Science degree covers all the key areas of the subject with particular specialities in computer graphics, artificial intelligence, data communications and business activities. The applications of computers in the marketing of goods and services and computers in industry and business are also offered, respectively, with courses in Internet Systems and E-Commerce and Information, Computer Science for Business and Communications Technology. The Creative Technologies course is one of the first of its kind and covers the applications of TV and radio, film and video. Degrees in Electronics also have options in Hardware Systems and Software.

Bath* Studies cover a range of subjects both theoretical and practical, including computer science, software engineering, multimedia and human–computer interaction, with options in computer graphics and computer music, depending on career intentions. Courses are offered in Computer Information Systems, Computing with Mathematics, Business or Computer Systems Engineering. Four-year sandwich courses are available with placements in the UK or study abroad.

Bedfordshire A wide range of subjects are offered including Computer Science, Computing, Computer Networking or Games Development, Graphics, Internet Computing, Artificial Intelligence and Software Engineering. There is a common first year for all courses.

Birmingham* The School of Computer Science offers several courses including Computer Science, Artificial Intelligence and Computer Science, Computer Science with Business Management and combinations with one of a range of subjects including Business Studies, Arts subjects, Software Engineering and Civil Engineering. There are options to study in continental Europe. A course in Bioinformatics bridges the disciplines of biology and computing. See also **Combined Courses**.

Birmingham City Ten degrees with sandwich placements are offered by the School of Computing. These cover Information Systems, Computing, Software Engineering, Business Information Technology, Computer-aided Design, Computing Games Technology, Computer Networks and Security. Sandwich placements are offered in most subjects and in E-Commerce. The university is a Cisco Systems and Microsoft Academy Centre, allowing students to take Cisco qualifications alongside their degree studies.

Bolton A number of courses are offered, including Internet Communications and Networks, Business Software Development and Computer Technology and Computing. Courses in Games Art and Games Design are also available.

Bournemouth A four-year sandwich course in Computing is offered, in addition to which there are courses in Business Computing, Information Systems Management and Business Information Technology. There is also a Software Engineering Management degree covering product development, with a 40-week placement in Year 3. In addition there are also courses in Multimedia Communications, IT Management and Applied Computing and Electronics. The university's Media School is the home to the National Centre for Computer Animation (NCCA), making it a leading centre for the study of computer animation.

Bradford A range of courses is offered including Computer Science, Computing and Information Systems, Internet Computing, Business Computing, Mobile Computing, Multimedia Computing, and Software Engineering. The four-year courses provide the opportunity for those wishing to have a year in industry. Courses are accredited by the British Computer Society (BCS). There are also courses in Computer Animation, Games or Computational Mathematics.

Brighton The Computer Science programme has a common first semester leading on to a wide range of specialisms including Computer Systems, Computer Architecture, Software Design and Planning and Games Development.

Bristol* The curriculum adopts four main themes: software, hardware, applications and cross-disciplinary themes. BSc, MEng and MSc courses are offered including the opportunity to study in Europe. Throughout, there is a balance between theory and practice. Fourth-year options include artificial intelligence, databases, systems architecture and computer networks. A three- or four-year course in Mathematics and Computer Science is also offered and a four-year course with Electronics.

Bristol UWE A wide range of topics is offered in Computer Science, which can be studied as either a three-year or four-year sandwich course. The course carries BCS accreditation and graduates will have met the educational requirements for registration as a Chartered Information Technology Professional (CITP). Other computing courses involve information systems, forensics, security, games technology and software engineering. Some overseas placements are available.

Brunel Computer Science and Information Systems courses can be taken as three-year or four-year courses. The former focuses on the design and development of software, while the latter prepares students for the application of computing in commercial and industrial organisations. There are specialist routes in both degree programmes including Artificial Intelligence, Digital Media Games, Network Computing and Software Engineering.

Buckingham A two-year course in Computing is offered starting in January or September. Several specialisms are offered in Year 2. Computing can also be studied with Accounting and Finance, Business Studies, Communication Studies, and Economics.

Bucks New Courses are offered in Computing, Web Development and Games Development.

Cambridge* The first year of the Computer Science Tripos introduces basic principles. All students take the Mathematics course and one Natural Sciences subject. The second year covers core technologies and themes and the third year graphics, digital communication and artificial intelligence.

Cardiff Computer Science is a broad course in Parts I and II, with modules on artificial intelligence, graphics, parallel computing, object-oriented languages and software engineering. The course in Computer Systems Engineering integrates with electronic engineering involving software and hardware pathways. Computing is offered with Physics or Mathematics. There is also a Business Information Systems course. Degree schemes are accredited by BCS and the Institute of Engineering Technology. There is also a Business Information Systems course.

Cardiff Met (UWIC) Several courses are offered, including Business Information Systems, Computing and Software Development.

Central Lancashire Fourteen computing courses are offered including Business and Computing, Computer-aided Design, Business Information Systems, Forensic Computing, Computer Games Development, Multimedia Networks and Software Development. All are focused on vocational and practical skills.

Chester Computer Science is a broad course available as a BA (Hons) combined honours or BSc (Hons) single or combined honours, involving all aspects of the subject with a six-week work placement in Year 2. Several specialist courses are offered.

Chichester IT Management is offered as a full-time or sandwich course with professional placement. The programme can be taken as a single or joint honours course. There are also joint courses linked with E-Business.

City There is a common first year for all courses, with specialist modules in the chosen course in Years 2 and 3. A one-year placement is possible between Years 2 and 3. The course is BCS- and CITP-accredited. There are courses in Business Computing Systems, Computer Science, Games Technology and Software Engineering.

Colchester (Inst) Computing Solutions degrees are offered specialising in internet and network computing.

Coventry Twelve degree courses are offered including Computer Science, which carries BCS accreditation, Computer Systems, Ethical Hacking and Security Studies, Games Technology, Computer Network Communications and Creative Computing and Software Engineering with optional third-year paid placements in industry.

Creative Arts Computer Games Design is offered. See also **Art and Design**.

Cumbria There are courses in Applied Business Computing and in IT.

De Montfort The three- or four-year sandwich course in Computer Science emphasises the uses and applications of the computer in commercial, industrial and scientific roles in the areas of software engineering and systems analysis and design. There are also courses in Multimedia Computing, Internet Computing, Business Information Systems, Software Engineering, Games Design, Robotics and Artificial Intelligence.

Derby The Computer Science degree focuses on the practical and theoretical aspects of developing and maintaining software systems. Other courses cover Computer Networks, Computer Forensics, Games and Business Programmes and Internet Computing.

Dundee After Years 1 and 2 in the Applied Computing course, which includes a subject of the student's own choice (e.g. Accountancy, Psychology or Mathematics), students may proceed to an honours degree in Years 3 and 4. A degree in Computing Science is available. Several joint courses are also offered including Computing and Economics. Third-year options include software engineering, computer systems and internet programming.

Durham* Courses offered are Computer Science, available as a three-year BSc or a four-year MEng, and Computer Science (Europe). All have a common first year followed by the chosen specialisation. There are also joint courses in Computer Science with Mathematics or Physics.

East Anglia* The course in Computing Science aims to establish an appreciation of the theoretical foundations that underlie computing as a scientific discipline and to develop practical skills. The Applied Computing course comprises a study of computing and its applications, including computer graphics, commercial information systems and operational research. The Business Information Systems BSc aims to give a broad understanding of information system theory and technology. Software Engineering, Computer Graphics and Computing for Business are also offered as three-year full-time courses. There is an opportunity to study for a year in North America or Australasia, or in industry.

East London Several courses are offered, including Computing, Business Information Systems, Information Technology, Internet Technology, Games Development and E-Commerce.

Edge Hill Computing is offered with specialisms in business information technology, information and software systems. A four-year sandwich course is available. Students can also design their own course.

Edinburgh BCS-accredited BSc or BEng Computer Science courses are offered, depending on the student's preferences. The BSc courses focus on Computer Science, which can be combined with Mathematics, Physics, Electronics, Artificial Intelligence or Management. The BEng courses in Software Engineering also have options in the same subject areas.

Edinburgh Napier A wide range of BSc, MSci and BEng courses is available, including Computing, Computer-aided Design and Computing, Networks Computing, E-Business, Electronic Computer Engineering, Information Systems and Software Technology. Some modules carry BCS accreditation. Sandwich courses are available.

Essex Computer Science is a modular course in which eight foundation units are chosen in Year 1 leading to a choice of 16 degree courses including Computer Science, Artificial Intelligence, Artificial Intelligence and Robotics, Internet Technology and Software Engineering. There are also degrees in Computer Games and Internet Technology and Internet Engineering.

Exeter Computer Science is a broad course comprising software development, artificial intelligence and hardware, and gives opportunities to debate the effects on society of new developments in computer science. Optional summer industrial placements contribute towards the degree. There is also a four-year course with industrial placement. A course is also offered in Computer Systems Engineering.

Glasgow* This highly rated research department offers courses in Computing Science and Software Engineering that require no previous experience of computing. BCS accreditation is carried. They are offered with a range of subjects such as Physics, Mathematics, Business Management, Physiology, Psychology and Statistics. An Arts and Media Informatics degree focuses on IT and digital media.

Glasgow Caledonian Several computer degrees are on offer including Animation, Games and a four-year course in Computer Aided Engineering.

Gloucestershire The three-year Computing degree is essentially vocational and aims to equip students with a range of software development skills. There are also courses in E-Business, E-Marketing, Forensic Computing, Business Information Technology and Multimedia. There is optional work placement on the four-year course.

Glyndŵr There is a degree in Computer Games Development. Students are assessed by way of coursework and the demonstration of competence in the delivery of practical work. A BSc in Creative Media Computing is also available.

Greenwich Computing Science is a three- or four-year (sandwich) course involving business skills, data systems and computer information systems. Specialisms in the final year include information systems, software engineering, computer networking, multimedia and artificial intelligence. Courses are also offered in Software Engineering, Multimedia and Business Technology, Internet Systems and Games Development. In all there are 29 BEng and BSc courses offered in Computing.

Heriot-Watt No previous computing experience is required for the nine Computer Science courses. The four-year courses cover language theory, graphics, data processing and various topics in artificial intelligence. Computer Science courses are also offered with specialisms in Information Technology, Software Engineering, Games Programming, Artificial Intelligence and Human Computer Interaction. It is possible to transfer to other courses at the end of Year 1.

Hertfordshire A wide range of degree courses is offered covering Computing, Computer Science (with options in Artificial Intelligence, Networks and Software Engineering), Computer and Network Technology, Information Systems, Interactive Systems, Multimedia Communication and Software Engineering. Psychology with Artificial Intelligence is also offered as well as a course in Software Systems for the Arts and Media. In addition, the Computing joint honours programme has 12 optional subjects.

Huddersfield A very wide range of courses is on offer, including Business Computing with Artificial Intelligence, and with Software Development, Virtual Reality Systems, Computing Science and Computer Games Programming. Many of these are four-year courses with Year 3 being supervised professional experience.

Hull Several degree programmes are offered that cover Software Engineering, Internet Computing, IT Management, Computer Music, Games Development, Computer Systems Engineering, Computer Science and Computer-aided Engineering. All are available as three-year BSc or four-year MEng degrees. A complementary subject can also be studied. There is a common first year for all courses, after which students can choose their specialism or transfer to other courses.

Imperial London* The Computing Integrated Engineering Study Scheme offers a common two-year course leading to specialist four-year MEng courses in Artificial Intelligence, Computational Management and Software Engineering.

See *Heap 2015: University Degree Course Offers* (Trotman Publishing) for details of offers

Keele The Computer Science course is designed to give students an understanding of the logical structure and organisation of computers and the theory and practice of computer operation and programming. Final-year options include software engineering (also a freestanding degree), communications, graphics and artificial intelligence. There are also dual honours programmes in Computer Science, Creative Computing, Information Systems and Smart Systems.

Kent A Computer Systems Engineering course is offered with a year in industry, as well as a BCS-accredited Computer Science course with a bias towards Artificial Intelligence, Consultancy or Networks. There are also several joint honours courses in which computing can be combined with Accounting, Business, Philosophy or Film Studies, focusing on the application of computers rather than theoretical aspects of computer science. There is also a degree in Information Technology.

Kingston Several courses are on offer focusing on Computer Science with specialisms in Network Communications, Games Programming, Digital Imaging, Digital Microelectronics and also Information Systems with Multimedia and Business Information options. Other courses include Business Management, Mobile Computing and Software Engineering.

Lancaster The degree in Computer Science has a strong emphasis on practical computing with a balance between hardware and software aspects. A common first-year course leads to specialisms in Software Engineering, Multimedia Systems or Embedded Systems. There is also an option to study abroad or spend a year in industry.

Leeds The Computing course offers a broad range of opportunities relevant to the design of computer systems. Artificial Intelligence is also offered with Mathematics, Philosophy and Physics. A large number of BCS-accredited Computer Science and Computing joint courses are offered and also degrees in Informatics, Artificial Intelligence and Information Systems. All programmes offer a year in placement or study abroad.

Leeds Beckett Courses in Computing have a common first year, after which students select their degree specialisation from a general computing course or Computer Communications and Forensics, Software Development, Multimedia Systems, Database Systems or Artificial Intelligence. Computer Security and Ethical Hacking, Business Computing and various computer animation courses are also offered.

Leicester A three-year Computer Science course, accredited by the BCS, can be taken with Management. There are also four-year courses to enable students to study in Europe or with a year in industry.

Lincoln A wide range of Computing courses is offered, including Computer Science, Information Systems, Software Engineering and Games Design.

Liverpool* Fourteen BCS-accredited courses are offered including Computer Information Systems, E-Business and Electronic Commerce Systems, Artificial Intelligence and Software Development. The Arts and Science combined programmes also include Computer Science. A year in industry is also an option.

Liverpool Hope Single and combined honours courses are offered in Information Technology and Computing with specialisation in Gaming Technology, Web Development or Computing Graphics. Both subjects can be studied jointly with such courses as Accountancy, Education and Law.

Liverpool John Moores Computer Studies with four main themes can be studied (business information systems, computer systems, software development and systems analysis and design). Other courses include Computer Technology, Internet Computing, Animation, Computer Forensics, Computer Games Technology and Software Engineering.

London (Goldsmiths) Courses are offered in Computer Science or Computing and Information Systems, Internet Computing or Creative Computing. Another creative option is offered through the BMus/BSc (Hons) in Music Computing. Industrial placements are arranged.

See *Heap 2015: University Degree Course Offers* (Trotman Publishing) for details of offers

London (King's)* Computer Science courses have a mainly common first year. Thereafter the course unit system permits a large element of choice and leads to courses including Computer Science with Management, Intelligent Systems and Robotics or with Mathematics or Electronics. Courses involving a year in industry or a year abroad are also offered.

London (QM) The Computer Science course emphasises the role of software. Years 1 and 2 cover the theory of program construction and software engineering. Project work and options follow in the third year, including computer graphics, multimedia and artificial intelligence. Computer Science can be studied with several other subjects including Business Management, Mathematics and Multimedia and is offered with industrial experience.

London (RH) The flexibility of the course unit systems in Computer Science means that students are not committed to any particular course but may choose their course from year to year as their interests develop. Students may choose three main options including management, a year in industry and artificial intelligence. Computer Science can be studied with Management or Mathematics and a course in Computing and Business is also available.

London (St George's) The degree in Biomedical Information is a healthcare information science and computing course providing experience of the interface between technology and health and patient care.

London (UCL)* All Computer Science degrees have a common core in Years 1 and 2. The first year gives a broad training (including programming and mathematics) with some optional courses, for example, Languages and Psychology. BEng and MEng courses occupy Year 3. An International Programme in Computer Sciences is also offered, allowing a year's study in Europe, the US, Asia or Australasia. A course in Mathematical Computation is also available and Information Management for Business is offered in the Faculty of Engineering.

London Met Computer Animation, Digital Media Design, Computer Networking and Computer Games Programming are among the range of computing courses offered.

London South Bank The Computing course has a common first year with all other computing specialisms covering software design and development, business information technology, computer networks and multimedia technology. Specialisms in such areas as Business Information Technology, Computer-aided Design, Digital Media Arts and Electronic Business follow in Year 2. There is also a course in Computer Systems Management.

Loughborough* Three-, four- and five-year MComp Computer Science courses are offered. After a broad introduction, specialisation is possible in database systems, networks and artificial intelligence, and many other areas. These courses came top in a survey on student satisfaction. Courses include Artificial Intelligence and Software Engineering, Computer Science, E-Business, Computing and Management, IT Management and Business. Computer Science can also be studied with Mathematics.

Manchester* Five courses are offered in Computer Science including one with Business and Management. Courses are modular but a free choice of units allows for study in other subjects, for example Languages, Psychology and Economics. Industrial placement options are available. Courses are also offered in Artificial Intelligence, Modern Telecommunications, Computer Engineering and Internet Engineering.

Manchester Met Computing courses allow students to build their own programme to suit their interests. Courses include Computation and Artificial Intelligence, Business Information Technology, Multimedia and Web Computing, Software Engineering, Computer and Information Systems, and Games Technology.

Middlesex Computing Science is offered as a three-year full-time degree and with optional work placement. Courses are also offered in Business Information Systems, Computer Networks, Internet Applications Development, Information Technology and Forensic Computing.

Newcastle All Computing Science degrees share first- and second-year courses. This gives considerable flexibility for change of course, for example to or from joint honours, at the end of the first year. Courses with Computing Science include Economics, Mathematics and Statistics. Courses are also available in Information Systems with joint courses in Business Studies. Industrial placements are available.

Newman Computer Science and ICT are offered for intending Secondary teachers and Information Technology is offered as part of a joint honours programme.

Northampton Computing course specialisms cover Communications, Computer Studies, Computer Systems Graphics, Internet Technology, Mobile Computing and Software Engineering. There are also 20 joint courses from which to choose.

Northumbria A very large portfolio of computer-based programmes is on offer. These cover Computer Games, Forensics, Computer Networks, Business, Software Engineering, Informatics, the Internet and Ethical Hacking. There is also a course in Information Studies, focusing on the organisation, retrieval, design and marketing of information. The Computer Sciences BSc (Hons) carries full exemption from BCS examinations.

Nottingham* The Computer Science course is available as a three-year BSc or a four-year MSci and involves software and hardware systems with a range of optional modules in each year. There are also courses in Computer Science and Management Studies, Artificial Intelligence, Robotics, Software Engineering, and E-Commerce and Digital Business.

Nottingham Trent Courses include Computer Games Systems, Computer Science, Information and Communication Technology, Software Engineering and Information Systems.

Oxford* BA (three years) and MCompSci (four years) courses are offered, the decision being made in Year 3 as to the choice of degree. The Computer Science course provides a bridge between theory and practice, hardware and software. The first-year course is shared with Mathematics. Final year options include computer graphics, artificial intelligence and computer security. A course in Computer Science and Philosophy is also offered.

Oxford Brookes Computing Science is a three-year full-time or four-year sandwich course in software engineering design and programming with over 30 modules from which to choose in Year 2 of the course, thus giving maximum flexibility in the choice of specialisms. There are also courses in Communication Network Software Engineering and Multimedia Production. A large number of combined courses can be taken with these subjects. Students are able to undertake a work placement or study abroad.

Plymouth Computing Informatics is a four-year sandwich course. In Years 1 and 2 students cover programming, systems analysis and design and software production. In the final year an individual project is undertaken along with two optional courses. Nine degree courses are also offered including Computing, Computer Science, Computer Systems and Networks, Digital Art and Web Development and Information Technology. There are also joint courses with Geography, Geology and Mathematics.

Portsmouth A very flexible scheme is offered with a common first year for all courses, after which the final degree choice is made. Degree subjects include Computer Science, Computing Software Engineering, Digital Forensics, Internet Systems, Computer Animation and Games Technology, Creative Computing Technologies, and Computer Network Management and Information Systems. Sandwich placements are available.

Queen's Belfast The aim is to produce graduates wanting to become software engineers although the course also covers programming and fundamental aspects of computer hardware in the first and second years. In addition to single honours courses, the subjects can also be taken in major/minor programmes. Courses in Business Information Technology, Computer Games Design and Development are also available.

See *Heap 2015: University Degree Course Offers* (Trotman Publishing) for details of offers

Reading The Computer Science degree offers a practical grounding in the subject, teaching programming languages including C++, C# and Java, but the course unit system allows great flexibility. Other courses include Applied Computer Science (with industrial placement), Information Technology, Computer Engineering, Robotics, Artificial Intelligence and Cybernetics.

Robert Gordon The BCS-accredited Computer Science course includes a one-year work placement. The Computing for Business course covers operations management, data communications and software engineering. Courses are also offered in Computing for Internet and Multimedia, Information and Business Systems and Graphics and Animation.

Roehampton Computing Studies can be studied as a single subject or combined with seven other options. There are single honours courses in Computing with Database Systems, Information Management and Computing with Web and Multimedia.

St Andrews* Courses are offered in Computer Science and Internet Computer Science, with 12 other subjects including Language and Management. Direct entry to Year 2 is possible with an appropriate academic background.

Salford The BCS-accredited Computer Science course has a bias towards the software aspects of the subject and can be taken as a three-year full-time or four-year sandwich course. Courses in Business Information Systems, Software Engineering, E-Commerce Systems, Internet Computing and Mobile Computing are also available.

Sheffield* Computer Science has an emphasis on theoretical principles and their applications. Computer Science can also be taken with Mathematics, Modern Languages and Physics, and courses are available in Artificial Intelligence and Information Technology Management for Business.

Sheffield Hallam The Computing programme has a professional placement in Year 3 and focuses on business and IT systems. There is a foreign language option in Years 2 and 4. Courses are also offered in Business and ICT, Games Software Development and Information Systems Security.

South Wales The BCS-accredited Computer Science course is one of breadth and includes the option to spend a year in industry. Other courses include Software Engineering, Information Communication Technology, Computer Forensics, Computer Games Development and Computer Security. The Computer Animation degree is internationally recognised.

Southampton* The BSc Computer Science course includes elements concerned with the engineering background to the design and application of computer systems, software and hardware in industry. Options in Year 3 include artificial intelligence, computer graphics, multimedia systems and programming language design. The MSc course includes work placements. Joint courses with Computer Science include Artificial Intelligence, Distributed Systems and Networks, and Image and Multimedia Systems. A course in Software Engineering is also available.

Southampton Solent In addition to Computer Studies, several programmes are on offer in Computer Networks with options in Communication, Management and Web Design, Video Games, Digital Media, Software Engineering and Business Information Technology. All programmes are BCS-accredited.

Staffordshire BSc honours courses are grouped into Business Computing and IT, Computing and IT, each providing a range of specialisms. Computing Science is available as a BSc (Hons) or a BEng (Hons). In addition there is a large number of joint courses covering Business Computing, Computer Games, Computer Graphics, Computer Science, Forensic Computing, Mobile Computing and Network Systems. Placement options are available.

Stirling Computing Science covers artificial intelligence, programming, software engineering, communications and networks. Eighteen courses are on offer including Modern Languages (French or Spanish), Marketing and Psychology.

See *Heap 2015: University Degree Course Offers* (Trotman Publishing) for details of offers

Strathclyde Computer Science is available as a three-year BSc (Hons) or four-year MEng course. In the first and second years courses are selected from programming, software design and artificial intelligence. The third year of the honours course covers communication and software development, with project work in Year 4. Other courses include Business Information Systems, Software Engineering, Computer Science with Law and Computer and Electronic Systems.

Sunderland Business Computing is a three-year full-time course or a four-year full-time extended course with a foundation year covering computer systems analysis and design and business studies. There are also degree courses in Computer Studies (and with joint courses), Computing, Information Technology, Business Computing, Forensic Computing, Software Engineering and Network Computing. A placement year is offered.

Surrey* The first two years of the Computer Science programme offer a wide range of modules and are followed by an optional placement in Year 3. Three- or four-year courses are offered in Computer Modelling and Simulation, Computer Science Engineering, and Computing and Information Technology.

Sussex The Computer Science degree includes the five core strands of programming, software engineering, computer systems, foundations and professional issues. There are options in web computing, computer graphics and animation, robotics and intelligent systems. Courses are also offered in Artificial Intelligence, Internet Computing, Games and Multimedia Environments and Music Informatics.

Swansea There are several schemes involving Computer Science, including options in Mathematics and Finance or with a modern language. In addition, there are several joint degrees with options in Geoinformatics, Physics and a language.

Teesside The Computer Science degree leads to specialisations in computer applications and computer science, while Business Computing focuses on the commercial world. Other degree courses include Software Engineering, Web Development, Visualisation, Business Information Technology, and Computer Games Design. Professional placements are available.

Trinity St David (Swansea) All aspects of the computer industry are covered in the degree courses on offer. These include information technology, games, networks software and web development. The university faculty is a Cisco Regional Academy.

Ulster Four-year sandwich courses are offered in Computing Science, Games Development, Software Systems and Computing with specialisms. In addition there are over 20 joint courses in subjects such as Business, Film and a range of languages including Irish.

Warwick* BSc and MEng courses are offered. The first-year Computer Science course consists of four core courses covering programming, architecture, mathematics and professional aspects of computing. In the second year more advanced work in programming, languages and computer systems takes place. Third-year options include artificial intelligence and psychology, robot technology and computers in business. Courses also include Computer Systems Engineering and Computer Science and Business Studies or Management Science.

West London Six courses include Network and Mobile Computing, Business Information Systems, Games Design and Computing Science and Network Management.

West Scotland Computing Science students choose their specialisms at the end of the first year. All programmes have a strong practical bias with team projects introduced from the first year. Other courses include Business Information Technology, Computer Games Technology, Computing Science, Digital Arts and Computer Animation, Information Systems, Multimedia Technology and Software Engineering.

Westminster A large number of courses are offered covering Computer Science, Computer Systems Engineering, Computer Visualisation, Computer Communications and Networks, Computing, E-Business, Internet Computing, Multimedia Computing, Mobile and Web Computing, Software Engineering and Design for the Digital Media. Sandwich placements are available.

See *Heap 2015: University Degree Course Offers* (Trotman Publishing) for details of offers

Wolverhampton The Computer Science degree scheme allows specialisation in Multimedia Technology, Information Systems, Business or Software Engineering. All decisions can be delayed until Year 2. There are also several courses covering Multimedia Computer Games and the Web.

Worcester In addition to the Computing degree there are specialist degrees in Business Information Technology, Computer Networks, Computer Games, Web Innovation and Entrepreneurship and Web Development.

York* Computer Science is offered as a three-year full-time or four-year sandwich course, transfers being possible at the end of Year 1. About a third of sandwich placements are outside the UK, others being in industry. Other courses include Computer Science and Mathematics or with Embedded Systems, and Software Engineering.

OTHER INSTITUTIONS OFFERING COMPUTER COURSES

Bath City (Coll), Blackburn (Coll), Blackpool and Fylde (Coll), Bradford (Coll Univ Centre), Bridgwater (Coll), Bristol City (Coll), Central Nottingham (Coll), Chichester (Coll), Cornwall (Coll), Coventry City (Coll), Craven (Coll), Dearne Valley (Coll), Doncaster (Coll Univ Centre), Dudley (Coll), Durham New (Coll), East Riding (Coll), Farnborough (CT), Gloucestershire (Coll), Grimsby (Univ Centre), Guildford (Coll), Havering (Coll), Hopwood Hall (Coll), Hull (Coll), Kirklees (Coll), Lakes (Coll), Leeds City (Coll), Lincoln (Coll), Llandrillo Cymru (Coll), Neath Port Talbot (Coll), Nescot, NEW (Coll), North Lindsey (Coll), Northbrook (Coll), Norwich City (Coll), Nottingham New (Coll), Pembrokeshire (Coll), Ravensbourne, Riverside Halton (Coll), St Helens (Coll), Sheffield (Coll), Shrewsbury (CAT), Sir Gâr (Coll), Solihull (Coll), Somerset (Coll), South Cheshire (Coll), South Devon (Coll), South Essex (Coll), Southport (Coll), Staffordshire Reg Fed (SURF), Stephenson (Coll), Stockport (Coll), Stourbridge (Coll), Suffolk (Univ Campus), Sunderland City (Coll), Swindon (Coll), Tameside (Coll), Truro (Coll), Tyne Met (Coll), UHI, Uxbridge (Coll), Wakefield (Coll), Walsall (Coll), Warrington (Coll), Warwickshire (Coll), West Anglia (Coll), West Cheshire (Coll), West Thames (Coll), Worcester (CT), York (Coll).

ALTERNATIVE COURSES

Business Studies, Economics, Electrical and Electronic Engineering, Mathematics.

DANCE

(*indicates universities with entry requirements over 340 UCAS points)

SUBJECT REQUIREMENTS/PREFERENCES

GCE A level: No specific A levels. **GCSE:** English usually required. Practical dance experience usually required.

SUBJECT INFORMATION

Every aspect of dance may be covered in Dance courses so be prepared for a study of the theory, educational, historical and social aspects of dance as well as practical studies.

Bedfordshire Studio-based and practice-led, the Dance and Professional Practice course focuses on the development of students as performers but also offers modules on marketing and entrepreneurship to develop transferable employment skills.

Bucks New Courses in Dance and Performance and Dance and Fitness offer a range of dance disciplines from performance on stage to the importance of dietetics and nutrition.

Canterbury Christ Church The Dance course offers development of dance skill, technique and choreography. Offered as a combined course with a choice of 10 related subjects or as a pathway in the Performing Arts programme.

Chichester The Dance course has a core of choreography and performance, with daily practical classes and involvement in ongoing rehearsal and choreography of peers.

Leeds Beckett A course in Creative Dance is offered for those aiming for a career in the profession.

Liverpool Hope In addition to degrees in Dance and Drama and Theatre Studies, the Creative and Performing Arts degree has options in dance, performance skills and technical theatre.

Surrey Dance and Culture is a three-year full-time or four-year sandwich course that encompasses both practical and theoretical studies of a wide variety of dance styles: African, Indian, Western classical ballet, and contemporary dance. In the third year, students gain practical professional training in one of the following career areas: dance administration/management, anthropology/community work, criticism/media education, notation and reconstruction, resources and archive work, work therapy. The degree in Theatre Studies covers performance and dance. A two-year foundation degree in Dance, Drama and Music is also available.

OTHER INSTITUTIONS OFFERING DANCE COURSES
Bath Spa, Cardiff Met (UWIC), Central Lancashire, Chester, Coventry, Cumbria, De Montfort, Derby, East London, Edge Hill, Falmouth, Gloucestershire, Greenwich, Hertfordshire, Kingston, Leeds Beckett, Lincoln, Liverpool (LIPA), London (RAc Dance), London Met, Middlesex, Northampton, Plymouth, RConsvS, Roehampton, Salford, South Wales, Staffordshire, Sunderland, Teesside, Trinity Laban Consv, Trinity Saint David, Ulster, Winchester, West London, Wolverhampton, Worcester.

ALTERNATIVE COURSES
Drama, Performing Arts.

DENTISTRY

(* indicates universities with entry requirements over 340 UCAS points)

SUBJECT REQUIREMENTS/PREFERENCES
GCE A level: Preference given to three subjects from science/Mathematics. Chemistry usually essential.

SUBJECT INFORMATION
Courses in Dentistry cover the basic medical science, human disease and clinical dentistry. The amount of patient contact varies between universities. All dental schools stress that work shadowing and experience beyond that of the ordinary patient are essential.

Aberdeen The new graduate entry course is based around a series of themes to meet the requirements of the General Dental Council. The school is in partnership with Dundee Dental School.

Birmingham* The Dentistry course lasts five years (with five terms of pre-clinical studies), biology forming an important part of the first year. A study of oral biology and human and oral diseases continues through the course. Clinical studies begin in the sixth term and specialist studies at the start of the third year. Part of this clinical studies course involves attachments in oral surgery at local hospitals. There is also a BSc in Dental Hygiene and Therapy and a BMedSc programme in Biomedical Materials.

See *Heap 2015: University Degree Course Offers* (Trotman Publishing) for details of offers

Bristol* A six-year pre-dental course is offered (previous knowledge of chemistry and physics strongly advised). Features of the course include early clinical experience, integrated teaching and self-directed learning. Academically able students are encouraged to intercalate two years of extra study to obtain a BSc honours degree. Regular clinical placements take place from Year 1.

Buckingham This is a five-year course which takes place in Leicester and is specially designed for the international student market. Applications through UCAS are normally submitted in June. Check with university.

Cardiff* The Dentistry pre-clinical year (or two years for students without the preferred A level combination) is undertaken at the Cardiff School of Biosciences. The course offers early contact with patients, teaching based on whole patient care, newly equipped areas for children and adult dentistry and an opportunity to pursue an intercalated BSc honours degree. In the final year there is an elective where students choose to work for at least six weeks in a medical centre, research unit or community practice anywhere in the UK or abroad. There is also a BDS foundation course, and a BSc in Dental Therapy and Dental Hygiene.

Cardiff Met (UWIC) Students taking the BSc course in Dental Technology work with trainee dentists and consultants in Years 2 and 3.

Dundee* A pre-dental year is offered for those without science subjects at Scottish Highers/Advanced Highers or A level, extending the length of the course to five and a half years. The first professional year of the four-and-a-half-year course covers anatomy, physiology and biochemistry, with practical experience in hospital in the third professional year and students becoming responsible for patients' dental health in the fourth and fifth professional years. Intercalated degrees are available in a range of subjects including Forensic Medicine and an Oral Health Sciences course unique to Scotland. Ten medically related subjects can be taken by selected students on a one-year course in Year 3.

Edinburgh The four-year Oral Health Science degree leads to a qualification in dental hygiene and dental therapy and provides a platform for those aiming for a graduate course in Dentistry. A professional placement is included.

Glasgow* The Dentistry course extends over five years. The first two years cover anatomy, physiology, pharmacology and also an environment, behaviour and health course. In April of the third year, students embark on the practical aspects of clinical dentistry with patients. Students who show a particular ability in basic science subjects may interrupt their dentistry course for a year and study for a BSc on a one-year or two-year course in one of 15 Life Science subjects. Study abroad options are offered.

Leeds* Clinical dentistry is introduced at the beginning of the course with the development of personal and professional skills. Community and practice-based education occur throughout the course. Child-centred and complex adult dentistry are introduced in Year 4 when optional courses are also offered. Courses are also available in Hygiene and Therapy, Dental Technology and Dental Nursing.

Liverpool* As elsewhere in the UK, Dental Surgery is a five-year course divided into three phases covering basic medical sciences, human disease and clinical studies. The opportunity to take a one-year BSc is open to most students. There is a strong emphasis on basic medical sciences, preventive dentistry and dental clinical practice. A course in Dental Hygiene and Dental Therapy is also available.

London (King's)* The first two years of the five-year BDS degree concentrate on the basic medical and dental sciences, with early patient contact. In the third and subsequent years more emphasis is placed on clinical dentistry, with supervised treatment of patients. Some students may opt to take the one-year BSc degree at the end of the second year. There is also a foundation course in Natural Sciences/Dentistry.

London (QM)* The BDS course lasts five years and the curriculum is organised in three phases: fundamentals of dentistry, clinical studies and vocational training. The opportunity to intercalate a one-year BSc degree is open to most students. A BEng in Dental Materials is also offered.

Manchester* Theory and practice are integrated in the dental course leading to enquiry-based learning with traditional lectures not forming a major part of the learning experience. There is also a pre-dental foundation course open to those with arts subjects and one science subject at A level. The Dental School is on the university campus. There is also a three-year course in Oral Health Sciences. Clinical work with children and adults commences in Year 2.

Manchester Met A three-year course is offered in Dental Technology, available with a sandwich placement year.

Newcastle* Dentistry has an introductory integrated five-term course in basic sciences and an opportunity for an intercalated Science degree course with options in Genetics, Microbiology and Pharmacology. The Dentistry course lasts five years. Contact with patients occupies half of every day in the final three years. Purpose-built premises adjoin the city's major teaching hospital.

Plymouth The Peninsula Schools of Medicine and Dentistry offer a four-year BDS course.

Portsmouth A three-year degree course is offered in Dental Hygiene and Dental Therapy. A Certificate of Higher Education in Dental Nursing is also offered. See also **Health Studies/Sciences**.

Queen's Belfast* This is a patient-focused, student-centred course. The majority of students are involved in Clinical Dentistry from the third year. There is an intercalated degree option in Year 3 leading to degrees in Anatomy, Biochemistry, Microbiology, Physiology and Pharmacology. Cadetships in the Dental Branch of the Armed Services can be obtained. A pre-dental course is also available for students not offering science subjects.

Sheffield The Dentistry course lasts five years. Students treat patients under supervision from the third year onwards. A special feature of the Sheffield course is the transitional training unit where final-year students work in an authentic working environment. A three-year course in Dental Hygiene and Dental Therapy is also offered.

ALTERNATIVE COURSES

Anatomy, Biochemistry, Biological Sciences, Medicine, Nursing, Pharmacy, Physiology, Speech Therapy.

DRAMA

(including Performance Arts/Studies)
(* indicates universities with entry requirements over 340 UCAS points)

SUBJECT REQUIREMENTS/PREFERENCES (DRAMA)

GCE A level: English, Theatre Studies, Drama, a foreign language and History are relevant for some Drama courses. **GCSE:** English usually essential; Mathematics may be required.

SUBJECT INFORMATION

Your choice of Drama course will vary depending on your preferences. For example, how much theory or practice do you want? It is worth remembering that by choosing a different subject degree course your interest in drama can be maintained by joining amateur drama groups. Performance Arts courses should also be considered, as well as courses offered by the stage schools.

QUESTIONS TO CONSIDER

  ✳ Am I interested in a purely performance-based course, or am I keen to learn about other practical stagecraft skills, such as technical set and lighting design, scriptwriting and costume?

See *Heap 2015: University Degree Course Offers* (Trotman Publishing) for details of offers

✳ Do I want to learn about the literary, theoretical and cultural context of drama through written work and seminars, as well as performance work?

✳ At the interview stage, will I need to prepare an audition piece or take part in a group performance workshop?

Aberystwyth The Drama Department (one of the largest in Britain) is characteristically a 'performing unit' but also offers an intellectually demanding course covering an historical perspective and a study of selected periods and playwrights. Film and TV studies (set, costume, lighting and sound, theatre administration and directing) are also covered in the course. In addition to Drama and Theatre Studies there are degrees in Performance or Scenographic Studies.

Anglia Ruskin A course in Drama is offered for students to study the subject from a practical or academic standpoint, or both. There are also joint courses with English and Film Studies. There is also a Performance Arts degree covering drama and music. The department regularly stages theatrical productions from leading playwrights, allowing students to gain performance and technical experience.

Bangor There are courses in English with Theatre Studies, incorporating performance workshops, and in Theatre and Media Studies. The Media Centre at Bangor houses TV and radio studios used by the BBC and the students' radio Storm FM. There is also a parallel course in the Welsh medium.

Bath Spa The non-vocational Drama Studies degree offers practical workshops in a range of performance styles, including stand-up comedy, physical theatre and children's theatre. Courses are offered in Dance (practical choreography), Drama (academic and practical), Performing Arts (production and performing). The Acting course is specifically a training course for actors and directors.

Bedfordshire A three-year degree is offered in Performing Arts covering studies-based, practice-led contemporary dance, theatre and performance. There are also courses in Theatre and Professional Practice and English and Theatre Studies.

Birmingham The programmes in Drama and Theatre Arts cover directing, playwriting, physical theatre, costume, stage management and lighting. The programme is also available as a joint honours course with a range of arts and humanities subjects including Music, French and Classical Literature.

Birmingham City Three courses are offered in Acting with an emphasis on Performance, Community and Applied Dance Theatre, and in Stage Management. English and Drama is also available.

Bishop Grosseteste A course is offered in Drama in the Community, a theoretical and practical studies programme. Applied Drama Studies can be combined with Music or as a major/minor degree.

Bournemouth Arts A highly practical Acting course is offered.

Bristol* The Theatre course covers the theory and history of dramatic literature and performance and has an introduction to practical aspects of dramatic art. The course includes radio, TV and film drama, playwriting and American theatre. Drama is also offered with English or one of six modern languages (all these are highly competitive courses).

Bristol UWE Drama is offered as a single honours or joint honours course or with English and Creative Writing. The Drama component is a balance between practical and theory. Trips to stage productions and film screenings form part of the study.

Brunel The course in Theatre involves production and practical studies. There are joint honours courses in Creative Writing, Film, TV and Games Design.

Bucks New The course in Performing Arts covers film, TV and stage work and dance.

Central Lancashire Courses in Acting and Theatre and Performance are highly practical. There is also a course in Musical Theatre.

Chester A combined honours course in Drama and Theatre Studies is offered emphasising practical work and featuring modules in digital performance. Some applicants may be required to audition.

City The university validates the Stage Management and Technical Theatre degree at the Guildhall School of Music and Drama. The Cultural and Creative Industries degree covers professional and managerial skills for careers in the arts sectors.

Colchester (Inst) There is an Acting course (Creative Performance) available and technical Theatre Studies course which covers backstage crafts.

Cumbria A range of programmes includes Drama, Performance and Production and Performing Arts (Acting; Singing; Dancing).

De Montfort Performing Arts applicants indicate a choice of options between arts management, dance or drama. In addition there are degrees in Performing Arts, Arts and Festival Management, Dance and Drama Studies, the latter combining practical performance work with study of theatrical traditions and scriptwriting.

Derby The Theatre Arts programme covers acting, directing, technical theatre, theatre in education, playwriting and production. Students participate in festivals and collaborative performances.

East Anglia* Drama is taught with a strong practical emphasis, supported by the theory and history of the subject. This is complemented by a close study of dramatic literature. Overall, the course has a distinctive vocational element. Courses are also offered in English Literature and Drama and in Scriptwriting and Performance, which covers theatre, cinema, television and radio. There is also a European exchange programme.

East London The Acting degree covers voice, movement and singing. Courses are offered in Dance and Theatre Studies, the latter involving both theoretical and practical studies. Applicants must participate in a performance workshop.

Edge Hill Courses are offered in Drama (which can be studied as a joint honours course with Creative Writing, English or Media), Dance, and Drama with Physical Theatre and Dance or with Music and Sound.

Edinburgh Queen Margaret The university offers a range of courses from the highly practical and vocational Acting for Stage and Screen, Drama and Performance, Theatre and Film Studies, to Costume Design and Construction degrees. Other opportunities exist in costume design, lighting, sound and set design, and there is a Performing Arts Management course.

Essex Courses are offered in Drama and in Drama and Literature. Both courses have practical strands and theoretical studies in theatre. The East 15 Acting School is also part of the university and offers professional training for those wishing to enter theatre, film, TV or radio. Practical performance courses in Acting are available, with specialisms in Community Theatre, Physical Theatre, Technical Theatre Studies and Stage Combat. The course is accredited by the National Council for Drama Training (NCDT).

Exeter The Drama course is based on a study of the medium of theatre from 'the inside' as a dramatic participant, rather than as a critic, and aims to explore and develop the physical and intellectual resources that are the basis of any serious creative acting and directing. The course also aims to develop drama-teaching skills through the Northcott Theatre and the local Theatre-in-Education.

Falmouth A wide range of courses is on offer including Screen and Media Performance, and Theatre Studies including Performance and Writing and Music Theatre.

Glasgow* Theatre Studies covers various aspects of the arts of the theatre including production, play construction and play spaces. It also deals with the place of the theatre in contemporary society and historical approaches to a play text. It is offered in combination with 30 subjects. Students are offered the opportunity to study in North America or Australia.

Gloucestershire A flexible course in Performing Arts has optional pathways in dance, drama and singing.

Glyndŵr The degree in Theatre, Television and Performance covers practical skills, stage management, and television and radio production work as well as a study of dramatic literature. Special topics include mime, puppetry, mask work and improvisation.

Greenwich Drama is offered as a major/minor or joint honours course with options in Education, English, History, Philosophy or Politics. The Modern American Drama course can be taken as part of a joint or combined honours degree.

Huddersfield Technical Drama and Music Theatre courses provide opportunities to work with professional practitioners and to undertake a third-year project in an area of vocational interest. Drama and English is also available.

Hull The Drama course offers a study of drama in all its aspects – literary, historical, aesthetic and presentational – with equal stress on formal teaching and practical work. Performance Studies is also offered with Drama, Music or Theatre. Drama can also be taken with Languages, English and Film Studies.

Kent The Drama and Theatre Studies course is available as a four-year MDrama (with a year of study in Europe or the US) or a three-year BA (Hons) and combines theoretical and practical studies involving acting, directing, community and educational theatre and management. Drama is also available as a joint subject with subjects such as Art, Film Studies and History. There is also a Visual and Performing Arts course (see under **Art and Design**) as well as a unique course in Creative Events devising live events and covering practical and managerial aspects.

Kingston Drama (practice, history and theory) includes a range of optional studies in areas including postmodernism, Gothic drama and song lyrics, and is available as a single honours degree or as a joint honours course with a range of subjects including Psychology, Film Studies and Applied English Language and Literature.

Lancaster The Theatre degree covers all aspects of theatre and offers courses within it in acting, directing, playwriting, lighting and sound, set and costume design, theatre administration and TV drama as well as historical studies. The course can also be combined with languages and English Literature.

Leeds Theatre and Performance provides opportunities for the study of Acting, Music Theatre, Performance Design and Arts Education. Options in Years 2 and 3 include modules from the English Literature programme.

Leeds Trinity An intensive programme of practical study is offered in the BA Acting degree, while the four-year Drama and Theatre Studies degree covers practical and theoretical disciplines. There is also a course in Theatre Design and Productions.

Lincoln The three-year single honours Drama course includes acting, directing, dramatic theory and literature and theatrical history. There are opportunities for short work placements. There are separate degrees in Dance, and Dance and Drama.

Liverpool John Moores The Drama course focuses on practical skills and theoretical studies. Courses are also available in Drama and Creative Writing, and Drama and English.

London (Goldsmiths) The Drama course provides a broad study of theatre, radio, film and TV as well as drama in the community. It has a good balance of practical experience and theatrical study. Drama is also offered with English.

London (QM)* Drama with English, Film Studies, Hispanic Studies or a range of modern languages are offered. The degree offers practical and theoretical studies.

See *Heap 2015: University Degree Course Offers* (Trotman Publishing) for details of offers

London (RH)* Drama and Theatre Studies balances the theory and practice of drama which is considered from different perspectives and includes a two-year course on film. In the second year several options are offered including direction, TV and radio drama, scene design, music and theatre and electronics and sound. Professional placements in the arts sector are encouraged. There are joint courses with Languages, Philosophy and Creative Writing.

London South Bank The Drama and Performance course covers theory, technique and creative theatre.

Loughborough The Drama course begins with practice in movement, speech and the art of acting and play construction plus seminars in drama and theatre. Television technique, lighting, sound, wardrobe studies, theatre practice and historical studies follow the project work in the third year. Throughout the course, theoretical studies support the practical aspects with historical and analytical elements of European and American theatre. A programme with a study of English or Business as a minor subject is also possible.

Manchester* Drama can be taken as a single subject or with Screen Studies or English Literature. It is primarily for the academic study of drama and is not an acting course.

Middlesex The Theatre Arts programme is available with specialisms in Performance, Solo Performance, Directing and Design.

Newman Drama is available as a single, joint or minor course with another subject. The Creative Arts degree also includes drama modules.

Northampton Single and joint honours degrees are offered in Drama. There is also a separate Acting course which is highly practical.

Northumbria The Performance course involves a study of styles and approaches in drama, integrating theory and practice. Performance-based modules involve sound, movement, music, song and visual imagery.

Oxford Brookes Drama, focusing on performance and history, is offered with a wide range of subjects in the modular degree scheme, including Fine Art, Theology, Sports and Coaching Studies, and Music.

Plymouth Theatre and Performance is offered as a three-year course that focuses on theatre, dance, ritual, performance arts and community arts. There are also several foundation degrees in theatre and performance.

Portsmouth The Drama course includes strands in musical theatre, theatre in the community, and theatre criticism and philosophy. The English and Drama combined honours course concentrates on the study of literary texts and their interpretation, and on practical and academic approaches to the study of various aspects of drama. Students are strongly encouraged to develop their skills in dramatic performance. Other courses include Drama with Creative Writing, or Performing Arts, Film Studies and Media Studies.

Queen's Belfast Drama is offered as a single, major/minor or joint honours course. Students in Stages 2 and 3 may focus their studies on the practical or academic aspects of drama.

Reading The Film and Theatre course covers the history of the cinema and drama with practical working in drama, film and video. A courses in Theatre Arts Education and Deaf Studies is also offered.

Roehampton Courses are offered in Drama, Theatre and Performance Studies. The Drama course covers performance studies, as well as modules including writing and approaches to directing in Years 2 and 3.

St Mark and St John The Acting course combines theory and practical studies with repertory vocational training. There is also a Theatre course with a study abroad option.

St Mary's Practical and theoretical studies are followed in the Drama course. There are special studies in applied theatre, physical theatre or theatre arts. Applicants must take part in a short practical workshop or perform an audition piece.

See *Heap 2015: University Degree Course Offers* (Trotman Publishing) for details of offers

Salford Performance features pathways in Drama and Theatre, Media Practice, Dance Theatre, Contemporary Theatre Practice, and Comedy. The Media Performance course integrates elements of media production and performance and includes dance, singing, scriptwriting, directing and producing. There is also a new course in Contemporary Theatre Practice, focusing on 20th- and 21st-century theatre and performance studies.

South Wales The Performing Arts course focuses on acting for theatre, screen and radio while the Theatre and Drama course offers a good balance between practical creative work and theory across a range of platforms. There are courses in Lighting Design and Technology, and Performance and Media, which focuses on creating performances for the screen and electronic media.

Southampton Solent A course is offered in Performance, combining theory and practice in physical theatre. There is also a degree in Dance, while the Screenwriting degree covers feature film, drama documentary, sitcom and television writing.

Staffordshire The degree in Drama Performance and Theatre Arts combines both theory and practice. A course in Theatre Studies and Technical Stage Production is also offered.

Sunderland A Performance Arts Studies degree offers study of more than one art form from dance, drama, music, performance or visual arts. Dance and Drama are also offered as part of the combined honours scheme.

Sussex Drama Studies can now be taken with languages, English and Film Studies. The course equips students with both theoretical and practical skills.

Swansea Metropolitan The Performing Arts course offers special studies in arts management, directing, acting and technical aspects of theatre production. Vocational Drama courses are also offered with Counselling, Educational Studies and Psychology.

Ulster Drama is a broad course that offers specialist options in stage management, theatre technologies and administration, press and publicity. Applicants must undertake a workshop audition at interview.

Warwick* The main emphasis of the Theatre and Performance Studies course lies in a study of the modern theatre (the last 100 years). It also introduces dramatic skills in the first year, leading on to the second and third years that allow students to specialise in either practical work or historical and analytical studies. Options include the moving image, marketing theatre and courses offered in the Faculties of Arts and Social Sciences. Other subjects including English, Advertising, International Politics and Languages are also offered with Theatre Studies as a major/minor scheme.

West London Courses are offered in Acting, Acting for Stage and Media, Musical Theatre, and Dance.

Winchester In addition to the Drama Studies degree, a course is offered in Applied Theatre involving theoretical studies and practical skills in theatre and video production. There are also degrees in Performance Management and Performing Arts, Stage and Arts Management, combining music, dance, theatre and management. Drama can be studied with a wide range of other subjects including Business Management, Education Studies, History and Law.

Wolverhampton Drama is offered as a single honours course. Several joint courses are offered, including Film Studies, English and Creative Professional Writing.

Worcester A wide-ranging practical course in Drama and Performance can be taken as a single or joint honours course. A Screenwriting course is also available.

York* There is a degree in Writing, Directing and Performance.

See *Heap 2015: University Degree Course Offers* (Trotman Publishing) for details of offers

OTHER INSTITUTIONS OFFERING DRAMA COURSES
Birmingham Met (Coll), Doncaster (Coll Univ Centre), East Surrey (Coll), Farnborough (CT), Gloucestershire (Coll), Hereford (CA), Liverpool (LIPA), Liverpool City (Coll), London (Royal Central Sch SpDr), Manchester (Coll), Newcastle (Coll), Northbrook (Coll), Nottingham New (Coll), Rose Bruford (Coll), Rotherham (CAT), Royal Welsh (CMusDr), St Helens (Coll), Shrewsbury (CAT), South Devon (Coll), Truro (Coll), UHI, Wakefield (Coll), West Thames (Coll).

ECONOMICS

(* indicates universities with entry requirements over 340 UCAS points)

SUBJECT REQUIREMENTS/PREFERENCES
GCSE: Mathematics, English and a foreign language may be required.

SUBJECT INFORMATION
If you haven't taken economics at A level, be prepared for study involving some mathematics, statistics and, depending on which course you choose, economic and social history, industrial policies, the British economy and labour history, money, banking and regional economics.

QUESTIONS TO CONSIDER
* Does the course carry industry accreditation which will help me progress towards a professional status, for example in accounting or insurance?
* Can I combine the course with another subject relevant to my career aspirations, such as Politics, International Relations or Surveying?

Aberdeen The honours degree in Economics offers a wide choice of topics including financial management, regional labour economics, public policy and natural resources. There are 26 joint honours courses including Languages, Management Studies, Politics and Real Estate.

Abertay The subject is offered as part of the Social Science degree.

Aberystwyth A modular Economics course is offered consisting of core subjects and electives in complementary subjects, for example computing, accountancy, marketing, human resource management or small business management. Economics is offered as a joint honours or major/minor scheme with a range of other subjects including Languages, Management, Politics and Law. A course in Business Economics is also offered.

Anglia Ruskin The Business Economics course includes modules in environmental and international economics. Option modules include environmental and international economics, business English and Japanese economics. Economics can also be studied as part of the combined honours course.

Aston* The course in Economics and Management is offered as a four-year sandwich course with one year set aside for either international study or industrial placement. Economics is also offered with a choice of 14 other subjects in the joint honours programme.

Bangor Business Economics is available as a single honours course or a joint honours degree with subjects such as Accounting, Social Policy and languages.

Bath* Economics is offered as a three-year or a four-year sandwich course with a one-year placement in industry or commerce worldwide. There is a choice of optional units each year. Joint courses with Economics are offered with Politics or International Development, including optional placements in Year 3.

Birmingham* The Economics degree is ranked first out of the Russell Group Universities and may be followed as a single or joint honours course. Joint honours courses are offered with Political Science, International Relations, German, Italian, Japanese, Portuguese, Spanish or Geography. There is also a new single honours course in Policy, Politics and Economics covering real-world issues as well as a course in Mathematical Economics and Statistics.

Birmingham City Economics and Finance can be studied as a three-year joint degree or as a four-year sandwich course. Joint courses include Accountancy, Advertising, Business, Finance or Marketing. A course in International Management and Economics is also offered. The Business School is a Platinum Approved learning partner of the ACCA.

Bradford The Economics course places less emphasis than most on mathematics and has major electives in management, politics, history and development studies. Economics is also offered with International Relations, Marketing, Sociology and Psychology or with an emphasis on business or finance. The course carries accreditation from ACCA and the CII.

Brighton See under **Finance**.

Bristol* Tuition is given in economics and econometrics (the use of statistical methods in economics), accounting, finance and management. There are several joint courses including Economics and Mathematics, Politics and Philosophy. There are also language options to support the course, which includes study in continental Europe (language qualification required).

Bristol UWE A course in Economics is offered with placements or study abroad in Europe or the US. Students choose a specialist option in Year 2 and two further options in Year 3. There are optional modules in money, banking and finance, labour economics and international trade.

Brunel The Economics course focuses on the applications of economics to business, finance, industry and government. Joint courses are offered with Accountancy, Business Finance and Management, each with placements available.

Buckingham Economics and Business Economics (start dates in January, July or September) have modules in labour economics, international economics, business psychology and financial management. There are joint honours courses with Politics, Spanish or Business Law.

Cambridge* Economics Part I (Year 1) covers economics, economic history, politics and statistics. In Years 2 and 3, Parts IIa and IIb of the Tripos provide a sound understanding of the core of pure and applied economics, and the workings of economic systems and links with social and political issues. There is also a degree in Land Economy covering law, the environment and economics. It is also possible to combine Economics with another subject, transferring at the end of Years 1 or 2. Not available at Corpus Christi College. See also **Property Management and Surveying**.

Cardiff* The Business School offers courses in Economics and in Business Economics. Modules can be chosen from a wide range of subjects including accounting, management and a modern language (French or Spanish with Year 3 spent abroad). Economics can also be taken with Management.

Cardiff Met (UWIC) Economics is offered as part of the Business programme. Accountancy courses carrying industry accreditation are also offered.

Central Lancashire Economics and Business Economics are offered as single honours courses. An optional industry placement in Year 3 is offered. There are also joint courses with Accounting and International Business.

Chester Economics can be taken as a single honours course or combined with appropriate subjects such as Accounting, International Development Studies, Politics, History, Sociology or Law. Accounting and Finance is also available.

City* The Economics degree combines theory and real-world applications. There is also a course in Financial Economics. Optional placement years are available on both courses. Year-long and summer placements are available. Economics can be combined with Accountancy.

Coventry Four Economics pathways are offered. A common first year leads on to a specialised study in Part II in Economics, Business or Financial Economics or International Economics and Trade.

De Montfort Courses are offered in Economics with Finance or Politics, each with a one-year placement in industry or commerce. There are also courses in Business Economics or with History or Finance. Courses are accredited by ACCA and the CIMA.

Dundee In the Economic Studies courses the principles of economics are covered and their applications to current problems. It also emphasises the broad outlines of national and international economic issues. Over 20 MA and BSc degree courses are offered covering Economics, Financial Economics and Business Economics.

Durham* Single and joint honours Economics students follow the same first-year course in economics. This allows flexibility in the choice of combined degree at the end of the first year, leading on to courses in Economics, Business Economics or Economics with French or Politics. Overseas study through an exchange programme is offered. There is also a course in Philosophy, Politics and Economics (PPE), a combined honours programme in Social Sciences and joint honours courses with Mathematics, Politics and Psychology.

East Anglia Economics students take a common programme of courses in the first two terms, Introducing economics, economic and social history, sociology, philosophy and politics. They then proceed to the honours programme. Economics can be taken with Accountancy, Business Economics or PPE.

East London Part I (first year) Economics offers a broad introduction, followed by Part II specialisms (second and third years). Continuous assessment accounts for up to 50% of the marks. Placements and overseas study are offered. There is also a course in Business Economics.

Edinburgh In the first two years of the four-year single honours course a third of the work is economics, plus two other subjects. Courses in Economics include the study of economic theory and institutions, the organisation of firms and the banking world, and economic policy-making. Eleven joint courses are offered with Economics, including Business Studies and Philosophy.

Edinburgh Napier Two-year full-time courses are offered in Accounting and Economics – accredited by the Institute of Chartered Accountants of Scotland (ICAS) – and Business Economics.

Essex A range of single honours Economics degrees is offered, including Management Economics, Financial and International Economics, and nine joint courses. A course in Philosophy, Politics and Economics and a four-year European exchange Economics course with French, German, Portuguese, Italian or Spanish are also available.

Exeter* The first year of the Economics course covers a study of economics and statistics and two other social science subjects chosen from a list of options, with more advanced studies in the second and third years. Economics is also offered with Econometrics, Finance and Politics. Several courses can also be taken with European Studies in which students spend Year 3 abroad. See also **Business**.

Glasgow* Economics can be taken to general and honours levels as a single subject and also by way of a wide range of joint courses. Overseas exchanges and placements are available. Courses in Business Economics are also offered.

Glasgow Caledonian Major and joint honours courses in Economics are offered as part of the BA Social Sciences programme. Other available modules include media and languages.

Greenwich Students taking the Economics degree may choose options in international trade and financial markets, business economics and finance. Economics is available as a major/minor programme with options including Law and Mathematics. Courses are also offered in Business Economics and Economics and Banking.

Heriot-Watt Six Economics courses are offered, including options in Business Law, Marketing, Business Management, Finance and Accountancy. There are opportunities to study abroad.

Hertfordshire The Economics sandwich course provides a firm background in computing, quantitative methods and modelling. There is also a Business Economics degree with an optional year in industry. Economics is also offered as a joint subject with one other subject, including Geography, Law, Mathematics and a range of languages.

Hull All students taking the BSc Economics degree follow a largely common course and a definitive choice of specialism need not be made until the beginning of the second year. Various streams are offered including mainstream economics, business economics, finance and development, accountancy and economic history. Joint, combined and major/minor options are offered, as well as a foundation year with Politics and Philosophy. BA students choose their specialism in Year 3.

Keele The Economics dual honours programme is taken with a second subject from 30 options. Final-year specialisms include finance, ecological economics, labour and public economics. A Business Economics course is also offered as a single honours degree.

Kent The Economics course has a strong European flavour and a European course enables students to spend a year in France, Germany or Spain. Economics is also available with Econometrics, Computing, Financial Economics, or a year in industry.

Kingston The Economics degree is constructed around a set of core courses in each year, covering micro- and macroeconomics, government and politics, and mathematics. This enables students to select from a number of routes throughout the course. There are also courses in Applied, Global, Financial and Business Economics.

Lancaster The first year of the Economics course comprises an introduction to economics and economic history plus two other subjects. The third year offers students a choice from a number of specialised options including international trade and business enterprise. The International Business course also has an economics focus. Economics can also be taken with Geography, International Relations, Mathematics, Politics or with study abroad.

Leeds* The BA Economics programme is a generalist course focusing on the application of economics to a broad range of topics. Courses are also offered emphasising business and financial economics. Specialist modules can be taken in other business subjects, such as Management, Finance and Transport Studies, and from other university departments including foreign languages.

Leicester Four degrees are available as BA and BSc programmes, in Economics, Business Economics, Financial Economics and Banking and Finance. All students share a common core of economic subjects that cover economic theory and its applications.

Liverpool* The Economics course focuses on theoretical and applied economics backed up by mathematics and statistics and a wide range of options. Students on the BSc course can follow either a general pathway or a financial route. Opportunities to study abroad are offered in Europe, Hong Kong, the US and Australia. There is also a degree in Business Economics. Economics is also one of 16 subjects offered in the combined honours programme.

London (Goldsmiths)* Economics is offered with Politics in a three-year full-time degree which examines international modern economic history, and there is also a degree in Economics, Politics and Public Policy.

London (King's)* A course is offered in Political and International Economy.

See *Heap 2015: University Degree Course Offers* (Trotman Publishing) for details of offers

London (QM)* Single honours degrees are offered in Economics, Economics and Finance, and Economics, Finance and Management. A wide range of joint study options are offered, and there are also exchange programmes with Latvia, Italy, Spain and the US.

London (RH)* The Economics course deals with all aspects of the subject including financial and industrial economics, economic and econometric and game theory, and analytical political economy. Ten courses are also offered with Economics as a major subject, including Politics, Mathematics and Languages, and there is a separate degree in Financial and Business Economics.

London (UCL)* Degree courses with Economics are based on the course unit system and some courses can be chosen from other departments. A certain amount of maths is compulsory and an A* at A level is required. The single honours course provides specialisation in economics with an emphasis on economic policy. There are courses in Economics and Statistics, Philosophy and Economics, Economics and Business, with East European Studies including a year abroad option. The BSc (Econ) international programme includes a year of study in North America.

London LSE* Two single honours three-year BSc degrees are offered in Economics and Econometrics and Mathematical Economics. Economics can also be taken with Environmental Policy, Geography, Government, Mathematics, Philosophy or Social Policy.

London Met The CIMA-accredited single honours Economics course gives an in-depth knowledge of methods, theory and application in Economics. Other courses include Economic Studies, Financial and International Economics and Politics, Philosophy and Economy. A large number of joint courses are offered with Economics and Business Economics.

London NCH This is a wide-ranging course. The introductory modules include statistics and mathematics, and proceed through econometrics and studies of both micro- and macroeconomics. Further modules cover topics such as corporate finance, economics of labour and international political economy.

Loughborough* Economics may be offered as a single honours degree, or it may be taken with a minor subject (e.g. Accounting, Geography, Politics, Sociology or Social Policy) or in combination with Accounting, which is designed as a more vocational degree. The course aims to provide a balanced package of theoretical and applied studies with an exceptional range of options in the final year. A year abroad is offered. There are also courses in Business Economics and Finance and International Economics.

Manchester* The Economic and Social Studies course is designed to give maximum flexibility and choice, with specialisation in Accounting, Business Studies, Criminology, Finance, Economic and Social History, Economic Studies, Politics, Social Anthropology, Sociology or Development Studies. There is also a BEconSc (Hons) degree in which half of the course units are compulsory and the remaining units are chosen from a range of options.

Manchester Met Over 50 joint courses are offered with either Economics or Business Economics. A course in Financial Services, Planning and Management is also offered.

Middlesex There are degrees in Business Economics, Business Economics, Banking and Finance, each with optional work placements. Special options can be chosen in the third year of each course. An industrial placement year is optional.

Newcastle* A range of courses is offered by the Faculty of Social Sciences. In the first and second year of the Economics course students also choose one other subject from a list of options including Accounting, Marketing and History. Other courses offered include Economics and Business Management or Mathematics, and Politics and Economics.

Northampton Thirty joint honours courses are offered with Economics, covering micro- and macroeconomic theory, historical and current events, and international issues.

See *Heap 2015: University Degree Course Offers* (Trotman Publishing) for details of offers

Northumbria Economics is offered as a specialism within the Business degree. There is also a degree in Business with International Trade. A four-year sandwich course is offered.

Nottingham* The first two years of all School of Economics degrees provide a basic foundation of theoretical and applied knowledge. Specialist options are chosen in Year 3. Economics is also offered with Philosophy, Modern Languages, and Chinese Studies. There are also courses in Industrial and International Economics.

Nottingham Trent A broad course in Economics, Finance and Banking is provided with an introduction to politics in the first year; options in politics, accounting and computing are available in the third year. There is also a Business Economics degree.

Oxford* In the first year of the Philosophy, Politics and Economics course, the three subjects are studied equally; in the second and third years, two or three subjects may be studied and also Sociology. There is also a course in Economics and Management that allows a choice from six subjects in Economics and two in Management or vice versa. Economics is also offered with History and with Engineering and Management.

Oxford Brookes Economics is offered as a four-year (optional) sandwich course jointly with over 40 other subjects including languages and science subjects. A course in Economics, Politics and International Relations is also available. Business Economics can also be taken as a single honours subject.

Plymouth Joint courses are offered with Economics and in addition there are degrees in Financial Economics and International Business Economics. Courses share common core modules in micro- and macroeconomic theory, business and growth cycles, and government policy.

Portsmouth The Economics degree is an extremely flexible course that allows students to move between various Economics schemes in the Business School. These include Business Economics (which can also be studied with Law), Applied Economics and Economics, Banking and Finance. Each course offers an optional work placement.

Queen's Belfast A BSc (Econ) course occupies one-third of the first year and two-thirds of the course in subsequent years, with modules in the economics of the workplace, the environment or the public sector and political studies. Opportunities exist for summer and year-long placements. The faculty offers a very wide range of courses including Business Economics, Economics and Accounting and Economics with International Studies, Accounting, Finance, Modern Languages or Management.

Reading For the first university examination, the Economics course has two parts. All students take units in mathematical economics and in economic theory. Optional subjects in the third year include money and banking, business economics, and European urban and regional economics. Economics can also be studied with History, International Relations, Politics, Econometrics, Business Economics and European Languages.

St Andrews* Degrees are offered in Applied Economics, Financial Economics, and Economics, which can be studied singly or in combination with another subject including Arabic, International Relations, Middle East Studies and Russian. Optional papers at honours level include financial markets, labour economics and industrial relations.

Salford This Economics degree has an applied focus. It offers the student a wide choice of optional areas including the pursuit of specialist streams in business economics, world economy and quantitative techniques. A sandwich course with an industrial placement in Canada is available. Courses are also offered in Business Economics, Business Economics with Gambling Studies, and Economics and Sports Economics.

Sheffield* For the foundation year, BA and BSc Economics students take microeconomics and macroeconomics and additional modules in other subjects. Single and dual honours degrees offer considerable flexibility and several subjects can be combined with Economics, including Accounting and Financial Management, Econometrics, Mathematics, Social Policy and Russian. An industrial sandwich placement is optional.

See *Heap 2015: University Degree Course Offers* (Trotman Publishing) for details of offers

South Wales The BA in Business and Economics focuses on the practical aspects of business and economic principles and offers flexibility in allowing students to change their pathway after the first year.

Southampton* Economics, mathematics and statistics are compulsory units in Year 1 with options in managerial systems, political systems and modern languages. Microeconomics and macroeconomics follow in Years 2 and 3 with a wide range of options in each year. Economics is also offered with Actuarial Studies, Financial Accounting, Philosophy, Politics and Management Sciences.

Staffordshire Economics, maths, statistics, politics and economic history are taken in the first year of the Economics course, plus sociology, international relations, accounting, geography or a language. These studies lead to a range of options in the second and third years that include managerial economics, poverty, income and wealth and the economics of sport and recreation. Economics courses are also offered with Actuarial Science, Management and Finance. Several Business Studies courses are also available.

Stirling Economics can be taken as general, single or joint honours. Students follow a sequence of core courses covering all aspects of economics, with a choice of a number of options towards the end of the course. Stirling also offers a course in Politics, Philosophy and Economics, and combined degrees can be taken with a range of subjects such as Accountancy, Environmental Science, Marketing and Mathematics.

Strathclyde The four-year Economics course assumes no previous study of the subject and is presented in two major parts: consumers, enterprises and industries; and markets and governments. Business Economics degrees are also available.

Surrey* Business Economics courses focus on real world issues and are highly applied and vocational. In the first and second years a study is made of economics and related subjects including computing, maths, statistics, sociology, politics and history. The third year is spent on an industrial or commercial placement and the final year devoted to specialist topics chosen by the student. Opportunities exist for an exchange scheme in the US for the students following the four-year course. There are also programmes in Business Economics and Economics and Finance with good employer contacts.

Sussex The focus is on the practical application of economics and an analysis of contemporary issues and problems. Other courses include Management Economics with Development Studies and Economics and International Relations. A Finance and Business course is also available.

Swansea Courses are offered in Business Economics (and with Accounting), Financial Economics and Economics. Joint honours courses are also available with Geography, History and Languages, and a year abroad is optional. (High research rating.) See also **Philosophy**.

Ulster Economics is a three- or four-year course with commercial placement in Year 3. The course offers modules from a wide range of options including international trade, small business and the economics of poverty. Economics can also be taken with Accountancy, Marketing or Politics.

Warwick* Economics degree courses are based on a core of courses in economic analysis, quantitative techniques and economic and social history. Optional subjects taught within the department include business studies, politics and international studies, law, accounting, industrial relations and marketing. There is the possibility to transfer to another Economics degree course at the end of Year 1. Other courses cover Industrial Economics, Economics and Economic History, Languages including Arabic, Japanese and Russian, Economics, Politics and International Studies and MORSE (Mathematics, Operational Research, Statistics and Economics – grade A in Mathematics required).

West Scotland The Economics course offers modules covering industrial, international, labour, public and social economics and economic techniques. Eight months of overseas study are offered.

Westminster Economics can be studied as a specialism in the Business Management degrees. Professional placements and overseas study are offered.

See Heap 2015: *University Degree Course Offers* (Trotman Publishing) for details of offers

York* Courses are offered in Economics, Economics and Finance, Econometrics and Economic History, as well as a range of joint courses with subjects from other departments. In the first year all Economics students are required to take four modules in Part I (economics, economic and social history, statistics and one other social science subject), with flexible options in Years 2 and 3. Students decide on a course pathway at the end of the first year.

OTHER INSTITUTIONS OFFERING ECONOMICS COURSES
Bradford (Coll Univ Centre), Euro Bus Sch London, Richmond (Am Int Univ), Ruskin Oxford (Coll), South Devon (Coll).

ALTERNATIVE COURSES
Accountancy, Banking, Business Studies, E-Commerce, Estate Management, Financial Studies, Marketing, Quantity Surveying, Valuation Surveying.

EDUCATION

(teaching and non-teaching courses)
(* indicates universities with entry requirements over 340 UCAS points)

SUBJECT REQUIREMENTS/PREFERENCES
GCE A level: In chosen major subjects. **GCSE:** English and Mathematics and Science.

SUBJECT INFORMATION
There are two types of courses under the title Education, those which cover the history, philosophy and theory of education and educational administration, which are not necessarily teacher-training courses, and those which are specifically designed for people wishing to enter the teaching profession.

It should be noted that students taking first degrees in National Curriculum subjects can, on graduation, take a one-year course leading to the Postgraduate Certificate in Education (PGCE) that will provide a teaching qualification. Grants are awarded for students taking these courses.

Aberdeen A BA course is offered in Primary Education (3–12 years). Core courses cover the practice of education, expressive arts, language studies, mathematics, environmental studies and religious and moral education. Courses in Childhood Practice and Music Education are also offered.

Aberystwyth The degree in Education explores the development of children and adolescents through learning and teaching. The course involves the psychology of learning and thinking, language and literacy, health and education and multicultural education. Education can also be studied as a joint honours or major/minor programme with a choice of up to 22 other subjects. A degree in Early Childhood Studies offers training in early years education.

Anglia Ruskin Courses focus on the Early Years and Early Childhood Studies with professional practice.

Bangor BEd Primary courses are offered in Art, Design and Technology, English Literature, Geography, History, Mathematics, Music, Physical Education, Religious Studies, Science and Welsh (first and second language). There is also a Secondary Teaching course in Design and Technology and a second course focusing on Product Design, and a degree in Childhood Studies. Courses are also offered in the Welsh medium. A secondary education course in Design and Technology is also available.

See *Heap 2015: University Degree Course Offers* (Trotman Publishing) for details of offers

Bath The degree in Childhood, Youth and Education Studies is taught by staff from the Department of Education and Psychology. There is an optional placement year in a professional setting. See also **Combined Courses**.

Bath Spa The degrees in Education Studies focus on Early Years and Primary teaching.

Bedfordshire Physical Education (Secondary) and Primary Education Teaching courses are offered along with foundation degrees in 14–19 Education and several Education specialities including child and youth and disability studies.

Birmingham Psychology, sociology, philosophy and social policy are disciplines studied in the Education degree.

Birmingham (UC) Early Childhood Studies involves the development, welfare and education of very young children.

Birmingham City A BA course is offered in Primary Education. Students choose one subject from art, design and technology, drama with English, English, geography, history, mathematics, music, science or religious studies with compulsory core subjects in mathematics, science and English. Education is also offered as part of the combined honours programme or with English Literature, History or Sociology. Degrees are also offered in Early Years, Children and Integrated Professional Care and Early Childhood Studies.

Bishop Grosseteste Courses are offered in Applied Studies in Early Childhood, covering education and youth work with options in Maths, Music or Primary Teaching. There are also joint honours and major/minor courses with Special Educational Needs.

Brighton Courses are offered in Primary Education (Early or Later Years), Upper Primary and Lower Secondary (Mathematics; Science; Design and Technology; Religious Studies; Geography; Physical Education; Information Technology; Science; English BA/QTS). Placements are offered through the department's partnership office. There is also a degree course in Education.

Bristol There is a degree in Childhood Studies studying child development from birth to teenage years.

Bristol UWE Initial Teacher Education BA courses are offered in Primary Education and in Early Childhood Studies, which includes child development, communication, behaviour, hearing and psychology. The Education Studies course focuses on systems, approaches and political aspects.

Bucks New Foundation degree courses are in Primary Education, Early Years and Working with Children.

Cambridge* The education degree focuses on the academic study of education through philosophy, psychology, sociology and history.

Canterbury Christ Church Single, joint and combined courses are offered in Early Childhood Studies. Primary Teaching courses leading to QTS, a degree in Education Studies and courses in Physical Education and Maths Education at Secondary Level are offered. A course in Education Studies (not a teaching course) is also available.

Cardiff The Education degree places an emphasis on the social and psychological development of children from birth to adolescence and on national and international policies in education. Practical issues in teaching, learning and school management are also covered.

Cardiff Met (UWIC) Courses offered include Primary and Secondary Teaching (Music and Welsh), Education Studies with pathways in Early Childhood Studies, English, Psychology, Sport and Exercise Science, Welsh and Youth and Community Work.

Central Lancashire Education can be taken as a major, joint or minor degree programme or combined with Sociology or History, and offers overseas study options in Europe and the US. Courses are also offered in British Sign Language and Deaf Studies.

Chester Courses are offered in Education Studies and Teacher Education covering Early Years (3–7 years) or Primary Education with QTS (5–11 years). There is also a course in Early Childhood Studies focusing on child development and working with children and families.

Chichester Courses in Education include Adventure Education and Childhood Studies, including health, child development and special needs. A BA in Mathematics and Teaching for Key Stages 2 and 3 is also available. Teacher-training courses are offered in Primary Education, Secondary and Physical Education and Sport Coaching.

Colchester (Inst) A BA Early Years course is offered covering child development, learning, playwork and safeguard and health issues.

Cumbria In addition to Primary and Secondary Education courses with specialist options (ICT; English; Maths; RE), there are also several options covering outdoor education and leadership.

De Montfort The Education Studies degree is a child-centred course. The joint degree can be taken with a National Curriculum subject that allows students to go on to take a PGCE. Overseas study opportunities are offered. Education Studies can also be taken with Languages or Psychology.

Derby A BEd Primary course is available in which all students study core subjects (mathematics, English and science). Degrees are also offered in Early Childhood Studies and Education Studies (also joint courses).

Dundee A BEd course is offered in the Primary range (3–12 years). Elective subjects cover information technology, modern languages, science and Scottish studies. Professional placements are offered. There is also a four-year degree in Community Education with a professional qualification.

Durham* Primary and Secondary PGCE courses are offered and Education Studies can be taken with English, Geography, History, Music, Philosophy, Sociology, Theology and Psychology (BPS accredited). Students cover core modules in English, maths, science and education studies, as well as an option from humanities, the arts, modern foreign languages or information and communication technology. An additional year leading to a PGCE provides entry to the teaching profession.

Durham (Stockton) A BA (Ed) Primary Teaching (General) course is offered leading to QTS. It includes 32 weeks of school experience.

East Anglia The Educational Studies degree offers a flexible pathway enabling students to tailor their degree to their own interests. It involves a balance between theory and practical experience and a study of the whole field of education in the UK and abroad, including modules in teaching, learning and assessment. Physical Education and Sport is also available as a BA or BSc.

East London A degree in Education and Community Development Theory is offered with pathways in health, early childhood studies, special needs and playwork with youth studies. Other degrees include Community Studies, Early Childhood Studies (with practitioner options) and Education Studies.

Edge Hill Primary Education with specialisms in language, communication and literacy, humanities, creative and expressive arts, foreign languages, or personal, social and health education, mathematics, PE and science are offered. There are also courses in Early Years Education, English Key Stage 2 and 3 with QTS, and courses in Secondary Design and Technology, ICT, Mathematics, and Childhood and Youth Studies.

Edinburgh The education degrees focus on three pathways. Four-year MA (Hons) teacher education (primary and secondary) courses offer specialism in Earth Sciences, History, German, Mathematics, Physical Education, Religious Studies or Scottish Studies. The community education courses focus on adult education, community work and youth work, while the BA in Childhood Practice prepares you for childcare management work.

Exeter The degree in Education Studies enables students to choose a first degree in a relevant subject before proceeding to a qualification (PGCE) for both primary and secondary teaching. There is also a course in Child and Youth Studies, covering gender, creativity, citizenship, health and relationships. Sports Science and English are also offered with Education.

Glasgow The Faculty of Education comprises departments of Curriculum Studies, Educational Studies, Religious Education and Adult and Continuing Education. There are teaching courses covering Primary, Religious, Technological, Music and Community Education. Courses in Childhood Practice and Community Development are also offered.

Gloucestershire Courses are offered in Early Childhood Studies, Education and Learning (with a QTS top-up available at Level 3) and Nursery (Key Stage and Primary Education (Early Years 3–7 and Later Years 5–11)).

Glyndŵr Courses focus on childhood care and education by way of degrees in Early Childhood Studies, Education Studies, Post-Compulsory Education and Training, and Play and Playwork.

Greenwich Primary Teaching courses leading to the BEd and BA Honours course leading to QTS are offered in English, French, Design Technology, Art and Early Years. Education is available as a major/minor or joint option with Psychology or Child Development. Secondary education courses are available in Design and Technology. There is also a course in Childhood Studies.

Hertfordshire In addition to Primary and Secondary Education courses a degree in Education Studies presents a broad picture of educational issues. Education Studies can also be taken with a modern foreign language or with Mathematics.

Huddersfield For those wishing to work with children there is a Childhood Studies degree. For pro-spective teachers there are Primary and Secondary Education courses with QTS.

Hull BA/BSc Primary courses are offered in Biology, English, Information and Communications Technology and Mathematics. There are also courses in Children's Inter-Professional Studies, Education (with Early Years, Society or Social Inclusion and Special Needs), Psychology and Urban Learning.

Keele Educational Studies is offered as a dual honours or major subject with a choice of 28 other subjects.

Kent The course in Intellectual and Developmental Disabilities covers behaviour problems, learning disabilities, work-based learning and person-centred support. There is also a unique degree in Autism Studies covering studies in behaviour, ethics and professional practice and periods of work-based learning with children and adults in Years 2 and 3.

Kingston BA courses are offered leading to primary school teaching, with the core subjects Art, English, Mathematics Science, ICT and Humanities, followed in Years 2 and 3 with specialisation. A one-year top-up BA in Early Years: Education and Childcare is also offered, and courses are available in Children's Special Educational Needs and Early Years: Management and Leadership.

Leeds There is a course in Childhood Studies covering education, sociology and psychology. A BA (Hons) in English, Language and Education is also offered, which allows the study of a foreign language.

Leeds Beckett Courses are offered leading to degrees in Education Studies, Childhood Studies, Primary Education (Design Technology; French; Maths; Spanish; English; History; PE) and Secondary Physical Education. A two-year BA in Early Childhood Education leads to QTS.

Leeds Trinity New courses in Education and Early Child Studies have been introduced, and the former can lead to a Primary teaching qualification with further study. Teaching courses in Primary, Primary PE and Secondary PE are also available.

Liverpool Mathematics or Science can be studied with Education, which includes a school placement.

Liverpool Hope Single and combined honours degrees are offered in Education Studies, Inclusive Education, Special Educational Needs and Early Childhood Studies, focusing on Early Years education and childcare provision. A BA/QTS Primary programme (with specialist subjects) is also offered and there are single and combined honours degrees in Childhood and Youth Studies.

Liverpool John Moores Education Studies can be studies with Early Years, Maths, Physical Education, and Special and Inclusive Needs. The Primary Education course can lead to QTS status. There is also a course in Outdoor Education.

London Met Courses are offered in Early Childhood Studies, and also Education Studies (with seven joint courses) and Education Studies with English Literature.

Manchester Met BEd Primary and Secondary courses are offered. In the Primary course one main subject is taken from science, English, history, information technology and physical education. BA/BSc Secondary courses are offered in Business, Communication Technology, Physical Education, Design and Technology and Mathematics. Over 24 other subjects are also offered with Education in the combined honours or joint honours programmes. There is also a new course in Arts and Humanities Education which includes creative work.

Middlesex A Primary programme is offered for the 5–11 age range. Modules are offered in English, mathematics and science. There are also degrees in Education Studies, with a short placement offered in Year 3, and Early Childhood Studies.

Newman Specific non-teaching courses are offered in Education and Early Childhood Education. Teaching courses are offered at Primary (Art, English, Languages) and Secondary (Computer Science and ICT, English, Mathematics, Languages, PE and Religious Studies) level.

Northampton BA honours courses leading to QTS in Early Years Education (3–8 years) and Primary Education (QTS General Primary) are offered along with joint courses in Education. Courses in Early Childhood Studies and Special Educational Need and Inclusion are also offered.

Northumbria Primary Education courses are offered concentrating on Early Primary (3–8 years) or Late Primary (7–11 years). There are also courses linked with Care and Education, Disability Studies, and Health and Social Care programmes.

Nottingham Trent A specialist Primary Education course is offered with students taking modules in a wide range of subjects. Subject specialisations are available in English, mathematics, science, art, music, design and technology, information technology, humanities, physical education and Early Years. There are also degrees in Early Years Psychology and Sport and Leisure Education with Education. A BA (Hons) in Childhood Studies is also available, with opportunities for UK and overseas placements.

Oxford Brookes A large number of courses are offered including Primary Teaching and Early Childhood Studies.

Plymouth General Primary courses are offered in Art and Design, Early Childhood Studies, Education Studies, English, ICT, Mathematics, Music, Physical Education and Science. There is also a course in Steiner Waldorf Education. Some work experience abroad is possible in the State of New York, Finland and Denmark.

Portsmouth Courses are offered in Early Childhood Studies and in Education with English or Languages. Foundation courses in Education Administration and Learning Support are also offered.

Queen's Belfast A four-year BEd course is offered for those intending to teach in primary schools. Alternatively, a PGCE course is available for graduates wishing to specialise in the secondary field. The BEd course takes place at either St Mary's University College Belfast or Stranmillis University College.

Reading A BEd degree (Primary) is offered with QTS with specialisms in Art, English, Mathematics, and Music. There are also BA programmes in Theatre Arts, Education and Deaf Studies and in Children's Development and Learning.

See Heap 2015: *University Degree Course Offers* (Trotman Publishing) for details of offers

Roehampton Primary Education courses are offered in Art and Design, Design and Technology, Early Childhood Studies, English, Geography, History, Music, Physical Education, Religious Education and Sciences. A flexible programme in Education is offered as a single or combined course, with specialisms in ages from young children to adult in various educational settings. Courses in Early Childhood Studies and in Childhood in Society are also offered as single or combined courses. There is also a foundation degree in Supporting Learning and Teaching.

St Mark and St John Courses offered include Children's Physical Education, Education Studies, Primary Teaching and Secondary Teaching (Physical Education).

St Mary's There is a theoretical Study of Education and Employment course with modules for those wishing to train to teach. A BA (Hons) Primary Education with QTS is available as a three-year or advanced four-year course.

Sheffield Hallam Courses are offered in Education Studies, available with Psychology and Counselling, and Primary (3–8 years and 5–10 years) Teaching. There are also Secondary Education courses in Design and Technology, Maths and Science Teaching, and a BA (Hons) in Education and Disability Studies.

South Wales Primary and Secondary teaching courses are available, with the latter offering specialisms in design and technology, mathematics and science. The course in Early Years Development and Education covers psychological, educational and sociological perspectives, while the BA in Education coves a range of topics including Child Development, Professional Practice, Learning in the Outdoor Environment, and Child Abuse Context and Recognition.

Staffordshire Work placements are part of the degree in Early Childhood Studies. The BA (Hons) in Education is recommended for students who have completed a related foundation degree.

Stirling Primary and Secondary courses are offered, the former with two pathways in languages, Early Years and environment.

Stranmillis (UC) Two BEd courses are offered in Primary and Post-primary Studies.

Strathclyde A Primary Education course is offered in which all students take core programmes in a range of subjects and select a range of elective programmes. A nursery placement forms part of the course. A four-year course is also offered in Community Education. There are also courses leading to Maths and Science Teaching.

Sunderland Four-year courses are offered in Primary Education with specialisms in ages 5–11 and in the secondary sector, covering design and technology, English, geography, information technology, mathematics and science. There is also a course in Early Childhood Studies.

Swansea There are courses in Early Childhood Studies, Educational Studies and Drama and Educational Studies.

Teesside A degree in Early Childhood Studies covers health and well-being, children's services and language and literacy. A BSc in Childhood and Youth Studies is also offered.

Trinity St David Degrees are available in Youth and Community Work, and Social Inclusion. There is also a Primary Education Studies course that leads to QTS.

Trinity St David (Swansea) There is a BA in Education Studies which focuses on the history, psychology, sociology and philosophy.

Ulster Education can be taken as a minor subject with 10 other subjects.

West Scotland A BA in Education is offered with students focusing on the main areas of: languages, literacy, maths, and science. There is also a course in Community Learning and Participation.

See *Heap 2015: University Degree Course Offers* (Trotman Publishing) for details of offers

Winchester Courses are offered in Education Studies and Education Studies (Early Childhood). When taken as combined degrees, these can be an excellent preparation for students wishing to take the primary teaching qualification (PGCE). There is also a BA Primary Education programme with QTS recommendation.

Wolverhampton Primary Education courses focus on English, mathematics and science. There is also a highly specialised degree in Conductive Education directed at children and adults with motor disorders, and courses in Early Childhood Studies and Special Needs.

Worcester Primary Teaching courses with Early Years (3–7) and Later Years (5–11) specialisation are offered. There are also several joint honours courses with Education Studies, as well as in Childhood and Family Studies (with practitioner options).

York Key themes of the Educational Studies course include literature and art, learning and education and primary education. An optional placement is offered in an educational service in or near York. A Deaf and Hard-of-Hearing Teaching programme is also offered. Other courses include Sociology/Education and Language and Literature in Education.

OTHER INSTITUTIONS OFFERING EDUCATION COURSES
Blackburn (Coll), Blackpool and Fylde (Coll), Bradford (Coll Univ Centre), Cornwall (Coll), Doncaster (Coll Univ Centre), Farnborough (CT), Guildford (Coll), Havering (Coll), Leeds City (Coll), London (RAc Dance), Neath Port Talbot (Coll), Northbrook (Coll), Norwich City (Coll), Peterborough (Reg Coll), South Devon (Coll), Southport (Coll), Truro (Coll), UHI, Warrington (Coll), Warwickshire (Coll), West Anglia (Coll), Wigan and Leigh (Coll).

ALTERNATIVE COURSES
Occupational Therapy, Psychology, Social Policy.

ENGINEERING

(* indicates universities with entry requirements over 340 UCAS points)

ENGINEERING (GENERAL)/ENGINEERING SCIENCES

SUBJECT REQUIREMENTS/PREFERENCES
GCE A level: Mathematics and Physics usually essential (except for Engineering foundation courses).
GCSE: Grade A–C may be required in English, Chemistry or a language for some courses. Mathematics essential.

SUBJECT INFORMATION
Engineering courses provide the opportunity to study two, three or four engineering specialisms and enable students to delay their choice of specialism. Mathematics and physics provide the foundation of engineering subjects. Several universities and colleges offer one-year foundation courses for applicants with non-science A levels. Extended Engineering courses are available in institutions throughout the UK; in some cases courses are open to applicants without the normal science A levels. After the initial foundation course they move on to the degree programme. Many sponsorships are available in engineering subjects.

AERONAUTICAL ENGINEERING

SUBJECT REQUIREMENTS/PREFERENCES
See under **Engineering (General)/Engineering Sciences**.

SUBJECT INFORMATION
Courses cover the manufacture of military and civil aircraft, theories of mechanics, thermodynamics, electronics, computing and engine design and manufacture.

CHEMICAL ENGINEERING

SUBJECT REQUIREMENTS/PREFERENCES
GCE A level: Chemistry with Mathematics and possibly Physics. Biology may be required for some university courses. See also **Engineering (General)/Engineering Sciences**.

SUBJECT INFORMATION
Courses are based on maths, physics and chemistry and lead to studies in energy resources, nuclear energy, pollution, petroleum engineering, bio-process engineering and biotechnology.

CIVIL ENGINEERING

SUBJECT REQUIREMENTS/PREFERENCES
See under **Engineering (General)/Engineering Sciences**.

SUBJECT INFORMATION
Specialist courses in this field may cover traffic and highway engineering, water and waste engineering, construction management, explosives and public health engineering. Essential elements in all courses, however, include surveying, design projects (for example Channel Tunnel, suspension bridges) and building technology. Aesthetic design may also play a part in the design of some structures (for example motorway bridges).

COMPUTER ENGINEERING

SUBJECT REQUIREMENTS/PREFERENCES
See under **Engineering (General)/Engineering Sciences**.

SUBJECT INFORMATION
The design and application of modern computer systems is fundamental to all these courses, which will also include electronic engineering, software engineering and computer-aided engineering. Several universities offer sufficient flexibility to enable final course decisions to be made in the second year. Applicants should note that many of these courses overlap with Computer Science and Electronic Engineering courses.

ELECTRICAL/ELECTRONIC ENGINEERING

SUBJECT REQUIREMENTS/PREFERENCES
See under **Engineering (General)/Engineering Sciences**.

SUBJECT INFORMATION

Options to specialise should be considered when choosing courses, so read the prospectuses carefully. In this field, options could include opto-electronics and optical communication systems, microwave systems, radio frequency engineering and circuit technology.

MANUFACTURING ENGINEERING

SUBJECT REQUIREMENTS/PREFERENCES

GCE A level: Physics may be required; check prospectuses. See also **Engineering (General)/Engineering Sciences**.

SUBJECT INFORMATION

Manufacturing engineering is sometimes referred to as production engineering. It is a branch of the subject concerned with management aspects of engineering such as industrial organisation, purchasing and the planning and control of operations, and at the same time provides an overview of engineering design systems. Engineering personnel are key staff in most manufacturing firms. These courses are often combined with Mechanical Engineering or with Business/Management Studies.

MECHANICAL ENGINEERING

SUBJECT REQUIREMENTS/PREFERENCES

See under **Engineering (General)/Engineering Sciences**.

SUBJECT INFORMATION

All courses involve the design, installation and maintenance of equipment used in industry. Thermodynamics, computer-aided design, fluid mechanics and materials science are subjects fundamental to this branch of engineering. Many universities offer students the opportunity to transfer to other Engineering courses in Year 2.

MINING ENGINEERING

SUBJECT REQUIREMENTS/PREFERENCES

See under **Engineering (General)/Engineering Sciences**.

SUBJECT INFORMATION

Mining Engineering covers geology, surveying and mineral processing and offers opportunities to enter careers in petroleum engineering as well as coal and metalliferous mining.

UNIVERSITY COURSE INFORMATION

Aberdeen Separate courses are available in Engineering and also Chemical, Civil (and Structural), Mechanical and Petroleum Engineering. The first two years have a common core of subjects for all students, after which the choice has to be made between BEng and MEng specialities.

Abertay Civil Engineering involves both practical and theoretical studies, with optional industrial experience in Year 3. Courses are offered in Civil and Environmental Engineering and Civil and Structural Engineering, and courses with European Studies and Management can also be taken.

Anglia Ruskin Degree courses are offered specialising in Integrated, Civil, Mechanical and Electronics, covering Audio Technology and Computer Science.

See *Heap 2015: University Degree Course Offers* (Trotman Publishing) for details of offers

Aston Courses in the School of Engineering are offered in Chemical, Communication and Design, Electrical and Electronic, Electronic, Mechanical Communications, Internet and Mechanical Engineering. There are also several Product Design courses. Most courses incorporate optional paid professional placements.

Bangor The School of Electronic Engineering and Computer Systems offers a number of Electronics courses including Electrical/Electronics Engineering and Computer Systems (BEng) which covers hardware systems or software programming. The Computer Systems BEng course covers hardware engineering and software programming. The school has extensive industrial links leading to industrial placements. A degree in Music Technology is subject to approval.

Bath* The university offers several Engineering courses covering Computer, Communications, Chemical, Civil and Architectural, Electronic and Electrical, and Mechanical (Aerospace, Automotive, Innovation and Design, Manufacturing, Mechanical, Medical or Sports) Engineering. All are MEng programmes which share the first two years, allowing students to change their route. Full-time or sandwich courses are offered and language (French or German) options are available.

Birmingham* There are five Schools of Engineering and courses on offer which cover Chemical, Biomedical, Civil, Electronic and Electrical, Mechanical and Materials, and Computer and Communications Systems Engineering. Three-year and four-year programmes are offered and in each discipline the first two years are common to both the BEng and MEng programmes. Civil Engineering can also be studied with Business Management. A year of industrial training in the UK or abroad is optional.

Birmingham City The Faculty of Engineering offers a range of courses in Automotive Engineering, Electronic Engineering, Electronic and Audio, Communications, and Mechanical Engineering, Sound Engineering, Manufacturing Systems and Motorsport Technology, most offering sandwich placements. Courses follow the requirements of UK-SPEC (UK standard for professional engineering competence). There is also a unique course in Horology (the art and science of time measurement) covering the design, maintenance and repair of both mechanical and electronic time pieces.

Bolton Full-time and part-time courses are offered in various engineering disciplines, including Automobile, which meets the requirements leading to chartered engineer (CEng) status, Civil and Mechanical Engineering.

Bournemouth The Design Engineering and Engineering courses have an optional 40-week placement included. There is also a course in Software Engineering.

Bradford A range of engineering disciplines is offered. These include Automotive, Civil and Structural, Electrical and Electronic, Mechanical and Medical and Clinical Technology, and Engineering Technology.

Brighton A general programme in Engineering embraces a broad range of subjects combined with business skills and management. There are also specialist courses in other fields of engineering covering Aeronautics, Automotive, Civil, Environmental, Electrical and Electronic, Mechanical and Manufacturing Engineering, Product Design and Sports Technology. Most courses carry industry body accreditation. Courses are offered on a three-year full-time or four-year sandwich basis.

Bristol* Three-year (BEng) and four-year (MEng) courses are offered in Engineering Design, Aeronautical Engineering, Avionic Systems, Computer Systems, Civil, Electrical and Electronic and Electronic and Communications Engineering, Mechanical Engineering and Engineering Design and Engineering Mathematics. Several have the option to study in continental Europe.

Bristol UWE Degrees are offered in 13 engineering disciplines: Aerospace Design, Aerospace Manufacturing, Aerospace Systems, Architecture and Environmental, Building Services, Civil, Computer Systems, Electrical, Electronic, Mechanical Engineering, Music Systems, Motorsport, and River and Coastal Engineering. Both BEng and MEng programmes are accredited by the Institution of Mechanical Engineers (IMechE). There is also a broad BSc Engineering course and a degree in Robotics.

See *Heap 2015: University Degree Course Offers* (Trotman Publishing) for details of offers

Brunel* Computer Systems Engineering and Internet Engineering are offered, in addition to which Electronic and Electrical Engineering can be studied with specialisms in Communications Systems and Renewable Energy Systems. There are also full-time and sandwich courses in Multimedia Technology and Design. There are also courses in Industrial Design, Product Design, Aerospace, Aviation (with Pilot Studies), Mechanical and Motorsport Engineering. A Foundations of Engineering year is offered.

Bucks New Courses in Mechanical Engineering Design are offered full and part time, covering design and manufacture with a focus on computer-aided tools.

Cambridge* The four-year Engineering course is divided into Parts I and II, each of two years. Part I provides a broad education whilst in Part II (Years 3 and 4) specialisation begins in one of the following areas: Aerospace and Aerothermal Engineering; Civil, Structural and Environmental Engineering; Electrical and Electronic Engineering; Electrical and Information Sciences; Energy and the Environment; Engineering for the Life Sciences; Information and Computer Engineering; Instrumentation and Control; Mechanical Engineering. There are also courses in Chemical Engineering and Manufacturing Engineering.

Cardiff* The School of Engineering offers courses in Architectural, Civil, Civil and Environmental, Computer Systems, Electrical and Electronic, Manufacturing, Mechanical and Medical Engineering. There is also an Integrated Engineering course, a broad-based education covering electronic, electrical, manufacturing and mechanical disciplines. The degree schemes cover MEng, BEng, and Year in Europe courses. All programmes carry CEng accreditation.

Central Lancashire Degrees are offered in Computer, Electronic, Computer-aided, Mechanical, Fire and Building Services Engineering, Robotics and Mechatronics, and Motor Sports. Two other significant courses involve Fire Engineering and Fire Safety and Risk Management.

City Courses offered cover Aeronautical Engineering, Air Transport Engineering, Automotive and Motorsport Engineering, Biomedical Engineering, Civil Engineering and Civil Engineering with Architecture, Computer Systems Engineering, Electrical and Electronic Engineering, Energy Engineering, Mechanical Engineering and Telecommunications. Many courses have placements in Europe and North America and sponsorships may be offered.

Coventry The School of Engineering offers a wide range of BEng, MEng and BSc courses including Automotive Engineering Design, Civil and Mechanical Engineering, Electrical and Electronic Engineering, Aerospace Systems and Technology and Motorsport Engineering. Disaster Management and Product and Industrial Design Engineering are also offered.

Cumbria A Sustainable Energy Technology degree is offered covering mathematics, modelling and renewable energy technologies.

De Montfort Courses offered include Electronic, Mechanical and Mechatronic Engineering and Engineering Design. Courses carry accreditation from the Institution of Engineering and Technology (IET). Audio and Recording Technology and Creative Sound Technology are also now available.

Derby The School of Engineering offers courses in Electrical, Electronic, Mechanical and Motorsport Engineering (IMechE-accredited), Music Technology with Audio Systems Design, Design Technology, and Product Design.

Dundee Courses are offered in Civil, Electronic and Electrical and Mechanical Engineering, Microelectronics and Photonics, and Engineering with options in Management. There are also courses in Electronics and Computing, Product Design, Electronic Media and Renewable Energy.

Durham* BEng and MEng Engineering students take a common course for the first two years, covering computing, applied mechanics, CAD and laboratory projects. In the third year, courses are available in Civil, Electronic, Electrical, Mechanical, Design Manufacture and Management or General Engineering. A BEng course in General Engineering is also available.

East Anglia The Software Engineering course covers all aspects of hardware and software. Specialist courses in Year 3 include Advanced Digital Design, Computer Networks and Computer Architecture.

East London Full-time and sandwich courses are offered in Civil Engineering, Computing and Electronics, Electrical and Electronic, Communications, Control and Power Engineering and Product Design. Two-subject degrees can be taken.

Edinburgh The School of Engineering and Informatics offers degree courses in Chemical, Civil, Structural and Environmental, Electrical and Mechanical Engineering and Electronics. Students taking Engineering courses defer their choice of specialism until the second half of Year 1, or to the beginning of Year 2 or even Year 3. All MEng programmes lead to CEng status. Two new degree programmes have been introduced in Electronics with Bioelectronics and Electrical Engineering with Renewable Energy.

Edinburgh Napier Engineering courses offered include Civil Transportation and Timber, Communication, Electronic and Electrical, Computer, Energy and Environmental, Mechanical, Mechatronics, Polymer and Product Design Engineering, as well as Materials Technology and Sports Technology. Degree programmes share common first two levels; up to the end of Level 2, transfer between programmes is possible. A BEng in Engineering with Management is also available.

Essex BEng, MEng or BSc courses are offered in Computer Science and Systems Engineering, Telecommunications, Electronic and Internet Engineering.

Exeter All General Engineering students attend the same classes for the first two semesters, followed by specialisation. Students choose from one of four specialist subjects – Civil, Electronic, Materials, Mechanical, and Engineering and Management. Students can transfer between three-year BEng and four-year MEng programmes. The Camborne School of Mines also offers courses in Mining Engineering and Engineering Geology.

Glasgow This School of Engineering teaches the main branches of the subject: Aero Engineering with avionics options (including a flight-testing course on the MEng option); Biomedical Engineering; Civil Engineering, which can be combined with Architecture; Electronics and Electrical Engineering with options to specialise in software engineering or with a European or international emphasis. There are also courses in Mechanical Engineering (which also has a European option), Naval Architecture, Marine and Ocean Engineering, in which one can specialise in fast-ship design or small-craft design, and Product Design Engineering.

Glasgow Caledonian CEng-accredited courses are provided in Computer, Building Services, Electrical Power, Electronic, Telecommunication, Environmental and Civil, Fire Risk, Computer-aided Manufacturing Systems and Mechanical Engineering. Summer school courses in Mathematics are provided for prospective students.

Glyndŵr Various industry-accredited Engineering courses are offered including Automotive, Aeronautical and Mechanical, Electrical and Electronics, Avionics and Broadcast Engineering. Speciality degrees include Motorsport Design Management and Performance Car Technology and Product Design. The Renewable Energy degree focuses on project management in Year 3.

Greenwich The School of Engineering offers over 70 course variations in the following programmes: Civil Engineering, Computing and Communications Engineering, Electrical and Electronic Engineering, Mechanical Engineering. Several courses lead to chartered or incorporated engineer status. General engineering can be studied with Business Management.

Harper Adams Courses focus on Agricultural and Off Road Vehicle Design.

Heriot-Watt Courses are offered in Automotive Engineering, Chemical Engineering (with options in oil and gas technology and pharmaceutical engineering), Architectural, Civil and Structural, Electrical and

Electronic, Mechanical Engineering and Software Engineering, Microwave and Photonics, Materials and Ocean Engineering, and Engineering with Management. Students taking Electronic and Photonic Engineering may also opt for a degree in Physics (during the course).

Hertfordshire The Faculty of Engineering offers degrees in Electronic and Electrical, Mechanical, Automotive, Aerospace and Computing. Engineering can also be studied with another subject in the combined modular scheme.

Huddersfield Industrial training forms part of all Engineering courses, which include a MEng route via all BEng courses. Options include Automotive and Motorsport Engineering, Chemical Engineering, Digital Systems, Electronic, Mechanical, Software and Manufacturing Engineering. Courses in Multimedia Design, Virtual Reality Design and Music Technology, which involves acoustics and electronics, are also offered by the School of Engineering. Industrial placements are optional.

Hull All students follow a similar path of study with specialisms being chosen in Years 2 and 3. Courses are offered in Chemical Engineering, Computer-aided Engineering, Electronics, Mechanical, Telecommunications Engineering and Design Technology. All MEng programmes are CEng- and IMechE-accredited.

Imperial London* The Faculty of Engineering offers courses in Aeronautics, Bioengineering, Biomedical Engineering, Chemical Engineering and Chemical Technology, Civil and Environmental Engineering, Computing, Earth Science and Engineering, Electrical and Electronic Engineering (with an option in management), Materials or Mechanical Engineering. Most are available as both BEng and MEng programmes and include the option to study abroad. (Modules can also be taken in history, philosophy, music, creative writing and a range of languages). (High research rating.)

Kent The Electronic Engineering programme offers courses in Electronics and Communications, the latter covering radio and satellite specialisms and medical electronics. The course is highly rated by students. In addition there is a course in Computer Systems Engineering with the option of a year in industry. A foundation year is also offered.

Kingston CEng-accredited degrees are offered in Aerospace, Aircraft, Automotive Systems, Building Services, Civil (and Construction Management), Communication Systems, Mechanical and Motorcycle, Motorsport and Product Design Engineering.

Lancaster* Several Engineering options are available covering Engineering (study abroad), Chemical, Eletronic and Electrical Engineering, Mechanical, Mechatronics and Nuclear Engineering. In collaboration with other departments, it is also possible to study Computer Systems Engineering. MEng and BEng courses with options to undertake 12–15-month paid placements or study in the US or Canada are also offered.

Leeds* Engineering courses are offered in the following specialisms – Aeronautical and Aerospace, Architectural, Automotive, Chemical, Civil and Environmental or Structural, Communications, Computer, Electronics and Communications, Energy, Environmental, Fire and Explosion, Mechanical, Mechatronic and Robotic, Medical, Materials Science and Engineering, Product Design, Pharmaceutical Chemical Engineering, Mining, Medical and Safety Engineering. Industrial placements and study abroad options are offered.

Leeds Beckett BSc courses are offered in Civil, Electronic and Electrical, Environmental Design, Manufacturing and Building Control Engineering.

Leicester A broad-based general Engineering degree programme is offered, with a common first year covering mechanical and materials engineering, electrical and software engineering; a mechanical or electrical pathway is taken in Year 2. Other courses include Aerospace Communications and Electronics, Software and Electronic Engineering, Electrical and Electronic Engineering, General Engineering and Mechanical Engineering degrees. BEng and MEng courses are offered with sandwich courses offering placements in the UK and Europe or the US.

Lincoln Courses are offered in Mechanical Engineering, Electrical and Electronic Engineering, Control and Systems Engineering and Materials Engineering.

See *Heap 2015: University Degree Course Offers* (Trotman Publishing) for details of offers

Liverpool* The Faculty of Engineering offers courses in Aerospace (with Pilot Studies), Avionic Systems, Civil and Structural, Environmental, Biomaterials and Materials Science, Metallurgy, Mechanical, Electrical and Electronic Engineering and Mechatronics. There is also a BEng course in Engineering that enables students to study mechanical, electrical and materials engineering.

Liverpool John Moores The IET-accredited School of Engineering has a strong multicultural and international base. Most students are offered the opportunity to take an industrial placement during the course. Degree courses in the main engineering disciplines are offered: Auto, Building Services, Broadcast, Civil, Computer, Electrical and Electronic, Mechanical and Marine, Mechatronics and Networks and Telecommunications Engineering. There are also courses in Nautical Science and Navigation and Marine Technology.

London (Goldsmiths) There is a BEng/MEng honours degree in Design and Innovation offered through the Engineering Department of Queen Mary College.

London (King's)* Courses are offered in Biomedical Engineering, (based at St Thomas's Hospital) and Robotics and Intelligent Systems.

London (QM) The Department of Engineering offers a wide range of degree programmes covering Aerospace, Audio Systems, Computing, Biomedical, Design and Innovation, Engineering Science (and with Business Management), Internet, Telecommunications, Materials Science, Electrical, Medical and Electronic, and Mechanical Engineering. Industrial placements are offered.

London (UCL)* The Faculty of Engineering Sciences offers courses in Biochemical, Chemical, Civil, Computer Science, Environmental (with Chartered Institution of Water and Environmental Management (CIWEM) accreditation), Electronic and Electrical Engineering, Engineering Information Management, Mechanical Engineering, Medical Physics and Naval Architecture and Marine Engineering. There are opportunities for sponsorship in a number of these areas as well as the opportunity to study abroad.

London Met There are degrees in Electronic and Communication Engineering and Telecommunication and Network Engineering.

London South Bank Degrees are available in Architectural, Building Services, Civil, Computer, Electrical and Electronic, Internet and Telecommunications, Chemical, Mechanical, Petroleum and Mechatronic Engineering.

Loughborough* All Engineering courses (very highly rated by students) lead to professional recognition and are supported by well-organised industrial placements. Students can graduate in Aeronautical and Automotive, Architectural, Chemical, Construction, Civil, Electronic and Electrical, Manufacturing and Management, Materials and Management, Mechanical and Manufacturing, Engineering Systems or Engineering Physics. A BEng is also offered in Product Design and Manufacturing.

Manchester* The School of Engineering offers BEng and MEng degree programmes in Aerospace, Mechanical, Chemical, Communication Systems, Civil, Computer Systems, Electrical and Electronic Engineering, Electronic Systems, Mechatronics, Materials Science and Petroleum. These studies will cover design, manufacture, research, development, marketing and sales. There are also courses in Engineering and Business. Industrial experience is available on most courses, as well as study in North America and Europe.

Manchester Met IME- and IMET-accredited degree courses are offered in Automotive Engineering, Electrical and Electronic Engineering, Communication and Electronic Engineering, Virtual Design in Engineering, Mechanical Engineering, Engineering and Automation and Control on full-time or sandwich course options. In addition, there are several specialised Technology courses including the media, special effects and robotics.

Middlesex Courses are offered in Computer Systems Engineering, Design Engineering (Digital, Electronic, Mechatronic) and in Product Design Engineering.

Newcastle* The faculty is one of the largest in the country and offers more than 30 CEng-accredited Engineering degree programmes. These cover Chemical and Process Engineering, Civil and Environmental

Engineering, Civil and Structural Engineering, Computer Systems, Electrical and Electronic Engineering, Marine Engineering and Technology, including Naval Architecture, Offshore Engineering and Small-craft Technology, Mechanical and Systems Engineering.

Northampton Courses are offered in Engineering covering Mechanical Engineering, Manufacturing and Electrical Engineering fields.

Northumbria Building Services Engineering, Communication and Electronic Engineering, Computer-aided Engineering, Electrical and Electronic, and Mechanical Engineering are offered. There are also courses in Manufacturing Systems Engineering, Electronic Design Technology and Mechanical Design and Technology. Courses are IMechE-accredited.

Nottingham* Over 30 courses are offered in Chemical and Environmental, Civil, Electrical, Electronic, Mechanical, Materials and Manufacturing Engineering.

Nottingham Trent BEng and MEng courses are offered in Civil Engineering and Civil and Environmental Engineering.

Oxford* The Engineering Science degree integrates the study of the subject across several areas. The first year is common to Engineering Science and Engineering Economics and Management. In Years 3 and 4 specialisation takes place in one of six branches of Engineering in Mechanical, Civil, Electrical, Information, Chemical, or Biomedical Engineering.

Oxford Brookes Courses are offered in Automotive, Electronic Systems Design, Motorsport Technology, Manufacturing Technology, Telecommunications and Mechanical Engineering. Most courses carry Incorporated Engineer status.

Plymouth Engineering courses are available in Civil, Civil and Coastal, Clinical Technology, Communication, Electronic and Electrical Engineering, Computer Systems, Robotics and Automated Systems, Composite Materials, Marine Technology, and Mechanical Engineering specialisms, in three-year and four-year sandwich courses. A BEng in Robotics is also available.

Portsmouth Degrees are offered in Communication Systems, Computer, Electronic, Mechanical and Manufacturing Engineering. There is also a BEng course in Petroleum Engineering.

Queen's Belfast* BEng Engineering courses are offered in the following specialisms: Aerospace, Chemical, Environmental and Civil, Electrical and Electronic, Electronic and Software, Manufacturing and Mechanical Engineering and Product Design and Development. Four-year enhanced courses are offered in the same subjects with sandwich placements and overseas study.

Reading Degrees are available covering Artificial Intelligence, Biomedical Cybernetics, Computer, Electronic, Robotic and Systems Engineering. Four-year courses are offered in each of these disciplines.

Robert Gordon In addition to BEng and MEng Engineering courses there are several CEng-accredited degrees with specialisms including in Electronic and Electrical Engineering, Computer and Communications, Mechanical Engineering and Offshore Engineering.

Salford BSc, BEng and MEng courses are offered in Acoustics, Aeronautical, Audio and Video and Broadcast Technology, and Civil, Digital Electronics, Mechanical, Software and Structural Engineering.

Sheffield* Degrees are offered in Aerospace, Architectutral, Bioengineering, Chemical, Civil, Computer Systems, Electrical, Electronic, Materials Science, Mechanical, Mechatronics, Software and Motorsport Engineering.

Sheffield Hallam BEng (Incorporated Engineer-accredited) and MEng (CEng-accredited) courses are offered in Computer-aided Engineering and Design, Electrical and Electronic Engineering, Environmental Engineering, Mechanical Engineering, Auto Engineering and Design Communications and Information Engineering.

See *Heap 2015: University Degree Course Offers* (Trotman Publishing) for details of offers

South Wales A wide range of Engineering degrees, some of which carry IMechE accreditation, are offered in subjects including Aeronautical, Automotive, Civil, Computer Systems, Electrical and Electronic, Fire Safety and Mechanical. Several of the courses give students the opportunity to undertake a sandwich year between Years 2 and 3.

Southampton* The large Faculty of Engineering and associated departments offer a wide range of BEng, BSc and MEng courses covering Acoustical, Audiology, Aeronautics, Civil, Environmental, Computer, Electrical, Electronic and Mechanical Engineering. Degrees in Ship Science, Naval Architecture and Engineering Management are also available.

Southampton Solent In addition to Electronic and Mechanical and Marine Engineering, there is a course in Audio Technology. BEng courses are also available in Engineering with Business and Mechanical Design.

Staffordshire IMechE-accredited courses are offered in Auto Engineering, Electronic, Electrical and Forensic Engineering, Mechanical, Mechatronics and Network Engineering.

Strathclyde* Forty-six BEng and five-year MEng courses cover Aeromechanical, Architectural, Chemical, Civil and Environmental, Computer and Electronic Systems, Electronic and Electrical, Manufacturing, Mechanical and Sports Engineering, Offshore specialisms and Naval Architecture. Product Design and Prosthetics and Orthotics (see under **Health Studies/Sciences**) Engineering are also offered with Business Management.

Sunderland Automotive Engineering is offered, whilst the broad course in Engineering Design includes Electrical, Electronics, Manufacturing, Renewable Energy and Mechanical Engineering.

Surrey* A large Engineering programme offers courses in Engineering Business Management, Chemical, Civil, Electronic, Aerospace, Media, Medical and Mechanical Engineering. Some courses are offered with a European language. Electronics courses comprise audio media engineering, digital broadcasting, mobile communications, radio frequency, satellite and systems engineering. There are also specialisms in offshore and maritime engineering, power/aerospace studies and information systems engineering. A year-long training placement is available.

Sussex There is considerable flexibility between most Engineering degree programmes. MEng and BEng degrees are offered in the following Engineering courses: Computer Systems, Electrical and Electronic, Electronic and Communication, Mechanical and Automotive Engineering. A BSc in Product Design is also available. Some courses can also be combined with European, North American and Business Studies.

Swansea A large selection of Engineering courses includes Aerospace, Chemical and Biological Process, Communication, Civil, Electrical and Electronic, Environmental, Materials, Mechanical, Medical, Nanotechnology and Product Design. Most courses offer a year in industry or overseas study.

Teesside Courses are offered in Chemical or Mechanical Engineering, Construction, Control and Process, Electrical and Electronic, Manufacturing and Civil Engineering, also with Disaster Management. Some courses include an integrated foundation year.

Trinity St David (Swansea) Automotive Engineering is a special subject at the university. A Design course is also offered. In addition, other Engineering courses cover Civil, Mechanical, Motorsport and Manufacturing Engineering. The university is a Motorsport Academy UK recognised educator.

Ulster Courses are available in the following disciplines: Civil, Electrical/Electronic and Mechanical Engineering. There is also a General Engineering course and a BEng (Hons) in Clean Technology. Some courses can be taken with German.

Warwick* BEng and MEng degree courses are offered in Auto, Civil, Electronic, Manufacturing, Mechanical and Computer Systems Engineering, and also in Engineering Business Management or with Business Studies. The general degree in Engineering enables students to defer their choice of specialisation in one of the options above until the end of Year 1.

See *Heap 2015: University Degree Course Offers* (Trotman Publishing) for details of offers

West London Courses are offered in Electronics, Mechatronics and Computer Systems Engineering.

West Scotland There are three- and four-year courses in Aircraft, Mechanical, Motorsport, Chemical and Civil Engineering, Mechatronics and Engineering Management. Four-year sandwich options are available.

Westminster BEng courses are available in Digital and Mobile Communications, Electronic Engineering and Computer Systems. Sandwich placements are available.

Wolverhampton BSc, BEng and MEng courses are offered in Automotive Systems, Civil, Electrical and Electronic, Mechatronics and Mechanical Engineering. A General Engineering course is also available.

York* Thirteen courses are offered including Electronic Engineering, Electronic and Communication Engineering, Computer Systems Engineering, Avionics, Business Management and Music Technology Systems. MEng courses are also available in Media Technology and Radio Frequency Engineering. Scholarships available.

OTHER INSTITUTIONS OFFERING ENGINEERING COURSES

Barking (Coll), Bath City (Coll), Blackburn (Coll), Blackpool and Fylde (Coll), Bradford (Coll Univ Centre), Bristol City (Coll), Central Nottingham (Coll), Chesterfield (Coll), Colchester (Inst), Cornwall (Coll), Doncaster (Coll Univ Centre), Dudley (Coll), Exeter (Coll), Farnborough (CT), Gower Swansea (Coll), Grimsby (Univ Centre), Havering (Coll), Highbury Portsmouth (Coll), Hopwood Hall (Coll), Lakes (Coll), Lincoln (Coll), Liverpool (LIPA), Llandrillo Cymru (Coll), Loughborough (Coll), Mid-Cheshire (Coll), Myerscough (Coll), Neath Port Talbot (Coll), Nescot, Northbrook (Coll), Norwich City (Coll), Pembrokeshire (Coll), Ravensbourne, St Helens (Coll), Sandwell (Coll), Shrewsbury (CAT), Sir Gâr (Coll), Solihull (Coll), Somerset (Coll), South Cheshire (Coll), South Essex (Coll), South Tyneside (Coll), Staffordshire Reg Fed (SURF), Stephenson (Coll), Stockport (Coll), Tameside (Coll), Truro (Coll), Tyne Met (Coll), UHI, Uxbridge (Coll), Warrington (Coll), Warwickshire (Coll), West Anglia (Coll), West Thames (Coll), Wigan and Leigh (Coll), Worcester (CT).

ALTERNATIVE COURSES

Architecture, Building, Chemistry, Mathematics, Physics, Surveying.

ENGLISH

(* indicates universities with entry requirements over 340 UCAS points)

SUBJECT REQUIREMENTS/PREFERENCES

GCE A level: English. **GCSE:** A foreign language may be preferred.

SUBJECT INFORMATION

English courses are an extension of school studies in literature and language and may cover topics ranging from Anglo-Saxon literature to the present day. Many courses will focus on certain areas such as the medieval or Renaissance periods of literature or English language studies. Admissions tutors will expect students to have read widely outside their A level syllabus. (Sunday newspaper book reviews will give a useful introduction to contemporary writing.)

QUESTIONS TO CONSIDER

 ✳ Do I have a preference for literature or language, or am I keen to combine the study of both?
 ✳ Do I want to produce my own creative written work, as well as studying existing texts?
 ✳ Does the course offer a study of relevant vocational subjects, such as Publishing or Journalism?

＊ Which areas of literature especially interest me – a particular historical period, other cultures, poetry, drama?

Aberdeen The courses in English cover English, Language and Linguistics, Language and Literature, Scottish Literature and World Cultures. A major department offering literature of the British Isles courses, involving critical and historical study of British and American authors from the Middle Ages to the present day. The English Language courses are concerned with the development of the English language up until the present day. There are 25 joint honours courses with English and 20 with Literature.

Aberystwyth English Literature focuses on texts from different periods, the genres of poetry, drama and the novel. In Part II topics explore the Renaissance and modern drama, the 20th-century novel and poetry. Specialisation follows in a range of subjects, including medieval and Victorian literature, 20th-century British, Anglo-Welsh and American literature and creative writing. English Literature is also offered with Creative Writing and as a combined honours course with a range of humanities subjects. Aberystwyth is also at the forefront for facilities in information and library studies and management and offers degrees in these subjects.

Anglia Ruskin The English course strikes a balance between the study of leading writers (Wordsworth, Milton, Dickens etc.) and less traditional areas such as modern science fiction. Modules include film and contemporary writers. There is also the option to take a course in practical writing. An English Language degree with Communication Studies is also offered, as well as English Language and Linguistics, and English Literature. Degrees in Writing and English Literature and Writing and Film Studies offer professional writing skills covering fiction, drama, radio and poetry.

Aston English Language can be taken as a single, joint or combined honours subject with International Relations, Politics, Psychology and a range of modern languages. This is the only English course in the UK which includes a placement year. There are opportunities to specialise in Business English, Legal Language or Teaching.

Bangor English degrees cover a wide range of subjects ranging from Old English to 20th-century literature. Studies in creative writing and plays in performance, film studies, journalism, theatre studies and linguistics are also offered. There is also a broad course that covers literature, history and society, offered on a part-time basis. Bangor is an internationally recognised centre for work on Arthurian literature. English can be combined with Creative Writing, Film Studies, Journalism and Theatre Studies and in addition there are courses in Linguistics.

Bath Spa The English Literature course allows a wide choice of modules, some period-based (17th century), others on modern topics and specialist subjects including environment, film and postcolonialism. There is also a Creative Writing programme with strands in prose, poetry and scriptwriting.

Bedfordshire Courses in Creative Writing (and with Journalism) and English for Business or Theatre are offered along with several English Language courses. The English Studies degree covers literary genres and periods in the context of language and society, and English and Theatre Studies is also available. Several Journalism courses are offered.

Birmingham* Single honours students choose between literature and some language or literature and language equally. Joint honours students choose between all literature or all language. English can also be taken as a major or minor subject with American Literature or Creative Writing.

Birmingham City Twelve courses in English Language and Literature are offered in joint or minor programmes with Creative Writing, Media, Drama and Psychology. There is also a degree in English and Drama.

Bishop Grosseteste The English Literature course covers Chaucer to the present day and in addition focuses on American and Children's literature. There are many joint and major/minor courses.

Bolton English courses focus on literary studies from the Renaissance period to the present day. Courses are also offered in Creative Writing and Media Writing and Production.

See *Heap 2015: University Degree Course Offers* (Trotman Publishing) for details of offers

Bournemouth The English degree covers a range of literary genres and their application in traditional and new media, with practical modules in journalism and publishing. The Communication and Media degree also includes English literature and creative writing modules. There is also a course in Multimedia Journalism available.

Bradford A course is offered in Creative Writing which covers gender, ethnicity, popular culture, mass media, film and literature. There is also an English degree offering theoretical study of a range of genres and periods alongside social and cultural issues.

Brighton Several courses are offered in English Language, English Literature and Linguistics. There are also joint courses with Education, Sociology and Media. A broad course in Cultures, Histories and Literatures can also be taken.

Bristol* The English course focuses on English literature from 1200 to the present day. A special subject from a very wide range of options is taken in each semester in Year 2. English is offered with Drama, Classical Studies, Community Engagement and Philosophy.

Bristol UWE The English course focuses on a range of topics with additional modules offered in history, media studies, women's studies, children's literature, modern languages and American literature. A complementary module can be taken in Year 1 in the humanities, psychology, sociology, international relations, politics, French, German or Spanish. There are also degrees in English Language jointly with several other subjects.

Brunel The English course emphasises personal response to English literature rather than a chronological historical survey. A wide range of options allows students to select choices of specialisms from poetry, creative writing, drama, fiction and literatures from across the world. The Creative Writing BA offers the option to study a modern foreign language. There is also a degree in English with Creative Writing, a central feature of the English programme at Brunel, and joint courses with Film/TV Studies, Drama and Music.

Buckingham English (comprising both language and literature) is a two-year course offering a broad programme from Shakespeare, Romantic literature and the Victorians to American literature, film studies and modern drama. English Language programmes are offered for overseas students. English Literature is also offered with Journalism, Media Communications, French, Spanish, History and Psychology.

Bucks New Scriptwriting for Film, TV and Stage and Creative Writing degrees are offered.

Cambridge* The English degree offers a study of English literature from the Middle Ages to the present day. Literature is also studied in an historical and cultural context with comparisons offered as options in Anglo-Saxon, Early Norse, Welsh and Irish. Various options including classical and other literatures are offered in Year 2. In addition to English, applicants for the course are reminded that Classics, Modern Languages, and History are among the most relevant A levels. There is also a degree in Linguistics. Not available at St Catharine's College.

Canterbury Christ Church The English course, which includes pre-1800 literature, is unique in that a double degree is offered combining study in Canterbury with a year in Lille. There is also a course in English Language and Communication with Teaching English as a Foreign Language as a module in Year 3.

Cardiff* Part I of the English Literature course covers English literature, medieval English and language and communications. In Years 2 and 3, nearly 100 modules of specialist themes are available. English Language is also available as a single honours degree or joint honours with English Literature. English Literature and Language Studies can also be taken with a humanities subject.

Cardiff Met (UWIC) The English and Contemporary Media course covers a range of literary genres including myth, gothic and science fiction, as well as practical journalism skills and contemporary culture theory. English can also be taken with Creative Writing or Drama.

Central Lancashire English Literature is offered singly or combined with other subjects or as a joint course with Film and Media. The English Language Studies course covers English language with options in linguistics and literature. In addition there are courses involving Linguistics, Communication and Popular Culture, American Literature, Theatre Studies and Creative Writing.

Chester Courses are offered in English Literature, including American and Irish Literature, and in Creative Writing, exploring prose, journalism, poetry, reviews and essays.

Chichester English and English with Creative Writing are offered as single and joint courses with a range of subjects, sharing Year 1 modules in literary history, literary theory and language.

Coventry English is offered (with specialisms in Literature or Language) as a single or joint honours programme with six options. There are also courses in English and Creative Writing, and Journalistic Studies.

Cumbria A three-year programme is offered in Creative Writing in addition to the English degree or joint degree. Both provide a wide range of options in Year 3, including assessed portfolios of creative writing.

De Montfort The English course covers English literature and literature in translation as well as literature in a social context. English can also be taken with Media Studies, or is available as a joint honours programme with a range of subjects. There is a separate Creative Writing degree.

Derby Students may take English as a full-time degree or major or joint subject. The programme covers critical theory of literature from a range of historical periods and nationalities. Creative Writing is also offered in the combined and single honours programmes.

Dundee All periods of literature are studied in the English course, from Chaucer to the present time. Modules are offered in film studies, comics and graphic novels and creative writing. Eleven joint honours courses with English are available including English with Theatre Studies and English with Film Studies.

Durham* English Literature is a wide-ranging course focusing on poetry, drama and the novel in Year 1 with modules on selected themes. Years 2 and 3 enable students to follow their special interests. Two additional modules from another department may also be studied. Joint courses are offered with History and Philosophy and the subject can be studied in combined honours in arts.

East Anglia* The School of English Literature and Creative Writing offers flexibility to study a wide range of different but related courses including American and English Literature, Literature and History, English Literature and Drama. There are also courses in English Literature with Creative Writing, English and Comparative Literature, and Literature and joint courses with History, Drama, American Literature, Politics, Film, Philosophy and Art History. Degree courses in Linguistics are also offered.

East London English Literature is offered as a joint course with Linguistics, Cultural Studies, Law and History. An extended degree BA or BSc course is also available. There are also courses in English Language, Linguistics, Languages in Education and Creative and Professional Writing.

Edge Hill Courses are offered in English Language and Literature. Vocational modules are offered, such as Teaching English to Speakers of Other Languages (TESOL). Creative Writing is also available and can be taken with Drama, English, Film Studies, History or Media. English can also be taken with Chinese Studies (Mandarin).

Edinburgh Students follow courses in either English or Scottish Literature in Years 1 and 2 followed by courses of special interest in Years 3 and 4. English Language covers pronunciation and grammar and examines the historical background to language through Anglo-Saxon English, medieval English, Elizabethan English and older Scots. There are also courses in Linguistics, Mind and Language, English Language and History or Linguistics.

Edinburgh Napier English examines literature in a social and historical context, and can be taken alongside Communication, Film, Publishing and Journalism.

Essex English Language and Linguistics is offered with options in linguistics and the role of language in society. It is possible to switch courses between language and linguistics. There are also degrees in

English Language and Literature, and a BA in Teaching English as a Foreign Language. Several Literature courses are also offered, including Comparative Literature and a course combined with Creative Writing.

Exeter* The English course provides a knowledge of the major texts, literary forms and periods of English literature and allows for considerable specialisation. The basic courses are the Renaissance, Shakespeare, the Restoration and the 18th century, and the 19th and 20th centuries. In Levels 2 and 3, specialisation takes place, with options including creative writing, American literature and postcolonial studies. English can also be taken with study in North America, or with Film Studies.

Falmouth English can be taken with Media Studies or Creative Writing, with modules covering literary and cultural theory and criticism across a range of periods and media. There are also three Writing courses.

Glasgow* The English Language course covers the history of the language from the earliest times to the present day. Phonetics and grammar are included and there are specialist options including dialectology, sociolinguistics and Scots language. The English Literature course concentrates on the Romantic period with optional subjects covering the Renaissance period and European literature in translation in poetry, drama and prose. Scottish Literature is also offered. There are also courses in Comparative Literature which covers literature across cultural and national boundaries.

Gloucestershire English Language and Literature are offered with a range of joint courses. There is also a course in Creative Writing.

Glyndŵr In addition to English degrees with options in history, screen studies, creative writing, broadcasting and journalism, there are special degrees in Writing and Media Communications.

Greenwich English is a broad course that includes Victorian studies, ideas in the modern world, American film and writing, drama in performance and video production. Electives include theatre studies and film studies. English is also offered with Creative Writing (which can be studied as a separate degree or as part of the combined honours course), Media Writing, Modern Languages, Law and Legal Studies. There is also a degree in Linguistics.

Hertfordshire English is offered as part of the Humanities programme in which English Literature and English Language and Communication can be studied as single, joint or combined honours subjects, with options including Acting and Screen Performance, Philosophy and a range of modern foreign languages. Several courses are available in English Language and Teaching, and Creative Writing is offered in the combined honours programme.

Huddersfield The English courses cover language, literature and writing. Optional modules include language or literature, media studies, information technology, desktop publishing, creative writing and a European language. English is also offered with Creative Writing, Journalism and Modern Languages.

Hull A modular course is offered in English Language and Literature that covers modern literature, criticism, medieval language and a subject from another department, with a similar course covering both English and American Literature and Culture. A wide range of specialist options is available, in addition to which there are 15 joint honours programmes. A Creative Writing single honours course and joint courses are also offered with American Studies, English, Philosophy and Theology.

Keele English is taken with a second subject from a choice of 30 subjects including American Studies, Law, Finance and International Relations. The course provides a good general grounding in literary criticism. English and American Literature is offered as a single honours subject. A Creative Writing course is also available.

Kent* The School of English offers a range of subjects. English and American Literature can be taken with a bias towards history, philosophy or politics. There is also a single and joint honours course in Comparative Literary Studies, with Drama, Film Studies or Philosophy, whilst courses in English Language Studies can have options in History, Linguistics, Philosophy or Politics.

See *Heap 2015: University Degree Course Offers* (Trotman Publishing) for details of offers

Kingston The emphasis of the English and American Literature course is on 19th- and 20th-century Anglo-American literature and women's writing; there is also the opportunity to study in Europe and America. The course is offered with specialisms in postcolonial literature or as a joint honours course with a range of subjects. There is also a course in Applied English Language and Linguistics, and Creative Writing is offered as a joint course with several subjects.

Lancaster* Courses in English Language, English Literature and Creative Writing can be taken, together with several joint options, including English Language and the Media, and English Literature and Languages. Some students spend part of the course in a European country or in the US. Single and combined Linguistics courses are also available with study abroad options.

Leeds* A course in English Language and Literature is combined with an extensive range of options covering English, American and Commonwealth literature. Students have a choice from a list of over 70 options in Years 2 and 3. These courses are combined with 'core' courses that involve a study of English from the Middle Ages to the present day. English can also be taken with Theatre Studies. There is also an English Language programme and a degree in Linguistics and Phonetics, and Classical Literature can be studied with a range of languages.

Leeds Beckett Courses are offered as three-year full-time study in English Literature, with theoretical readings of Shakespearean, gothic and postcolonial texts, and in English with History.

Leeds Trinity English is offered as a joint course with Film Studies, History, Journalism, Media and Writing.

Leicester English is a diverse and flexible course with lectures and small-group teaching. A modular course is provided with a chronological approach to the major periods of English literature. Language is part of the curriculum in Years 1 and 2 and there is an optional year in Europe. Optional modules from other departments include Film Studies, Languages and History of Art and there are sever joint honours courses available with English. See also **Combined Courses**.

Lincoln English covers literature and creative writing, and is offered as a joint course with Drama, History and Journalism.

Liverpool The English degree offers work placements in teaching, the media and in other fields. English Language and Literature can be studied from their origins in the Anglo-Saxon period to the modern period, covering all the major literary and linguistic developments. Optional courses are available in the second and third years. There are also seven joint courses with English including Communication Studies, Languages, History and Philosophy.

Liverpool Hope The English degrees enable students to study the foundations of both language and literature. A large number of joint courses with arts, humanities and social sciences subjects are offered.

Liverpool John Moores The English degree offers work placements in teaching, the media and in other fields. There are three-year courses in Creative Writing and English (Literature) with Media and Cultural Studies, History or Drama.

London (Goldsmiths) All aspects of literature are covered in the English degree, including Shakespeare, Gothic literature, the Victorians, Caribbean women writers and the English detective story. English can also be studied with American Literature, History, Drama, Comparative Literature, Creative Writing, Drama or History. A BA (Hons) in Media and Modern Literature is also offered.

London (King's)* English Language and Literature covers a study of language and all the major periods of English literature from Old English to the 20th century. Optional courses in the second and third years allow specialisation in such fields as American literature, creative writing, modern theatre and sociolinguistics. There is also a degree in Comparative Literature spanning nine languages and over 2,500 years, and a degree in English Language and Communication.

London (QM) The English course covers the study of both English language and literature from the earliest periods to the present day, plus a wide range of options. English is also offered with Drama,

European Law, Film, Linguistics, History, a language or Hispanic Studies. Courses are also offered in Comparative Literature and Linguistics with either Language or Literature.

London (RH)* The English course is common to all students for the first two terms, comprising literature, critical ideas, aspects or periods of literature and introductory language courses. This enables students to plan the remainder of their course to suit their own particular interests. Classics, Creative Writing, Drama, Philosophy and European Languages are offered with English.

London (SOAS) Single and combined courses are available in Linguistics.

London (UCL)* After the first-year foundation studies course, students are encouraged to build their own programme. There is an emphasis on one-to-one tutorials. A four-year course in English can be taken with Dutch, French, German or Scandinavian Studies. There is also a course in Linguistics.

London Met English Language Studies is a modular programme offered as a single or a joint degree or a minor subject. Courses in Creative Writing and English Literature are also available. Study abroad options include universities in North America and Japan.

London NCH This course begins with a survey of literature since Homer and an overview of approaches to text. The remaining modules are drawn from a rich optional list ranging from medieval literature through Renaissance and Restoration literature to the Victorians and moderns, and include studies of the novel, Shakespeare, 19th-century and modern American literature, drama, Romanticism, Irish literature, and much more.

London South Bank The English degree covers literature spanning American, Caribbean, African, Canadian and Australian texts as well as those of British origin. Film and detective fiction are included. English can also be taken with Media Studies or Creative Writing.

Loughborough* The English course concentrates on modern English literature starting with the Renaissance although there is an option in medieval literature. It also includes a wide range of subsidiary subjects in the second year including publishing and marketing, politics, languages and art history.

Manchester* There are 19 courses offered involving English Language and Literature. The courses focus on language and the entire range of English literature. A large number of joint courses are offered with American Studies, Drama, Languages, Philosophy and Linguistics. There is also a course in Language, Literacy and Communication.

Manchester Met English includes modules in Romanticism, drama, minority writing and creative writing options, and is available as a single subject degree or with other subjects involving American Literature, Creative Writing or Film. (Subject to approval.)

Middlesex Thirteen English courses are offered covering English Language, English Literature and Creative Writing.

Newcastle* All courses include compulsory and optional modules. The English Literature course offers a traditional angle and a variety of options (including film, American literature, and the Russian novel). English Language and Literature is distinctive and occupies one-third of the student's workload in Year 1, with greater freedom in Year 2 and 3 choices. English Language covers both historical and descriptive approaches and also medieval English literature. Subsidiary subjects, e.g. psychology or computer science, can be taken in the English course. Several courses in Linguistics are also offered, and English can also be taken as part of the Combined Studies in Arts programme.

Newman English covers literature, language, creative writing and film, and is offered as a single, joint or major course with another subject.

Northampton Degrees in English, English Literature, Creative Writing and American Literature and Films are offered as single courses and joint honours.

See *Heap 2015: University Degree Course Offers* (Trotman Publishing) for details of offers

Northumbria The English Language and Literature BA offers a study of the relationship between language and the development of major phases of literature from the medieval to modern periods. English can be studied with Creative Writing, Film Studies, History and Sociology. There is also a Scriptwriting course with Drama.

Nottingham* The English Studies course covers the entire range of English literature from its beginnings to the 20th century and also medieval and modern English language, and includes study of dramatic texts. English Studies can also be taken with, for example, Latin, Philosophy, Theology or Hispanic Studies. A course in English Language and Literature is also offered. There is also a unique course in Viking Studies covering language, literature, history and archaeology.

Nottingham Trent A flexible English course is offered with a free choice of areas of study from traditional English and colonial cultures. Linguistics, Heritage Studies, History and International Relations and Creative Writing can also be studied with English, and there is a wide choice of English and Communication Studies joint courses. A course in Print Journalism is also available. See also **Media Studies**.

Oxford* The course in English Language and Literature covers the whole range of English writing from the beginnings to the present day. The first year covers Old English and Middle English literature and English literature 1832–1960, while the second and third years offer alternatives in a range of periods of literature, Shakespeare, English language, special authors and special topics. There is also a course in English and Modern Languages.

Oxford Brookes English is offered as a study of language and literature with a wide range of specialisations including medieval, modern literature and theatre literature. Combined honours courses are also offered in English. There is also a degree in English and Communication with modules in language, culture, communication, media, psychology and linguistics and an option to study for two semesters in Europe, North America or Australia. Work placements are offered in organisations with literary and cultural connections.

Plymouth English is offered jointly with a range of other subjects including Creative Writing, History and Modern Languages.

Portsmouth A very wide range of courses is offered including English (covering 19th-century to contemporary literature), English and Creative Writing, and English with Media Arts, History and Languages.

Queen's Belfast Literature and Language courses are offered with over 30 specialist modules in Year 3 for the former, including Theology, Philosophy and Irish. Major, joint and minor courses are available. A course in Linguistics is also available.

Reading Several individual units are taken in the English Language and Literature course, four of which are compulsory core subjects covering literature from the Elizabethan period to the mid-19th century. The remaining five courses are chosen from a long list of humanities and languages options. Other courses include English and Classical Studies. See also **European Studies**.

Roehampton English Language and Linguistics, English Literature and Creative Writing can be studied in joint degrees with another subject from a wide choice. There is also a course in TESOL (Teaching English to Speakers of Other Languages).

St Andrews* The single honours English degree offers several specialist topics, which include creative writing and speech writing. There are also 24 courses combining English with a second subject including Management, Psychology and Modern Languages. There is also a programme of English Language Teaching.

St Mark and St John Separate courses are offered in English Language and Literature, Language and Linguistics and Creative Writing.

Salford English Literature with English Language offers a study of both language and literature with an emphasis on modern (post-1750) literature and its connections with society, which is central to the degree. Courses are also offered with Journalism, Cultural Studies, Drama and Creative Writing.

Sheffield* English Literature and Language are offered as a dual honours with nine other subjects, including Modern Languages, Management and Music.

Sheffield Hallam The English Studies course covers literary studies (16th–19th centuries), linguistics and creative writing skills, English and American fiction, biography and autobiography and teaching English as a foreign language. A Creative Writing course is also offered.

South Wales The English course covers language, literature and creative writing with options in language and society, women's writing and the writing media. There are separate courses in English Literature, and English and Creative Writing. A course in Creative and Professional Writing offers modules covering various genres and formats as well as print journalism and radio production.

Southampton* The English degree introduces the major genres of English literature, after which students form their own course by choosing topics out of the whole range of English literature, from the medieval period to the present day. During the first year, English language and an additional subject may be taken from another department. English with Modern Languages and with History, Music or Philosophy are also offered.

Southampton Solent English Literature and English Language are studied on a 50/50 basis in joint courses with Journalism, Screenwriting and Writing Popular Fiction, and Writing, Fashion and Culture, which introduces students to the broad field of magazine journalism. Industry placements relating to both chosen subject areas are available.

Staffordshire There is a degree in English Language, Literature and Culture. Creative Writing and Scriptwriting courses are offered.

Stirling A study of the novel, drama and poetry occupies the first three semesters of the English Studies course. Thereafter, in the next three semesters, studies focus on the literary tradition, critical theory, language and literature, Renaissance drama and the 19th-century novel. During this time, and in the final year, a range of 18 options allows students to choose their own specialist areas to study, including creative writing and poetry writing. A degree in English Studies and Scottish Literature is also offered.

Strathclyde Single and joint courses are offered in English. There is also a Journalism and Creative Writing course which can be taken as a second subject.

Sunderland In the English single honours course a range of topics is on offer including 20th-century literature and poetry, and American literature. English can also be taken with Creative Writing, Practical Drama, Film or Literature.

Surrey* Several degree courses are offered in English Literature, including a four-year course with professional training, and can be combined with Creative Writing, French, Spanish, Dance and Theatre.

Sussex* The English Language programme is one of considerable breadth and presents the subject in terms of intellectual, moral, religious, political, social and aesthetic contexts. The first term introduces the range of approaches to the study of English in addition to giving the student a choice of options. English Literature is offered with English. English is also offered with Drama and Languages and in English Language Teaching.

Swansea In the English Literature syllabus, tragic drama, lyric poetry, theories and monsters (Dracula and Frankenstein) are studied in Part I. For single honours during Years 2 and 3 there are two core courses – literature from Chaucer to the present day and criticism – plus a choice of options. English with Gender covers the representation of gender in literary culture. English Language is also offered in a wide range of joint courses including with Welsh, Politics, European Languages and Geography. Language Studies courses are offered with subjects such as Latin, Ancient History and Italian.

Teesside Core modules in the English Studies course introduce English prose and poetry and creative writing. In the second and third years students construct their own programme, which includes historical periods, women's writing, drama and children's literature. English can also be taken with Creative Writing, Media or History.

Trinity St David The single honours English degree offers a wide range of courses from the Renaissance to Contemporary Writing. A wide range of English joint courses are offered, including with Medieval Studies, Chinese Studies and Anthropology. Courses in Creative Writing can also be taken.

Ulster English is offered as a single honours course and as minor and major subjects in combination with 25 other subjects.

Warwick* Degrees include English and European Literature, English and American Literature, and English and Creative Writing (which covers poetry and writing for the theatre and film, as well as an introduction to journalism). Students take the same modules in Year 1 before specialising. There are also several joint degrees including Theatre Studies, a range of European languages and Creative Writing with English.

Westminster Joint degrees with English are offered in Creative Writing (also offered with Linguistics), Modern History, International Relations and Politics.

Winchester This is a wide-ranging programme covering old and new literature, creative writing and critical analysis. Courses are also offered in English Literature and English Language and also English with American Literature. A degree course in Creative Writing is also offered involving fiction, poetry, short stories, screenplays, features and film-writing, and a Journalism degree is available.

Wolverhampton English can be taken in specialist, joint, major or minor programmes of study. The course covers Shakespeare, the novel, journalism and American literature. Degree courses in Linguistics and English, Creative and Professional Writing and English as a Foreign Language are also offered. There is also a course in British Sign Language, and Deaf Studies can be taken with English.

Worcester Single and joint courses are offered in English and Literary Studies.

York* English can be studied as a single subject or in combination with seven other subjects, including History of Art, Philosophy and Politics. Single subject students must take at least one course involving the study of literature in a foreign language. All students follow the preliminary course for one term before choosing their subject or subjects. Courses are examined by continuous assessment. A work placement module is offered.

OTHER INSTITUTIONS OFFERING ENGLISH COURSES
Blackburn (Coll), Blackpool and Fylde (Coll), Burton (Coll), Doncaster (Coll Univ Centre), Falmouth, Grimsby (Univ Centre), Havering (Coll), North Lindsey (Coll), Norwich City (Coll), Peterborough (Reg Coll), Suffolk (Univ Campus), West Anglia (Coll), Wigan and Leigh (Coll).

ALTERNATIVE COURSES
Combined Arts, Drama, Information Management/Sciences, Journalism.

ENVIRONMENTAL SCIENCE/STUDIES
(including **Ecology**)
(* indicates universities with entry requirements over 340 UCAS points)

SUBJECT REQUIREMENTS/PREFERENCES
GCE A level: Sciences, Biology and Chemistry usually preferred. Geography may be required. **GCSE:** English, Mathematics and a science (often Chemistry) usually required.

See *Heap 2015: University Degree Course Offers* (Trotman Publishing) for details of offers

SUBJECT INFORMATION

Environmental Science can cover a range of subjects with options to specialise that may include biology, geography, geology, oceanography or chemistry. Environmental Science/Studies could also involve town and country planning or environmental health options, thus leading to two quite different careers. Environmental Health courses usually lead to qualifications as an environmental health officer.

Aberdeen The course in Environmental Science covers animal and plant biology, ecology, chemistry, geography and geology in the early years with a strong/chemistry/biology element in Year 2. Aberdeen is also ideally situated for a study of marine environments and has a Marine Resource Management course.

Aberystwyth Part I of the Environmental Bioscience course covers physical and biological processes and support studies involving environmental chemistry and biology. These studies are extended in Year 2 with field modules covering mid-Wales, the Low Countries and the Rhine delta. Optional modules in Year 3 include freshwater biology, soil science and ecology. There is a degree course in Environmental Earth Science, covering aspects of geology and oceanography.

Bangor Access to the coastlines, forests and mountains of the Snowdonia National Park provides ideal opportunities for those following one of the eight courses covering environmental sciences, including a four-year Environmental Science MEnvSci, ocean sciences management, conservation, and marine ecology. Studying in Canada or Finland in Year 2 may also be part of the Forestry degree, whilst the four-year course includes work placement in industry.

Bath Spa Geographical and biological issues are covered in the very flexible Environmental Science degree, which includes a work placement and field investigation in Year 2.

Birmingham Specialisation in four pathways (applied ecology, water in the environment, atmospheric processes and earth surface processes) follows a broad first-year Environmental Science course. Professional placements or a study year in Australia are offered. There are also courses in Environmental Management and Environmental Geoscience.

Bournemouth An Environmental Science course is offered with options in river/water/waste management, health and industrial safety and coastal protection. The Heritage Conservation course with professional placements focuses on architectural heritage, landscapes, education services and tourism. Courses are also available in Environment and Coastal Management and Environment Conservation Biology, Heritage Conservation and Tourism, and Ecology and Wildlife Conservation.

Bradford Environmental Science is offered as a three-year full-time or four-year sandwich course. There is also a course in Geography and Environmental Management.

Brighton The Environmental Sciences course involves a study of the human and physical environment, ecology, energy and pollution. There are also degrees in Environmental Hazards, covering geography, health, pollution and human hazards, and Earth and Ocean Science, Environmental Biology and Ecology and Biogeography. A course in Environment and Media Studies is also available.

Bristol See under **Geology/Geological Sciences**.

Bristol UWE The Environmental Science course has special options that cover ecology, toxicology, environmental biotechnology, pollution and waste management. An optional placement year is included. There is an Environmental Health course leading to professional qualification as an environmental health officer.

Cambridge* Ecology can be studied in the Natural Sciences Tripos. The Land Economy course covers the Environment, Law and Economics. See also **Property Management and Surveying**.

Canterbury Christ Church The Environmental Science course covers the biological, chemical and physical aspects of the environment. A four-year course with a foundation year is available. There are also courses in Ecology and Conservation and in Environmental Biology. (High research ratings.)

Cardiff A course in Ecology and Environmental Management follows a common first year covering seven biological sciences. There is also a course in Environmental Geoscience, available as a four-year sandwich course.

Cardiff Met (UWIC) The professional course in Environmental Health covers food safety, housing, health and safety and environmental protection.

Central Lancashire The Environmental Management courses cover geography, ecology, law, chemistry and planning. Scientific emphasis is provided in the three-year Environmental Science degree. There are also courses in Ecology and Environmental Hazards and Management.

Chester A combined honours course in Natural Hazard Management focuses on geography, geology and people.

Coventry The Environmental Health course is available as a BAS or BSc and covers food, health and safety and leads to professional status as an environmental health officer.

Derby There is a course in Environmental Hazards offered by the Geology Department, covering geographical and earth sciences with field studies in volcanology in Tenerife and earthquake studies on the San Andreas fault in California.

Dundee The first year of the Environmental Science course covers global environmental processes, geography, geology and natural environmental systems. Second-year topics include ecosystems and resource monitoring and management while the third-year themes cover environmental geoscience, remote sensing and resource management. The course is also offered with Geography. Courses in Environmental Management and Renewable Energy are also offered.

Durham A course is offered in Environmental Geoscience, with a choice of elective modules in each year, as well as courses in Earth Sciences and Natural Sciences.

East Anglia* An extensive range of courses and fieldwork opportunities are offered including Meteorology and Oceanography along with Environmental Sciences, Environmental Chemistry, Earth Sciences and Ecology, with the opportunity to study in Europe, Australasia or North America or to work in industry.

Edge Hill Environmental Science is a comprehensive course involving fieldwork in the UK and Mallorca and optional visits to Europe and the Far East. A careers guidance module forms part of Year 3. There is also a degree in Ecology.

Edinburgh Ecological Science is divided into four degree programmes covering Conservation and Management, Ecology, Environmental Science and Forestry. It is possible to change degree programmes up until the end of the third year. Environmental Studies can also be studied alongside Economic and Social History. There are also courses in Ecology and Ecology with Environmental Science.

Edinburgh Napier A BSc ordinary and honours course is available in Environmental Biology.

Essex The course in Environment, Lifestyle and Health focuses on human disease, public health, conservation and environmental issues. There are also degrees in Ecology, including a year abroad, and in Biodiversity and Conservation.

Glasgow Courses are offered in Environmental Chemistry (reclamation, pollution, pesticides), Environmental Biogeochemistry (interactions of water in different environments) and Earth Science. The Environmental Stewardship degree covers renewable energy sources and applied ecology and conservation. A degree in Environmental Stewardship is offered at the Crichton campus in Dumfries.

Glasgow Caledonian In Year 3 of the Environmental Management course, students undertake a six-month placement. Specialist modules include waste management, water quality and urban regeneration. A course in Environmental Civil Engineering is also available.

See *Heap 2015: University Degree Course Offers* (Trotman Publishing) for details of offers

Gloucestershire Ecology and Environmental Science can be studied with a work placement. There is also a course in Water Resource Management.

Glyndŵr Fieldwork, IT skills and a study of GIS are included in the Environmental Science degree. Tutorial support is available through the medium of Welsh.

Greenwich The Environmental Science course offers three options from a choice of 12 in Year 3, including geological and scientific topics, and planning and landscape issues. A sandwich placement year is optional. There is also a course in Ecology.

Harper Adams Degrees include Agricultural and Countryside Environmental Management.

Heriot-Watt The Environmental Management and Planning course is a multidisciplinary programme with modules in coastal biology and offshore technology, and can be taken with other science subjects such as Physics.

Hertfordshire Environmental Studies covers biological, physical and social aspects. In Year 2, environmental planning, landscape development and pollution issues are covered. Supervised work experience takes place in Year 3. There is also a course in Environmental Management which can include study abroad. Environmental Studies can also be taken with Business, Communication, Geography, Human Biology and Sport Studies.

Hull The course in Environmental Science covers biology, geography and anthropology, and offers overseas study in the Caribbean, Egypt and the Mediterranean. There is also a degree in Ecology.

Imperial London* A course is offered in Environmental Geoscience. The course, which is part of the Geology programme, leads to the associateship of the Royal School of Mines. A two-week field trip to Spain is included.

Keele The Applied Environmental Science dual honours course covers biology, geology and chemistry and is taken with Physical Geography. Over 20 dual honours combinations are possible. An optional field trip to the European Alps is offered in Year 2.

Kent The course in Environmental Studies covers anthropology, economics, law, social policy and sociology. There is also a course in Wildlife Management involving modules in biodiversity, climate change, species conservation and human and wildlife conflict.

Kingston Pathways in Environmental Science include ecology, conservation and resource management. Options include languages, business and human geography. Environmental Studies is offered with a range of subjects including Business Management. There are also degree courses in Environmental Studies and Environmental Hazards and Disaster Management. Industrial placements are offered.

Lancaster The Environmental Science Department is a major centre in this subject field. Specialisation is introduced in the final year when a choice is made between aquatics and atmospheric systems, applied earth science or environmental assessment and management. Final-year topics include pollution, water resources management, earth science and geophysics. Study abroad options are available. Degrees in Ecology, Earth and Environmental Science and Environmental Biology or Chemistry are also offered.

Leeds Environmental courses are offered with variations in Business, Ecology, Energy Science, Conservation, Management and Sustainability. An Environmental MEnv with a year abroad or industrial placement is available.

Leeds Beckett The Environmental Health course involves five study areas, comprising environmental science, technology, management, the environment, methodology and practice. Topics include occupational health, food safety control and public health. Year 3 is spent in practical experience. The course leads to qualification as an environmental health officer. Courses in Environmental Science are also available, with an industrial placement option, and a year abroad offered on the MEnv.

See *Heap 2015: University Degree Course Offers* (Trotman Publishing) for details of offers

Leicester See under **Geology/Geological Sciences**.

Liverpool The Environmental Science degree offers options in Climate Study, Oceans and Maritime Studies. The course in Ecology and Environment has a main focus on Ecology.

Liverpool Hope The Environmental Science BSc includes studies in urban regeneration, glacial geomorphology and coastal management, and Environmental Management is offered as part of a combined honours (BA/BSc) programme. Popular combinations include Geography, Sport Studies and Sport Development.

Liverpool John Moores The accredited Environmental Health degree covers issues in society, housing and food safety. There is also a Wildlife Conservation degree.

London (QM) Environmental Science is an interdisciplinary course offered by the Departments of Geography and Biology that studies the natural environment, covering physical geography, geology, environmental biology and chemistry. There is some emphasis on marine aspects, for example oceanic, river and coastal environments, and marine biology. Specialisms include conservation, ecology management, chemistry and environmental quality. Overseas fieldwork destinations include Los Angeles, Iceland and Florida. A course can also be taken with Business Management.

London (RH) Courses are offered in Ecology and the Environment, Human and Physical Geography, Environmental Geology and Geography with Environmental Archaeology.

London (UCL)* Courses are offered in Environmental Geography, Environmental Biology and Environmental Geoscience, with three-year BSc and four-year MSci programmes available.

London LSE The Environmental Policy course covers the natural environment, geography, economics and sociology. A second subject can be studied in Year 1. Final-year options include management, transport, urban planning or geography. The Geography and Environment course allows specialisation in physical or human geography. There is also a course in Environmental Policy focusing on Economics.

Manchester The Environmental Science degree programme enables students to specialise in their particular fields of interest within biology, earth sciences, chemistry or biology. The course in Environmental Studies offers similar topics but deals more with the relationship between humans and their environment. A four-year MEarthSci in Earth Sciences is available.

Manchester Met The Environmental Health course leads to a career as an environmental health officer. The Climate Change degree covers geomorphological changes and issues in consumption and sustainability. Courses are also available in Environmental Management and Environmental Protection, together with Environmental Studies and Ecology and Conservation. All courses provide the option to study in North America or Australia.

Middlesex Courses are offered in Environmental Health, covering food safety, housing, flood control and health and safety.

Newcastle The Environmental Science course covers management, ecology, tropical environments and biological conservation. An optional work placement is offered. Courses are also offered in Countryside Management and Rural Studies.

Northampton A BSc course is available in Environmental Science with separate pathways in Climate Change, Landscape Ecology and Wastes Management. A course in Applied Conservation Biology is also available.

Northumbria The Environmental Management degree is accredited by the Chartered Institute of Environmental Health (CIEH) and focuses on the sustainability of natural and human systems, e.g. wildlife, landscapes or industry. The Environmental Health degree leads to careers in food science and public health.

Nottingham Degrees are offered in Environmental Biology and Environmental Science (available as a BSc or four-year MSci), focusing on the management of ecosystems. A wide range of options is offered in Year 3.

Nottingham Trent Courses include Environmental Biology, Environmental Health, and Environmental Science with Business, Environmental Conservation or Countryside Management. Environmental courses cover ecology, conservation, countryside management and business.

Oxford Brookes Environmental Sciences can be taken as a BA or BSc degree. The subject is offered by the Department of Biological and Medical Sciences.

Plymouth The Environmental Science and Policy degree course includes a study of environmental biology, chemistry, geology and the human environment, environmental management, food and water resources, pollution and land reclamation. Pathways are offered in community and environment or environmental science. There are also courses in Wildlife Conservation and several courses focusing on Marine Studies including pathways in merchant shipping, navigation and ocean exploration.

Portsmouth The Environmental Science course is a blend of biology, chemistry, physics, geology and conservation. There is also a course in Marine Environmental Science with industrial placements, and courses in Environmental Biology, Environmental Hazards, Environmental Forensic Science and Environmental Health. Courses carry accreditation from the Institution of Environmental Sciences (IES).

Queen's Belfast For Land Use and Environmental Management, see under **Agricultural Sciences/ Agriculture**. Environmental Biology is offered from Stage 0, and after Stage 1 students may transfer to pathways leading to degrees in Biological Sciences, Plant Science Genetics, Marine Biology or Zoology. See also **Town Planning and Urban Planning Studies**.

Reading Environmental courses follow different themes. Part I prepares all students with a basic core of subjects and thereafter specialisms follow. Programmes offered cover biology, chemistry, earth science, geology or earth and atmosphere. Courses include Environmental and Countryside Management, Environmental Science or Forensics, and Applied Ecology and Conservation.

St Andrews* A four-year course in Environmental Biology and Geography is offered. There is also a single honours course in Sustainable Development, covering ecological, social, economic and environmental issues, and a Marine Biology course.

Salford The Environmental Studies foundation year aims to provide an understanding of environmental problems and professional practice. This leads on to courses in Environmental Health, Environmental Management, Geography and Wildlife.

Sheffield* The first year of the Environmental Science course covers geography, geology, environmental biology and ecology. A more specialised treatment of the subject follows in the second year while in the third year specialist areas include global change, hydrology and biology in the environment. There are also courses in Human and Physical Geography and Environmental Mathematics.

Sheffield Hallam Environmental Management is a four-year sandwich course with a European language option. The course involves environmental quality engineering, landscape management and water engineering. A residential trip to Croatia is offered. Other courses cover Environmental Studies and Environmental Conservation.

Southampton* Environmental Sciences is an interdisciplinary course comprising options from biology, geography, geology, chemistry and oceanography. Students have the opportunity to design their courses in groups of units. The groups cover the physical and the biological environments, chemistry and human

See *Heap 2015: University Degree Course Offers* (Trotman Publishing) for details of offers

sciences within the environment and water in the environment, hydrology and hydrobiology. There are also courses in Environmental Engineering.

Southampton Solent Environmental Studies is offered with options in Tourism, Geography and Media Communications. Courses are also available in Coastal Conservation or Marine Environmental Science.

Staffordshire The degree in Environment and Sustainability has a vocational emphasis with work placement opportunities.

Stirling Environmental Science focuses attention on the surface and near-surface environments of the earth. Final-year options include environmental hazards, remote sensing, pollution, rivers and tropical environments. Several joint courses are also offered. There is also a course in Environmental Science and Outdoor Education. The Primary Education course has an environmental pathway.

Sussex The Environmental Science course establishes the link between chemistry, biology and geography. The emphasis is on scientific investigation, although social and economic aspects are also considered. A field trip to Portugal is available. Ecology and Conservation is also offered.

Swansea Environmental Biology can be taken as part of the Biological Sciences group of subjects. A course in Marine Biology is also available.

Trinity St David (Swansea) The Environmental Conservation courses can be taken focusing on scientific, legal, political and social aspects. Specialisation follows in BSc routes after a common first year.

Ulster After a common first year for all Environmental Science students aiming for the ordinary and the honours degrees, Years 2 and 3 offer a choice between a study of geological aspects including natural resources and society's exploitation of them, and a course with a geographical emphasis. There are also courses in Environmental Health and over 20 joint courses in Environmental Science.

West Scotland Environmental Science is offered with Applied Bioscience. The course covers biochemistry and biotechnology and can be taken with a year's industrial placement. A degree in Environmental Health is also offered.

Wolverhampton The CIEH-accredited course in Environmental Health provides training as an environmental health officer. There is an optional year's placement. There is also a degree in Environmental Science and Management.

Worcester There is a degree in Water and Environmental Management, which focuses on the rural environment and is available with Leadership.

York Courses are offered in Environmental Science, Environmental Geography and Environment, Economics and Ecology, with specialisations taking place in Year 2.

OTHER INSTITUTIONS OFFERING ENVIRONMENTAL SCIENCE/STUDIES COURSES
Blackpool and Fylde (Coll), Cornwall (Coll), Farnborough (CT), Pembrokeshire (Coll), SRUC, UHI, Warwickshire (Coll), Writtle (Coll).

ALTERNATIVE COURSES
Agricultural Sciences, Agriculture, Applied Natural Sciences, Biological Sciences, Countryside Management, Earth Resources, Estate Management, Forest Resources, Garden Design, Geography, Geology, Landscape Architecture, Maritime Environmental Management, Meteorology, Ocean Sciences, Soil Science, Underwater Studies.

EUROPEAN STUDIES

(* indicates universities with entry requirements over 340 UCAS points)

SUBJECT REQUIREMENTS/PREFERENCES

GCE A level: Two or three appropriate languages. **GCSE:** English for all courses and possibly Mathematics.

SUBJECT INFORMATION

European Studies is an increasingly popular subject and offers the language student the opportunity to study modern languages within the context of a European country (for example economic, political, legal, social and cultural aspects). On these courses there is usually a strong emphasis placed on the written and spoken word. There are also European Business Studies courses available.

Aberdeen First-year European Studies students follow courses in modern and contemporary European history, comparative European politics and two languages from Gaelic, French, German and Spanish, as well as elective subjects including economics, history and law. Language study continues over three years. The third year is spent abroad. Courses in European Management Studies, European Languages, 20th-century Culture and European Cultural Studies are also offered.

Aston The four-year European Studies programme is a joint or combined honours course offering a choice between French or German and topics covering the history and development of the European Union, European law, current affairs and international relations. European Studies is also offered with Business Administration, Public Policy and Management, and Sociology. There is a one-year placement year following Year 2.

Bath See under **Languages**.

Birmingham A course in European Politics, Society and Economics provides a broad study of European development. A course in Russian Studies with Central East European Studies is offered, with options to spend Year 3 in Moscow, St Petersburg and Petrozavodsk.

Cardiff European Union Studies offers an integrated four-year programme in which students choose one or two modern European languages (from French, German, Italian or Spanish with an option in Catalan) in the context of the contemporary political, economic, legal and social structure of Western Europe. Emphasis is placed on the practical (non-literary) aspects of language. The third year is spent in study abroad. A Cardiff-Bordeaux joint diploma degree in Politics is split between the UK and France.

Central Lancashire Courses in International Business Studies and International Business Communication (with a modern foreign language) are offered.

Coventry European Law is offered with French, German, Italian, Russian and Spanish. A BEng in European Engineering Studies is also offered.

Dundee During the first two years of the European Studies course, students normally take at least two courses from French, German and Spanish. A two-year honours course in French, German or Spanish is compulsory for single honours students. In the third and fourth years five courses on Europe are chosen from a wide range of subjects. The whole or part of Year 3 may be spent in France, Germany or Spain through an Erasmus exchange scheme.

East Anglia The European Studies programme is one of the most flexible on offer, starting with a foundation year and progressing to a wide range of options including languages and exchanges with European universities. International Relations is available with European Politics or Modern History, and the Culture, Literature and Politics degree covers European media and the EU.

THINK PSYCHOLOGY
THINK BANGOR

PRIFYSGOL
BANGOR
UNIVERSITY

There are lots of reasons why we think you should consider studying Psychology with us. Here are just a few:

- Regularly ranked in the top 5 for **'Student Satisfaction'** in the NSS

- Ranked 7th in UK for **'Research Power'** based on the most recent RAE

- Bangor Psychology is ranked 16th by **THE TIMES** 2014 Good University Guide

- Last Year over **70%** of students graduated with a 1st or 2:1

- Bangor Psychology provides students with an excellent mix of transferable skills and **employability** courses giving access to a varied range of professions

- A compact **friendly city** dominated by over 11,000 students and in a stunning location

- **Easy to reach:** 20 minutes from the Holyhead ferry terminal, about 90 minutes from Liverpool & Manchester and around 3 hours on the train from London

Student Views

"The staff and lecturers are absolutely outstanding, helpful, dedicated, passionate and always friendly."

"The lecturers are easy and friendly to talk to, attention is paid to me as an individual and I have always had advice when I needed it."

"It has prepared me for the work in skills as well as information, which is great for me as I am not planning on being a psychologist when I graduate."

Contact us for more information:

School of Psychology, Bangor University, Gwynedd LL57 2AS
t. +44(0)1248 382629 **e.** psychology@bangor.ac.uk

 @PsychBangor

SEICOLEG
BANGOR
PSYCHOLOGY

www.bangor.ac.uk/psychology

PRIFYSGOL
BANGOR
UNIVERSITY

College of Health and Behavioural Sciences

"The School of Psychology at Bangor is producing some of the best quality psychology graduates in the UK". – External Examiners Report

Bangor has an unusual combination of qualities, which make our department uniquely well positioned to offer undergraduates an exceptional learning experience and a degree which carries with it the reputation of an exceptional department.

What makes Bangor Unique?

- One of only 5 departments in the UK to be ranked in the top 20 by The Times 2014 League table for Student Satisfaction, Research Quality and Graduate Prospects
- Established in 1963 Bangor Psychology is one of the oldest and largest in the UK with over 1100 students
- Our world-class research focused academics are involved in undergraduate teaching, which is lead by a research active Teaching Team who focus on delivering the undergraduate programmes. This dual emphasis provides students with a skill set that is second to none and a degree which carries with it our worldwide research reputation
- We have developed sophisticated systems that ensure our students achieve their full potential in a department that combines excellence with accessibility.
- We have a large number of laboratories including a research dedicated 3T fMRI scanner.

Psychology gives students an excellent mix of key skills and access to a varied range of professions, flexibility which is very valuable in today's economic climate and Bangor University, with the School of Psychology in the vanguard, has been at the forefront of the drive to embed employability into academically rigorous degrees.

Entry Requirements

Our normal offers are in the range of 340-280 points. General Studies/Key Skills are not accepted and applicants are strongly preferred to have at least 1 relevant science A level (Maths, Biology, Human Biology, Physics, Chemistry, Statistics, Psychology, Science) GCSE Maths & English are required. Applications from those with other qualifications are welcomed.

Undergraduate Courses

BSc Psychology
BSc Psychology with Clinical & Health
BSc Psychology with Neuropsychology
BSc Psychology with Child & Language Development
BSc Psychology and Business*

What's Bangor Like?

Bangor is situated on the north Wales coast between the mountains of Snowdonia and the sea, making it one of the most attractive university towns in the UK. Bangor has a reputation as a multi-cultural, multi-lingual, safe and friendly city, which hosts over 11,000 students drawn from across the globe.

If you require any further information, please do not hesitate to contact us.

*subject to validation

Contact us for more information:
School of Psychology, Bangor University, Gwynedd LL57 2AS t. +44(0)1248 382629
e. psychology@bangor.ac.uk   @PsychBangor   www.bangor.ac.uk/psychology

Essex European Studies is offered with a range of subjects including French, German, Italian, Spanish, (one or two languages can be studied), Politics and Economics. Beginners' courses are possible and it is possible to transfer between courses.

Glasgow* A course in Central and East European Studies covers Russia, Poland, Hungary, Czech Republic, Bulgaria and Romania and deals with the geography and the social, political and cultural development of the areas. Fields trips are offered. There is also a general humanities course in European Civilisation.

Hertfordshire The European Studies programme offers courses with 12 other subjects such as Business, Health Studies, Biology, Geography, Law, Sport Studies and Tourism.

Kent A range of degrees in European Studies is available, covering politics, history and culture and including specialisations in French, German, Italian, Spanish and combined languages.

Lancaster The European Studies four-year degree scheme enables students to aim for a high proficiency in two European languages (from French, German, Italian or Spanish), of which one can be taken from beginners' level. Joint courses are available with subjects including Computing, Mathematics and Music. Topics cover European ideas, regions, cinema and society. There is also a course in European Languages and Management Studies.

Lincoln European Business Studies, European Marketing and European Tourism are offered.

Liverpool John Moores Three-year courses in European Studies are offered in which a European language is taken with a study covering the history, politics, geography and economics of contemporary Europe. A four-year European Studies course includes a year in France, Germany, Italy or Spain. The International Journalism course covers European law and ethics and offers overseas study.

London (King's)* The four-year European Studies humanities course has a focus on politics, history and the culture of modern Europe with French, German or Spanish pathways.

London (QM) The course unit system enables European Studies students to select courses in French, German, Russian or Hispanic studies, combined with at least two courses in linguistics and/or literature, and a wide choice of other subjects such as law, politics or mathematics. A year abroad is normally undertaken.

London (RH) European Studies courses are offered with French, German, Italian and Spanish. Year 3 is spent in the relevant country. The final year consists of core courses in social sciences, international relations and a language.

London (UCL)* European Social and Political Studies is a four-year degree that combines the study of one or two European languages (from Dutch, French, German, Italian, Russian, Scandinavian languages and Spanish) with a chosen humanities or social science specialisation, e.g. Anthropology, Economics, Geography, History, Law, Philosophy or Politics. The third year is spent abroad. Degree courses are also offered in Slavonic and East European Studies with Bulgarian, Czech, Slovak, Finnish, Hungarian, Polish, Romanian, Serbian and Ukrainian, or with courses in East European history, culture and social sciences.

London Met European Studies is offered as a joint honours course studied with subjects such as Economics, History, Law, Politics or Spanish. Courses are also available in International Relations, International Development, European Business Studies and European Banking and Finance.

London South Bank The European Policy Studies degree covers European and British history and politics, European issues and international relations. French, German or Spanish language units are also available.

Loughborough European and International Studies is a three-year course combining social sciences with fluency in one or more European languages (French, German and Spanish). International Relations can be studied with History.

Manchester European Studies and Modern Languages covers French, German, Italian, Russian and Spanish, with one major language being studied and one at subsidiary level, plus the government and politics of Western Europe. Russian Studies is offered with subjects including History, Film and Media Studies.

Manchester Met European Studies is offered as a joint course with several other subjects including Business Mathematics, Computing Science, Multimedia Technology, Languages and Communications.

Newcastle Government and European Union Studies is offered as a four-year course, including options in the study of Italian and Russian politics. European Studies can also be studied with Chemistry with French, German or Spanish specialisation.

Nottingham The Modern European Studies course is a four-year course with the third year being spent abroad. Taught jointly by the Departments of History and Modern Languages, it is designed to enable students to study aspects of modern European history, the contemporary societies and institutions in Eastern and Western Europe and at least two European languages. A degree in International Studies can also be taken with Spanish, German, French, Chinese or Japanese.

Nottingham Trent There are several European Studies courses with a study of a language from beginners', intermediate or advanced level. Joint courses include History, International Relations or Politics.

Portsmouth European Studies is a three-year course covering European history, culture and a specialist knowledge in chosen aspects of EU policy of a particular European country. Language study is optional. European Studies can be taken with International Relations, Law or Languages. An Applied Languages course is also offered.

Queen's Belfast The European Studies course involves the study of one European language (French, German or Spanish). The course covers history and politics with language fluency, with a placement in Europe between Years 2 and 3. A course in International Politics and Conflict Studies is also offered, and can be taken with Spanish.

Reading In the European Studies degree one or two languages are taken from French, German and Italian, with minor studies offered in Spanish, Dutch, Swedish or Greek. Specialisms follow in language and culture, politics, history, economic and social studies. There is also a course in European Cultures and History.

Southampton* The Contemporary Europe degree comprises a study of the history and politics of Europe and European Union institutions, with options in economics, history, law or politics. Two European languages are studied from French, German and Spanish. Portuguese is also offered as a minor language. International Relations and Modern History with Politics are also available.

Sussex There are degrees in International Relations and Contemporary European Studies. The latter can be taken as a joint degree or as a minor subject. International Development is also available.

Ulster European Studies can be taken as a Combined Arts course combined with over 25 other subjects. The course covers Western and Eastern Europe.

ALTERNATIVE COURSES

European Business Studies, European Languages, History, International Studies/Relations, Sociology.

FILM, RADIO, VIDEO AND TV STUDIES

(* indicates universities with entry requirements over 340 UCAS points)

SUBJECT REQUIREMENTS/PREFERENCES
GCE A level: English, Media Studies. History may be required. **GCSE:** English usually required. Courses vary, so check prospectuses.

SUBJECT INFORMATION
Many of these courses are mainly theoretical and historical in approach, but they may involve practical studies, the media in general and video work.

QUESTIONS TO CONSIDER
* Am I looking to gain practical experience of creating my own work, or am I more interested in theoretical and critical study?
* Which technical skills do I want to learn about – camera work, sound, editing, scriptwriting?
* I have a keen interest in world cinema; can I study a language with the course?

Aberdeen There is a course in Film and Visual Culture exploring all aspects of this art form in the 20th century, available as a joint degree with a range of humanities and languages subjects. This is not a practical film-making course.

Aberystwyth Film and TV Studies is a degree scheme covering aspects of history and analysis. Practical work in video production, scripting and editing is also included with the added advantage of access to the National Screen and Sound Archive of Wales.

Anglia Ruskin Film Studies is a popular course with options including practical work with camcorder, video documentary and internet communications. Optional language programmes are available. Other courses include Film and TV Production and Film and Media.

Bath Spa The course in Film and Screen Studies covers theory and practice and some practical and creative film-making.

Birmingham City Film Production Technology and Production are offered as three-year full-time, four-year sandwich or five-year sandwich courses with a foundation year. A course in Film Technology and Special Effects is also available.

Bolton The Film and Media course covers a wide range of topics relating to the cinema and the use of film in the media. A specialist BSc in Film Production for the Advertising and Music Industries is offered.

Bournemouth A BA (Hons) in Film Production and Cinematography is delivered at the Wiltshire (Salisbury) campus. The courses cover advertisements, videos, drama and documentaries.

Bournemouth Arts There is a practical degree course in Film Production.

Bradford Film studies is a largely theoretical course, with 20% of the time spent on practical work. Courses are also offered in Television Production, or Media Studies with Cinematics or Television.

Bristol See under **Drama**.

Bristol UWE The single honours courses in Film Studies provide special studies in the field of documentary films, Hollywood and world cinema. Joint courses are available with Media Studies, Drama and English. There are also courses in Film-making and Creative Media and Screen-writing.

See *Heap 2015: University Degree Course Offers* (Trotman Publishing) for details of offers

Brunel Single and joint honours courses are offered in Film and Television Studies, covering history, theory and practice in both video and still photography. Work placements are optional. A degree in English and Film and TV Studies is also available.

Bucks New The Film and TV Production course covers camera work, lighting, sound and editing. A creative production-based course is also offered in Digital Film Art. There is also a scriptwriting course, and a course in Performing Arts (Film, TV and Stage).

Canterbury Christ Church The course in Film, Radio and Television Studies offers the opportunity to develop and practise production skills in each of the three media, additional pathways in broadcasting and animation.

Central Lancashire Single and joint honours courses are offered in Film and Media and involve the mass media, television, the press, cinema, advertising and photography. A short work placement is optional. Other courses cover Film Production and Screenwriting.

Chester Film Studies is a combined honours degree. A single honours degree is being validated.

Chichester There are courses in Digital Film Production and Film and TV. Both have a strong practical element and are ideal for intending film-makers and creative writers.

Creative Arts Courses are offered in Film Production, Digital Film and Screen Arts, and Creative Arts for Theatre and Film.

Cumbria Film Studies (joint honours) has a theoretical approach to the subject. An industry-acclaimed practical course in Television Production is also offered.

De Montfort The Film Studies degree is offered as a joint course, with subjects including Journalism. The course is largely theoretical but there is a practical option to explore the techniques of video-making. There are also courses in TV and Film Production Technology, Film Studies, Photography and Video and a Radio Production course.

Derby The course in Film and Video offers 75% practical work, while some work placements are offered in the Film and Television degree course. There are also Photography courses.

Dundee See under **English**.

East Anglia Courses in Film and English Studies or American Studies are offered. There is also a course in Film and Television Studies with an emphasis on film history and options to spend the third year in North America or Australasia. Some practical work is also offered.

East London Courses are offered in Film and Video (Cinematics) Theory and Practice, Animation, Moving Image, and Film Studies taken with a second subject.

Edge Hill Courses are offered in Film Studies and Film and Television Production. There are also nine joint courses including Creative Writing, Media and English.

Edinburgh Napier Photography, Film and Imaging is available either as a three-year or four-year full-time course. Film can also be taken with English.

Edinburgh Queen Margaret Film and Media combines a study of the industry with many specialisms including video production, documentaries, media management and world cinema.

Essex Film Studies is a broad course focusing on the social and historical aspects of the media. It is offered as a joint programme with History of Art, Literature or History and American Studies. A course in Film and Creative Writing is also offered.

Exeter The Film Studies course has an emphasis on European, Latin American and African cinema in addition to Hollywood. Joint courses with modern languages are also available. There are opportunities for practical film-making. Film Studies can be taken with languages.

See *Heap 2015: University Degree Course Offers* (Trotman Publishing) for details of offers

Glasgow* The Film and Television course studies both cinema and TV as major forces within 20th-century culture. An introduction to video techniques is available to students. Overseas study options include North America and Australia.

Gloucestershire The major, minor or joint course in Film Studies focuses on genre topics in film history and the Hollywood film industry. There is an optional placement period on the Film Management course. A Film Production course is also offered.

Glyndŵr The Film and Photography course specialises in understanding the key elements of still and moving imagery and includes location and studio work. There is also a degree in Television Production.

Greenwich Practical courses are offered in Film Studies, Film and TV Production and Digital Film Production.

Hertfordshire Three degrees are offered in Film and Television specialising in Fiction, Fiction Documentary or Entertainment. There are also degrees in Screen Cultures with Media Practices, and a course in Special Effects.

Huddersfield There is a course in Digital Film and Visual Effects Production. Film Studies is available as a single and joint honours course with English, Drama, History and Music Technology.

Hull Film Studies is part of a joint programme and focuses mainly on British and American cinema. A course in Media, Culture and Society is also offered.

Keele The Film Studies course is a critical study of film history. There are opportunities to study abroad.

Kent The Film Studies single and dual honours course provides a theoretical study of film history and production. Practical photography, video and film modules are only available to single honours students. A degree in European Arts (Film Studies) is also available.

Kingston The Film Studies course is theoretical and focuses on the history of film and contemporary European and American cinema. It can be studied with French or Spanish and other subjects. Courses are available in Film-making, Television and New Broadcasting Media, Media Technology, and History of Art, Design and Film.

Lancaster The Film Studies course explores the links between theory and practice. It is not a vocational course preparing students for media. It is offered as a combined course with Philosophy, Sociology and English Literature.

Leeds A three-year course is offered in Cinema and Photography with a practice-based study of both art forms supported by historical and critical analysis. World cinema is available as a joint honours course with a language.

Leeds Beckett A course is offered in Film and Moving Image Production requiring a portfolio of art or film work. Courses are also offered in Animation, Broadcast Media Technologies, Computer Animation and Special Effects, and Media, Communication and Cultures.

Leeds Trinity The Film course is largely theoretical although there are practical modules in Years 2 and 3. There are also practical TV Studies and Production courses.

Leicester Film Studies and Visual Arts comprises a study of the history of film and art. Film Studies can also be taken with English or Modern Languages.

Lincoln Film and TV Studies includes modules on Scriptwriting, Production Planning and Camera Work.

Liverpool Film Studies is available as a joint or minor subject, offered with over 30 humanities subjects.

Liverpool Hope Film Studies is offered as a combined honours subject and combines theory and practice. The Film and TV Production degree combines practical and theoretical work.

See *Heap 2015: University Degree Course Offers* (Trotman Publishing) for details of offers

Liverpool John Moores The hands-on Film Studies course spans the histories and practices of film and television with some practical work. The Screen Studies course spans the histories and practices of film and television. It has a critical rather than creative approach.

London (King's)* Film Studies is offered as a single honours degree. The department has excellent facilities and lies in close proximity to the British Film Institute, Southbank and the London Film Museum.

London (QM)* Film Studies can be taken with Comparative Literature, a course comprising a study of fine arts, music, literature and film.

London (RH) The Film Studies course covers the theory and history of the moving image.

London (SOAS) See under **Media Studies**.

London Met Film Studies is a single or joint honours course with practical modules. There are also courses in Film and Broadcast Production, Film and Television Studies and in Cinematics.

London South Bank The Film and Media Studies degree is a theoretical study of contemporary issues in cinema and broadcast media; there is no practical element. Practical courses are offered in Digital Film and Video.

Manchester Courses are offered in Film Studies which can be combined with Drama, Art History, Media and Cultural Studies, Creative Writing or Video. There are also courses in TV Journalism and Production.

Manchester Met Courses are offered in Film and Television Studies, Film and Media Studies, European Film and Contemporary Film and Video. There is an assessed work placement in Year 2, and overseas exchange options are offered.

Middlesex The Film Studies course covers film theory, history and criticism. A practical Television Production course is also offered.

Newcastle Film Studies can be taken with Modern Languages. Film modules are also taken in the Media, Communications and Cultural Studies and the English Literature, Language and Linguistics degrees.

Northampton There is a degree course in American Literature and Film, as well as a study of the history, theory and cultural significance offered in the Film and Television Studies degree.

Northumbria Film and Television Studies can be studied with English or the History of Modern Art and Design.

Norwich Arts The Film and Moving Image degree includes an industrial placement.

Nottingham Film and TV Studies is offered with American Studies, Art History, Music, Cinema, Theology, French, German, Hispanic Studies or Russian. See also **Sociology**.

Nottingham Trent There is a course in Design for Film and TV. There are several courses on offer assisted by work experience opportunities.

Oxford Brookes Film Studies is a theoretical course that can be taken as a single honours degree or with 16 other subjects. Modules include scriptwriting and production management.

Portsmouth There is a single honours course in Film Studies, including modules in web journalism, fashion in film and screenwriting, and combined programmes with Creative Writing or Drama. There are also courses in Television Broadcasting or with Film Production.

Queen's Belfast The Film Studies course is offered as a single, joint, major or minor subject, with options including Theatre Studies. Students can specialise in creative practice, scriptwriting, cinematography or direction and production.

See *Heap 2015: University Degree Course Offers* (Trotman Publishing) for details of offers

Reading The Film and Theatre course integrates practical work, a critical study of film and theatre and the historical and cultural significance of television.

Roehampton Film can be studied as a single honours course or in joint degrees with another subject from a choice of 12, such as Journalism and News Media, Media and Culture. Roehampton runs partnership events with the British Film Institute.

St Andrews* Film Studies is a joint course with a strong bias in European film-making. Many courses offer a year abroad.

St Mary's A theoretical course in Film and Popular Culture can lead to pathways in creative writing, media arts or sociology.

Sheffield Hallam Courses are offered in Film Studies, Film and Screenwriting or Media Production, covering history and criticism with several options in photography or film production.

South Wales The Film degree focuses on film-making practice and creative storytelling across a range of genres, while the Film Studies degree is theoretical, focusing on critical and analytical skills. Both courses offer screenwriting modules.

Southampton* A degree in Film covers European and US studies and some practical work. Students opt for specialist studies each year. A year in Korea is available. Students have the option to take an alternative subject for 25% of the course.

Southampton Solent Courses are offered in Film Studies and Television Production. The Film, TV and Radio degree has a substantial element of practical work. Field trips to film festivals in the UK and Europe are offered.

Staffordshire Courses are offered in Film Production Technology and Film, Television and Radio Studies, Scriptwriting, Screenwriting with Film Studies, and Music Broadcasting, all involved largely with practical studies.

Stirling The focus of the two courses in Film and Media Studies and European Film and Media lies in the very wide range of options. In the latter, students opt for either Media or Film.

Sunderland See **Media Studies**.

Surrey The Film Studies degree offers the study of audiovisual media and focuses on film (theory and industry). Film Studies can also be taken with Creative Writing.

Sussex The Film Studies course provides a foundation in film genre and theory and the range of film-making worldwide. It can also be taken with Languages, Drama, Music and English. A course in Media Practice covers video-editing, scriptwriting and production skills.

Swansea There is a degree in Media Studies covering film and TV.

Trinity St David The Film and Visual Culture course combines the study of film with practical work where students create their own pieces.

Trinity St David (Swansea) A range of courses is offered including Digital Film and Television Production, Documentary Video and Video Arts. Work experience is available and students pitch programme ideas to a BBC commissioning Editor as part of their final year project.

Ulster Film Studies can be taken with 18 other subjects.

Warwick* Five courses are offered. Film and Literature and Film with Television Studies and three Film Studies programmes. The first offers a study of English, European and American literature linked to aspects of film, and includes an Introduction to Theatre module, while the second provides wider coverage of film and develops TV studies.

West London Video Production courses are offered including Advertising with Video Production and Film, Video Production with Film Studies. Film is also covered in the Media Studies course.

West Scotland The course in Film-making and Screenwriting is mainly practical and is available as either a three-year or four-year course. The course is delivered as part of the Skillset Media Academy.

Westminster The three-year Film and Television Production degree covers film-making, TV drama and documentary, screenwriting, film theory and criticism.

Winchester A theoretical Film Studies course is offered and also a large number of joint courses with Film and Cinema Technologies, which includes cinematography, lighting and set design.

Wolverhampton The Film Studies degree can be combined with one or two other subjects from 10 options. The course focuses on production, language and aesthetics of the cinema with specialist options that include the British, French, Spanish and American cinema. Short placements are offered during term time. There is also a practical course in Video and Film Production.

Worcester Courses are offered in Film Studies, which is largely theoretical, and in Digital Film Production.

OTHER INSTITUTIONS OFFERING FILM, RADIO, VIDEO AND TV STUDIES COURSES

Bradford (Coll Univ Centre), Central Nottingham (Coll), Cleveland (CAD), Cornwall (Coll), Croydon (Coll), Edinburgh (CA), Exeter (Coll), Falmouth, Grimsby (Univ Centre), Hereford (CA), Hull (Coll), Kirklees (Coll), Manchester (Coll), Nescot, Newham (CFE), Northbrook (Coll), Sandwell (Coll), Solihull (Coll), South Cheshire (Coll), St Helens (Coll), Stockport (Coll), Suffolk (Univ Campus), Sunderland City (Coll), Truro (Coll), Walsall (Coll), Warwickshire (Coll), Wiltshire (Coll).

ALTERNATIVE COURSES

Media Studies, Photography, TV and Video, Visual Communication.

FINANCE

(including **Banking** and **Insurance**)
(see also **Accountancy/Accounting**)
(* indicates universities with entry requirements over 340 UCAS points)

SUBJECT REQUIREMENTS/PREFERENCES

GCSE: English and Mathematics required.

SUBJECT INFORMATION

These are specialised courses leading to careers in banking, building societies, insurance companies, pension funds etc. Major banks offer sponsorship. Most courses follow a similar curriculum; many Finance courses are combined with Accountancy.

Aberdeen The degree in Finance involves a broad study of aspects of accounting, corporate banking and personal finance, treasury and international management, and property investment. Part of the degree may be taken abroad. A course in Finance and Investment Management is also available.

Abertay This is a four-year course in the applications of finance and accounting in business. ACCA and CIMA accreditation is held.

Aberystwyth Broad courses in Banking, Financial Services and Business Finance introduce investment fundamentals, portfolio management and global finance. Finance can also be combined with Accountancy.

Bangor The course in Banking and Finance provides a study of financial services and markets. Banking can be studied with a range of subjects including Mathematics, Accounting, Italian, Spanish, French and German. Financial Economics is also available as a BA or BSc.

Bedfordshire There are degrees in Business Studies (Finance and International Finance).

Birmingham* Single and major/minor courses in Money, Banking and Finance are offered.

Birmingham City Finance is offered as a joint degree of three years or with an additional year on a business placement after Year 2. Some ACCA and CIMA exam exemptions are included.

Bournemouth Courses are offered in Finance and Business and Finance and Economics, allowing flexibility to specialise in options in law, accounting and taxation. ACCA, CIOT, CIMA and ICAEW accreditation is included. There is also a European language option. Finance is also offered with Law.

Bradford There are courses in Financial Economics and Financial Planning which offers specialisms in accountancy, human resource management, international business, management and marketing.

Brighton The degree course in Finance and Investment (three-year full-time or four-year sandwich) covers both the UK and international economics. The course involves economics, corporate law and risk management. This course has a common first year with Economics and Finance. A transfer is possible in Year 2. Courses are also offered in Business Management with Finance and Accounting and Finance.

Bristol See under **Accountancy**.

Bristol UWE See under **Accountancy**.

Brunel Business Finance is offered with Economics as a three-year of four-year sandwich course. Courses are also available in Finance and Accounting and Financial Mathematics.

Buckingham A course in Financial Services is offered starting in January or July. It is aimed at students seeking careers in banking, finance, investment analysis and other financial services. Courses in Accounting and Financial Management, and Finance with Information Systems are also available. ACCA and CIMA accreditation is held.

Cardiff* Banking and Finance is an economics-based course that includes training relevant to the practice of banking. Optional courses include accounting and management with a foreign language and a year spent abroad. ICAEW- and ACCA-accredited.

City* In the Banking and International Finance course economics, statistics, computer programming and introductions to law and accounting are studied with banking and international finance in the first year. There are options in two subjects to be chosen in the second and third years, including French or German. Study abroad and work placements are an option. Financial Economics also offers a year-long placement. The degree in Investment, Finance and Risk Includes international investment policies in Europe, North America and Japan. A course is also offered in Actuarial Science. See also **Mathematics**.

Coventry The Finance and Investment courses can be taken on a full-time or part-time basis. Finance can also be taken with Accountancy or Economics. An industrial placement year is offered. There is also a course in Banking and Insurance.

De Montfort Finance is offered, covering finance and accountancy, business investment, risk management and investment and international finance.

Dundee The BFin and BIFin (the latter covering international topics) Finance courses carry ACCA, CIMA and AIA accreditation. Modules include financial economics, and they can also be taken with eight other subjects including Psychology, Political Science and German. See also **Accountancy/Accounting**.

Durham A range of Finance courses can be selected, including Finance with pathways in Accountancy and Finance, International Financial Economics, Investment, Banking and Finance and Money Banking and Finance.

East London There is a modular course in Finance, Money and Banking with options in asset pricing, political economy and corporate finance. See also **Accountancy/Accounting**.

Essex Banking and Finance and Finance and Financial Economics courses are available. Options are offered with a year on a placement or studying abroad.

Exeter* Finance can be studied with Accounting and Economics. Both have a European study option. A four-year course in Accounting with Leadership is also available.

Glasgow* The course in Financial Statistics includes a study of Financial Accounting and Financial Management.

Glasgow Caledonian Options on the four-year Finance, Investment and Risk course include business management, social security, languages, insurance, banking, building societies, international banking and underwriting. There is also a course in Risk Management relating to insurance with topics involving fire, employee injury, pollution and computer fraud, and a four-year full-time course in Financial Mathematics.

Greenwich Banking can be studied with Economics. A degree in Finance and Financial Information Systems is offered and covers banking, insurance, securities and investments.

Heriot-Watt Several Finance courses are offered with specialisms in Business Law, Business and Finance, Economics and Mathematics.

Hertfordshire There is a three-year full-time or four-year sandwich course in Finance which covers business and international finance, global economy and taxation. The course carries exemptions from CIMA and ACCA examinations.

Hull Several ICAEW- and ACCA-accredited courses are offered in Financial Management focusing on business, economics, logistics or marketing.

Keele The dual honours degree in Finance focuses on financial markets and can be combined with over 25 subjects including Languages, Management, Computer Sciences and Business Economics. Overseas study is offered.

Kent The university offers one of the few courses in Actuarial Science. The Accounting and Finance degree is available with a year in industrial placement.

Kingston The course in Financial Economics covers accountancy, corporate management and risk management. There is also a joint course in Financial Mathematics and Business.

Lancaster* Finance is offered as a three-year degree course and can also be taken in combination with Accounting or Economics. The four-year Ernst & Young degree in Accounting, Auditing and Finance includes a salaried placement with Ernst & Young.

Leicester A three-year degree is offered in Banking and Finance.

Lincoln A course in Accountancy and Finance can be taken as a single subject or in combination, for example with Management, Public Relations or Marketing. Four-year sandwich placement courses are available.

Liverpool John Moores The course in International Banking and Finance covers economics, statistics, accounting and law, with final year options in personal finance, international economics, money and banking. There is a modern language option in Year 2. See also **Accountancy/Accounting**.

London (QM)* Courses in Finance are offered with Mathematics and Business Management or with Physics or Economics. Courses are flexible, allowing for a range of choices in modules, and placement and overseas study options are available.

London (RH)* Two three-year courses are offered: Finance and Mathematics and Financial and Business Economics.

London (UCL)* Business Finance is offered with Engineering in three-year and four-year full-time honours degree courses.

London LSE* Finance is offered with Accounting and there is also a course in Actuarial Science. Some ACCA and IPCAS accreditation is included.

London Met Courses are offered in Banking, Banking and Finance, Financial Mathematics, and Financial Services.

London South Bank A three-year honours degree is offered in Accounting and Finance, which covers taxation, company law, auditing, corporate finance and economics. The course is fully accredited by the ACCA, the CIMA and the ICAEW. There is also a four-year sandwich option where the student will spend a year in a work placement.

Loughborough* Banking, Finance and Management is a four-year sandwich course covering managerial, financial, legal and economic aspects of banking and finance. Optional subjects include French, German, computing, personnel work, marketing and economic history. Other courses offered include Financial Management, International Economics and Financial Mathematics. Economics can also be taken as a combined honours course with Geography or Politics.

Manchester* A single honours BA Econ course is offered in Finance, or it can be taken in combination with International Business and Economics.

Manchester Met There are courses in Financial Services and Financial Sector Management. AAT accreditation is included in the Accounting and Finance course.

Middlesex The Accounting and Finance degree carries accreditation from ACCA, CIMA, ICAEW, AIA and AAT. A course in Banking and Finance is offered with optional industrial placements in Year 3.

Newcastle Courses are offered in Finance Business and Economics and Financial Mathematics.

Northampton The Banking and Financial Planning degree covers banking, insurance, building society operations, fund management and treasury operations.

Northumbria A three-year degree is offered in Finance and Investment Management that covers economics, accounting, marketing, International finance and taxation. Business with Finance is offered as a four-year sandwich course.

Nottingham* A unique course is offered in Industrial Economics and Insurance and there is also a course in Finance, Accounting and Management, which allows graduates exemption from all CIMA examinations, Parts 1 and 2 of the ACCA examination scheme and three ICAEW papers.

Nottingham Trent An 'in company' Retail Banking degree is offered. The Accounting and Finance course offers an industrial placement and carries exemption from various industry examinations.

Plymouth International Financial Services is offered as a three- or four-year sandwich course. See also **Accountancy/Accounting**.

Portsmouth Finance and Management is a three-year or four-year sandwich course covering building society and banking operations and the marketing of financial services. A degree is also available in International Finance and Trade.

Queen's Belfast The course in Finance covers accounting, capital investment decisions, management of stock, debtors, company and international finance. Year 3 is a placement year in a financial institution in the UK or abroad. It can also be studied with French, German or Spanish.

Reading* Courses are offered in Finance and Investment Banking or Property Investment, delivered at the ICMA Centre. Internships can be arranged during summer vacations.

Robert Gordon Management is offered with Finance. A sandwich placement is optional.

Salford The Finance and Accounting degree carries ICAEW, CIMA and ACCA accreditations. Property Management and Investment is available as a three-year full-time degree.

Sheffield Hallam A four-year sandwich course in Business and Financial Services is offered. Core subjects include economics, business accounts, international finance, financial and management accounting, quantitative analysis, information systems, financial institutions, law and marketing. There is also a degree in Banking with Finance, with international options.

Southampton* Finance is offered with Accounting, Mathematics and Economics.

Southampton Solent Degrees are offered in Accountancy and Finance with either Business Management or Entrepreneurship.

Staffordshire Degree courses are offered in Finance (including a two-year fast-track option) and Business and Financial Economics.

Stirling Several courses are offered with Finance including French, Management, Law, Marketing, Sports Studies and Spanish. There is also a degree in Money, Banking and Finance. Semesters 1 and 2 focus on accounting. Study abroad in Europe, North America, Asia or Australia is an option.

Strathclyde A Finance course is offered jointly with Management, Marketing, International Business and Mathematics.

Surrey The course in Financial Services Management is designed to match the needs of industry and can be taken to include a professional training year, adding considerably to employment prospects.

Swansea There is a Finance specialisation in the Business and Management Science programmes and there is also a degree in Actuarial Studies. Finance is also offered with Computing.

Teesside A BA (Hons) in Accounting and Finance is offered along with a broader BA (Hons) in Applied Accounting and Business Finance.

Ulster Finance and Investment Analysis is offered as a three-year full-time degree. There are also courses in Financial Services and Financial Engineering.

Westminster A finance pathway is available in the three-year Business degree and in the four-year Business Studies sandwich course. The new Finance with Management course offers a year in a placement or overseas study.

OTHER INSTITUTIONS OFFERING FINANCE COURSES

Blackburn (Coll), Bradford (Coll Univ Centre), Cornwall (Coll), Dudley (Coll), Euro Bus Sch London, Grimsby (Univ Centre), Guildford (Coll), Highbury Portsmouth (Coll), Hopwood Hall (Coll), London Regent's, Manchester (Coll), Newcastle (Coll), Northbrook (Coll), Norwich City (Coll), Nottingham New (Coll), Peterborough (Reg Coll), Richmond (Am Int Univ), Sandwell (Coll), Sheffield (Coll), South Essex (Coll), Suffolk (Univ Campus), Swindon (Coll), Truro (Coll), Warwickshire (Coll), Wigan and Leigh (Coll).

ALTERNATIVE COURSES

Accounting, Ac--tuarial Studies, Business Studies, Economics, Retail Management.

FOOD SCIENCE

(including **Nutrition** and **Dietetics**)
(see also **Agricultural Sciences/Agriculture**)
(* indicates universities with entry requirements over 340 UCAS points)

SUBJECT REQUIREMENTS/PREFERENCES

GCE A level: Sciences, usually including Chemistry and Biology. **GCSE:** English, Mathematics and a science.

SUBJECT INFORMATION

Biochemistry, microbiology, human nutrition, food processing and technology are components of these courses. The study depends on its understanding on a secure foundation of several pure sciences: Chemistry and two subjects from Physics, Mathematics, Biology, Botany and Zoology. Only students offering such a combination can be considered. Food Technology covers the engineering aspects of food processing and management.

Abertay Three courses are offered, all with common first and second years, leading to a choice of degree in Food and Consumer Science, Food Science and Technology, or Food, Nutrition and Health. Opportunities exist for one-semester or year-long exchanges with students from a university in Toronto or on work placement.

Bath Spa The central theme of the Food Science course is the study of the food chain, nutrition and consumer protection. The course is actually suitable for students from a non-science background. Food and Design focuses on food product development, whilst the Food, Nutrition and Consumer Protection and the Human Nutrition courses emphasise food chain and nutritional issues.

Birmingham (UC) The Culinary Arts Management course involves food and beverage studies and kitchen management. A work placement scheme is also included.

Bournemouth The BSc Nutrition course includes a study of the molecular, physiological and biochemical aspects of nutrition, psychology, health promotion, public health, food production and safety. Students undertake a 20-week placement on the three-year course or a 40-week placement on the four-year sandwich option. A foundation degree in Professional Culinary Arts is also offered.

Cardiff Met (UWIC) The four-year Human Nutrition and Dietetics course includes clinical training in Years 2, 3 and 4. There are also degrees in Food Science and Technology, Food Production Management and Public Health Nutrition with pathways in Sport Nutrition and Health Promotion. A year-long or summer work placement is optional.

Chester Courses are offered in Nutrition and Dietetics, leading to the career of dietician, and also a single honours course in Human Nutrition.

Coventry The Food and Nutrition BSc covers food analysis, food safety and human nutrition. Opportunities are available for long- and short-term placements and study abroad.

Edinburgh Queen Margaret The degree in Nutrition provides expertise in areas such as health promotion, clinical sciences, epidemiology, international health and research. Years 1 and 2 are shared with the Applied Pharmacology and Human Biology courses, allowing students to change course before Year 3. The course is accredited by the Association for Nutrition.

Glasgow Caledonian Year 1 of the Human Nutrition course includes sociology and information studies in addition to nutrition, physiology and chemistry. Community studies, management, food science and clinical dietetic studies follow. There are also four-year courses in Food Technology, Food Bioscience, Applied Nutrition and Human Nutrition and Dietetics leading to professional qualification.

Greenwich The Human Nutrition degree is available as a four-year sandwich course and includes options in medical biochemistry, immunology, and nutrition in sport and exercise.

Harper Adams Food, Nutrition and Well-being and Food and Consumer Studies are both offered with a placement year in the industry.

Heriot-Watt The university offers one of the very few Brewing and Distilling courses available in the UK. The course is organised in collaboration with representatives of the brewing, malting and distilling industries.

Hertfordshire A Dietetics degree is offered with placements throughout the course. A new course in Nutrition carries accreditation from the Nutrition Society and the Association for Nutrition.

Huddersfield The Food and Nutrition course leads to technical management careers in the food and related industries. Specialisms include food processing, applied nutrition, food safety and food science. Courses in Food, Nutrition and Health, Diet and Health, and Food Science Technology Management are also offered. The Nutrition and Public Health degree can be taken over three years or as a four-year sandwich course with a placement year.

Kingston The degree in Exercise, Nutrition and Health has an emphasis on sport and exercise with modules in physiology, sport and exercise and psychology. A four-year sandwich course is offered.

Leeds The Food Studies and Nutrition degrees include options to spend Year 3 in a salaried position in industry, or to study abroad in Europe (including spoken language training for six months followed by industrial placement), or to spend a year at a university overseas, e.g. in the US. Courses are also offered in Nutrition and Food Science.

Leeds Beckett There are three degrees focusing on Public Health, one of which centres on nutrition with an emphasis on the relationship between nutrition and nutrition-related health and disease. A four-year Dietetics course is also available, from which graduates are eligible to apply for registration with the Health Professions Council.

Leeds Trinity The degree in Nutrition and Food includes two placements, each of six weeks. The course covers health and well-being, food culture and behaviour, eating disorders, food safety and quality, and community health. Nutrition can also be studied on the combined honours programmes with Psychology or Sport, Health and Exercise.

Lincoln Courses are offered in Food Manufacture (Operations Management) and Food Manufacture (Quality Assurance and Technical Management).

Liverpool Hope Nutrition is taken as a combined honours degree or with Health Promotion as a single honours programme. Other appropriate combined subjects could include Child and Youth Studies or Human Biology.

See *Heap 2015: University Degree Course Offers* (Trotman Publishing) for details of offers

Liverpool John Moores The Food and Nutrition course focuses on food design and technology. There is also a unique course in Home Economics leading to careers in food production and development.

London (King's) The BSc course is a modular programme with specialised options including diet, disease, obesity and antioxidants and cancer. Graduates may apply for the UK Voluntary Register of Nutritionists. There is also a four-year Nutrition and Dietetics course with clinical placements in Years 2, 3 and 4, leading to qualification as a dietician.

London Met The scientific emphasis of the course in Nutrition, Exercise and Health covers cell biology, biochemistry and human physiology and focuses on the importance of the links between nutrition and exercise. There is also a course in Food and Consumer Studies.

London South Bank Food Design and Technology covers all aspects of the study of food including chemistry, hygiene, processing and preservation. There are also degrees in Food and Nutrition and Human Nutrition.

Manchester Met There is a course in Nutritional Sciences which covers nutrition, dietetics, sports nutrition, food science and food technology. The course is also available as a four-year sandwich option.

Middlesex The Sport and Exercise Science course focuses entirely on sports nutrition with opportunities for work placement.

Newcastle Students taking the four-year course in Food and Human Nutrition, which includes a year's placement in Year 3 in the UK or abroad, are able to take options in economics, marketing or a foreign language.

Northumbria In the Human Nutrition degree (three or four years) the fundamentals of biochemistry and physiology are studied in addition to the nutritional composition of foods and diets. The course is accredited by the Association for Nutrition. There is also a degree in Food Science and Nutrition.

Nottingham Three-year courses are offered in Nutrition, Nutrition and Food Science with industrial placements and Nutrition Biochemistry, focusing on health and agriculture. Industry placement and study abroad options are offered. There is also a four-year course leading to Master of Nutrition (Dietetics). Courses are also offered in Food Science and Food Microbiology.

Nottingham Trent The degree in Exercise, Nutrition and Health offers an industry placement and allows students to become a member of the Nottingham Trent University Health Forum. Placements are offered in a variety of organisations, such as: Slimming World, Jamie Oliver's Ministry of Food and Nottingham City Council.

Oxford Brookes Two courses are offered: Nutrition (accredited by the Nutrition Society) and Public Health Nutrition. Both courses have work experience modules and provide the opportunity in Year 2 for students to study abroad in Europe, the US, Canada or Australia.

Plymouth Problem-based learning features throughout the three-year Dietetics degree. Other courses offered include Applied Biosciences (Food and Nutrition), Nutrition, Exercise and Health, and Health and Social Care Studies.

Queen's Belfast The Food Quality, Safety and Nutrition degree has a 16-week work placement period in Year 3 or a one-year placement in the four-year, sandwich course leading to qualification as a dietician.

Reading The Nutrition and Food Science course is taken over three years with a four-year option involving professional placement in Year 3. Food Science degrees are also offered with Business and with industrial training, as well as a Nutrition with Food Consumer Sciences course.

Robert Gordon Four-year degree courses in Nutrition and Nutrition and Dietetics are offered with placements integrated in Years 2, 3 and 4. Courses are accredited by the Association for Nutrition.

Roehampton The degree in Nutrition and Health is offered on a full-time or part-time basis. The course encompasses physiology and biochemistry as well as aspects of psychology and sociology which may influence food intakes. Graduates are eligible to become a Registered Associate Nutritionist.

Royal Agricultural Univ The Food Production and Supply Management courses covers processing, manufacturing, ingredients, suppliers, marketing organisations, wholesalers, retailers and the food supply chain.

St Mary's The Nutrition degree offers options in clinical nutrition, obesity, public health nutrition and sports nutrition. The course is accredited by the Association for Nutrition.

Sheffield Hallam A degree is offered in Food and Nutrition, with a year spent on an industry placement. There is some emphasis on food quality, technology and consumer studies, and also a focus on health promotion in the community.

South Wales The degree in Nutrition, Physical Activity and Community Health prepares students for work in the public health sector by focusing on theory and its practical application. Students have the opportunity to spend a short placement in the community or in a developing country.

SRUC The degree in Food Technology covers quality, production and marketing.

Surrey Food Science and Nutrition and Dietetics degrees are offered, the former on a three- or four-year basis. As with the Dietetics option, the four-year degree courses include a year's placement with an employer. The Nutrition and Dietetics programme is commissioned by the NHS, which pays student tuition fees and offers a means-tested bursary. Graduates may apply for registration as a dietician.

Teesside Food, Nutrition and Health Science is a three-year course with the option to extend it by including a professional placement in the UK of one year.

Ulster There is a course in Consumer Studies, with a four-year sandwich course available, and a course in Food and Nutrition. See also **Biology**.

West London Nutritional Medicine is offered as a part-time degree course lasting five or six years. The start dates are in October, February and June.

Westminster A free-choice subject module is offered in each year of the degree course in Human Nutrition. Relevant topics include public health, physiology and psychology. There are also courses in Nutrition and Exercise Science and Nutritional Therapy.

Worcester Human Nutrition can be taken as a single, joint or major/minor course. It may be combined with other biological subjects or with most other subjects in the modular scheme, e.g. health, psychology or sports subjects.

OTHER INSTITUTIONS OFFERING FOOD SCIENCE COURSES
Bradford (Coll Univ Centre), Suffolk (Univ Campus).

ALTERNATIVE COURSES
Biological Sciences, Biomedical Science, Food Science, Health Science, Psychology.

FORESTRY

(*indicates universities with entry requirements over 340 UCAS points)

SUBJECT REQUIREMENTS/PREFERENCES
GCE A level: Two science subjects are usually stipulated.

SUBJECT INFORMATION
Forestry is concerned with the establishment and management of woodlands and forests for timber production, environmental, conservation and amenity purposes.

Aberdeen Taught at Aberdeen since 1907 the four-year course in Forestry covers aspects of forestry, ecology, zoology, and plant science. It is accredited by the Institute of Chartered Foresters with options for a professional placement year and study abroad. Other related courses include Forest Sciences.

Bangor The Forestry course covers studies in silviculture, forest operations, practical forestry, zoology, plant science and estate planning. It is accredited by the Institute of Chartered Foresters.

Cumbria There are vocational courses in Forestry, Woodland Conservation, and Outdoor Studies with the option for a professional placement year.

OTHER INSTITUTIONS OFFERING FORESTRY COURSES
Myerscough (Coll), Sparsholt (Coll), UHI, Worcester.

ALTERNATIVE COURSES
Biological Sciences, Conservation, Ecology, Environmental Science.

GEOGRAPHY

(* indicates universities with entry requirements over 340 UCAS points)

SUBJECT REQUIREMENTS/PREFERENCES
GCE A level: Geography is usually the highest grade shown in the offers made. One or more science subjects may be required for BSc courses. **GCSE:** Mathematics often required for BSc courses.

SUBJECT INFORMATION
These courses cover the human, physical, economic and social aspects of geography. Each institution offers its own particular emphasis. Check the prospectuses for all courses, with particular attention to the specialist options in the second and third years.

Aberdeen Geography honours students have the opportunity to specialise in topics chosen from human, physical and environmental geography. In Level 2, courses are offered in Environmental Systems, Space Economy and Society, and Mapping. Student exchange programmes are also available. A field trip to the Alps is included. There are many joint courses and also a course in Geographical Information Systems.

Aberystwyth Degrees in Human and Physical Geography are offered in the Faculties of Arts or Science. Specialist modules can be taken in both Physical and Human Geography courses. A residential field course is offered in New Zealand, New York, Spain, Ireland or Wales. Several joint honours schemes link Geography with other subjects. There are also courses in Geographical Information Systems and Environmental and Earth Sciences.

Bangor A three-year course in Geography is offered leading to BA or BSc degrees with a specialist stream for those aiming to teach. There is an emphasis on practical work. Specialist BA streams are available in Planning, Housing, Transport and Environmental Management whilst BSc options include Coastal Geography, Oceanography, Agriculture and Atmospheres.

Bath Spa Human and physical geography are the main features of this degree. Both courses can be taken as part of the combined award. There is also a course in GIS. School and voluntary placements are also organised, and an optional field course in Barcelona is offered.

Birmingham* In the first year of the Geography (BSc and BA) courses, students cover human and physical geography. In the second year, single honours students choose three from five elective courses that determine the final degree and which include conservation, settlements, planning and resource management and physical geography. There is a free choice of options in Year 3 including a year abroad. Joint courses with Archaeology, Economics and Urban and Regional Planning are also offered. See **Combined Courses**.

Bournemouth The Applied Geography course aims to focus on geographical skills relating to real world issues and covering resources, GIS, planning, countryside management and environmental matters.

Brighton Human environmental and physical geography are offered at Level 1 of the Geography degree followed by specialist topics in Levels 2 and 3. These include water resources, medical geography and environmental studies. Language studies are offered. Geography can also be taken with Geology and with subjects in the joint science field. A Biogeography course is also offered.

Bristol* The Geography course is offered as a three-year BSc or a four-year MSci, and covers a wide range of geographical interests and related problems concerning the environment and the regions. After Stage I (first year), three different syllabuses are offered allowing specialisation in human and/or physical geography. Complementary subjects are offered as minor courses occupying one-third of Year 1. A course involving study in continental Europe is also offered.

Bristol UWE Both human and physical geography are covered in the Geography course, with joint courses in environmental management, planning and tourism. Associated courses are also offered in Planning and Communities and Transport Planning.

Cambridge* Part IA of the Geography course covers physical, human and historical geography, environment and resources and geographical methods. In the second year (Part IB) there are options in human or physical and environmental geography. In the third year, four topics are chosen from a wide range of subjects. Not available at Peterhouse or Pembroke Colleges.

Canterbury Christ Church Geography students can choose course specialisations from Human or Physical Geography or Planning and the Environment. There is a strong emphasis on regional geography and in Year 2 an opportunity to study in Canada. Courses are offered with PGCE options for students who wish to teach Geography.

Cardiff The Marine Geography course focuses on the ocean as a maritime frontier and human beings' socio-economic relationship with the physical environment and the principles of maritime transport, the maritime industries and ocean and coastal management. Topics covered include geology, the ocean atmosphere, cartography, coastal hydrography and coastal zone management. The third year may be spent in industrial training. A course in Human Geography and Planning is also available.

Central Lancashire The BA/BSc Geography courses offer specialisms in physical, human, social and industrial geography or urban planning. There is a language option available. The subject is also offered on the combined honours programme and can also be studied with Sociology and Environmental Management. See also **Environmental Science/Studies**.

Chester Human and physical geography are key features of this course which includes GIS and useful joint courses in Urban Studies and International Development Studies. Residential field trips to Spain, New York and Norway are offered.

Coventry Both a BA programme and a BSc Geography course are offered; the latter is a three-year or four-year sandwich course. A unique feature of this course is the third year spent in professional training in which students have placements related to geography such as hydrology, forestry, offshore surveying, marketing and transport, in the UK and abroad. Four geography modules are selected from a choice of 10 in the final year. There are also courses in Natural Hazards, Global Sustainability and Climate Change.

Cumbria Courses are offered in Geography covering human and physical geography. Teaching courses in Geography are also available.

Derby The Geography course is offered with the option to study abroad. There are also pathways in Third World Development and International Relations.

Dundee The emphasis in the first two years of the Geography course is population geography, urban and regional development, physical geography and the evolution of Europe's landscape. In Year 3, students select from a range of physical, human and regional courses. A BSc course is also offered that includes a study of two other science subjects in Years 1 and 2. It is also possible to study Geography with Environmental Science as a joint honours degree.

Durham* The first-year courses in Geography cover human, physical and regional geography with field-work in the UK and abroad and practical classes. In the second and third years a choice of specialist options enables students to choose their own emphasis to the subject, either social or science research. Continuous assessment is used for one-third of the degree. Geography is also part of the Natural Sciences and combined honours programmes in social sciences.

East Anglia Environmental Geography is combined with International Development Studies, a subject with a social science perspective focusing on social analysis, economics and the management of natural resources and the environment. There is also a degree in Meteorology and Oceanography, with options to study in Europe or North America, and a course in development studies covering international, social and environmental perspectives. A joint honours course in Natural Sciences offers options in Geology, Biology, Mathematics, Psychology and Statistics.

East London The university offers three-year full-time degrees in GIS, Global Change: Environment, Economy and Development, and Surveying and Mapping Sciences.

Edge Hill Honours courses in Geography, Human Geography, Physical Geography and Physical Geography and Geology are offered. Fieldwork locations include Hawaii, Norway, Morocco and India. There is also a course in Geotourism focusing on environments, communities, culture and lifestyles.

Edinburgh Geography may be studied as a natural science or a social science. The main distinction lies in the entry qualifications, which must include the basic sciences for the BSc course. There is a range of options including the economic and social landscape, disease and the environment and leisure studies.

Exeter* The undergraduate Geography programme extends over three years and offers alternative courses that lead to single or combined honours degrees in the Faculties of Arts, Science or Social Studies. There is a choice of field courses in the UK and abroad. Each student can therefore make his or her own specialist studies. Geography with European Study is a four-year course involving a year abroad. Joint honours courses are taken at the Cornwall campus.

Glasgow* Physical and human geography are covered in Year 1, followed by the study of a major world area, statistics, computing and mapping. Study abroad opportunities include Brazil, Iceland and Tanzania. Geography may be studied in the Arts, Social Science or Science Faculties, and is available as a joint course with a wide range of subjects.

Glasgow Caledonian Geography is offered as part of the Social Science degree.

Gloucestershire Human Geography and Physical Geography are studied over three years. Nine other subjects are available in the joint degree programme, including Biology, Psychology and English. Optional modules include Teaching English as a Foreign Language.

Greenwich Geography students elect to follow the BA or BSc courses at the end of the first year. Options include environmental or natural resources management and human geography. Sandwich course students go on industrial or commercial work placements in Year 3.

Hertfordshire A broad Geography degree (including the option of a work placement) is available with specialism in human or physical geography. It is also offered as a sandwich course and with the opportunity to study in Europe or North America and as a joint degree with up to 15 subjects.

Hull A modular course leading to a BA (Human Geography) or BSc (Physical Geography) is offered. The first year is common to both courses. Some modules can be taken in other subjects. Geography is also offered as a joint honours programme with History, Archaeology, Business or Marketing.

Keele The Geography (single honours), Human Geography and Physical Geography (both dual honours) courses offer field courses in the UK, Europe and further afield. Dual honours courses are taken with a second subject from more than 20 options.

Kingston The Geography courses offer a choice of options in both human and physical geography. These include regional geography and GIS. GIS can be studied with Business or Computing/Web Development.

Lancaster* All Geography students follow courses in human and physical geography and geographical techniques in Year 1. These, and environmental themes, develop in Years 2 and 3. There are also separate courses in Physical and Human Geography. Specialisms in North America and Australasia are also offered. Many of the courses have a strong applied theme, giving a broad picture of social, economic and environmental problems. In Year 2 there is an option of teaching Geography in a local school. Exchanges with the US may be arranged.

Leeds* Courses in Geography cover both social and natural science interests with one or two subsidiary subjects. The former offers a wide range of options with particular strength in urban and resources studies, and with compulsory field weeks and visits to France in Year 2. The BSc course aims to provide a broad base in geography while emphasising the scientific study of the environment. Geology or Transport Planning can also be studied with Geography.

Leeds Beckett Human Geography is offered, as a single honours course and also with Planning. International field trips are offered.

Leicester The Geography course has a common first year for BA and BSc students. Thereafter the BA students follow a human geography course, and a bias towards physical geography exists for BSc students, with a high degree of flexibility in option choice and specialisation. Year 1 supplementary subjects include archaeology, computer science, history and politics. A separate degree in Human Geography is offered whilst Geography can also be studied with Archaeology or Geology. See also **Combined Courses**.

Liverpool* Geography is offered as a BA or BSc course. Students follow first-year courses in physical and human geography and an introduction to the planet earth. Options are available in the first and second years. The physical geography element has a strong science bias. A course in Geology and Physical

Geography is also available. Archaeology, Biology or Management are additional options. Scholarships available.

Liverpool Hope The BSc Geography single honours course provides a mix of human, physical and environmental geography. Several combined honours combinations are also on offer. See also **Environmental Science/Studies**.

Liverpool John Moores The Geography course combines modules from both environmental and human geography. The course has a vocational emphasis, with core modules in GIS and overseas field projects. There is a BSc course which covers both human and physical geography.

London (King's)* Physical and human geography and geographical techniques are covered in the first year of the BA and BSc courses. Second-year and third-year students follow optional course units and present an independent geographical study.

London (QM) Geography is taught under the course unit system, enabling students to combine their own choice of geographical studies with a wide variety of other disciplines, for example economics, history, politics, geology or a modern language. There are separate courses leading to BA, BSc or BSc (Econ) degrees, including Human Geography.

London (RH) Geography courses cover physical and human geography and involve the interactions between people and their natural, economic and social environments. In Years 2 and 3 students have a free choice in the selection of specialist courses and are encouraged to acquire career-related skills. There is also a course combined with Environmental Archaeology.

London (SOAS)* This is the only Geography degree course that is specific to regions of the world, namely Asia and Africa. Various joint honours combinations are also available with 10 other subjects. There is also a course in Development Studies and there are eight joint courses with Geography including Law, Politics and History.

London (UCL)* Geography may be studied as either an arts or a science subject with students being offered both human and physical geography in the first year. All students have the same wide choice of options, designing their own second-year and third-year programmes. The International programme includes a year of study at an overseas university. Geography may also be studied as a joint degree with Economics. There is also a course in Environmental Geography.

London LSE* The BA Geography course focuses on human geography and the environment. There is also a course in Geography and Economics.

Loughborough Modular programmes in human, physical and environmental geography are taken in the first year of the Geography course followed by a wide range of options in the second and third years. Subsidiary options can be taken from non-geographical subjects including languages. Geography can also be studied with Economics, Management, Sport Management, Sport Science and History.

Manchester* Geography courses are offered in both the Faculties of Arts and Sciences, with a variety of subsidiary courses in Years 2 and 3. Geographical issues cover social, economic, historical and political topics, with 20 options in the final year. Optional modules include languages, arts and social sciences. Geography can also be studied with Archaeology or International Study, with the possibility of studying abroad, worldwide.

Manchester Met Several courses can be taken including Human or Physical Geography. Similar programmes are offered in GIS, with study in North America or Australia. Geography is offered with several subjects in the combined honours programme.

Newcastle Geography is offered in both the Faculties of Arts and Sciences. This is a modular course in which two modules can be taken from the Combined Studies or Arts programmes. Second-year and third-year courses offer similar optional and core topics. There is a BSc in Physical Geography, and Geography can also be taken with Planning, Mathematics or Statistics.

Northampton A BSc degree can be taken as a single honours subject with pathways in human geography or physical geography and as joint honours courses. Physical Geography is also available as a BA or BSc.

Northumbria The Geography BA/BSc course introduces human, environmental and physical geography. A wide range of options is available in the third year, including a Geography in Education module for students wishing to take a PGCE course. Geography is also offered with Environmental Management or Sports Studies.

Nottingham* BA and BSc students follow a common first-year Geography course in human and physical geography and also a course in GIS. Specialised topics begin in the second year, including meteorology, industry and transport, environmental studies and geomorphology. Geography can also be taken with Chinese Studies or Business.

Nottingham Trent A BSc degree in Physical Geography can be taken as a specialised study. A sandwich placement year is offered. Geography is taught at the Brackenhurst campus.

Oxford* The first-year Geography course introduces human and physical geography, and offers optional subjects (ethnology, geomorphology, sociology, political history or plant ecology), from which one must be selected. During the second and third years three geography papers are common to all students and there are optional topics, depending on students' geographical interests.

Oxford Brookes Geography (BA or BSc) combined honours courses are offered with a very large number of other subjects and courses. A compulsory field course abroad takes place in Year 2.

Plymouth The BA and BSc courses include optional work experience for a year, the latter with a further option to travel in Europe, the US or Australia. Geography is offered with Geology and Ocean Science, as well as a range of combined BA subjects.

Portsmouth The BA/BSc Geography honours degree is a single-subject, broad-based degree programme, offering a balance between both physical and human fields of interest. Degrees in Human and Physical Geography are also offered.

Queen's Belfast Human and physical geography are taken in the first year. In the second year, courses vary depending on the type of degree course chosen. Regional geography is studied in the second and third years alongside modules including social, human, economic, urban or physical geography with an introduction to earth science. BA programmes are offered in Environmental, Human and Physical Geography and BSc programmes in Physical Geography and GIS.

Reading Geography is offered with specialisation in human or physical geography, or both combined, or as geography and economics combined in the Regional Science degree course. A rare course in Meteorology with scholarships available can also be taken.

St Andrews* Geography is taught in the Arts and Science Faculties, the first two years being common to all students and allowing two other subjects to be studied. A system of teaching in small option groups follows for the next two years. Students may specialise in human or physical geography or may study groups of courses concerned, for example, with landscape processes, land and water resources. Some exchanges take place with European institutions.

St Mary's Geography is offered as a single or joint degree and provides an overview of physical, social, cultural and political aspects. A field trip to the Caribbean is offered in Year 3.

Sheffield* The BA Geography course focuses on human geography (population and environmental resources). The BSc course lays emphasis on physical geography (geomorphology, soil formation and vegetation) throughout. Geography can also be taken as a dual honours course with Mathematics, Politics, Sociology or Planning.

Sheffield Hallam A Human Geography course can be followed with options in urban, social and economic geography and modern languages. There is also a degree in Geography and Planning.

South Wales The course in Geography covers both the human and physical aspects of the subject. Human Geography and Physical Geography are available as single honours degrees, and there is a course in Natural History. Work experience and some sponsorships for Welsh-language students are available.

Southampton The BA and BSc Geography courses provide a common broad foundation until midway through the second year. Thereafter students begin to specialise and have considerable opportunity to select courses in transport geography, urban development, environmental change, remote sensing and hydrology. Physical Geography can also be taken with Geology or Oceanography.

Southampton Solent Courses in Geography with Environmental Studies or Marine Studies are offered and in addition there is a BSc course in Marine Geography and a large Maritime Operations programme covering topics from shipping and port management to yachting.

Staffordshire The BA Geography course emphasises human aspects of the discipline while the BSc course focuses on environmental and physical subjects. There is a broad range of options in Years 2 and 3. There are also degrees in Geography with Mountain Leadership, a foundation degree and two-year accelerated degrees.

Stirling The BSc Geography course is available as a four-year programme. Environmental Geography courses are offered as pathways in the Environmental Science programme.

Strathclyde The course specialises in Human Geography including population dynamics, society and nature and natural hazards. Joint courses are offered including German, Law, Psychology, Sociology and Human Resource Management.

Sunderland Geography is offered with over 25 other subjects including American Studies, Criminology, Business Studies, Human Resource Management and Journalism or as a single honours subject covering both human and physical geography. A career placement is offered for Geography students. A PGCE course specialising in Geography is also available.

Sussex* The subject emphasis of the Geography course depends on the school chosen. It can cover environmental, social, physical or urban issues and historical geography, physical geography, resource development and geographical analysis. Six joint courses can be followed.

Swansea Geography is offered in the Faculties of Arts, Science and Economic and Social Studies. The first-year course is common to all three faculties and deals with human, physical, economic and social issues in the practice of geography, computing, four compulsory courses and a selection from a very wide range of options. There are 10 joint honours programmes with subjects including Languages, Social Policy, Biological Sciences and Geoinformatics. Geoinformatics can also be studied as a joint honours course with Computer Science or Mathematics.

Ulster The Geography course covers human and physical geography and includes work experience or study abroad. Honours courses with DIS/DAS are available. Geography can also be taken as part of a modular programme with over 20 subjects.

Westminster The Human Geography course includes specialisms in European, UK and Third World geography and is taken as part of the Social Science programme.

Wolverhampton The Geography BSc course offers topics in soil management, pollution and the alpine environment, while the BA course focuses on Britain, the US and Eastern Europe. There is a common first year for both degrees. Eleven joint courses are also on offer.

Worcester BSc courses can be taken in Geography or Physical/Human Geography, with work placement opportunities.

OTHER INSTITUTIONS OFFERING GEOGRAPHY COURSES
Havering (Coll), Staffordshire Reg Fed (SURF), UHI.

ALTERNATIVE COURSES
Development Studies, Earth Sciences, Environmental Studies/Sciences, Estate Management, Town and Country Planning.

GEOLOGY/GEOLOGICAL SCIENCES

(including **Earth Sciences**)

(* indicates universities with entry requirements over 340 UCAS points)

SUBJECT REQUIREMENTS/PREFERENCES
GCE A level: Two to three subjects from sciences/Mathematics usually required. **GCSE:** English and Mathematics required.

SUBJECT INFORMATION
Geology is the science of the earth. Topics covered include the physical and chemical constitution of the earth, exploration geophysics, oil and marine geology (oceanography) and seismic interpretation.

Aberdeen Geology is offered with Petroleum Geology and is designed for those whose career intentions are with the petroleum industry. Geoscience degrees are also available. Geology can be taken with Physics. Students are able to take one year of study at an overseas institution.

Aberystwyth A degree course in Environmental Earth Science is offered covering the fields of earth science and physical geography. The subject can be taken with Education. There is also a course in Earth, Planetary and Space Science.

Bangor For all degree programmes in Ocean Science, including Geological Oceanography, students are sought with a good scientific background. In Year 1, all Oceanography students take core courses in ocean and earth science. In Years 2 and 3, the degree has a dominant oceanographic perspective. Oceanography can be studied with Computing. Courses in Coastal Geography and Marine Environmental Studies are available.

Birmingham Courses are offered in Geology, Environmental Geoscience (pollution and hazards) and Geology and Archaeology, Geography or Biology. Core courses and specialisms in the chosen degree are offered in Years 2 and 3. See also **Combined Courses**.

Brighton The BSc (Hons) Geology is accredited by the Geological Society of London, and is offered as a three-year course or with an optional placement year. It can also be taken combined with Geography. A new course in Earth and Ocean Science is awaiting accreditation.

Bristol* The Geology course in this leading research department is aimed at those who wish to practise geology professionally and the degree is regarded as the basic foundation for further training in industry or research. Two subsidiary subjects are taken. One other subject from the Faculty of Science is also taken in the first year with specialism in geology in Years 2 and 3. A degree in Environmental Geoscience is offered, as well as MSc courses with study in North America or continental Europe.

Cambridge* See under **Combined Courses**.

Cardiff* The Geology programme is open to those with no prior knowledge of geology. There is a strong fieldwork element and up to two modules per year can be taken possibly from other departments. Topics covered include the physical and chemical constitution of the earth, exploration geophysics and seismic interpretation, geological time and earth history. Courses in Environmental Geoscience, Exploration and Resource Geology, Earth Sciences, and Marine Geography are also offered; these are choices in Years 2 and 3.

Derby Geology is offered with a pathway in Environmental Hazards. The course is accredited by the Geological Society.

Durham* The first year of the Geology course introduces the basic principles and methods of geology and recent advances. Single honours students then continue through the second and third years with a study of special branches of the geological sciences, for example economic geology, lunar geology, geochemistry and geophysics. Geology is also offered as part of the Natural Sciences programme and there are also courses in Natural Sciences, Environmental Geoscience and Geophysics with Geology.

East Anglia The Geological Sciences course applies mathematics and physics to a range of natural phenomena such as floods, earthquakes and weather systems. There are also courses allowing study in continental Europe or North America or in industry. Courses are also offered in Meteorology and Oceanography.

Edinburgh The foundation of geological and other subjects is laid down in Years 1 and 2 with specialised studies following in Years 3 and 4. Courses in Geology, Geophysics, Geology and Physical Geography and Environmental Geoscience are offered. Overseas fieldwork takes place in Cyprus, Jamaica and Spain. A five-year MEarthSci Geology programme is available.

Exeter (Camborne School of Mines) Applied Geology (accredited by the Geology Society) and Engineering Geology and Geotechnics are offered as three-year full-time courses. Training courses are offered in Cornwall, Wales, Scotland and Spain. Excellent employment prospects.

Glasgow* The four-year degree in Earth Science offers an extensive range of options and has close links with geography and environmental management. Geology can be studied with a second subject such as Astronomy, and there is a Geological Science course. There is also a four-year course in Environmental Biogeochemistry.

Imperial London* The department offers three- and four-year BSc and MSci courses in Geology and Geophysics. A year abroad programme is offered with both courses.

Keele The dual honours in Geology is offered jointly with over 30 subjects. No previous knowledge of geology is required. The course covers rocks, minerals, fossils, geophysics and computing. A single honours course in Geoscience and a four-year MGeoscience are also available.

Kingston The courses in Geology and Applied and Environmental Geology assume no previous knowledge of the subject. Fieldwork is an important element of the courses. The Earth Sciences course is a broad study covering rocks, air, water and life systems and there is also an Earth Systems course together with a four-year degree with a foundation year in Earth and Planetary Sciences.

Lancaster The Earth Science and Environmental Science courses are integrated programmes covering land, weather, geographical and science topics. Earth Science can also be taken with Geography. There are options to study in North America or Australasia.

Leeds* The first two years in Geological Sciences cover a basic training in geology and the principles of geophysics plus a first-year study of two other relevant sciences. In the final year, students choose from a range of options that includes environmental geochemistry, global geophysics and engineering geology. Geophysical Sciences and Environmental Geology are also offered as three-year degrees or with an additional year in Europe or further afield. As of 2012, all fieldwork courses are free of extra costs for students.

Leicester* Nine courses are offered in the Geosciences programme with opportunities to study in Europe, the US or New Zealand. In the Geology course a supplementary subject is studied in the first year. Geology can also be taken with Environmental Geology, Geophysics, Paleobiology and Geography. All courses are accredited by the Geological Society of London.

Liverpool* A range of well-integrated courses in Geology and Geophysics can be followed in this Geology programme and there is a four-year course that includes a year in North America. Field courses take place in Scotland, Wales, Greenland and the Alps. Oceanography, Climate Studies and Earth Sciences courses are also offered.

Liverpool John Moores A three-year full-time course in Geology is offered with a four-year sandwich course option. Geography or Geology at A2 are preferred subjects. Programmes are accredited by the Geological Society or the Institute of Physics.

London (RH) Geology is offered as single or joint honours. The single honours course introduces geology, earth materials and earth structure. Second- and third-year options include marine geology, fossil fuels, mineral deposits and engineering geology. There are also courses in Geology with a year in industry or a year of international study and courses in Petroleum or Environmental Geoscience and Planetary Geology.

London (UCL) Geology is a broad-based three-year or four-year course covering all the major aspects of geological sciences. Introductory courses are available in maths, physics, chemistry or biology. Theoretical and practical skills are developed through the programme and students are encouraged to take a computing course. A year in industry programme is offered. There are also courses in Planetary Science, Environmental Geoscience, Paleobiology and Geophysics. The Department of Earth Sciences has the only Regional Planetary Image Facility of NASA images.

Manchester The Department of Earth Sciences offers degree courses in Geology, Earth Sciences and Petroleum Engineering. The common first year of the Earth Sciences course covers most aspects of geology and a basic training in physical science. Students select which stream to follow in the second year and have a choice of specialist options in the third year, including geochemistry, geology and environmental and resource geology. Geology can also be taken with Planetary Science or Geography, and a four-year MEarthSci course is available.

Oxford* The first year of the four-year Earth Sciences course is designed to cater for students with a variety of A level subjects (a good foundation is Chemistry and Physics with Maths, Geology or a biological subject). The course covers the main aspects of geology, geophysics and geochemistry.

Plymouth Students who enter the Geology course are expected to have an interest in geology, but not necessarily previous geological experience or qualifications. The degree in Applied Geology follows the same programme as Geology in Stages 1 and 2 but leads on to specialist modules in Stage 3, including mining geohazards, engineering geology, and volcanology. The programme is accredited by the Geological Society of London. There are also degree courses in Geology with Physical Geography, Computing or Geography.

Portsmouth Fieldwork forms a major part of the Geology course. Throughout the three years, the practical work is continually assessed and makes up to 25% of the total assessment in each year. There is a clear emphasis on the economic significance and practice of geology. There are also courses in Earth Sciences, Engineering Geology and Geotechnics, Geological Hazards and Paleobiology and Evolution. Courses are accredited by the Geological Society of London.

St Andrews* The Geoscience degree provides training across the earth sciences, geology and physical geography and can be studied as a single honours degree or it is offered with several subjects including Spanish, French and Management. There is also Environmental Geoscience.

See *Heap 2015: University Degree Course Offers* (Trotman Publishing) for details of offers

South Wales The Geology degree, which can be taken with a sandwich year, includes minerals surveying and exploration. A course in Geology with Physical Geography is also offered. Geology is also offered as part of the combined degree course.

Southampton* The Master of Geology degree offers the option of a year in North America. In the first year, Geology students take five units including geochemistry, map interpretation, mineralogy and petrology and paleontology. Additional subjects in the second year include geotechnics and geophysics, while third-year students choose options according to their interests. Geophysics, and Ocean and Earth System Science are also offered. There is also a degree in Geophysical Sciences with a common first year enabling students to transfer to degrees in Physics, Geology or Oceanography.

ALTERNATIVE COURSES

Chemistry, Civil Engineering, Earth Sciences, Environmental Science, Geography, Mining Engineering, Soil Science, Surveying and Geophysics.

HEALTH STUDIES/SCIENCES

(including **Occupational Therapy**, **Optometry**, **Podiatry**, **Radiography** and **Physiotherapy**)
(see also **Nursing** and **Sports Science/Studies**)
(* indicates universities with entry requirements over 340 UCAS points)

SUBJECT REQUIREMENTS/PREFERENCES

These vary according to the specific course and university.

Anglia Ruskin Three-year courses in Optometry and Ophthalmic Dispensing are offered from the Department of Vision and Hearing Sciences. Other courses include Healthcare Science, Health and Social Care, Primary and Community Care and Public Health.

Aston Degrees in Optometry and Healthcare Science are offered with clinical placement in Year 3.

Bangor A broad Health and Social Care course is offered covering care and counselling management and focuses on specific areas of practice with optional specialisation in nursing. These areas include mental illness, housing policy, personal social services, poverty and welfare law. In addition there is also a vocational course in Diagnostic Radiography and Imaging. See also **Nursing**.

Bath Spa The Health Studies degree offers a study of health issues related to social, cultural, economic and environmental factors. There is also a degree in Human Nutrition focusing on nutrition, food safety and health promotion and a separate course in Food with Nutrition.

Bedfordshire A course is offered in Health and Social Care, focusing on community care and health education. There are also degrees in Healthcare and Practice and Health Psychology.

Birmingham* Physiotherapy, a very popular course in all universities, comprises both university and clinically based modules. There is also a course in Dental Hygiene and Therapy.

Birmingham City Degree courses with placements are offered by way of the pathways Health and Well-being (Exercise Science; Individuals and Communities; Nutrition). There are also courses in Radiography and Radiotherapy, Speech and Language Therapy.

Bolton The Health Studies course focuses on the study of contemporary health issues relating to healthcare practice and has a range of specialist options.

See *Heap 2015: University Degree Course Offers* (Trotman Publishing) for details of offers

Bournemouth The Exercise Science course focuses on health and rehabilitation for the healthy, ill, disabled and sporting sub-populations. There are also professional practice courses in Occupational Therapy and Physiotherapy. see also **Nursing**.

Bradford Optometry, Occupational Therapy, Diagnostic Radiography and Physiotherapy are offered. Additional courses include Health and Social Care (part time) and also a part-time course in Dementia Studies.

Brighton Several courses are offered including Physiotherapy, Podiatry and Occupational Therapy.

Bristol UWE There are courses in Healthcare Science (Life Sciences) with specialisms in Blood Science, Genetic Science, Infection Science and Tissue Science. A further Healthcare Science course focusing on Physiological Science is also available and all courses have placements included.

Brunel* Degree courses are available in Occupational Therapy and Physiotherapy. Both courses place an emphasis on preparing students for working life by promoting autonomy and clinical practice.

Bucks New See under **Nursing**.

Canterbury Christ Church The Health Studies degree is a joint or combined honours programme with options in health promotion, education or psychology, public health nutrition and holistic health promotion. There are also degrees in Operating Department Practice and in Occupational Therapy leading to professional practice. There is also a degree in Diagnostic Radiography. The Paramedic Science degree has an April intake with applications submitted the previous year. Check with the university.

Cardiff* The degree in Optometry leads to registration by the General Medical Council, as do other courses in this subject. Courses are also offered in Occupational Therapy, Physiotherapy, Radiotherapy and Oncology, Radiography and Imaging and Intra and Perioperative Practice (a development of Operating Theatre practice), and Diagnostic Radiography and Imaging. There is also a Diploma in Higher Education award in Operating Department Practice Education.

Cardiff Met (UWIC) Courses are offered in Podiatry, Speech and Language Therapy and Complementary Therapies and Dental Technology. Clinical competence is assessed by examination of practical skills.

Central Lancashire A new course is offered in Strength and Conditioning covering biomechanical studies and psychology. The Health Studies degree covers politics, sociology, economics, philosophy, history and a study of health concepts and health service provision. The Stage 2 programme can focus on Community Health, Health Promotion or Health Policy and Management. There are also courses in Counselling and Psychotherapy, Occupational Therapy, Operating Department Practice and Physiotherapy.

Chester Courses are offered in Human Nutrition, Osteopathy, Health and Social Care, and Nutrition and Dietetics, some of which give full professional status. The Health and Social Care programme prepares students for work in diverse environments.

City The university is a major provider of education and training in health-related subjects. Courses offered include Speech and Language Therapy, Optometry and Diagnostic Radiography and Radiotherapy and Oncology. There are also degrees in Human Communication, which focuses on speech, language and hearing, and in Health Science, which is a course for practitioners to develop management roles.

Colchester (Inst) Health and Social Care is a broad course introducing students to the range of studies relating to career opportunities open in the health field, such as anatomy, physiology, mental health education and legal issues.

Coventry Degrees are offered in Dietetics, Occupational Therapy, Operating Department Practice and Physiotherapy. The Occupational Therapy course allows students to study Neurology and Paediatrics in Year 3.

Cumbria Courses cover Health and Social Care, Health Improvement, Occupational Therapy, Physiotherapy, Diagnostic Radiography, Health Assessment, Human Health and Pathophysiology and Complementary Therapies.

De Montfort The Health Studies degree course provides a preparation for careers in health service administration, education and promotion. There is also a degree in Human Communication leading to a qualification in speech and language therapy and a vocational course in Audiology. Several Youth and Community courses are also offered.

Derby Courses are offered in International Spa Management and Spa Therapies. Health can also be studied with Information Technology, Diagnostic Radiography and Occupational Therapy. The Health and Social Care course explores social policy, equality and mental health services.

Durham A course in Health and Human Sciences covers the biological sciences and cross-cultural approaches of social and cultural anthropology. There are opportunities to study abroad in Iceland, Czech Republic, Slovenia and Malta. There is also a course in Health and Wellbeing.

East Anglia Allied Health Professional courses are offered in Occupational Therapy, Physiotherapy, and Speech and Language Therapy. The courses include work placements, which are elective. Teaching groups are small and there is the chance to meet with students from other health disciplines.

East London The courses offered cover Health Studies, Health Fitness, Health Promotion and Health Services Management, Public Health, Acupuncture, Herbal Medicine, Physiotherapy and Podiatry, with many courses offering the opportunity for extended study.

Edge Hill Work-based experience takes place in Year 3 of the course in Health and Social Well-being, which focuses on community work. There are also degrees in Nutrition and Health and Public Health.

Edinburgh Napier The Acupuncture with Health Studies is a distance-learning course and is taught through a combination of online lectures, virtual tutorials, correspondence, group work and independent study.

Edinburgh Queen Margaret* BSc courses cover Audiology, Diagnostic and Therapeutic Radiography, Dietetics, Occupational Therapy, Physiotherapy, Podiatry, and Speech and Language Therapy, all leading to professional status.

Essex The courses offered are Health Studies and Social Psychology and Sociology. Both courses include elements of psychology with the latter offering a bias towards sociology

Exeter A BSc (Hons) course is offered in Medical Imaging (Diagnostic Radiography) and covers the areas of radiography, fluoroscopy, computed tomography, ultrasound, nuclear medicine and magnetic resonance imaging.

Glasgow A Health and Social Policy course is offered at the Dumfries campus with the opportunity to study abroad in Year 3. The course involves work placements.

Glasgow Caledonian Courses are offered in Diagnostic Imaging Science, Radiotherapy and Oncology, Optometry and Ophthalmic Dispensing (vision sciences), Occupational Therapy, Oral Health Sciences, Physiotherapy, Podiatry, Human Nutrition (also offered with Physiology and Sport Science), Dietetics and Radiography.

Gloucestershire Work-based experience takes place in the Health, Community and Social Care honours course which includes modules such as human lifespan development, addictive behaviour and criminal justice.

Glyndŵr The course in Complementary Therapies for Healthcare includes massage, aromatherapy and reflexology. There are also degrees in Occupational Therapy, Occupational Health and Safety, Health Studies and Acupuncture.

See *Heap 2015: University Degree Course Offers* (Trotman Publishing) for details of offers

Greenwich In addition to the Health BSc, which focuses on health systems and management, courses are also offered in Osteopathy, Health and Well-being, Acupuncture, Public Health, Health and Safety and Nutrition.

Hertfordshire The first Paramedic Science with Paramedic Award degree with work placement is offered with topics ranging across biosciences, pharmacology, psychology, law, ethics and health promotion. Placements constitute 40% of the course. Degrees in Dietetics, Nutrition, Paramedic Science, Radiography (Diagnostic or Therapeutic), Radiotherapy and Oncology and Physiotherapy can be studied. Health Studies is also offered as a joint course.

Huddersfield Courses are offered in Health and Community Studies or Nutrition and Public Health, Occupational Therapy, Physiotherapy, Podiatry.

Hull The degree in Global Health and Humanitarian Relief covers world health issues, health service systems and some aspects of biological science.

Keele The single honours degree in Physiotherapy includes clinical placements and modules focusing on health and well-being as well as rehabilitation.

Kent A course is offered in Health and Social Care that will appeal to potential employees in the NHS or social service departments and to potential managers in the voluntary and private social and healthcare sector.

Kingston Physiotherapy, Diagnostic and Therapeutic Radiography are studied at Kingston in Year 1 and at St George's for practical applications. In addition to a single honours course in Nutrition there is also a degree in Exercise, Nutrition and Health with an optional sandwich year.

Leeds The School of Healthcare Studies offers single honours courses in Audiology, Diagnostic Radiography, Cardiology, and Food Science and Nutrition.

Leeds Beckett Courses in Health include degrees in Sport, Physical Activity and Health, Physiotherapy, Dietetics, Nutrition, Public Health, and Clinical Language Sciences, which leads to qualification as a speech therapist. See also **Nursing**.

Leeds Trinity There is an interdisciplinary course in Nutrition, Food and Health.

Leicester A Physiotherapy course awarded by Coventry university is offered. Teaching takes place on two campuses at Leicester and Coventry, however while students are admitted to the department at Coventry, they mostly live and study in Leicester.

Lincoln The Health and Social Care course covers physical and social services, management and education and international health issues. There is also a course in Herbal Medicine leading to full professional qualification and also a degree in Acupuncture.

Liverpool Courses are offered in Nursing, Orthoptics, Physiotherapy, Physiology, Radiotherapy, Occupational Therapy, Dental Hygiene and Dental Therapy and Diagnostic Radiography. Courses are taught via lectures, seminars and tutorials.

Liverpool Hope The Health degree has a strong foundation in health, sociology, psychology and geography. Nutrition can be studied on the combined honours programme or as a minor pathway leading to a postgraduate study in Dietetics. There is a separate degree in Disability Studies, and a single honours course in Health Nutrition and Fitness.

Liverpool John Moores The School of Health is a major provider of healthcare education in the UK. Courses include Health and Social Care for Families and Food and Nutrition.

London (King's)* Courses are offered in Nutrition, Dietetics and Physiotheraphy. See also **Nursing**. The Nutrition course shares the same syllabus as the degree in Nutrition and Dietetics except that the latter has a dietetic research project and a 28-week placement in Years 3 and 4.

London (St George's) Courses are offered in Diagnostic and Therapeutic Radiography and in Physiotherapy. Courses are taught at both Kingston University and St George's. There is also a course in Healthcare Science (Physiological Sciences) available. See also **Computer Courses**.

London (UCL) There is a four-year course in Speech Sciences with clinical placements in London and the South East. A course is also offered in Audiology which leads to a qualification to practise as an audiologist in the NHS and elsewhere.

London Met The Health and Social Policy course covers a range of contemporary health and social policy issues. Courses are also offered in Herbal Medicinal Science, Human Nutrition and in Public Health and Social Care.

London South Bank Diagnostic Radiography, Occupational Therapy and several other health courses are offered including Acupuncture, Therapeutic Radiography and Chinese Medicine. Assessment is made through a variety of methods including placement competencies, essays and exams.

Manchester A degree is offered in Speech and Language Therapy (four years) leading to professional registration. There are also courses in Nursing, Optometry and Oral Health Science.

Manchester Met Health Studies involves sociology, psychology, biology and health promotion with specialisations in management, public health, physiology and complementary therapy. There is also a full-time degree in Speech Pathology and Therapy and courses in Environmental Health, Acupuncture, Nutritional Science and Physiotherapy.

Middlesex Complementary Health courses predominate with degrees in Herbal Medicine, Ayurveda and Traditional Chinese Medicine. Study is enhanced by placements in the university's partner clinics.

Newcastle Speech and Language Sciences covers anatomy, psychology, linguistics and child language and leads to qualification as a speech therapist. Clinical practice increases throughout the four years of the course. There is also a course in Nutrition and Psychology.

Northampton Degrees are offered in Health and Social Care, and in Health Studies (joint honours) comprising biology, sociology, psychology and nutrition. Podiatry and Occupational Therapy can also be studied.

Northumbria Occupational Therapy and Physiotherapy courses are offered amongst various health courses including Public Health Practice and Practice Development. Assessment varies from essays and practice to exams.

Nottingham* Courses are offered in Physiotherapy, Dietetics and Nutrition and Healthcare Science, which prepares students to enter a number of disciplines in the NHS.

Nottingham Trent The Health and Social Care course offers work experience and the opportunity to study abroad.

Oxford Brookes* Opportunities exist to study Physiotherapy, Occupational Therapy, Osteopathy, Nutrition, Health and Social Care, Hearing Aid Audiology and Public Health Nutrition. Funding and scholarships available.

Plymouth Courses offered include Food Science, Nutrition and Dietetics, Physiotherapy, Podiatry, Occupational Therapy and Health and Social Care Studies. Funding is available from the NHS.

Portsmouth Degrees offered include Diagnostic and Therapeutic Radiography, Dental Hygiene, Dental Therapy and Healthcare Science. There are three clinical placements over the three years which are assessed.

Reading The degree in Speech and Language Therapy is a training course leading to speech therapy careers. There are also courses in Nutrition and Food Science and Nutrition with Food Consumer Sciences.

See *Heap 2015: University Degree Course Offers* (Trotman Publishing) for details of offers

Robert Gordon Courses in Occupational Therapy, Physiotherapy and Diagnostic Radiography are offered by the School of Health Sciences. Nutrition and Dietetics courses are also offered.

Roehampton Nutrition and Health is offered as a single honours course and covers subject areas including vitamins, minerals and health, dietary change and public health.

St Mark and St John Courses in Speech Sciences and Speech Language and Therapy lead to professional status. Other courses include Health and Social Welfare and Health, Exercise and Physical Activity.

St Mary's Health, Exercise and Physical Activity is a theoretical study of health promotion focusing on lifestyle and behaviour. There is also a course in Clinical Exercise Science.

Salford Several courses are available including Counselling, Health and Well-being, Diagnostic Radiography, Exercise and Health Sciences, Occupational Therapy, Sports Rehabilitation, Prosthetics and Orthotics, Physiotherapy and Podiatry.

Sheffield A course in Speech Science is offered (leading to work as a speech and language therapist). Health and Human Sciences, and Orthoptics are also offered.

Sheffield Hallam Degrees are offered in Occupational Therapy, Physiotherapy, Diagnostic Radiography, Radiotherapy and Oncology, Health and Social Care Professions, Health and Social Care Service Management and Human Bioscience.

South Wales A four-year full-time course is offered in Chiropractic leading to professional registration. Degrees in Medical Sciences and Health and Social Care are also offered.

Southampton* Courses are offered in Audiology, Occupational Therapy, Physiotherapy and Podiatry. The courses are designed to challenge students practically, academically and personally and can be studied full or part time.

Southampton Solent There are courses in Health and Fitness Management and Fitness and Personal Training, each with a six-week placement at the end of Year 1.

Staffordshire A course is available in Health Studies which includes a foundation year which can lead to a number of options including Nursing, Midwifery and Social Work.

Strathclyde There are courses in Speech and Language Pathology and also Prosthetics and Orthotics, a highly practical course dealing with clinical biomechanics and limb replacements.

Sunderland Health and Social Care offers a broad multidisciplinary study of health covering biological, psychological and sociological perspectives. There are also degrees in Community and Public Health and in Social Care.

Teesside There are courses in Diagnostic Radiography, Physiotherapy, Food and Nutrition, Occupational Therapy and Social Work with Nursing. On completion, students are eligible for registration with the Health and Care Professions Council.

Trinity St David There is a degree in Health Nutrition and Lifestyle with an exchange programme available in Year 2. Courses in Health and Exercise and Sports Studies are also available.

Ulster Courses are available in Health and Social Care Policy, Health and Well-being, Dietetics, Human Nutrition, Occupational Therapy, Optometry, Radiography (Diagnostic and Therapeutic), Physiotherapy, Podiatry and Speech and Language Therapy.

West London There are courses in Health Promotion and Public Health, Operating Department Practice, Nutritional Therapy and Nutritional Therapeutics. There are also various Nursing courses available.

West Scotland A three- or four-year degree in Environmental Health covers public health, physiology and medical chemistry. The Health and Lifestyle course includes nutrition and stress management. There is also a course in Occupational Health and Safety.

See *Heap 2015: University Degree Course Offers* (Trotman Publishing) for details of offers

Westminster Complementary therapy courses are available in Human Nutrition, Herbal Medicine, Nutritional Therapy and Acupuncture. There is also a BSc honours course available in Herbal Medicine which is fully accredited by the National Institute of Medical Herbalists.

Wolverhampton Health Studies, Public Health, Rehabilitation Studies and a degree in Complementary Therapies are offered. The latter can follow a general course or alternatively there is a choice of a specialist route in Aromatherapy or Reflexology or both. There are also degrees in Conductive Education, dealing with children with motor disorders, and Deaf Studies.

Worcester Health and Social Care is offered with modules including understanding health, work-based learning and politics, policy and empowerment. The course is assessed through coursework, reflective practice and portfolio work, presentations, case studies, reports and practical assessment.

OTHER INSTITUTIONS OFFERING HEALTH STUDIES/SCIENCES COURSES
Blackburn (Coll), Blackpool and Fylde (Coll), Bradford (Coll Univ Centre), Bristol City (Coll), Brit Coll Ost Med, CAFRE, Chesterfield (Coll), Cornwall (Coll), Duchy (Coll), European Sch Ost, Exeter (Coll), Filton (Coll), Grimsby (Univ Centre), Hopwood Hall (Coll), Leeds City (Coll), Loughborough (Coll), Neath Port Talbot (Coll), Nescot, Newcastle (Coll), Norwich City (Coll), Sheffield (Coll), South Devon (Coll), Sunderland City (Coll), Truro (Coll), Tyne Met (Coll), UHI, Wakefield (Coll), Walsall (Coll), Warwickshire (Coll), West Anglia (Coll), Wigan and Leigh (Coll), Worcester (CT), Writtle (Coll), York (Coll).

ALTERNATIVE COURSES
Biological Sciences, Biomedical Sciences, Dietetics, Food Science, Medical Sciences, Nursing, Nutrition, Sports Science.

HISTORY

(including **Medieval Studies**)
(* indicates universities with entry requirements over 340 UCAS points)

SUBJECT REQUIREMENTS/PREFERENCES
GCE A level: History usually required.

SUBJECT INFORMATION
History is a very broad subject, with most courses covering British and European history. There is, however, a wide range of specialist topics on offer, for example American, Scottish, Welsh, Irish, East European and Far Eastern history.

QUESTIONS TO CONSIDER
* Does the course focus on the period of history I want to study?
* Are there diverse or unusual modules which I may find stimulating?
* If I choose a combined degree, how closely does that faculty work with the history faculty?

Aberdeen The degree in History includes coverage of European and British history, medieval history, Scottish history and modern world history. In Years 3 and 4, options cover a wide range of topics. In addition, there is a course in Scottish Studies and also one in Celtic Studies covering literature, music, language and the Gaelic community. The degree in Cultural History covers social relations, resources, beliefs and values. There is an option to take joint honours with a variety of subjects including Anthropology, Languages and Politics.

See *Heap 2015: University Degree Course Offers* (Trotman Publishing) for details of offers

Aberystwyth A very wide range of single honours courses is offered including History, European and Welsh History and Medieval and Early Modern History. There are also 25 joint courses with History and the option to study abroad in the US, Czech Republic, Germany and Hungary.

Anglia Ruskin British, European and American History is offered with a wide range of topics including American and Latin American history, politics and war studies. History is also offered with English and Sociology.

Bangor A general introduction to the History course includes four modules covering early and modern history with optional modules from other subject areas including archaeology. In Years 2 and 3 a range of specialist history topics can be taken including medieval, modern and British political history, archaeology, Renaissance art, Arthurian Britain and Celtic heritage. History courses are also offered with Archaeology, Film Studies, Journalism, Heritage Studies and Welsh History.

Bath Spa The degree in History is a modular course with a very wide range of options allowing students to choose their own field. Modules include politics and literature, early modern witchcraft and the Third Reich. There is also a degree in Heritage which can be studied as a joint or minor course with History.

Birmingham* History courses offered cover the range of studies from Ancient and Medieval History to Modern History. The former extends from the classical world to its Western medieval and Byzantine successors. Modern History offers a thematic approach from 1500 to the present day. There is also a course in Economic and Social History.

Bishop Grosseteste Single and joint honours History courses are offered.

Bradford Modern European History is offered and includes elements of political theory and international relations with a focus on European history. There are also courses in History and Politics and Economics and History.

Brighton The degree course in Cultures, Histories and Literatures covers critical traditions in Western thought, nation and identity, history, narratives and gender and local history. Culture forms include novels, newspapers, films and photographs. Modern History is also offered as part of the Humanities course. There are also courses in Community and Family History and Museum and Heritage studies.

Bristol* The course covers medieval and modern history in Europe and offers a wide range of specialised units. Language options are available in the first two years. There is a separate degree in Ancient History focusing on the Greek and Roman world which can combine the study of ancient languages.

Bristol UWE The History course focuses on Early Modern and Modern History covering British, European, imperial, international, American and women's history. Complementary modules in other subjects are offered. There is also a course in History and Politics.

Brunel The History course involves a core curriculum and optional modules with an emphasis on social, political, intellectual or cultural history and offers an optional work placement module. The courses offered cover British, European, American and Russian history. History is also offered with Politics and Professional Development.

Buckingham Two main paths can be followed in the History programme, covering British History from the earliest times to the present day and International History from 1800. History is combined with French, Spanish, Politics, English Literature, Economics and the History of Art as a joint, major or minor subject.

Cambridge* The History course offers a flexible timetable with a choice of five from 22 periods of history in Years 1 and 2 and a focus on cultural and social history and politics and economic development. A wider range of courses can be taken in Year 3. Year 2 offers shared options with faculties such as Modern and Medieval Languages and Classics.

See *Heap 2015: University Degree Course Offers* (Trotman Publishing) for details of offers

Canterbury Christ Church The History course covers medieval and early modern history with the option to study modern history in Year 2 and a pathway in archaeology in Years 2 and 3. A wide range of options can be selected in Years 2 and 3. Joint and combined courses are possible.

Cardiff* The History course introduces medieval history and contemporary history. Specialist topics are offered in the second and third years covering British, European and Asian history. There are specialist degree courses offered in Welsh History, Ancient History and Ancient and Medieval History, and with Archaeology as well as various joint honours combinations.

Central Lancashire The History course covers Britain and Europe and also focuses on North America and Asian history. Joint subjects include Law, Politics, Film and Media and American Studies. Other courses include Modern World History and History, Museums and Heritage. There are also joint courses with English Literature, Education, Law, Sociology and Politics.

Chester Single and combined honours courses are offered in History with options in world, American, Irish and British history. Popular combinations include Archaeology, English, Law and Theology.

Chichester History is a broad course covering a range of subjects covering British European, American and African Political history as well as education, local history, the heritage industry, film, the 1960s and early modern art. During Year 2 some students have the opportunity to undertake a placement in a heritage institution.

Coventry The History course focuses on the 20th century. Students can specialise in North American history, European history, social history or the history of organised crime.

De Montfort A broad course in History is offered covering the period from the French Revolution to the modern world with modules ranging from US ethnic history in Year 2 to Yugoslavia and beyond in Year 3. Joint honours subjects include Education, Film Studies, Politics and International Relations.

Derby History is offered as part of the Humanities programme and covers modern British, European and international history from the Renaissance to the modern day. The course focuses on social, economic, cultural, military and political history and is assessed by 100% coursework.

Durham* The History course focuses on the history of the West from the fall of the Roman Empire. In the first year, all students read early European history from the fourth to the 11th century and later choose two courses from a selection of history topics. In the second and third year specialist topics are followed. BA History can be combined with Ancient History, English and Modern European Languages. Courses are also offered in Ancient History and the History and Philosophy of Science.

East Anglia* The School of History offers courses in History and Modern History with over 100 units offered including Anglo-Saxon England, the history of Norwich, and madness and medicine. A minor or joint subject can be taken as one-third of the degree; subjects offered include English, Politics, Law and Languages. There are also courses in History and History of Art and Landscape Architecture.

East London The History course covers Britain and cultural imperialism and the development of British society from the 18th century. There is the option to take joint honours with a range of subjects including English Literature and International Politics.

Edge Hill History is offered as a single, major/minor or joint honours course with eight other subjects. In the single honours course, specialisation is possible in British political, social and economic history or in European or American history.

Edinburgh History is a two-part course with the division coming at the end of the second year. In the first year, students focus on British and European history, plus two other courses from history or social science subjects. Specialised history courses are chosen by the student in the third and fourth years. A range of History degree courses are offered, including Ancient, Architectural, Scottish, Medieval, and Economic and Social History.

Essex This programme offers a comparative approach to history with an emphasis on the modern period. Courses are also offered in Modern, Contemporary, American and Social History and there are joint courses with Politics, Criminology, Languages, Law and Geography.

Exeter* Single and a wide range of joint honours courses are offered including International Relations and Ancient History. Ancient History can also be taken with Archaeology. Single honours History is available on both the Streatham and Cornwall campuses.

Glasgow* The History course covers medieval, modern and Scottish and European history. Scottish History is also offered as a single honours with topics including medieval society and 20th-century Scotland. There are also degree courses in a range of subjects which can be studied with Economic and Social History. Courses are also offered in Gaelic, Celtic Studies and Celtic Civilisation. See also **Archaeology** and **History of Art and Design**.

Glasgow Caledonian History is offered as part of the Social Science degree.

Gloucestershire History is offered with a wide range of subjects including Creative Writing, Education Studies and Psychology. The staff have expertise in American, British, European and Russian history and offer modules including the Victorians, black America and Soviet history. There is an optional work placement module. History can also be taken with Religion, Philosophy and Ethics.

Glyndŵr History degrees can be combined with English, Creative Writing and Welsh Language Studies. Study themes cover medieval, Renaissance and modern history in a Welsh, British, European and international context.

Greenwich Early modern and modern British, European and world history are the main features of the BA History course. History can be combined with English, Politics or a foreign language or as part of the combined honours programme. Studies include Britain at war, early modern England and magic and witchcraft.

Hertfordshire History is offered as a single honours subject and also with one of several subjects including Journalism, New Media Publishing and Film. The course focuses on history from 1500 onwards with modules including Britain and Africa c 1750–2000, women in Britain and public history, memory and heritage.

Huddersfield The modular course in History covers medieval, modern, British, European and world history. The course includes a work placement in the second year. History can also be combined with English, Journalism, Politics and Heritage, Media and Sociology.

Hull The first year of the History degree has seven modules covering a range of periods and options in social, maritime and art history. A special subject is chosen in Year 3. There is also a course in 20th century History and 10 joint courses. The department also incorporates Archaeology and the History of Art, providing opportunities to specialise.

Keele The single honours History degree offers modules in historical research and writing, medieval Europe, early modern Europe and modern Europe.

Kent Courses include British History, European History (with one year in France or Germany) and History joint degrees including Drama, Film, Archaeology or Politics. There is also a separate course in Ancient History which can be combined in 13 joint courses.

Kingston The History course has a focus on 19th- and 20th-century British, European and American history. Opportunities are provided to study an additional language and to study in Europe and the US. History can also be studied with another subject, ranging from Languages, History and Ideas, Journalism and Creative Writing to Criminology.

Lancaster* The History course offers a very wide selection of topics including medieval and modern history, British, European, American and Russian history. Some exchanges with the US and with European universities are possible. A course in Medieval and Renaissance Studies is also offered. There are also 10 combined courses with History.

Leeds* The size and structure of the school enables it to offer a wide range of History options over the whole of European, British and world history, from ancient to contemporary. The International History and Politics course sets the international events of the recent past firmly into their historical context. Taking the first-, second- and third-year courses together, all students will have studied international history from 1494 to the present day. Joint courses include Economic and Social History.

Leeds Beckett History is offered as a single honours degree or with English. With four areas of focus the course covers European history, social and cultural history, empire and migration, and working with history.

Leeds Trinity History is a single honours course covering Roman Britain to the present day with additional studies covering American and Chinese history.

Leicester In the first year of the History course modules include medieval, early modern, modern and global history. In the second and third years subjects are chosen from British, European (a year in Europe is an option) and non-European history. Other degree courses cover Contemporary History and combinations with Politics, Ancient History, Archaeology and International Relations. See also **Archaeology**.

Lincoln A single honours History course covering historical skills, society and popular culture with first-year modules focusing on the social history of medicine, American histories and the English Civil War.

Liverpool* A broad-based History course enables students to develop their interests within a wide range of periods and geographical areas. These cover medieval history, modern history and 20th-century Britain in Year 1 plus a module from another department. Students select options in Year 2 and follow a comparative course in Year 3. There are opportunities to study abroad, currently in the US, Hong Kong and Australia. Ancient History is also offered with Archaeology, and there are also courses in Irish Studies and History, and Modern History and Politics and History with Languages.

Liverpool Hope The History degree is offered as a single or combined honours course. The course involves extensive fieldwork activities and runs study visits to Berlin. Popular combinations with History include Politics, Theology and World Religions.

Liverpool John Moores History is offered as a single honours degree or in conjunction with other subjects including Human Geography, English, American Studies, Politics and Sociology. A study is made of British, European and non-European history (1700 to present day). See also **Social Sciences/Studies**.

London (Goldsmiths) History students take a compulsory course in concepts and methods, with a choice of three other foundation courses. In the second year they choose a selection of courses from a related discipline, and in the final year concentrate on a special subject. Other degree courses include History and History of Ideas, Anthropology, English and Politics.

London (King's)* History students can develop their interests in ancient, medieval or modern history in this course by way of a very large range of modules. Combined Studies courses in War Studies are offered with 12 subject choices.

London (QM)* The History course is aimed at those students who do not wish to specialise in any one period. The programme covers British, European and American history with options in other periods. Specialised subject areas are covered in other degrees such as History and Comparative Literature, History and German and History and Politics.

London (RH)* In addition to the single honours course in History, courses are offered in Ancient History, Modern History and Politics with an option to study in Europe. There are also courses in History with International Relations and History with a year studying abroad.

London (SOAS)* Seven regional and thematic pathways are offered in the History course covering Africa, the Near and the Middle East, the Indian sub-continent, South East Asia, China and Japan and the modern Third World. Over 20 joint courses in Far Eastern languages are also offered.

See *Heap 2015: University Degree Course Offers* (Trotman Publishing) for details of offers

London (UCL)* Courses include modules covering Ancient History, Medieval or Early Modern History and Modern History. A year abroad in North or Latin America can be taken and also History with a European language. There are also degree courses in Jewish Studies, Jewish History, Egyptology and the Ancient World.

London LSE* The school offers a range of historical studies including degrees in History, Economic and Social History, Government and History, and International Relations and History. Modules in single honours History include the history of Russia and modernity and the state in East Asia.

London Met History can be taken as a single or joint degree and covers British, imperial, Caribbean, Irish and European history. The degree is flexible and can be studied in the day or in the evening.

London NCH This course provides a structured route into the past in all its guises. The subject matter ranges from an introduction to ancient history to civil rights in 1960s America, and from ethnicity, identity and citizenship in modern British life to the interpretation and writing of history. The foundation units provide a general introduction to the subject and its methodology; in the remainder of the course, students study their chosen areas in more detail.

Manchester* A broad History course includes options covering all the major historical periods with the option of joint honours with American Studies, Sociology and a range of European languages. There are also opportunities to spend part of the degree studying abroad. There is also a course in Ancient History and Archaeology.

Manchester Met Students have the chance to study History, Medieval History and Modern History, Modern History, Political History, Social History and American History for the first year before deciding on which area to specialise in. History is also available as a combined honours degree.

Newcastle* In the first year of the History course students can choose to study British, European or American history alongside core modules which offer an introduction to studying History. There is also a course in Politics and History, Classics, Classical Studies and Ancient History.

Newman History is offered as a single, joint or minor course with another subject. There are also courses in Local History, Classical Civilisation and Ancient History.

Northampton The university offers a single honours course and a wide range of joint courses with History. Areas of study include witchcraft trials, the Holocaust and modern medical history.

Northumbria The History programme offers a breadth of historical knowledge covering Britain, Europe and world history from the medieval period to the present day. History is also offered with Politics.

Nottingham* The History course covers the period from AD500 to the present day and is offered as a single honours subject and also in a range of joint courses including with Art History, Politics and Contemporary Chinese Studies. There are also courses in Ancient History and there is a unique course in Viking Studies covering language, history, literature and archaeology.

Nottingham Trent In the History course, foundation modules are taken in medieval and modern history leading to a wide range of units covering British, European and American history. History is also offered as a joint course with 14 other subjects.

Oxford* The Modern History course covers the history of the British Isles and European history. In the first year, students take papers in a period of British history, but thereafter there is considerable choice at all stages. Other degree courses offered include Ancient and Modern History and Classical Archaeology and Ancient History and joint courses with Economics, English, Politics and Modern Languages.

Oxford Brookes The first year of the History course introduces the study of history with modules including modern Europe and the age of revolutions, followed in Years 2 and 3 with modules on British and European history. History can also be studied with other subjects in the modular degree scheme including Publishing, Geography and Leisure and Tourism. There is also a course in the History of Medicine. There is also the opportunity for students to earn credits learning a foreign language.

Plymouth The History degree has an emphasis on British, American, European, African and Asian history with the option to study modules from History of Art. There is also a wide range of History joint courses which include English and International Relations.

Portsmouth History is offered as a single honours course or can be studied in joint courses with Politics and English. The course places emphasis on the social and cultural history of Europe between 1450 and 1990 with modules including outlaws at sea and British society in the 1930s.

Queen's Belfast The History course covers periods from early Greece and the later Roman Empire to the early Middle Ages up the 20th century. Although it covers Great Britain and Ireland, there are also modules on North America, China and Africa.

Reading In the first year, two themes are introduced in approaches and landmarks in history. This provides a foundation for the more specialised topics chosen in the third year, covering British and European history. Joint courses are also offered and there is also a course in Ancient History.

Roehampton History can be taken as a single honours subject or in joint courses with subjects including Art History, Classical Civilisation, English and Philosophy. Modules include a study of Muslims, Jews and Christians in medieval Iberia.

St Andrews* An integrated single honours course in History is available for students who wish to take a degree course covering various types of historical subject matter. Specialist modules are taken from ancient history, history or Scottish history. Courses are also offered in Medieval, Modern and Scottish History.

St Mary's History can be studied as a single or joint honours course with pathways in general history or in modern, early modern or military history. There is also a course in Irish Studies.

Salford A degree in Contemporary Military and International History is offered, which covers the period from World War I to the present day. There is also a programme leading to a degree in Contemporary History and Politics.

Sheffield* At Level 1 of the History course a study is made covering the period from the fall of Rome to the present day with options in European or American history. Options across these fields continue in Level 2 and special studies on selected themes follow in Level 3. Other courses include Archaeology and History, and History and Politics.

Sheffield Hallam The History course concentrates on the 19th and 20th centuries in Britain with modules which look at the history of Europe, Africa, India, Australia and the US. History can also be studied with Criminology or English.

South Wales The History courses cover the social, economic, political and cultural history of British, Welsh, European and American history, sourcing information from film and media, literature and archaeology. The course can be studied with a combination of subjects including Professional Welsh and English.

Southampton* A general introduction in the first year of the History course covers both medieval and modern periods. Units available in the second year are: European and British history, economic, social, political, religious, intellectual and art history, and American civilisation. The third year is dominated by the study of a special subject. There are also joint courses available with History.

Staffordshire Courses in Modern and International History both as single or joint honours courses can be taken. The courses focus on the political, cultural and social history of the modern world from 1750 to the present day.

Stirling The History course covers British and European history from the 18th century and Scottish history from 1513. Specialist options are available as are opportunities to study in the US.

Strathclyde History is a principal subject in the Faculty of Arts and Social Sciences. Year 1 is designed as an introduction for students with no recent history qualifications as well as those with a history background. From Year 2, students choose from a very wide range of history subjects and periods which may include Scottish history and modern European history.

Sunderland History is offered as a joint honours course with subjects such as Comparative Literature, History of Art and Design, Media Studies, Photography and Psychology and focuses on modern history since 1500.

Sussex* The History degree is strong in early modern intellectual and contemporary history and enables students to explore a variety of subject areas alongside other subjects related to history. Degree courses are also offered in Contemporary European Studies and in Cultural Studies, and several joint courses are also available.

Swansea Specialist themes commence in Year 2 covering British, European and American history. In addition to single honours History, degrees are offered in Ancient and Medieval History, European History with a range of European languages and also with Latin.

Teesside The History course covers the 16th century through to the late 20th century with a wide range of optional modules. Degree courses are also offered in History with English, Media Studies or Politics. There are also courses in contemporary European History and Social and Cultural History.

Trinity St David The first year introduces the study of history through a range of case studies by investigating how the past was recorded, through visits to archives and museums. The second and third years cover British, European and American history. Courses are also offered in Ancient History, (scholarships offered), Ancient History and Archaeology, Ancient and Medieval History, Medieval Studies and Modern Historical Studies covering the Victorians, 20th-century Britain and the American Frontier.

Ulster History and Irish History may be taken as a single honours course or in combination with other subjects in the Humanities programme. History modules cover British, Irish and world history.

Warwick* Particular strengths include Renaissance, early modern British and European history. Courses offered include History (Renaissance/Modern; Modern) and History, Literature and Cultures of the Americas.

Westminster History is taken as a course within Social Sciences focusing on economic, social and political history and can be combined with English Literature, Politics or Sociology.

Winchester Courses are offered in History, and History and the Medieval or Modern World, and a number of joint courses are on offer including Criminology, Law and Theology.

Wolverhampton History is a modular course covering 20th-century Europe, early modern England, women's history, British social history from 1530, the Americas post-1860 and the West Midlands from 1600. There is also a degree in War Studies.

Worcester The History degree offers a study of significant political and cultural movements of the recent past covering British, European and world history. A range of joint courses can be taken.

York* The courses in History offer study in depth and a wide range of individual choice throughout. Students study many types of history from a wide geographical and chronological range. Teaching is mainly by individual tutorial and small-group seminar. Each student also undertakes an independent research project as well as a paper in historical methodology. History can be combined with English, Politics, Economics, Education, History of Art, Philosophy and French. Heritage Studies and Historical Archaeology are also available.

See *Heap 2015: University Degree Course Offers* (Trotman Publishing) for details of offers

York St John History can be studied as a joint degree with American Studies or English Literature. Modules include war and society, China 1911–1997 and conflict on the East Asian mainland.

OTHER INSTITUTIONS OFFERING HISTORY COURSES

Blackburn (Coll), Blackpool and Fylde (Coll), Bradford (Coll Univ Centre), Burton (Coll), Havering (Coll), North Lindsey (Coll), Peterborough (Reg Coll), Richmond (Am Int Univ), Ruskin Oxford (Coll), Suffolk (Univ Campus), Truro (Coll), UHI, West Anglia (Coll), Wigan and Leigh (Coll).

ALTERNATIVE COURSES

Archaeology, Economic and Social History, International Relations, Politics, Public Administration.

HISTORY OF ART AND DESIGN

(* indicates universities with entry requirements over 340 UCAS points)

SUBJECT REQUIREMENTS/PREFERENCES

GCE A level: No specific subjects required.

SUBJECT INFORMATION

Art History covers a very wide range of topics that involve a study of classical Greek and Roman art and architecture through to modern 20th-century art and design. The main focus is usually on painting and sculpture with a specialised study of the European schools of painting. Some courses, however, diversify into textiles, furniture, ceramic design, photography and film.

Aberdeen The History of Art course provides a broad introduction to the history of painting, sculpture, architecture and the decorative arts from classical times to the modern period. There is a focus on the Western European tradition and options in Latin American art.

Aberystwyth The university offers courses in Art History. Options range from the Renaissance to contemporary work including the history of graphic design and photography and Mannerism and Baroque. There is also an unusual degree scheme in Museum and Gallery Studies that includes new technologies and changes in display and the management of collections.

Birmingham* History of Art is offered as a single honours or a joint major/minor programme and covers Western art from the Renaissance to the present day. Part of the Easter vacation in Year 2 is spent abroad.

Brighton The History of Design, Culture and Society course specialises in the manufacturing and design aspects of modern industrial society and its beginnings from the 17th century. The History of Decorative Arts and Crafts course is a study of artefacts from 1880 to the present day in Britain, touching on 'exotic' and non-European art and design. There is also a course on Fashion and Dress History.

Bristol* The History of Art course provides a broad study of European and British art and architecture from the medieval period to recent 20th-century movements. There are opportunities to study abroad in Year 2 in the US and joint degrees with languages (French, German, Italian, Russian, Portuguese and Spanish) are also offered. Part-time study is available.

Buckingham The Art History course (January and September start dates) focuses on the visual arts and is offered as a joint honours course with French, Spanish, History, Heritage Management and Journalism.

See *Heap 2015: University Degree Course Offers* (Trotman Publishing) for details of offers

Cambridge* History of Art is a flexible course covering areas from classical antiquity to modern art but aiming to foster a deep understanding of Western European art and architecture. There is a compulsory paper on the display of art in Year 3. Not available at the following Colleges: Girton, Robinson and St Catharine's.

East Anglia* History of Art can be studied as a single course or with another subject such as Literature, History, Archaeology or Anthropology. There are options to study abroad.

Edinburgh The History of Art and Architectural History course topics include the art, sculpture and architecture of the Western world from late antiquity to the present day. In Year 3 students are placed within a gallery or similar institution or undertake a major project, e.g. writing exhibition reviews or cataloguing works of art, Scottish painting and American art. Other courses include Fine Art and Architectural History.

Essex This non-practical History of Art course includes the European Enlightenment and Case Studies in the History of Art. These are followed by a study of Tuscan art from 1330 to 1500. Topics also include Russian art, industrial design and the fine arts in England. There are also courses with Literature, Film and Modern Languages.

Exeter* The course in Art History and Visual Culture covers both traditional and contemporary art with opportunities to study abroad.

Glasgow* First-year studies in the History of Art provide an introduction to the history of art by analysing trends. This is followed by short courses concentrating on aspects of modern art, medieval art and architecture and Scottish art. The third and fourth years are devoted to special studies on specific artists. Travel grants available.

Hull History of Art is offered as a minor subject with History. The course covers a wide range of art subjects including museum work and auction studies. A travel fund is available to visit art in Italy.

Kent* Part I of the History and Philosophy of Art course covers history, media and genres, followed in Part II by historical studies and special options. There is also a multidisciplinary course in the Visual and Performed Arts and a degree in Art (History) and Film.

Kingston The History of Art, Design and Film course involves four main areas of study: art, architecture, design and film. The course can be combined with a range of subjects including English Literature, Film Studies and History.

Leeds There are courses in the History of Art and Museum Studies, the latter covering country house and museum collections and a study of the decorative arts.

Leicester History of Art is offered as a three-year course or over four years including a year in Europe. Practical art classes are available. Combined degrees can include History, Archaeology and Languages.

Lincoln The course in Conservation and Restoration covers drawings, photography and the decorative arts. The course builds confidence gradually for students who do not come from a science background.

Liverpool Hope The Art and Design History course covers the study of visual artefacts and museum and gallery organisations.

Liverpool John Moores The History of Art course involves collaboration with the Tate Liverpool and focuses on a practical as well as a theoretical framework involving the organising and designing of exhibitions.

London (Courtauld)* This specialist degree in the History of Art covers classical, Byzantine, medieval, Renaissance, early modern and contemporary art. The course is assessed through formal assessments and on an ongoing basis which involves contribution in class, presentations and written work.

See *Heap 2015: University Degree Course Offers* (Trotman Publishing) for details of offers

London (Goldsmiths) Fine Art and the History of Art consists of fine art studio practice, history of art courses and interdisciplinary studies which explore the relationship between the history of art and art practice.

London (SOAS) History of Art is offered as a single honours subject and also with Archaeology and has an emphasis on Asia, Africa and Europe. Joint courses with several other subjects can be selected.

London (UCL)* History of Art single honours students take two course units in either anthropology, history or philosophy to support their studies. The course focuses on Western art with specialised studies following in Years 2 and 3. Joint courses are offered with Dutch, French, German, Italian, Philosophy or Spanish. There is also a course in History of Art and Materials Studies involving conservation.

London Met The Conservation and Restoration course has work placements in leading galleries and museums. The course covers an introduction to conservation with the second year focusing on a study of historical and scientific methods of treatment and care and the third year involving an eight-week placement and dissertation.

Manchester History of Art is offered as a single subject or with another subject including a modern language and Archaeology. The course covers art history and visual culture from antiquity to the present. History of Art can also be taken with Music or Social Anthropology.

Manchester Met Contemporary Art History is a modular degree programme looking at contemporary art and interpretation. The course has links with local galleries and involves a work placement in Year 2.

Newcastle* History of Art is offered as part of the Combined Studies in Art degree and looks at art from 1945 onwards (previous experience of the subject preferred).

Nottingham The Art History degree focuses on painting, sculpture and graphic arts, photography and architecture in Western Europe from classical times to contemporary art. Joint courses are offered with subjects including Classical Civilisation, English and German.

Oxford* In Year 1, the History of Art course covers visual culture, Renaissance art to postmodernism, classical art and an extended essay on a building, object or image in Oxford. In Years 2 and 3, seven elements are taken involving the whole field of Western art from classical times to the present day.

Oxford Brookes History of Art focuses on Western Art from the 15th to 20th century and is offered as a single or joint honours course and can be combined with 12 subjects including Japanese Studies and Anthropology.

Plymouth Art History is offered as part of the Art and Design programme with Fine Art and also as a single honours course. The course includes a field trip to a major European city.

Reading The course in History of Art covers Western art and architecture with options to specialise in the history of painting, sculpture or architecture. Joint courses and Museum courses are also offered.

St Andrews* First-level courses in Art History cover the Renaissance and art in Britain from the early Middle Ages to the 19th century. This is followed by a study of European art from 1800 and the Modern Movement. Students then select specialist studies from a range of 25 modules. Over 20 joint courses are offered.

Sussex Art History focuses on Western art from Byzantium to the Renaissance to the present day. A study of special periods takes place in Year 2 and options in several specialisms are available in Year 3, including museum studies. Joint courses are offered with Modern Languages, Cultural Studies and Film Studies.

Warwick History of Art is a wide-ranging course covering the major periods of the history of art. A wide choice of options is offered throughout the course. A full term is offered in Venice.

See *Heap 2015: University Degree Course Offers* (Trotman Publishing) for details of offers

York In Year 1 History of Art students take modules focusing on critical readings, encounters with material objects and art-historical skills. The course is taught through lectures which provide an overview of art history and seminars which allow students to explore subjects in detail.

ALTERNATIVE COURSES

All practical Art and Design courses; Archaeology, Architecture, Classical Civilisation, Communication Studies, Film Studies, Landscape Architecture.

HOSPITALITY MANAGEMENT

(including **Hotel and Catering Management, Tourism** and **Events Management**)
(see also **Leisure, Recreation Management and Tourism**)
(* indicates universities with entry requirements over 340 UCAS points)

SUBJECT REQUIREMENTS/PREFERENCES

GCSE: English and Mathematics usually required plus a foreign language for International Hospitality Management courses.

SUBJECT INFORMATION

All courses provide a comprehensive preparation for entry into the hotel, catering, tourism and leisure industries.

QUESTIONS TO CONSIDER

* Are there opportunities for me to gain work experience in the relevant sectors?
* Is there a variety of modules, ensuring I learn about all areas of hospitality?
* Is there a specialist degree available?

Birmingham (UC) The Hospitality and Tourism Management course includes a year's industry placement. The Events Management course prepares students for work in conventions, conferences, music and festival events, exhibitions and media and product presentations.

Bournemouth The course in Hospitality Management involves a 40-week placement in the industry in Year 3 in the UK and overseas. Students can expect to study areas ranging from financial reporting and market economy through to food and beverage management and management decision-making.

Bournemouth Arts A degree in Arts and Events Management is offered.

Brighton The International Hospitality Management degree has optional modules including e-commerce, niche tourism, wine marketing and ecotourism. Progress is assessed through individual and group tasks throughout the degree. There are also courses in Hospitality and Event Management and International Event Management.

Canterbury Christ Church A course in Events Management covers entertainment and the arts, cinema, tourism and leisure marketing, heritage and festivals. There is no formal placement but students are encouraged to gain events work experience from a range of opportunities.

Cardiff Met (UWIC) There are degrees in International Hospitality with specialisms in Event, Marketing and Tourism Management. The courses in Events Management are vocationally oriented and students take a mandatory work-based module in the second year. The course is comprised of core management and specific events management modules.

See *Heap 2015: University Degree Course Offers* (Trotman Publishing) for details of offers

Central Lancashire Hospitality and International Hospitality Management are four-year sandwich courses which provide management education for those wishing to enter the hotel and leisure industries. The third year is spent on sandwich placement in the UK or overseas. There are also courses in Event Management and Tourism Management, both with options for a one-year placement in the industry.

Chester The Events Management course covers groups playing in local venues to Chester Races. The course is three years or four if a work placement is undertaken.

Colchester (Inst) The International Hospitality Management course covers general management studies, food and beverage studies, consumer behaviour and small business management.

Coventry The course in Event Management involves practical workshops and the opportunity to gain first hand experience in a range of events with international workshops focusing on sporting events in the Netherlands and Germany.

Derby The Events Management course can be studied as a single or joint honours. Courses are also offered in Culinary Arts, Hospitality Management (joint honours) and International Spa Management.

East London There are courses in Hospitality and International Tourism and the Events Management course offers the opportunity to study abroad.

Edinburgh Napier Hospitality Management is a modular course that includes options and electives. A foreign language option is available. Particular emphasis is given to personal development and transferable skills. There is a strong information technology resource base. There are also courses in Festival and Event Management with Languages, Tourism, Hospitality and Human Resources Management.

Edinburgh Queen Margaret The International Hospitality and Tourism Management course covers food service and preparation in Years 1 and 2 with a nine-month work placement. There is also a course in Events Management.

Glasgow Caledonian The International Tourism and Travel Enterprise degree aims to develop students' skills in the travel and hospitality sectors with the opportunity for students to choose which sector to pursue.

Gloucestershire Hospitality Management is offered with a range of subjects in the modular degree scheme including Events Management and Tourism Management. There is a compulsory placement for honours Event Management students.

Hertfordshire A degree is offered in Event Management with an optional year in paid work placement. Teaching is mainly through lectures, seminars and tutorials and assessment is through coursework and examinations.

Huddersfield The Hospitality Management course requires entrants to have skills and knowledge in Hospitality Management to HND level or similar and can be taken with a modern language. There is also an Events Management sandwich course.

Kent The course in Creative Events provides the opportunity to explore the options in organising and the management of events such as product presentations in industry and commerce and a wide range of social, sporting and professional meetings.

Leeds Beckett The sandwich course in Hospitality Business Management covers all aspects of the industry: food and accommodation studies, tourism, European business, management and manpower studies, finance, law and business policy. Other relevant courses include Events Management and Sport Event Management, Hospitality Leadership and Management, and Conference and Exhibitions Management.

Liverpool John Moores There is a course in Events Management which includes a year-long industrial placement.

London Met Events Management and Events Marketing Management are offered.

See *Heap 2015: University Degree Course Offers* (Trotman Publishing) for details of offers

Manchester Met Hospitality Management covers operations management (catering and accommodation) and includes management and business, which are the core subjects in Years 1, 2 and 4. Industrial placement occupies the third year. There is also a course in International Hospitality Management and other courses in Events Management.

Oxford Brookes There is a four-year single honours course in International Hospitality Management with industrial placements in the UK and abroad. There is an emphasis placed on professional and personal development.

Plymouth Hospitality Management is a modular programme that includes hospitality, the consumer, food and beverage services, front office and accommodation services. There is also a sandwich course in International Hospitality Management with French and German modules. Optional industrial placements are available following Year 2. There are also courses in Cruise Management, Events Management and Tourism and Hospitality Management.

Portsmouth Hospitality Management is a four-year sandwich course with industrial experience taking place in Year 3. The course covers catering and accommodation studies, behavioural science, personnel work, law, marketing and finance. Similar courses emphasise tourism or marketing. The degree can also be combined with Tourism.

Robert Gordon International Hospitality Management is offered as a four-year full-time course with the chance to study abroad. There is also a course in Events Management which includes guest lectures.

Salford Hospitality Management is a modular course with shared units which can be taken as a three-year degree or over four years with a placement. There is also a course in Hospitality and Tourism Management. Both courses come with the option of study abroad.

Sheffield Hallam Hospitality Business Management with the Conference and Events or the International options share a common first year with the BSc course in Hospitality Business Management and with the BSc course in Hospitality Business Management with Culinary Arts. The courses are accredited by the Hotel and Catering International Management Association.

South Wales The course in Event Management covers the social and cultural aspects of tourism and the leisure industry as well as practical business experience. It is available as a sandwich course.

Strathclyde Hospitality and Tourism Management courses cover hotel operations with options in tourism, food and beverage, and leisure management and planning. In the first and second years, one class is normally chosen from business-related subjects such as marketing, business law, computing and accounting and finance.

Surrey Courses with a worldwide reputation are offered in International Hospitality Management (four years) and International Hospitality and Tourism Management with placements in the UK and abroad.

Ulster International Hospitality Management and Tourism Management are four-year sandwich courses that cover food and accommodation studies, tourism, accounts and marketing. There are also four-year sandwich degrees in International Hospitality Studies with languages.

West London The Hospitality Management course covers the business environment, operations (food/beverage/wines/spirits/room division) and includes information technology and accounting. There are also courses in Culinary Arts Management, Hospitality Management and International Hotel Management.

Winchester Event Management is studied in the context of leisure, business and tourism. The third-year final project can take the form of a work placement or a dissertation.

Wolverhampton Courses are offered in International Hospitality Management and Event and Venue Management. Both courses can be studied over three years full time or four years with a placement year.

See *Heap 2015: University Degree Course Offers* (Trotman Publishing) for details of offers

OTHER INSTITUTIONS OFFERING HOSPITALITY MANAGEMENT COURSES

Bedford (Coll), Blackburn (Coll), Blackpool and Fylde (Coll), Bradford (Coll Univ Centre), Bristol City (Coll), Chichester (Coll), Cornwall (Coll), Doncaster (Coll Univ Centre), Ealing, Hammersmith and West London (Coll), Euro Bus Sch London, Grimsby (Univ Centre), Guildford (Coll), Highbury Portsmouth (Coll), Leicester (Coll), Liverpool City (Coll), Llandrillo Cymru (Coll), Loughborough (Coll), Menai (Coll), Neath Port Talbot (Coll), NEW (Coll), Newcastle (Coll), North Lindsey (Coll), Norwich City (Coll), Nottingham New (Coll), South Devon (Coll), Stratford upon Avon (Coll), Suffolk (Univ Campus), Tameside (Coll), UHI, Walsall (Coll), Warrington (Coll), Warwickshire (Coll), Westminster Kingsway (Coll), Wigan and Leigh (Coll), Worcestershire (CT), York (Coll).

ALTERNATIVE COURSES

Consumer Sciences, Consumer Studies, Dietetics, Events Management, Food Science.

INFORMATION MANAGEMENT AND LIBRARY STUDIES

(* indicates universities with entry requirements over 340 UCAS points)

SUBJECT REQUIREMENTS/PREFERENCES

GCE A level: Subject requirements may apply to joint courses. **GCSE:** English, Mathematics and occasionally a foreign language.

SUBJECT INFORMATION

This subject area involves the study of information systems. These cover retrieval, indexing, computer and media technology, classification and cataloguing.

Aberystwyth This leading department offers courses in Information and Library Studies by way of 10 specialist joint subjects. There is also a unique course in Historical and Archival Studies in addition to courses in Museum and Gallery Studies.

Brighton The Museum Heritage course offers students an overview of the histories of art and design as well as engaging them in the ever-changing world of museums and galleries. It is offered full and part time.

Central Lancashire There is a course in History, Museums and Heritage. The course incorporates history with modules such as insight into museums and insight into archives, with work placements available.

Chester The Information Systems Management course is offered by the Department of Computer Science. Modules include data analysis, e-society and website production and development. There is a work placement in the second year.

De Montfort The BSc in Business Information Systems equips students to observe, manage, process, analyse, present and evaluate information. It focuses on databases, information systems and systems building.

Edinburgh Napier Business Information Systems offers a highly industry-focused, systems-oriented course set in the context of modern business. The course can be taken with a work placement, to last three and a half years (four and a half for honours) or three years without (four years for honours).

Gloucestershire Optional placements are offered on the Information Technology course through the Degree+ scheme, a year on a paid placement which counts towards the degree. Modules include network design and database application development.

See *Heap 2015: University Degree Course Offers* (Trotman Publishing) for details of offers

Glyndŵr The course in Library and Information Management is supported by the Chartered Institute of Library and Information Professionals (CILIP), CyMAL (Museums, Archives and Libraries Wales) and the Society of Chief Librarians (Wales).

Huddersfield A four-year sandwich course in ICT is offered with placement opportunities available locally, nationally and within Europe. The course aims to develop the student's transferable skills.

Keele There is a single honours degree in Information Technology Management for Business and a dual honours course in Information Systems.

Kingston Museum and Gallery Studies is offered as a joint honours course and can be combined with History of Art, Design and Film. The degree is aimed to equip students with the skills to move into the museum and gallery sectors as well as the larger sector of heritage and culture.

Lancaster IT for Creative Industries is offered with or without industrial placements.

Liverpool Hope The Information Technology course allows students to develop their specialist interests in aspects of information technology. The course will equip students with skills in SQL, Java, JavaScript, HTML and PHP.

London (QM) Courses are offered in Information and Communication Technology and with Business, including a year in industry.

London (UCL)* Information Management for Business has core courses in accounting, management and information. The degree is endorsed by e-skills UK and assessed through coursework and examinations.

Loughborough The Information Management course is offered with Computing or Business Studies and can be studied three years full time or four years as a sandwich course. It covers informatics, statistics, accounting, financial management, databases, systems modelling, knowledge management, electronic media and strategic management.

Manchester Met Information and Communications is a modular course, which is recognised by the Chartered Institute of Library and Information Professionals, and offers the basic core subjects covering management, information systems, retrieval and information technology. Special studies in Year 3 provide flexibility to cover areas of special interest to students. These include working in academic, business and commercial communities. Students are required to undertake placements.

Newman Information Technology can be taken as a single, joint or minor course with another subject. The course aims to develop the student's skills in both hardware and software and ensures recent developments in the industry are covered.

Northumbria Several courses in Information Technologies are offered as three-year full-time or four-year sandwich programmes. There is also a course in Librarianship which aims to aid students in furthering their careers in a library and information service environment.

Nottingham Trent The Information Communication Technology course has industrial placements following the second year.

Reading There are courses in Management and Information Technology and in IT with an industrial placement.

Sheffield Information Management is offered as a single subject course or with Accounting and Financial Management or Business Management and is accredited by the Chartered Institute of Library and Information Professionals.

Stirling A full-time and part-time degree is offered in Information Systems. The single honours degree is given full accreditation by the British Computer Society, the Chartered Institute for IT.

See *Heap 2015: University Degree Course Offers* (Trotman Publishing) for details of offers

West Scotland Information Technology is offered as a three-year or four-year full-time course or four-year or five-year sandwich degree. The degree is flexible with a range of modules to choose from.

Wolverhampton Information Technology Management is a modular course with a bias towards business and management and human factors over purely technical design. Business Information Systems and Management of IT are also offered.

OTHER INSTITUTIONS OFFERING INFORMATION MANAGEMENT AND LIBRARY STUDIES COURSES

Blackburn (Coll), Blackpool and Fylde (Coll), Bradford (Coll Univ Centre), Bristol City (Coll), Cornwall (Coll), Craven (Coll), Croydon (Coll), Havering (Coll), Hopwood Hall (Coll), Lincoln (Coll), Llandrillo Cymru (Coll), Neath Port Talbot (Coll), Nescot, Newcastle (Coll), Northbrook (Coll), Nottingham New (Coll), Pembrokeshire (Coll), Peterborough (Reg Coll), Richmond (Am Int Univ), Shrewsbury (CAT), Sir Gâr (Coll), South Essex (Coll), Staffordshire Reg Fed (SURF), Swindon (Coll), Truro (Coll), UHI, Warrington (Coll), Warwickshire (Coll), West Anglia (Coll), Wirral Met (Coll).

ALTERNATIVE COURSES

Communication Studies, Cultural Studies, Information Science, Information Systems, Publishing, Technical Communication.

LANGUAGES

(* indicates universities with entry requirements over 340 UCAS points)

SUBJECT REQUIREMENTS/PREFERENCES

GCE A level: French and German courses: the chosen language is almost always required at A level (or equivalent). Spanish courses: most universities require the language at A level (or equivalent) although some offer Spanish courses ab initio.

Aberdeen In addition to the European Studies course, degrees are offered in French, German and Hispanic. Gaelic Studies and Celtic Studies are also available. There are also courses in the Languages and Literature of Scotland.

Aberystwyth Single and joint honours courses are offered in French, German, Italian and Spanish. There is also a European Language degree scheme that combines the study of any three languages (two at major level, one at minor level) from French, German, Italian and Spanish. A degree scheme combining Modern Languages with Business Studies has also been introduced. Courses are also offered in Celtic Studies, Irish and Welsh.

Aston French and German can be studied as single honours degrees or as a joint programme. Spanish can be studied as a joint course only with a range of subjects. Courses are also offered in European Studies, Translation Studies, International Business and International Relations.

Bangor The School of Modern Languages offers honours degrees in French, German, Spanish, Italian and Welsh. There are one-, two- and three-language courses available and several joint courses with non-language subjects. Welsh Language courses are also available, including one with Media Studies and Creative Writing.

Bath The course in Modern Languages and European Studies focuses on high-quality spoken and written language learning combined with units devoted to cultural studies and the politics and society of individual countries in Europe as a whole. Equal weighting is given to two languages from French, German,

Italian and Russian and Spanish. A year abroad is compulsory. There is also a course in European Language and Politics. See also **Combined Courses**.

Birmingham* French, German, Italian, Russian, Spanish and Portuguese are offered and, in the Hispanic Studies course, Galician and Catalan. There are also degrees with Modern Languages and European Studies.

Bristol Single and joint courses can be followed in Czech, French, German, Italian, Portuguese, Spanish or Russian. The Modern Languages programme allows for a study of two of these languages with the possibility of a third (Catalan in Year 1).

Bristol UWE French, Chinese and Spanish can be studied in joint honours courses. French and Spanish are also offered with Law.

Buckingham Joint courses are offered in French and Spanish and can be studied with subjects such as English Literature, Accounting, Art History and Law.

Cambridge* Modern and Medieval and Oriental Language courses are offered. Greek and Latin are taken as part of the Classics course while the Modern and Medieval Languages Tripos offers a high level of linguistic training in two languages. The languages available are French, German (including a course for beginners), Italian, Portuguese, Russian and Spanish. Classical Latin or Classical Greek may be combined with any one of these languages. Languages from the Faculty of Asian and Middle Eastern Studies are available in Arabic, Chinese, Hebrew, Japanese and Persian. Also, there is the unique course in Anglo-Saxon, Norse and Celtic covering history, languages and literature.

Canterbury Christ Church French can be taken as a joint or combined subject. Students are encouraged to spend a year studying abroad and students on a combined course must spend 10 weeks in a French-speaking environment during the course.

Cardiff French, German, Italian and Spanish are offered as single or joint honours courses. There is also a flourishing school of Welsh. Modern languages are also offered with Accounting, Banking, Business Administration, Business Economics, Economics, Japanese and Law.

Central Lancashire Degree courses are offered in Chinese, French, German, Japanese and Spanish. In addition, some languages can be studied by way of Languages with Tourism or International Business and Law (French or German) and also on the Modern Languages degree in which two languages are chosen. There are also courses in Asia–Pacific Studies and Islamic Studies.

Chester Courses are offered in French, German and Spanish and include an introduction to European studies and cinema. Placements abroad take place between Years 2 and 3. It is also possible to study two of these languages.

Coventry Modern Language programmes offer French and Spanish (not ab initio). There are optional placements of one year.

Dundee French, German or Spanish can be taken as part of any degree alongside the main subject choice.

Durham* The modern languages offered are French, German, Russian, Spanish, Arabic, Italian and Hispanic Studies with the option to study up to three. All courses involve a year spent abroad.

East Anglia Four-year Modern Language courses are offered in French, Japanese and/or Spanish. In addition, Translation and Media can be taken with Languages and there are also courses with Management Studies, Spanish with International Development, and Translation and Interpreting with double honours Languages.

Edinburgh Language courses are offered in Arabic, Celtic, Chinese, French, German, Italian, Japanese, Persian, Portuguese, Russian, Scandinavian Studies (Danish, Swedish, Norwegian) and Hispanic Studies. There is also an Islamic Studies course, which includes the option to study Arabic, Persian or Turkish and a Middle Eastern Studies course.

See *Heap 2015: University Degree Course Offers* (Trotman Publishing) for details of offers

Essex A number of Modern Language courses are on offer at various levels, including French, German, Italian, Portuguese and Spanish. There are also courses in European Studies and Modern Languages.

Exeter Courses are offered in French, German, Italian, Latin, Russian and Spanish. Arabic is also available. Several joint courses are available with European languages, including French and Latin, and German and Drama.

Glasgow* French, German, Greek, Italian, Latin, Russian, Hispanic Studies, Spanish and Slavonic Studies are offered. There are also courses in Gaelic and Celtic.

Greenwich French, English, Italian and Spanish are offered as part of the International Studies degree which looks at historical and contemporary Europe alongside language study.

Heriot-Watt The university is one of the leading centres in the UK for the training of interpreters and translators. The courses involve intensive language training with complementary studies in administration, politics, economics, current affairs and international organisations. Joint language courses are offered in combinations with French, German and Spanish. A course in British Sign Language (Interpreting and Translation) is also offered.

Hertfordshire Degrees in French, Spanish, Chinese, Italian, Japanese and German are offered as part of joint or combined courses and can be studied with subjects such as Economics, Tourism and Business.

Hull Combined language programmes are offered with Chinese, French, German, Italian and Spanish. Subject to availability, it may be possible to study Arabic, Japanese, Dutch or Portuguese. There is also a minor course in Translation Studies and a course in Modern Language Studies.

Keele Modern Language courses are available to students at Keele and include Chinese, French, German, Spanish, Russian and Japanese. Classes are taught by native speakers.

Kent French, German, Italian and Hispanic Studies single and joint honours courses are offered. The courses offer an optional year abroad and can be studied full or part time. European Studies courses focusing on France, Germany or Spain are also offered.

Kingston Languages offered cover French and Spanish in joint courses only with subjects including Journalism, Film Studies, Television and New Broadcasting Media and Criminology.

Lancaster French, German and Spanish Studies courses are offered, combined with a large number of other subjects including Politics, Linguistics, Management and Mathematics. The European Languages course allows students to study up to two languages.

Leeds Courses offered include Arabic, Asia Pacific Studies, Chinese, French, German, Greek, Italian, Japanese, Latin, Portuguese, Russian, Spanish and Latin American Studies. The courses include a work placement abroad.

Leeds Beckett Courses in Arabic, French, German and Spanish can be taken. Joint honours including combinations with Marketing, Public Relations, Tourism and Business are available as well as a degree in Language Studies with a choice of two languages studied on a major/minor basis.

Leicester The School of Modern Languages offers French, Italian and Spanish. There are also courses in Modern Languages and with Management, Film and History of Art.

Liverpool The Modern European Languages course offers three languages in Year 1 from French, German, Spanish and a beginners' language from Catalan, Irish, Italian or Portuguese. There are also courses in Hispanic Studies and Latin American Studies.

Liverpool Hope French and Spanish are studied in the first two years of the Primary teaching specialist course in Languages.

See *Heap 2015: University Degree Course Offers* (Trotman Publishing) for details of offers

Liverpool John Moores French, Spanish, Chinese and Japanese are offered as joint courses on the four-year International Business degree course focusing on language skills.

London (King's)* A wide range of single and joint honours courses are offered in French, German, Hispanic Studies and Portuguese, and Brazilian Studies, Turkish and Modern Greek Studies, as well as the classical language of Greek. See also **European Studies**.

London (QM) Language options include French, German, Hispanic Studies and Russian. These can be taken as single or joint courses and with History, Drama, Economics, Geography, European Studies or Film Studies.

London (RH) Languages are offered in French, German, Greek, Italian, Latin and Spanish. There are also major/minor degrees in Modern Languages and another subject, such as Philosophy, Management or Drama. Multilingual courses are also offered.

London (SOAS)* The School offers the widest range of African and Asian languages in the UK. These cover Amharic (Ethiopia), Hausa (Niger, Ghana, Cameroon), Somali (Horn of Africa, Djibouti, Ethiopia), Swahili (East Coast of Africa, Tanzania, Kenya), Yoruba (Nigeria), Zulu (South Africa), Chinese (Modern and Classical), Tibetan, Japanese, Korean, Ancient Near East, Arabic, Hebrew, Persian, Turkish, Georgian, Bengali (Bangladesh, West Bengal), Gujarati (North West India), Nepali (Nepal, Sikkim), Pali (Classical Middle Indo-Aryan), Panjabi (Panjab), Sanskrit (Classical Indian), Sinhalese (Sri Lanka), Tamil (South India), Urdu (Pakistan), Burmese, Indonesian, Malay, Tagalog (Philippines), Thai and Vietnamese. Linguistics is also offered as a single- or two-subject degree.

London (UCL) Language courses are offered in Dutch, French, German, Greek, Hebrew, Italian, Latin, Polish, Russian, Scandinavian Studies, Icelandic, Viking Studies, Finnish, Hungarian, Romanian, Serbian, Hispanic Studies, Ukrainian, Czech, Bulgarian and Slovak. The degree in Language and Culture includes the study of a main and second language. Linguistics is also offered.

London LSE French, German, Mandarin, Russian and Spanish languages are offered relating to a specific interest in one of the social sciences.

London Met There is a course in Translation Studies which offers French, Spanish, Italian, Russian, German, Arabic and Portuguese combined with English Studies. The course is accredited by the Chartered Institute of Linguists.

Manchester A single honours degree can be taken in Arabic, Chinese, French, German, Greek, Hebrew, Italian, Japanese, Latin, Russian, Portuguese, Spanish and Middle Eastern Languages. Scholarships available. There are also courses in Latin American Studies and in European Studies with Languages.

Manchester Met Language courses are offered in French, German, Italian and Spanish with Linguistics. There are over 20 degree courses covering Business, Economics and Engineering in which options in languages are available.

Middlesex Arabic, Chinese, Russian and Spanish are offered on the International Business and Language course and Spanish can be studied with Tourism. There is also a course in Translation which can be studied with English and another language.

Newcastle The Modern Languages degree covers French, Chinese, German, Japanese, Portuguese and Spanish. Some joint honours subjects can be taken alongside other courses such as Business, European Studies, Politics, Chemistry and Engineering.

Northampton French is offered as a joint degree only and can be combined with subjects such as Sociology, Film and Television Studies, Politics and Popular Music. There is an optional year abroad where students can apply for a post as an English-language assistant in a French primary or secondary school in France, Belgium, Senegal or Quebec.

Northumbria Degrees are offered in French and Spanish as well as in a large number of joint courses in the Modern Foreign Language Studies programmes, in which one or two languages can be combined with English Language, European Studies or International Business Management.

Nottingham Portuguese, Chinese, Dutch, French, German, Ancient Greek, Hispanic Studies, Latin, Russian, Spanish and Serbian and Croatian Studies are available. There is also a unique course in Viking Studies covering language, literature, history and archaeology.

Nottingham Trent Joint courses are on offer with Chinese (Mandarin), French, German, Italian and Spanish. There are also courses in Latin American Studies, Linguistics and Spanish Studies.

Oxford* Courses are offered in Modern Languages (two languages), European and Middle Eastern Languages and Modern Languages and Linguistics. There is also a course in History and Modern Languages. The range of languages offered is considerable and the Modern Language course covers French, German, Medieval and Modern Greek, Italian, Portuguese, Russian, Spanish and Czech (with Slovak). The course in European and Middle Eastern Languages involves Arabic, Hebrew, Persian or Turkish and the Oriental Studies options cover Chinese, Egyptology and Japanese. Modern Languages can also be studied with Linguistics.

Oxford Brookes There is a single honours course in Japanese with a year in Japan, a BA combined honours programme in French Studies and similar language courses in French, Japanese or Spanish, which can be added as a minor subject to a major subject.

Plymouth French and Spanish are offered with Modern Language degrees as major or minor subjects with English, Geography, International Business, International Relations and Human Resource Management.

Portsmouth Degrees are offered in Applied Languages in which two languages are chosen from French, German, Spanish, Italian, Mandarin and English as a Foreign Language. There are options in translation theory and practice in Year 2 and the option to start a new language including British Sign Language, Arabic, Mandarin, Portuguese or Japanese. Degrees are also available in Languages and International Relations, Journalism, American or European Studies.

Queen's Belfast Courses are offered in French, Spanish, and Irish and Celtic Studies, which includes modules in Irish, Old Irish and Scottish Gaelic language.

Reading Single and joint honours courses are offered in French, German and Italian. Programmes include a year abroad and can be combined with subjects such as Philosophy, Classical Studies and Politics.

Roehampton French, Spanish and English are offered as main foreign languages in a new four-year programme with Year 3 as a year abroad. They are offered as single and combined honours courses with a range of other subjects. There is also a degree course in Translating and Interpreting between French, Spanish and English and in TESOL (Teaching English to Speakers of Other Languages.)

St Andrews Courses are offered covering Arabic, French, Greek, Latin, German, Italian, Russian and Spanish, which can be taken from scratch.

Salford The Modern Languages Studies with TESOL programme can be studied with a range of languages from French, German, Italian, Spanish, Chinese, Arabic or Portuguese. There are also courses in Translation and Interpreting Studies and European Languages. There are vocational courses available with paid industrial placements in the EU.

Sheffield The Modern Language course allows for three languages to be studied from a wide range of languages including Catalan, Chinese, Czech, Dutch, Japanese, Korean, French, German, Hispanic Studies, Polish and Russian.

Sheffield Hallam French, German and Spanish can be taken with International Business Studies, Marketing or Tourism. Eighteen months of the course are spent abroad.

See *Heap 2015: University Degree Course Offers* (Trotman Publishing) for details of offers

South Wales Professional Welsh can be taken as part of the Combined Studies programme and can be studied alongside a range of subjects such as history, Law and Education.

Southampton* Degrees in French, German, Spanish, Portuguese and Latin American Studies are offered, mainly as joint courses. In addition, there is also a four-year Language and Linguistics degree offering a choice of three languages: Chinese, Japanese and Russian.

Stirling Degree courses are offered in French and Spanish and Latin American Studies as single or joint honours courses. French and Spanish can also be studied with several other subjects including Politics and Psychology.

Strathclyde Degrees are offered in French, Italian and Spanish. Modern Languages can also be studied with Law and International Business, which includes spending the fourth year abroad.

Surrey Language courses focus on contemporary language in business, culture and society and cover French, German, Russian and Spanish. Languages can be combined with Translation and International Communication.

Sussex French, German, Italian and Spanish are available in several joint courses including Anthropology, English Language Teaching and Media Studies. There is also a language studies opportunity open to students on a wide range of single honours degrees.

Swansea French, German, Greek, Italian, Latin, Spanish and Welsh are offered as major languages with a large number of joint courses in each case. Catalan can also be taken alongside Spanish with Business Studies. There are also courses in Translation.

Trinity St David Arabic, Greek (Ancient), Latin and Welsh are offered on a range of courses. There is also a course in Chinese Studies with the opportunity to visit China.

Ulster French, German, Irish and Spanish are available in the Combined Arts course and as joint courses with other subjects. A study of language is also possible in the Language and Linguistics degree. Applied Languages and Translation can be combined with two languages from French, German and Spanish.

Warwick Single honours and joint courses are offered in French, German Studies and Italian. The courses are four years in length with the fourth year spent abroad.

Westminster Degrees are offered in Arabic, Chinese, French, German, Spanish and Translation Studies. For all students at the university there is a Polylang scheme in which language study can continue throughout their courses. There are also courses in Professional Language Studies.

Wolverhampton Language courses cover Linguistics, British Sign Language (English) and Deaf Studies, including courses on interpreting. Courses can be studied full or part time.

York French, German and Spanish joint courses are offered and can be combined with Linguistics. The university also offers a Languages for All scheme enabling any student to continue the study of a language.

OTHER INSTITUTIONS OFFERING LANGUAGE COURSES
Blackburn (Coll), Blackpool and Fylde (Coll), Doncaster (Coll Univ Centre), Euro Bus Sch London, London (Inst Paris), Northbrook (Coll), UHI.

ALTERNATIVE COURSES
English, Linguistics.

See *Heap 2015: University Degree Course Offers* (Trotman Publishing) for details of offers

LAW

(* indicates universities with entry requirements over 340 UCAS points)

SUBJECT REQUIREMENTS/PREFERENCES

GCE A level: Good grades in languages for courses combined with a foreign language. **GCSE:** English. The National Admissions Test for Law (LNAT) may be required.

SUBJECT INFORMATION

Law courses are usually divided into two parts. Part 1 occupies Year 1 and introduces the student to criminal and constitutional law and the legal process. In order to gain exemption from the Common Professional Examination, students must have studied a number of core subjects. These are constitutional and administrative law, contract, criminal and land law, laws of tort, equity and law of trusts and European Union law. Thereafter, many different specialised topics can be studied in Years 2 and 3. The course content in most Law degrees is very similar, although students not intending to practise in Scotland are recommended to limit their applications to universities south of the border.

QUESTIONS TO CONSIDER

* Will I gain a qualifying Law degree?
* Will I have to undertake further study or training to qualify as a solicitor or barrister?
* Is there an opportunity for me to undertake work experience?
* If I study in Scotland will I be qualified to practise law in England and Wales and vice versa?

Aberdeen Topics covered include constitutional law, legal systems, contract, civil liberties, delict and computing. Over 40 honours options are offered including European law and international law. In addition, there are degrees in Law and French, German, Spanish and Belgian Law and with European Studies. The Law degree is based on Scots law therefore a conversion course must be taken to qualify as a solicitor in England. The course offered in Legal Studies does not qualify students to enter the legal profession.

Abertay A BA Law degree is offered accredited by the Scottish Law Society. It has a strong practical focus, business and business law being important features of the course. In addition there is a course in European Business Law covering business law of the UK and one other European Union country, European Union law, a European language (Spanish), commercial property and employment law, international trade and dispute settlement.

Aberystwyth The LLB scheme is offered for those wishing to concentrate entirely on law while a broader course is offered in the BA degree by way of a major in Law plus a minor in another subject. LLB and BA degrees in Law are also offered with a European language, French, German or Spanish (not for beginners), with opportunities to study abroad. There are also courses in Criminal, European and Business Law, and in Human Rights Law.

Anglia Ruskin The LLB degree is a qualifying law degree for students seeking to qualify as a solicitor and aims to combine the academic and practical aspects of law to prepare students to enter a legal career.

Aston The Law with Management programme is a qualifying Law degree focusing on business skills. The course is three years full time or four years with an integrated placement year.

Bangor The Law degree addresses the Welsh, British, European and global dimensions of contemporary legal developments. There are also courses in Law with Accountancy, Business, Criminology, Social Policy and Modern Languages.

Birmingham* The Law course aims to provide thorough grounding in the main areas of English law in addition to the vocational training. Core subjects taken in the first two years provide students with exemptions from certain professional examinations should they wish to practise law. European Union law is a compulsory second year (Part I finals) course. The third year offers a wide range of subjects including labour law, human rights and international law. Other degree courses offered by the Faculty of Law include Law with French or German and Law with Business Studies.

Birmingham City The Law course aims to provide a broad-based legal education sensitive to the social, economic and political contexts of modern society. Students have the opportunity to take part in simulated legal disputes by way of moots, mock trials and 'clinical' legal exercises. An emphasis is placed on the wide range of options available in Years 2 and 3, which include medicine, company, consumer and European Union law and also American legal practice. There are also courses in Law with American Legal Studies, Criminology and Legal Practice and Business Law.

Bolton BA and LLB courses are provided to give students a thorough grounding in the discipline of law. Real scenarios are studied allowing students to understand the application of law. A part-time course is available.

Bournemouth The four-year LLB Law degree with a professional placement (40 weeks) in Year 3 offers a range of specialist Law options in Year 4. The theme of the European Union is taken in Year 2. A study of information technology for lawyers and accounting is also offered. This is a four-year course, with a year in professional practice. Taxation and Law courses are also available.

Bradford The LLB course enables graduates to apply for exemption from the Common Professional Exam and, if successful, proceed directly to training as lawyers in England and Wales. Law can also be taken with Business, History or Politics.

Brighton Law is offered with Business or Criminology. Modules include law of tort, criminal law, land law and consumer law and practice. Students have the option to undertake a work placement in the third year.

Bristol* The three-year course includes up to 10 mandatory units taken in Years 1 and 2 to meet the requirements for exemption from the Common Professional Examination. Optional units include criminology, women and the law, and medical and family law, human rights and UN law. Six programmes of study are offered and at the end of Year 1 it is possible to transfer from the LLB course to European Legal Studies. Law can also be studied with French or German or with study abroad.

Bristol UWE This is a comprehensive Law course comprising four law subjects in the first year and four in the second and third year, with an option to take one or two non-law subjects, for example forensic science or economics. Additional subjects are taken in the third year along with a number of options. There is also a course in European and International Law.

Brunel Three-year and four-year Law courses are offered. For the latter, students spend three periods of approximately 20 weeks each year in law-related work placement. The study of law is placed in a wide context, and in Year 1 a small number of non-law modules are taken.

Buckingham The Law course (an English qualifying law degree), lasting two years, starting in January, July or September, comprises the six essential core subjects – public law, criminal law, contract, tort, land law and law of trusts – plus three other legal subjects. Law is also offered with Business Finance, Economics, English Language Studies, Management Studies, French, Spanish and Politics. There is also a part-time course.

Bucks New LLB (Hons) courses are offered in Law and Business Law and lead to exemption from the academic stage of qualifications as a solicitor or barrister. The courses emphasise criminal law, contract law, tort, public law, European Union law, land law and equity and trusts.

Cambridge* The emphasis in the Law course is on principles and technique although, as in other courses, many students do not intend to practise. While the courses focus mainly on English law, the law of the European Union and French law can be studied. The sociological aspects of law such as jurisprudence and sentencing and the penal system are covered. Exchange schemes exist with universities in France, Holland, Germany and Spain.

Canterbury Christ Church Law is offered as a single honours LLB course in addition to which there is a Legal Studies course offered within the joint or combined honours programme.

Cardiff* The Law degree scheme is designed to give students a wide choice of subjects to suit their professional interests. The first year consists of standard core subjects: contract, tort, the legal system, constitutional and administrative law. This is then followed in the second and third years with a choice of eight courses from a list of over 20 options including maritime law and international trade and finance. Law can also be taken with French, German, Welsh, Sociology, Criminology and Politics.

Central Lancashire Law is offered at the Burnley campus. Second- and third-year options include copyright and trademark law, media law and medicine and the law. Students have the opportunity to go on placements with local solicitors and abroad.

Chester Core subjects are offered to fulfil the requirements for a qualifying Law degree, covering contract, land, European Union, constitutional and administrative law, crime and tort. Students studying combined law can apply for partial exemption.

City Core subjects are studied in the first two years of the Law course, followed in Year 3 with a choice from a range of options that currently includes company law, media law, family law and public international law. There are opportunities for study abroad.

Coventry Three-year and four-year Law courses are offered with opportunities for national and international work experience. The university has a moot room giving students the opportunity to develop their advocacy skills. There are courses in Commercial Law and Legal Studies also offered.

Cumbria In addition to the seven foundation subjects required for legal professional purposes there are a number of taught options including media, medical, human rights and family law.

De Montfort The Law course is a qualifying degree recognised by the Law Society and the Bar. The School of Law promotes the use of computer-assisted learning. Joint courses are also offered with Criminal Justice and there are single honours courses in Law, Human Rights and Social Justice and Business Law.

Derby An LLB course is offered with foundation areas of European Union law, contract, tort, criminal, constitutional and land law and trusts. In the final year students may specialise in Business Law, International Law or Social and Public Law. Law can also be taken with Criminology.

Dundee This unique course offers two main streams: Scots Law and English Law. Since many of the subjects are common to all students, both courses lead to qualifications as a lawyer in Scotland, England or Northern Ireland. There are also degrees in English or Scots Law with History, Philosophy, Politics, European Studies or Modern Languages.

Durham* Core courses in the first year of the Law course leading to the examination (preliminary honours) at the end of the first year cover contract, tort, UK and EU constitutional law and civil liberties. Eight full subjects are then taken in the second and third years from 20 law topics or nine non-law subjects. There are courses on international, European and French law as well as English law. Students on the single or joint honours degree courses can obtain exemption from the Common Professional Examination.

East Anglia* The preliminary programme of the Law course (Year 1) covers criminal, constitutional and land law. The honours programme (Years 2 and 3) in Part I covers a study of the laws of land, tort, trusts and EU law. Part II comprises a range of optional subjects. Degree courses in Law with French Law and Language, European Legal Systems and the American Legal System are also offered.

East London Compulsory subjects are taken in Years 1 and 2 of the Law course, with a range of options offered in Years 2 and 3 that give the necessary exemptions from professional examinations. Topics include medicine and law, European Union law, pension funds and international law. Law can also be studied as part of a two-subject degree.

Edge Hill The degree course in Law gains exemption from the Legal Practice course and Bar finals. Law can also be studied with Criminology or Management.

Edinburgh In the first year of the Law course compulsory subjects include the Scottish legal system, contract, family and constitutional law. It is also possible to take a course outside the Law Faculty, for example French, German or History. The decision to follow the honours courses is taken at the end of the second year when the required courses for those wishing to enter the profession will have been taken. In the third and fourth years further professional courses and options are taken. There are exemptions from stages of professional training. Students wishing to practise in England and Wales are recommended to apply to law schools south of the border. There are 13 joint honours courses with Law.

Edinburgh Napier A broad legal education is offered in the LLB Law course helping students take their first step towards a career in the Scottish legal profession. Law with Accounting or Business Management or Entrepreneurship is also available. The LLB course is accredited by the Law Society of Scotland.

Essex The Law course is in three parts, each covering one year. The Law qualifying examination is taken at the end of the first year, and Parts I and II of the final LLB at the end of the second and third years. In the second year it is possible to take a non-law subject as an option. There is also a degree in English and French Laws with Year 3 abroad and also Law with an international exchange. Several academic departments also combine to offer degrees in Human Rights.

Exeter* In the first year of the Law course five modules are taken, including criminal law. Examinations take place at the end of each year, LLB Parts I and II being taken at the end of the second and third years. The LLB (European) is a four-year course covering French or German law which includes modules taught in French and German and a year spent abroad.

Glasgow* Ordinary (three-year) and honours (four-year) Law courses are available. A wide range of degrees are available that can give appropriate exemptions from professional examinations. The Scottish legal system and Scottish law occupy an important place in the first-year course. Law can also be studied with a range of subjects including Gaelic, Slavonic Studies and Philosophy. Students wishing to qualify in England or other member states of the EU need to pass additional examinations.

Glasgow Caledonian Law (accredited by the Law Society of Scotland) and Business with Business Law are offered as four-year full-time degrees and focus on Scots law.

Gloucestershire The LLB course is a qualifying Law degree and includes options in criminal, medical, employment and family law. There is a two-year fast-track course.

Greenwich BA and LLB courses are offered in Law and Business Law. Law is also offered with a range of other subjects as a combined degree.

Hertfordshire The Law course offers several interesting third-year options including medical law, jurisprudence, company and international law. Joint honours courses are offered with a choice of other subjects. There is also an LLB (Hons) course in Commercial Law.

Huddersfield There is a Law (Exempting) course enabling students to qualify as a solicitor by incorporating the legal practice course in Years 3 and 4 (subject to an appropriate training contract). Degree courses are also offered in Law and Business.

Hull The first two years of the Law course introduce legal techniques and the English legal system. A significant emphasis is placed on the law relating to the European Union. Years 2 and 3 include options in more than 20 subjects including information technology law, government law, international law, American public law, admiralty law and media regulation. Suitable students may spend their third year abroad in France, Germany, Belgium or Holland, which extends their course to four years. Law is also offered with French and German Law and Language and courses are offered in International Law and Commercial Law.

Keele Law and Law with Criminology or Politics can be taken as either single honours or dual honours courses. The Law course qualifies for exemption from the Law Society Common Professional Examination.

Kent The Law course is designed to enable students to gain the necessary exemptions from the Law Society examinations. Other Law courses include Law with a year in China/Hong Kong, English and French/German/Spanish/Italian Law, European Legal Studies (which includes a year in Europe) and Law with a Language. There is a law clinic enabling students to practise law under the supervision of solicitors.

Kingston All the major aspects of law are covered in this Law course, with a wide choice of subjects in the final year. These include revenue and family law, the law of international trade, EU, medical and welfare law. Law with Business is also offered and a degree in International Law is available. The Law BA can be combined with arts and social science subjects.

Lancaster* Part I of the Law course introduces the principles of law and provides a detailed study of constitutional and administrative law. The units cover various aspects of law and some are compulsory to comply with the examinations of the Law Society. A course in European Legal Studies is also on offer with a year abroad between Years 2 and 4 and there are courses in Law and Criminology, Law and Politics and Law (International).

Leeds* Four compulsory subjects are taken in the first year of the Law course and five in Years 2 and 3, with optional subjects chosen from a wide range of topics. Courses are also offered in Criminal Justice and Criminology, and Law with French.

Leeds Beckett Core subjects of the Law course give exemptions from professional legal examinations for the Bar and Law Society. Law can also be studied with Criminology.

Leicester* Students on the LLB course taking certain options are guaranteed a place at the College of Law on graduation. There are also courses in English and French Law and Law with French Law and Language.

Lincoln The LLB Law course is a qualifying degree giving professional exemptions. Joint honours courses are also offered with Politics, Business, Criminology or Finance. Legal Studies is also offered.

Liverpool The first year of the Law course (intermediate) covers the core courses of criminal and constitutional law and an introduction to English law and EU law. Final Part I covers the second year with three compulsory subjects (tort, land law and equity) plus one optional subject. The third-year course (Final Part II) provides a wide range of options from which students select five subjects. Law and Business Studies can also be studied with modules in resources management, banking and commercial law. Law can be studied with Accounting and Finance, Business Studies, Criminology, French, German, Italian, Philosophy and Spanish.

Liverpool Hope The BA combined honours Law degree covers some of the key aspects of law including business law, criminal law, European law and UK parliamentary decision-making.

Liverpool John Moores The course in Law (LLB) is the standard qualifying Law degree. There is also a joint degree with Criminal Justice. Students are assessed through examination, coursework and skills-based assessments such as undertaking a moot, dispute resolution or mediation.

London (King's)* The Law course provides a grounding in the basic areas of legal knowledge, methods and technique in the first two years and permits a greater degree of specialisation in the final year. King's also offers English and French or American, Australian, German or Hong Kong Law. There is also a course in European Legal Studies.

London (QM)* A leading Law Department offering a standard Law course with many options in Year 3. There is also a course in Law and Politics.

London (SOAS)* The Law course is unique; instruction comprises English law subjects, including those required for professional purposes, and also aspects of law relating to a particular region in Asia or Africa, and comparative law. The second and third years involve eight courses. Law can be combined with 27 other subjects.

London (UCL)* The large Law Faculty offers an LLB course with specialist areas covering labour law, media and communications law. Law is also offered with French, German or Hispanic Law or with another legal system (Australia or Singapore). See also **European Studies**.

London LSE* Public law, the English legal system, contract, tort and property law are studied for the intermediate examination at the end of the first year of the Law course. Parts I and II follow in the second and third years and include compulsory and optional subjects. Anthropology and Law is also offered.

London Met The Business Law and LLB Law degrees are recognised by the Bar and the Law Society as giving full exemption from the academic stage of professional education. There is also a course in International Relations and Law.

London NCH This is the LLB degree in its traditional three-stage format. It provides students with a solid grounding in the concepts and frameworks of the English legal system.

London South Bank The Law course is recognised by the Law Society. It aims to develop the student's skill in the use of legal materials and their relation with the social environment. Optional units include company law, jurisprudence, medical law and ethics. Other courses cover Family Law, Human Rights and Legal Studies. Law can also be combined with Psychology, Criminology and Sociology.

Manchester* Law students wishing to become solicitors and graduating with a lower second class degree are guaranteed a place at a branch of the College of Law to do the legal practice course. A very wide range of options, including human rights, criminal justice, youth justice and child law, can be chosen in Years 2 and 3 following a study of the basic subjects in Year 1. Law is available to study with Criminology and Politics.

Manchester Met The first qualifying year of the Law course is made up of basic legal subjects followed by a series of options that are chosen in Years 2 and 3. A large number of joint courses with Legal Studies are offered.

Middlesex The Law course is offered as a BA and LLB. The LLB degree involves compulsory law subjects which, with a wide range of options, lead to exemption from professional examinations.

Newcastle* This is a flexible Law course with constitutional and administrative law, land law, contract and tort, and judicial process in the first two years. With the option to join the European Legal Studies programme in the second year, students have the opportunity to study at a European university. Throughout the course there is an emphasis on the relationship between law and other social sciences.

Northampton A very large number of joint degrees with Law are offered in addition to an LLB qualifying Law degree. Courses in International Business Law and International Criminal Law and Security are also available.

Northumbria The LLB degree is taken in three years, four years for students wishing to be exempt from the barristers' or solicitors' vocational awards, or five years for full qualification as a solicitor.

See *Heap 2015: University Degree Course Offers* (Trotman Publishing) for details of offers

Nottingham* BA and LLB courses are offered and students can defer their final choice until their arrival at the university. The LLB follows the traditional route of four compulsory courses in the first year, followed by compulsory and optional subjects in the second and third years. In the BA course, legal subjects are studied in each year along with two subsidiary non-law subjects. Law can also be studied with French and French Law, Spanish and Spanish Law, or German and German Law.

Nottingham Trent The qualifying LLB degree in Law is offered as a three-year full-time and four-year sandwich course with paid placements with a law firm in Year 3. The last six and nine months respectively of each course are spent in practical training in a solicitor's office at the end of Year 1 and during Year 3. Both courses give exemptions from professional examinations. Law can be studied with Business, Criminology, Psychology and Professional Practice.

Oxford* Three-year and four-year Law courses are offered, the latter with one year of Law Studies in Europe. The courses are identical except that after Year 2 students on the longer course may study in a university in France, Germany or Italy studying French, German or Italian Law or in the Netherlands studying European and International Law.

Oxford Brookes Law (single or combined honours courses) is a flexible degree scheme within the modular degree course. By taking a prescribed combination of modules, students may obtain exemption from the first stage of the Law Society professional examinations. Law is also offered as a combined course with subjects including Anthropology, History, Business Management, Japanese Studies, Politics and Religion and Theology.

Plymouth The LLB course offers the basic course subjects required for professional practice. Options in Year 3 include employment law, the media and company law. Courses are also offered in Law with International Relations, Criminal Justice Studies, Psychology, Economics and Business Studies. There is also a course in Maritime Business with Maritime Law.

Portsmouth Degrees are offered in Law as single honours or with Business, Business Communication (BA), Criminology, European Studies and International Relations. The university features an exact replica of the Crown court where students can be part of mock trials and moots.

Queen's Belfast* Students study the law as it relates to Northern Ireland (similar to English law) and are offered courses in European Union and Community law and the sociological aspects of the subject. Law can be taken with Politics and there are courses in Common and Civil Law with French and Spanish.

Reading* The Law course is modular and 12 modules are taken for the first university examination. Thereafter, the course comprises the traditional compulsory and optional subjects leading to qualification through the Law Society or Bar Council. Law with Legal Studies in Europe is also offered.

Robert Gordon The BA Law and Management course combines both subjects. There is a 24-week placement for home students. There is also an LLB Law degree. Students with the BA degree may transfer to the LLB course in Year 3.

Salford An LLB course is offered, whilst Law can also be studied with Criminology, Finance, Spanish or Business and Management Studies. The course is accredited by the Solicitors Regulation Authority and Bar Standards Board.

Sheffield* In the first year, Law students take courses in contract and public law and an introduction to law and the legal system. This leads to the intermediate examination. Thereafter there is considerable freedom of choice in planning the programme of study for the final two years. For those students not aiming for a law career it is possible to transfer to the BA Law course. European and International Law can be studied and Law is also offered with Criminology or with French, German or Spanish.

Sheffield Hallam LLB courses are offered and in addition there are joint courses with Business or Criminology. There are also opportunities to study with European institutions in countries such as Holland, Turkey and Poland.

See *Heap 2015: University Degree Course Offers* (Trotman Publishing) for details of offers

South Wales Law is taken as a modular course divided into semesters. Options are available in Years 2 and 3 and include languages, environmental law, international trade, criminology, media law and intellectual property law. Courses in Criminology and Business and Law can also be taken. The award is a qualifying Law degree.

Southampton* The LLB course consists of a core of seven compulsory subjects studied in the first and second years, together with a wide range of optional subjects. These range from admiralty law and carriage of goods by sea to law and medicine, environmental law and EU law, including legal French, medical ethics and law, and information technology law. There are also degrees in European and International Legal Studies and Maritime Law.

Southampton Solent A qualifying Law degree can be taken with options including Criminology, Social Law and Commercial Law, covering topics such as criminal justice, family law and sports law.

Staffordshire All Law students follow a common course of compulsory subjects in the first and second years. Several specialist options can also be taken including employment law, human rights and sports law. Advisory work in the field of social studies can be studied on the LLB Advice Work degree.

Stirling An LLB programme is offered whilst BA Law is offered with Accountancy, Business Studies, Criminology, French, History, Human Resource Management, Marketing, Politics or Spanish. A single honours Business Law course is also available.

Strathclyde The Law course (which focuses on Scottish law) includes law and legal processes, public law and Scottish law. Commercial and criminal law are combined with Scottish law in the first and second years, with a choice of options in the second and third years that include computer, society and the law, international law and Roman law of property.

Sunderland The LLB course has options in employment, environmental, land and international law. BA/BSc Law is also offered with a range of subjects including Management, Marketing and Media Studies. The degree is recognised by the Bar and Law Society.

Surrey* Law is offered with Criminology and International Studies. Courses have opportunities for legal work placements in the UK, Europe and North America.

Sussex* Law course students are examined in Law and also in contextual subjects taught within their schools of studies. The degree carries exemption from the Bar and Law Society examinations. Other Law courses offered include Languages, Contemporary European Studies, American Studies and International Relations.

Swansea All Law students follow a first year with four compulsory law modules. Eight law modules are taken in Years 2 and 3. Law is also offered with other subjects including Politics, Economics, Spanish and Welsh, and courses in Legal Studies are also available.

Teesside As well as the core subjects of a standard Law degree, students can choose optional modules in the second and third year. European law and land law is compulsory for students wishing to gain a qualifying Law degree. Other courses offered include Law with Criminology and Law with Politics.

Ulster Law is offered as a single honours degree or with a range of other subjects including Criminology, Accounting, Politics, Irish, Human Resource Management and Marketing.

Warwick* Three-year and four-year Law courses are available. Both types of course allow the student to choose 'full' or 'half' courses in a wide range of legal subjects. In the four-year course, second-, third- and fourth-year students may take up to a total of four non-law subjects. Law is studied in the context of wider social, political and theoretical practice – with expertise from all around the globe. There is also a four-year course in European Law that requires students to have a good knowledge of French or German. Three-year courses combining Law with Sociology or Business Studies are also offered.

See *Heap 2015: University Degree Course Offers* (Trotman Publishing) for details of offers

West London The LLB course provides a traditional legal education with a wide range of options in Years 2 and 3, including European Union law, public international law, civil litigation and the government and politics of Britain. It is recognised by the Bar and Law Society. Criminology courses are also offered with Law, Psychology and Policing and Forensics.

West Scotland Law is offered as a BA course and can be studied as a three-year full-time course or over four years with a sandwich year. The degree focuses on the Scottish legal system with a range of specialist areas available.

Westminster The seven compulsory law subjects required to gain necessary exemptions from professional law examinations are taken in Years 1 and 2 of the Law course with additional options in Years 2 and 3. Other courses include Commercial Law, European Legal Studies, Law with French, and Law and Solicitor's Exempting.

Winchester The LLB Law course is single honours only and is a qualifying Law degree. Optional modules available in the second and third year include evidence, company law, employment and family law.

Wolverhampton The Law course is approved by the Law Society and the Bar Council for exemption from Law Society final examinations. It covers the required compulsory core subjects plus a wide range of options from which seven must be chosen in Years 2 and 3. There are also BA courses in Accounting and Law, Business and Law, Criminology, Criminal Justice and Law, and Human Resource Management and Law.

York* A new Law course (LLB) has been introduced comprising three streams: foundation, law and society, and law and practice, which reflect the core subjects needed to pass a qualifying Law degree, the interdisciplinary nature of the programme and the development of practical skills.

OTHER INSTITUTIONS OFFERING LAW COURSES
Blackburn (Coll), Bradford (Coll Univ Centre), Croydon (Coll), Doncaster (Coll Univ Centre), Euro Bus Sch London, Exeter (Coll), Grimsby (Univ Centre), Kaplan Holborn (Coll), London Regent's, Newcastle (Coll), Nottingham New (Coll), Peterborough (Reg Coll), Ruskin Oxford (Coll), South Devon (Coll), Staffordshire Reg Fed (SURF), Truro (Coll), Warrington (Coll), Warwickshire (Coll), Worcester (CT).

ALTERNATIVE COURSES
Government, History, International Relations, Politics, Social Sciences, Social Studies, Sociology.

LEISURE, RECREATION MANAGEMENT AND TOURISM

(see also **Hospitality Management**)
(* indicates universities with entry requirements over 340 UCAS points)

SUBJECT REQUIREMENTS/PREFERENCES
GCSE: English and Mathematics and for some courses a foreign language.

SUBJECT INFORMATION
Courses in these subjects are generally quite similar. However, the applicant should note the specialist options offered, for example recreation management, countryside management and heritage studies.

See *Heap 2015: University Degree Course Offers* (Trotman Publishing) for details of offers

Anglia Ruskin Courses are offered in Tourism Management with modules/specialist studies in management, heritage, ecotourism and international business. Optional modules include wildlife and tourism, dark tourism and cross-cultural issues in international management.

Bedfordshire An International Tourism Management degree is available and modules are also offered in Marketing and Finance. There is also a Travel and Tourism degree.

Birmingham (UC) The Adventure Tourism Management course involves studies in commercial and risk management. Options include modern languages and sports, international and nature tourism.

Bournemouth The Leisure Marketing course offers modules in accounting, leisure planning and marketing. The third year consists of a 40-week placement in the UK and overseas. This leads on to the fourth year which focuses on the dissertation and modules in strategy and leadership and international leisure marketing.

Brighton Sport and Leisure Management is offered in which social, scientific and management subjects are studied. The International Travel Management course covers travel geography, operations and retail studies. There is an industrial placement or dissertation in Year 3. There are also courses in Tourism Management and International Tourism Management with language studies in French, German or Spanish.

Bucks New Two courses are available in International Travel and Tourism Management including one with Air Travel. The courses include field trips at each level and the opportunity to study abroad.

Central Lancashire International Tourism Management is a four-year sandwich course with a placement abroad in Year 3. Other courses are offered in Tourism Management and there are several courses involving outdoor leadership, recreation and education.

Chichester A course is offered in Tourism Management covering rural, sport, events and heritage studies. It includes the opportunity to gain certification in a range of training programmes accredited by VisitBritain.

Cumbria A course is offered in Adventure Media which includes modules such as travel writing, professional development, social issues in the outdoors and outdoor adventure skills.

East London Third World Development and International Tourism Management are two subjects offered in the BA/BSc combined honours degree, which covers modules such as urban tourism management and fundamentals of finance.

Edinburgh BSc Sport and Recreation Management is offered as a three-year or four-year full-time degree with a 10-week placement in the third year.

Edinburgh Napier Tourism Management is offered with Human Resource Management, Entrepreneurship and Hospitality Management. Courses are also offered in Tourism Marketing and Festival and Event Management.

Glasgow Caledonian Courses in International Tourism and Travel/Hospitality Enterprise are offered. The degrees are accredited by the Institute of Travel and Tourism, the Institute of Hospitality, the Tourism Management Institute and the Tourism Society.

Gloucestershire Leisure and Sports Management with a compulsory placement year is offered with a wide range of subjects in the modular degree scheme. Events Management is also offered.

Greenwich A BA course is offered in Tourism Management with French, German, Italian or Spanish and covers subjects including health and safety, marketing and strategy. Events Management is also available.

Harper Adams Leisure and Tourism Management is available and covers a range of key subjects including tourism policy, strategy and destination management. Options are available in Outdoor Adventure Design and Visitor Management.

See *Heap 2015: University Degree Course Offers* (Trotman Publishing) for details of offers

Hertfordshire A large number of joint courses in Tourism are offered, including Tourism and Management Sciences, Business and Tourism, Event Management and Tourism and Human Resources.

Huddersfield Travel and Tourism Management is offered as a three-year full-time or four-year sandwich degree. Tourism and Leisure are also part of the Hospitality programme.

Leeds Beckett Courses are offered in Sport, Leisure and Culture and Tourism Management, which can be studied with French, German or Spanish. There is also a course available in International Tourism Management.

Lincoln Single and joint courses are offered in International Tourism Management which cover topics including the travel industry, tourism in the UK and Europe, economics, marketing and heritage management. There is an optional year in industry and a choice of languages from French, German and Spanish. There is also the opportunity to spend a semester at an overseas university.

Liverpool Hope The Tourism degree looks at the subject from both management and academic perspectives. There is fieldwork throughout the course and a work placement can be undertaken at Level 3. It can be studied as a three-year honours degree or as part of a combined honours programme with a wide rage of subjects such as Accounting, Drama and Theatre Studies, Marketing and Special Educational Needs. There is also a three-year single honours Tourism Management degree available.

Liverpool John Moores The Tourism and Leisure Management course includes data management, accounting, economics, marketing, consumer studies and personnel management. The course can be taken with a sandwich year.

London Met Courses are offered in International Tourism Management and Tourism and Travel Management, and in Events and Sports Management. There is also a degree in International Hospitality Management.

Loughborough Sport Management is offered as a three-year full-time or four-year sandwich course. Geography can also be studied with Sports Management on a three-year full-time degree.

Manchester Met Tourism Management can be studied as a single honours degree and is also offered with 28 other subjects including Events. The course can be studied as a three- or four-year sandwich degree.

Middlesex International Tourism Management is available with a range of subjects including Hospitality Management, Marketing, Business, Spanish and Human Resource Management. There is the chance to study in Dubai.

Plymouth Courses are offered in Tourism Management, Hospitality, Events and Tourism Management, Business and Tourism and International Tourism Management. The Tourism Management degree involves spending the third year in a paid work placement.

Robert Gordon The International Tourism Management course offers 28 weeks of paid placement at the end of Year 2 and the option to study abroad. The course is four years with the option to follow a taught or placement route.

St Mark and St John Single and combined courses can be taken with Outdoor Adventure. The single honours option can be tailored to the student with options in Sport and Leisure Management and Education Studies.

Salford Leisure and Tourism Management is a three-year full-time course that covers sport, recreation, tourism and health promotion, and includes languages with options for a placement in Europe. There are also courses in Events Management, and in Hospitality and Tourism Management.

Staffordshire Industry-facing degree courses are Events Management and Tourism Management. Both courses are three years full time or four years full time with a placement.

See *Heap 2015: University Degree Course Offers* (Trotman Publishing) for details of offers

Strathclyde Hospitality and Tourism is offered in several joint courses from the Business School including Accounting, Business Enterprise, Economics, Human Resource Management, Marketing and Business Law.

Sunderland Large numbers of joint, major and minor courses with Tourism are on offer. A BSc in International Tourism and Hospitality Management is also available.

Teesside The top-up degree in Tourism Management offers students a broad understanding of current issues and developments in tourism. The events management modules give students the opportunity to organise and stage their own event.

Trinity St David A broad course in Outdoor Education is available which includes a work placement.

Trinity St David (Swansea) Courses are offered in Events, Tourism and Sports Management and an International Travel and Tourism Management BA is also available. Placement opportunities on these courses are available across the world, including at Disney World (US) and the CN Tower (Canada).

Ulster International Hotel and Tourism Management and International Travel and Tourism Management are offered. International Travel and Tourism Studies can be taken with French, German or Spanish.

West London Courses are offered in Travel and Tourism Management. The course covers areas including European travel, geography, legislative framework, inclusive tour operations, attractions management and ecotourism.

West Scotland There is a BA course offered in Events Management and a third-year entry course in Events and Tourism Management offered at the Ayr campus.

Westminster Courses in Tourism are offered with options in planning, travel and business. Courses are offered on a full-time basis only and are taught in central London.

Winchester The vocationally oriented Event Management course is offered with opportunities to take part in visits to venues, live events and trade exhibitions. See also **Hospitality Management**.

Wolverhampton Tourism Management and Sport Management degrees are offered. There is also a course in Event and Venue Management available as a full-time or sandwich degree.

OTHER INSTITUTIONS OFFERING LEISURE, RECREATION MANAGEMENT AND TOURISM COURSES

Blackburn (Coll), Cornwall (Coll), Craven (Coll), Duchy (Coll), Grimsby (Univ Centre), Liverpool City (Coll), Loughborough (Coll), Northumberland (Coll), Norwich City (Coll), Nottingham New (Coll), Riverside Halton (Coll), Sheffield (Coll), Solihull (Coll), Somerset (Coll), Southport (Coll), SRUC, Staffordshire Reg Fed (SURF), Suffolk (Univ Campus), Truro (Coll), UHI, Warwickshire (Coll), Wirral Met (Coll).

ALTERNATIVE COURSES

Amenities Management, Arts Management, Facilities Management, Hotel Management, Leisure Boat Design, Physical Education, Sports Studies.

MATERIALS SCIENCE/METALLURGY/ MATERIALS ENGINEERING

(* indicates universities with entry requirements over 340 UCAS points)

SUBJECT REQUIREMENTS/PREFERENCES
GCE A level: Two or three science/mathematics subjects required for most courses. **GCSE:** Science/ mathematics subjects. **Brunel:** Grades A–C in Physics and Chemistry if not offered at A level. **Swansea:** Predominantly grades A and B.

SUBJECT INFORMATION
This is a subject that covers physics, chemistry and engineering at one and the same time! From its origins in metallurgy, materials science has now moved into the processing, structure and properties of materials – ceramics, polymers, composites and electrical materials. Materials science and metallurgy are perhaps the most misunderstood of all careers. Thus applications for degree courses are low and offers are very reasonable. As with other careers in which there is a shortfall of applicants, graduate employment and future prospects are good.

Aberdeen A BEng course is offered in Mechanical Engineering with Materials. All Engineering courses at Aberdeen are recognised worldwide as an accredited route to professional engineering status.

Birmingham* Courses are offered in Materials Science and Engineering and Materials Science and Technology with opportunities to link the subject with Biomedical Materials, Business Management, Energy Engineering and Nuclear Science.

Cambridge* See **Combined Courses**.

Edinburgh Napier A four-year sandwich course in Polymer Engineering is offered with 12 months' supervised work experience between Years 2 and 4. The course covers the most recent developments in the subject including liquid crystal polymers, flame-retardant materials and recycling.

Heriot-Watt Fashion Technology is offered covering areas including fashion product development, textiles, commercial context and management. Projects aim to develop a broad range of essential skills and there is an optional year in industry which provides an additional award.

Imperial London* The department offers three-year BEng courses in Materials Science and Engineering, Materials with Management, and Materials with a year abroad, and four-year courses in Aerospace Materials, and Materials Science and Engineering. Students are encouraged to gain practical experience during two summer vacations; some are spent abroad. There are also opportunities for industrial sponsorship. A course in Biomaterials and Tissue Engineering is also offered.

Leeds* The School of Process, Environmental and Materials Engineering offers a course in Chemical and Materials Engineering with modules across four years including engineering materials, materials, structures and characterisation and extractive metallurgy.

Liverpool Mathematics, computing, corrosion and oxidation are common core courses for the Mechanical and Materials Engineering course. Other modules include aeroengines, construction materials and microstructure and strengthening mechanisms.

London (QM) The course in Materials Science and Engineering provides a bridge between pure and applied sciences and covers polymers, biomaterials, metals and ceramics. There are also specialised courses in Automotive, Aerospace and Dental Materials.

London (UCL) History of Art with Material Studies is offered as a three-year full-time course and focuses on questions of materiality both at the time the art was created and as it deteriorates.

London Met Three-year degree courses are offered in Polymer Engineering and in Polymer Science and cover core areas including mathematics, IT for engineers and an introduction to materials.

Loughborough The Materials Engineering programme allows students to develop either Materials Engineering or Business Management options in the final year. There is an optional third year in Europe or in industry. There are also courses in Automotive Materials.

Manchester* The Materials Science and Engineering programme focuses on engineering aspects whilst the Biomedical Materials Science programme can be taken with or without industrial experience. The Biomedical Materials Science course covers cell structure, anatomy, tissue interaction and drug-release systems. There are also courses in Textile Sciences and Technology.

Manchester Met There is a degree course in Dental Technology. The first year acts as an introduction to the techniques and materials used in the dental laboratory.

Newcastle* Mechanical Engineering is offered in a three-year full-time degree. There is also a new course available in Mechanical Design and Manufacturing Engineering which meets the standards of international bachelor's degrees from the US and Commonwealth countries.

Northampton The university has always been one of the main centres for the study of Leather Technology. A Leather Technology BSc top-up can be taken following the completion of the Leatherseller's Diploma.

Nottingham* A course is offered in Biomedical Materials Science that allows students to specialise in cell biology, materials design and processing and pharmaceutical applications. The course is only available full time.

Oxford* The study of the Materials Science is interdisciplinary, involving the physics and chemistry of solids and their engineering applications. The course lasts four years and the final year involves research in the department or in industry leading to the thesis. This subject area is undersubscribed. A degree course is also offered in Materials, Economics and Management that has a common first year with the previous course.

Sheffield In this Materials Science and Engineering course modules exist in biomaterials, mathematics and material chemistry. Admission can also be by way of Physical Sciences since final degree course decisions between Materials Science or Physics or Chemistry can be delayed. Various Engineering courses are also available as well as a course in Aerospace Materials.

Southampton* Courses are offered in Aeronautics and Astronautics with specialist modules in materials. There is also a course offered in Fashion and Textile Design.

Staffordshire Three-dimensional Design for Ceramics is a comprehensive study of ceramic materials' manufacture and design and benefits from being located in the heart of the Potteries, the UK's centre for the ceramic industry.

Strathclyde There is a course in Mechanical and Materials Engineering with options in Aeromechanical Engineering, Mechanical Engineering and Mechanical Engineering with International Study.

Swansea Scholarships are available in the Materials Science and Engineering course, in which specialist topics include polymer engineering, microelectronics, materials technology and failure analysis. The course is also offered with a year in North America. A course in Resistant Materials Design is also offered.

See *Heap 2015: University Degree Course Offers* (Trotman Publishing) for details of offers

OTHER INSTITUTIONS OFFERING MATERIALS/METALLURGY COURSES
Bradford (Coll Univ Centre), Hull (Coll), Warwickshire (Coll).

ALTERNATIVE COURSES
Aerospace Materials Technology, Biomedical Materials Science, Chemistry and Applied Chemistry, Engineering Design, Geology, Geophysics, Materials Engineering, Mechanical, Mineral Exploitation, Mining and Production Engineering, Paper Science, Physics and Applied Physics, Polymer Chemistry, Polymer Science, Textiles, Wood Science.

MATHEMATICS

(including **Statistics**)
(* indicates universities with entry requirements over 340 UCAS points)

SUBJECT REQUIREMENTS/PREFERENCES
GCE A level: Mathematics subjects, normally the highest grade in the offers made. **GCSE:** English often required.

SUBJECT INFORMATION
Mathematics degree courses are an extension of A level Mathematics, covering pure and applied mathematics, statistics, computing, mathematical analysis and mathematical applications. Research ratings below include Pure and Applied Mathematics and Statistics unless otherwise indicated.

QUESTIONS TO CONSIDER
 * Does the university offer specialist courses or modules in the area of mathematics I am interested in?
 * Are there opportunities for a work placement?
 * Do I need to have a Statistics A level to gain entry to this course?

Aberdeen Students can aim to choose between focusing their attention on Mathematics or spreading their interests to combine it with other subjects such as Computing, Economics and Physics.

Aberystwyth Mathematics is offered as a modular course for students wishing to specialise in Pure or Applied Mathematics or Statistics. It is possible to delay the final choice of specialisation until the end of Year 1. The course in Financial Mathematics draws together modules in economics, accounting, business law and mathematics. A wide range of joint courses can be taken including with Education, Welsh History, European Languages, Fine Art and Geography.

Aston Mathematics can be studies as both a single and joint honours course.

Bath* In the School of Mathematical Sciences a number of three-year and four-year courses, all with a common first year, are offered covering Mathematics and Statistics, with some transfers possible at the end of Year 1 to pathways in pure and applied mathematics, probability and statistics. There are four-year courses with a job placement or study abroad. See also **Combined Courses**.

Birmingham* The Mathematical Science courses offer a broad framework of subjects with a wide choice of specialisms in Year 3. An additional year of computer science is possible. Joint courses with Business Management, Philosophy, Psychology, Sports Science or an arts subject are possible. There are courses in Applied, Pure and Management Mathematics. See also **Combined Courses**.

Bolton The degree offers a broad education in Mathematics with plenty of pure and applied mathematics. The course can be studied jointly with a range of subjects.

Bradford There is a course in Computational Mathematics with a foundation year in informatics for applicants with non-standard qualifications. Students are offered a broad education with the opportunity to specialise in the third year.

Brighton A BSc Mathematics course is available with over 15 options in the third year including mathematics, statistics and operational research, and an optional placement year. Joint courses are also offered with Computing, Education, Business or Finance.

Bristol* A particular feature is the flexibility of the Mathematics course structure at every undergraduate stage, with most of the programmes having a common structure in the first year. From Year 2 a wide range of options can be chosen. Students may also choose to spend one-third of their time on subjects outside the Mathematics Department in either or both of their second or third years, for example computer science, psychology, economics or philosophy. This is particularly useful for students moving into the business world who may wish to study financial mathematics or alternatively a career in education. Mathematics can also be taken with Statistics.

Bristol UWE Mathematics is a modular programme covering mathematics, statistics and computing. There is also a separate degree in Statistics which shares modules in Years 1 and 2 with the Mathematics programme.

Brunel* The Department of Mathematics and Statistics caters for all possible interests with a wide range of courses that includes Mathematics, Mathematical and Management Studies, Mathematics and Computing, and Mathematics and Statistics with Management. These courses are also offered on a sandwich basis, which leads to a high proportion of successful graduate employment placements.

Cambridge* In Part IA of the Pure and Applied Mathematics Tripos there are two options: (a) Pure and Applied Mathematics; and (b) Mathematics with Physics. In Part II there is a choice of alternatives that lead either to practical applications of the subject or to research applications. About 10% of students change from Mathematics to Physics each year after having taken option (b).

Cardiff* The core modules are taken by all Mathematics students in Year 1 with the opportunity to change degree programmes at the start of Year 2. The Mathematics course allows students to specialise in pure or applied mathematics, operational research, computing or statistics. The Mathematics and its Applications course provides opportunities for specialisation in several branches of the subject and professional placements and study in Europe. Mathematics can also be taken with Operational Research and Statistics, Computing and Physics, while Pure Mathematics can also be taken with a humanities subject.

Central Lancashire The BSc course in Mathematics provides an excellent foundation in modern mathematics and covers statistics, applicable mathematics, computing and programming. Mathematics can also be taken with Economics, Psychology, Computer Science and Statistics.

Chester Single and combined honours courses are offered involving Pure and Applied Mathematics, Statistics and Operational Research. Assessment is through examinations and coursework with modules often placing an emphasis on examinations.

Chichester Mathematics is offered as a teaching programme for Key Stages 2 and 3 (7–14 age range). Specialist placement in the second year provides students with the opportunity to experience working in an educational environment.

City* The Mathematical Sciences course gives an excellent grounding in mathematics, statistics and computer science, with options in finance and economics, statistics and computing in Years 2 and 3 leading to specialist degrees. Good opportunities exist for transfer across courses. There is an optional third year in industry or abroad. See also **Actuarial Sciences/Studies**.

Coventry Courses are offered in Mathematics, Mathematics and Theoretical Physics and Mathematics and Statistics with modules focusing on the applications of mathematics in engineering, finance, computing, business and statistics.

Cumbria Mathematics is studied as part of the BA Primary Education with Advanced Curriculum Specialism with QTS, which qualifies students to teach children aged 5–11.

Derby Mathematical Studies and Mathematics with Education follow similar courses at the outset before specialisms are decided. Mathematics and Computer Studies is also offered with an industrial placement.

Dundee Schemes are offered in which students can take Mathematics for one year only or to honours level. The department teaches a broad-based Mathematics syllabus in Levels 1 to 3 leading on in Level 4 to a set of options. Joint courses in Mathematics are offered and, additionally, further joint courses in Statistics.

Durham* Maths courses cover Pure and Applied Maths and Statistics with optional modules, e.g. finance, education, arts and social science. The BSc and MMaths courses are common with the choice being made later.

East Anglia* The course unit system gives considerable flexibility for studying Mathematics. The preliminary programme in Mathematics includes two compulsory units and one optional unit. By taking certain optional units students may then choose to follow one of several joint courses in Mathematics (with Computing, Economics, Environmental Sciences, Management, Meteorology or Statistics) or single honours Mathematics. The second and third years are planned on a unit system, allowing students further flexibility in the choice of options. A four-year degree programme also offers a year in Australia or North America.

Edinburgh The first two years of the Mathematics course cover pure mathematics (mainly in the Faculty of Arts) and applied mathematics (Faculty of Science) and two other courses in science, arts or social sciences. The third and fourth years specialise in Mathematics with a wide range of options in the fourth year. There are degrees in Mathematics and Statistics, Applied Mathematics and Mathematics with Management or Music.

Essex Students follow common first-year courses that can then lead on to degrees in Mathematics or Mathematics with Computing and Economics or with a teaching qualification. Courses in Mathematics and a humanity are also available.

Exeter* Most first-year modules are common to all single honours courses. Transfers to other courses are possible from Year 2 and options to take modules in other subjects are also available. There is a wide range of degrees including combinations with Environmental Studies, Management, Physics and Finance and Accounting.

Glasgow* The Mathematical Sciences course involves the study of three disciplines: maths, statistics and computing science. There is also a degree course in Pure Mathematics and Applied Mathematics. Further courses are offered in Accounting and Mathematics and Finance and Mathematics.

Greenwich Several full-time and sandwich courses in Mathematics are offered, covering Mathematics, Statistics, Mathematics and Computing, Financial Mathematics and Mathematics for Decision Science. There are also opportunities for combined degrees with subjects such as Business and Languages.

Heriot-Watt Nine courses are offered in Mathematics including Mathematical, Statistical and Actuarial Science and Statistical Modelling with options in computer science, economics, finance, education, nanoscience, physics, languages and management. Late transfers to other degrees in Mathematics are possible.

Hertfordshire The main feature of the Mathematics course is that a choice may be made between a broad BSc course in Mathematics or more specialised courses in Computing Mathematics or Financial

Mathematics at the end of Year 1. Mathematics is also offered in the modular degree scheme with subjects including Economics, Human Geography and Digital Media Technology.

Imperial London* Twelve courses are offered with considerable flexibility to transfer between courses and between BSc and MSci. Options include Applied Maths, Statistics, Computer Science and a year in Europe. There is also a new course in Mathematics and Computer Science (Pure Maths and Computational Logic).

Keele Mathematics can be taken as a single honours course or in combination with one from over 15 other subjects. In the first and second years the principal course covers pure and applied mathematics and statistics, while the third year offers a wide choice of topics, depending on the student's interests.

Kent* Three-year programmes are offered in Mathematics, Financial Mathematics, and in Mathematics and Statistics, all of which may be taken with a year in industry.

Kingston Courses in Mathematical Sciences and Actuarial Mathematics and Statistics are offered along with Statistics and Statistics with Business degrees, including joint honours options. Scholarships available.

Lancaster* Courses are offered in Mathematics, Mathematics and Statistics and with Philosophy. A course is also offered in Financial Mathematics with core courses covering finance, corporate finance, computing, quantitative methods and economics.

Leeds* The School of Mathematics is one of the largest in the country. Flexible degree schemes are offered, including opportunities to study in Europe. Study of non-mathematical subjects is possible alongside Mathematics. The Mathematics course is for those wishing to concentrate on maths (with up to two non-maths modules). Mathematics Studies allows more time to be spent on non-maths subjects (including management, physics, chemistry, economics, geography, music and English), with the choice of a BSc or MMaths at the end of Year 2, and European options in both. Courses are also offered in Mathematics with Finance and also in Statistics.

Leicester* There are 10 BA, BSc and MMaths courses offered in Mathematics, Financial Mathematics, Mathematics with Economics and Mathematics with Management. The MMaths Mathematics degree comes with the opportunity to study abroad.

Liverpool Over 20 courses are available in Mathematics, the department also being responsible for courses in Statistics and Computing. Core studies form the basis of first-year programmes followed by specialisation in Years 2 and 3. Computer Science can be studied alongside Mathematics in Year 2. Mathematics can be studied with Ocean and Climate Studies, Finance, Education, Statistics and Business Studies. Mathematics is also offered as part of the combined honours programme for students with or without A level Mathematics.

Liverpool Hope Mathematics is offered as a BSc combined honours or as a BA with Education and covers applied mathematics in the area of scientific computing.

Liverpool John Moores The course in Mathematics focuses on the use of mathematical and statistical methods in industry and business. Professional placement takes place in Year 3. There is also a BA degree offered in Mathematics and Education Studies.

London (King's)* The Mathematics curriculum is flexible and allows for a change of direction according to ability and interest. Specialist mathematicians in their third year follow courses of their own choice from a range of options in pure and applied mathematics and mathematical physics. Computer Science, Management and Finance, Physics and Philosophy can also be taken with Mathematics.

London (QM) The School of Mathematical Sciences embraces pure mathematics, probability, statistics and computing. Joint degrees are also offered involving other departments. A course unit system is in operation that enables students to choose from a large number of courses, both within Mathematics itself and also combining Mathematics with another subject, including Discrete Mathematics, Mathematical Sciences and Statistics. Mathematics can also be studied with Business Management, Finance, Accounting and Statistics.

London (RH)* Mathematics can be taken on its own or with a range of options including Management, Music, Physics, Languages and Philosophy. There is also a course in Mathematics with Statistics.

London (UCL)* A range of courses, including Economics, Statistical Science and Theoretical Physics, is offered with Mathematics and some sponsorships are possible. Small-group tutorials and computer-assisted learning are important features of this course. There is a range of options in Years 3 and 4. There are also several Statistics degree courses.

London LSE* Mathematics is offered with Economics and there is also a course in Business Mathematics and Statistics. The latter has a common first year with Actuarial Science.

London Met There are single and joint degrees in Mathematics, Financial Mathematics and Mathematical Sciences, which includes statistics and operational research. Mathematics can also be studied with Computer Science and as an extended degree alongside Computing and Communications Technology.

Loughborough* BSc and MMaths programmes are common over Years 1 and 2. All students study calculus, linear algebra, applied mathematics, mathematical computing and probability and statistics. Courses are offered in Mathematics, Mathematics with Accounting, Economics, Education, Sport Science or Statistics.

Manchester* Three-year and four-year courses are offered with modules taken in subjects from other departments. Modern Languages, Management, Philosophy and Statistics are offered in joint courses with Mathematics.

Manchester Met In addition to a very flexible degree course in Mathematics, the subject can be taken as part of the combined honours programme focusing on core modules including mathematical fundamentals and programme skills.

Newcastle* The Mathematics course structure allows students to defer their choice of final degree course until the end of Year 2. In addition, a significant amount of time can be spent studying a minor subject, e.g. accounting, music or languages. There are degrees in Statistics, Mathematical Sciences, Financial Mathematics and Economics and Mathematics. Opportunities exist to take non-mathematical options including accounting, economics, computing and languages. Changing between the various degrees offered by the department is a routine matter at the end of the first and second years.

Newman This teaching course is taken in collaboration with Aston University, with Years 1 and 2 taken at Aston.

Northampton Mathematics is offered as part of the Primary Education (QTS) degree, which qualifies students to teach children aged 5–11. The degree comprises taught sessions and school placements.

Northumbria The course in Mathematics is a strongly vocational three-year or four-year programme with Year 3 spent on optional placement in industry or commerce. Mathematics is also offered as a joint honours course with Business Management.

Nottingham* Mathematics is a flexible course in which students take optional modules in statistics and pure and applied maths in the first year, in addition to mathematics. Transfer is possible between single and joint courses. Mathematics can also be taken as a joint honours course with six other subjects, including Engineering, Philosophy, Management Studies, Economics and Computer Science. There is also a course in Mathematical Physics offered.

Nottingham Trent The Mathematics degree covers mathematics, statistics and computing. Sport Science and Computer Science can also be taken with Mathematics and there is a course in Financial Mathematics.

Oxford* The three-year course in Mathematics is designed for students who require a sound analytical and numerical training. The four-year option leads to advanced research areas. There is a common first year for both courses. In addition, Mathematics is offered with Statistics, Computer Science or Philosophy.

Oxford Brookes Mathematics is offered jointly with a wide range of subjects. Mathematical Sciences is a broad course including computing and statistics. A range of courses with Statistics and Medical Statistics is also available.

Plymouth Five Mathematics courses are offered including combinations with Statistics, Education, Computing and Finance. Applied Statistics can also be taken with Management Science and a BEd in Primary Mathematics is available.

Portsmouth Several Mathematics courses are on offer, including Mathematics for Finance or Management or with Statistics. The flexibility of the courses allows students to change between Mathematics degrees after the first year.

Queen's Belfast* Three departments teach Applied Mathematics, Pure Mathematics, Statistics and Operational Research. All courses and all students register initially for Mathematics. Thereafter, depending on the student's interest and progress, transfers can take place to the other three specialisms at the end of Year 1 and from the BSc to the MSc course.

Reading Courses are offered in Mathematics, Applied Statistics and Computational Mathematics. For each degree there is a set of compulsory units and optional units. Students taking Mathematics also take a third subject in the first year that could include geometry or scientific writing.

St Andrews* The three departments, offering 60 courses in Mathematics, Pure Mathematics, Applied Mathematics and Statistics, co-operate within a very flexible joint honours course structure. Mathematics can be studied as an arts or science degree, and combined with a range of subjects including, for example, Psychology, Logic and Philosophy of Science, Languages, Scottish History and Hebrew. Mathematics is also offered as a single honours course where students can study for a BSc (Hons), MA (Hons) or MMaths (Hons) degree.

Sheffield* The single honours degree in Mathematics provides a balance between pure and applied mathematics and statistics in all years. Mathematics is offered with a number of second subjects including Philosophy, Physics, Languages and Economics.

Sheffield Hallam The three main strands of Mathematics cover modelling, analysis and statistics. Mathematics, information technology and statistics are taken in Year 1. There are placement options in Year 3. Mathematics is also available with Education and Qualified Teacher Status.

South Wales Mathematics is offered as part of several degree programmes and as a single BSc Mathematics course. There are also courses in Financial and Computing Mathematics, and Mathematical Sciences.

Southampton* A common first year for Mathematics students includes calculus, geometry, mechanics, statistics and computing, followed in Years 2 and 3 by a wide range of options. This enables students to build a course best suited to their interests and needs. There are also degrees with Mathematics including Languages, Astronomy, Statistics, and Actuarial Studies. Biology, Computer Science and Operational Research are also available.

Staffordshire Mathematics and Applied Statistics brings together the two subjects to deliver a highly numerate and analytical honours degree. The main focus of the degree is to develop students' problem-solving skills. There is also a course in Business Data Analysis available.

See *Heap 2015: University Degree Course Offers* (Trotman Publishing) for details of offers

Stirling The Mathematics and its Applications course includes statistics and provides graduates with a strong base for many careers. A range of subjects can be studied with Mathematics including French, Environmental Science, Psychology and Management Science.

Strathclyde Mathematics students are offered a range of single and joint honours courses involving Mathematics and Statistics, Computer Science, Accounting, Economics, Finance and Management Science. A flexible modular structure allows students to tailor their own courses. A course in Mathematics with Teaching is also offered.

Sunderland A teacher-training course (11–18 years) is offered in Mathematics. On successful completion of the course, students will have gained Qualified Teacher Status.

Surrey* The Mathematics programme covers a broad range of mathematical subjects, with all students following the same lecture course for the first two terms, after which there is some degree of specialisation. Mathematics may be studied with Statistics, Computing Science or Music and there is a course in Financial Mathematics.

Sussex* The Mathematics course provides a broad mathematical education. The degree structure is based on a core of mathematics combined with another subject. Second subjects include Computer Science, Economics, Education and Management Studies.

Swansea* There are several Part I courses in Mathematics. For non-specialists the Part I course in mathematical methods includes practical training in the use of computers. Part II courses include both single and joint honours courses including Applied Mathematics and Pure Mathematics. Mathematics is also offered with Sport Science and with a language (French, German, Italian, Spanish or Welsh) and with Geoinformatics.

Warwick* A number of Mathematics degree courses are offered, including Mathematics with Economics, Business and Philosophy, and Mathematics, Operational Research, Statistics and Economics (MORSE), as well as several joint honours combinations. Depending on individual choice, the Mathematics programme contains 75% mathematics in Year 1 and between 50% and 100% in Years 2 and 3. The balance is made up from an extensive range of options. Statistics degrees are offered with Mathematics and the MORSE course.

Winchester Mathematics can be chosen as a specialist subject as part of the Primary Education with Recommendation of Qualified Teacher Status BA. The course offers a common first year with students then able to follow a three- or four-year route.

Wolverhampton The BSc in Mathematics aims to develop students' theoretical understanding of the subject while also employing a range of practical applications which place a particular emphasis on statistics and operational research.

York* A balanced foundation of general mathematical knowledge occupies the first year of Mathematics courses, with flexibility for course transfer. The second and third years provide a wide choice of options including Mathematics with a year in Europe or in industry. Joint honours courses include Mathematics with Economics, Philosophy or Physics or Statistics, Linguistics and Computer Science.

OTHER INSTITUTIONS OFFERING MATHEMATICS COURSES
Staffordshire Reg Fed (SURF).

ALTERNATIVE COURSES
Accountancy, Actuarial Studies, Astronomy, Computing, Engineering, Management Science, Meteorology, Operational Research, Physics, Statistics.

MEDIA STUDIES

(including **Communication Studies**, **Journalism** and **Photography**)
(* indicates universities with entry requirements over 340 UCAS points)

SUBJECT REQUIREMENTS/PREFERENCES

GCE A level: Language requirement for appropriate language course. Communication Studies, English and Media Studies may be preferred. **GCSE:** English and Mathematics often required.

SUBJECT INFORMATION

Check prospectuses carefully since subject content differs considerably between universities. Media courses generally focus on radio, television, journalism and the effects of the media on society. Communication Studies courses are not necessarily a training for the media but extend to management, international communications, design and psychology. The courses listed here are those with the title 'Communications' and the reader is strongly advised to recognise the distinction that different universities and colleges give to this title and to research the courses carefully.

Abertay Media, Culture and Society is a theoretical study of the media focusing on social and political issues and the emerging possibilities of new media technology.

Aberystwyth A Media and Communications Studies course offers both theory and practice in both traditional and new media including film, journalism and the information society.

Anglia Ruskin There is a Media Studies degree involving radio, TV, video and film. There are also courses in Film Studies and Media Studies and Media and Internet Technology.

Bangor The BA in Creative Studies enables students to pursue a variety of related subject areas including creative writing, film studies, theatre studies, media and journalism or to combine modules from these programmes. These subjects are also offered as separate degrees.

Bath Spa The Creative Media Practice course offers a choice of two options from interaction design, digital photography, music technology, media production for TV and radio, PR and marketing for publishing and scriptwriting for TV and radio. There is also a degree in Media Communications.

Bedfordshire The Media Practices and Public Relations course covers marketing and public relations. There are also courses in Journalism, Moving Image, Radio, Scriptwriting, Mass Communications, Public Relations and Media and TV Production.

Birmingham* The Modern Languages and European Studies BA focuses on culture, society and communication in Europe with some modules in media, culture and communication. The course involves the study of a modern language.

Birmingham City Media and Communication courses have specialisms in events and exhibitions, journalism, media photography, web and new media, public relations, radio production and television and music industries. There is also a separate course in Television Technology and Production with a sandwich placement and Multimedia Technology.

Bolton The Media Writing and Production course covers screenwriting and digital video production with work in film studies. Bolton University is a BBC Educational Partner. Work placements are offered.

Bournemouth The Multimedia Journalism course involves news and feature writing, radio and TV journalism, shorthand, and information technology. The professional placement module places students in a working environment alongside print, radio or television journalists. Other Media courses include

Film Production, Television Production and Scriptwriting for Film and Television. There are also courses in Communications with Media, Advertising, Film Production and Marketing and a Public Relations degree.

Bradford The Media Studies course offers options in several subjects including web, computer games, three-dimensional animation, film and TV. Courses cover technical, social and cultural aspects. The course can be taken with Cinematics or Television.

Brighton The Media Studies degree covers visual communication, marketing, video and film with work placements in the industry. Education or Sociology can also be taken with Media Studies. There is also a Digital Media course that introduces the underlying technologies of the media industry, and courses in Moving Image, Sport Journalism, Film and Screen Studies, Broadcast Media and joint courses with English, Education, Environment and Sociology.

Bristol UWE* The Media Culture and Practice degree is an integration of theory and practice with a focus on digital media. There are also courses in Animation, Photography and Marketing Communications.

Brunel A course is offered in Communications and Media Studies focusing on the social aspects of the media and new communications and information technologies. A substantial amount of the course involves practical work. A rigorous and demanding course in Journalism is also offered.

Buckingham Two-year degrees are offered in Communications and Media Studies for EFL/ESL overseas students. There is also a degree in Journalism which can be studied with Communication Studies.

Bucks New Practical courses include Radio, Film and TV Production and Advertising. Media can be studied with Football Business and there is also a course in Advertising Management and Digital Media Communications available.

Canterbury Christ Church The Media and Communications programme is a study of how communication has developed through the use of media. Courses in Journalism and Digital Media are also offered.

Cardiff In one of the largest media departments in the UK, the Journalism, Media and Cultural Studies course is an academic scheme with some practical work aiming to provide an understanding of the media industries and of mass communications in society. There is also a course in English Language and Communication, which emphasises the study of language as a means of human communication.

Central Lancashire The Journalism course also covers radio and television skills. This well-established course is aimed at those wishing to become professional journalists and introduces the broader study of related areas such as law, politics and history. There are also courses in Film and Media, TV Production, Sports Journalism and International Journalism. There is also a degree in Communication and Popular Culture.

Chester Several media programmes are offered, including Journalism and Media Studies with specialisations in Radio and Television Production. There is also a course in Advertising which combines critical analysis with practical projects.

Chichester Courses are offered in Media Cultural Studies (including media writing) and practical studies in Digital and Film Studies and Film and TV.

City* The Journalism course emphasises practical journalism with a focus in print, broadcast and web journalism. A four-year course is offered with a school of journalism abroad. Journalism can also be combined with Sociology, Economics, Psychology or Contemporary History. Media Studies is offered with Sociology.

Coventry A course in Media and Communications offers modules in film, television, photography, journalism, public relations and video. There are also courses in Media Production and Journalism.

Creative Arts Courses are offered in Journalism focusing on fashion, music and sport. The general Journalism degree includes modules which focus on reporting skills, production skills and feature writing

Cumbria There are courses in Journalism, Film and Television Production and Mass Communications. In the first year of the journalism degree students learn the fundamentals of good journalism with a focus on finding stories, interviewing people and writing. Courses can be studied full or part time.

De Montfort Year 1 of the Media and Communication course focuses on close analysis of media texts including advertisements, news media, films and television programmes. Options in Year 2 include television studies, video production and photography (for single honours students) and a study of journalism and new media. Other courses include Audio Recording, Journalism (single and joint honours), Radio Productions and Digital Video and Broadcast Production, Media Production and Media Technology.

Derby Three-year full-time courses are offered in Media Production, Media Writing, Broadcast Media, Journalism, Interactive Media Production and Film and Television Studies. The course in Journalism offers specialist studies in sport, fashion and music journalism. Many courses can be studied as joint honours.

East Anglia A broad course is offered in Society, Culture and the Media which covers social studies and political aspects. It is an academically rigorous media course. Media can also be studied with Politics.

East London The courses in Media Studies and the Creative Industries cover aspects of the media including film, print, recorded music and the TV industry. Media Studies can be studied as part of a two-subject degree. Other courses include Journalism and Sports Journalism.

Edge Hill Courses are offered in Media specialising in advertising, film and TV or music and sound. There are also joint courses in Media with Drama, Creative Writing, English or Film Studies.

Edinburgh Napier A very vocational course in Journalism is available for students totally committed to a career in this field. The Digital Media course focuses on animation, audio, video and two- and three-dimensional graphics.

Edinburgh Queen Margaret The Media courses of three- or four-year duration offer a study of the media industries with specialist media topics in Years 3 and 4. Film and Media and Theatre and Film Studies courses are also offered.

Essex There is a very broad course covering Media, Culture and Society.

Falmouth Courses are offered in Creative Computing, including games design and animation, and also in Digital Animation and Digital Media.

Glasgow* Film and Television Studies is a theoretical study of the cinema and TV within modern culture. There are opportunities to study abroad in Canada, the US and Australia.

Glasgow Caledonian There are courses in Multimedia Journalism and Media and Communications which includes a wide range of modules from radio and video production and web design to public relations and event management.

Gloucestershire Courses are offered in Advertising, Journalism, Radio Production, Media Communications, Digital Film Production, Popular Music and TV Production with optional and compulsory work placements.

Glyndŵr A course is offered in Studio Recording and Performance Technology which covers theatre sound, radio production, computer music programming and studio planning. There are also courses in Digital Media and Media Communications and in Broadcasting and Journalism.

Greenwich The Media Culture and Communication course covers communication studies, media studies, cultural studies and options in each of the three years. Courses are also offered in Media Writing, Creative Writing, Media Arts Production and Film and Television Production. Courses are also offered in Public Relations and Marketing.

See *Heap 2015: University Degree Course Offers* (Trotman Publishing) for details of offers

Hertfordshire Courses are offered in Media Cultures, Mass Communications, Film, Journalism, and Digital Media Technology or Production and Film and TV. Joint honours courses are also offered with Journalism, Digital Media Technology and Media Cultures.

Huddersfield Journalism and Media and Popular Culture can be taken with options in film, gaming, music, radio and sport. There are also specialist courses in Broadcast, Music and Sport Journalism.

Hull The course in New Media and Political Communication specialises in studying the effects of new social media on modern political practices, culture and society.

Keele A dual honours course is offered in Media, Communications and Culture focusing on theoretical issues surrounding television, film, literature and music. More than 25 subject combinations are available.

Kent The Journalism and the News Industry degree includes history, politics and law, learning radio and TV skills with specialist modules in documentary-making and journalists in fiction and film. There are opportunities for work placements.

Kingston Several joint courses are offered with Media and Cultural Studies including Psychology, Media Technology, Film, Journalism, Sociology and Television Studies, all of which can also be studied as single honours.

Lancaster The course in Media and Cultural Studies is largely theoretical with practical components covering such topics as celebrity culture, war and terror, visual representation, media and marketing.

Leeds The very popular Broadcast Journalism course is aimed at those seeking a career in the industry. Communications is also taken at degree level and four electives are taken in Years 1 and 3 from another subject area. A course is also offered in New Media.

Leeds Beckett Media, Communication and Cultures is a creative and academic course with a focus on mass communication. There are also courses in Broadcast or Creative Media Technologies and Journalism.

Leeds Trinity There is a new course in Broadcast Journalism offering practical skills in written, audio and camera work. There are also courses in Journalism, Magazine Journalism and a Media course with a strong practical emphasis.

Leicester The Communications, Media and Society course is multidisciplinary, covering all aspects of the media, with modules in radio and TV production. Media Studies can be taken with Sociology or Film.

Lincoln Journalism can be taken jointly with Public Relations. Other courses include Media Production, Film and Television and Creative Advertising.

Liverpool Communication Studies is offered with Italian or Business Studies or as Communication, Media and Popular Music, and as part of the BA combined honours programme. The course is theoretical in emphasis and includes topics on TV analysis, popular music, public media and the politics of language. There are also courses in European Film Studies with a modern language.

Liverpool Hope Media and Communication (single or combined) is a highly vocational programme covering TV, film, radio, digital photography, marketing, PR, print journalism and web design.

Liverpool John Moores The Media, Culture and Communication course examines media practice to understand and study new media and cultural trends. There are also vocational courses in Journalism, Media Professional Studies, International Journalism and Broadcast and Media Production.

London (Goldsmiths)* The Media and Communications course combines media practice and communication theory. The media element involves TV, radio journalism, animation, photography, creative writing and scriptwriting. Other courses offered combine Media with Anthropology, Sociology and English. The course in Journalism offers a strong basis of practical experience.

London (QM) Courses are offered in Film Studies with Drama, English and Languages. The degree looks at international cinema with modules in genre, auteurism, scriptwriting and production skills.

See *Heap 2015: University Degree Course Offers* (Trotman Publishing) for details of offers

London (RH) The Media Arts course covers both theory and practice and includes screen drama, screenwriting, documentary, creative sound and film and TV production. There is also a separate degree in Film and TV Studies with an emphasis on Hollywood, UK TV and European film as well as non-Western cinema.

London (SOAS) The BA Cinema Cultures course is studied with another subject chosen from a list of 29. The course looks at cinema cultures in Africa, Asia and the Middle East and their complex relationships with European and American cinema.

London Met Mass communications is offered in a range of courses including Media and Communications, Media Business Management and Journalism. There are also joint courses available in Media Practice with specialisms in animation, film and broadcast and lenscraft.

London South Bank The Media and Cultural Studies course covers the history, politics and sociology of mass media. Media Studies can also be taken as a joint course with Film Studies. The Communications course covers drama, creative writing, arts and festival management, journalism and film studies.

Loughborough The Communication and Media Studies course examines the social, political and economic impact of communication and the media. Publishing with English is also available.

Manchester Screen Studies is available with Drama and focuses more specifically on the study of film. Students study modules such as the art of film, screen culture and society and transnational Chinese cinema alongside compulsory drama modules.

Manchester Met Courses are offered covering Media Technology and Film and Media Studies. Film, Television and Cultural Studies is also available with opportunities for an exchange visit to the US in Year 2.

Middlesex Media and Cultural Studies covers sociology, politics, history and economics and there is also a course in Publishing and the Media. More practical courses include Media Writing, Journalism, Advertising, Publishing, Television Production and Public Relations.

Newcastle Media, Communication and Cultural Studies covers the study of communication from psychological, sociological, managerial and cultural aspects. The course focuses on media studies, film and television and the heritage and museum sectors.

Newman Media and Communication is offered as a minor or joint course with another subject and combines theoretical with practical work.

Northampton A very large number of joint courses in Media Production are offered including a course in Journalism. Journalism is also offered as a single honours degree alongside Film and Television Studies.

Northumbria There are courses in Media Production enabling students to specialise in scriptwriting, film/video production or animation, advertising and journalism. Courses are also offered in Film and Television Studies and Mass Communications and Business.

Nottingham Film and TV Studies can be taken with American Studies, French, German, Hispanic Studies and Russian. The International Media and Communication course is a theoretical study of global communications and can be taken with French, Russian, German or Spanish.

Nottingham Trent Broadcast Journalism covers studio practice and microphone technique. Practical studies can take place with Central TV Midlands, radio and Sky Sports. There is also a course in Communication and Society covering linguistics, psychology and sociology, and courses in Media and Print Journalism as well as Linguistics Communication and Society.

Oxford Brookes Publishing Media is offered in combination with a range of subjects including Business Management, Communication, Media and Culture and Music. A Media Technology degree is also offered providing a study of electronics as applied to the media industry and there are also courses in Communications, Media and Culture or Languages.

Plymouth The Media Advertising course covers theory and practice in the fields of photography, film and video. There are also courses in Media Arts, TV Arts, Science and the Media.

Portsmouth Courses are offered in Media Studies, with a range of subjects including Journalism, Sociology and Entertainment Technology. There are also several courses with Journalism.

Queen's Belfast The degree in Film Studies can be studied as a single, major, minor or joint subject. The course looks at world cinema focusing on countries including Germany, France, Italy, Ireland, the US and Asia.

Robert Gordon Journalism covers areas including print journalism, magazine journalism and photojournalism. Courses are also available in Media, with a focus on digital media, and Public Relations.

Roehampton Courses are offered in Journalism with an emphasis on practice. There is also a broader study of the media by way of the degree in Mass Communications and Media and Culture, which includes modules such as media narratives, ways of looking and mapping the field.

St Mark and St John There is a Media Production degree and courses in Journalism and Sports Media and Journalism.

St Mary's There is a practical and theoretical course in Media Arts which allows students to learn about media literacy, film and television, popular culture and journalism. The course can be combined with 11 subjects including Drama, History and Tourism.

Salford Courses are offered in Journalism, TV and Radio, Media Technology, Media Production and Film Studies. Courses focus on the new digital age and have work placement opportunities.

Sheffield The Journalism Studies course covers theoretical and practical aspects of reporting and sub-editing and includes radio work and special journals and can be studied with French, Russian, Germanic and Hispanic Studies.

Sheffield Hallam Media Studies offers a study of mass media from social, political and economic aspects. Journalism and radio reporting also feature in the course. There is also a separate Journalism degree. Other degrees include Public Relations and Film and Media Production and Digital Media Production.

South Wales The degree in Media, Culture and Journalism offers a theoretical study of the media with practical options. Courses in Journalism, Radio and Media Technology are also offered.

Southampton Solent Students in Year 2 of the course in Journalism may specialise in print or broadcast journalism and may take part in an exchange scheme in a European country. There are also courses in Magazine and Multimedia Journalism, Film and TV Studies, Media Technology, and Media, Communication and Culture.

Staffordshire There are degrees in Journalism, Media Studies, Film Production, and Music Journalism and Broadcasting. Specialist Journalism courses are available in Sports, Broadcast and Celebrity.

Stirling Journalism is offered and also Film and Media Studies, which concentrates on critical and theoretical work based on film, television, radio and the press. A limited amount of practical work is available. Students may choose to specialise in film or media. European Film and Media and Global Cinema and Culture are also offered.

Sunderland There are degrees in Journalism, TV, Public Relations and Video. The Media Culture and Communication course is also offered as a joint honours programme and covers the social and historical aspects of mass media, radio, video, computing and photography, with options in American film, British cinema, radio and print journalism. Over 40 joint courses are offered, also with Photography.

See *Heap 2015: University Degree Course Offers* (Trotman Publishing) for details of offers

Surrey Media Studies is offered either as a three-year full-time or four-year sandwich course focusing on TV, radio, print and the internet. A course in Sociology, Culture and Media is also available.

Sussex A theoretical course in Media Studies is offered with Sociology, Cultural Studies and Modern Languages. A practical course is offered in Media Practice and a further course is available in Computing for Digital Media.

Swansea Media Studies (theory and practice) can be taken as a single honours course or with languages including Welsh. There is also a course in Language and Communication.

Teesside In addition to a broad Media Studies degree, technologies covered in the Creative Digital Media course include virtual reality, networking, the internet, computer games, medical computing and knowledge-based systems. There are also degrees in Broadcast Media Production, Journalism and Television and Film Production.

Trinity St David The New Media Production course is a multidisciplinary subject which allows students to explore areas such as electronic publishing, online film-making, blogging and online journalism.

Trinity St David (Swansea) Media topics are covered in courses involving Video and Documentary Video Studies, Design for Advertising, Photojournalism and Digital Media. Courses are also offered in Interactive Digital Media and Multimedia.

Ulster Media Studies is a modular course, designed to promote a critical understanding of mass media (film, TV, radio, photography and the press). Students spend time on both academic and practical projects. In addition there are several Communications courses with joint subjects including Advertising, Counselling and Public Relations.

Warwick Film and Television Studies covers history, Hollywood, the silent cinema and TV studies. Film can be studied as a single subject or with Literature, French or Italian.

West London Degree courses are offered in Advertising, Broadcast Journalism, Broadcasting, Media Studies, Photography, Acting for Stage and Media, Practical Film-making, Radio Broadcasting and Public Relations.

West Scotland Three degree courses are offered in Broadcast Production (theoretical and practical), Journalism and Sport Journalism. The courses can be studied for three or four years (honours).

Westminster Courses in Journalism, Medical Journalism, Public Relations, Radio Production and Television Production are offered from the School of Journalism and Mass Communications. The courses are not available part time.

Winchester The Media Studies course is an academic degree focusing on cultural studies and media practices. A work placement opportunity exists in Year 2. There are also courses in Journalism, Journalism Studies and Media Production.

Wolverhampton Media and Communication Studies is a broad study of the media, its management and impact on society. Some opportunities exist for practical work and work experience. Other courses include Broadcasting and Journalism, Media and Cultural Studies, Film Production and Film Studies.

Worcester There are courses in Advertising, Public Relations and Journalism, with joint pathways in English, Politics, American and Film Studies, and a theoretical Media and Cultural Studies degree.

York St John Media is offered as a single honours course or with English Literature, Film Studies or Creative Writing. The course covers areas such as film, TV, art and advertising to provide a broad education.

See *Heap 2015: University Degree Course Offers* (Trotman Publishing) for details of offers

OTHER INSTITUTIONS OFFERING MEDIA STUDIES COURSES
Blackburn (Coll), Blackpool and Fylde (Coll), Bournemouth Arts, Bradford (Coll Univ Centre), Bristol City (Coll), Central Nottingham (Coll), Chesterfield (Coll), Colchester (Inst), Cornwall (Coll), Croydon (Coll), Durham New (Coll), Ealing, Hammersmith and West London (Coll), East Riding (Coll), Exeter (Coll), Farnborough (CT), Gower Swansea (Coll), Grimsby (Univ Centre), Guildford (Coll), Hereford (CA), Highbury Portsmouth (Coll), Hopwood Hall (Coll), Hull (Coll), Liverpool City (Coll), Llandrillo Cymru (Coll), Neath Port Talbot (Coll), Nescot, NEW (Coll), Newcastle (Coll), North Warwickshire and Hinckley (Coll), Northbrook (Coll), Norwich City (Coll), Peterborough (Reg Coll), Plymouth (CA), Ravensbourne, St Helens (Coll), Sheffield (Coll), Somerset (Coll), South Devon (Coll), South Essex (Coll), South Leicestershire (Coll), South Tyneside (Coll), Staffordshire Reg Fed (SURF), Stephenson (Coll), Stratford upon Avon (Coll), Suffolk (Univ Campus), Swindon (Coll), Truro (Coll), Tyne Met (Coll), Walsall (Coll), Warwickshire (Coll), West Cheshire (Coll), Wiltshire (Coll), Wirral Met (Coll), Worcester (CT).

ALTERNATIVE COURSES
Advertising, Communication Studies, English, Politics, Psychology, Public Relations, Publishing.

MEDICINE

(* indicates universities with entry requirements over 340 UCAS points)

SUBJECT REQUIREMENTS/PREFERENCES
In almost all cases, three A level grades are expected including A* grades, with Chemistry at A level normally required, plus one or two other science subjects. If only two sciences are offered, then a third 'rigorous' academic subject should be included in the choice of A levels. Some medical schools also stipulate subjects at AS level. Pre-medical courses do not require science A levels: contact medical schools for their requirements.

SUBJECT INFORMATION
Candidates are required to limit their applications to four choices and submit their UCAS forms by 15 October. Applicants to Oxford, Cambridge and the Royal Free and University College Medical School are required to take the Biomedical Admissions Test (BMAT). All courses will offer the same components leading to a career in medicine. Many medical schools have moved away from an emphasis on lectures and factual learning to a system based on acquiring appropriate skills and understanding as well as knowledge. This system is referred to as the 'New Curriculum', which introduces communication, problem-solving and more directed self-learning. While there is a core curriculum of knowledge, the first three years integrate scientific and clinical experience, and there are fewer formal lectures and more group and individual work.

For outstanding students without science A levels some pre-medical courses are available. Thereafter, for all, a period of pre-clinical studies leads on to clinical studies. Intercalated courses of one year leading to a BSc are also offered and elective periods abroad in the final years can sometimes be taken. All courses are very similar in content. Other courses in the medical field include Dentistry, Nursing, Pharmacy and Pharmacology, Biological Sciences, Microbiology, Genetics, Anatomy, Physiology, Medical Sciences (a branch of biological science), Physiotherapy, Occupational Therapy, Osteopathy, Chiropractic, Podiatry and Radiography. Deans of medical schools have decided unanimously to adopt a policy of 'no detriment' for applicants to Medicine who list one non-medical course on the UCAS application. However, applicants should know if they receive four rejections for Medicine and accept an offer for a non-medical course, they are not officially allowed to change their decision and attempt to re-open negotiations with medical schools if they achieve higher A level grades than expected.

When selecting applicants, admissions tutors first look for evidence of academic excellence, not just for its own sake but because a medical course is long and demanding, and the ability to apply oneself and to survive is extremely important. Secondly, a longstanding interest in medicine is always an advantage, together with evidence that the applicant has a well-rounded personality, a wide range of interests, imagination, research potential, and is socially aware. A year out is also becoming an asset with some medical schools. A history of mental illness – even the mildest form – can be a bar to entry, and students' physical and mental stability is often under review. The confidential report from the applicant's school is very important. In addition to A level applicants, most medical schools have a small annual intake (four to eight) of graduates (usually dental or science). Early applications are advantageous and very serious consideration is given to the overall GCSE grades achieved. The fact that applicants have four choices does not mean that they will receive equal consideration from all the institutions named on their UCAS application. In Medicine this is especially so: applicants receiving one or two offers will often be rejected by other medical schools. Therefore medical applicants receiving even one offer and three rejections have little cause for concern, since any other offer they might have received would have demanded the same, or a very similar, high level of attainment.

Letters have been received from medical schools indicating that they continue to receive applications from candidates who are not predicted by their schools to achieve grades above DDD. They stress the futility of such applications.

QUESTIONS TO CONSIDER
 * Does the university teach under the 'New Curriculum' with an emphasis on work-based learning?
 * Is a pre-medical course or foundation year available if I do not have the relevant qualifications?
 * Will there be an opportunity to gain a BSc as an intercalated degree?

Aberdeen* Phase 1 covers the fundamentals of medical sciences followed in Phase 2 by the principles of clinical medicine. Clinical teaching and patient contact take place from Year 1. An intercalated BSc Biomedical Sciences degree is offered with placements across the Highlands and Islands.

Birmingham* A curriculum based on student-centred learning and teaching combines the basic sciences and clinical experiences in the Medicine and Surgery MBChB. The modular system of learning enables students to focus on their personal preferences. Further courses are available including Biological Sciences, Biomedical Materials Science, Clinical Science, Healthcare Ethics and Law and Dental Surgery.

Brighton* Brighton and Sussex Medical School students are members of both universities. The course offers an integrated programme of academic and clinical experience with students working with patients from the first term. From Year 3, students are based at the Royal Sussex County Hospital in Brighton. Experience of medical practice in different medical settings in the UK or abroad takes place in Year 4.

Bristol* The majority of applicants embark on the five-year course which is divided into three phases, with early patient contact in the first two terms. Each year students have the opportunity to intercalate in a medical science or humanities subject. Bristol operates a European Credit Transfer scheme with 14 other schools in which a student may spend not less than three months in a participating medical school. A preliminary year of study is available for students without science A levels.

Cambridge* The course of study in Medical Sciences falls into two periods: the two- or three-year pre-clinical period spent in Cambridge and the clinical course of three years and one term in the Cambridge Clinical School at Addenbrooke's Hospital. About half the students, however, choose to go to other medical schools, usually Oxford or London. Some students may devote the third year of the pre-clinical course to reading one of a variety of subjects for Part II of the Natural Sciences or Medical Science Tripos leading to a BA degree, before embarking on the clinical course. Applicants are required to take the BMAT test.

Cardiff* Students have direct patient contact from Year 1, the science curriculum extending throughout the course. A core course occupies approximately 75% of the curriculum and student-selected components form the rest, enabling students to explore topics to greater depth. The pre-medical course plus the main course totalling six years is available for those without the required A level subjects.

Dundee* A pre-medical course is available for those students who do not have the necessary science qualifications. The medical course is 'problem-oriented, student-centred and community-based'. Promising students may, after the second year, take a one-year in-depth course leading to a degree in Anatomy, Biochemistry, Biomedical Engineering, Developmental and Molecular Medicine, Forensic Medicine, Medical Microbiology, Psychology, Pharmacology or Physiology. Dundee also offers special modules such as Sports Medicine and Human Rights and Travel Medicine.

Durham* The university is now jointly offering a five-year medical course through Newcastle University. The first two years of study take place at the Stockton campus after which students are based at NHS regional centres in the North East. It is designed to provide a broad medical education leading to later career specialisation. Much of the learning is 'case led', involving the presentation and study of a patient case. See under **Newcastle** (to which applications are made).

East Anglia* The course includes clinical and life sciences as well as socio-economic aspects (e.g. sociology, psychology, epidemiology, management, health economics, law and ethics). Clinical presentations are grouped into units of learning based on body systems. Students spend a substantial part of each year gaining clinical experience with patients.

Edinburgh* In the five-year course, Years 1 and 2 cover principles for practice, Year 3 introduces clinical medicine, Year 4 focuses on a major research project, and Year 5 preparations for practice. Important vertical themes in the curriculum include clinical skills, public health, pharmacology and therapeutics and the psychological aspects of medicine.

Exeter* This is a new Medical School accepting students from 2013. Check website (www. exeter.ac.uk/medicine) for course details. See also under **Peninsula Medical School**.

Glasgow* The MBChB programme introduces clinically based exercises from Year 1. Learning takes place in small groups. Studies involve care and vocational modules and attachments with opportunities for study abroad available in Years 3 and 4. Students who do well in the first three years have the chance to undertake an intercalated BSc programme.

Hull* The Hull-York Medical School was established in 2003 to offer a standard medical programme leading to entry to the medical profession. Years 1 and 2 are based in either Hull or York but all students follow the same course. In Years 3, 4 and 5 the groups combine to follow a programme of community and hospital-based study.

Imperial London* The course consists of three main elements that run throughout five of the six years and leads to both a BSc and MBBS. These are the scientific basis of medicine, doctor and patient, and early clinical experience from the first year. The final phase of the course consists of three senior rotations designed to prepare students for their final written and practical examinations.

Keele* The five-year course has five themes which run through the course: (a) scientific basis of medicine; (b) clinical communication; (C) individual communication and population health; (d) quality and efficiency in healthcare; and (e) ethics, personal and professional development. There is also a health foundation year.

Leeds* The course has three main phases: 'Preparing for clinical practice' (Years 1, 2 and 3), 'Clinical practice in context' (Year 4) and 'Becoming a doctor' (Year 5).

Leicester* The five-year medical course is divided into two phases: Phase 1 – foundations, clinical skills, medical sciences, social and behavioural medicine, learning how to learn, learning to integrate, rational practice; Phase 2 – developing skills, the learning environment, the elective, preparing for postgraduate training, testing skills, intercalating year and life after medical school.

Liverpool* The main themes of the medical course cover structure and functions in health and disease, individuals and society, public health and professional practice. Clinical skills are introduced in Year 1. A problem-solving approach is used with small-group teaching support.

London (King's)* The integrated programme of study in Medicine comprises basic medical science and clinical teaching over the first four years including special study modules in medical and non-medical areas (for example arts subjects). Students are encouraged to take an intercalated BSc degree course of one year after the end of the pre-clinical period. Subjects offered include Anatomy, Biochemistry, Pharmacology and Physiology. A foundation course in Natural Sciences (Medicine) is offered for candidates with no science A level background. The course covers chemistry, biology, physics and maths and successful completion guarantees a place on the medical degree.

London (QM)* The curriculum for the five-year course at Barts and the London Medical School is based on six stages: fundamentals of medicine, systems in health, disease, specialities, integrated clinical studies, and preparation for practice. A student-centred teaching approach is used, introducing early patient contact from the first term.

London (St George's)* The MBBS has been designed to enhance the integration between scientific and clinical disciplines and to develop self-directed learning skills. A six-year course is available with the foundation year taught mainly at Kingston University. See also **Health Studies/Sciences**.

London (UCL)* The degree is organised in three main phases: science and medicine (Years 1 and 2), science in medical practice (Years 3 and 4) and preparation for practice (Year 5). Promising students can take an additional year at the end of their pre-clinical course to take a BSc degree and highly motivated students have the opportunity to gain a PhD.

Manchester* The curriculum is organised around problem-based learning and incorporates early patient contact from Year 1. Intercalated degrees are available after either Year 2 or Year 4 leading to a BSc. From Year 3, students are assigned to one of four major teaching hospitals. A pre-medical programme is available for students without science subjects and a European Studies option enables students to study abroad for part of the medical course.

Newcastle* Phase 1 (two years) of the medical course is taken either at Newcastle or Stockton. Students come into contact with patients at the start of the course, being attached to a GP and accompanying them on some of their rounds. Clinical applications are emphasised throughout the course alongside basic sciences. Students not taking science subjects may apply for the pre-medical course. See also **Durham**.

Nottingham* The medical course is fully integrated and includes early patient contact. It covers a two-year study of basic medical sciences (Years 1 and 2) and a special medical sciences course (Year 3) lasting one year and leading to the BMedSci degree. Clinical practice takes place during Years 3, 4 and 5. This is followed by clinical practice lasting 26 months, which includes the last term of the third year.

Oxford* The course in Medicine lasts six years. The pre-clinical course lasts three years. This is followed by the clinical course, which is based in the John Radcliffe Hospital. A significant part of this course is examined by continuous assessment.

Peninsula Medical School From 2013 new students have studied for either University of Exeter or Plymouth degrees.

Plymouth* This is a new Medical School accepting students from 2013. Check website (www.plymouth.ac.uk/peninsula) for course details.

Queen's Belfast* An integrated five-year course (system-based and student-centred) is offered linking the basic sciences with clinical experience (the latter from the second semester). Students achieving high marks in the second MB examination can take a one-year course leading to the BSc in Anatomy, Biochemistry, Medical Genetics, Medical Microbiology, Pathology or Physiology.

St Andrews* Medical Sciences is a three-year degree course and leads to the ordinary degree of BSc in three years or to an honours degree in four years. Studies cover molecular biochemistry, human anatomy and human physiology. Half of all graduates progress to a clinical place at Manchester University Medical School to follow the three-year clinical course; the remainder have a place at one of the four medical schools in Scotland, almost a third at Edinburgh.

Sheffield* There is a foundation science year in Medicine for those who do not have the required combination of A level subjects. The medical course aims to integrate the basic and clinical sciences and to cultivate in students a desire for intellectual curiosity and to equip students with the essential personal and professional skills. The three main stages of the course cover basic sciences (Stage 1), acquisition of clinical skills (Stage 2), and the refinement of skills (Stage 3).

Southampton* The first three years of the course are planned as a single exercise with integrated teaching programmes. In addition, there are courses in Psychology and Sociology, and patient contact in the early stages in either the hospital or the home. The first clinical attachments take place in the third year. There are various entry routes and the chance to intercalate.

Sussex* See under **Brighton**.

Swansea The Medical Sciences degree has elective modules in biological sciences, clinical sciences, the philosophy and social sciences of medicine and the history or literature of medicine. The course can lead to the graduate entry scheme for Medicine.

Warwick* Warwick Medical School is the only all-graduate medical school in the UK and offers a four-year MBChB programme for graduates in the biological, health, natural or physical sciences.

York* See under **Hull**.

ALTERNATIVE COURSES
Anatomy, Biochemistry, Biological Sciences, Dentistry, Nursing, Pharmacy, Physiotherapy, Speech Therapy.

MUSIC

(* indicates universities with entry requirements over 340 UCAS points)
(scholarships are offered by most institutions)

SUBJECT REQUIREMENTS/PREFERENCES
GCE A level: Music is usually the highest grade in the offers made.

SUBJECT INFORMATION
Theory and practice are combined in most of these courses to a greater or lesser extent. The menu of options is varied – choose with care!

Aberdeen Music is offered in the MA and BMus degree programmes. Topics covered include musical history (Baroque, classical and 19th century), composition, style and performance. Opportunities exist for study abroad. Music Studies is also offered as the minor part in several major/minor degrees including Religious Studies, Divinity, History of Art and Philosophy.

Abertay The top-up degree in Creative Sound Production aims to develop skills in music industry knowledge and general business awareness. It involves the study of production techniques for drama, radio, film and animation.

Anglia Ruskin Subject areas in Music are taught through issue-based modules which consider music in a wider context not defined by historical period or geography. There are also degree courses in Popular Music, Creative Music Technology and Audio and Music Technology. Music can also be taken with Drama and English. The Performing Arts degree covers drama and music.

Bangor BA and BMus courses are offered. The department is active in the following areas: music history, composition, performance and interpretation, music cultures of the world, popular culture and music in Western society, music technology including electro-acoustic composition. There is also a degree in Music Technology and Electronics.

Bath Spa In addition to the highly practical Music degree, which includes classical, jazz, musical theatre and world music, programmes are offered in Music Production, Creative Music Technology and Commercial Music.

Birmingham* The Music course provides a wide general grounding in musicology (music as an academic discipline). Studio composition and performance offer each student the opportunity to develop special interests. There is also an introductory course in electro-acoustics and studio techniques. There are several joint honours courses with Music available, including Drama. The university has a strong music tradition enhanced by the musical life of Birmingham.

Birmingham City The Music course is offered jointly at the Millennium Point and Birmingham Conservatoire and provides the opportunity for specialisation and diversification. Options include early music, chamber music, folk, jazz, electronic and world music. The music industry can be studied through the Media and Communications course and a BMus course in Jazz blends academic and practical content.

Bournemouth The Music and Audio Technology course focuses on the application of hardware and software technologies to create music. There is a 40-week placement in Year 3. There is also a foundation degree in Popular Music.

Brighton The course in Music and Visual Art utilises the visual art/music interface with close links between dance, theatre and music. There is also a Digital Music and Sound Arts degree in which music is studied relating to computers and electronic instruments.

Bristol The two main aims of the Music course are to give a wide understanding of the European musical tradition from medieval times to the present day and to enable students to develop their own individual interests in historical, creative and practical fields. The modular syllabus allows for an extensive choice of options. There are also Music and Language courses (French, German and Italian) with Year 3 spent abroad. Part-time courses are available.

Brunel Single and joint honours courses are offered in Music, with a special focus on 20th-century and contemporary music encompassing Western classical, jazz, rock/pop and world music. Music is offered with Film and Television Studies, English, Games Design and Theatre, and there are also courses in Sonic Arts introducing music technology as a creative tool. Other courses cover Musical Composition and Musical Performance.

Bucks New Courses can be followed in Audio and Music Production, Music Management (with Artistic Development, Branding and Public Relations and Studio Production), Music and Live Events Management and Musical Theatre.

Cambridge* Performance has an important place in the Music course and is one of several aspects of study in which music is covered in a very broad syllabus, giving weight to the appreciation and history of the subject as well as practical techniques.

Canterbury Christ Church The Music degree covers performance studies, written musicianship, critical studies and ensemble and practical musicianship. There are also courses in Commercial Music, Creative Music Technology, Music Industry Management, Music Performance and Music Production.

See *Heap 2015: University Degree Course Offers* (Trotman Publishing) for details of offers

Cardiff The Department of Music aims to provide a musical education that achieves an equal balance between theoretical and practical studies and the pursuit of vocal and instrument study. The BMus degree is the most specialised with students taking 360 credits in music modules, while the BA scheme offers a wider selection of modules. A second-year placement in a European university is possible through the Erasmus-Socrates scheme. Music can also be studied with Languages, English Literature, History, Mathematics, Physics, Philosophy, Welsh and Religious Studies.

Central Lancashire Courses are offered in Music Practice, Music Production and Music Theatre, with an emphasis on voice and acting.

Chester A theoretical study of Popular Music (Performance) with practical options involving live performance, musicianship, improvisation and digital recording is offered. There is also a course in Commercial Music Production at the Warrington campus.

Chichester The Music degree has three strands: Performance and Direction; Composing, Arranging and Improvising; and Style and Genre. There are also courses in Musical Theatre, Performing Arts and Commercial Music.

City* The Music course is concerned with music in today's multicultural and technological society and is intended to bridge the gap between music as art and music as science. Topics include African-American music studies, music therapy, performance and sound recording and studio techniques. There are also links with the Guidhall School of Music for those aiming to be solo performers.

Colchester (Inst) The Music degree involves practical studies, composing, education and arts business. There are also studies in Film Music, Soundtrack Production and Pop Music.

Coventry A course in Music Composition and Music Performance is offered that includes performance and administration. There is also a course in Music Technology covering sound and acoustics, recording technology and music analysis and composition and Music Production for Online Industries.

Cumbria Musical Theatre Performance is offered and can be studied with Drama or Dance Performance. There are many opportunities to take part in shows and to improve confidence and technique.

De Montfort A single, joint or combined degree in Music Technology can be taken. The course covers creative projects (digital music and sound), studio techniques, sound recording, audio engineering, musicianship and performance.

Derby There are courses in Popular Music and Music Technology which are also offered with Music Production. Creative Expressive Therapies is also available in which students can choose to specialise in music, art, dance or drama.

Durham* The Music course aims to provide a wide and critical knowledge of music and to develop the basic skills. Provision is made for students to develop their own special interests, with flexibility in the third year for specialisation. Options include electro-acoustic compositions, ethno-musicology and historical musicology. Music is also offered as part of the Arts combined honours course.

East London Music Culture, Theory and Production is offered as a comprehensive study of performance and composition. There are also degrees in Musical Theatre and Dance, Music Industry Management and Music Performance.

Edinburgh Music is a three-year or four-year honours course. In each year the curriculum is broadly divided between composition, history and practical studies. Options are introduced in the third year and include electronic music but also cover music technology and acoustics. There is also a BMus course in Music Technology.

Edinburgh Napier The Music course allows students to take a principal study (either instrument, voice or composition) and core academic studies and focuses solely on classical music. There is also a three-year or four-year degree in Popular Music which covers contemporary genres.

See *Heap 2015: University Degree Course Offers* (Trotman Publishing) for details of offers

Falmouth Popular Music and a BA in Music are offered with options in performance, composition and music technology. There is also a course available in Music Theatre.

Glasgow* The MA degree is for students with some musical ability and an interest in cultural aspects. The BMus course is for those aiming for a career in music at ordinary (three years) or honours (four years) level and includes performance on the piano, organ, any orchestral instrument or voice, writing from dictation and harmony. Courses in Electronics with Music and a BEd in Music for intending teachers also offered.

Gloucestershire The course in Popular Music covers history, music production and creative work and a study of the music industry and professional practice. There is also a Music and Media Management degree.

Glyndŵr Music and Sound Technology courses are offered which include practical music production skills, sound recording work and video production.

Greenwich A HND degree in Music Technology is offered to school leavers with relevant qualifications. There is also a Creative Production and Technology top-up course for students who have completed a HND in Music and who intend to pursue careers in the music industry.

Hertfordshire Courses are offered in Music Composition and Technology, Sound Design Technology and Music and Entertainment Industry Management, which has three pathways in studio production, entertainment industry and the classical music industry. There are also courses in Audio Recording and Sound Design Technology.

Huddersfield In Year 1 of the Music course equal weight is given to performance, composition and the history of music. In Year 2, students take music history and choose two other subjects as their major areas of study, with a third subject being their minor study. In Year 3 two subjects are chosen (a major and a minor) plus up to three other optional modules. The course encourages increasing specialisation throughout its three years. Music is offered with Drama, Modern Languages or English. There are also Popular Music degrees and degrees in Creative Music Technology and Music Production and Sound Recording.

Hull The first year of the Music course is devoted to an intensive basic course in harmony, counterpoint, history, set works, analysis and aural work and performance. In the second year, students select two special options. In the final year there is a wide range of choice including composing for stage and screen and music and critical thinking. Music is offered with four modern language subjects as well as Drama, English and Film Studies. There are also courses in Music and Theatre, Jazz and Popular Music and Creative Music Technology.

Imperial London* A four-year BSc course is offered jointly with the Royal College of Music in Physics and Musical Performance. The course is equal to a three-year Physics course but incorporates musical training in one instrument to the highest international standards.

Keele Music or Music Technology is taken as a single honours course or with a second subject from a choice of over 15 options including Educational Studies, American Studies, International Relations, History, Neurosciences and Accounting. Specialisation is offered in European and American 20th-century music. Pathways are offered in musicology, performance, non-Western music and composition.

Kent The course in Music Technology combines music and computer technology, exploring sound design in the context of new media applications. A BMus degree in Music is also available covering both history and performance.

Kingston Two alternative Music courses are offered. The BA Music concentrates on performance, theory and musicianship, and complementary studies such as psychology, world music and music technology. The Creative Music Technologies is more concerned with music and technology, and covers electronic music,

See *Heap 2015: University Degree Course Offers* (Trotman Publishing) for details of offers

recording technology and business studies. (The Gateway School of Music Technology, based at Kingston, has recording facilities onsite.) There are also BMus courses in Music and Creative Music Technologies.

Lancaster A BA (Music) course is offered, to enable students to develop their artistic and intellectual potential. Music is offered jointly with Computer Science, English Literature and History and is also taught in Creative Arts, Theatre Studies and Film Studies.

Leeds* The Music course is designed with topics common to all students in the first year (analysis, aural training, counterpoint, harmony, and historical studies). From the second year it is possible to concentrate increasingly on one of four main options – performance, notation, composition, or history and criticism. Throughout the course there is a balance between theoretical and practical, academic and vocational aspects of music, irrespective of the options taken. There are also courses in Music, Multimedia and Electronics, Theatre and Performance and joint courses with Languages, Philosophy and Mathematics.

Leeds Beckett Courses are offered in Music Production and Music Technology with placement opportunities. The courses can be studied full time, part time or with a sandwich year.

Lincoln The Audio Technology degree covers all aspects of the study of music in the context of audio production.

Liverpool The three-year Music/Popular Music course strikes a balance between academic and practical work. Musical history is central to many of the complementary studies in style, composition, analysis, orchestration and practical musicianship, with pathways giving a popular or classical emphasis. During the first year of the single honours course all students take an additional subject of their choice. Proficiency in performing is not absolutely necessary.

Liverpool Hope Music can be studied as a single course or combined with a large number of other courses. Students can specialise in popular or classical music. A BA/QTS is also offered.

Liverpool John Moores A very broad course in Popular Music Studies includes modules such as popular music genres, digital music production and cultural themes and aesthetics. There is also a course in Audio and Music Production.

London (Goldsmiths) The Music course aims to develop music skills and associated areas of study. There is a strong emphasis on the study of contemporary music, electronic music and advanced musical analysis. There is also a course in Popular Music Studies and Music Computing.

London (King's)* Music can be studied as a single honours course or in combination with German (a four-year course with a year spent abroad). The BMus course aims to provide students with a knowledge of the history and theory of music, composition and techniques of analysis. Singing instruction is studied through the Royal Academy of Music.

London (RH) Music can be offered as a single or combined honours course. The course offers a detailed study of the historical, theoretical and practical aspects of music with a wide range of second- and final-year options including practical and performance work. Students can follow programmes in Performance, Composition or Music Studies.

London (SOAS) The Music course has a strong focus on Asian and African music. The programme includes vocal and instrumental performance, although to a lesser extent in joint rather than single honours courses.

London Met In addition to the courses in Event Management and Music and Media Management, the university offers courses in the Repair of Musical Instruments. There are also courses in Music Technology with specialisations in production, audio systems or sound for media.

Manchester* The aim of the Music course is to give students a thorough grounding in the theoretical, practical and historical aspects of the subject. The final year is spent in performance analysis, history and criticism. Drama is also offered with Music.

See *Heap 2015: University Degree Course Offers* (Trotman Publishing) for details of offers

Manchester Met A very large number of combined courses are offered which include Music and Popular Music. Music, Creative Music Production and Popular Music can also be studied as single honours courses.

Marjon The course in Live Music provides a programme of study focusing on performance technology and media work. There are opportunities to focus on practical music-making and, in the third year, the opportunity to gain industry experience.

Middlesex There are courses in Music focusing on theory, performance and historical and cultural contexts and in Jazz with modules in performance and improvisation. Courses are also offered in Music and Arts Management and Popular Music.

Newcastle Practical tuition takes place throughout the Music course, which also covers the history of music, compositional techniques, acoustics, electro-acoustic music and, in the BA, a subsidiary subject. Courses in Folk and Traditional Music and Popular and Contemporary Music are also offered.

Northampton The Popular Music degree includes a study of the music industry and focuses on the relationship between theory and performance. The course can be combined with a range of other subjects.

Northumbria A Performance degree is offered which has courses on music and song available. Assessment for the course is through practical (75%) and written (25%) work.

Nottingham The Music course is wide ranging and offers the chance to specialise at an early stage. The course covers both practical and historical studies as well as offering options in such topics as the music of the Middle and Far East, electronic music and the music of the 20th century. Philosophy is also offered with Music.

Oxford* The purpose of the Music course is not simply to offer professional training but to produce musicians who are proficient in the technique of the art and its history and criticism. It is a broad-based course which allows students the opportunity to specialise as they proceed through the course.

Oxford Brookes Music is offered with a range of subjects (including Film, Psychology, History and English) or as a single honours course. There is also a course in Sound Technology and Digital Music and in Sound and Media Technology.

Plymouth Sound and Music Production can be taken as a single honours subject. Music is offered as a stand-alone subject and as a combined course. BA Music students have the opportunity to visit Gambia in West Africa where they focus on cultural music. Courses are also offered in Contemporary World Jazz and Primary Music.

Queen's Belfast The BMus course provides a thorough grounding in Western music from medieval times to the present day, together with keyboard skills, conducting, history, traditional Irish music, compositional technique and styles. There is a flexible course structure in Years 2 and 3 that enables students to choose their own options in practical work, as well as 20th-century and electronic music. The BA course is taken with one or more other subjects. There are also degrees in Music Technology and Sonic Arts.

Roehampton Music can be studied as an Education specialism and aims to prepare students for curriculum leadership in music. Instruments and resources that are found in schools are used and Years 2 and 3 include a school-based placement.

Salford The Music course focuses on performance, composition and history with pathways in popular music and recording, popular musicology, interactive music and studio production and modular options. Courses in Audio Technology, Performance and Acoustics are also available.

Sheffield The broad-based course in Music aims to develop practical as well as academic interests. A wide range of options provides students with the chance to specialise. Music is also offered with East Asian Studies, Chinese Studies, Hispanic Studies or Korean Studies and with English, French, German, Russian and Theology.

See *Heap 2015: University Degree Course Offers* (Trotman Publishing) for details of offers

South Wales A wide range of courses are offered, including: a BSc course in Music Technology, involving practical electronics and business practices; a Popular Music BA, focusing on the historical and cultural aspects of music as well as the practical; and a Sound Technology degree, covering acoustics and sound for radio and TV. There is also a degree in Creative Music offering courses in practice, performance, media and business.

Southampton History, analysis and composition are integrated throughout this Music course. The history of Western music is studied from the Middle Ages to the present day. In Years 2 and 3 students choose historical periods for special emphasis, along with a considerable choice of other topics ranging from classical to jazz. Acoustics, French, German, Management, Philosophy, Mathematics and English are also offered with Music.

Southampton Solent Five Music courses cover Popular and Digital music, Music Promotion, Journalism and Performance. There are also courses in Live and Studio Sound and Outside Broadcast Production Operations.

Staffordshire The Creative Music Technology degree focuses on audio recording, acoustics, multimedia, and the design of recording studios. Courses are also offered in Music Technology and Management. Some students spend a year in the US.

Sunderland Music is offered with a wide range of subjects, including Business Law, European Studies, Journalism, Management, Education and Psychology. The majority of music modules include practical work and creative exploration.

Surrey* The Music course is taken by students who have a particular interest in performance, conducting, composition or musicology. Music and Sound Recording (Tonmeister) is followed by those whose main concern is with the theory and practice of recording and the reproduction of music (a year is spent in industrial training in a studio, with a manufacturer or broadcaster). Creative Music Technology prepares students for careers in the contemporary and computer-based music industry.

Sussex Music is offered singly or joint with Film Studies, Cultural Studies and with French, German, Italian or Spanish. Performance can be taken as an option in all years providing students hold the grade 8 music qualification. Music Informatics and Music Technology are also offered.

Teesside Music Technology allows students to perform and engineer live performances, set up an internet radio station and create dub music, sound effects and foley to video and media. Students use the same technology used in the industry and have the chance to undertake exams in the hardware.

Ulster The BMus course combines academic study with practical training on one or two instruments. Music can also be taken in a modular framework with other subjects.

West London The BMus course focuses on music performance and recording. There are also courses in Music Technology, Music Performance and Composition, Musical Theatre and Applied Sound Engineering.

West Scotland Commercial Music with work experience and Commercial Sound Production are offered as three-year full-time degrees. The latter includes computer technology, recording, and editing in the fields of audio and video production. A course is also offered in Musical Theatre.

Westminster Commercial Music is a unique course that combines the production of commercial music based on rock and pop with a strong grounding of business, law and cultural studies. There is also a BMus in Commercial Music Performance available.

Winchester Vocal and Choral studies can be taken as part of the combined honours programme. Study includes singing, speaking and vocal work alongside a grounding in vocal anatomy and physiology.

Wolverhampton Music may be studied as a specialist award or as a joint, major or minor programme. Practical experience is offered over a range of instruments, singing and keyboard. Modules cover multi-track recording and computers, popular and non-European music. Courses are also offered in Popular Music, Sound Production, Musical Theatre and Music Technology.

York The Music course is designed to enable students to explore music from various aspects and is concentrated in a series of projects. Projects cover history and musicological topics, written techniques, analysis and composition, solo and ensemble performance, electronic and computer music. Music Technology and Music Technology Systems courses are also offered.

York St John The Music course encourages students to experience various genres in an eclectic manner and offers a broad spectrum of modules in which students perform and study various music types. There is also a course in Music Production.

OTHER INSTITUTIONS OFFERING MUSIC COURSES

Bath City (Coll), Blackpool and Fylde (Coll), Central Nottingham (Coll), Coventry City (Coll), Doncaster (Coll Univ Centre), Durham New (Coll), East Surrey (Coll), Exeter (Coll), Great Yarmouth (Coll), Grimsby (Univ Centre), Havering (Coll), Hereford (CA), Hull (Coll), Leeds (CMus), Leeds City (Coll), Liverpool (LIPA), London (RAcMus), London (RCMus), London (Royal Central Sch SpDr), Manchester (Coll), Mid-Cheshire (Coll), Neath Port Talbot (Coll), Newcastle (Coll), Newham (CFE), Nescot, NEW (Coll), North Lindsey (Coll), Northbrook (Coll), Norwich City (Coll), Nottingham New (Coll), Ravensbourne, RConsvS, RNCM, Rose Bruford (Coll), Rotherham (CAT), Royal Welsh (CMusDr), St Helens (Coll), South Downs (Coll), South Essex (Coll), South Tyneside (Coll), Staffordshire Reg Fed (SURF), Stratford upon Avon (Coll), Suffolk (Univ Campus), Trinity Laban Consv, Truro (Coll), UHI, Wakefield (Coll), West Anglia (Coll), West Thames (Coll), Wiltshire (Coll), Worcester (CT).

ALTERNATIVE COURSES

Acoustics, Anthropology, Band Musicianship, Drama and Theatre Studies, Electronic Music, Music and Sound Recording, Music combined courses, Music Technology, Performance Studies, Popular Music, Recording.

NURSING

(including **Midwifery**)
(see also **Health Studies/Sciences**)
(* indicates universities with entry requirements over 340 UCAS points)

SUBJECT REQUIREMENTS/PREFERENCES

GCE A level: Two to three subjects may be required. **GCSE:** English, Mathematics and a science subject. All applicants holding firm offers are required to provide documentary evidence that they have not been infected with hepatitis B.

SUBJECT INFORMATION

Nursing courses, usually covering the social sciences as well as practical work, lead to state registration in the chosen specialism. Pre-registration nursing degrees are offered within four main branches: adult, child (paediatric), mental health and learning disability. Students will need to decide on their specialty before applying for a degree course and work experience can help in deciding which branch of nursing is best suited to you. In order to become a registered nurse, students are required to hold a degree in pre-registration nursing which leads to registration with the Nursing and Midwifery Council and the right to practise within your speciality. Financial support is given by way of a means-tested bursary and all tuition fees for student nurses are paid by the Department of Health. This list does not include diploma courses or degrees for already qualified and registered nurses.

See *Heap 2015: University Degree Course Offers* (Trotman Publishing) for details of offers

QUESTIONS TO CONSIDER
* Is the specialisation I want to study offered?
* Can I decide on my specialisation at the end of the first year?
* Which hospitals are my placements likely to be at?

Abertay Nursing is offered as a pre-registration course integrating academic studies with clinical experience. Degrees are also offered in Adult and Mental Health Nursing with opportunities to undertake work-based learning.

Anglia Ruskin There is a common element of Nursing for all specialised areas that cover nursing fields in Child, Adult and Mental Health areas. There is also an International Nursing Studies course and a BSc Midwifery degree course.

Bangor After a common foundation programme of 18 months, branch programmes are offered in Adult, Child, Mental Health and Learning Disability Nursing. There is also a course in Midwifery with theoretical studies taking place in Wrexham and Bangor.

Bedfordshire Obstetrics, midwifery, the midwife practitioner, women's health, ethics and law are all covered in the Nursing degree. Specialisation is offered in Adult, Children's and Mental Health Nursing. A Midwifery course is also provided. There is also an Overseas Nursing programme.

Birmingham The BNurs degree covers biological, social and medical sciences along with clinical placements with choice of specialism being made at the end of the first year. More clinical placements and specialised studies continue in Years 3 and 4. Specialist studies in Adult, Child or Mental Health Nursing commence in Year 2. An overseas elective period is also available.

Birmingham City Degree courses are offered in Midwifery and Nursing, the latter with specialist studies in Adult, Mental Health, Child Nursing and Learning Difficulties. A fast-track course in Midwifery is also available.

Bolton Nursing specialisations are offered in District, General and Health Visiting Nursing and Social Care.

Bournemouth Clinical Nursing and Midwifery are both three-year courses and include five clinical placements. Clinical Nursing students decide whether to seek registration in Adult, Learning Disabilities, Mental Health or Child Health Nursing. A range of BSc courses and diplomas is offered. There is also a foundation degree in Paramedic Studies available. See also **Health Studies/Sciences**.

Bradford A BSc (Hons) course in Midwifery Studies is offered and there is also a three-year BSc in Nursing Studies with options in Adult, Child or Mental Health Nursing.

Brighton The BSc degree in Nursing has pathways in Adult, Children's and Mental Health Nursing. The course is split equally between theoretical and practical learning. There is also a BSc course in Midwifery.

Bristol UWE Three-year pre-registration degree programmes are offered in Adult, Children's, Mental Health or Learning Disabilities Nursing. There is also a degree in Midwifery and a range of specialist degrees covering Emergency Care and Child Health.

Bucks New The Nursing degree has specialist avenues in Adult, Child and Mental Health Nursing. The courses consist of a mix of generic and field content.

Canterbury Christ Church Courses are offered leading to Adult, Child and Mental Health Nursing. There is also a course in Midwifery which has intakes in April (Canterbury campus) and September (Medway campus).

Cardiff The Nursing course covers Adult, Children's or Mental Health Nursing (to be stipulated on the application form). Placements usually take place in the local area. A course in Midwifery is also offered.

See *Heap 2015: University Degree Course Offers* (Trotman Publishing) for details of offers

Central Lancashire The Midwifery course leads to full registration and involves clinical placements covering 50% of the course. A Nursing (pre-registration) course is offered focusing on Adult Nursing, Mental Health or Paediatric Nursing. There is also a course in Specialist Community Public Health Nursing.

Chester The BSc Nursing degree has branch programmes in Adult, Child Health, Learning Disability and Mental Health. Practice is undertaken throughout Cheshire and Merseyside. There is also a degree in Midwifery.

City Nursing is part of a modular scheme (50% practice based) that includes psychology, sociology and philosophy. Specialisms cover Adult, Mental Health and Children's Nursing. A degree course in Midwifery is also offered and a BSc in Primary Care (Practice Nursing) is available.

Coventry Specialisation covers Adult, Children and Young People, Learning Disabilities and Mental Health Nursing. A three-year course in Midwifery is also offered which includes online assessment in some modules.

Cumbria There are degrees in Nursing (Adult; Child; Learning Disabilities; Mental Health) and Midwifery is available as a diploma or a BSc.

De Montfort Nursing courses are offered with specialisms in Adult, Children's, Learning Disability or Mental Health Nursing. Degree courses in Midwifery, Health Studies and an International Nursing Studies course for internationally qualified nurses are also available.

Derby BSc (Hons) Nursing courses are offered, specialising in Adult and Mental Health Nursing. In addition there are degrees in Community Practice and in Public Health.

Dundee Bachelor of Nursing courses are offered. They cover nursing, applied biological sciences, applied social sciences, applied healthcare ethics, care management and health promotion. The degree course provides specialism options in Adult, Child and Mental Health Nursing.

East Anglia Three-year Nursing degree courses are offered and lead to Adult, Child and Mental Health Nursing and Learning Disability specialisms. There is also a degree in Midwifery.

Edge Hill Courses are available in Adult, Children's and Mental Health Nursing, in Learning Disabilities and in Midwifery. A course in Children's Nursing and Social Work is also offered.

Edinburgh The four-year Nursing course enables graduates to qualify for registration in General or Mental Health Nursing. Clinical practice is integrated with theoretical teaching throughout the four years and parts of the third and fourth years are spent in hospital training. Students are also introduced to the wider social, economic and organisational issues in healthcare. Supporting courses can be selected from a very wide range of subjects in the Faculties of Social Sciences, Arts and Science.

Edinburgh Napier Nursing courses are offered in Adult, Child, Mental Health and Learning Disability specialisms. There is also a degree in Midwifery which offers a non-means-tested bursary.

Edinburgh Queen Margaret A four-year Nursing degree is offered with a period of clinical practice. The course focuses on adult nursing. Some students may be entitled to a bursary in Years 1 to 3.

Essex Nursing degrees are offered with Adult and Mental Health specialisms.

Glasgow The common Nursing foundation programme also includes a community care scheme. This course focuses on adult nursing with plenty of opportunities for work experience.

Glasgow Caledonian Nursing Studies is a broad course preparing graduates for employment in a variety of healthcare settings with specialisms in Adult, Child, Learning Difficulties and Mental Health. There is also a Midwifery course and a BSc in Operating Departments Practice.

Greenwich Several Nursing courses are offered with specialisms in Midwifery, Adult, Mental Health and Children's Nursing. Courses are also offered in Health and Nutrition. There is also a degree in Midwifery. See also **Health Studies/Sciences**.

See *Heap 2015: University Degree Course Offers* (Trotman Publishing) for details of offers

Hertfordshire The Nursing degree covers Mental Health, Adult and Child Nursing. Midwifery, Specialist Community Nursing and Contemporary Healthcare courses are also available. See also **Health Studies/ Sciences**.

Huddersfield After a basic course in Year 1, the Nursing degree offers specialisms in Adult and Child Nursing, Learning Disabilities and Mental Health. Midwifery Studies is also available.

Hull Nursing is a three-year programme of theoretical and practical work leading to a BSc degree in Mental Health, Children's, Adult and Learning Disability Nursing. There is also a BSc Midwifery degree.

Keele Adult, Children's, Mental Health and Learning Disability are the specialisms on the Nursing degree, which is taught through a case-based approach. A course in Midwifery is also offered.

Kingston A BSc course is offered in Nursing with the four specialisations: Adult, Children's, Mental Health and Learning Disability. Midwifery is also available.

Leeds A Midwifery course is offered that leads to registration and there is also a BSc programme in Adult and Child Nursing and Mental Health Nursing.

Leeds Beckett A three-year Nursing course provides a foundation in nursing and natural and social sciences in Year 1. In Years 2 and 3 students develop their technical skills, including nursing in adult and mental health areas.

Lincoln A three-year course (each year of 45 weeks) leads to a qualification in Adult or Mental Health Nursing. Almost two-thirds of placements are in primary care with the rest in secondary care across the East Midlands.

Liverpool The Adult Nursing degree is a three-year course leading to the degree (BNurs), with modules covering physiology, pathophysiology, behavioural sciences, communication skills, clinical skills and curative, rehabilitative and palliative care.

Liverpool John Moores The three-year Nursing degree covers Adult and Mental Health Nursing. The Midwifery course is divided between theory and practice and includes options in the management of professional practice, law and ethics.

London (King's) Nursing Studies focusing on Adult, Children's and Mental Health Nursing is based on three main areas of study – the biological, medical and social sciences. A substantial amount of practical work forms an integral part of the course (80 weeks in total) through St George's School of Nursing. Graduates qualify as Registered General Nurses at the end of the course. Midwifery with registration is also offered.

London South Bank Nursing courses cover Mental Health, Child Care, Adult Health and Learning Disabilities. Midwifery and courses in Primary and Social Care are also offered.

Manchester The BNurs degree course (covering Adult, Child and Mental Health Nursing) has a strong theoretical basis of nursing and midwifery practice, together with aspects of behavioural, social and biological sciences. There is also a degree in Midwifery.

Manchester Met There is a full-time course in Adult Nursing which is divides time equally between theoretical work and clinical practice.

Middlesex Special features of the three-year Nursing course lead to Adult, Mental Health or Children's Nursing. Clinical experience can be taken anywhere in the UK or abroad. A three-year full-time course in European Nursing is offered, introducing European nursing methods. Diploma and degree courses in Midwifery can also be taken.

Northampton There are courses covering all aspects of nursing (Adult, Child, Mental Health and Learning Disability), in addition to which there is a Midwifery degree offered as a long or short programme as well as a BSc degree in Cancer Care.

Northumbria Nursing Studies is offered with specialism in Child, Mental Health, Learning Disabilities or Adult Nursing. There is also a Midwifery Studies course leading to registration.

Nottingham The Master of Nursing (MN) course leads to a qualification in nursing and a professional qualification. The three-year course has a strong research foundation and provides pathways in Adult, Mental Health, Learning Disabilities and Child Nursing. There is also a pre-registration degree (shortened) in Midwifery.

Oxford Brookes Nursing is offered with specialisms in Adult, Children's and Mental Health. There is a Midwifery course and a specialist distance-learning Nursing degree.

Plymouth The three-year full-time Nursing course leads to specialisms in Adult, Mental Health and Child Nursing. There is also a pre-registration BSc offered in Midwifery.

Queen's Belfast The BSc Nursing course offers specialisation in Adult, Children's, Learning Disability and Mental Health Nursing in Year 2. There is also a BSc Midwifery degree.

Robert Gordon This four-year Nursing course has a common foundation programme followed by specialist studies in Adult, Children and Young People, or Mental Health Nursing. A Midwifery course is also offered.

Salford The three-year Nursing course provides programmes in Adult, Child and Mental Health Nursing. There are also three-year degrees in Midwifery and in Professional Studies in Nursing and Social Work.

Sheffield The BMedSci course in Health and Human Sciences offer students a basis in the healthcare profession with options to go on to study Nursing at postgraduate level.

Sheffield Hallam Three-year courses in Nursing Studies are offered with specialisms in Adult, Child and Mental Health Care Nursing. A BSc in Midwifery is also offered and a BA in Applied Learning (Learning Disability) and Generic Social Work is available.

South Wales Degrees are offered in Adult, Child, Learning Disabilities and Mental Health Nursing. There is also a degree course in Midwifery and degrees are available in Acute and Critical Care and Cancer Care.

Southampton Nursing degrees in Adult, Child, Mental Health, Adult and Child, or Adult and Mental Health Nursing are available and a degree in Midwifery is also offered.

Staffordshire Courses in Nursing focus on Adult, Child and Mental Health Nursing. There is also a degree in pre-registration Midwifery Practice with placements at Royal Shrewsbury Hospital.

Stirling The BSc Nursing degree covers the adult and mental health fields of nursing.

Surrey Nursing Studies degree courses lead to Child, Adult and Mental Health Nursing. Placements take place in Surrey, West Sussex, Middlesex or North Hampshire. There is also a Midwifery course.

Swansea Nursing students in Wales are paid by a bursary from the NHS Wales Bursary Scheme. It is not means tested. The course covers Adult, Child and Mental Health Nursing, prior to which a common foundation course is offered. There is also a Midwifery degree.

Teesside There are courses in Nursing specialising in Adult, Child, Mental Health and Learning Disabilities and also in Midwifery. There is also a course offered in Nursing in the Home/District Nursing.

Ulster Years 1 and 2 and the final year of the Nursing course are suitable for students aiming for an Adult Nursing or Mental Health qualification. Thirty-six units are studied, with both theory and practical placements in every year of the course. Theoretical units cover biological sciences, behavioural sciences (psychology and sociology), research and nursing.

West London Degree courses are offered in Learning Disability, Mental Health, Child Health and Adult Health Nursing and also in Midwifery (also available as a shortened course).

West Scotland Midwifery and Nursing courses (Adult and Mental Health) are offered at various campuses (Ayr, Dumfries, Hamilton and Paisley). Placements take place across the region and are dictated by the campus the student is studying at.

Wolverhampton Three-year courses are offered in Midwifery and Nursing covering the areas of Children, Adult, Mental Health and Learning Disabilities. A BSc course is also offered in Emergency Practitioner Nursing.

Worcester Midwifery is offered as a three-year degree course and also Nursing in Adult, Child and Mental Health. There is also a Nursing Studies course for overseas students.

York Degrees are offered in all four branches – Adult, Children, Mental Health and Learning Disability – with the option to take the course as an extended degree (four years). There is also a three-year Midwifery Practice degree.

OTHER INSTITUTIONS OFFERING NURSING COURSES
Suffolk (Univ Campus), York (Coll).

ALTERNATIVE COURSES
Anatomy, Biochemistry, Biological Sciences, Biology and Applied Biology, Environmental Health, Health and Community Studies, Occupational Therapy, Physiotherapy, Psychology, Radiography, Social Administration, Speech Therapy.

PHARMACOLOGY

(including **Toxicology**)
(* indicates universities with entry requirements over 340 UCAS points)

SUBJECT REQUIREMENTS/PREFERENCES
GCE A level: Two to three science subjects. Chemistry usually required. **GCSE:** English and Mathematics.

SUBJECT INFORMATION
Pharmacology is the study of drugs and medicine in which courses focus on physiology, biochemistry, toxicology, immunology, microbiology and chemotherapy. Pharmacologists are not qualified to work as pharmacists.

Aberdeen First year studies focus on chemistry and biology leading on to a range of specialised topics, including neuropsychology, physiology and the principles of chemotherapy. The teaching rating is 'Excellent'.

Bath* Pharmacology is a four-year sandwich course in which the third year is spent on industrial placement. In the first year the core subjects are cell biology, physiology, pharmacology and pathology, chemistry and computing skills. The second year develops these subjects more fully, and in the final year pharmacology is combined with a research project. Transfers are possible between the three- and four-year courses up to the end of Year 2. See also **Combined Courses**.

Birmingham* Pharmacology can be taken as part of the degree in Medical Science or as a minor subject with Chemistry. Year 1 covers an introduction to Pharmacology with a deeper study of drug kinetics in Year 2 and specialist choices in Year 3.

Bristol* Subjects covered in the Pharmacology course include chemistry, anatomy and biochemistry. In the second year, pharmacology is taken with anatomical science, human anatomy or molecular genetics and one other course, and in the final year, pharmacology is studied throughout the year. There is a strong research base involving neuropharmacology and cell signalling with training in a wide variety of modern techniques. The MSci course includes a year in industry.

Cambridge* Pharmacology is offered as part of the course in Natural Sciences and Medicine. It is accompanied by two related sciences in the second year. See also **Combined Courses**.

Cardiff* The first year of the Medical Pharmacology course deals with chemistry, biochemistry and physiology, pharmacology and toxicology. In Part II, practical experience is combined with theory in a number of specialised areas, which include an insight into the philosophical implications of drugs and society.

Central Lancashire Pharmacology is offered with Physiology and consists of 18 modules in the three years. Year 1 provides a theoretical and practical framework in areas such as biochemistry, physiology and pharmacology, data handling and laboratory skills. The second year develops critical skills with the final year consisting of specialist modules.

Coventry The course in Medical and Pharmacological Sciences focuses on a study of pharmacology and physiology and applications in medicine. It can be taken with a year in professional placement.

Dundee The Pharmacology degree begins in Year 2 after a first year in allied sciences with biology or chemistry, and is taken as a single honours or joint honours with Biochemistry or Chemistry. During the third year students focus on pharmacology with additional optional subjects. The rapidly developing area of neurosciences features strongly in Year 4, when students research their chosen area. Four-year full-time degree courses are also offered in Pharmacology and Physiological Sciences and Biochemistry and Pharmacology. See also **Biological Sciences**.

East London The first year of the three-year full-time or four-year sandwich course in Pharmacology is taken in common with Applied Biology and Medical Biotechnology, and transfer between courses is possible. Second-year students take pharmacology, human physiology and biochemistry. The third year is spent in optional industrial training. Final-year students take pharmacology and toxicology and undertake a research project. Toxicology and Pharmacology can also be taken as extended degrees.

Edinburgh Biology and physiology are taken by all students specialising in Pharmacology. Pharmacology and three other subjects are taken in Year 3 and pharmacology is studied throughout in Year 4. See also **Biological Sciences**.

Edinburgh Queen Margaret Applied Pharmacology is a three-year single honours degree. The course covers areas such as the effects of drugs on the brain, treatments of cancer and the use of drugs to treat arthritis. The first two years of the course are shared with Human Biology and Nutrition.

Glasgow* Pharmacology students enter the honours course after studying biology, chemistry and related subjects for the first two years. Students may register for an MSci degree with a year in work placement in research or industry in the UK or abroad.

Glasgow Caledonian Specialist studies in Pharmacology are chosen in Year 3 after a common first and second year with students aiming for Food Bioscience, Microbiology and Cell Biology.

Hertfordshire Pharmacology is offered as a three-year full-time or four-year sandwich course and there are also options for a year in North America or Europe.

Kingston Pharmacology is offered as a three-year full-time or four-year sandwich course. Final-year topics include toxicology, molecular genetics and biotechnology in healthcare. Joint courses are also offered.

Leeds Pharmacology is a broad scientific course as opposed to an applied study and is taken with physiology and biochemistry in the first year. This is common to all students, who can delay their choice between single or combined courses until the end of Year 1. A year in industry can be taken between the second and final year.

Liverpool Pharmacology is studied as part of the Life Science scheme. A basic core of units is studied followed by a choice of other units to suit the student's interests. At Liverpool the emphasis is given to the physiological, biochemical, toxicology and clinical aspects of Pharmacology. There are also three-year full-time and four-year sandwich MChem courses in Medicinal Chemistry with Pharmacology.

London (King's)* A single honours degree is offered in Pharmacology and also a joint degree with Molecular Genetics. In the first two years the focus is on physiology, biochemistry and pharmacology. In the third year, specialist topics include toxicology, immunology and environmental pharmacology. An optional year in industry is available. See also **Biological Sciences**.

London (UCL)* Students take physiology, biochemistry, and toxicology in their first year. A range of advanced courses in the final year allows students to concentrate on particular aspects of the subject and undertake a research project.

London Met A single honours course is offered in Pharmacology. The first year gives students a broad understanding of life sciences going into greater depth in the second year. The final year consists of an independent research project in which students carry out pharmacological investigation.

Manchester Five courses are offered in Pharmacology, including joint courses with Physiology with Industrial Experience and with a Modern Language. Pharmacology with Industrial/Professional Experience is also offered.

Newcastle* Pharmacology is a modular course with a wide range of biological sciences studied in Stage 1. More advanced topics of pharmacology follow in Stages 2 and 3 covering anti-cancer drugs, cardiovascular pharmacology and toxicology. There is also a degree in Physiological Sciences. See also **Biology**.

Nottingham Trent Pharmacology is offered with the option to take a 12-month placement. Final-year options include clinical pharmacology, toxicology and current topics in pharmacology, physiology and neuroscience. There is also a course in Pharmaceutical Chemistry. See also **Biological Sciences**.

Portsmouth The Pharmacology course has a common first year with Biomedical Science. This is a three-year full-time course and includes a study of physiology and chemistry to support studies in pharmacology. Overall, the course has a biochemical focus towards modern pharmacology with an emphasis on pharmacology in all three years.

St Andrews Pharmacology is offered with Chemistry and is studied over four years. Students are provided with a broad base of chemical knowledge with core modules studied in the first two years. Years 3 and 4 offer research-led learning.

Sheffield Physiology with Pharmacology is one possible route of the BSc Biomedical Science course, working from the level of the gene, protein, cell and organ to the whole body.

Southampton The Pharmacology degree is based on both physiology and biochemistry and looks at the design of drugs and their biological effects. A one-year placement is possible.

See *Heap 2015: University Degree Course Offers* (Trotman Publishing) for details of offers

Strathclyde In the Biochemistry and Pharmacology degree course, physiology and chemistry are taken in the first year with bioscience and pharmacology, followed by advanced studies in biochemistry and pharmacology in the second and third years. Final-year modules include genes and cancer, glycobiology and oxidative stress. A four-year full-time degree is offered in Immunology and Pharmacology.

Surrey* Pharmacology and Toxicology are offered as a pathway in the three-year full-time or four-year Biochemistry degree. An optional placement year can be taken between the second and final year of the course.

Westminster Pharmacology can be studied in a joint three-year degree with Physiology. The course can also be taken with a foundation year. Final-year modules include immunopharmacology, bioinformatics and central nervous system pharmacology.

Wolverhampton A three-year course is available in Pharmacology focusing on immunology, human physiology and microbiology with a research project in the third year. There is also a Pharmaceutical Science degree.

ALTERNATIVE COURSES

Agricultural Sciences, Biochemistry, Biological Sciences, Chemistry, Dietetics, Food Science, Pharmacy.

PHARMACY

(including **Pharmaceutical Sciences**)

(* indicates universities with entry requirements over 340 UCAS points)

SUBJECT REQUIREMENTS/PREFERENCES

GCE A level: Two to three science subjects. Chemistry usually required. **GCSE:** English, Mathematics and a science subject.

SUBJECT INFORMATION

All Pharmacy courses are very similar and lead to qualification as a pharmacist who may then work in hospitals or private practice. All the Pharmacy degree courses listed below lead to an MPharm degree. They are all of at least four years' duration. Programmes are fully accredited by the Royal Pharmaceutical Society. In order to practise as a fully qualified pharmacist an additional pre-registration year must be completed, supervised by a registered pharmacist, followed by passing the Society's professional examinations. Pre-registration experience is an integral part of Pharmacy courses and leads to membership of the Royal Pharmaceutical Society of Great Britain. **Pharmaceutical Science courses do not prepare students for careers as pharmacists.**

Aston* The Pharmacy course covers the basic sciences and includes communication skills and computing in Year 1. In Year 2, pharmacology occupies one-third of the total time along with biological chemistry. In Years 3 and 4, a core course includes chemotherapy, medicinal chemistry, toxicology and professional practice. There is an emphasis on professional studies and patient-oriented care.

Bath* Pharmacy is a four-year full-time course introduced by basic studies in biology, human biology, pharmaceutical and medical chemistry, pharmacology, pharmaceutics and practical pharmacy with an optional placement in Year 3. Pharmacy practice takes place in the second and third years with clinical pharmacy being the focus in Year 4 leading to the MPharm degree.

Birmingham* Pharmacy is offered as a four- or five-year course, with the latter including the professional pre-registration year. Clinical placements take place throughout the course.

Bradford The course in Pharmacy includes two six-month practical training periods in two different areas of practice in the third and fifth years as part of this five-year sandwich course. There is also a four-year full-time course. Both courses satisfy the training and registration requirements for practice as a pharmacist. A degree in Pharmaceutical Management is also offered involving marketing, human resource management and language options (French, German or Spanish).

Brighton The Pharmacy degree covers microbiology, clinical pharmacology, pharmacy practice and health psychology. In Years 3 and 4, core subjects involve immunology and pharmaceutics, and an opportunity is provided to gain work experience in hospital and in community pharmacy. There is also a course in Pharmaceutical and Chemical Sciences covering chemistry, biology and biochemistry.

Cardiff* The Pharmacy course with an intake of 120 students each year covers topics including: pharmaceutical chemistry; pharmaceutics (design, production and control of all medical preparations); and clinical pharmacy (the law and practice of pharmacy). All subjects are covered in each year of the four-year course.

De Montfort A degree is offered in Pharmacy in which pharmaceutical science subjects are taken in Years 1 and 2. In Years 3 modules cover physiology and patient treatment and, in the final year, two elective topics are offered combined with patient care, medicine and a project. A degree course is also offered in Pharmaceutical and Cosmetic Science.

Durham (Stockton)* There is a new, innovative MPharm course, accredited by the General Pharmaceutical Council. Work placements are available.

East Anglia* The four-year degree in Pharmacy covers pharmaceutical chemistry, physiology, genetics and pharmacy practice, leading to the MPharm degree and full professional registration. Professional placements take place in the community, in hospitals and in industry. There are also degrees in Pharmaceutical Chemistry, Biomedicine and Biological and Medical Chemistry.

Greenwich An MPharm degree at the Medway School of Pharmacy is offered leading to full registration in Pharmacy. The degree in Pharmaceutical Sciences lays a foundation in chemistry, biology, physiology, product formation and process technology. Further studies include micro-organisms, drug testing, pharmacokinetics and quality assurance. Professional recognition is available for the Pharmaceutical Sciences course which can be taken as a four-year sandwich course.

Hertfordshire Pharmaceutical Sciences, with or without a year in Europe or North America or work placement, is offered as a three- or four-year course. There is also a four-year MPharm degree with placements in Years 1, 2 and 3.

Huddersfield A Pharmacy degree is offered and also a course in Pharmaceutical Science can be studied as a three-year full-time course or with industrial placement for one year.

Hull Courses are offered in Pharmaceutical Science, with optional industrial experience, studied over three (BSc) or four years (MPharmSci).

Keele The Pharmacy course can include a foundation year for those without science A levels and includes many opportunities for scheduled visits and placements in hospital, community and industrial settings.

Kent The Medway School of Pharmacy offers a four-year MPharm degree, which includes placements in hospitals and in the community. The course is based on three interlinked themes: practitioner and patient; medicinal products; and the patient, disease and drug action.

Kingston Three-year BSc and four-year MPharmSci courses in Pharmaceutical Science are offered with common first two years.

See *Heap 2015: University Degree Course Offers* (Trotman Publishing) for details of offers

Liverpool John Moores The accredited four-year Pharmacy course includes study of the scientific basis of therapeutics, dosage form design, pharmaceutical chemistry and pharmacy practice. There are also courses in Pharmaceutical Science.

London (King's)* The Master of Pharmacy course commences with a two-week pharmacy orientation course. This is followed by an integrated programme covering the principles of pharmacy, pharmacy and therapeutics, and pharmacy into practice.

London (UCL)* Pharmaceutical science and the scientific basis of pharmacy are studied in Year 1 of the Pharmacy course; these subjects are developed in Year 2 with a study of drug development. In Years 3 and 4 students take specialist options and undertake a research project followed by preparation for practice.

London Met Pharmaceutical Sciences is offered as a single honours course. General chemistry and cell biology are covered in the first year followed by practical studies and a double project in the third year. Pharmacology is also offered as a BSc.

Manchester A standard four-year Pharmacy course is offered that leads to a full qualification recognised by the Royal Pharmaceutical Society (RPS) to work as community, hospital or industrial pharmacists. A foundation year is also offered.

Medway School of Pharmacy See under **Greenwich** and **Kent**.

Northumbria Pharmaceutical Chemistry involves the design, preparation and metabolism of drugs with a strong emphasis on practical laboratory skills. The course is offered as a three- or four-year programme.

Nottingham* In the MPharm Pharmacy course the main subjects taught are pharmaceutics, chemistry, biology and physiology, and pharmacology and therapeutics. In each of the two summer vacations, students are encouraged to take posts in some branch of pharmacy, the department assisting students to find suitable posts. The course is biased towards careers in industry, hospital pharmacy and research. There is also the opportunity to study in Malaysia. Scholarships available.

Nottingham Trent Courses can be taken in Pharmaceutical and Medicinal Chemistry, which covers the biological chemistry of drugs, their synthesis, analysis uses and mode of action.

Portsmouth The four-year course in Pharmacy covers three main subject areas: pharmacy practice; pharmaceutical science; and life science. Advanced and professional studies plus electives are followed in Years 3 and 4.

Queen's Belfast* In the first year of the four-year course, students are introduced to pharmaceutical microbiology including disinfection and sterilisation, and to the principles of physical and analytical chemistry. These lead on to a study of the traditional subjects (pharmaceutics, pharmacology and pharmaceutical chemistry). Topics are included that reflect the pharmacist's wider role as a member of the healthcare team and involve visits to hospitals, health centres and industrial pharmacies.

Reading Professional experience is gained by way of short placements throughout the MPharm course. Modules in pharmacy practice run in all years of the degree alongside topics such as medicinal chemistry, human physiology and pharmacognosy.

Robert Gordon The Pharmacy course develops the scientific basis of pharmacy through the study of pharmaceutics, pharmacology and pharmaceutical chemistry. It also develops the application of this knowledge to practical situations and the communication skills necessary to perform competently as part of the healthcare team in the clinical situation.

Strathclyde This accredited degree provides several themes throughout the course including pharmacology, physiology and pharmaceutical practice and care. Students have the opportunity to choose from a list of elective modules in the first year.

See *Heap 2015: University Degree Course Offers* (Trotman Publishing) for details of offers

Sunderland In the Pharmacy course a knowledge of the action and uses of drugs is achieved by a study of pharmaceutical chemistry, pharmaceutics and associated subjects. Topics include drug information handling, clinical pharmacy, toxicology, health education and quality control. A course is also offered in Chemical and Pharmaceutical Sciences.

Ulster* An MPharm degree is offered leading to professional recognition. The first year consists of an introduction to the subject with modules covering pharmacy practice, human physiology and anatomy, medical cell biology and biochemistry.

Wolverhampton A four-year MPharm course in Pharmacy has practice placements in Years 1, 2 and 3. The final year remains clinically focused while students undertake substantial research.

ALTERNATIVE COURSES
Biochemistry, Biological Sciences, Chemistry, Pharmacology.

PHILOSOPHY

(* indicates universities with entry requirements over 340 UCAS points)

SUBJECT REQUIREMENTS/PREFERENCES
GCE A level: No specific subjects required. **GCSE:** English and Mathematics. **Aberdeen, Dundee, Edinburgh, Glasgow, St Andrews:** English, Mathematics or a science and a foreign language. **Oxford, Cambridge:** Grade A in most subjects preferred. **Sussex:** Grade B in a foreign language.

SUBJECT INFORMATION
Philosophy is a rigorous logical study of the most fundamental and general problems that arise in human thought. What is knowledge? What is the nature of truth? Contemporary philosophy covers political, educational, psychological, aesthetic and religious issues. Some reading of the works of the leading philosophers is recommended before applying for the courses.

Aberdeen The single honours course in Mental Philosophy provides a grounding in the history of the subject and an understanding of its contemporary development. Topics cover political, social, moral, scientific and religious philosophy. Joint courses are offered with a range of options including Languages, Physics, Sociology, Anthropology and Psychology. The history of philosophy is a key element of the course.

Anglia Ruskin Metaphysics, aesthetics, moral and political philosophy are covered in the single honours degree. Philosophy can also be taken with English Literature.

Bangor There are courses in Philosophy and Religious Studies with additional subjects taken from History and Welsh History, Languages, Physical Education and Sport Science.

Bath Spa Philosophy and Ethics can be taken as a major, joint or minor component with another subject, e.g. English, Sociology or History. Religion, Philosophy and Ethics is also offered.

Birmingham Central areas of philosophy including ethics, logic, moral, political philosophy and the philosophy of the mind are studied in the first year of Philosophy. These courses provide a basis for later and more advanced studies in analytical philosophy, ethics and visual arts. Optional courses are also available in the second and third years when students design their own programme. There is also a course in Philosophy, Religion and Ethics and Joint courses offered.

See *Heap 2015: University Degree Course Offers* (Trotman Publishing) for details of offers

Bristol* The Philosophy course aims to present a thorough understanding of contemporary philosophical issues (political, psychological, linguistic and aesthetic) and provides a grounding in the subject covering philosophy in antiquity and from the 17th century onwards. Course choices and specialised topics give students considerable freedom to select those areas of philosophy that are of particular interest to them. Transfer from any one of the 15 joint courses to the single honours course may be possible in Year 2 depending on aptitude and departmental numbers.

Bristol UWE Philosophy is offered as a single or joint honours course with over 12 other subjects. The degree places emphasis on the broad historical range, from Ancient Greek thought through to Nietzsche and contemporary issues.

Cambridge* The Philosophy Tripos is divided into three parts, each taking one year. In the first year a study is made of logic, ethics and metaphysics, followed in the second year by a choice of two subjects from the philosophy of science, historical philosophy, politics and experimental psychology (which includes some lab work). A range of options in Part II (third year) allows for a closer study of topics studied in the first two years. Philosophy of Science can be studied with History in the Natural Sciences Tripos. See also **Combined Courses**.

Cardiff No previous knowledge of philosophy is required for the degree in Philosophy, which begins with the practical relevance of political and moral philosophy and the theory of knowledge in Part I. In Part II the main branches of philosophy are covered, with a wide choice of courses available. Joint courses are also offered including Philosophy and Ancient History, Music, Politics and Welsh.

Central Lancashire Modules in critical thinking, epistemology, crime and morality form part of the degree in Philosophy. Philosophy is also offered as part of the combined honours programme as a joint or minor course with English Literature, Health Studies, Politics, Sociology or Religion and Culture.

Dundee A four-year course in Philosophy is offered leading to an MA. The degree covers the history of philosophy in the first two years, ethics, moral problems and other specialised studies. General courses follow on continental philosophy and other options including the philosophy of religion (Christian or Indian), aesthetics and the philosophy of science, European politics and history, international relations and fine art. The department also offers a course in Art, Philosophy and Contemporary Practices (60% Fine Art, 40% Philosophy).

Durham* Philosophy can be studied as a single honours course, a joint course or in the combined honours Arts or Social Science or Natural Sciences programmes. All students take a common first-year course. In the second and third years of the honours course students choose from a wide range of topics. A course in Philosophy, Politics and Economics is also offered.

East Anglia Single and joint courses are offered with considerable flexibility. The courses have an emphasis on the links between Philosophy and other subjects in the humanities and social sciences. Over 20 modules are offered covering art, science, religion, history, the leading philosophers and mental health. Joint courses can be taken with History and Politics.

Edinburgh A first-year course in philosophy is taken by all students on all Philosophy courses, and has options in logic and the philosophy of science. This continues in the second year with options to take courses in sociology and politics, while in Years 3 and 4 specialisation begins. There is a range of joint courses with Philosophy including Economics, Greek and Theology.

Essex In the Philosophy course, the main topics covered include an introduction to philosophy and logic, reason and experience and 20th-century continental philosophy. Other specialisms involve the philosophy of religion, the arts, law, literature, rights, Freud and psychoanalysis and ethics. There is also a course with an international exchange.

Exeter* A large number of combined honours courses are offered in Philosophy including options with modern languages in which a year is spent abroad. Other programmes also allow for a year of study in Europe, North America and Australia.

See *Heap 2015: University Degree Course Offers* (Trotman Publishing) for details of offers

Glasgow* Philosophy is studied within the Social Science programme and includes general and moral philosophy and the work of the leading philosophers. A very large number of joint courses are also offered including Celtic Civilisation, Scottish Literature, Polish, Computing, Anthropology, Mathematics and Management Studies. The honours course contains 20 core and optional papers.

Greenwich The combined Philosophy course covers aspects of the Western philosophy tradition from the Greeks to the present day and includes literature, political science and language. Philosophy is offered with, for example, English, Politics, Creative Writing or Sociology.

Hertfordshire Philosophy can be taken as a joint or minor subject in the Combined Studies programme and also as a major or single honours course in the Humanities modular scheme. Computing, Psychology, Law, and Journalism and Media Cultures can be studied with Philosophy.

Hull The first two terms of the Philosophy course are devoted to an introduction to the subject – its history, methods and problems. Over the next six terms, courses are taken in epistemology (theory of knowledge), moral philosophy and metaphysics. Students then choose courses to develop their own interest. A range of joint honours courses are also offered, and also Politics, Philosophy and Economics (PPE).

Keele Philosophy can be taken with a choice of over 20 dual honours options, including Mathematics, Educational Studies, Politics, English and Psychology. The course aims to develop the student's analytical and critical abilities. Final-year options include the philosophies of mind, religion and politics.

Kent After an introduction to Philosophy in Part I, core courses in Part II cover moral philosophy, theory of knowledge, logic and social philosophy, aesthetics and meta-ethics. Optional courses are also offered as specialised studies in the second and third years, as is the opportunity to spend a year abroad. Philosophy can be studied in over 14 honours programmes, including Business Administration, Drama, Religious Studies, Social Anthropology, European Languages, Computing and Social Policy.

Lancaster Philosophy in Year 1 covers knowledge and reality, freedom of the will, critical thinking, political philosophy and ethics. These are followed in Years 2 and 3 with a range of options covering various aspects of philosophy. Philosophy is also offered with Religious Studies or Politics and there is also a PPE course. Exchange programmes with European and American universities are possible.

Leeds* In Year 1 of Philosophy, 10 philosophy courses are taken (introduction to ethics and reason and argument) plus two other subjects. In Years 2 and 3, courses include the history of ancient and modern philosophy, ethics and social philosophy and logic. There is also a course in Philosophy, Ethics and Religion and a wide range of combined courses.

Leeds Trinity A new course has been introduced in Philosophy, Ethics and Religion.

Liverpool The Philosophy course provides a solid foundation in core areas of Western analytical philosophy and involves ethics, epistemology and logic plus two other subjects in the first year. The non-philosophy subjects can be continued in the second year along with further compulsory philosophy topics. In the third year, students choose areas of special interest to them taken from a wide range of options.

Liverpool Hope Philosophy and Ethics has a focus on applied ethics. Students are encouraged to think deeply about issues such as human rights in order to develop their own powers of critical reasoning and decision-making. A separate course is offered in Philosophy, Ethics and Religion.

London (Heythrop) Philosophy students follow courses in logic, epistemology, metaphysics, ethics or political philosophy and the history of philosophy, as well as two courses from a wide range of options, and produce a dissertation on a special topic. Philosophy may be combined with Theology, Religion or Ethics.

London (King's)* Fifteen compulsory subjects are taken through the Philosophy course, covering logic and methodology, Greek philosophy, modern (17th/18th-century) philosophy, ethics and political philosophy, epistemology and metaphysics. Students also choose options from a wide range including in-depth studies of the great philosophers. Philosophy can also be studied with Hispanic Studies and Physics.

London (UCL)* First-year Philosophy students attend introductory courses in logic, the history of philosophy, and moral and political philosophy. These studies can continue in the second and third years with a wide range of subject options. Philosophy can also be taken as a joint subject with Economics, Greek or the History of Art.

London LSE* Philosophy, Logic and Scientific Method focuses on a commitment to clarity of expression and argumentative rigour and the links with the social and natural sciences. Several 'outside' options are offered including anthropology, economics, history, linguistics, politics, psychology and sociology. The courses offered are in Philosophy and Economics, and Politics and Philosophy, as well as Philosophy, Logic and Scientific Method.

London NCH The course provides a thorough grounding in the central areas of philosophy. It introduces historical and contemporary issues in the subject and encourages students to make connections between the ideas and arguments that inform philosophical debates. A range of philosophical works from classical times to the present day are covered. Optional units enable students to focus on areas that may be of particular interest such as political philosophy, aesthetics and philosophies of mind and language.

Manchester Philosophy is a broad course covering the main subject topics such as the philosophy of modern religion, modern political thought, psychology, law and a language. Philosophy is also offered with Politics or Criminology.

Manchester Met Philosophy, focusing on European philosophy, is offered as single, joint and combined honours programmes and can be studied with, for example, Sport, Cultural Studies, Health Studies and Languages.

Newcastle There is a course in Philosophical Studies: Knowledge and Human Interests, which can be taken as a single honours course or as part of the Combined Studies (BA) programme.

Newman Philosophy with either Theology or with Religion and Ethics can be taken with a focus on topics such as God and the philosophers and science and the cosmos.

Nottingham The Philosophy course provides a rigorous training in analytical philosophy. The department's strengths include metaphysics, self, mind and body. Subsidiary subjects can also be taken from other departments and optional choices form the entirety of the third year.

Oxford* Philosophy is offered as part of several joint courses that share a common structure. For the course in Philosophy, Politics and Economics, all three subjects are studied equally in Year 1. In Years 2 and 3, all three subjects can be continued or two main subjects can be chosen. Philosophy is also offered on its own or with Theology, with nine options in Modern Languages, or with Computer Science, Mathematics, Physics, Physiology and Linguistics or Psychology.

Oxford Brookes Philosophy can be studied as a single subject or with a range of joint subjects including Anthropology, Film Studies, Mathematics, Psychology, Sociology and Religion and Theology.

Queen's Belfast Philosophy can be studied as a single, joint or major/minor subject with other subjects including Theology, Sociology, Psychology and Ancient History. In both cases a study is made of the works of leading philosophers over the last 2,500 years, on debates relating to truth, proof, meaning and value, science, aesthetics and law.

Reading Philosophy offers modules in logic and theory of knowledge and moral philosophy which are subject-centred rather than author-centred. Thereafter, other courses follow, covering a range of specialisations that could include the philosophy of law, language, mind, natural science or religion. Students can spend a year abroad by combining Philosophy with a modern language. There is also a

See *Heap 2015: University Degree Course Offers* (Trotman Publishing) for details of offers

course in Ethics, Values and Philosophy. At the end of the first year students may transfer to the Philosophy degree.

Roehampton Philosophy is offered as a single or combined honours course with subjects such as Classical Civilisation, History and Theology and Religious Studies. Years 2 and 3 provide a choice of modules in the main areas of philosophy such as ethics, metaphysics and moral and political philosophy.

St Andrews* Degree courses are offered with Philosophy as both single and joint honours in the Faculty of Arts or Science. Programmes of study in Year 1 include reasoning and argument, knowledge and learning, logic, morals and political philosophy, with more specialist topics following in subsequent years.

St Mary's The Philosophy degree draws on Christian, Islamic, Jewish and Indian traditions. The course can be taken jointly with subjects including Film and Popular Culture, Sport Science and Theology and Religious Studies.

Sheffield* Philosophy in Year 1 is organised around the self, knowledge, ethics, religion, society, existentialism and science. A generous system of optional courses provides a wide choice of specialist subjects in Years 2 and 3.

Southampton* Single and combined Philosophy honours courses are offered, the latter available with Economics, English, Politics, French, German, Film, History, Mathematics or Sociology. The course is designed for students who are new to philosophy as well as those who have some previous knowledge.

Staffordshire The main focus of the Philosophy course lies in modern European philosophy. A range of other subjects can be studied with Philosophy, including Creative Writing, English Literature, Sociology, Modern History and International History. There are also courses in Fine Art: Philosophy and Ethics, and Philosophy and Society.

Stirling Philosophy is taken with two other subjects in Part I with semesters in introduction to philosophy, the justification of behaviour, and the individual and society. Part II involves logic and language, rationalism and empiricism and a choice from a wide range of options. Combined Studies courses are also offered with over 10 subject choices including Film and Media Studies, Politics and French. A course is also offered in Politics, Philosophy and Economics.

Sussex* Students specialise in two of the central areas of moral and political philosophy – modern continental philosophy and analytical philosophy. Philosophy can be studied with History, Cognitive Science, English, French, Italian, Music, Sociology, Spanish or Politics.

Swansea The three core disciplines, philosophy, politics and economics, are strongly represented throughout the PPE course. It offers an examination and critique of the traditions of thought that pervaded modern Europe.

Trinity St David Western philosophy can be studied on the three-year Philosophy course. Options include ancient philosophy, phenomenology and existentialism and mind and metaphysics. There is also a course in Applied Philosophy.

Warwick* Philosophy can be offered as a single honours or a joint course with Mathematics, Literature, Psychology, or Classical Civilisation, or as Philosophy, Politics and Economics. In Year 1, students wishing to broaden the scope of their degree can take courses in other subjects, for example Economics, Film Studies, French Studies, History, History of Art, Mathematics and Politics.

Winchester Philosophy, ethics and spirituality are studied within Theology and Religious Studies and can be taken as part of a combined honours degree with subjects including Archaeology, Drama and Creative Writing.

Wolverhampton The Philosophy course covers ethics, law, logic, philosophy of science, political philosophy and the philosophy of the mind. Religion, feminism, ecology and history also feature. Philosophy is studied with English, Film Studies, Law, Creative Professional Writing, Sociology, Politics, Religious Studies or War Studies.

York* A single honours and a range of integrated courses can be studied on an equal basis in which Philosophy is taken with English, French, German, History, Linguistics, Sociology, Mathematics or Physics. A Politics, Philosophy and Economics course is also offered. See also **Combined Courses**.

ALTERNATIVE COURSES
Psychology, Religious Studies, Social Sciences.

PHYSICS

(including **Applied Physics**)
(* indicates universities with entry requirements over 340 UCAS points)

SUBJECT REQUIREMENTS/PREFERENCES
GCE A level: Mathematics and Physics usually required. Check prospectuses for foundation courses.

SUBJECT INFORMATION
There is a considerable shortage of applicants for Physics courses. Many courses have flexible arrangements to enable students to follow their own interests, for example circuit design, microwave devices, cosmology, medical physics and solid-state electronics. (Research ratings below also include **Astronomy**.)

Aberdeen The Physics (Natural Philosophy) course starts with a broad introduction at Level 1, including astronomy, the physical universe, mechanics, electricity and magnetism, with practical studies in physical computing. In Level 4 specialisms are offered. Physics is also available with Geology, Gaelic, Mathematics and a number of other subjects.

Aberystwyth Honours courses are offered in Physics and physics-based courses with specialisation in other areas, for example Planetary and Space Physics, or Astrophysics. Part I of these courses includes similar modules that allow for specialisation in Year 2, ranging from optics and nuclear physics through astronomy, stars and galaxies to meteorology and global warming, depending on degree choice. Physics with Business Studies (two-thirds Physics, one-third Business Studies) is also offered as well as other subjects. There is also a degree in Space Science and Robotics.

Bath* Physics is a three-year full-time or four-year enhanced sandwich course, the latter having a placement year in industry in the third year, possibly in a European country. Several degrees are offered in which all students follow a common course for the first two years with final choices between the BSc or MPhys courses and study abroad or full-time university study in Years 1 or 2. See also **Combined Courses**.

Birmingham* The first two years are common to both BSc and MPhys degrees, and cover basic physics and maths, after which a study of the major areas of physics continues with a wide choice of options allowing considerable flexibility for students to build their own course. Personal tutorials and small-group teaching takes place throughout the three years of the course. Physics can also be taken with Astrophysics, Particle Physics and Cosmology, Nanoscale Physics and Theoretical Physics or with a year in Europe (France, Germany, Italy, Spain or Portugal). See also **Combined Courses**.

Bristol* Physics is a mathematically oriented course with core subjects being taken in the first and second years. In the third year, students choose from a wide range of options. The Physics first year is arranged so that students can transfer from joint courses to single honours courses and also transfer between the BSc and MSci at the end of Year 1. Several complementary subjects can be taken including Geography, Psychology or Philosophy. An MSc with Astrophysics is also offered, as are courses in Chemical Physics.

Cambridge* See under **Combined Courses**.

Cardiff First-year studies in Physics include physics and another science subject (astrophysics, chemistry, computing, geology or mathematics). Transfer to another degree in a similar field is possible at the end of the year. In Years 2 and 3 the course is physics-based in addition to students completing a substantial physics-based project in the final year.

Central Lancashire The first year of the Physics course provides a firm foundation in applied physics, mathematics and laboratory skills. At the end of the second year, students choose from applied physics, physics/astronomy or physics, or applied physics with another subject on a combined honours programme.

Dundee BSc and MSci courses in Physics are taken with a focus on mathematics in Years 1 and 2, with a single honours or joint honours course following in Years 3 and 4. Physics can be studied with a range of other subjects.

Durham Physics (BSc/MEng) is designed to prepare people in the understanding and use of knowledge and techniques in any branch of physics. A transfer to other Physics courses is possible at the end of Year 1. In addition to joint honours courses there are programmes involving Physics and Astronomy, Natural Sciences and Theoretical Physics.

East Anglia* Chemical Physics is offered as a three-year degree and courses in Environmental Sciences give opportunities for a year in Europe, Australasia or North America.

Edinburgh Physics students take the subject in each of the four years with modules in thermodynamics, electronics and computing and general relativity. The second-year course in mathematical physics is aimed at students whose interests lie in the more theoretical aspects of the subject. There are also courses in Computational Physics and Astrophysics, and Physics with Meteorology or Music can also be taken.

Exeter Four courses are offered with Physics, covering Astrophysics, Professional Experience and Mathematics and with the opportunity to study in Australia, New Zealand and North America. The first year is common to all courses, allowing transfers to other courses in Year 2.

Glasgow Core courses are studied by all Physics students, with specialised courses in the final year. Technological applications in laser physics, electronics and semiconductor physics and devices can be followed in the single honours course. Courses are also available in, for example, Theoretical Physics, Chemical Physics and Physics with Astrophysics, Mathematics and Computer Science.

Heriot-Watt The first year of the four-year course is common to all Physics degrees, with elective options in other subjects. Physics is developed in Year 2 and specialised pathways follow in Years 3 and 4 covering Computational and Engineering Physics, Nanoscience, Photonics and Lasers, Energy Science and Mathematics.

Hertfordshire An optional sandwich year or study abroad is offered on each of the Physics courses, which include Physics, Extended Physics and Aerospace Engineering with Space Technology.

Hull The first two years are common to all courses followed by specialisms in Physics and Applied Physics, Astrophysics, and Physics with Nanotechnology. Physics can be studied with Philosophy.

Imperial London* The department offers three-year BSc courses in Physics and Physics with Theoretical Physics, four-year BSc and MSci courses in Physics, Theoretical Physics and Physics with a year in Europe or with Studies in Musical Performance. There is also a new course in Physics with Science Education.

Keele Physics can be taken with a second subject from 30 options including Business Management, Music Technology, and Media, Communications and Culture. The course covers concepts of both classical and modern physics.

Kent The Physics course allows considerable flexibility and enables students to defer their choice between Physics and other degree programmes in the faculty until the end of the first year. Physics can also be studied with Astrophysics and with a year in the US.

Lancaster* Separate Physics degree schemes are possible, including Astrophysics and Cosmology, Physics with Particle Physics and Space Science and Theoretical Physics. There is also an option to combine Physics with study in North America. Scholarships available.

Leeds* Mathematics is taken in the first two years of the Physics course. At the end of the first year there is the opportunity to transfer between Physics courses (e.g. Physics, Physics/Astrophysics). Optional subjects include polymer and particle physics, bionanophysics, and quantum computation. Courses in Nanotechnology and Theoretical Physics are also offered.

Leicester Physics, Physics with Astrophysics, Physics with Space Science and Technology or with Planetary Science, or Nanotechnology can be studied. Specific core subjects are studied in all the degrees, supplemented by a wide range of optional courses. An optional year in Europe is offered.

Liverpool* Several Physics courses are offered in addition to the single honours programme. These include Mathematical Physics and Physics with Ocean and Climate Studies. Students opting for Physics and Mathematics can study these subjects equally or defer a choice between the two until the end of the first or second year. There are degree courses in Astrophysics, Nuclear Science, Physics and Astronomy, Geophysics and Medical Applications.

Liverpool John Moores Physics with Astronomy is available as a three-year full-time honours course. This is a joint course with the Department of Physics at Liverpool University. The course provides a grounding in physics and computing alongside astronomy. There is also an MPhys course in Astrophysics.

London (King's)* The Physics course gives a thorough grounding in the concepts and techniques of physics and the essential elements of mathematics and computing. The course unit structure provides for a wide choice in the second and third years. Joint honours combinations are also available including a year abroad and, for example, Physics with Medical Applications, with Theoretical Physics, Mathematics or Philosophy.

London (QM)* The flexibility of the course unit system in Physics, and the wide range of options in the final year, allow students to change their choice of course as their interests develop. In addition to Physics, Theoretical Physics, Particle Physics and Astrophysics courses are also offered.

London (RH) All Physics courses have a common first year and provide a wide range of classes from applied physics and theoretical physics topics. Further options are courses in Astrophysics, Mathematics or Music, and a possible year abroad.

London (UCL)* Study is based on the course unit system in which Physics students can select units appropriate to their interests. Courses offered include Astrophysics, Medical Physics and Theoretical Physics.

London South Bank The Integrated Science course, available as three years full time or four years with a placement year, focuses on the physical sciences. Modules include the physical environment and physical science for sustainability.

Loughborough Three-year and four-year full-time and sandwich Physics courses are offered, the latter being either with industrial training or an MPhys. Breadth of studies continues through to the final year, and there are optional courses from other departments including French or German, Management or Environmental Science. Industrial placements abroad are a feature of the course. Three-year and four-year courses are also available in Engineering Physics, Physics with Mathematics, Sports Science, Management and Cosmology.

See *Heap 2015: University Degree Course Offers* (Trotman Publishing) for details of offers

Manchester* There are several Physics courses, including Physics with Astrophysics, with a wide range of options including several from the Mathematics Department. Physics can also be combined with Theoretical Physics or Philosophy or with a study in Europe or industrial experience, while the four-year master's course involving study in Europe includes language tuition and exchange arrangements with France, Germany, Italy, Spain and Belgium.

Nottingham* In the Physics degree all single and joint honours students take physics, maths and a third subject. This allows for flexibility for transfers between single and joint courses at the end of the first year. Other courses offered include Physics with Astronomy or a European language or with Nanoscience or Medical Physics. Chemistry and Molecular Physics and Mathematical Physics can also be studied.

Nottingham Trent Five degrees in Physics are offered including Forensic Science (Physical), Physics with Astrophysics, Physics with Forensic Application and Physics with Nuclear Technology.

Oxford* The first year of the Physics course is equally divided between maths and physics, with an introductory course in computing. At the end of Year 1, it may be possible to transfer to another degree course in the Mathematical and Physical Science Division. The second year covers all the main areas of modern physics. In the final year there is a choice of options including particle physics, atmospheres and oceans, modern laser physics, and astrophysics. Physics is also offered with Philosophy.

Queen's Belfast Courses in Physics and Theoretical Physics are offered. Physics can also be studied with Applied Mathematics, Astrophysics and Computer Science, and with opportunities for an extended study in Europe. All students take a common course in Level 1 after which they can choose which Physics degree course they wish to follow, or proceed to a degree in another science subject.

St Andrews* Courses include Physics, Astrophysics, Physics with Photonics and Theoretical Physics. The final choice between BSc and MPhys can be postponed until the third level. Institute of Physics bursaries worth £1,000 are available based on academic merit and financial need.

Salford The first year of the Physics course covers subjects ranging from electricity and opto-electronics to thermodynamics and quantum mechanics. Industrial training between Year 2 and Year 3 is considered very important and leads on to a comprehensive study of solid state physics in the final year. A number of Physics joint courses are available including Physics with Acoustics and Pilot Studies or with opportunities to study in Europe or North America. Pure and Applied Physics is also offered.

Sheffield* A broad course in Physics is offered covering both theoretical and experimental aspects including electronics. Physics can be studied with Astrophysics, Medical Physics and Computer Science. There are opportunities to study in North America or Australasia and a degree in Theoretical Physics is also offered.

Southampton* Most of the core course material occupies the first two years, leaving the final year for a selection of advanced topics. These include lasers, cosmology, solid state and advanced quantum mechanics. Options in other scientific subjects can also be taken (chemistry, biology, electronics, geology and computation). Physics courses with Astronomy, Space Science and Nanotechnology are also available.

Strathclyde The first year is common to all courses and provides a foundation in physics, mathematics, electronics, computational physics and experimental measurement. Students may then take a further two years to complete one of the honours degree courses or transfer to the MPhys degree or a BSc award. A BSc course in Physics with Teaching is also offered.

Surrey In addition to the BSc and MSci Physics single honours course, Physics can be taken with Satellite Technology, Finance or Nuclear Astrophysics. All BSc programmes can be taken as a three-year course or a four-year course including a period of professional training at a research laboratory or in industry in the UK, Europe or North America. Students have access to excellent computing facilities and well-resourced teaching laboratories. Optional modules in a broad range of topics are available in all academic years. There is also a degree in Space Technology and Planetary Exploration with hands-on experience in space engineering.

See *Heap 2015: University Degree Course Offers* (Trotman Publishing) for details of offers

Sussex Physics can be studied as a three-year BSc or a four-year MPhys honours course. Both provide a wide range of options in addition to the core subjects, and give students the opportunity to either specialise in a single science strand or to sample a variety of maths and science topics. Other Physics courses include Physics with Astrophysics, Astronomy and Theoretical Physics.

Swansea Courses are offered in, for example, Physics, Physics with Particle Physics and Cosmology with Mathematics, Sports Science and Nanotechnology. In the core course common to each degree there is an intensive study of the main branches of both classical and modern physics, which is continued beyond Level 1. This is supplemented by one of the specialised courses appropriate to the chosen degree.

Warwick* A central core of physics and mathematics is taken by all Physics students, ensuring flexibility and freedom of choice in the courses that follow in the second and third years. Mathematics and Physics and Physics and Business Studies courses are also available.

West Scotland Physics is part of the Science and Technology degree scheme which offers students maximum flexibility in their course specialisms. An optional sandwich placement is included. Physics with Nuclear Technology is also offered.

York* A common first-year course allows for considerable flexibility to change courses. For those not fully committed to a particular course, this enables students to leave their final choice of course until the end of the first year. Other courses include Physics with Business Management, Physics with Astrophysics and Physics with Philosophy.

OTHER INSTITUTIONS OFFERING PHYSICS COURSES
South Devon (Coll).

ALTERNATIVE COURSES
Astronomy, Astrophysics, Computing, Electronics, Geophysics.

PLANT SCIENCES

(including **Botany**)
(*indicates universities with entry requirements over 340 UCAS points)

SUBJECT REQUIREMENTS/PREFERENCES
GCE A level: One or two science subjects are usually required. **GCSE**: Mathematics, if not offered at A level.

SUBJECT INFORMATION
Plant Sciences is concerned with the scientific make up and function of plants. Areas of research can include plant biochemistry, plant genetics, plant conservation and geography. As with other biological sciences, some universities introduce Plant Sciences by way of a common first year with other subjects.

Aberystwyth After a common first year, focusing on plant structure, function, physiology and classification, students can tailor their degree scheme through their choice of module options. Field studies in northern Spain and western Ireland are available.

Birmingham Plant Biology is an option in the Biological Sciences programme. Specialisation can take place at the beginning of the course or in Year 2.

Durham* Two courses are offered in Plant Sciences, one of four years including an industrial placement.

Edinburgh A course in Plant Science including a field course module is offered.

Manchester Three courses in Plant Science are offered, one with industrial experience.

Nottingham The three-year course in Plant Science includes a study of the application of plant sciences in the agricultural, biotechnological, horticultural and food industries. The course offers the option for professional placement and to study abroad at partner universities across the world.

Sheffield Three-year and four-year degrees in Plant Science can be followed with the option of undertaking field courses in the UK or overseas.

OTHER INSTITUTIONS OFFERING PLANT SCIENCES COURSES
Cambridge*, Canterbury Christ Church, East Anglia, Glasgow, Worcester.

ALTERNATIVE COURSES
Biological Sciences, Horticulture.

POLITICS

(including **Government**, **International Relations** and **Peace Studies**)
(* indicates universities with entry requirements over 340 UCAS points)

SUBJECT REQUIREMENTS/PREFERENCES
GCE A level: Foreign languages for courses with a language option. History or English may be required.

SUBJECT INFORMATION
Politics courses have become increasingly popular in recent years and usually cover the politics and government of the major powers. Through the degree courses on offer it is possible to study the politics of almost any country in the world.

QUESTIONS TO CONSIDER
  * Does the course look at politics outside the UK and the US?
  * Are there placement opportunities?
  * Can I study complementary subjects, either as a combined degree or as optional modules?

Aberdeen The course in Politics and International Relations covers Europe and the comparative politics of the US and Britain and political theories and behaviour. At Level 3, options include Scottish politics, Green politics, international peace and international security. Study abroad options in Year 2 are offered in Europe, Hong Kong, Japan and North America.

Aberystwyth A course in International Politics is a multidisciplinary course covering history, sociology, economics and psychology. In addition, there are courses in Political Studies and European Politics and joint courses with International Politics that include Strategic Studies, Intelligence Studies and Military History.

Aston Politics is offered as a joint honours course or as Politics with International Relations. The courses combine history and politics with a strong present-day focus. A placement year is included.

Bangor Political and Social Sciences is offered as a three-year course, which includes modules in psychology, economic and social issues, crime and US history and politics.

Bath* Politics is offered as a joint course with Economics, the main focus being on politics. Three- and four-year schemes are offered in Politics and International Relations whilst Politics can also be studied with French, German, Italian, Russian or Spanish.

Birmingham The first year of the Political Science course consists of social science courses and political core modules. In the second and third years, students take either political theory or political analysis, with a choice of options from British, European, American and comparative European politics. Courses in International Relations are also available, together with courses in Politics, and Political Science, Political Economy and International Relations with Languages or Economics. There is also a degree in War Studies.

Bradford Courses in Peace Studies and Politics provide opportunities to specialise in conflict resolution, international relations and defence and security studies. There are also courses in International Relations and Security Studies.

Brighton Politics can be studied alongside Social Policy, Philosophy with Ethics or Sociology and as part of the Globalisation: History, Politics and Culture BA degree which looks at global society, global networks and global communication to understand the defining issues of our age.

Bristol* Previous study of politics is not necessary for this degree course, which offers a very wide range of specialisms. The course includes a study of political institutions in specific countries and in world politics. It can be studied with Modern Languages – French, German, Italian, Portuguese, Russian or Spanish – and with Philosophy, Sociology, Economics or Policy.

Bristol UWE Politics (joint honours) is part of the Social Science undergraduate modular programme. The course covers European, British and world politics, political philosophy and justice. A degree in International Relations is also offered which can be combined with a variety of subjects including Journalism and Politics.

Brunel Politics and International Politics are offered including joint courses with History, Economics, Professional Development and Sociology. Work placements are arranged in local and national government and abroad.

Buckingham Two-year courses in Politics can be taken with Economics, History and Law. A wide range of options is offered in the Economics and Law programmes. A course in International Studies is also offered.

Cambridge* See under **Social Sciences**.

Canterbury Christ Church The Politics and Global Government course offers an overview of national, international and global political developments. There are separate courses in International Relations and Politics, Politics, and Politics and Government.

Cardiff* Part I of the Politics course covers the foundation of Western political theory, electoral systems, party systems, and internal and international war. Part II offers a number of optional subjects including European Union policy and the comparative systems of Britain, France, Germany, Italy, Sweden and the US. Joint degrees are also offered in European Politics, International Relations, Law and Medieval History.

Central Lancashire Politics is offered as part of the combined honours programme and can be taken with History, Philosophy or Social Policy. There is also a course in Human Rights.

Chester The International Development Studies course focuses on socio-economic, political, cultural and environmental aspects, exploring the Third World and comparisons between rich and poor, urban and rural, and contemporary and historical. Politics is also offered as a single or combined honours course and covers subjects such as British government, political thinkers and social policy.

See *Heap 2015: University Degree Course Offers* (Trotman Publishing) for details of offers

City The International Politics degree includes global policy-making, and intergovernmental organisations such as the United Nations, the European Union and the World Bank. A wide range of elective modules is offered in each year of the course. There is also a course in International Politics and Sociology.

Coventry The Politics single honours course covers topics including political theory and key world events. There is also a separate programme in International Relations.

De Montfort The new Politics BA looks at global comparative policies, policy and society and the British government in the first year with a wide range of options available in the second and third years of the course. The degree in Politics and Government covers British and global politics including modules on the government, public sector topics and healthcare. A course in International Relations is also offered.

Derby Courses are offered in Third World Development and in International Relations and Global Development; both are available as joint honours with subjects including Geography, Law and Psychology.

Dundee Politics is offered as a single or joint honours course with 11 subjects in the Arts and Social Sciences or combined honours programmes. The course covers British and European politics and has a wide range of options including Scottish politics. There are also courses in International Relations that can be combined with American or European Studies or History, and courses in European Politics and Geopolitics.

Durham* All first-year Politics students take an introduction to politics course followed by a further eight courses, two of which may be taken from other subject areas, usually within the Faculty of Social Sciences. There are opportunities to specialise in non-Western politics. Politics can be taken with a year in Europe. Courses are also available in PPE and with Sociology, Philosophy, Economics.

East Anglia The Politics course is extremely flexible and allows students to customise their course. There are currently over 20 specialised modules from which to choose, ranging from Russian and American politics to conflict resolution and Big Brother. Courses in European Politics and International Relations are also available. There are opportunities for parliamentary and other internships.

East London The Politics course includes a study of politics in its social and economic settings, political theory and historical ideas, government in Britain and other European countries, the law, human and civic rights and local government. There are also courses in International Third World Development and International Politics.

Edinburgh The four-year (leading to an MA) Politics degree course offers an introduction to political theory, British government and administration. In the third and fourth years, options are offered in European politics, political parties and the politics of the former Soviet Union, Eastern Europe, the US and Africa. Politics is also offered with Persian and Arabic in addition to a range of other subjects. There is also a degree in International Relations.

Essex The Department of Government offers a wide range of courses in two main degrees: Politics and International Relations and Politics. A range of specialist options are available covering world politics, democracy and human rights. Twelve other joint courses are also available. There is also a course in Philosophy, Politics and Economics.

Exeter Single honours Politics students take courses in all branches of the subject. Opportunities to study in Europe, the US, Canada or Australia are offered. Courses are offered in a range of subjects including Economics and Politics, Philosophy and Political Economy and International Relations.

Glasgow* The Politics course is distinctive in concentrating on ideas and ideologies, liberalism and socialism while looking at political institutions and parties. Political organisations' behaviour in the UK and the US is studied as well as an optional 30 courses.

See *Heap 2015: University Degree Course Offers* (Trotman Publishing) for details of offers

Greenwich The Politics course focuses mainly on British and European politics and aspects of society. Spanish, History, Philosophy and International Studies can also be studied with Politics.

Huddersfield The Politics course involves British government and politics, European politics and American politics. In addition there is a degree in International Politics. Politics can also be studied with Contemporary History, Criminology and Sociology.

Hull An imaginative and broad Politics programme, allowing several specialist options from the single honours course, is provided. Politics, Philosophy and Economics or Law are also offered. There is also a course in International Relations and a four-year course in British Politics and Legislative Studies. There are also courses in Globalisation and Governance and War and Security Studies.

Keele Politics can be taken as a single or dual honours subject with over 25 courses including Philosophy, Economics and History. There is also a single or joint course in International Relations.

Kent The department offers two main programmes, Politics, and Politics and International Relations, which can be taken with French, German or Italian and an optional year in countries including Finland, Japan or the Czech Republic. Other courses include Social Policy, Economics and Politics, Conflict, Peace and Security and Politics and Social Anthropology. The highly reputed War Studies course covers military history, warfare and the new technology and propaganda.

Kingston Politics is offered as a single honours course (Politics and International Relations) or as part of the modular scheme that offers a choice from more than 15 subjects including Journalism, Psychology and Languages. There are several joint courses with International Relations.

Lancaster In the first year of Politics with International Relations, students take politics (including British and American government and international relations) and two other subjects, for example law, religious studies, history or economics. In Years 2 and 3 a wide range of political topics is covered including political thought, government, comparative politics, international relations and strategic studies. Other degree courses include Peace Studies and International Relations and Politics with a year abroad. A course in Philosophy, Politics and Economics is also offered.

Leeds In the first year of the Political Studies course, compulsory subjects cover an introduction to politics and British government and an explanation of political ideas. Second-year subjects cover foreign governments and comparative world governments and political and social history. A wide range of final-year optional subjects are available. Politics and Parliamentary Studies is a unique course involving five months working as an intern in a Congress member's or senator's office in Ottawa or Washington DC, and a similar period in the House of Commons. There are also courses in European Politics, Politics and Parliamentary Studies, International Development and International Relations.

Leeds Beckett Relevant courses include Global Development, Peace Studies and International Relations. The BA in Politics covers world politics from parties and elections through to political participation and engagement.

Leicester Politics is offered as a single honours course with an opportunity to spend a second-year semester in Europe, or the subject can be studied with Economics, Management or Sociology. Courses in International Relations (or with History) are also available.

Lincoln The single honours degree in Politics covers all aspects of British politics and government and introduces international politics in the US, EU and Middle East. It can be taken as a joint honours course with a range of other subjects. There are also degrees in International Relations with Politics or Social Policy.

Liverpool The Politics course covers British politics in Year 1 and, later, Western European, Russian, American, Latin American and South American politics. Special subjects include the media, immigration and environmental politics. Communication Studies and International Business can be studied with Politics. There is also a course in International Politics and Policy.

See *Heap 2015: University Degree Course Offers* (Trotman Publishing) for details of offers

Liverpool Hope The course covers British politics, political ideas and the politics of international relations. In Year 3, a study is undertaken of American and European politics. There are also several joint courses in Politics and a course in Politics and International Relations is offered.

London (Goldsmiths)* Politics is offered with Economics, International Studies or Public Policy, or as a single honours subject. European politics, political ideas and public administration also feature in the course.

London (King's)* A BA programme in War Studies can be followed either as a three-year course or for four years with an optional year abroad. The subject focuses on the impact of war on human society from ancient times to the present day. A course in International Politics is also offered.

London (QM)* The Politics course focuses on specialisation in modern Western political institutions, theory and ideas. There are also several joint honours programmes including Russian, French or German, Hispanic Studies, Business Management and Economics. There is also a course in International Relations.

London (RH)* Politics can be taken as a single honours or joint honours subject with International Relations or Philosophy. All first-year students take a common package of courses leading to optional courses in Year 2.

London (SOAS)* Single-subject and joint degree Politics students all take an introduction to political study and comparative politics focusing on Africa and Asia. Students then follow a programme with an increasing optional element. Courses taught at SOAS stress the issues and problems more specific to the non-European world, but the opportunity exists to choose courses at other colleges within the university. Politics is also offered with a wide range of African and Far Eastern languages.

London (UCL)* Politics and East European Studies is offered as a three-year full-time degree. Compulsory courses are taken in Years 1 and 2 in politics, government and international relations, with a wide range of options available in the third year.

London LSE The first-year Government course covers an introduction to the study of politics and political theory. Years 2 and 3 offer courses in the politics and governments of other countries. Options in other subjects are offered each year. International Relations courses are also offered. There are also courses in Government and Economics and Government and History.

London Met Politics is offered as a single or joint subject with an introductory Year 1 and the chance to specialise in Years 2 and 3. Other parallel courses include International Relations and Peace and Conflict Studies.

London NCH The Politics and International Studies course involves 12 course modules, in addition to which students choose five further modules from other subjects including Art History, Classical Studies, Economics, English, History, Law, Philosophy or Psychology.

London South Bank The Politics course provides a sound understanding of contemporary political issues and covers a wide range of social science subjects and political issues in Europe, the US and the Third World.

Loughborough* Three-year and four-year Politics and International Relations courses are available with minor subjects in Economics, Social Psychology, French, German, Spanish, Sociology or English. The Politics element provides a thorough grounding in political science with particular reference to Western and Eastern European states, the European Union, the US and the former Soviet states. Language students may opt to spend the third year in, for example, France or Germany. Politics may also be studied with History or International Studies.

Manchester The Department of Government is one of the largest in Britain, enabling students to build a good foundation in the study of politics, covering Anglo-American, European and international politics, with opportunities to specialise in the final year. Politics can be studied with Criminology or International Relations and there is also a degree in PPE.

Manchester Met A three-year Politics course covers politics, sociology, social administration and economics. There are also courses in International Politics, Political History and Public Services.

Middlesex A degree in International Politics covering aspects of the subject across the world, including issues of globalism and disasters development, is offered as a single or joint course.

Newcastle The Politics course covers British politics, world politics, an introduction to democratic politics and political ideas, together with one or two from a range of other subjects including languages, history, law and psychology. In Stages 2 and 3 the focus is on political studies that cover Western Europe, Africa, East Asia, the US and China. Politics can also be studied with Economics, History or Sociology. There is also a degree in Government and European Union Studies that includes language study as part of the course (French, German, Spanish or Portuguese) and involves a year abroad.

Northampton Politics is offered as a single or joint course. The first year focuses on politics in the UK with the second-year compulsory modules focusing on European politics. There is a wide range of optional modules to choose throughout the three-year degree.

Northumbria The Politics course covers British politics, political institutions and behaviour and international relations. The course has a strong European and international focus. History can also be studied with Politics.

Nottingham* This degree concentrates on three key areas within the study of politics: comparative politics, political theory, and international relations. A wide selection of optional modules allows students to specialise in a variety of different areas, such as the European Union, British politics, the government and politics of the US, terrorism and security, and globalisation. There is also a degree in European Politics and a BA in International Relations.

Nottingham Trent Politics is studied as a three-year single honours programme, and is also offered with International Relations and History. There are also several joint courses in International Relations.

Oxford* Politics is offered with Philosophy and Economics or with History. In the first year of the PPE course all three subjects are studied equally; the decision to focus on two or all three of the subjects is made in the second year. Scholarships available.

Oxford Brookes Politics is offered with over 40 separate subjects including Communications, Media and Culture, Sociology and Philosophy. There is also a wide range of International Relations courses.

Plymouth The Politics course can be taken as a joint honours, major or minor subject. It largely covers British and European politics but provides options in the politics of Eastern Europe and Third World issues. The subject is also combined with Economics, History, International Relations and Criminology and Criminal Justice Systems. There is also a range of joint courses with International Relations.

Portsmouth In the first year, Politics is studied alongside political economics, political thought and current politics. In Years 2 and 3, core courses are accompanied by options. There are also degrees in International Relations with Politics, History and Sociology.

Queen's Belfast All students take four basic courses: politics of Britain and Ireland, contemporary Europe, world politics and politics in a media culture. In Years 2 and 3 students choose from over 25 modules covering all aspects of the subject. Politics can be studied with another subject from a wide range including International Studies, Irish and Celtic, Law, Social Policy, Modern History and Psychological Studies. There are also courses in International Studies emphasising conflict resolution, Politics, Philosophy and Economics, and European Integration.

Reading The degree course in Politics and International Relations covers the politics of the UK, the US, former Soviet states, Africa and Northern, Southern and Western Europe. There are also courses in Politics with International Relations or Economics and in War, Peace and International Relations.

See *Heap 2015: University Degree Course Offers* (Trotman Publishing) for details of offers

St Andrews* Degree courses are offered in International Relations either as single or joint honours courses. Programmes of study include themes in 20th-century international relations, power and violence, and peace and governance in world politics.

Salford Politics can be taken as a single honours or joint degree with Contemporary History, Journalism, Arabic and several other subjects. There are opportunities for placement in Westminster.

Sheffield* The Politics course introduces British politics, moving on to international politics and political ideas. Specialised modules follow at Level 3. There are also courses with International Relations and Philosophy.

Sheffield Hallam The course focuses on politics, political structures and recent developments on a UK, European and global scale looking at issues such as environmental damage, the impact of technology and human rights.

Southampton All Politics students in the Social Sciences Faculty take an introductory first-year course in politics and may also take a course in another subject. In Years 2 and 3 students become progressively more specialised and may opt for such topics as arms control. Politics and International Relations or Languages, Philosophy or Modern History are also offered.

Stirling The first three semesters (Part I) introduce the practical and theoretical aspects of politics and survey different political systems. Part II is designed to develop analytical skills and there are courses in nationalism, political philosophy and environmentalism. There is also a course in Politics, Philosophy and Economics and a separate degree in International Politics, and also joint courses including Politics and Business Studies, Psychology or Sociology.

Strathclyde Politics is offered as part of the Arts and Social Studies programme. Honours students select from a wide range of options in Years 2 and 3.

Sunderland Politics can be taken jointly with a wide range of subjects including American Studies, Criminology, Health and Social Care, Media Studies, Music, Photography, Tourism and Public Relations.

Surrey* Students are able to choose from a range of programmes including Politics, International Politics, Politics with Policy Studies, International Politics with English for International Communication, and Politics with French, German or Spanish.

Sussex* Politics is available as a single honours course and in combination with nine other subjects including International Relations, which is also available as single honours and in other joint courses. Students are increasingly encouraged to become independent and self-directed learners.

Swansea A degree in Politics and International Relations is offered, leading to specialist studies in Years 2 and 3. There are also several joint courses in both these subjects. A course in Political Communication is also available. See also **Philosophy**.

Ulster The degree in International Politics can be taken with 12 other subjects. There is also a three-year Politics degree available singly or with combinations.

Warwick* The courses in Politics have been designed to cater for a wide range of interests. There is the opportunity to spend the second year in an overseas university. As well as the single honours degree, Politics may be combined with Economics, History, Philosophy, Sociology, French or International Studies and there is a course in Philosophy, Politics and Economics.

West Scotland Politics is available as a joint degree and can be studied with Psychology, Social Policy or Sociology. The course focuses on British, American, European and Scottish politics.

Westminster The Politics course covers British, American and European politics. It involves four core modules and more than 12 options. Politics can also be studied with Arabic or Chinese. Courses are also available in International Relations.

Winchester The Politics and Global Studies course focuses largely on international issues and applies the study of fixed historical and cultural contexts to the analysis and consideration of contemporary issues.

Wolverhampton Politics can be taken as part of the modular degree programme. The main focus is on British, European and American politics, and degrees include Politics and Religious Studies, History, Social Policy or Media and Communication Studies. War Studies and Politics is also offered.

Worcester Politics, People and Power offers a 'people-centred' view of politics with the opportunity to study for one semester in Europe, Canada, the US or Australia.

York* A wide spectrum of subjects is covered in the degree course in Politics. These include the major governmental systems of a range of countries. Subject strengths include Third World and British politics and political philosophy. Politics can also be studied with Economics, English, Philosophy and History. Social and Political Sciences and Philosophy, Politics and Economics are also offered. See also **English** and **Combined Courses**.

OTHER INSTITUTIONS OFFERING POLITICS COURSES
Blackburn (Coll), Euro Bus Sch London, Richmond (Am Int Univ), Staffordshire Reg Fed (SURF), Truro (Coll), Worcester (CT).

ALTERNATIVE COURSES
Economic History, Economics, Government, History, International Relations, Public Administration, Public and Social Policy, Social Administration, Social Sciences, Social Studies, Sociology.

PROPERTY MANAGEMENT AND SURVEYING

(including **Housing Studies**)
(see also **Town Planning and Urban Planning Studies**)
(* indicates universities with entry requirements over 340 UCAS points)

SUBJECT REQUIREMENTS/PREFERENCES
GCSE: English and Mathematics required, and for some institutions a science subject (for professional body registration).

SUBJECT INFORMATION
Surveying is a very broad subject (and career) that includes several specialisms, for example building surveying, quantity surveying, land valuation surveying and architecture, which could also be considered as alternative courses. Most courses cover very similar topics and lead to professional qualifications, giving exemptions from the examinations of the RICS.

Aberdeen A degree in Real Estate is offered as a joint honours degree with Economics.

Anglia Ruskin The range of programmes includes Building Surveying, Real Estate Management and Quantity Surveying. The surveying courses are in partnership with the RICS, providing students with exemption from RICS academic requirements.

Birmingham City The course in Real Estate covers building structures and environmental and planning issues. The course is fully accredited by the RICS for those aiming for a career as a chartered surveyor.

Bishop Grosseteste Some joint honours courses are available.

See *Heap 2015: University Degree Course Offers* (Trotman Publishing) for details of offers

Bolton A course in Building Surveying and Property Management is offered with work placements included.

Brighton The first and second years of the Building Surveying course cover building performance, built environment, building surveying practice and the professional environment. The third year covers a range of options, including a dissertation.

Bristol UWE There are courses in Business in Property and Property Investment and Management, Property Development, Town and Country Planning and Real Estate (Valuation and Management). Quantity Surveying and Commercial Management is a three-year or four-year sandwich course with professional placement in the third year. Topics include construction technology and measurement, contract and legal studies. Final-year studies cover project and conflict management, value and risk management and cost modelling. Maximum exemptions are afforded to graduates from relevant professional body examinations for this and the Building Surveying course.

Cambridge* The Land Economy course covers environment, law and economics and is concerned with the use of land and property and with the protection of the environment. Students take courses in law and economics relating to the ownership, exploitation, planning and protection of land, and explore the issues raised. The degree gives full exemption from RICS examinations. Not available at the following Colleges: Churchill, Corpus Christi, Emmanuel, King's and Peterhouse.

Central Lancashire Courses are offered in Building Surveying, Construction Project Management and Quantity Surveying, all of which can be taken with an industrial placement of one year.

City* Real Estate Finance and Investment is designed to meet the needs of qualified specialists in the field of property, finance and investment, law and taxation. Valuation is studied throughout the course, along with building design and construction, company structure and planning. The course has an optional placement year and professional body recognition. See also **Engineering**.

Coventry Building Surveying is a three-year or four-year (sandwich) course in the built environment. There is the option to spend the placement year abroad with an International partner institution. Courses are also offered in Quantity Surveying and Commercial Management.

Derby Joint courses are offered in Property Development.

East London A course in Surveying and Mapping Sciences covers environmental science and information technology, mathematics and physics to equip students with the skills to map, measure and analyse spatial measurements.

Edinburgh Napier Courses are offered in Building and Quantity Surveying. Both courses are accredited by the RICS, making graduates eligible for chartered surveyor status following industry experience.

Glasgow Caledonian The Quantity Surveying course includes a six-month period of supervised work placement with private offices, contractors and local authorities. Building Surveying, Construction Management and Property Management and Valuation are also offered.

Glyndŵr The Estate Management degree covers both natural and built environments with options in housing, planning and surveying. The Estate Agency course involves the investment and marketing of property. There is also a degree in Housing Studies and Housing and Sustainable Communities.

Greenwich The Building Surveying (Commercial Management) course can be studied on a three-year full-time or four-year sandwich basis. The main subjects cover construction technology, design, economics of land and building, law and management. Quantity Surveying is a three-year full-time, four-year sandwich or five-year part-time course with topics focusing on construction technology, measurement, law and economics. Professional practice on the sandwich course comes in Year 3. It has professional body recognition, as is the case with the degree in Estate Management.

Harper Adams Professionally accredited courses are offered in Rural Property Management and Rural Environmental Land Management.

Heriot-Watt In the first two years of the Quantity Surveying course, building technology, materials, management, measurement and valuation studies are included. Emphasis on quantity surveying studies begins in the third year and continues to the end of the final (fourth) year. Professional and industrial practice is also included. Urban Planning and Property Development is also offered. Courses are validated by the Town Planning and Chartered Surveying Professional bodies.

Kingston The four-year Quantity Surveying Consultancy sandwich course focuses on basic economic theory and the principles of law lead on to applications in building work in Years 1 and 2. The third year is spent in professional placement. Other studies cover construction technology and measurement. Exemptions from relevant professional body examinations are gained on graduation, similarly with the courses in Real Estate Management, Residential Property, Property Planning and Development and Building Surveying.

Leeds Beckett The Quantity Surveying course provides a thorough understanding of all aspects of quantity surveying and building economics. Distinct themes include measurement and contractual procedures, cost price, and various supporting studies. There is professional body recognition. A course in Building Surveying is also offered. See also **Building**.

Liverpool John Moores Quantity Surveying is a three-year full-time or four-year sandwich course. Industrial training takes place in the third year of the four-year course, which includes economic, quantitative and legal studies and construction management. There are exemptions from professional body examinations. There are also courses in Building Surveying and Real Estate Management.

London South Bank Building Surveying is a three-year full-time course. Subject areas cover construction, quantitative, economic, legal and management studies. The course should not be confused with Building Services Engineering. Quantity Surveying is also offered and shares a common first year with Building Surveying. The degrees give professional exam exemptions. A three-year degree course in Housing Studies is also offered.

Loughborough The Commercial Management and Quantity Surveying programme, sponsored by major contractors, covers construction technology, law, economics, management and professional practice. The course is studied over four years with a placement in the third year.

Northumbria* Commercial Quantity Surveying is a three-year full-time or four-year sandwich course with professional placement in Year 3. There is also a European route with one year of work and study abroad. Core subjects follow the set pattern prescribed by the RICS for exemptions from their examinations. Courses are also offered in Building Surveying and Estate Management.

Nottingham Trent Building and Quantity Surveying are offered from the Department of Surveying. Courses are also offered in Real Estate, Planning and Development, and Property Finance and Investment.

Oxford Brookes* The Real Estate Management course is designed primarily for those students aiming to become chartered surveyors in the general practice division. The curriculum focuses on subjects based on valuation, building technology, town planning, economics and law.

Portsmouth The three-year Property Development with Quantity Surveying course covers in depth all the aspects of quantity surveying practice. The course also introduces new themes for future development in the field such as computer use, cost planning and design management. Financial management is an important feature of the course. The course is accredited by the RICS.

Reading There are four themes that run through the programmes: development and planning, investment and finance in property, urban property management and valuation, and rural studies. These programmes are highly integrated. This gives students the opportunity to move between the programmes easily in the first or second year, when they may still not be certain which aspect of property or planning most appeals to them. The courses offered cover Real Estate, Investment and Finance in Property, Real-estate and Urban Planning and Rural Property Management. Quantity Surveying and Building Surveying are also offered.

Royal Agricultural Univ The courses in Property Agency and Management, Real Estate and Land Management and Rural Land Management all lead to professional qualifications.

Salford Building Surveying is a thee-year full-time or four-year sandwich course and incorporates elements common to the degree course in Quantity Surveying. There are three main study areas: professional, management and construction studies, leading to project work in the final year. Quantity Surveying is a four-year sandwich course, the third year being spent in approved professional experience. Construction technology is taken throughout Years 1, 2 and 4, with other aspects of science and design. Other subjects include management, finance and applied economics and mathematics and computing. A course is also offered in Property Management and Investment.

Sheffield Hallam Building Surveying is studied in common with Quantity Surveying, with transfers possible at the early stages. Years 2 and 4 cover construction technology, building services, law, economics, building surveying, design and refurbishment. The third year is spent in professional placement. Urban and Environmental Planning covers land administration, economics, valuations, planning and building. This is a four-year course in which the third year is spent in professional training. Other courses offered include Planning and Property Development.

South Wales Several courses are offered leading to professional qualification. These cover Quantity Surveying and Commercial Management, Project Management (Construction) and Surveying.

Ulster Surveying is offered with specialisms in Building and Quantity Surveying and there are also courses in Housing Management and Planning and Property Development and Property Investment, Appraisal and Development.

Westminster Degree courses in Building and Quantity Surveying are offered, giving professional body exemptions from examinations. Similarly, the degree in Real Estate also gives exemptions from RICS examinations. There are also courses in Business and Property and Property and Planning.

Wolverhampton A degree in Building Surveying is offered and there are also RICS-validated degrees in Quantity Surveying and in Commercial Management and Quantity Surveying.

ALTERNATIVE COURSES
Accountancy, Architecture, Building, Civil Engineering, Housing, Structural Engineering, Town Planning, Urban Studies.

PSYCHOLOGY

(including **Behavioural Science**)
(* indicates universities with entry requirements over 340 UCAS points)

SUBJECT REQUIREMENTS/PREFERENCES
GCE A level: One or two science subjects may be required for BSc courses. **GCSE:** English, Mathematics and/or a science may be required.

SUBJECT INFORMATION

Psychology is an ever-popular subject, covering studies in development, perception, learning, personality as well as social and abnormal psychology. (It is not training to enable you to psychoanalyse your friends!) **NB** All courses approved for future training as psychologists are listed in the publications of the British Psychological Society, St Andrews House, 48 Princess Road East, Leicester LE1 7DR.

QUESTIONS TO CONSIDER

　＊ Is the course accredited by the British Psychological Society and can it lead to registration as a chartered psychologist?
　＊ Can I specialise with either a more focused degree or choice of modules?
　＊ Is there a chance for work experience?

Aberdeen The honours course in Psychology is recognised by the British Psychological Society (BPS) and after Levels 1 and 2 there is a wide range of options available, including biological psychology, developmental psychology, memory, social psychology and perception. There are opportunities for study abroad in the second year.

Abertay The four-year Behavioural Science course integrates the study of psychology and sociology with specialised options that include health, sociology, psychology and human rights. There are opportunities for work placement in Year 4. There is also a course in Forensic Psychobiology and a Psychology degree covering biology, cognitive development and social psychology. Psychology is available with Sport or Counselling.

Aberystwyth Psychology is offered as a single honours programme or as joint honours degree schemes with Criminology, Education, English Literature or Marketing. Year 1 modules include social and developmental psychology, biological and cognitive psychology, individual differences psychology and applications of psychology.

Anglia Ruskin Psychology can be taken as a single or a combined honours subject. The course covers social, health, developmental and forensic psychology. Joint courses are offered with Criminology and a course in Abnormal and Clinical Psychology is also offered.

Aston The Psychology course is an applied programme with three-year and four-year sandwich courses. Students on the four-year course spend a year on work experience. Its emphasis is on the study of human behaviour and the underlying mental processes, with final-year options in health and forensic psychology, clinical neurosciences and developmental disorders. Psychology is also offered as part of the combined honours programme.

Bangor The range of academic specialisms within the school currently enables students to choose from courses as varied as Clinical and Health Psychology, Psychology with Neuropsychology and Psychology with Child and Language Development. The school has a number of prestigious research centres including the Wolfson Centre for Cognitive Neuroscience, the Centre for Experimental Consumer Research and the Wales Centre for Behaviour Analysis.

Bath* The Department of Psychology offers a BSc course in Psychology focusing on cognitive developments and health and social psychology. Compulsory worldwide industrial placements in Year 3 are in clinical, occupational, educational or research settings. See also **Combined Courses**.

Bath Spa The course in Psychology provides an introduction to the scientific study of human behaviour with an emphasis on real-world applications. Bursaries are available.

Bedfordshire The Psychology course has core modules in social, cognitive and developmental psychology and specialisms in counselling, child, sport and clinical psychology. In Year 1 an elective subject from another department can be taken, for example languages, anthropology or sociology. During Years 1 and 2, core subjects in psychology are taken. Other courses include Applied Psychology (a vocational degree with a one-year placement), Health Psychology, Psychology, Counselling and Therapies and Psychology with Criminology or Criminal Behaviour.

See *Heap 2015: University Degree Course Offers* (Trotman Publishing) for details of offers

Birmingham* The Psychology course provides a scientific study of behaviour in all its aspects related to developmental and child psychology, perception, learning, social, abnormal psychology and neuropsychology. In the final year, students choose from a number of options in contemporary psychology including forensic and clinical psychology. See also **Combined Courses**.

Birmingham City Psychology can be studied over three years full time or five years part time and is accredited by the BPS. There is also a course in Criminology combined with Psychology.

Bolton Work placements are offered on the Psychology degree, which includes modules in social, development and abnormal psychology and mental health. There are specialisms in Counselling and Psychology and Criminological and Forensic Psychology.

Bournemouth The Psychology course offers a study of human factors, social psychology and forensic psychology. In addition there is also a Sports Psychology and Coaching Sciences degree.

Bradford Specialisation takes place in Year 3 in this Psychology degree, in such subjects as forensic psychology, psychological health and treatment interventions and the psychology of health and eating behaviour. Psychology can be taken with Crime, Economics, Counselling or Management Psychology.

Brighton There are courses in Applied Psychology and Sociology or Criminology. The courses share modules such as developmental psychology, ICT for the social sciences and an introduction to research methods alongside specialist subjects.

Bristol* The emphasis in the Psychology course is on both human and animal behaviour. Courses in the first two years provide a basis for specialisation in the third year and cover perception, learning, motivation, personality, social and physiological psychology. One additional subject is taken from another department in the first year. Psychology is also available with Philosophy. A single honours degree in Neuroscience is also offered, studied alongside anthropology and physiology.

Bristol UWE The degree in Psychology is a single or joint honours programme and is accredited by the BPS. Various specialist modules are offered including social, health, biological and applied psychology. Psychology is also offered with Criminology, Law and Sociology.

Brunel During the first and second years of the Psychology course a broad approach is taken which covers the core areas of cognitive, biological, social, abnormal and development psychology. Options including autism, mental health and cognitive neuroscience are offered in Year 3. Brunel offers an integrated sandwich course with three placements. Psychology is also offered with Anthropology and Sociology.

Buckingham The two-year programme in Psychology (January and September start dates) includes cognition and perception and social psychology in Year 1 and specialist subjects in business, health and clinical psychology in Year 2 of the degree programme. Psychology can also be taken with Business and Management, English Literature, French, Information Systems, Media Communications, Spanish or Marketing.

Bucks New Psychology can be taken as a single honours degree or jointly with Criminology or Sociology. There are also degrees in Criminological Psychology and Sports Psychology.

Cambridge* See also **Combined Courses**.

Canterbury Christ Church Psychology is offered as a single or combined degree programme. Final-year modules include the psychology of work, psychology and the therapeutic process, media and applied psychology. There is also a degree in Sport and Exercise Psychology.

Cardiff* The Psychology degree is a modular course in which modules focus on social, biological and cognitive psychology in Year 1. In Part II (second and third years) core courses and options are taken, including social and occupational psychology, abnormal psychology and clinical and counselling psychology. Final-year options lead to vocational and professional areas of work. There is also a course which includes a professional placement.

Cardiff Met (UWIC) The course is accredited by the BPS with third-year options in media, forensic and health psychology; culture and identity development; psychological perspectives on reading; and applied human cognition.

Central Lancashire In the third year Psychology students take eight options from a wide range and also complete a project. The decision as to which course to follow is taken in Year 2. Psychology is also available on the combined honours programme with a choice from eight other subjects and there are also courses in Forensic Psychology, Neuropsychology, Health Psychology, Neuroscience and Sport Psychology, or in joint courses with Business, Education, Law, Health or Forensic Sciences. There is also a course in Counselling and Psychotherapy.

Chester The Psychology degree is approved for those wishing to become psychologists. The course emphasises the importance of practical work and involves interviewing, observation and experimentation with modules in specialist fields. There is also a vocational course in Counselling taken as part of the combined honours programme.

City* Psychology is studied as a three-year degree course and involves cognitive and social psychology, learning, and clinical and abnormal psychology. Specialist subjects include health psychology, organisational psychology, and memory, trends and issues.

Colchester (Inst) There is a BA course in Counselling in which students work with clients in Year 2.

Coventry A modular course in Psychology is offered with a focus on developmental, biological and social psychology and health. There are also courses with Criminology and Sport Psychology.

Cumbria The Applied Psychology degree includes options in forensics, health, community and organisational psychology. Core modules include physiological and cognitive psychology, issues and applications in contemporary psychology, and settings in psychology.

De Montfort This is a comprehensive Psychology course covering human communication, language development, developmental, social, educational and clinical psychology and counselling. Psychology is also offered as part of the joint/major/minor degree schemes and can be taken with Criminology, Health Studies and Education Studies.

Derby The course in Psychology leads to registration as a chartered psychologist. Child, cognitive and social psychology are studied in Year 1. Options in Year 3 include the psychology of emotion, criminology, sexuality and gender, psychotherapy, vision and psycholinguistics. Psychology can also be taken as a joint subject. A course is also offered in Sport Psychology.

Dundee Students gaining a second class honours degree will have satisfied the requirements of the BPS and can specialise in subjects including clinical, counselling, educational, forensic, health and occupational psychology. Psychology is also offered with French, German, Spanish, Mathematics or Computing.

Durham A course in Applied Psychology at Stockton focuses on everyday issues such as health, education and neuropsychological rehabilitation. The BSc Psychology degree at Durham covers cognitive, biological, social, developmental and abnormal psychology and perception. Psychology is also offered as part of the Social Sciences combined honours programmes.

East Anglia The Psychology course draws upon psychology and perspectives on human behaviour. Theoretical ideas are introduced from fields including developmental, social, cognitive and biological psychology.

East London The Psychology course is recognised by the BPS and covers mental health, counselling and families. Specialised courses are offered in Critical, Developmental and Forensic Psychology. Psychology can also be studied with Criminology, Biology or Health Studies. Degrees in Psychosocial Studies are also offered.

Edge Hill A broad introduction to Psychology takes place in Year 1 with electives being chosen in Years 2 and 3 depending on the student's particular interests and career objectives. There are also courses offered in Counselling, Educational Psychology, Health Psychology and Sport and Exercise Psychology.

See *Heap 2015: University Degree Course Offers* (Trotman Publishing) for details of offers

Edinburgh A general introduction to Psychology in Year 1 is followed by a mainly experimental and biological programme in Year 2. (Entry to the honours course is then conditional on obtaining grades A or B in Psychology in Year 2.) Compulsory core subjects in Year 3 combine with a range of options such as social psychology or animal behaviour. A wide range of options continues in Year 4. Research methods and analysis are included in the first three years.

Edinburgh Napier Psychology is offered as a single honours subject or as a joint honours with Sociology. The courses focus on both the theory and practice of psychology, preparing students for a professional career.

Edinburgh Queen Margaret Psychology can be taken as a single honours or jointly with Sociology. The course can be studied over three years (ordinary) or four years (honours) and enables students to take further training as a chartered psychologist.

Essex The schemes are identical for both BA and BSc courses in Psychology. Options taken in Year 2 dictate the final degree. The course has an emphasis on cognitive science, linguistics and the social sciences. Psychology can be combined with Criminology and there are also courses in Social Psychology. See also **Health Studies/Sciences**.

Exeter* Single honours Psychology courses are available in the Faculties of Science and Social Studies although the syllabus is much the same in both, only ancillary subjects being different. The course covers the whole field of psychology – comparative, physiological, social and abnormal – with students being introduced to clinical and other applications of the subject. There is a relatively high practical component to the course and considerable freedom in the choice of options.

Glasgow* Computation techniques, abnormal and developmental psychology and cognitive science are included on the Psychology course. Psychology can be studied with other subjects including Italian, Celtic Civilisation, English Literature and History of Art. See also **Social Studies/Science**.

Glasgow Caledonian There is a wide range of options in this Psychology course, which has an emphasis on small group teaching. Modules are offered in abnormal, health, and forensic and occupational psychology. There are also courses in Psychology and Interactive Entertainment and Human Biology with Sociology and Psychology.

Gloucestershire The Psychology course provides a broad basis for further training as a specialist psychologist. Joint courses are also offered including Psychology and Animal Biology, Criminology or Sociology.

Glyndŵr The Psychology degree covers cognitive, developmental and social aspects of the subject leading to specialisms in the work field such as educational and occupational psychology.

Greenwich Courses are offered in Psychology and Psychology with Counselling. The courses are accredited by the BPS, leading to registration for those holding a second class honours degree.

Heriot-Watt The course in Applied Psychology (recognised by the BPS) focuses on its uses in education, work and organisations, health and mental health, sport and crime. A course in Forensic Psychology is offered and a single honours Psychology course, which can also be combined with Human Health or Management.

Hertfordshire The Psychology course provides a grounding in all the major areas of psychology. In Year 3, 12 optional courses are offered. Courses in Counselling and a range of 18 Psychology joint courses are also offered.

Huddersfield The Behavioural Sciences course offers a firm grounding in psychology and sociology with an applied focus. Third-year options include psychology and sociology modules. A broad Psychology course is offered and in addition it is also possible to take degrees in Criminology and Counselling Studies.

Hull In Year 1 all Psychology students study core psychological theory, followed in Year 2 by social, developmental, biological and cognitive psychology and a course in clinical psychology. In Year 3 students choose their specialisms, which include occupational, educational, health, clinical and counselling psychology. There are four major/minor subjects available to study with Psychology: Criminology, Philosophy, Sociology and Sport Science.

Keele Single, joint or major/minor courses are offered in Psychology, with 31 subjects offered at joint honours and 11 offered as minor subjects. There is also a degree in Neuroscience.

Kent Psychology, Social Psychology and Applied Psychology courses provide a broad base from which to specialise. Clinical psychology features largely in some programmes. Psychology can be taken with Clinical Psychology, Law, Social Anthropology and Sociology.

Kingston Psychology is offered as part of the modular course with a choice of some 10 other subjects including languages (French or Spanish), Criminology, Journalism and Creative Writing.

Lancaster* Developmental, cognitive biopsychology and social psychology are taken in the first year of the BSc and BA Psychology course with one other subject. Second- and third-year studies include cognitive, social and neuropsychology. Other courses include Psychology in Education or Statistics.

Leeds* In the Psychology course, four major areas are covered – social psychology, learning and biological psychology, cognitive psychology and developmental and clinical psychology. Electives are offered in evolutionary and occupational health psychology. There is also a degree in Neuroscience.

Leeds Beckett Psychology is offered as a single or joint honours course, the latter with Criminology and Society. There is also a course in Counselling and Therapeutic Studies.

Leeds Trinity Psychology is a single honours course but can also be taken with Child Development or as Forensic Psychology.

Leicester* In the Psychology programme, courses are taken covering the biological bases of behaviour, cognitive psychology (learning, language and thinking) and abnormal, social and developmental psychology. There are also joint Psychology courses with Cognitive Neuroscience and Sociology. See also **Combined Courses**.

Lincoln In addition to the single honours Psychology course, joint courses are offered with Criminology, Marketing, Child Studies, Social Policy and Clinical Psychology and Forensic Psychology.

Liverpool In Year 1 of the Psychology course, psychology is introduced, along with brain cognition and behaviour. In Year 2, psychological themes include biological, abnormal, developmental and cognitive psychology. In Year 3, eight courses are taken from a range of options. The course is also offered on the combined honours programme.

Liverpool Hope The BSc Psychology single honours degree confers eligibility for registration with the BPS. There is also a Sport Psychology degree. Combined courses are also offered.

Liverpool John Moores The Applied Psychology course offers modules that include social problems and client rehabilitation and care. There are also options in counselling, criminal behaviour and mental health. A joint course in Psychology and Biology is also available. There are also courses in Forensic Psychology, Criminology and Criminal Justice and Applied Sports Psychology.

London (Goldsmiths) The Psychology degree is a laboratory-based programme studied through course units, which allows considerable flexibility in what can be studied. Final-year options focus on vocational applications or intellectual curiosity and include psychotherapy, psychological aspects of music and psychology and the law. Psychology is also offered with Criminal Psychology and Cognitive Neuroscience.

London (QM) The course focuses on psychology as a natural and experimental subject with a large range of core and module options from the biological sciences. Year 3 options include action and perception and behavioural ecology.

See *Heap 2015: University Degree Course Offers* (Trotman Publishing) for details of offers

London (RH)* The Psychology syllabus in Years 1 and 2 covers both theoretical and experimental work on a whole range of topics. These include research methods, social, developmental and cognitive psychology and aspects of clinical psychology. Occupational, health and social psychology are among several options offered in the third year. Psychology can also be taken with Biology, Mathematics or Music and courses in Applied Psychology and Applied Social Psychology are also available.

London (UCL)* Psychology is taken as part of the BSc programme in which students can take some modules in another subject. In the final year all courses are taken in Psychology and there is a compulsory research project.

London LSE Social Psychology is not offered as a degree but can be taken as an option with many other subjects offered by the School through modules such as self, others and society: perspectives on social and applied psychology, and societal psychology: theory and applications.

London Met The three-year degree in Psychology offers specialisation in Year 3 that includes applied, health, child and social psychology. Other courses include Psychology and Criminology and Sociology and Sports Psychology.

London South Bank Psychology is offered as a single honours degree course and covers biology, social sciences and philosophy. It also focuses on the psychology of learning and memory and behaviour. It can also be studied with a second subject, for example with Child Development, Clinical Psychology, Criminology or Law.

Loughborough The Psychology and Social Psychology courses qualify for professional status. Students choosing the four-year programme spend Year 3 on a placement in an approved occupation relevant to their degree. There are also courses in Ergonomics. See also **Biology**.

Manchester* A wide range of options can be taken in Year 3 of this comprehensive Psychology course, with particular reference to applied psychology practice 'in the real world'. There is also a course in Cognitive Neuroscience and Psychology.

Manchester Met Various aspects of the study of psychology are covered in the Psychology course, which has two major units: social and individual psychology and cognitive psychology. Psychology can also be taken with a large number of subjects including Speech Pathology, Health Studies, Childhood and Youth Studies, Crime Studies and Visual Arts. A course in the Psychology of Sport and Exercise is also offered.

Middlesex The three-year full time course in Psychology includes biological, social and developmental psychology and the opportunity for work placements. Psychology can also be taken with Counselling Skills, Criminology, Human Resource Management or Marketing.

Newcastle In Stages 1 and 2 of the Psychology course, students receive a broad foundation in the major areas of experimental psychology (abnormal, developmental, social and psychological) as well as animal behaviour, learning and language. Final-year options include evolutionary and consumer psychology and the psychology of health.

Newman The course covers biopsychology, social and developmental studies, educational, clinical and forensic psychology.

Northampton The Psychology degree is accredited by the BPS for further training as a psychologist. Psychology is also available as a joint honours degree or with Counselling.

Northumbria A general introduction to Psychology takes place in the first year of the course, followed by more specialised areas. These include social psychology, evolutionary psychology, behaviour, health and children's psychology. Psychology with Sports Science or Criminology is also offered.

Nottingham* Central topics of the Psychology degree include social and developmental psychology, and biological and cognitive psychology. In Year 3 there is a wide range of options and a year-long research project. There are also courses in Psychology and Neuroscience and Psychology with Philosophy.

Nottingham Trent This is a broad Psychology course with specialist options in criminology, cognitive behavioural therapy for trauma and evolutionary psychology. Psychology with Sociology, Sport Science, Criminology and Educational Development are also offered and there is a course in Equestrian Psychology and Sports Science.

Oxford* Experimental Psychology is a study of psychology as an experimental science and covers the whole range of research: human experimental psychology, animal and physiological development, behaviour and linguistics. Courses are also offered in Psychology and Philosophy and Psychology, Philosophy and Linguistics.

Oxford Brookes Psychology is offered as a single subject or jointly with over 15 other subjects including Anthropology, Business Management, Educational Studies, International Relations, Human Biosciences and Music.

Plymouth The broad-based Psychology course introduces students to a range of topics including cognition, learning, social development and applied psychology. There are special facilities for work in clinical psychology, and psychological and social psychology. This is a three-year course with an optional sandwich year (subject to a successful application to transfer to the four-year course). Other courses include Psychology with Criminal Justice Studies, Sociology, Human Biology, and Law.

Portsmouth Introductory courses in the first year of the Psychology degree lead on to a range of specialist topics, including developmental psychology, social psychology, cognitive psychology, clinical psychology and ecological psychology. The course emphasises human behaviour, and the final year contains options in applied psychology and counselling. There is also a course in Forensic Psychology with topics covering cybercrime, interviewing and offender profiling. Psychology can also be studied with Human Resource Management, Marketing, Criminology or English.

Queen's Belfast Psychology is offered as a BSc with accreditation by the BPS. Emphasis is laid on practical and experimental work throughout the course, which covers subjects including cognitive psychology, conceptual and historical issues and psychobiology.

Reading The basic subject matter of modern psychology is studied during the first four terms of the Psychology degree. This is followed by a choice of special options in the final year, covering a wide range of topics including clinical and neuropsychology and social psychology. Psychology can also be taken with Childhood and Ageing, Mental and Physical Health, Biology or Philosophy.

Roehampton Psychology is offered as a single or combined honours course which qualifies graduates for graduate membership of the BPS. In Year 2 there is a focus on cognitive, social and development psychology, along with personality psychology and abnormal behaviour. In Year 3 there is a supervised, year-long research project and also the opportunity to study a range of optional modules such as autism or criminal and forensic psychology. There is also a degree course in Psychology and Counselling and in Sport Psychology.

St Andrews* Psychology can be offered in the Faculties of Arts and Sciences. Decisions to specialise are made in Year 3. Single and joint honours are available in both faculties. Joint courses and major/minor degrees are also offered including Psychology and Art History, French, Philosophy or Social Anthropology.

St Mary's The Psychology course and the major route in the combined programme are accredited for registration by the BPS. The course can be combined with 13 subjects including Creative and Professional Writing, History and Sport Science.

Salford A single honours course in Psychology is offered, with an emphasis on the application of theory and skills. The course can be studied with Counselling Studies or Criminology.

Sheffield* Introductory modules cover biological, social and developmental psychology, neuroscience and psychological disorders in both the BA and BSc Psychology degrees. Specialist studies are chosen in Year 3 for the research project and extended essay. Courses are also available with Philosophy and in Human Communication Sciences.

See Heap 2015: *University Degree Course Offers* (Trotman Publishing) for details of offers

Sheffield Hallam Psychology specialisms are offered in social, behavioural and developmental psychology including communication disorders and mental health. In the second year, four routes can be followed including a work placement or a year abroad. Psychology can also be taken with Sociology or Criminology.

South Wales A course in Psychology (leading to registration) is taken on a three-year full-time basis. and covers cognitive, social, health, counselling and developmental aspects of the subject. Degrees are also offered in Developmental, Sport and Applied Psychology. Students can also take psychology as a major/minor subject in joint honours courses.

Southampton* Psychology students follow compulsory courses in psychology in Year 1 – introduction to psychology, thinking psychologically, research methods and data analysis and psychological research laboratory. Practical work is an important component of the course. Specialisation takes place in Year 3 in such topics as animal behaviour, human learning, attention and stress and health. A course in Education Studies and Psychology is also available.

Southampton Solent In addition to a single honours Psychology degree, there are four pathways: Education, Counselling, Criminal Behaviour and Health Psychology. Psychology can also be studied with Criminology, Criminal Investigation and Marketing.

Staffordshire This broad Psychology course provides options in the environment, crime, social psychology and counselling. Other courses include Psychology with Criminology, Counselling, Child Development and Sport and Exercise. A course in Forensic Psychology is also offered.

Stirling Psychology is introduced as a biological and social science. Other studies include learning, clinical and abnormal psychology, and the social and cognitive development in infants and young children. Part II covers psychological methods, animal behaviour, social psychology, perception and performance, clinical and counselling psychology, and occupational psychology. Psychology can also be studied with, for example, Film and Media, Marketing and Politics.

Strathclyde Psychology is offered as a single or joint honours course with another subject, including Mathematics, Sociology and Spanish. Joint courses are not accredited for qualification as a psychologist.

Sunderland In addition to the fundamentals of psychology and research methods there is a wide choice of options on the Psychology course, covering topics including mental health and illness, the psychology of ageing, counselling and health psychology. Psychology is offered with a wide range of courses including Journalism, Business and Media Studies.

Surrey* Psychology is a four-year sandwich course in which the third year is spent in professional placement. These placements are in hospitals and clinical schools, social survey companies, personnel and occupational guidance services, industry and commerce.

Sussex* Students interested in Psychology are taken from both arts and science backgrounds. A variety of degree programmes is offered with a common core of subjects, allowing students to specialise later. These cover applied, developmental and social psychology. Degrees with Cognitive Science, Neuroscience, American Studies and Sociology are also available.

Swansea* Psychology is offered by the School of Human and Health Sciences. The course looks at how the brain works and covers memory and language and the behaviour of people in social situations. The course can be taken as a four-year sandwich course with a year spent abroad.

Teesside The Psychology course provides a broad theoretical and practical base, together with computer skills, and is taught on the flexible modular system. Options include counselling, occupational psychology and neuropsychology. Other courses include Forensic Psychology, Sport and Exercise Psychology and Psychology with Counselling or Criminology.

Trinity St David (Swansea) The Counselling and Psychology course offers special studies in such topics as health and well-being, learning, behaviour and occupational psychology. Educational Studies and Psychology is also offered.

See *Heap 2015: University Degree Course Offers* (Trotman Publishing) for details of offers

Ulster The Psychology degree leads to specialisation in clinical, counselling, occupational or health psychology. There is also a separate degree in Social Psychology. Both courses are accredited by the BPS.

Warwick* In Year 1, Psychology students are introduced to the foundations of psychology and take an optional subject from a range of possibilities in science, mathematics, social sciences and humanities subjects. Core courses in Year 2 covering personality, perception, action, memory and language are followed by a choice of six courses in the final year.

West London Psychology is offered in the Humanities programme. It can be studied in combination with another subject or on a specialist route giving eligibility for graduate membership of the BPS. Psychology is also offered with Criminology and Counselling Theory.

West Scotland The BA in Psychology covers areas such as social policy and cross-cultural psychology. The BSc in Psychology offers a broad overview of scientific study. Both courses are accredited by the BPS.

Westminster The Psychology course covers cognitive, social, developmental and abnormal psychology as well as units in the psychology of women, prejudice, education and counselling. Courses are also offered in Cognitive Neuroscience.

Winchester The course is approved by the BPS and explores all aspects of human behaviour. Opportunities to specialise commence in Year 2. There are several joint courses from which to choose. Courses are also offered in Psychological Science, Psychology and Child Development and Psychology and Cognition.

Wolverhampton After a broad introductory first year, Psychology students choose from a range of optional modules such as social psychology, personality and abnormal psychology. They also complete an individual project and have the opportunity to combine studies with one or two other subjects. Psychology courses include Counselling Psychology and Criminal Behaviour.

Worcester The Psychology course has a practical emphasis with final-year options in a wide range of subjects. There is also a course in Business Psychology and Psychological Studies.

York* The Psychology course places particular emphasis on psychology as an experimental science and academic discipline. It attempts to avoid any strong bias in favour of, or against, any specific field or approach within psychology. Sociology with Social Psychology is also offered.

York St John The BSc course in Psychology is accredited for registration for a career as a psychologist. There is also a single honours programme in Counselling, Coaching and Mentoring.

OTHER INSTITUTIONS OFFERING PSYCHOLOGY COURSES
Blackburn (Coll), Bradford (Coll Univ Centre), Burton (Coll), Cornwall (Coll), Duchy (Coll), Grimsby (Univ Centre), Havering (Coll), Llandrillo Cymru (Coll), Northop (Coll), Norwich City (Coll), Richmond (Am Int Univ), Somerset (Coll), Staffordshire Reg Fed (SURF), Suffolk (Univ Campus), Truro (Coll), Warwickshire (Coll), West Anglia (Coll), Wigan and Leigh (Coll).

ALTERNATIVE COURSES
Advertising, Business Studies, Computer Science and Artificial Intelligence, Education and Teacher Training, Human Resources Management, Social Administration, Social Studies/Science.

RELIGIOUS STUDIES

(including **Biblical Studies**, **Theology** and **Divinity**)
(* indicates universities with entry requirements over 340 UCAS points)

SUBJECT REQUIREMENTS/PREFERENCES

GCE A level: Religious Studies may be preferred; check prospectuses. **GCSE:** English, Mathematics or a science may be required. For teacher training, English, Mathematics and Science.

SUBJECT INFORMATION

Religious Studies courses cover four degree subjects: Religious Studies, Divinity, Theology and Biblical Studies. The subject content of these courses varies and students should check prospectuses carefully. They are not intended as training courses for the church ministry; an adherence to a particular religious persuasion is not a necessary qualification for entry. (A level Religious Studies is an acceptable second or third A level for any non-scientific degree course.)

Aberdeen Degrees in Divinity and Religious Studies are offered, the latter covering topics in Judaism, Christianity, Islam, Buddhism, Sikhism and Hinduism. The degree in Divinity covers church history, history of religions, Hebrew Bible, New Testament and theology.

Bangor Religious Studies is offered with Philosophy.

Bath Spa A specialised course in Religion, Philosophy and Ethics is offered but it is also possible to study each subject separately. Philosophy and Ethics or Study of Religion can be taken as part of the combined degree programme.

Birmingham A very flexible Theology and Religion course is offered, focusing primarily on Christianity, Islam and Judaism but offering programmes on other major religions such as Sikhism and Hinduism. Core courses cover introductions to biblical studies, Christian theology and Christian history. Second- and third-year options include a range of biblical subjects, for example Hebrew, Greek texts, the Gospels and New Testament theology and the study of the Qur'an. Theology can also be taken with English Literature, Language or History.

Bishop Grosseteste There is a degree in Religion, Theology and Ethics in Society involving critical thinking and philosophical issues.

Bristol The course in Theology and Religious Studies has a strong focus on the study of religion both in the contemporary world and in the past. The basic subjects taught are biblical studies, Jewish studies, Christian history and theology with an emphasis on the early, medieval and modern periods. In Years 2 and 3 the course continues with interfaith studies, biblical studies, religion and gender, the New Testament, Judaism, Islam, Buddhism and Hinduism. Language options include Greek, Hebrew, Pali, Latin, Japanese, Chinese and Sanskrit.

Cambridge* The Theology and Religious Studies Tripos is taken in two parts. Part I is taken after one year and Part II after a further two years. The Part I course provides for a wide variety of interests: biblical, historical, philosophical and comparative religion, and students choose four out of 14 papers. The two core courses cover one scriptural language (Hebrew, New Testament Greek, Qur'anic Arabic or Sanskrit) and a paper on the New or Old Testament. Part II builds on the foundation laid by the Part I course and includes church history, the philosophy of religion, religious themes in literature, and world religions. Homerton College also offers Religious Studies for those aiming for a teaching qualification at primary level. Not available at Churchill College.

Canterbury Christ Church The Religious Studies course covers world religions, ethics and problems in philosophy of religion, followed in Years 2 and 3 by a wide range of options. There is also a course in Theology. Previous study of religions is not required.

Cardiff The Religious and Theological Studies course comprises a study of major faiths past and present, language and text theology and optional topics, including the history of the early church, the Crusades and Welsh history and religious literature. For the course in Theology, students cover the Holy Scriptures, the Old and the New Testaments, Christian doctrine, ethics, and church history. There are beginners' courses in Greek, Hebrew and Sanskrit, and practical theology involving fieldwork. A third pathway now covers Indian religions and includes Buddhism, Hinduism and Jainism, including Sanskrit language and texts.

Central Lancashire Ten courses are offered in Religion, Culture and Society including combined courses with Education, Philosophy, Politics, Archaeology, Sociology and Islamic studies.

Chester The courses in Religious Studies engage with religions such as Islam, Hinduism, Judaism and Christianity as well as modern religious movements. There is also a Theology degree exploring traditional ideas and concepts in the modern world.

Chichester The Theology and Religion degree covers biblical studies, philosophy, worship and ethics. The course can be combined with English, English and Creative Writing, History, International English Studies and Music.

Cumbria The Religious Studies degree introduces a wide range of world religions and covers theology, Christian ethics and biblical studies. Judaism, Islam, Hinduism, Buddhism and Sikhism are also studied in the first year.

Durham* The Theology course provides a broad study of the subject ranging from biblical studies and Christian theology to Jewish studies and the sociology and anthropology of religion. Theology is also offered with Philosophy, Education Studies and in the combined honours programme in Arts.

Edinburgh Divinity focuses on Christianity, its origins, historical development and its global spread. There is also a BA and MA course in Religious Studies focusing on Asian traditions, Christianity and Islam.

Exeter The Theology course provides an introduction to the subject by way of Old Testament studies (history and literature), church history and the development of Christian doctrine. Other modules include sexuality, criminal justice, feminism, martyrs, pilgrimage and life after death.

Glasgow Two degrees are offered leading to the Bachelor of Divinity (BD): General (focusing on the study of Christianity) and Ministry (a vocational course). The former is wide-ranging and interdisciplinary, covering religious beliefs and practices. There is also an MA degree in Religious Studies with specialist studies in Islam, Eastern religions, philosophy, literature, theology, women's studies and Holocaust studies. The BD and MA degrees are recognised teaching qualifications in Religious Studies. A degree in Religious and Philosophical Education is also offered.

Gloucestershire The degree in Religion, Philosophy and Ethics brings together the study of three subject areas and is also offered as a joint course with other subjects.

Hertfordshire Religious Education is offered as part of the Primary Teaching programme. Students spend 24 weeks in school placements over the course of three years.

Huddersfield The degree in Religion and Education is a study of major world religions and educational issues. The course covers religions such as Christianity, Islam, Hinduism, Sikhism and Buddhism.

Hull Courses are offered in Religion and Film Studies, Religion and Politics, and Religion and Sociology. Joint courses are also offered. The courses approach religion in an interdisciplinary way, looking at the relationships between religion, literature, culture, arts and society.

See *Heap 2015: University Degree Course Offers* (Trotman Publishing) for details of offers

Kent Religious Studies is offered at single and joint honours levels. Topics include applied theology, biblical interpretation, mysticism, and religious experience. A wide range of modules gives the course considerable flexibility with options in science, philosophy, psychology and theology and their impact on religion.

Lancaster* The Religious Studies course covers world religions, approaching religion from theological, sociological, anthropological, psychological and philosophical perspectives. The main studies include Judaism, Christianity, Islam, Hinduism, Buddhism and philosophy. Exchanges with the US are possible. Other courses include Ethics, Philosophy and Religion and Religious Studies with English Literature, History, Philosophy, Politics or Sociology.

Leeds In Year 1 of the Theology and Religious Studies course there is an introduction to Christian theological tradition, ancient Middle Eastern religion, New Testament Greek, early Indian religions or another subsidiary course. In the second and third years, students choose from a range of options. The course tends to stress the contemporary and 'lived' aspects of religions rather than their classical and theoretical aspects. A wide range of joint courses with Religious Studies are also on offer, including Arabic and Islamic Studies and Russian Civilisation.

Leeds Trinity A broad course is offered covering world religions, ethics and philosophical studies.

Liverpool Hope The degree in Religion and Philosophy is offered at single and combined honours levels. Other courses offered include World Religions, Christian Theology, Biblical Studies and Philosophy, Ethics and Religion.

London (Heythrop) Degree courses are offered in Theology, Philosophy and Theology, Philosophy, Religion and Ethics, Divinity and Abrahamic Religions (Islam, Christianity, Judaism). This small college is one of the largest schools of theology in the UK.

London (King's)* Religion can be studied with a focus on the contemporary world, with Philosophy and Ethics or with Politics and Sociology. There is also a course in Theology.

London (SOAS) Specialising in the religions of Asia and Africa, the three-year degree in the Study of Religions is taken as a joint course with a choice of over 40 subjects, including African and Asian languages.

Manchester The Study of Religion and Theology is a broad-based course providing an introduction to the different approaches of this field. These cover historical, theological, psychological, anthropological, philosophical and sociological aspects. There are also pathways focusing on Jewish Studies, Biblical Studies, and Religion and Society as well as a course in Theological Studies in Philosophy and Ethics.

Middlesex Education Studies and Religious Studies is offered with modules covering myth and society in the sacred and secular worlds, the world of Islam and world religions in modern debate.

Newman There are three degrees offered: Theology, Theology for Education and Religious Studies.

Nottingham The Theology course introduces a study of the Old Testament, Christianity, and faith and practice of Islam. Years 2 and 3 provide a wide choice of specialist options.

Oxford* The Theology and Religion course provides an informed and critical understanding of the Old and New Testaments, of the historical development of the role of the church and the contemporary meaning of the Christian faith. A large range of options includes the philosophy of religion, ancient and modern church history, Christian ethics, textual criticism and biblical Hebrew. Students have the opportunity to visit Israel on an archaeological dig, in a kibbutz, to study Hebrew in Jerusalem or to travel on a study tour. Theology may also be studied with Oriental Studies.

Oxford Brookes Religion and Theology can be studied as a single honours or as a first or second subject in a wide range of joint degrees. Three-year full-time degrees are also available in a range of combined subjects, including Philosophy, Education Studies, Anthropology and Sociology.

See *Heap 2015: University Degree Course Offers* (Trotman Publishing) for details of offers

Queen's Belfast Queen's University is free from association with any religious denomination. Degrees in Theology (non-denominational) and Divinity are offered with a common curriculum in Year 1 in which a study of languages (Greek or Hebrew) is possible.

Roehampton Theology and Religious Studies is offered as a single or combined honours course and explores the multifaceted nature of the subject. Topics range from biblical themes, world religions, philosophy of religion and mythology. There is also the opportunity to study the languages of sacred texts such as Greek, Hebrew, Latin, classical Arabic and Sanskrit. There is also a foundation degree in Ministerial Theology.

St Andrews* Biblical Studies and Theology can be taken as Arts or Divinity subjects. Within the Bachelor of Divinity (BD) course, an honours subject or group may be chosen from among Old or New Testament language and literature, ecclesiastical history, divinity and practical theology. There are also separate joint degree courses in a range of subjects including Greek, Latin or History with New Testament, Theological Studies, and Languages with Biblical Studies or Hebrew.

St Mary's The degree in Theology and Religious Studies covers biblical studies, world religions and contemporary world issues. The course can be studied as part of the combined honours degree with 11 subjects including Irish Studies, Sociology and Tourism.

Sheffield In Year 1, Biblical Literature and English comprises a wide-ranging survey of biblical history, languages and literature, also looking at the Qur'an and religion and science. Years 2 and 3 cover Old and New Testament texts, broader areas of biblical history, literature and theology. Students also take modules in English literature, language and linguistics. There are also courses in Religion, Theology and the Bible, and Theology and Music.

South Wales A BA degree in Religious Studies embraces all the main religions and includes an optional study tour of India and Nepal to experience its rich cultural diversity.

Stirling Part I (the first four semesters) of the combined honours Religion degree offers modules in: religion, ethics and society; religion, nationalism and colonialism; religion in culture; and theory and method. In Semesters 5–8 all students take courses in biblical studies and in historical and philosophical studies. There are also options in Part II, including Eastern religions and new religious movements.

Trinity St David Several courses are offered including Islamic Studies, Religious Studies and Theology. Islamic Studies is offered as a joint subject with Religious Studies. Scholarships available.

Winchester The course in Theology and Religious Studies examines aspects and traditions of the major religions by way of single or combined honours programmes. See also **Philosophy**.

Wolverhampton A degree in Religious Studies can be taken as a combined degree course with subjects such as English, History, Sociology, Philosophy and Education Studies.

York St John Christian Theology and Theology and Religious Studies courses are offered as single or joint courses. Both courses can be studied with Education Studies.

OTHER INSTITUTIONS OFFERING RELIGIOUS STUDIES COURSES
Havering (Coll), Nazarene Theological (Coll), UHI.

ALTERNATIVE COURSES
History, Philosophy, Psychology, Social Studies.

SOCIAL SCIENCES/STUDIES

(including **Criminology**, **Social Policy** and **Social Work**)
(see also **Law** and **Sociology**)
(* indicates universities with entry requirements over 340 UCAS points)

SUBJECT REQUIREMENTS/PREFERENCES
GCSE: Usually English and Mathematics; a science may be required for some courses.

SUBJECT INFORMATION
These courses are a good vocational preparation for careers in the social services. A wide range of topics is covered, for example housing policy, health services, mental illness, the family and prisons. New Social Work degrees are being introduced, which replace the Diploma in Social Work. Check with institutions and with the General Social Care Council (www.gscc.org.uk) and on www.skillsforcare.org.uk. (Research ratings are shown for **Social Work**.)

QUESTIONS TO CONSIDER
 * Can I gain relevant work experience?
 * Are there opportunities to focus on children, youth, adults, family or disabilities?
 * Is the course accredited by the General Social Care Council, allowing me to register as a profes
   sional care worker upon graduation?

Abertay A study of human behaviour from different aspects. Opportunities to specialise in one social science subject from Economics, Psychology, Sociology or Sport. Degrees are also offered in Criminology and Policing and Security.

Anglia Ruskin A degree is offered in Criminology, covering criminal psychology, law, politics, crime and the criminal justice system. In addition there are degrees in Social Work and Social Policy.

Aston Public Policy is offered with Management as a joint or combined honours programme with placement year opportunities. The course can be taken with English Language, International Relations, Politics, Business or Sociology.

Bangor The course in Health and Social Care involves a study of social policy, housing, poverty and family welfare. There is also a course in Criminology and Criminal Justice which enables graduates who are interested in careers in law or the police to proceed from the degree to the Common Professional Examination or the Postgraduate Diploma in Law or to a graduate training programme with the police.

Bath Courses are offered in Social Sciences, Social Work and Social Policy with optional units in economics, politics, psychology and languages. The courses in the Department of Social and Policy Sciences are highly flexible and it is often possible to move from one programme to another at the end of the first year. See also **Combined Courses**.

Bedfordshire The Applied Social Studies course is a vocational course preparing students for work in the social services and covers criminology, social policy, sociology and psychology. There are also courses in Social Work, Child and Adolescent Studies, and Youth and Community Studies.

Birmingham The Social Policy course covers politics, policy-making, sociology, economics, psychology and urban studies. There is a range of specialist modules on offer covering health and social care, housing, and policing and community justice. There is also a course in Social Work.

Birmingham City A degree in Social Work leads to eligibility to register with the General Social Care Council to practise as a professional social worker. There is also a three-year course in Criminology and

Policing, giving an in depth study of crime, punishment and victimisation, or with Psychology or Security Studies. There is also a unique course in Criminal Investigation.

Bolton The Community with Early Years and Youth and Community Work courses include modules in ethnicity and race, housing problems, poverty and the community and mental illness. Work placement takes place in local community groups.

Bournemouth The Social Work degree covers children and young people, adults, mental health, social exclusion and law. Students are taught through interprofessional learning and share modules with nurses, midwives, Sociology and Social Policy students. There is also a course in Vulnerable Adults and Community Care.

Bradford There are courses in Social Work and Working with Children, Young People and Families.

Brighton The degree in Social Science covers social psychology, criminology, health and criminal justice. Courses in Criminology, Social Policy and Social Work are also offered. There is also a course in Applied Social Sciences.

Bristol The Social Policy degree provides a broad picture of historical and contemporary issues leading to options in criminology, poverty, urban studies and violence against women. There is also a course on Childhood Studies which includes options in psychology and youth justice.

Bristol UWE Courses are offered in Public Health and Social Work, and in Housing Development and Management, which has elective topics in the history of architecture, urban conservation and safer communities.

Brunel The BA degree in Social Work includes modules in professional social work skills, theories and methods, law, social policy, social welfare and child observation. All students have to complete 200 days of practical placement (30 days in Year 1, 70 days in Year 2 and 100 days in Year 3). Specialist routes are offered in work with adults or children and families.

Bucks New Courses are available in Police Studies, Criminology and Social Work. The Social Work BSc focuses on the service users' and the carers' perspective in Year 1, statutory work in Year 2 and creativity in Year 3.

Cambridge* The relatively new course in Human, Social and Political Sciences offers the study of Politics and International Relations, Sociology, Anthropology and Archaeology in various combination courses with specialist subjects including Assyriology and Egyptology. See also **Combined Courses**.

Canterbury Christ Church Courses are offered in Social Work and Police Studies, the latter offered in conjunction with Kent Police. There are also courses in Childhood Studies and in Applied Criminology.

Cardiff The Social Sciences degree scheme provides full degrees and half degrees in Education, Sociology, Social Policy and Criminology, all of which can be studied jointly with a range of other subjects including Welsh and Journalism.

Cardiff Met (UWIC) Courses offered include Housing (Policy and Practice; Supported Housing), Health and Social Care and Social Work. A course is also offered in Youth and Community Work.

Central Lancashire Degree courses in Criminology and Philosophy, Police and Criminal Investigation, Deaf Studies and joint British Sign Language, Human Rights and Social Policy are offered on the combined honours and joint programmes. The university offers a unit degree scheme that includes courses from economics, psychology and sociology.

Chester A Social Work programme is offered at the Warrington campus leading to a career in the profession. Courses are also offered in Counselling and Criminology, which explores crime and punishment, discipline and deviance, mental health and crime and legal issues.

Chichester The Social Work course involves social policy, mental health and welfare, and child and adult services. Placements are undertaken in each year. A course is also offered in Counselling.

City Courses are offered in Criminology and Sociology with a focus on topics including media, crime and cultural practices, policing, security and human rights, and victims, crime control and security.

Coventry The Criminology degree focuses on the social aspects of crime and the workings of the police, sentencing and prisons. There are also degrees in Criminology and Law, Youth Work and a Social Work course with placements.

Cumbria A course in Social Science and Criminology is offered drawing on sociology, psychology, philosophy, cultural studies and social policy. There is also a course in Social Work.

De Montfort The Social Studies programme offers degrees in Criminology and Criminal Justice, Social Work and Youth and Community Development. Students are encouraged to undertake placements throughout the course.

Derby Courses are offered in Applied Community and Youth Work, Applied Criminology, Applied Social Work and Health and Social Care. The Applied Social Work degree is fully accredited by the General Social Care Council (GSCC).

Dundee There is a Community Learning and Development course which includes work-based studies.

Durham* The Criminology course covers crime, deviance, social control and criminal justice in society. Modules cover organised crime, punishment and forensic science. There are opportunities to spend part of the course abroad. There is also a separate course in Criminology with Criminal Justice.

East Anglia A degree in Social Work accredited by the GSCC is offered covering topics in psychology, sociology, social policy and legal context. The course focuses on provisions regarding child care, mental health and adult care.

East London Courses are offered in Criminology (with Psychology, Law, Sociology, Business and Criminal Justice), Social Work, Psychosocial Studies, Community Service and Enterprise. There are also specialist courses in Social Work with Adults and Special Needs and Inclusive Education.

Edge Hill There is a degree in Social Work leading to professional qualification, with 200 days of practice placement assessed as part of the degree. The course is accredited by the GSCC. There are also several degrees in Criminology.

Edinburgh* Courses are offered in Social Policy and Social Work and last four years. Social Policy can be studied with Economics, Geography, European Languages, Law, Politics, Social and Economic History, Social and Political Studies, Social Anthropology or Sociology.

Edinburgh Napier The Social Sciences course offers core subjects in psychology, British society and economics. It later focuses on various aspects of social problems including welfare, education, organisations and health. There are several combined courses with Criminology.

Glasgow Degrees in Community Development and Public Policy are offered, the latter focusing on the major social policy issues of the day. Applicants for the Social Work degree apply through Strathclyde University; the degree is also available at Glasgow's Crichton campus in Dumfries where a Liberal Arts programme is also offered.

Glasgow Caledonian In Years 1, 2 and 3 of the Social Sciences degree, module choices are made from economics, a foreign language, geography, history, politics, psychology and sociology. There is a degree in Social Work with placements throughout the four-year course.

Gloucestershire Degree courses are offered in Community Engagement and Governance, Community Care Practice with Vulnerable Adults, Social Work, Social Work with Adults, Criminology and Youth Work.

See *Heap 2015: University Degree Course Offers* (Trotman Publishing) for details of offers

Glyndŵr The degree in Public and Social Policy focuses on the welfare services including social and environmental aspects, drugs, youth problems, child abuse and community care. Social Work, Criminology and Criminal Justice and Youth and Community Work degrees are also offered.

Greenwich Courses covered by the Social Sciences include Criminology, and Social Care with Social Work. There are also degrees in Youth and Community Studies, and Criminology and Criminal Psychology.

Hertfordshire A course is offered in Social Work which provides professional registration with the GSCC. The course covers topics such as law, partnership working, assessment, planning, intervention and review, human growth and development, values and diversity, social science, social policy, communication skills, mental health, disabilities, family and children and European social work.

Huddersfield There are courses in Criminology, Health and Community Studies and Youth and Community Work. A three-year course is also offered leading to a degree and a Diploma in Social Work.

Hull This is a multidisciplinary Social Science Department covering Criminology, Sociology, Anthropology, Gender Studies, Social Work and Community and Youth Work Studies. Courses can be combined with a range of degree programmes, for example there are six courses combined with Criminology.

Keele A degree in Criminology is offered with over 30 other dual honours subjects and there is also a single honours course in Social Work.

Kent Degrees are offered in Social and Public Policy, Social Work and Sociology. Courses in Criminology and Criminal Justice Studies are also offered as single and joint honours programmes. Close links exist with criminal justice agencies. The Social Sciences BSc allows students to study social policy, sociology, criminal justice, history, politics, psychology and geography in this multidisciplinary subject.

Kingston Courses are offered in Social Work, Criminology and Human Rights, which can be studied with Applied Economics, Business, Creative Writing, Criminology, Drama, English Language and Communication and nine other subjects.

Lancaster Criminology students study social issues in the context of divisions of class, gender, race, age, disability and sexuality. There is also a Social Work course that has two placements over the course of the degree.

Leeds There is a Criminal Justice and Criminology course with a range of topics covering criminal law, punishment and society, crime prevention and community safety. Courses are also offered in Social Policy and Social Work.

Leeds Beckett Social Work and Youth Work and Community Development are offered in addition to several social science options including Criminology with Sociology or Psychology.

Leicester A course is offered in Criminology, covering the penal system, policing, terrorism, probation, punishment, the courts and all issues relating to crime and justice.

Lincoln Courses are offered in Social Science, Social Policy and Criminology, with joint subjects in Forensic Investigation, Politics, Social Policy and International Relations.

Liverpool Courses in Criminology and Sociology are offered. Sociology can also be studied with Social Policy, focusing on social theory and policy and the social groupings of class, gender and race.

Liverpool Hope Courses are offered in Social Policy and Social Work. The degree in Criminology (single and combined courses) runs parallel with Sociology and Psychology in Years 1 and 2, with options in Year 3.

Liverpool John Moores Degrees are offered in Criminal Justice, Criminology (with Sociology or Psychology) and Social Work. There is also a degree in Health and Social Care for Families, Individuals and Communities.

London (Goldsmiths) A three-year Social Work degree is open to students over 18. There are also courses in Applied Social Science, Community Development and Youth Work.

London (RH) A BSc course is offered in Social Work with 200 days of supervised practice. There is also a course in Criminology and Sociology which covers a wide range of topics including youth and crime, war and terrorism, restorative justice and forensic psychology.

London (St George's) The Social Work course provides an academic qualification and a passport to practice.

London LSE Social Policy is offered with Economics, Sociology, Government or Criminology, in addition to the single honours course. The course covers a broad range of fields including healthcare, education, housing, criminal justice, international development, social security and personal social services.

London Met A degree is offered in Public Health and Social Care dealing with public health, social care, health promotion and ethical issues. There are also degrees in Social Work, Social Sciences, Youth Studies, Youth Work and Criminology and Community Development.

London South Bank Criminology is offered as a single subject or with Law or Psychology. A BA in Social Work is also available with 200 days' placement split over the second and third year.

Loughborough A course is offered in Criminology and Social Policy examining current theories and the problems of society. Optional modules cover a range of topics including women and crime: victims and offenders; children, young people and risk; and human rights and civil liberties.

Manchester The Social Work course is integrated into the School of Nursing and Midwifery, providing the opportunity for interdisciplinary learning. There are also several courses linked with social sciences including Criminology.

Manchester Met Courses are offered in Social Work, Social Care, Criminology, Abuse Studies, and Childhood and Youth Studies and Youth and Community Work, which leads to a professional qualification validated by the National Youth Agency.

Middlesex Courses focus on Policing, Criminal Justice and Criminology, which can also be combined with Psychology or Sociology. A course in Youth Justice is also offered and there is also a Social Work course.

Newman Courses in Youth Work and Working with Young People are offered as single, joint or major course programmes. New for 2014 is a course in Criminology.

Northampton Courses are offered in Criminology, Social Welfare, Social Work, Social Care and Social and Community Development which can be studied over four years with an optional sandwich year.

Northumbria The Social Work course has an emphasis on practice and experience in different welfare settings. A specialised course is offered in Social Work with Children, Young People, their Families and Carers. A Criminology course can also be taken with Sociology, Forensic Science or Psychology.

Nottingham A course is offered in Cultural Sociology covering political and social issues under debate in Britain, Europe and North America. Courses are also offered in Social Work and Social Policy.

Nottingham Trent Courses are offered in Social Work, Youth Studies and Youth Justice. The course in Health and Social Care has pathways in criminal justice, guidance and counselling, community studies, policy and leadership, and practice.

Oxford Brookes The Social Work course prepares students for placement through the Fit for Practice module. There is also a student-designed Health and Social Care course.

See *Heap 2015: University Degree Course Offers* (Trotman Publishing) for details of offers

Plymouth There is a combined Social Science degree and courses in Health and Social Care Studies, Social Work, Community Studies, Public Services and Criminology and Criminal Justice with Law, Politics, Psychology or Sociology.

Portsmouth Courses are offered in Social Work and Criminology with Criminal Justice, Forensic Science or Psychology. There is the opportunity to undertake up to 30 days of the practical placement abroad in the third year of the Social Work degree.

Queen's Belfast The Social Policy course covers citizenship, the family in European society, health and social care, penal policies, and aspects of poverty, politics and protest. There are also courses in Social Work and Criminology.

Robert Gordon In the three-year BA Social Work degree, course entry in Year 2 is possible for applicants with appropriate qualifications. There is also a flexible course in Applied Social Sciences with several options in social issues, e.g. psychology, police work and health.

Roehampton Criminology is offered from the Department of Social Sciences and can be combined with Sociology, Psychology, Social Anthropology, Photography or Journalism. Students can specialise in Years 2 and 3 in modules covering prisons, domestic violence and victimisation.

St Mark and St John Community courses focus on solutions to societal problems, community development and youth work.

Salford Degrees in Social Policy are offered with core modules in sociology and psychology and a wide range of options. There are also courses in Social Work, Criminology and Counselling.

Sheffield A degree is offered in Sociology and Political Studies which offers special topics including crime and deviance, ageing and society, social values, the European Union, East and Central European democracy and territorial politics. There are also degrees in Social Policy and Criminology and Social Policy and Sociology.

Sheffield Hallam There is a Social Sciences programme with several Criminology courses which include criminal justice, law, policing and psychology. There are also courses in Social Work and Youth and Community Studies/Work.

South Wales Social Science programmes include Criminology and Criminal Justice, Police Sciences, Public Services, and Youth and Community Work. There is also a degree in Social Work with 200 days of placement over the three-year course.

Southampton Social Policy is offered with Sociology. Applied Social Science includes four pathways with options in general, anthropology, criminology, and criminology and psychological studies.

Southampton Solent Social Work and Criminology single honours courses are offered. Criminology can be studied with Psychology and a course in Criminal Investigation and Psychology is also offered.

Staffordshire There is a Social Work degree with a 90-day placement. At Level 1 students cover subjects including law for social work, social work skills, social work values and methods and social policy.

Stirling Courses are offered in Social Work, Sociology and Social Policy. Sociology, social policy and criminology modules are taken in the first year of the Criminology degree.

Strathclyde A BA in Social Work with two 80-day placements in Years 2 and 4 is offered. Modules cover families and carers, ethics and law and legal frameworks.

Sunderland Courses are offered in Health and Social Care, Criminology, and Community and Youth Studies. A degree in Social Work is also available with 200 days spent on a placement.

See *Heap 2015: University Degree Course Offers* (Trotman Publishing) for details of offers

Sussex There are three- and four-year full-time or part-time courses in Social Work. A BA in Working with Children and Young People is also offered with assessed work placements.

Swansea Criminology is offered with Psychology, Law or Social Policy. Single honours courses are also offered in Social Policy and Social Work from the College of Human and Health Sciences.

Teesside The Social Sciences degree covers sociology, politics, public administration, economics and social policy, with an option in nursing. There are also degrees in Youth Studies with Criminology, Childhood and Youth Studies, Crime Scene Science (with placements) and Crime and Investigation.

Trinity St David There are courses in Social Inclusion, and Youth and Community Work, taught in English or Welsh. Placements are in statutory and voluntary youth-work settings.

Trinity St David (Swansea) Public Administration and Public Services degrees cover finance, law, criminology, leisure, the emergency services and community work. Health and Social Care is also offered and covers childhood services, policy and practice, working with communities, learning difficulties and communication, health policy in the UK, Europe and internationally, mental health, leadership and management and applied practice.

Ulster There are courses in Social Policy, Social Work, Community Development and Community Youth Work. Placements are an important part of many of these courses and can lead to specialisms.

West Scotland There is a Social Sciences degree with a common first year. Students make a final choice of degree subject from Year 2 onwards from Social Policy, Psychology, Sociology, Politics or Economics. There are also degrees in Criminal Justice, Social Policy and Social Work.

Westminster Criminal Justice is a three-year full-time course with a free option module in Year 1 taken from anywhere across the university. Sociology and Criminology is also offered.

Winchester The Social Work degree leads on to careers in social services, health services, schools, day centres and residential homes. A work placement is built into the second and third years of the course.

Wolverhampton Courses in Criminal Justice, Social Policy, Special Needs and Deaf Studies are offered. A course is also available in Social Work accredited by the General Social Care Council.

Worcester There are courses in Youth and Community Services and Social Welfare covering a range of social issues including policy, crime, violence, criminal justice and disability.

York The course in Applied Social Science follows the same programme as that of Social Policy in Year 1. Thereafter, over 15 optional subjects are available, giving maximum flexibility to subject choice.

OTHER INSTITUTIONS OFFERING SOCIAL SCIENCES/STUDIES COURSES
Blackburn (Coll), Bradford (Coll Univ Centre), Cornwall (Coll), Durham New (Coll), Havering (Coll), Kirklees (Coll), Llandrillo Cymru (Coll), Norwich City (Coll), Ruskin Oxford (Coll), Solihull (Coll), Somerset (Coll), South Devon (Coll), South Essex (Coll), Staffordshire Reg Fed (SURF), Suffolk (Univ Campus), Stockport (Coll), Sunderland City (Coll), Truro (Coll), UHI, Wigan and Leigh (Coll), Wiltshire (Coll), Wirral Met (Coll), Worcester (CT), York (Coll).

ALTERNATIVE COURSES
See under **Sociology**.

See *Heap 2015: University Degree Course Offers* (Trotman Publishing) for details of offers

SOCIOLOGY

(see also **Social Sciences/Studies**)
(* indicates universities with entry requirements over 340 UCAS points)

SUBJECT REQUIREMENTS/PREFERENCES
GCSE: English and Mathematics usually required.

SUBJECT INFORMATION
Sociology is the study of societies in general, both in Britain and abroad. Elective subjects offered will include industrial behaviour, crime and deviance, health and illness.

Aberdeen A highly rated department offering a course which covers topics in social-life interaction, structures and institutions. Thereafter a study is made of self and society, modern lifestyles, work and industry, peace, religion and also European and Scottish issues.

Abertay The Sociology degree offers a study covering media, work, social movements, politics, sexuality and crime. At the end of the second year it is possible to transfer to the degree in Behavioural Science. Placements are offered in the fourth year.

Anglia Ruskin A wide range of modules are offered in the Sociology degree (which can also be studied as part of the combined honours course), ranging from gender studies, politics, popular cultures and class inequality to educational problems, race, deviance, health and illness and understanding crime. There is also an opportunity to spend a semester in Sweden.

Aston Sociology is offered as a joint or combined honours course with a number of subject options including Business, Psychology, Public Policy and Management, International Relations, Spanish, Politics, French and English Language. Some courses have sandwich options.

Bangor Each year of the Sociology course consists of core modules and a choice of optional subjects including subjects from social sciences. Sociology can also be taken as a joint subject with up to 13 other subjects.

Bath In each year of the three-year Sociology and Social Policy course some subjects are stipulated, and in Years 2 and 3 subsidiary subjects (psychology, history, politics, philosophy and economics) are offered. There is an optional placement in Year 3. See also **Combined Courses**.

Bath Spa Sociology is a flexible degree programme offering a range of modules which include topics related to business, health, psychology, education and the media. Optional modules in Year 1 include health, education and welfare in Britain and exploring childhood.

Birmingham The Sociology course offers a range of pathways focusing on politics, social policy, social history, work, youth studies, criminology and the media. There is the opportunity in all years to take modules from another subject.

Birmingham City Sociology is a modular course of three years allowing students to select courses with options in social policy, cultural and media studies, psychology and urban studies. Public Sociology and joint courses with Political Science, Education or Philosophy are also offered.

Bradford The course in Sociology is one of the options in the Interdisciplinary Human Studies programme, also combining philosophy, psychology and English in Year 1. There is also a degree in Sociology and Psychology.

Brighton Sociology is offered with Social Policy or Criminology. The course in Social Policy and Sociology covers topics such as contemporary social inequalities, social justice, welfare and well-being and social problems and human needs.

Bristol In the broad first year of the Sociology course students take four compulsory units leading to specialisations later in the course. There are joint programmes combining with Philosophy, Social Policy, Politics and Theology. Sociology can also be taken with study abroad.

Bristol UWE Sociology is part of the Social Science undergraduate modular programme and covers such subjects as deviance and crime, health and well-being, the family and political sociology.

Brunel Three-year full-time and four-year sandwich courses with professional development are offered with a wide range of topics related to theory, methods and specialisation in aspects of British and international societies. Sociology can also be taken with Politics, Media Studies, Psychology or Anthropology.

Bucks New Sociology is offered jointly with Criminology or Psychology. These three-year courses combine the two subjects, looking at criminology or psychology within a sociological context.

Cambridge* See under **Social Sciences/Studies**.

Canterbury Christ Church Sociology is offered with Social Science as a single, joint or combined honours degree. Sociology can be combined with subjects including Politics, History, American Studies, Criminology, Health Studies, Early Childhood Studies and Business Studies.

Cardiff Sociology is introduced in Part I of the Sociology course, with studies in education, health and medicine, modernity, environment, risk and time, occupational socialisation and science, technology and methodology as some Part II options. Sociology can be taken as a joint subject with Social Policy (also a single honours subject), which is concerned with social problems such as housing, ageing, crime and health.

Central Lancashire Sociology is offered in the combined honours course and also as a single honours subject in which students can follow courses in history, politics, race and ethnic studies and other subjects.

Chester The single and combined honours degrees provide a flexible curriculum offering a range of choices. First-year modules cover topics including welfare politics, sex scandal and society, and deviance, crime and society.

City Sociology can be taken as a single or joint subject within the Social Sciences programme. The course includes applied sociology, race and society, mass communications, the sociology of work and industrial relations. Joint courses with Criminology, Media Studies, International Politics and Psychology can be taken.

Coventry In addition to a single honours course, Sociology can be taken with Psychology or Criminology. All courses can involve a year's work placement if taken as a sandwich course or with study abroad.

De Montfort Media, gender, race, politics, health and illness are all included in this applied Sociology course. Government or Politics can also be taken with Sociology.

Derby Sociology is offered as a single honours course and with over 20 joint honours subjects.

Durham* Sociology can be taken as a single honours subject focusing on social control and change, or within the combined honours degree, or with Law or Anthropology.

East London Sociology courses make use of the East London location for research studies. The course can be taken as an extended degree or with professional development.

Edge Hill Sociology can be taken as a single subject or with Childhood and Youth Studies, Early Childhood Studies or Criminology. The course focuses on critical issues in contemporary society.

Edinburgh Sociology, the discipline which examines the relationship between individuals and society, is offered as a single honours course or with Social Anthropology, Politics, Psychology, South Asian Studies or Economic History.

Edinburgh Napier The Psychology and Sociology course is a flexible research-based degree. After studying the foundations of both subjects, students have the choice to specialise or to continue studying both.

Edinburgh Queen Margaret Sociology is studied with Psychology in a course which combines the study of the individual and society with the chance to specialise. The course can be taken as an ordinary degree over three years or an honours degree over four.

Essex There are four courses focusing on Sociology, including combinations with Criminology, Media Studies and Humanities. All include modules in sociology and the modern world. The BA degree in Sociology can be taken with options in such areas as politics, sociology, psychology, history, philosophy and literature.

Exeter Sociology is a modular course in which a range of topics is chosen, with further options taken from other subjects in the social sciences. There is also an opportunity to spend a year in a European country, the US or Australia.

Glasgow* Sociology is studied within the Faculty of Arts and Social Sciences. The study covers issues arising from the social relations of work, family, community and market, and from the distribution of wealth and power. Anthropology is included as part of the course.

Glasgow Caledonian See under **Social Sciences/Studies**.

Gloucestershire The degree in Sociological Studies includes social policy and the welfare state, disability, race, and a broad study of modern societies. The course can also be studied jointly with Criminology, English Literature or Language, Geography, History, Psychology and Religion, Philosophy or Ethics.

Greenwich The Sociology degree covers sociological debates, comparative sociology, sociological skills and reasoning, and science in society. Options are available in such subjects as society and politics in Africa and Asia, racism, contemporary popular culture and drug use.

Huddersfield The Sociology degree covers the study of race and ethnicity, sociological imagination and human rights. There is also a degree in Sociology and Criminology or Psychology.

Hull Degrees are offered in Sociology or with Anthropology with an option to study with a language or Gender Studies. Joint honours courses are also offered including Sociology and Film Studies or Media Studies.

Keele Sociology must be taken with a second subject in the dual honours programme. Students can choose from over 30 subjects including American Studies, Chemistry, Music Technology and Physical Geography.

Kent A single honours course is offered with the option of spending a year in Hong Kong, Finland, the Netherlands and Spain. In Part II, core courses are taken, including social analysis and research practices in sociology, as well as optional third-year courses such as the sociology of politics, education, food, work, gender and the family.

Kingston The single honours Sociology course is organised around four themes: sociological theory, practical research, the application of sociology to contemporary issues and the comparative analysis of societies. Modules include media, culture and society, slavery and race, and youth, conformity and transgression. Joint courses are also offered.

Lancaster In the Sociology course, Year 1 includes two options from the sociology of class and gender, power and capitalism plus two other subjects. In Years 2 and 3 these subjects can be continued with additional topics such as deviance and social control, education and society, health and illness, the sociology of sport, popular culture and race. Sociolinguistics focuses on aspects of sociology and anthropology. Some exchanges with the US are possible.

Leeds In the first year of the Sociology degree, social, intellectual and cultural trends in contemporary society are studied together with study and research skills. Central problems in sociology and social policy form the core subjects in Year 2, and in Year 3 options are taken from a wide range of topics from which students are asked to choose three for further research.

Leeds Beckett Sociology is offered as part of the Social Sciences programme or as a single honours subject. Core modules cover areas such as contemporary society, gender, crime and justice and the sociology of gender and feminist perspectives.

Leicester The Sociology course concentrates on sociological issues from Year 1. A wide range of modules provides flexibility for students to focus their interests. Sociology can also be taken with Media, Politics and Psychology. A semester may be spent at a university in Europe or the US.

Liverpool Students are able to build their own degree course and choose which theories to pursue. In Year 2 one or two of five specialist pathways are chosen from, for example, crime and deviance, gender and law and ageing and society.

Liverpool John Moores The Sociology course involves the structure of modern society, racial divisions, health, education, social policy and globalisation. The course can also be taken with Criminology.

London (Goldsmiths) Sociology core courses cover theory, methods of research and social structure. In addition, optional courses are offered in the sociology of race, sex and gender, culture and communications and vision, truth and knowledge. Sociology is offered with Anthropology, Media and Politics.

London LSE LSE offers a Social Policy and Sociology course planned on a unit system with core courses in sociology, social structure, statistical analysis and sociological theory. Year 3 students choose from a range of options in sociology, social policy and one outside subject. Sociology can also be studied as a single subject.

London Met Sociology is offered as a single or joint honours degree programme. A course is also offered in Social Work and there are several Criminology courses.

London South Bank Sociology is offered with modules in revolutions, war and social change, sociological imagination, gender, difference and equality, youth, crime and delinquency, and politics and protest.

Loughborough The honours course in Sociology allows students to take modules in other subjects as career interests develop. Sociology modules in the second year include the sociology of gender, the sociology of tourism and the sociology of religion.

Manchester Students may take either the BSocSc degree in Sociology or follow the BASS route, which allows specialisation in Sociology in Years 2 and 3. Sociology is also offered with Philosophy, Social Anthropology and Criminology.

Manchester Met Sociology can be taken as part of the Humanities or Social Studies programme and can be studied as a single subject or as part of the combined honours programme.

Middlesex In the Sociology degree, topics cover the family and society, health, religion and crime. Work experience opportunities are available. Sociology can also be taken with Criminology or Psychology.

Newcastle The Sociology course combines the fields of sociology and social anthropology. There is also a joint course with Politics. Compulsory modules in Year 1 cover the sociological imagination; knowing in society; comparing cultures; social justice and citizenship; and doing sociology.

Northampton Sociology is offered as a single or joint honours course. Joint courses are offered in a wide range of subjects including Equine Studies, International Development and Human Geography.

Northumbria Sociology is a broad-based course emphasising sociological aspects but including the related disciplines of economics, history, psychology and philosophy, with course units covering class, gender and race. Sociology is also offered with Criminology.

Nottingham The Sociology course aims to develop an awareness of the workings of social groups and organisations and to understand the theories and evidence about social and political problems. In addition to core courses, students select options each year from a range of subjects including the sociology of religion, science and technology, gender, transnationalism and urban life. There are also courses in Sociology with Social Policy and in Cultural Sociology in Film and TV.

Nottingham Trent Sociology covers contemporary areas such as sexualities, religion, spirituality, food and culture. A course in Communication and Society is also offered which draws on psychology and sociology.

Oxford* It is possible to specialise in sociology as part of the course in Philosophy, Politics and Economics. The course also covers international relations.

Oxford Brookes Sociology is offered as a joint course with a wide range of second subjects including Law, Communication, Media and Culture, International Relations, Psychology and Religion and Theology.

Plymouth The Sociology course can be taken in single honours, major or minor programmes. It offers a range of specialised studies covering media, drugs in society, tourism, health and illness, gender, music, the virtual society, art and culture and developing societies. Several joint courses are offered.

Portsmouth Social theory, analysis and statistics, politics and social life and families in society are included in the first-year course in Sociology. Joint courses are also offered with Criminology, Media Studies and Psychology.

Queen's Belfast Sociology is a broad course focusing on the study of individuals and the society in which we live. There is a wide range of modules in fields involving both theoretical and practical issues.

Roehampton Sociology is available as a full-time or part-time single or combined honours course, with a choice from five other subjects in the combined honours programme. Years 2 and 3 include courses in areas such as health and illness, the sociology of death, food and society and globalisation. There are opportunities for placement with voluntary organisations.

St Mary's Sociology is offered as a single honours course or can be combined with a choice from 13 other subjects including Business Law, Management Studies and Theology and Religious Studies.

Salford The Sociology programme has modules covering the sociology of the family, culture and urban imaginations. There are also courses with Cultural Studies and Criminology.

Sheffield The Level 1 modules of the Sociology course cover sociology and social policy with specialisms appearing in Levels 2 and 3. Several unrestricted units are offered as modules in Years 2 and 3. Sociology is also available with English Language, History and Politics in the dual honours programme.

Sheffield Hallam Sociology topics cover social change and the emerging global society, culture, media and consumption, social inequality, crime, the family and employment. Psychology and Criminology are also offered with Sociology.

South Wales Sociology can be studies as a joint honours course with Criminology, Education and Psychology.

Staffordshire The Sociology course offers a combination of specialist aspects of sociology and related subjects offered as options in Years 1 and 2, with a wide range of options offered in Year 3. The course is also available as a joint degree.

Stirling Sociology is offered with Social Policy. The programme is built around a core course in theory and methods with options to suit the student's field of interest.

See *Heap 2015: University Degree Course Offers* (Trotman Publishing) for details of offers

Sunderland The degree in Sociology offers a broad picture of British and global society covering such topics as politics, history, media studies, cultural studies, health factors, race, work, leisure and criminology.

Surrey Sociology is a three-year course or a four-year course with a year spent in professional training in industry, commerce or the public sector. There is also a course in Sociology, Culture and New Media, which explores print, digital, broadcast and mobile phone technology. The course in Criminology and Sociology studies the nature of crime and deviance and possible solutions.

Sussex The main emphasis of the Sociology course is on sociological theory, independent critical work, the opportunity for specialist studies in contextual courses and the practical approach to planning and conducting research. Study is offered with related subjects and it is possible to follow pathways through the programme in these subjects. Sociology can be studied with a wide range of other subjects.

Teesside Sociology is a modular course with specialisms in criminal justice, policing and social control, football, culture and society and understanding domestic and sexual violence. Psychology can also be combined with Sociology.

Ulster The emphasis in the second year covers contemporary industrial societies with Irish themes, and a variety of options follows in Year 3. There is also a modular programme with Politics and Criminology. A number of joint courses are also offered.

Warwick The aim of the Sociology course is to provide students with an insight into theoretical sociology, methods of social research and the problems of the society in which we live. In Year 1, in addition to sociology courses, students choose an option from a course in applied social studies, economics, education, history, languages or psychology. A range of different options are available in Years 2 and 3. Sociology can be taken with French, History, Law or Politics.

West Scotland Sociology is offered as part of the Social Sciences programme and can be studied with Politics or Social Policy. The course focuses on the social structure of modern Britain in relation to various institutional areas.

Westminster The Sociology degree has options in crime, politics, globalisation, race and ethnicity, health and illness, feminist theory and media. The course can also be studied with History, Criminology or Social Policy.

Wolverhampton Sociology is offered as part of the modular degree scheme and covers British social life, work and society, sexuality and identity and families. The course is also offered with History or Politics.

Worcester The Sociology course offers themes in social welfare, criminal justice, gender and race. Students studying Sociology as a joint honours are offered the opportunity to specialise through a major/minor structure in the second year.

York The Sociology course provides a wide structural choice of subjects and perspectives. It may be taken as a single subject or in combination with Economics, Social Psychology, Political Sciences, Philosophy, Education or Criminology. There are no compulsory courses in Years 2 and 3, which offer a wide range of options. See also **Combined Courses**.

OTHER INSTITUTIONS OFFERING SOCIOLOGY COURSES

Blackburn (Coll), Bradford (Coll Univ Centre), Burton (Coll), Colchester (Inst), Cornwall (Coll), Doncaster (Coll Univ Centre), Grimsby (Univ Centre), Havering (Coll), Norwich City (Coll), Richmond (Am Int Univ), Ruskin Oxford (Coll), South Essex (Coll), Suffolk (Univ Campus), UHI, West Anglia (Coll), Wigan and Leigh (Coll). See also **Social Sciences/Studies**.

ALTERNATIVE COURSES

Anthropology, Communication, Government, History, Politics, Psychology, Social Administration, Social Policy, Social Sciences/Studies, Social Work.

See *Heap 2015: University Degree Course Offers* (Trotman Publishing) for details of offers

SPORTS SCIENCE/STUDIES

(including **Physical Education**)
(* indicates universities with entry requirements over 340 UCAS points)

SUBJECT REQUIREMENTS/PREFERENCES

GCE A level: A science subject may be required; check prospectuses. **GCSE:** English and Mathematics and often a science subject; check prospectuses.

SUBJECT INFORMATION

These are very popular courses and are increasing in number. Ability and involvement in sport are obviously important factors.

QUESTIONS TO CONSIDER

 * What can I specialise in?
 * Does the course involve work experience or a placement?
 * Is the course mainly academic or vocational?

Aberdeen The programme in Sports and Exercise Science commences at Level 2 after a year following a course in chemistry, medical science and sports science. In the third year, three specialist courses are offered: in integrative physiology, exercise physiology and nutrition and biochemistry of exercise. There is also a course in Sports Studies based on the inter-relationships between science, sport, health and leisure.

Abertay At the end of Year 2, the Sport and Exercise programme leads to options in Sport and Exercise Science, Sports Coaching, Physical Activity and Health, Sports Development, and Strength and Conditioning. There are also separate Sports degrees with Nutrition, Management or Psychology. Courses in Golf Management and Performance Golf are also offered.

Aberystwyth The Sport and Exercise Science degree follows three themes, psychology, physiology and biomechanics, which are studied in Years 1 and 2. Year 3 consists of specialist modules.

Anglia Ruskin Courses are offered in Sports Science, Sports Science with a foundation year, and Sports Coaching with Physical Education. A course in Sports Journalism is also available.

Bangor Sport, Health and Physical Education (SHAPE) includes sport psychology, health promotion, information technology and counselling. It is a theory and practice course. The same department also offers courses in Sports Science with options to specialise in Outdoor Activities, Physical Education or Psychology.

Bath* A three-year or a four-year sandwich degree is offered in Sports Performance, and in Sport and Exercise Science. There are opportunities for professional placement or study abroad.

Bedfordshire Sports Studies covers general health, coaching and sports psychology. There is a very wide range of courses in sports subjects including Applied Sports Science, Clinical Exercise Physiology, Sport and Physical Education and Sports Science and Personal Training.

Birmingham* Sport, Physical Education and Coaching Science is offered as a three-year full-time course. The degree in Sport and Materials Science focuses on sports equipment design. Courses are also offered in Applied Golf Management Studies and Sport and Exercise Science. See also **Combined Courses**.

Birmingham (UC) There are courses in Sport Management and Sport Therapy with an emphasis on practical studies leading to a professional qualification.

See *Heap 2015: University Degree Course Offers* (Trotman Publishing) for details of offers

Bolton Courses are offered in Sport and Leisure Management, Sports Development, Sports and Exercise Science, Sports Rehabilitation and Sports Science and Coaching, the last two courses requiring PE or a science subject.

Bournemouth Courses are offered in Sport Development and Coaching, bringing together aspects of management and coaching. Courses are also offered in Sports Management and with an optional specialisation in Golf; both include industrial placement in Year 3.

Brighton There are courses in Sport and Exercise Science, Sport Coaching, Sport Journalism and Sport and Leisure Management. There is also a Physical Education degree leading to a teaching qualification. See also **Leisure, Recreation Management and Tourism**.

Bristol UWE Sports Coaching, Sports Business Management, Sport Studies and Sport, Equestrian Sport Science and Exercise Management demonstrate the strength, scope and facilities in this department.

Brunel At Level 1 a broad Sport Sciences course is followed, with specialisms in Levels 2 and 3. Students can choose a non-teaching or a teaching route with a study of physical education modules. Other Sport Sciences courses focus on Management of Sport Development, Coaching, Human Performance and Physical Education and Youth Sport. Sport Sciences can also be taken with Business Studies.

Bucks New Degrees are offered in Football Business and Finance, Marketing or Media; Golf Club Management; Sports Management and Coaching Studies, Football Studies, Golf Studies or Rugby Studies; Sports Nutrition; and Sports Psychology.

Canterbury Christ Church Courses are offered in Physical Education and Sport and Exercise Science, in Sport and Exercise Psychology or Exercise Science and Sport and Leisure Management.

Cardiff Met (UWIC) Degrees are offered in Sports Biomedicine and Nutrition, Sport Coaching, Sport and Physical Education, Sport Conditioning, Rehabilitation and Massage, Sport and Exercise Science and Sport Management.

Central Lancashire Core subjects in the Sport Science degree cover biomechanics, physiology and information technology. Optional studies follow in Years 2 and 3. There are also courses in Sports Psychology, Motor Sports, Outdoor Leadership, Sport Public Relations, Sports Therapy and Sports Coaching, Sports Technology and Sports Event Management.

Chester Sport and Exercise Sciences is offered at Chester as a single or combined honours with Sport Development and Sport Journalism offered at the Warrington campus. Optional modules include sports coaching, physical activity and aspects of management.

Chichester Several degrees in Sport are offered including Exercise Psychology, Sports Coaching Science, Sports Development, Sport Exercise Science and Sport Therapy. There is also a degree in Physical Education and Sports Coaching.

Colchester (Inst) The Sport Management course is aimed at students interested in working in gymnasiums and leisure centres.

Coventry Sport and Exercise Science is offered, with specialist studies in Year 3. Other courses include Sport Management, Sport Marketing, Sport Psychology, Sport, Exercise and Health Sciences and Sports Therapy.

Cumbria A very wide range of Sport degrees is available covering Sport Coaching, Sport and Exercise Therapy, Sport Studies (Sport and Physical Activity Development), Sport Therapy and Massage, and Sport and Exercise Science.

Derby A three-year degree is offered in Sport and Exercise Studies and there is a wide range of Sports Studies courses, including Massage and Exercise Therapies, Psychology, Sport Coaching and Sport Development.

Dundee A degree is offered in Sports Biomedicine. In addition to biological topics the course also covers psychology and the design and administration of coaching programmes.

Durham* The course in Sport, Exercise and Physical Activity covers social issues, sport development and psychology, coaching and performance, and health and rehabilitation. Students have the opportunity to take part in community-based sports activities.

East London Courses in Sport and Exercise Science, Sports Therapy, Sports Coaching, and Sport, Physical Education and Development are offered. They share a common first year with specialisation taking place in Years 2 and 3.

Edge Hill Courses include Sport and Exercise Science or Psychology, Sports Development, Sports Studies and Sport Therapy. There are also courses in Coaching Education and Physical Education and School Sport.

Edinburgh Courses are offered in Applied Sport Science, and Sport and Recreation Management, the former emphasising scientific aspects of sport, the latter with a 10-week placement with a leading sports organisation.

Edinburgh Napier Sport and Exercise Science is offered as a three- or four-year full-time degree. Specialisms can be taken in Exercise Physiology, Sport Psychology, Sports Coaching and Sports Injuries.

Essex The Sport and Exercise Science degree covers biology, biochemistry, physics and psychology with a focus on coaching and training. This degree and the joint programme with Biology have a strong practical component. There are sports bursaries for competing athletes.

Exeter Exercise and Sport Science covers anatomy, biomechanics, physiology, psychology and sociology, teaching, learning, leadership, communication skills, coaching sport and exercise. There are opportunities for some specialisation in Years 2 and 3.

Glasgow A degree in Sports Medicine is offered. It is also possible to study Physiology with Sport Science and with Nutrition. This course can be taken to MSci level and includes a year-long placement.

Gloucestershire Coaching, Development and Fitness are some of the specialisms offered with Sports. Courses are also available in Sport and Exercise Sciences, Sport Science, Sports Education, Sports Management, Strength and Conditioning and Sports Therapy.

Greenwich The Sports Science course covers human movement, the sociology of sport, sport physiology, competing, nutrition and performance. Sports Science is also offered with Coaching or Professional Football Coaching. A course in Physical Education and Sport is also offered.

Hertfordshire The Sports Therapy course includes psychology, physiotherapy, sports injury and treatments and can be studied with a sandwich year. Three-year Sport Studies and Sport and Exercise Science courses are also available in addition to several joint degree courses.

Huddersfield There are several Sports degrees with specialisations in Journalism, Marketing and Public Relations, and Promotion and Marketing. Courses are three years full time or four years with a sandwich year.

Hull Sport Science is offered as a minor subject with Psychology or Geography. There are also courses in Sport and Exercise Science, Sports Rehabilitation and Sports Coaching and Performance.

Kent Sports Therapy and Sport and Exercise for Health include health promotion, sport rehabilitation and event management. Other courses focus on Exercise Management and Psychology. Sport Science is also offered.

See *Heap 2015: University Degree Course Offers* (Trotman Publishing) for details of offers

Kingston Sports Science is offered as a three-year full-time course, a joint honours degree, or as a four-year extended degree that includes a foundation course. Courses are also offered in Sports Analysis and Coaching and in Exercise, Nutrition and Health.

Leeds Sports and Exercise Science and Physiology are offered covering biology, physiology, psychology and sports specialisms. Both courses can involve a study year taken between the second and final year.

Leeds Beckett Sport and Exercise Science is a modular course taken in the School of Leisure and Sports Studies, sharing Year 1 with Physical Education and Sport and Recreation Development. Other Sport courses include Exercise and Fitness, Physical Education, Leisure and Recreation, Coaching, Events Management and Marketing. The university is a leader in the field of sport courses.

Leeds Trinity The degree in Sport and Exercise Science can be followed with options in nutrition, psychology or strength and conditioning. There are also courses in Sport Journalism and in Health and Nutrition.

Lincoln Sport and Exercise Science, Sport Development and Coaching, Golf Science and Development, Sports Business Management and Equine Sports Science are offered as three-year degree courses.

Liverpool Hope Degrees are offered in Sport Psychology, Sport Studies, and Sport and Exercise Science. All Sports students have the opportunity to take part in a field trip to Hope's outdoor educational centre in Wales.

Liverpool John Moores Sports and Exercise Science covers research methods (including statistics), coaching and applied sports science. Topics include physiology, health science, psychology and recreational management. Science and Football, Coaching Development, and Applied Sport Psychology are also offered.

London Met Several courses are offered, including Sport Psychology and Coaching, Sports Business Management, Sports and Dance Therapy, Sports Science, Therapy and Physical Education.

London South Bank A three year course is offered in Sport and Exercise Science. The course is structured around four main themes: physiology, psychology, nutrition and biomechanics within the context of sport and exercise.

Loughborough* This is a leading university in this field and offers a range of Sports Science and Management courses. A course is also offered in Sports Technology covering equipment design and ergonomics and includes industrial training.

Manchester Met A wide range of courses is offered including Coaching and Sports Development, Physical Education and Pedagogy, Physiology (Physical Activity and Health), Psychology of Sport and Health, Sport, Exercise Science and Sport Management.

Middlesex Opportunities for work placements exist in the degree course in Sport and Exercise Rehabilitation. Other courses include Sport and Exercise Science, Teaching and Coaching Sport and Sports Performance.

Newman Sport Science and Sport Studies are offered as single, joint or minor courses. New for 2014 is a course in Sports Coaching.

Northampton Courses are offered in Sport Development, Sport Studies (joint honours) and Sport and Exercise Science. A course in Physical Activity and Health is also available.

Northumbria Courses are offered in Applied Sport Science with Coaching, Sport Management, Sport, Exercise and Nutrition and Sport Development. Psychology is also available with Sport Sciences.

Nottingham Trent Courses in Sport and Exercise Science, Sport Science with Management, Sport and Leisure, Psychology and Education, Equestrian Psychology and Sports Science, Exercise, Nutrition and Health are available.

See *Heap 2015: University Degree Course Offers* (Trotman Publishing) for details of offers

Oxford Brookes Courses in Sport and Exercise Science, Sport Science and Sport, Coaching and Physical Education are available with study abroad options in Europe, the US, Canada and Australia.

Plymouth A unique course in Applied Marine Sports Science is offered that covers sailing and navigation, diving and surfing. There are also courses in Sport Therapy, a teacher-training course in Physical Education and courses in Surf Science and Technology and Ocean Yachting.

Portsmouth The Sport and Exercise Science course offers students the opportunity to participate in sport and obtain a variety of coaching awards. The scientific elements of this course include physiology, nutrition and psychology. There are also courses in Sports Development and Sports Business Management.

Robert Gordon Applied Sport and Exercise Science is offered as a four-year full-time course with work placements in Years 2 and 3. The course covers human anatomy, exercise physiology, biomechanics and sport psychology.

Roehampton Sport and Exercise Science is a single honours course studying sport from a scientific and a cultural perspective. It allows focus on specific areas of personal interest or the study of a broad range of sport topics. There is also a single honours course in Sport Psychology and a foundation degree in Sports Coaching and Practice.

St Mark and St John A wide range of courses covers Coaching and Fitness, Rehabilitation, Sport Exercise Management and Therapy and Outdoor Activities.

St Mary's Courses are offered in Sport Science, Sports Coaching Science, Sport Rehabilitation, Physical and Sport Education, Health, Exercise and Physical Activity and Strength and Conditioning Science.

Salford A Sports Rehabilitation programme is available dealing with sports injuries and the psychology of sport. Hospital and clinical placements are included in the course. Exercise, Physical Activity and Health, Sport Science and Sport and Leisure Management are also offered as degree courses.

Sheffield The Sports Engineering degree focuses on the design of sporting equipment and is an extension of the Mechanical Engineering programme.

Sheffield Hallam The Sports Studies degree programme offers Sport and Exercise Science, Sports and Community Development, Coaching, Sport Business Management and Sport Science for Performance Coaching. There is a common first year for many of the degrees and the opportunity to change at the end of the year.

South Wales The Sports Studies course prepares students for the sports and leisure industry. There are also courses in Clinical Exercise Physiology, Football Coaching and Performance, Sports Development, and a degree in Rugby Coaching and Performance, which enables students to gain Welsh Rugby Union coaching qualifications.

Southampton Solent Courses are offered in Sport Coaching and Development, Sport Studies and Business, Applied Sport Science and Football Studies with Business. There are also Water Sports and Outdoor Adventure programmes.

Staffordshire A range of Sport courses is offered, including Sport and Exercise Science, Sports Therapy, Sports Studies, Sports Journalism, Sports Development and Coaching and PE and Youth Sport Coaching.

Stirling A course in Sports Studies is available covering sport policy and management, sport, exercise and health, and sport, society and culture. Sports Studies can also be studied with, for example, Business Studies, Psychology, Accountancy or Film and Media. Sports and Exercise Science is also offered.

Strathclyde Courses cover Sport and Physical Activity and Sports Engineering. The latter focuses on the development of high-performance sports equipment and the former on the promotion of and issues surrounding sport and physical activity.

See *Heap 2015: University Degree Course Offers* (Trotman Publishing) for details of offers

Sunderland The Sports courses include Exercise Sciences and Development, Coaching and Sport Studies. Sport can also be studied as a combined course and a course in Exercise, Health and Fitness is available.

Swansea The modular degree in Sports Science is centred around physiology, biometrics and psychology, leading to specialisms in exercise and health, diet and nutrition, and sports coaching. Sports Science can be studied with Management, Mathematics or Physics.

Teesside A range of courses is offered focusing on sport and exercise, including Sports Therapy and Outdoor Leadership, and with specialisms in Coaching Science, Applied Exercise Science and Psychology.

Trinity St David A degree in Physical Education includes work placements and an exchange scheme in the US. There is also a degree in Health and Exercise with Sport Studies.

Ulster During the first two years of the Sport and Exercise Sciences degree, students undertake an analysis of sport and leisure from both theoretical and practical perspectives. Topics include individual performance, psychology, interpersonal relations, issues in sport and vocational studies. The course can be taken with an optional sandwich year. There are also degrees in Sport Studies and Sports Technology.

West Scotland Applied Sport and Exercise Science, Sport Coaching, Sports Development and Sport and Exercise Science are offered. A course in Sports Journalism is also available over three or four years.

Winchester Courses are offered in Sports Science, Sports Studies, Sports Management and Sports Coaching and Development. They are offered as single or combined programmes with subjects including History, Law and Sociology.

Wolverhampton Sport Studies can be taken as a specialist award, joint, major or minor subject and covers a wide range of topics from community recreation and games performance to coaching, dance and European leisure policy. There are also courses in Sport and Exercise Science, Sports Coaching and Physical Activity, Exercise and Health.

Worcester Courses are offered including Sports Therapy, Sport and Exercise Science, Sport Business Management, Sports Studies and Sport Coaching Science. Courses are also offered in Physical Education and Cricket Coaching and Management.

York St John Courses are offered in Sport Science for Performance Conditioning; Sport, Society and Development; Physical Education and Sports Coaching, Sports Science: Exercise Practice; and Sport Science and Injury Management.

OTHER INSTITUTIONS OFFERING SPORTS SCIENCE/STUDIES COURSES
Basingstoke (CT), Bath City (Coll), Bishop Burton (Coll), Blackburn (Coll), Blackpool and Fylde (Coll), Bridgwater (Coll), Central Nottingham (Coll), Cornwall (Coll), Dearne Valley (Coll), Doncaster (Coll Univ Centre), Duchy (Coll), Exeter (Coll), Farnborough (CT), Filton (Coll), Grimsby (Univ Centre), Hopwood Hall (Coll), Hull (Coll), Leeds City (Coll), Lincoln (Coll), Llandrillo Cymru (Coll), Loughborough (Coll), Mid-Cheshire (Coll), Myerscough (Coll), Nescot, NEW (Coll), Newcastle (Coll), North Lindsey (Coll), Northop (Coll), North Warwickshire and Hinckley (Coll), Norwich City (Coll), Pembrokeshire (Coll), St Helens (Coll), Sheffield (Coll), Shrewsbury (CAT), Sir Gâr (Coll), South Cheshire (Coll), South Downs (Coll), South Essex (Coll), Southport (Coll), SRUC, Staffordshire Reg Fed (SURF), Suffolk (Univ Campus), Sunderland City (Coll), Truro (Coll), Tyne Met (Coll), Wakefield (Coll), Warwickshire (Coll), Wigan and Leigh (Coll), Worcester (CT), Writtle (Coll), York (Coll).

ALTERNATIVE COURSES
Anatomy, Biology, Human Movement Studies, Leisure Studies, Physiology, Recreation Management.

TOWN PLANNING AND URBAN PLANNING STUDIES

(* indicates universities with entry requirements over 340 UCAS points)

SUBJECT REQUIREMENTS/PREFERENCES
GCE A level: Economics and Geography are appropriate. **GCSE:** English and Mathematics.

SUBJECT INFORMATION
Courses in Town Planning, which are all very similar, lead to qualification as a member of the Royal Town Planning Institute (RTPI). Courses usually include a year out. (Students should check with universities.) This is an ideal course for the geographer. The employment prospects for graduate planners have undergone a remarkable transformation in recent years. There is now a considerable shortage of planners in view of the increased demand by local authorities and the private sector. Increasingly, consultants, developers and other property-related organisations, such as major retailers, are employing qualified Planning graduates, with the result that demand is far outstripping supply. In response, the Planning schools have increased their intakes but there would appear to be a significant shortage for the foreseeable future.

Additionally, the 3+1 format of courses provides an opportunity for students who are well trained in environmental matters to leave such courses after three years with an honours degree, but without the necessity of completing the Diploma in Town Planning (DTP) for professional qualification. There are also increasing job opportunities for such students.

Birmingham Urban and Regional Planning is offered combined with Geography. A joint degree in Planning is offered with Economics or Social Policy and a programme in Spatial Planning and Business Management is also available.

Bristol UWE Town and Country Planning is a three-year degree course with a further year to specialise in transport, urban design or spatial planning leading to a master's. There are also courses in Architecture and Planning.

Cardiff City and Regional Planning is a three-year, full-time or four-year sandwich course providing a comprehensive study of all aspects of town planning, including environmental design, economics, development, urban regeneration and transportation planning. Compared with other courses, Cardiff puts particular stress on social science approaches to planning and on analytical and computing skills. There is also a degree course in Human Geography and Planning.

Dundee Town and Regional Planning is a four-year course providing a broad study leading to two areas of specialised study: conservation and design, and environmental policy and practice. Final-year options include specialisms in community governance, climate change, environmental management and urban conservation. Planning is also offered with Economics or Geography.

Heriot-Watt Planning and Property Development is a four-year full-time or a five-year course with a sandwich year spent in practice between the second and third years. The course combines real-estate management with urban and regional planning. All aspects of planning are covered in this course, which leads to a BSc degree and full exemption from the final professional examinations of the RTPI.

Kingston Property Planning and Development is offered as a three-year full-time or four-year sandwich course. A special feature of the course is its emphasis on sustainable development.

See *Heap 2015: University Degree Course Offers* (Trotman Publishing) for details of offers

Leeds Beckett Human Geography and Planning is offered as a three-year full-time course offering students the chance to study contemporary social, economic and cultural geography with urban and local planning.

Liverpool The Environment and Planning (MPlan) course focuses on urban and regional planning, urban design and environmental planning. There are also courses in Town and Regional Planning and Urban Regeneration and Planning.

London (UCL) Two three-year courses are offered: Urban Planning, Design and Management, and Urban Studies. They share a common first and second year. The final choice of degree is made in Year 3.

London South Bank Urban and Environmental Planning is offered. The course covers planning history and principles, law, geography, transport, strategies, finance, policy and spatial planning. The course is accredited by the RTPI.

Manchester The four-year BA course in Town and Country Planning includes the option to study for three years, leading to the degree of Bachelor of Planning. The latter is recognised by the RTPI, giving exemptions from their examinations. There is also a course in Urban Studies.

Newcastle Town Planning is a three-year course. The course carries full exemption from the examinations of the RTPI. There is also a new course in Architecture and Urban Planning.

Nottingham Trent A three-year or four-year sandwich degree is offered in Planning and Development covering surveying, economics, law, construction, valuation, property management, development consultancy, planning consultancy and built environment research.

Oxford Brookes Two degrees, Planning and Property Development, and City and Regional Planning, are offered as single honours courses. The former is accredited by the RTPI when combined with the postgraduate Diploma in Planning and the postgraduate Assessment of Professional Competence.

Queen's Belfast The Environmental Planning course can lead to a one-year master's course with specialism in either Spatial Regeneration or Urban and Rural Design. Level 1 covers an introduction to key issues. Subsequent studies involve both design and the social implications of the planned environment.

Reading The BSc in Real Estate also leads to an MSc or Diploma in Planning and Development. The course provides exemptions from the examinations of both the RICS and the RTPI.

Sheffield Urban Studies and Planning covers major subject areas in Year 1 including development, planning and the state; data analysis and presentation; economics for spatial planning; and the environmental challenge. In the subsequent years compulsory subjects are studied covering areas such as profit, planning and context, urban design and place-making, development planning and critical perspectives. Courses are also offered in Landscape Architecture with Planning and Urban Studies.

Sheffield Hallam An Urban and Environmental Planning degree is offered with options to specialise in regeneration, environment and conservation and design. A course in Geography and Planning is also available.

Westminster One of the degrees in Architecture focuses on Urban Design. The award allows students the opportunity to continue study in planning and other disciplines such as urban renewal and regeneration.

ALTERNATIVE COURSES
Architecture, Development Studies, Geography, Housing, Landscape Architecture, Social Administration, Sociology, Transport.

See *Heap 2015: University Degree Course Offers* (Trotman Publishing) for details of offers

VETERINARY SCIENCE/MEDICINE

(see also **Animal Sciences**)
(* indicates universities with entry requirements over 340 UCAS points)

SUBJECT REQUIREMENTS/PREFERENCES
GCE A level: Three subjects in Mathematics/science subjects with Chemistry essential; check prospectuses.

SUBJECT INFORMATION
These are very popular and academically demanding courses for which some work experience prior to application is obligatory. Every course has much the same content, but check with prospectuses for all courses.

Bristol* The first three years of Veterinary Science cover the pre-clinical stage and include the basic sciences (anatomy, biochemistry and physiology) with animal management, breeding and genetics. Years 4 and 5 are the clinical years and include veterinary public health, pathology, farm-animal science, companion-animal science and clinical rotations. Degree courses are also offered in Animal Behaviour and Welfare and in Veterinary Nursing and Bioveterinary Science.

Bristol UWE The degree in Veterinary Nursing Science includes 70 weeks of work placement and leads to the RCVS qualification. This course and that of Foundation Veterinary Nursing Science take place at Hartpury College, Gloucester.

Cambridge* In the first and second years, students read for Part IA and Part IB of the Medical and Veterinary Sciences Tripos, with both parts including veterinary anatomy and veterinary physiology, pathology and pharmacology. Part II enables students to make a study of a single subject in depth, such as applied biology, biochemistry, genetics, psychology or zoology. The three years that follow the pre-clinical course include weekly practical experience with a vet in practice in Year 5. The final year is lecture-free and includes seven weeks of elective study and the final veterinary examination. Not available at the following Colleges: Christ's, Homerton, Hughes Hall, King's, Peterhouse or Trinity.

Central Lancashire A four year sandwich course is available in Veterinary Nursing linked with Myerscough College a few miles from the university. Applicants must spend six to eight weeks in a small veterinary practice before enrolling.

Edinburgh* The curriculum of the Veterinary Medicine course falls into two interrelated main parts. The first (pre-clinical) covers the biology and chemistry of the animal body, and the second (foundation clinical studies) deals with surgery, diagnostic imaging, anaesthesia and pharmacology. Students can interrupt their studies after Year 2 to take an intercalated degree in Biochemistry, Neuroscience, Veterinary Biological Sciences or Microbiology and Infection.

Edinburgh Napier There is a course in Veterinary Nursing with work placements.

Glasgow* In the first two years (the pre-clinical period) of the Veterinary Medicine and Surgery course, studies cover anatomy, biomolecular sciences, physiology and animal husbandry. The third year (para-clinical studies) covers pathology, bacteriology, virology, parasitology and pharmacology. The fourth year is lecture-intensive and the fifth year largely clinical, with practical lessons in medicine, surgery and pathology. Selected candidates may be admitted to an intercalated BSc degree course in one of eight subjects. There is also a course in Veterinary Biosciences with the option to study abroad.

Harper Adams There are courses in Veterinary Nursing or Veterinary Physiotherapy and in Bioveterinary Science.

Lincoln A degree in Bioveterinary Science covers animal health, infection, immunity and husbandry.

Liverpool* In Year 1 of the five-year Veterinary Science course, the structure and development of the animal body are studied. Animal maintenance, pathology, disease processes and disease-producing organisms are studied in Years 2 and 3. In Years 4 and 5 students undertake clinical rotations while studying clinical theory and electives. A six-year course including an intercalated one-year honours degree is also offered. There is also a course in Bioveterinary Science.

London (RVC)* Years 1 and 2 of the BVet Med course at the London campus are the pre-clinical years that introduce aspects such as anatomy, physiology, animal management and husbandry. In Year 3 students commence clinical studies involving pathology, toxicology, body systems and hygiene, and veterinary medicine. Vacation study lasting 26 weeks takes place in a veterinary practice, followed by rotations in small-animal medicine, equine medicine and farm-animal medicine. The final year is devoted to developing practical skills. There is also a Veterinary Gateway programme for students wishing to reach the required entry standard, a course in Bioveterinary Sciences and a Veterinary Nursing degree.

Nottingham* A School of Veterinary Medicine and Science is based on the Sutton Bonington campus, 10 miles south of the university. The five-year Veterinary Science course is divided into three stages: in Years 1 and 2 learning about normal animal-care studies; Years 3 and 4 involving professional skills; and the final year practising clinical skills. There is also a Pre-veterinary Science course leading to a four-year course in the West Indies.

Surrey* The degree in Veterinary Biosciences focuses on animal health and disease. There are opportunities for professional placements. The course lasts three years with an optional training year between the second and final year.

INSTITUTIONS OFFERING VETERINARY SCIENCE/MEDICINE COURSES
Askham Bryan (Coll), Barony (Coll), Brighton, Duchy (Coll), Greenwich, Harper Adams, Middlesex, Myerscough (Coll), Nottingham Trent, Warwickshire (Coll), West Anglia (Coll), Worcester.

ALTERNATIVE COURSES
Agricultural Sciences, Animal Sciences, Biological Sciences, Medicine, Nutrition, Pharmacology.

6 | **FINAL CAREER DESTINATIONS**

Deciding what career path to follow after leaving university or college is an important issue for you – and your parents. Unfortunately there's not much information available to prove that one university is better than another in helping you. Your professors and lecturers certainly do not consider it their main responsibility to find you work! That's your problem, they will say, pointing you in the direction of the university careers service.

If you do want a steer in the right direction, then it's very interesting to note that students who have been on sandwich courses, in which they have spent time with an employer, seem to be more successful than others in obtaining full-time employment on graduation. The likelihood is that if you impress an employer while you are on work placement he or she will often offer you a job when you've completed your degree.

Research done among employers about graduate employment and what they seek shows that they invariably say 'intelligence and transferable skills'. In other words, bright young people who can be trained to do a job, who can communicate with people, write reports, work in a team and perhaps use a computer or speak a foreign language.

Finally, remember that three, four or more years will elapse between the time you leave school and graduation day when you leave university, and your ideas and aspirations for your future career will develop and change during your studies.

It's also likely that there will be changes in the industries relating to your degree subject – particularly in areas such as media, economics and politics. In addition, it's worth bearing in mind that other factors, such as the economy, may affect competition for jobs and the type of careers which will be available when you graduate.

So it's not absolutely important to decide on a future career before commencing a degree course. However, the information below may give you some insight into graduate destinations and careers. The following statistics are provided by the Higher Education Statistics Agency (HESA) and Surrey University Careers Service, from 2011–12 graduates who were surveyed six months after course completion. While this information is intended to give you an idea of the range of careers and study paths available, it is not representative of all graduates, courses or universities. It is a snapshot of some graduate experiences, which may develop and change in the future. Graduate data is also usually collected only six months after graduation, so those who get jobs any later than this (which is a growing norm) are not included.

SUBJECT-SPECIFIC STATISTICS
Out of all the graduates surveyed by HESA, 53.8% were in full-time work (down from 54.8% in 2009–10).

The table overleaf will give you some idea of the subjects that lead most directly into employment.

Degree subject	Full-time work (%)	Part-time work (%)	Work and further study (%)	Further study (%)	Assumed to be unemployed (%)
Agriculture and Related Subjects	51.4	16.5	4.9	10.9	8.9
Architecture Building and Planning	60.4	10.2	6.4	8.4	10.2
Biological Sciences	41.9	17.9	7.5	19.7	8.0
Business and Administration	59.4	12.6	6.4	6.5	10.0
Combined Studies	48.9	14.9	7.3	13.8	8.0
Computer Science	60.7	10.8	2.9	7.8	14.4
Creative Arts and Design	47.2	25.0	4.2	7.6	11.2
Education	62.7	14.7	4.5	10.9	4.0
Engineering and Technology	61.1	8.9	3.3	12.1	10.5
Historical and Philosophical Studies	40.5	14.4	7.4	23.1	9.1
Languages	44.5	14.6	6.5	20.2	8.7
Law	34.9	11.1	12.0	30.4	7.2
Mass Communications and Documentation	53.2	21.2	2.8	5.5	12.4
Mathematical Sciences	47.1	7.9	8.2	22.9	9.1
Medicine and Dentistry	91.9	0.4	1.5	5.6	0.2
Physical Sciences	41.9	10.9	4.5	27.4	9.8
Social Studies	50.2	14.7	6.6	13.3	9.5
Subjects allied to Medicine	67.3	12.7	4.1	7.8	5.1
Veterinary Sciences	84.8	3.3	1.0	2.2	6.5

CAREER PATHS OF GRADUATES FROM THE MOST POPULAR SUBJECTS

The information below shows you the sectors into which graduates of certain subjects entered (taken from the 2011–12 graduate statistics). The figures given do not equal the total number of graduates surveyed as we have chosen only to include the most relevant or interesting areas.

Accounting (out of 3,830 respondents)
* Further study: 29.2% (1,120)
* Legal and accounting: 21.7% (830)
* Wholesale and retail trade: 12.8% (490)
* Finance and insurance: 9.4% (360)

Architecture (out of 2,105 respondents)
* Architecture and engineering: 37.1% (780)
* Further study: 24.5% (515)

* Wholesale and retail trade: 8.1% (170)
* Construction: 4.3% (90)

Art and Design (out of 13,160 respondents)
* Wholesale and retail trade: 23.7% (3,120)
* Professional, scientific and technical (including management and head office, legal and accounting, advertising and market research): 13.5% (1,780)
* Further study: 17% (2,235)
* Arts, entertainment and recreation: 6.6% (870)
* Information and communication (including computer programming, telecommunications, broadcasting, new media and publishing): 4.9% (645)

Business Studies (out of 9,910 respondents)
* Wholesale and retail trade: 17.3% (1,715)
* Further study: 24.8% (2,445)
* Finance and insurance: 7.9% (780)
* Manufacturing: 6.2% (615)
* Information and communication (including computer programming, telecommunications, broadcasting, new media and publishing): 4.8% (475)

Cinematography and Photography (out of 2,940 respondents)
* Further study: 18.4% (540)
* Arts, entertainment and recreation: 5.6% (165)
* Wholesale and retail trade: 21.8% (640)
* Information and communication (including computer programming, telecommunications, broadcasting, new media and publishing): 19% (560)

Computer Science (Broad) (out of 8,845 respondents)
* Information and communication (including computer programming, telecommunications, broadcasting, new media and publishing): 28.6% (2,530)
* Further study: 14.4% (1,275)
* Wholesale and retail trade: 10.8% (955)
* Professional, scientific and technical (including management and head office, legal and accounting, advertising and market research): 5.2% (460)

Drama, Dance and Performing Arts (out of 5,145 respondents)
* Arts, entertainment and recreation: 18.2% (935)
* Further study: 21% (1,080)
* Wholesale and retail trade: 13.9% (715)
* Education: 12.5% (645)

Economics (out of 4,235 respondents)
* Further study: 23.7% (1,005)
* Finance and insurance: 18.1% (765)
* Legal and accounting: 11.6% (490)
* Wholesale and retail trade: 7.8% (330)

Education and Teacher Training (out of 13,400 respondents)
* Education: 53.5% (7,165)
* Further study: 21.8% (2,920)
* Human health and social work: 7.6% (1,020)
* Public administration and defence; social security work: 7.8% (1,040)
* Administrative and support services: 3.5% (465)

English (out of 9,115 respondents)
* Education: 13.5% (1,230)
* Wholesale and retail trade: 11.8% (1,075)
* Information and communication (including computer programming, telecommunications, broadcasting, new media and publishing): 6.2% (565)
* Further study: 25.7% (2,345)
* Arts, entertainment and recreation: 3.1% (285)

History, including Theological and Philosophical Studies (out of 12,950 respondents)
* Further study: 17.2% (2,225)
* Wholesale and retail trade: 11.5% (1,490)
* Education: 9.6% (1,240)
* Professional, scientific and technical (including management and head office, legal and accounting, advertising and market research): 5.8% (755)

Hospitality, Leisure and Tourism (out of 3,825 respondents)
* Accommodation and food/beverage service: 19.2% (735)
* Further study: 6.7% (255)
* Sports activities, amusement and recreation: 5.8% (220)
* Travel agency, tour operator and other reservation service and related activities: 3.0% (115)

Law (out of 10,320 respondents)
* Further study: 39.5% (4,080)
* Wholesale and retail trade: 11% (1,135)
* Legal and accounting: 11.9% (1,225)
* Finance and insurance: 5.5% (545)
* Public administration and defence; social security work: 4.4% (450)

Management Studies (out of 4,525 respondents)
* Wholesale and retail trade: 17.2% (780)
* Further study: 10.8% (490)
* Professional, scientific and technical (including management and head office, legal and accounting, advertising and market research): 11% (500)
* Finance and insurance: 5% (520)

Mathematics (out of 4,770 respondents)
* Further study: 27.8% (1,325)
* Finance and insurance: 13.2% (630)
* Professional, scientific and technical (including management and head office, legal and accounting, advertising and market research): 11.1% (530)
* Wholesale and retail trade: 7.1% (340)
* Education: 7.8% (530)

Mechanical Engineering (out of 2,685 respondents)
* Manufacturing: 30.9% (830)
* Further study: 13.8% (370)
* Professional, scientific and technical (including management and head office, legal and accounting, advertising and market research): 19.7% (530)
* Wholesale and retail trade: 6.5% (175)

Medicine (Clinical) (out of 4,810 respondents)
* Human health and social work: 98.1% (4,720)
* Further study: 1.5% (70)

Nursing (out of 10,725 respondents)

* Human health and social work: 90.3% (9,690)
* Further study: 11.2% (1,205)

Politics (out of 4,255 respondents)
* Further study: 24.7% (1,050)
* Wholesale and retail trade: 9.6% (410)
* Professional, scientific and technical (including management and head office, legal and accounting, advertising and market research): 7.6% (325)
* Education: 6.3% (270)
* Finance and insurance: 5.3% (225)
* Public administration and defence; social security work: 6.6% (280)

Psychology (out of 10,080 respondents)
* Further study: 23.8% (2,400)
* Human health and social work: 18.4% (1,855)
* Wholesale and retail trade: 12.6% (1,270)
* Education: 11.4% (1,145)

Social Work (out of 5,800 respondents)
* Human health and social work: 28.1% (1,630)
* Public administration and defence; social security work: 30.9% (1,790)
* Further study: 9.7% (560)
* Education: 10.9% (630)

Sports Science (out of 7,190 respondents)
* Further study: 19.5% (1,405)
* Education: 20.1% (1,440)
* Sports, amusement and recreation activities: 14.2% (1,020)
* Wholesale and retail trade: 11.8% (850)

EXAMPLES OF CAREER DESTINATIONS IN THE MOST POPULAR SUBJECTS

The following information is provided by Surrey University Careers Service, from 2011–12 graduates of Surrey University who were surveyed six months after course completion. It shows the subjects studied, and the positions and locations of each graduate's job. We have chosen to show you a selection of the most popular courses and their graduate destinations, to give you a snapshot of careers.

Accounting and Financial Management
A24 Group *Payroll Administrator*
Asda *Cashier*
CBRE Hotels *Trainee Analyst*
Deloitte *Auditor*
Ernst and Young *Tax Adviser*
Gurkha Global Security Services Ltd *Accounting Assistant*
PWC *Trainee Accountant*
Snow and Rock *Warehouse Assistant*
TCC *Assistant Group Accountant*
Xpress Legal Services *Personal Assistant*

Acting
Apollo Theatre UK *Actor*
Invertigo Theatre *Assistant Producer*
Perform *Teacher*

Ripley's Museum *Exhibition Assistant*
Royal Shakespeare Company *Actor*
The Gordon Craig Theatre *Theatre Production*

Computer Science
Accenture *Programmer*
Allianz *IT Graduate*
Aveva Solutions Ltd *Technical Graduate – Software Engineer*
BAE Systems Detica *IT Consultant*
BP Oil International Limited *Software Developer*
Cap Gemini *Software Engineer*
Eagle Eye Technology *.NET Junior Developer*
Gatwick Hilton *Chef*
Northgate Information Solutions Ltd *Junior Software Developer*
OBS Logistics *Junior Programmer*

Economics
Aviva Investors *Graduate Analyst*
CMT Prooptiki *Economist*
Deloitte *Administrator*
Department for Business Innovation and Skills *Assistant Economist*
Halcrow Group Limited *Graduate Consultant (Economics)*
New Look *Sales Adviser*
Office for National Statistics *Classification Officer*
Paul Strank Roofing *Personal Assistant*
Unknown company *Bar Staff*

English Literature
Autoforms *Video Production Assistant*
Blackthorn Technologies *Marketing Analyst*
Cath Kidston *Senior Sales Assistant*
Cool Tan Arts *Researcher*
Daily Echo *Media Sales and Advertising Consultant*
Greenwich and Bexley Community Hospice *Community Fundraiser*
Lingfield Primary School *Teaching Assistant – Special Needs*
Quiller Publishing Ltd *Editorial Assistant*
TGI Fridays *Assistant Restaurant Manager*

Law
Boux Avenue *Visual Merchandiser*
Enterprise Rent-A-Car *Billing Assistant*
Evelyn Oldfield Unit *Volunteer Coordinator*
Global Trade Media *Sales Executive/Project Manager*
Griffin Law *Paralegal*
HMRC *Trainee Tax Professional*
Home Office *Home Office Caseworker*
Innocent Drinks *Office Administrator*
J D Wetherspoon *Team Leader*
KPMG *Trainee Accountant*
Macmillan Publishers *Customer Service*
Price Waterhouse Coopers *Tax Associate*
Self-employed *Piano Teacher*
Shergill & Co *Legal Secretary*
Specsavers *Dispensing Adviser*
The Partnership Limited *Paralegal/Legal Assistant*
Warner Goodman LLP *Conveyancing Executive*

Mathematics
3M *Accounts Assistant*
Allianz *Pricing Analyst*
Argos *Customer Assistant*
DFDS *Operations Co-ordinator*
ES Pipelines *Market Analyst*
Geokinetics *Processing Geophysicist*
News Quest *Trainee Financial Accountant*
OOCL *Operations Controller*
Self-employed *Tutor*
Waterstones *Bookseller*

Nursing
Berkshire Healthcare Foundation Trust *Community Staff Nurse*
Brighton and Sussex University Hospital NHS *Registered Nurse*
East Surrey Hospital *Community Health Nurse*
Frimley Park Hospital *Cardiac Nurse*
Royal Surrey Hospital *Staff Nurse (2)*
Southampton General Hospital *Staff Nurse*
Southern Health NHS Foundation Trust *Staff Nurse*
Springfield Hospital NHS *Psychiatric Nurse*
St Ashford & St Peter's NHS Hospital *Nurse*
St Helier Hospital *Staff Nurse*
St Mary's Hospital Imperial College *Paediatric Nurse*
Surrey Community Health NHS *Student Health Visitor*
Surrey and Borders Partnership NHS *Staff Nurse*

Politics
British Medical Association *Policy Adviser*
Chives Cafe *Catering Assistant*
House Builders' Federation *Research Assistant*
Manan Ltd *Marketing and PR Assistant*
Mount Grace School *Programme Manager Mount Grace Higher*
Office Broker *Receptionist*
Snapdragon Consulting Ltd *Public Affairs Consultant*
The Content Group Ltd *Service Delivery Specialist*

Psychology
All Saints School *Teaching Assistant*
Barnardo's Children's Charity *Project Worker*
Bookings Models *Fashion Model*
Brownbill Associates *Family Support Worker*
Civil Service Fast Stream *Government Statistician*
Estée Lauder Companies *HR Co-ordinator*
Genesis Housing, Cavendish Lodge *Support Worker*
Hounslow PCT *Speech Therapy Assistant*
King's College Hospital NHS Foundation Trust *Clinical Trial Coordinator*
Life Psychol *Assistant Psychologist*
Malmesbury Primary School *Teaching Assistant*
Private family *Nanny*
Queen Mary, University of London *Research Assistant*
Radlett Lodge *Teaching Assistant*
Sainsbury's Supermarkets Ltd. *Sales Assistant*
St George's Hospital *Healthcare Assistant*
St Mary's Primary School *Play Worker*
Surrey County Council *Assistant Primary Mental Health Worker*
Sussex Partnership NHS Trust *Assistant Psychologist*

Tourism Development
Hills Balfour *Sales and Marketing Account Executive*
Jet 2 Holidays/ Jet.com *Data Control Executive*
SG Hambros *Trust Administration Assistant*
Thamesview *Sales Negotiator*
University of Southampton *Alumni Relations and Event Assistant*

APPENDIX 1
DIRECTORY OF UNIVERSITIES
AND COLLEGES

SECTION 1: UNIVERSITIES

Listed below are universities in the United Kingdom that offer degree and diploma courses at higher education level. Applications to these institutions are submitted through UCAS except for part-time courses, private universities and colleges, and further education courses. For current information refer to the websites shown and also to www.ucas.com for a comprehensive list of degree and diploma courses (see Appendix 2).

Aberdeen This is a city-centre university on Scotland's east coast. (University of Aberdeen, Students Admissions and School Leavers, University Office, King's College, Aberdeen, Scotland AB24 3FX. Tel 01224 272090; www.abdn.ac.uk)

Abertay The University has a modern city-centre campus and a range of courses with an applied, practical focus. (Abertay University, Student Recruitment Office, Kydd Building, Dundee, Scotland DD1 1HG. Tel 01382 308000; www.abertay.ac.uk)

Aberystwyth This is a coastal university with an attractive campus. (Aberystwyth University, Undergraduate Admissions Office, Student Welcome Centre, Penglais Campus, Aberystwyth, Wales SY23 3FB. Tel 01970 622021; www.aber.ac.uk)

Anglia Ruskin The University has main campuses in Cambridge and Chelmsford and partner colleges throughout East Anglia. (Anglia Ruskin University, Bishop Hall Lane, Chelmsford, England CM1 1SQ. Tel 01245 686868; www.anglia.ac.uk)

Arts London Six distinctive and distinguished colleges make up University of the Arts London: Camberwell College of Arts, Central Saint Martins College of Arts and Design, Chelsea College of Art and Design, London College of Communication, London College of Fashion, and Wimbledon College of Art. The Colleges offer the University's 20,000 students a diverse range of courses at all levels from foundation and undergraduate to postgraduate and research. (University of the Arts London, 272 High Holborn, London, England WC1V 7EY. Tel 020 7514 6000; www.arts.ac.uk)

Aston This University has a green campus in the centre of Birmingham with academic, sporting and social activities on site. (Aston University, The Registry (Admissions), Aston Triangle, Birmingham, England B4 7ET. Tel 0121 204 4444; www.aston.ac.uk)

Bangor The University has a central site in Bangor on the Menai Straits with partner institutions (including the Welsh College of Horticulture) throughout North Wales. (Bangor University, The Student Recruitment Unit, Bangor, Wales LL57 2DG. Tel 01248 382017; www.bangor.ac.uk)

Bath The University is on a rural campus one mile from the centre of Bath, with partner colleges in Bath, Swindon and Wiltshire. (University of Bath, Claverton Down, Bath, England BA2 7AY. Tel 01225 383019; www.bath.ac.uk)

Bath Spa This University was created in 2005 and is located on two campuses near Bath, with partner colleges in Wiltshire. (Bath Spa University, Admissions Office, Newton Park, Newton St Loe, Bath, England BA2 9BN. Tel 01225 875875; www.bathspa.ac.uk)

Bedfordshire The University was formed in August 2006 from the merger of Luton University and the Bedford campus of De Montfort University. The main campus is in the centre of Luton, with two campuses in Bedford, and four partner colleges. (University of Bedfordshire, The Admissions Office, University Square, Luton, England LU1 3JU. Tel 01234 400400; www.beds.ac.uk)

Birmingham This is a 'red-brick' university at Edgbaston to the south of the city, with a second campus at Selly Oak. (University of Birmingham, Edgbaston, Birmingham, England B15 2TT. Tel 0121 415 8900; www.birmingham.ac.uk)

Birmingham (UC) A specialist institution offering courses in Hospitality, Tourism and allied studies. (University College Birmingham, Summer Row, Birmingham, England B3 1JB. Tel 0121 604 1000; www.ucb.ac.uk)

Birmingham City Part-time evening courses are offered for mature students wishing to read for first and higher degrees. Courses are offered in the Faculties of Arts, Science, Social Science and Continuing Education. (Birmingham City University, City North Campus, Birmingham, England B42 2SU. Tel 0121 331 5000; www.bcu.ac.uk)

Bishop Grosseteste A Church of England foundation offering single and joint honours courses in Childhood Studies, Drama, Education, English and Theology and Ethics. (Bishop Grosseteste University, Longdales Road, Lincoln, England LN1 3DY. Tel 01522 527347; www.bishopg.ac.uk)

Bolton The University was granted university status in 2005 and is based at Deane Campus, close to the town centre. The University has been a higher education provider since 1982 and can trace its roots back to the first mechanical institutes. It was the third in the country, opening in 1824. (University of Bolton, Recruitment and Admissions, Deane Road, Bolton, England BL3 5AB. Tel 01204 900600; www.bolton.ac.uk)

Bournemouth The University site is in a large coastal resort, with partner colleges in the region also offering courses. (Bournemouth University, Talbot Campus, Fern Barrow, Poole, England BH12 5BB. Tel 01202 961916; www.bournemouth.ac.uk)

Bournemouth Arts Arts University Bournemouth (formerly The Arts University College at Bournemouth) was established in 1885 as a specialist institution in art, design, media and performance. (Arts University Bournemouth, Wallisdown, Poole, England BH12 5HH. Tel 01202 533011; www.aub.ac.uk)

BPP Campuses in Birmingham, London and Manchester. (BPP University, 6th Floor Boulton House, Chorlton Street, Manchester, England M1 3HY. Tel 0330 060 3100; www.bpp.com)

Bradford The University's main campus is close to the city centre, with the School of Management two miles away. (University of Bradford, Course Enquiries Office, Richmond Road, Bradford, England BD7 1DP. Tel 0800 073 1255; www.bradford.ac.uk)

Brighton Situated on the south coast, the University has five campuses in Brighton, Eastbourne and Hastings. University-validated courses are offered at several partner colleges. (University of Brighton, The Registry (Admissions), Mithras House, Lewes Road, Brighton, England BN2 4AT. Tel 01273 600900; www.brighton.ac.uk)

Brighton and Sussex (MS) BSMS is a small medical school, based in Falmer, approximately five miles away from the centre of Brighton. There is frequent public transport from central Brighton to both sites, with 24-hour buses running seven days a week. (Brighton and Sussex Medical School, BSMS Admissions, University of Sussex, Brighton, England BN1 9PX. Tel 01273 643528; www.bsms.ac.uk)

Bristol A world-renowned university, one of the most popular in the UK. This is a city university with halls of residence in Stoke Bishop and Clifton. (University of Bristol, Senate House, Tyndall Avenue, Bristol, England BS8 1TH. Tel 0117 928 9000; www.bristol.ac.uk)

Bristol UWE The University has four campuses in and around Bristol with an associate Faculty at Hartpury, and regional centres in Bath, Gloucestershire and Swindon. It also has links with the Bristol Old Vic Theatre School and the Royal West of England Academy. (University of the West of England, Bristol, Admissions Office, Frenchay Campus, Coldharbour Lane, Bristol, England BS16 1QY. Tel 0117 965 6261; www.uwe.ac.uk)

Brunel The University has a compact campus to the west of London at Uxbridge. (Brunel University, Admissions Office, Uxbridge, England UB8 3PH. Tel 01895 265265; www.brunel.ac.uk)

Buckingham A small independent university, it has two sites within the town some 40 miles north of London offering two-year (eight-term) degrees. (University of Buckingham, Admissions Office, Hunter Street, Buckingham, England MK18 1EG. Tel 01280 814080; www.buckingham.ac.uk)

Bucks New It has two campuses in High Wycombe and one at Chalfont St Giles, and links with partner colleges; two of which are UCFB (Burnley and Wembley) offering football courses. (Buckinghamshire New University, Admissions, Queen Alexandra Road, High Wycombe, England HP11 2JZ. Tel 0800 056 5660; www.bucks.ac.uk)

Cambridge The University has 29 undergraduate Colleges located throughout the city: Christ's, Churchill, Clare, Corpus Christi, Downing, Emmanuel, Fitzwilliam, Girton, Gonville and Caius, Homerton, Hughes Hall (mature students only), Jesus, King's, Lucy Cavendish (mature, female students only), Magdalene, Murray Edwards (female students only), Newnham (female students only), Pembroke, Peterhouse, Queens', Robinson, St Catharine's, St Edmund's (mature students only), St John's, Selwyn, Sidney Sussex, Trinity, Trinity Hall, and Wolfson (mature students only). (University of Cambridge, Cambridge Admissions Office, Fitzwilliam House, 32 Trumpington Street, Cambridge, England CB2 1QY. Tel 01223 337733; www.cam.ac.uk)

Canterbury Christ Church The University was created in 2005 with the main campus located near Canterbury city centre and campuses also at Broadstairs, Medway University Centre and Folkestone. The University is the third highest in England for student employability. (Canterbury Christ Church University, Admissions, North Holmes Road, Canterbury, England CT1 1QU. Tel 01227 782900; www.canterbury.ac.uk)

Cardiff The main (Cathays Park) campus of the University is located in the city centre, with the Heath Park campus a mile to the south. (Cardiff University, Admissions, MacKenzie House, 30–36 Newport Road, Cardiff, Wales CF10 3XQ. Tel 029 2087 4000; www.cardiff.ac.uk)

Cardiff Met (UWIC) Cardiff Metropolitan University (formerly UWIC) sits in the heart of the capital and is made up of five academic schools: Cardiff School of Art and Design, Cardiff School of Education, Cardiff School of Health Sciences, Cardiff School of Management and Cardiff School of Sport. (Cardiff Metropolitan University, Llandaff Campus, Western Avenue, Cardiff, Wales CF5 2YB. Tel 029 2041 6044; Admissions Enquiries 029 2041 6010; www.cardiffmet.ac.uk)

Central Lancashire The University is located on a small campus close to Preston city centre. Single and joint honours are offered with subjects either studied equally or weighted towards one subject in a 75/25 split. (University of Central Lancashire, Admissions Office, Preston, England PR1 2HE. Tel 01772 201201; www.uclan.ac.uk)

Chester The University was formed in 2005 and is located on a campus in Chester with a second campus in Warrington and three partner colleges. (University of Chester, Undergraduate Admissions, Parkgate Road, Chester, England CH1 4BJ. Tel 01244 512528; www.chester.ac.uk)

Chichester One of the UK's smallest universities with just over 5500 students. Campuses are situated in Chichester and Bognor Regis. (University of Chichester, Admissions, Bishop Otter Campus, College Lane, Chichester, England PO19 6PE. Tel 01243 816002; www.chi.ac.uk)

City The University is situated in central London, with Nursing and Midwifery courses located at St Bartholomew's Hospital. (City University London, Undergraduate Admissions Office, Northampton Square, London, England EC1V 0HB. Tel 020 7040 5060; www.city.ac.uk)

Coventry The University has a 33-acre campus in Coventry and a number of teaching centres throughout the city with courses offered in several partner colleges. (Coventry University, The Student Centre, Gulson Road, Coventry, England CV1 2JH. Tel 024 7615 2222; www.coventry.ac.uk)

Creative Arts The University has five colleges: three in Kent (Canterbury, Maidstone and Rochester) and two in Surrey (Epsom and Farnham). (University for the Creative Arts, Enquiries Service, Falkner Road, Farnham, England GU9 7DS. Tel 01252 892960; www.ucreative.ac.uk)

Cumbria This University was founded in 2007 by the merger of three institutions: Cumbria Institute of the Arts, St Martin's College and University of Central Lancashire's Cumbria site (including the campus at Newton Rigg). The University of Cumbria's four campuses are located at Carlisle Fusehill Street, Carlisle Brampton Road, Lancaster and Ambleside and it also has sites at Energus Workington, Newton Rigg College Penrith, Tower Hamlets London and Furness College Barrow-in-Furness. (University of Cumbria, Fusehill Street, Carlisle, Cumbria, England CA1 2HH. Tel 0845 606 1144; www.cumbria.ac.uk)

De Montfort The University has two sites in Leicester and nine associated colleges. (De Montfort University, Students Admissions, The Gateway, Leicester, England LE1 9BH. Tel 0116 255 1551; www.dmu.ac.uk)

Derby The University has two campuses: one close to Derby city centre and the second at Buxton. (University of Derby, Admissions, Kedleston Road, Derby, England DE22 1GB. Tel 01332 591167; www.derby.ac.uk)

Dundee A city-centre campus, with the Medical School and School of Nursing located at Ninewells Hospital to the west of the city. (University of Dundee, Admissions and Student Recruitment, Nethergate, Dundee, Scotland DD1 4HN. Tel 01382 383838; www.dundee.ac.uk)

Durham The University has 15 colleges admitting undergraduates, split between the main site in Durham city and on the Queen's campus, Stockton. Durham city colleges: Collingwood, Grey, Hatfield, Josephine Butler, St Aidan's, St Chad's, St Cuthbert's, St Hild and St Bede, St John's, St Mary's, Trevelyan, University, Van Mildert. Stockton colleges: John Snow, Stephenson. Durham University is the third oldest university in England. Undergraduate students have access to teaching by world experts, award-winning study facilities, extensive collections of books and learning resources and a unique collegiate system offering a distinctive student experience. (Durham University, The Palatine Centre, Stockton Road, Durham, England DH1 3LE. Tel 0191 334 6128; www.dur.ac.uk)

East Anglia The University is set in parkland close to Norwich. (University of East Anglia, Admissions Office, Norwich Research Park, Norwich, England NR4 7TJ. Tel 01603 591515; www.uea.ac.uk)

East London The University has campuses in London at Stratford and Docklands. Courses are also offered at several colleges in Greater London. (University of East London, Docklands Campus, 4–6 University Way, London, England E16 2RD. Tel 020 8223 3333; www.uel.ac.uk)

Edge Hill The University is situated on a spacious campus in Ormskirk near Liverpool and offers a wide range of three-year degrees. (Edge Hill University, St Helens Road, Ormskirk, England L39 4QP. Tel 01695 575171; www.edgehill.ac.uk)

Edinburgh The University's Central Area is located on the south side of the city centre. The King's Buildings (the main science and engineering campus), Medical School and Vet School are all to the south of the city centre, within easy travelling distance. (Edinburgh University, Old College, South Bridge, Edinburgh, Scotland EH8 9YL. Tel 0131 650 1000; www.ed.ac.uk)

Edinburgh Napier The University has three main campuses in Edinburgh: the Business School is based in Craiglockhart Campus, the Faculty of Engineering, Computing and Creative Industries is based at Merchiston Campus and the Faculty of Health Life and Social Sciences is based at Sighthill Campus. (Edinburgh Napier University, Information Office, Craiglockart Campus, Edinburgh, Scotland EH14 1DJ. Tel 0845 520 3050; www.napier.ac.uk)

Edinburgh Queen Margaret This new university (2007) is located on a new, purpose-built campus on the Firth of Forth, east of Edinburgh, with student accommodation on site. (Queen Margaret University, Edinburgh, The Admissions Office, Queen Margaret University Drive, Musselburgh, Edinburgh, Scotland EH21 6UU. Tel 0131 474 0000; www.qmu.ac.uk)

Essex The University has a parkland campus two miles from Colchester. The University and the South Essex College Partnership also provide degree schemes at the new Southend campus. (University of Essex, Undergraduate Admissions, Wivenhoe Park, Colchester, England CO4 3SQ. Tel 01206 873666; www.essex.ac.uk)

Exeter The University has two sites in Exeter: the Streatham campus is the largest, and the St Luke's campus is a mile away. A third campus (the Cornwall campus) is situated at Penryn near Falmouth in Cornwall. (University of Exeter, Admissions Office, 8th Floor, Laver Building, North Park Road, Exeter, England EX4 4QE. Tel 0844 620 0012; www.exeter.ac.uk)

Falmouth Falmouth University specialises in arts-based subjects and is split between two campuses at Falmouth and Penryn. (Falmouth University, Admissions Office, Woodlane, Falmouth, England TR11 4RH. Tel 01326 213730; www.falmouth.ac.uk)

Glamorgan The University of Glamorgan and the University of Wales, Newport merged in 2013 to create the University of South Wales. Please see **South Wales** for more information.

Glasgow The University has three campuses: two on the outskirts of Glasgow and one on the Crichton campus at Dumfries. Glasgow School of Art and the Scottish Agricultural College in Ayr are associated institutions. (University of Glasgow, Recruitment and International Office, 71 Southpark Avenue, Glasgow, Scotland G12 8QQ. Tel 0141 330 2000; www.gla.ac.uk)

Glasgow Caledonian The University has a city-centre campus. (Glasgow Caledonian University, Cowcaddens Road, Glasgow, Scotland G4 0BA. Tel 0141 331 3334; www.gcu.ac.uk)

Gloucestershire Three campuses in Cheltenham and one in Gloucester form the University. It also has partner colleges in Gloucestershire, Herefordshire, Wiltshire and Worcestershire. Many students are home-based. (University of Gloucestershire, Admissions Office, The Park, Cheltenham, England GL50 2RH. Tel 0844 801 0001; www.glos.ac.uk)

Glyndŵr This is a new university (2008), formerly North East Wales IHE, and is situated in Wrexham town centre. (Glyndŵr University, Mold Road, Wrexham, Wales LL11 2AW. Tel 01978 293439; www.glyndwr.ac.uk)

Greenwich The main campus of the University is at Greenwich, a second is at Avery Hill in south London and a third is at Medway at Chatham Maritime, Kent. There are also partner colleges in east London and Kent. (University of Greenwich, Old Royal Naval College, Park Row, London, England SE10 9LS. Tel 020 8331 9000; www.gre.ac.uk)

Harper Adams A specialist institution offering courses in Agriculture and allied subjects. (Harper Adams University, Admissions Office, Newport, England TF10 8NB. Tel 01952 815000; www.harper-adams.ac.uk)

Heriot-Watt The University has a large parkland campus seven miles west of Edinburgh and a second campus in the Scottish Borders at Galashiels 35 miles to the south. (Heriot-Watt University, Admissions Unit, Edinburgh Campus, Edinburgh, Scotland EH14 4AS. Tel 0131 449 5111; www.hw.ac.uk)

Hertfordshire The University has two campuses in Hatfield. Courses are also offered through a consortium of four Hertfordshire colleges and the University has links with all Hertfordshire further education colleges. (University of Hertfordshire, University Admissions Service, College Lane, Hatfield, England AL10 9AB. Tel 01707 284800; www.herts.ac.uk)

Huddersfield This is a town-centre university with University Centres at Barnsley and Oldham and links to colleges of further education throughout the north of England. (University of Huddersfield, Admissions Office, Queensgate, Huddersfield, England HD1 3DH. Tel 01484 473969; www.hud.ac.uk)

Hull The main campus is in Hull, two miles from the city centre, with a smaller campus at Scarborough. (University of Hull, Admissions Service, Cottingham Road, Hull, England HU6 7RX. Tel 01482 466100; www.hull.ac.uk)

Hull York (MS) The Medical School is a partnership between the Universities of Hull and York, with teaching facilities on the main campuses of both universities. (Hull York Medical School, Admissions Office, University of York, Heslington, York, England YO10 5DD. Tel 0870 124 5500; www.hyms.ac.uk)

ifs (UC) The *ifs University College* is a registered charity, incorporated by Royal Charter and has a remit to provide the financial services industry with a skilled and competent workforce while also promoting a better understanding of finance amongst consumers. The *ifs* has a heritage in the provision of financial education spanning 130 years. (*ifs University College*, 8th Floor, Peninsular House, 36 Monument Street, London, England EC3R 8LJ. Tel 01227 829499; www.ifslearning.ac.uk)

Imperial London The College became an independent university, separate from the University of London, in 2007. The central site is in South Kensington. Medicine is based mainly at St Mary's Hospital, Paddington, Charing Cross Hospital and Hammersmith Hospital. (Imperial College London, Registry, Level 3 Sherfield Building, South Kensington Campus, London, England SW7 2AZ. Tel 020 7589 5111; www.imperial.ac.uk)

Keele This is a small university on a green campus five miles from Stoke-on-Trent. (Keele University, Academic Registry, Keele, England ST5 5BG. Tel 01782 734005; www.keele.ac.uk)

Kent The University is a leading research-led university in the south-east of England. It has two main campuses in Canterbury and Medway, with two associate colleges (South Kent College, Mid-Kent College) and is the lead sponsor of Brompton Academy. (University of Kent, Enrolment Management Services, The Registry, Canterbury, England CT2 7NZ. Tel 01227 827272; www.kent.ac.uk)

Kingston With four campuses in and around the town and 10 partner colleges, the University has easy access to London. (Kingston University, River House, 53–57 High Street, Kingston upon Thames, England KT1 1LQ. Tel 0844 855 2177; www.kingston.ac.uk)

Lancaster The University has a parkland site three miles south of Lancaster city centre. It is collegiate with each student being a member of one of the eight colleges. (Lancaster University, Undergraduate Admissions Office, Bailrigg, Lancaster, England LA1 4YW. Tel 01524 592028; www.lancaster.ac.uk)

Leeds The University is sited on a campus in the centre of the city. (University of Leeds, Undergraduate Admissions Office, Leeds, England LS2 9JT. Tel 0113 343 3999; www.leeds.ac.uk)

Leeds Beckett The University (formerly Leeds Metropolitan) has two campuses, one in the city and a second in Headingley on the outskirts of Leeds, and partner colleges throughout the region. (Leeds Beckett University, City Campus, Leeds, England LS1 3HE. Tel 0113 812 3113; www.leedsmet.ac.uk)

Leeds Trinity Originally established as a Catholic teacher training college, now offering a wide range of courses. (Leeds Trinity University, Student Enquiries Office, Brownberrie Lane, Horsforth, Leeds, England LS18 5HD. Tel 0113 283 7100; www.leedstrinity.ac.uk)

Leicester The compact campus is located on the southern edge of the city. (University of Leicester, Admissions Office, University Road, Leicester, England LE1 7RH. Tel 0116 252 2522; www.le.ac.uk)

Lincoln The Brayford and Cathedral campuses are in the city, with the Riseholme Park campus some five miles away. There is also a campus in Hull and associated colleges in Lincolnshire. (University of Lincoln, Academic Registry, Brayford Pool, Lincoln, England LN6 7TS. Tel 01522 886644; www.lincoln.ac.uk)

Liverpool The University has a large city-centre campus. (University of Liverpool, Student Recruitment and Admissions Office, Foundation Building, Brownlow Hill, Liverpool, England L69 7ZX. Tel 0151 794 5927; www.liv.ac.uk)

Liverpool Hope Liverpool Hope University has two campuses: one four miles from the city centre, the other a brisk walk from the city centre. Liverpool is a vibrant student city offering plenty of cultural, sporting, musical and social opportunities to students. (Liverpool Hope University, Admissions Office, Hope Park, Liverpool, England L16 9JD. Tel 0151 291 3000; www.hope.ac.uk)

Liverpool John Moores Liverpool John Moores University is a thriving, vibrant university located at the heart of Liverpool, consisting of three large campuses. (Liverpool John Moores University, Kingsway House, 2nd Floor, Hatton Garden, Liverpool, England L3 2AJ. Tel 0151 231 5090; www.ljmu.ac.uk)

London (Birk) The College is situated in Bloomsbury in the London University precinct and provides part-time and evening higher-education courses. (Birkbeck, University of London, Malet Street, London, England WC1E 7HX. Tel 020 7631 6000; www.bbk.ac.uk)

London (Gold) The College is located on a single campus in south-east London. (Goldsmiths, University of London, New Cross, London, England SE14 6NW. Tel 020 7919 7171; www.gold.ac.uk)

London (Hey) The College is on a site in central London, offering specialist studies in Philosophy or Theology. (Heythrop College, University of London, Registry, Kensington Square, London, England W8 5HN. Tel 020 7795 6600; www.heythrop.ac.uk)

London (Inst Ed) (Institute of Education, University of London, 20 Bedford Way, London, England WC1H 0AL. Tel 020 7612 6000; www.ioe.ac.uk)

London (Inst Paris) The Institute's Department of French Studies and Comparative Studies is located in central Paris and operates in partnership with Queen Mary and Royal Holloway, University of London. (University of London Institute in Paris, 9–11 rue de Constantine, 75340, Paris, France Cedex 07. Tel +33 (0) 1 44 11 73 83/76; www.ulip.lon.ac.uk)

London (King's) The College has campuses in central and south London (Strand, Waterloo and London Bridge) and includes the School of Medicine, the Dental Institute and the School of Biomedical and Health Sciences. (King's College, University of London, Enquiries, Strand, London, England WC2R 2LS. Tel 020 7836 5454; www.kcl.ac.uk)

London (QM) There is a city campus in the East End of London. (Queen Mary, University of London, Admissions Office, Mile End Road, London, England E1 4NS. Tel 020 7882 5511; www.qmul.ac.uk)

London (RH) There is a large campus with halls of residence situated at Egham, 19 miles west of central London and three miles from Windsor. (Royal Holloway, University of London, Egham Hill, Egham, England TW20 0EX. Tel 01784 434455; www.rhul.ac.uk)

London (RVC) The College has campuses in London and Hertfordshire. (Royal Veterinary College, University of London, Royal College Street, London, England NW1 0TU. Tel 020 7468 5147; www.rvc.ac.uk)

London (St George's) Located on a compact site in south-west London, St George's is a specialist health sciences university, having extensive links with many hospitals and practices, and also with Kingston University and Royal Holloway London. (St George's, University of London, Cranmer Terrace, London, England SW17 0RE. Tel 020 8672 9944; www.sgul.ac.uk)

London (SOAS) The School of Oriental and African Studies (SOAS) is a college of the University of London and the only higher education institution in the UK specialising in the study of Asia, Africa and the Near and Middle East. (School of Oriental and African Studies, University of London, Thornhaugh Street, Russell Square, London, England WC1H 0XG. Tel 020 7637 2388; www.soas.ac.uk)

London (UCL) The College is located in Bloomsbury in the London University precinct. (University College London, University of London, Gower Street, London, England WC1E 6BT. Tel 020 7679 2000; www.ucl.ac.uk)

London (UCL Sch Pharm) The School has a central London site close to the London University precinct. (UCL School of Pharmacy, University of London, 29–39 Brunswick Square, London, England WC1N 1AX. Tel 020 7753 5831; www.ucl.ac.uk/pharmacy)

London LSE The School is located in the heart of London and specialises in the whole range of social science subjects (from Economics, Politics and Law to Sociology, Accounting and Finance). (London School of Economics and Political Science, Undergraduate Admissions Office, Houghton Street, London, England WC2A 2AE. Tel 020 7955 7125; www.lse.ac.uk)

London Met The University has two campuses: one in north London (with the largest (new) science laboratory in Europe) and one in the City, and several partner colleges. (London Metropolitan University, Admissions Office, 166–220 Holloway Road, London, England N7 8DB. Tel 020 7133 4200; www.londonmet.ac.uk)

London NCH NCH is an independent university college, centrally located in Bloomsbury, which is dedicated to providing high academic experience. (New College of the Humanities, 19 Bedford Square, London, England WC1B 3HH. Tel 020 7637 4550; www.nchum.org)

London Regent's The University has now been established as the UK's second private university offering a range of degree courses to the 4500 students based at it's central London location in Regent's Park. (Regent's University London, Inner Circle, Regent's Park, London, England NW1 4NS. Tel 020 7487 7700; www.regents.ac.uk)

London South Bank The main campus of the University is in Southwark on the south bank of the Thames in London. Other campuses are at Whipps Cross in east London and at Havering in Essex. (London South Bank University, Admissions Office, 90 London Road, London, England SE1 6LN. Tel 0800 923 8888; www.lsbu.ac.uk)

Loughborough On a large rural single-site campus, the University is a mile from the town centre. (Loughborough University, Undergraduate Admissions Office, Loughborough, England LE11 3TU. Tel 01509 263171; www.lboro.ac.uk)

Manchester The University has a large precinct one mile south of the city centre. The University of Manchester has a long tradition of excellence in higher education. (University of Manchester, Student Recruitment and Admissions, Rutherford Building, Oxford Road, Manchester, England M13 9PL. Tel 0161 275 2077; www.manchester.ac.uk)

Manchester Met The University has five sites in Manchester and one in Cheshire. It offers a wide choice of vocational and non-vocational courses, the former with industrial and commercial placements. (Manchester Metropolitan University, Admissions Office, All Saints Building, All Saints, Manchester, England M15 6BH. Tel 0161 247 2000; www.mmu.ac.uk)

Middlesex This is a multi-campus university in north London with associate colleges in the region. (Middlesex University, Hendon Campus, The Burroughs, London, England NW4 4BT. Tel 020 8411 5555; www.mdx.ac.uk)

Newcastle The University has a single campus in the city centre. (Newcastle University, Admissions Office, 6 Kensington Terrace, Newcastle-upon-Tyne, England NE1 7RU. Tel 0191 222 6000; www.ncl.ac.uk)

Newman This Catholic foundation offers a wide range of courses to undergraduates of all religions. (Newman University, Admissions Registrar, Genners Lane, Bartley Green, Birmingham, England B32 3NT. Tel 0121 476 1181; www.newman.ac.uk)

Newport The University of Glamorgan and the University of Wales, Newport merged in 2013 to create the University of South Wales. Please see **South Wales** for more information.

Northampton The University (created in 2005) has two campuses close to the town centre. (University of Northampton, Admissions Office, Park Campus, Boughton Green Road, Northampton, England NN2 7AL. Tel 0800 358 2232; www.northampton.ac.uk)

Northumbria The University has two campuses in and around Newcastle. (Northumbria University, Ellison Place, Newcastle-upon-Tyne, England NE1 8ST. Tel 0191 243 7420; www.northumbria.ac.uk)

Norwich Arts Courses focus on Art and Design and Media Studies (Norwich University of the Arts, Admissions, Francis House, 3–7 Redwell Street, Norwich, England NR2 4SN. Tel 01603 610561; www.nua.ac.uk)

Nottingham This is a large, campus university to the west of the city with a second campus two miles from the city centre, and a third at Sutton Bonington for the new School of Veterinary Science and Medicine, 10 miles south of University Park. (University of Nottingham, University Park, Nottingham, England NG7 2RD. Tel 0115 951 5559; www.nottingham.ac.uk)

Nottingham Trent The University has three campuses: City site, in the centre of Nottingham, Clifton and Brackenhurst. The Clifton campus of the University is four miles from Nottingham city centre and caters for Education, Humanities and Science, whilst Brackenhurst, near Southwell, focuses on land-based subjects. (Nottingham Trent University, Registry Admissions, Dryden Centre, Burton Street, Nottingham, England NG1 4BU. Tel 0115 941 8418; www.ntu.ac.uk)

Open University This is the UK's largest university for part-time and distance-learning higher education, providing support for students who must be aged over 18 years. Application and registration is made direct to the OU, and not through UCAS (at present). (Open University, Walton Hall, Milton Keynes, England MK7 6AA. Tel 0845 300 6090; www.open.ac.uk)

Oxford The University has 30 colleges and five private halls admitting undergraduates. Colleges: Balliol, Brasenose, Christ Church, Corpus Christi, Exeter, Harris Manchester (mature students only), Hertford, Jesus, Keble, Lady Margaret Hall, Lincoln, Magdalen, Mansfield, Merton, New, Oriel, Pembroke, St Anne's, St Catherine's, St Edmund Hall, St Hilda's, St Hugh's, St John's, St Peter's, Somerville, Queen's, Trinity, University, Wadham, Worcester. Permanent Private Halls: Blackfriars, Regent's Park College, St Benet's Hall, St Stephen's House, Wycliffe. Whilst many universities offer reduced fees or bursaries, Oxford provides both in addition to generous support to those on a family income of less than £16,000. (University of Oxford, Undergraduate Admissions Office, University Offices, Wellington Square, Oxford, England OX1 2JD. Tel 01865 288000; www.ox.ac.uk)

Oxford Brookes The University has three main campuses in and around Oxford. (Oxford Brookes University, Admissions Office, Headington Campus, Gipsy Lane, Oxford, England OX3 0BP. Tel 01865 484848; www.brookes.ac.uk)

Peninsula (MS) From 2013 new students are studying for University of Exeter or Plymouth University degrees. Please see these institutions for more information.

Plymouth The University has two main campuses: one in Plymouth and a second, the Peninsula Allied Health Centre, is four miles north of the main campus. Courses are also offered at eight partner colleges. (University of Plymouth, Central Admissions, Drake Circus, Plymouth, England PL4 8AA. Tel 01752 585858; www.plymouth.ac.uk)

Portsmouth The main campus of the University is close to the town centre; courses are also taught at colleges in Hampshire and Surrey. (University of Portsmouth, Academic Registry, University House, Winston Churchill Avenue, Portsmouth, England PO1 2UP. Tel 023 9284 8484; www.port.ac.uk)

Queen's Belfast The University has a large campus in the south of the city. (Queen's University Belfast, Admissions Service, University Road, Belfast, Northern Ireland BT7 1NN. Tel 028 9024 5133; www.qub.ac.uk)

Reading Situated on 320 acres of landscaped parkland, the campus won the Green Flag Award in 2011 as the highest-rated university campus in the Scheme's national People's Choice Awards. There are three campuses in the University, with the main (Whiteknights) on a rural campus at the edge of the city, and two others within walking distance. Foundation degrees are taught at two partner colleges. (University of Reading, Student Recruitment Office, PO Box 217, Reading, England RG6 6AH. Tel 0118 378 8619; www.rdg.ac.uk)

Richmond (Am Int Univ) Richmond, The American International University in London, is an independent, not-for-profit, international, liberal arts and professional studies university established in 1972. It educates a multi-cultural student body in the American liberal arts tradition. (Richmond, The American International University in London, Queen's Road, Richmond-upon-Thames, England TW10 6JP. Tel 020 8332 8200; www.richmond.ac.uk)

Robert Gordon The University has two campuses in and near Aberdeen city centre. (Robert Gordon University, Admissions Office, Administration Building, Schoolhill, Aberdeen, Scotland AB10 1FR. Tel 01224 262728; www.rgu.ac.uk)

Roehampton Roehampton, London's only campus university, is located in south-west London, close to Richmond Park, and has four colleges: Digby Stuart, Froebel, Southlands and Whitelands. (Roehampton University, Enquiries Office, Erasmus House, Roehampton Lane, London, England SW15 5PU. Tel 020 8392 3000; www.roehampton.ac.uk)

St Andrews Founded in 1413, and the third oldest university in the English-speaking world, this is a town-centre university on the east coast of Scotland. (University of St Andrews, Admissions Application

Centre, St Katherine's West, 16 The Scores, St Andrews, Scotland KY16 9AJ. Tel 01334 462150; www.st-andrews.ac.uk)

St Mark and St John A teacher training institution by tradition but now offering a range of courses. (University of St Mark and St John, Admissions Office, Derriford Road, Plymouth, England PL6 8BH. Tel 01752 636890; www.marjon.ac.uk)

St Mary's A small, picturesque university located between Richmond and Kingston-on-Thames in south-west London. Combined courses offer two subjects in Year 1, a major/minor choice in Year 2 and the final degree subject in Year 3. Originally founded for the training of teachers it now offers a wide range of additional subjects for its 3700 full-time students. (St Mary's University Twickenham, Registry, Waldegrave Road, Strawberry Hill, Twickenham, England TW1 4SX. Tel 020 8240 4000; www.smuc.ac.uk)

Salford This is a city-centre campus university. All courses are taught in the central campus, except for Midwifery which is taught at Bury and Nursing which is at Eccles. (University of Salford, Admissions Officer, The Crescent, Salford, England M5 4WT. Tel 0161 295 4545; www.salford.ac.uk)

Sheffield The University campus is close to Sheffield's city centre. (University of Sheffield, Western Bank, Sheffield, England S10 2TN. Tel 0114 222 2000; www.shef.ac.uk)

Sheffield Hallam The University has two campuses: one in the city centre, and the second two miles away. (Sheffield Hallam University, Admissions Office, City Campus, Howard Street, Sheffield, England S1 1WB. Tel 0114 225 5555; www.shu.ac.uk)

South Wales The University of South Wales was formed by the merger of the University of Glamorgan and the University of Wales, Newport. (University of South Wales, Treforest Campus, Pontypridd, Wales CF37 1DL. Tel 0845 576 7778; www.southwales.ac.uk)

Southampton The University has five main campuses in Southampton and Winchester. (University of Southampton, University Road, Southampton, England SO17 1BJ. Tel 023 8059 5000; www.southampton.ac.uk)

Southampton Solent Southampton Solent University first became a university in 2005 but has a well-established background in higher education which can be traced back to 1856. Situated close to Southampton city centre, the University has two partner colleges. (Southampton Solent University, Student Recruitment, East Park Terrace, Southampton, England SO14 0YN. Tel 023 8031 9039; www.solent.ac.uk)

Staffordshire The University has campuses at Stafford, Stoke, Lichfield, Shrewsbury and several regional colleges. (Staffordshire University, Admissions, C117 Cadman Building, College Road, Stoke-on-Trent, England ST4 2DE. Tel 01782 294400; www.staffs.ac.uk)

Stirling A campus-based university close to the centre of Stirling. (University of Stirling, UG Admissions Office, Stirling, Scotland FK9 4LA. Tel 01786 467044; www.stir.ac.uk)

Strathclyde The University's main campus is in Glasgow city centre, with the Jordanhill campus to the west of the city. (University of Strathclyde, 16 Richmond Street, Glasgow, Scotland G1 1XQ. Tel 0141 552 4400; www.strath.ac.uk)

Sunderland The main campus of the University is in Sunderland city centre, with the Sir Tom Cowie campus across the river accommodating the Business School and Informatics Centre. (University of Sunderland, Edinburgh Building, City Campus, Chester Road, Sunderland, England SR1 3SD. Tel 0191 515 3154; www.sunderland.ac.uk)

Surrey The University has a modern campus a mile from Guildford city centre. Some foundation-year teaching takes place in local colleges. (University of Surrey, Stag Hill, Guildford, England GU2 7XH. Tel 01483 300800; www.surrey.ac.uk)

Sussex The University has a single-site campus four miles from Brighton. (University of Sussex, Student Recruitment Services, Sussex House, Falmer, Brighton, England BN1 9RH. Tel 01273 876787; www.sussex.ac.uk)

Swansea The University is situated in a parkland campus outside Swansea. (Swansea University, Admissions, Singleton Park, Swansea, Wales SA2 8PP. Tel 01792 205678; www.swan.ac.uk)

Teesside This is a city-centre university, with its campus in Middlesbrough. It has links with colleges in the region. (Teesside University, Admissions Office, Middlesbrough, England TS1 3BA. Tel 01642 218121; www.tees.ac.uk)

Trinity Saint David This university was created by the merger of the University of Wales, Lampeter, Trinity University College Carmarthen and, more recently, Swansea Metropolitan, with courses run in all locations. (Trinity Saint David, University of Wales, Academic Registry, Lampeter, Wales SA48 7ED. Tel Carmarthen 01267 676767; Lampeter 01570 422351; Swansea 07192 481000; www.trinitysaintdavid.ac.uk)

Trinity Saint David (Swansea) Formerly Swansea Metropolitan, this University merged with Trinity Saint David in 2013 and is situated in the centre of Swansea. (Trinity Saint David (Swansea), Admissions Office, Mount Pleasant Campus, Swansea, Wales SA1 6ED. Tel 01792 481000; www.trinitysaintdavid.ac.uk)

UHI The University of the Highlands and Islands is based on a partnership of colleges and research centres. Courses are offered thoughout Scotland at various centres including Argyll, Lews Castle, Moray, Perth, Orkney and Shetland. (University of the Highlands and Islands, Course Information Unit, Executive Office, Ness Walk, Inverness, Scotland IV3 5SQ. Tel 01463 279000; www.uhi.ac.uk)

Ulster The University has four campuses: Belfast, Coleraine, Jordanstown, and Magee in Londonderry. (University of Ulster, Belfast Campus, York Street, Belfast, Northern Ireland BT15 1ED. Tel 028 701 23456; www.ulster.ac.uk)

Univ Law (formally the College of Law) The University offers specialised law courses across the country with centres in Birmingham, Bristol, Chester, Guildford, London, Manchester and York. (University of Law, Braboeuf Manor, St Catherines, Guildford, England GU3 1HA. Tel 0800 289997; www.law.ac.uk)

Warwick The University has a single-site campus situated three miles outside Coventry. (University of Warwick, Student Admissions Office, Coventry, England CV4 7AL. Tel 024 7652 3723; www.warwick.ac.uk)

West London (formerly Thames Valley University) The University has campuses at Ealing, Reading, Slough and Brentford, and links with four sites in west London and associated colleges. (University of West London, Learning Advice Centre, St Mary's Road, London, England W5 5RF. Tel 0800 036 8888; www.uwl.ac.uk)

West Scotland This university was formed in 2007 from the merger of the University of Paisley and Bell College. There are four campuses: Paisley, Ayr, Hamilton and Dumfries. UWS, which is unique due to its geographical spread, provides local university access for over 30% of Scotland's population. (University of the West of Scotland, Admissions Office, High Street, Paisley, Scotland PA1 2BE. Tel 0141 849 4101; www.uws.ac.uk)

Westminster The University has four campuses (Cavendish, Marylebone and Regent in central London and Harrow) and associated colleges including the British Academy of New Music. (University of Westminster, 309 Regent Street, London, England W1B 2HW. Tel 020 7915 5511; www.westminster.ac.uk)

Winchester A university close to the centre of Winchester with additional sites in Basingstoke and Bournemouth. (University of Winchester, Course Enquiries, West Hill, Winchester, England SO22 4NR. Tel 01962 827234; www.winchester.ac.uk)

Wolverhampton The University has two campuses in Wolverhampton and others in Walsall and Telford. (University of Wolverhampton, Wulfruna Street, Wolverhampton, England WV1 1LY. Tel 0800 953 3222; www.wlv.ac.uk)

Worcester This new university (2005) is located on a campus a short distance from Worcester city centre. (University of Worcester, Admissions Office, Henwick Grove, Worcester, England WR2 6AJ. Tel 01905 855111; www.worcester.ac.uk)

York The University has a landscaped campus on the outskirts of York and a smaller central site, the beautiful medieval King's Manor in the city centre. The University aims to select not only students who have the ability and motivation to benefit from the programmes they intend to follow but also students who will make a contribution to University life. (University of York, Admissions and School Liaison, Heslington, York, England YO10 5DD. Tel 01904 320000; www.york.ac.uk)

York St John The University is based on an award-winning campus in the centre of York with almost 6000 students studying a wide range of subjects. (York St John University, Lord Mayor's Walk, York, England YO31 7EX. Tel 01904 624624; www.yorksj.ac.uk)

SECTION 2: UNIVERSITY COLLEGES, INSTITUTES, AND SPECIALIST COLLEGES OF AGRICULTURE AND HORTICULTURE, ART, DANCE, DRAMA, MUSIC, OSTEOPATHY AND SPEECH

University colleges and institutes provide undergraduate and postgraduate courses in a wide range of subjects and are university-sector institutions. While many universities and university colleges offer courses in art, design, music, drama, agriculture, horticulture and courses connected to the land-based industries, the specialist colleges listed below provide courses at many levels, often part time, in these separate fields.

It is important that you read prospectuses and check websites carefully and go to open days to find out as much as you can about these colleges and about their courses which interest you. Applications for full-time courses at the institutions listed below are through UCAS.

Abbreviations used below A = Art and Design; **Ag** = Agriculture, Animals and Land-related courses; **C** = Communication; **D** = Drama, Performing and Theatre Arts; **Da** = Dance; **F** = Fashion; **H** = Horticulture and Landscape-related courses; **M** = Music.

Academy of Live and Recorded Arts (ALRA) Studio 24, Royal Victoria Patriotic Building, John Archer Way, London, England SW18 3SX. Tel 020 8870 6475; www.alra.co.uk [**D**]

Anglo-European College of Chiropractic 13–15 Parkwood Road, Bournemouth, England BH5 2DF. Tel 01202 436200; www.aecc.ac.uk

Anniesland College Hatfield Campus, 19 Hatfield Drive, Glasgow, Scotland G12 0YE. Tel 0141 272 9000; www.anniesland.ac.uk

Architectural Association School of Architecture 36 Bedford Square, London, England WC1B 3ES. Tel 020 7887 4051; www.aaschool.ac.uk

Arts Educational Schools London Cone Ripman House, 14 Bath Road, London, England W4 1LY. Tel 020 8987 6666; www.artsed.co.uk [**A**]

Askham Bryan College Askham Bryan, York, England YO23 3FR. Tel 01904 772277; www.askham-bryan.ac.uk [**Ag**]

Berkshire College of Agriculture Hall Place, Burchetts Green, Maidenhead, England SL6 6QR. Tel 01628 824444; www.bca.ac.uk [**Ag**]

Bishop Burton College Learner Services, York Road, Bishop Burton, England HU17 8QG. Tel 01964 553000; www.bishopburton.ac.uk [**Ag**]

Bristol Old Vic Theatre School Bristol Old Vic Theatre School is an affiliate of the Conservatoire for Dance and Drama and is an Associate School of the University of the West of England. 2 Downside Road, Clifton, Bristol, England BS8 2XF. Tel 0117 973 3535; www.oldvic.ac.uk [**D**]

British College of Osteopathic Medicine Lief House, 120–122 Finchley Road, London, England NW3 5HR. Tel 020 7435 6464; www.bcom.ac.uk

British School of Osteopathy 275 Borough High Street, London, England SE1 1JE. Tel 020 7407 0222; Student Admissions 020 7089 5316; www.bso.ac.uk

Camberwell College of Art, University of the Arts London Peckham Road, London, England SE5 8UF. Tel 020 7514 6302; www.arts.ac.uk/camberwell **[A]**

Capel Manor College Administrative Office, Bullsmore Lane, Enfield, England EN1 4RQ. Tel 0845 612 2122; www.capel.ac.uk **[H]**

Cavendish College London 35–37 Alfred Place, London, England WC1E 7DP. Tel 0800 881 5232; www.theeducators.com/cavendish

Central Saint Martins College of Art and Design, University of the Arts London 1 Granary Square, King's Cross, London, England N1C 4AA. Tel 020 7514 7023; www.arts.ac.uk/csm **[A]**

Chelsea College of Art and Design, University of the Arts London 16 John Islip Street, London, England SW1P 4JU. Tel 020 7514 7751; www.arts.ac.uk/chelsea **[A]**

City and Guilds of London Art School 124 Kennington Park Road, London, England SE11 4DJ. Tel 020 7735 2306; www.cityandguildsartschool.ac.uk **[A]**

City College Norwich Ipswich Road, Norwich, England NR2 2LJ. Tel 01603 773311; www.ccn.ac.uk **[A]**

Cleveland College of Art and Design Green Lane, Linthorpe, Middlesbrough, England TS5 7RJ. Tel 01642 288000; www.ccad.ac.uk **[A]**

Colchester Institute Course Enquiries, Sheepen Road, Colchester, England CO3 3LL. Tel 01206 712000; www.colchester.ac.uk

College of Agriculture, Food and Rural Enterprise (CAFRE) Greenmount Campus, 45 Tirgracy Road, Antrim, Northern Ireland BT41 4PS. Tel 0800 028 4291; www.cafre.ac.uk **[Ag]**

College of Estate Management Whiteknights, Reading, England RG6 6AW. Tel 0800 019 9697; www.cem.ac.uk

Courtauld Institute of Art, University of London The Courtauld Institute of Art is one of the world's leading centres for the study of the history and conservation of art and architecture, and its gallery houses one of Britain's best-loved collections. Based at Somerset House, The Courtauld is an independent college of the University of London. Somerset House, Strand, London, England WC2R 0RN. Tel 020 7848 2645; www.courtauld.ac.uk **[A]**

Drama Centre London (part of Central St Martin's, University of the Arts London). Saffron House, 10 Back Hill, London, England EC1R 5LQ. Tel 020 7514 8760; Auditions 020 7514 7156 or 020 7514 8769; www.csm.arts.ac.uk/drama **[D]**

East 15 Acting School Hatfields, Rectory Lane, Loughton, England IG10 3RY. Tel 020 8508 5983; www.east15.ac.uk **[D]**

Edinburgh College of Art Academic Registry, Lauriston Place, Edinburgh, Scotland EH3 9DF. Tel 0131 651 5800; www.ed.ac.uk/eca **[A]**

European School of Osteopathy Boxley House, The Street, Boxley, Maidstone, England ME14 3DZ. Tel 01622 671558; www.eso.ac.uk

Glasgow School of Art 167 Renfrew Street, Glasgow, Scotland G3 6RQ. Tel 0141 353 4500; www.gsa.ac.uk **[A]**

Gray's School of Art, Robert Gordon University Garthdee Road, Aberdeen, Scotland AB10 7QD. Tel 01224 262728; www.rgu.ac.uk/grays **[A]**

Guildford School of Acting, GSA Conservatoire Stag Hill Campus, Guildford, England GU2 7XH. Tel 01483 684052; www.conservatoire.org **[D]**

Guildhall School of Music and Drama Silk Street, London, England EC2Y 8DT. Tel 020 7628 2571; www.gsmd.ac.uk [**M**]

Hartpury College Hartpury House, Hartpury, England GL19 3BE. Tel 01452 702345; www.hartpury.ac.uk [**Ag**]

Heatherley School of Fine Art 75 Lots Road, London, England SW10 0RN. Tel 020 7351 4190; www.heatherleys.org [**A**]

Hereford College of Arts Folly Lane, Hereford, England HR1 1LT. Tel 01432 273359; www.hca.ac.uk [**A**]

Leeds College of Art Blenheim Walk, Leeds, England LS2 9AQ. Tel 0113 202 8000; www.leeds-art.ac.uk [**A**]

Leeds College of Music 3 Quarry Hill, Leeds, England LS2 7PD. Tel 0113 222 3416; www.lcm.ac.uk [**M**]

Liverpool Institute for Performing Arts The Liverpool Institute of Performing Arts provides courses in Acting, Community Drama, Dance, Music, Theatre and Entertainment Management, Sound Technology, Theatre and Performance Design, and Theatre and Performance Technology. For the past four years LIPA has traced 85% of each year group who have graduated, of these an average 93% are in work with 82% working in the performing arts. Mount Street, Liverpool, England L1 9HF. Tel 0151 330 3000; www.lipa.ac.uk [**D**]

London Academy of Music and Dramatic Art 155 Talgarth Road, London, England W14 9DA. Tel 020 8834 0500; www.lamda.org.uk [**M**]

London College of Communication, University of the Arts London Elephant and Castle, London, England SE1 6SB. Tel 020 7514 6599; www.arts.ac.uk/lcc [**C**]

London College of Fashion, University of the Arts London 20 John Princes Street, London, England W1G 0BJ. Tel 020 7514 7563; www.arts.ac.uk/fashion [**F**]

Mountview Academy of Theatre Arts Mountview is situated in Wood Green, in the Borough of Haringey, north London; home of Alexandra Palace. It is well placed for easy access to West End theatres, fringe theatres and London nightlife. Founded in 1945, Mountview offers extensive and stimulating training for those interested in pursuing a performance, directing or technical theatre career. Ralph Richardson Memorial Studio, Kingfisher Place, Clarendon Road, London, England N22 6XF. Tel 020 8881 2201; www.mountview.org.uk [**D**]

Myerscough College Six miles north of Preston, Myerscough College is a higher and further education college dating back to the 19th century. It specialises in education and training for the land-based and sports industries, offering more than 20 different subjects. Myerscough Hall, St Michael's Road, Bilsborrow, Preston, England PR3 0RY. Tel 01995 642211; www.myerscough.ac.uk [**Ag**]

Northern School of Contemporary Dance 98 Chapeltown Road, Leeds, England LS7 4BH. Tel 0113 219 3000; www.nscd.ac.uk [**Da**]

Northop College (part of Coleg Cambria) Holywell Road, Northop, Wales CH7 6AA. Tel 01352 841000; www.cambria.ac.uk [**H**]

Plymouth College of Art Tavistock Place, Plymouth, England PL4 8AT. Tel 01752 203434; www.plymouthart.ac.uk [**A**]

Ravensbourne 6 Penrose Way, London, England SE10 0EW. Tel 020 3040 3500; www.rave.ac.uk [**C**]

Reaseheath College Reaseheath, Nantwich, England CW5 6DF. Tel 01270 625131; HE Enquiries 01270 613284; www.reaseheath.ac.uk [**Ag**]

Rose Bruford College Lamorbey Park Campus, Burnt Oak Lane, Sidcup, England DA15 9DF. Tel 020 8308 2600; www.bruford.ac.uk [**D**]

Royal Academy of Dance 36 Battersea Square, London, England SW11 3RA. Tel 020 7326 8000; www.rad.org.uk [**Da**]

Royal Academy of Dramatic Art (RADA) 62–64 Gower Street, London, England WC1E 6ED. Tel 020 7636 7076; www.rada.ac.uk [**D**]

Royal Academy of Music, University of London This is Britain's senior conservatoire, founded in 1822. Marylebone Road, London, England NW1 5HT. Tel 020 7873 7373; www.ram.ac.uk [**M**]

Royal Ballet School 46 Floral Street, London, England WC2E 9DA. Tel 020 7836 8899; www.royal-ballet-school.org.uk [**Da**]

Royal Central School of Speech and Drama The School's main campus is at the Embassy Theatre, 15 minutes by Underground from Central London. Royal Central School of Speech and Drama, Eton Avenue, London, England NW3 3HY. Tel 020 7722 8183; www.cssd.ac.uk [**D**]

Royal College of Music Prince Consort Road, London, England SW7 2BS. Tel 020 7591 4300; www.rcm.ac.uk [**M**]

Royal Conservatoire of Scotland (formerly Royal Scottish Academy of Music and Drama) 100 Renfrew Street, Glasgow, Scotland G2 3DB. Tel 0141 332 4101; www.rcs.ac.uk [**M**]

Royal Northern College of Music 124 Oxford Road, Manchester, England M13 9RD. Tel 0161 907 5200; www.rncm.ac.uk [**M**]

Royal Welsh College of Music and Drama Castle Grounds, Cathays Park, Cardiff, Wales CF10 3ER. Tel 029 2039 1361; www.rwcmd.ac.uk [**M**]

Ruskin School of Drawing and Fine Art 74 High Street, Oxford, England OX1 4BG. Tel 01865 276940; www.ruskin-sch.ox.ac.uk [**A**]

Scotland's Rural College Student Recruitment and Admissions Office, SAC Riverside Campus, University Avenue, Ayr, Scotland KA8 0SR. Tel 0800 269453; www.sruc.ac.uk [**Ag**]

Slade School of Fine Art, University College London Part of UCL, The Slade School of Fine Art is concerned with contemporary art and the practice, history and theories that inform it. Gower Street, London, England WC1E 6BT. Tel 020 7679 2313; www.ucl.ac.uk/slade [**A**]

Sparsholt College Hampshire Westley Lane, Sparsholt, Winchester, England SO21 2NF. Tel 01962 776441; www.sparsholt.ac.uk [**H**]

Stranmillis University College Academic Registry, Stranmillis Road, Belfast, Northern Ireland BT9 5DY. Tel 028 9038 1271; www.stran.ac.uk

Trinity Laban Conservatoire of Music and Dance Creekside, London, England SE8 3DZ. Tel 020 8691 8600; www.trinitylaban.ac.uk [**M**]

University Campus Suffolk Admissions Office, Waterfront Building, Neptune Quay, Ipswich, England IP4 1QJ. Tel 01473 338000; www.ucs.ac.uk

University College of Football Business (partner college of Bucks New University) Campuses in Burnley and Wembley. Burnley Football Club, Turf Moor, Harry Potts Way, Burnley, England BB10 4BX. Tel 0843 208 2222; www.ucfb.com

Wimbledon College of Art, University of the Arts London Merton Hall Road, London, England SW19 3QA. Tel 020 7514 9641; www.wimbledon.arts.ac.uk [**A**]

Winchester School of Art, University of Southampton Park Avenue, Winchester, England SO23 8DL. Tel 023 8059 7141; www.wsa.soton.ac.uk [**A**]

Writtle College Lordship Road, Chelmsford, England CM1 3RR. Tel 01245 424200; www.writtle.ac.uk [**H**]

SECTION 3: UNIVERSITY CENTRES, FURTHER EDUCATION AND OTHER COLLEGES OFFERING HIGHER EDUCATION COURSES

Changes are taking place fast in this sector, with the merger of colleges and the introduction in 2009 of University Centres. These are linked to further education colleges and to one or more universities, and provide foundation and honours degree courses (often part time) and sometimes postgraduate qualifications.

The following colleges appear at the end of the tables in Chapter 6 and are in UCAS for some of their courses. See prospectuses and websites for application details.

University centres
Barony College SRUC Barony Campus, Parkgate, Dumfries, Scotland DG1 3NE. Tel 01387 860251; www.barony.ac.uk

Blackburn College Feilden Street, Blackburn, England BB2 1LH. Tel 01254 55144; Student Hotline 01254 292929; www.blackburn.ac.uk

Bradford College University Centre Admissions Office, Great Horton Road, Bradford, England BD7 1AY. Tel 01274 433333; www.bradfordcollege.ac.uk

College of West Anglia King's Lynn Centre, Tennyson Avenue, King's Lynn, Norfolk, England PE30 2QW. Tel 01553 761144; www.cwa.ac.uk

Doncaster College and University Centre High Melton, Doncaster, England DN5 7SZ. Tel 0800 358 7474; www.don.ac.uk

University Campus Oldham Cromwell Street, Oldham, England OL1 1BB. Tel 0161 334 8800; www.uco.oldham.ac.uk

University Centre Folkestone Mill Bay, Folkestone, England CT20 1JG. Tel 01227 782900; www.canter bury.ac.uk/AboutUs/Findus/Folkestone.aspx

University Centre Grimsby Nuns Corner, Laceby Road, Grimsby, England DN34 5BQ. Tel 0800 315002; www.grimsby.ac.uk

University Centre Milton Keynes 200 Silbury Boulevard, Milton Keynes, England MK9 1LT. Tel 01908 688223; www.mkcollege.ac.uk

University Centre Yeovil 91 Preston Road, Yeovil, England BA20 2DN. Tel 01935 845454; www.ucy.ac.uk

Other further education colleges
Abingdon and Witney College Abingdon Campus, Wootton Road, Abingdon, England OX14 1GG. Tel 01235 555585; www.abingdon-witney.ac.uk

Accrington and Rossendale College Broad Oak Campus, Broad Oak Road, Accrington, England BB5 2AW. Tel 01254 389933; Information and Care 01254 354354; www.accross.ac.uk

Andover College Charlton Road, Andover, England SP10 1EJ. Tel 01264 360000; www.andover.ac.uk

Angus College Keptie Road, Arbroath, Scotland DD11 3EA. Tel 01241 432600; www.angus.ac.uk

Argyll College (UHI partner college – see Section 1) West Bay, Dunoon, Scotland PA23 7HP. Tel 0845 230 9969; www.argyll.uhi.ac.uk

Aylesbury College Oxford Road, Aylesbury, England HP21 8PD. Tel 01296 588588; www.aylesbury.ac.uk

Ayrshire College Dam Park, Ayr, Scotland KA8 0EU. Tel 0300 303 0303; www.ayrcoll.ac.uk

Banff and Buchan College Main Campus, Henderson Road, Fraserburgh, Scotland AB43 9GA. Tel 01346 586100; www.banff-buchan.ac.uk

Barking and Dagenham College Rush Green Campus, Dagenham Road, Romford, England RM7 0XU. Tel 020 8090 3020; www.barkingdagenhamcollege.ac.uk

Barnet and Southgate College Wood Street, Barnet, England EN5 4AZ. Tel 020 8266 4000; www.barnet-southgate.ac.uk

Barnfield College New Bedford Road Campus, New Bedford Road, Luton, England LU2 7BF. Tel 01582 569569; http://college.barnfield.ac.uk

Barnsley College Church Street, Barnsley, England S70 2AN. Tel 01226 216165; www.barnsley.ac.uk

Basingstoke College of Technology Worting Road, Basingstoke, England RG21 8TN. Tel 01256 306237; www.bcot.ac.uk

Bedford College Cauldwell Street, Bedford, England MK42 9AH. Tel 01234 291000; www.bedford.ac.uk

Bexley College Tower Road, Belvedere, England DA17 6JA. Tel 01322 442331; www.bexley.ac.uk

Bicton College East Budleigh, Budleigh Salterton, England EX9 7BY. Tel 01395 562400; www.bicton.ac.uk

Birmingham Metropolitan College (incorporating Matthew Boulton College of Further and Higher Education and Sutton Coldfield College) Jennens Road, Birmingham, England B4 7PS. Tel 0845 155 0101; www.bmetc.ac.uk

Bishop Auckland College Woodhouse Lane, Bishop Auckland, England DL14 6JZ. Tel 01388 443000; www.bacoll.ac.uk

Blackpool and The Fylde College Ashfield Road, Bispham, Blackpool, England FY2 0HB. Tel 01253 504343; www.blackpool.ac.uk

Borders College Head Office, Scottish Borders Campus, Nether Road, Galashiels, Scotland TD1 3HE. Tel 01896 662600; www.borderscollege.ac.uk

Boston College Skirbeck Road, Boston, England PE21 6JF. Tel 01205 365701; www.boston.ac.uk

Bournemouth and Poole College Customer Enquiry Centre, North Road, Poole, England BH14 0LS. Tel 01202 205205; www.thecollege.co.uk

Bournville College Longbridge Lane, Longbridge, Birmingham, England B31 2AJ. Tel 0121 477 1300; www.bournville.ac.uk

Bracknell and Wokingham College College Information Centre, Church Road, Bracknell, England RG12 1DJ. Tel 0845 330 3343; www.bracknell.ac.uk

Bridgend College Cowbridge Road, Bridgend, Wales CF31 3DF. Tel 01656 302302; www.bridgend.ac.uk

Bridgwater College Bath Road, Bridgwater, England TA6 4PZ. Tel 01278 455464; www.bridgwater.ac.uk

Brockenhurst College Lyndhurst Road, Brockenhurst, England SO42 7ZE. Tel 01590 625555; www.brock.ac.uk

Bromley College of Further and Higher Education Rookery Lane, Bromley, England BR2 8HE. Tel 020 8295 7000; www.bromley.ac.uk

Brooklands College Weybridge Campus, Heath Road, Weybridge, England KT13 8TT. Tel 01932 797797; www.brooklands.ac.uk

Brooksby Melton College Melton Mowbray Campus, Ashfordby Road, Melton Mowbray, England LE13 0HJ. Tel 01664 850850; www.brooksbymelton.ac.uk

Burnley College Princess Way, Burnley, England BB12 0AN. Tel 01282 733373; Student Services 01282 733333; www.burnley.ac.uk

Burton College Student Services, Lichfield Street, Burton-on-Trent, England DE14 3RL. Tel 01283 494400; www.burton-college.ac.uk

Bury College Woodbury Centre, Market Street, Bury, England BL9 0BG. Tel 0161 280 8280; www.burycollege.ac.uk

Buxton and Leek College Part of University of Derby, the college has campuses in Leek, Buxton and on the main campus of the university. Stockwell Street, Leek, England ST13 6DP. Tel 0800 074 0099; www.blc.ac.uk

Calderdale College Francis Street, Halifax, England HX1 3UZ. Tel 01422 399399; www.calderdale.ac.uk

Cambridge Regional College Kings Hedges Road, Cambridge, England CB4 2QT. Tel 01223 418200; www.camre.ac.uk

Canterbury College New Dover Road, Canterbury, England CT1 3AJ. Tel 01227 811111; Learning Advice/Courses 01227 811188; www.cant-col.ac.uk

Carlisle College Information Unit, Victoria Place, Carlisle, England CA1 1HS. Tel 01228 822700; www.carlisle.ac.uk

Carmel College Prescot Road, St Helens, England WA10 3AG. Tel 01744 452200; www.carmel.ac.uk

Carnegie College (formerly Lauder College) Pittsburgh Road, Halbeath, Dunfermline, Scotland KY11 8DY. Tel 0844 248 0155; www.carnegiecollege.ac.uk

Carshalton College Nightingale Road, Carshalton, England SM5 2EJ. Tel 020 8544 4444; www.carshalton.ac.uk

CECOS London College 59 Crompton Road, London, England N1 2YT. Tel 020 7359 3316; www.cecos.co.uk

Central Bedfordshire College (formerly Dunstable College) Kingsway, Dunstable, England LU5 4HG. Tel 0845 355 2525; www.centralbeds.ac.uk

Central College Nottingham A multi-campus college, with 11 locations across the city of Nottingham. Jesse Boot Avenue, Science Park, University Boulevard, Nottingham, England NG7 2RU. Tel 0115 914 6414; www.centralnottingham.ac.uk

Chelmsford College 102 Moulsham Street, Chelmsford, England CM2 0JQ. Tel 01245 265611; www.chelmsford.ac.uk

Chesterfield College Infirmary Road, Chesterfield, England S41 7NG. Tel 01246 500500; www.chester-field.ac.uk

Chichester College Westgate Fields, Chichester, England PO19 1SB. Tel 01243 786321; www.chichester.ac.uk

City and Islington College The Marlborough Building, 383 Holloway Road, London, England N7 0RN. Tel 020 7700 9200; www.candi.ac.uk

City College Brighton and Hove Pelham Street, Brighton, England BN1 4FA. Tel 01273 667788; Course Advisers 01273 667759; www.ccb.ac.uk

City College Coventry Swanswell Centre, 50 Swanswell Street, Coventry, England CV1 5DG. Tel 024 7679 1000; Course Information 024 7679 1627; www.covcollege.ac.uk

City College Plymouth (formerly Plymouth College of Further Education) Kings Road, Devonport, Plymouth, England PL1 5QG. Tel 01752 305300; www.cityplym.ac.uk

City of Bath College Student Advice Centre, Avon St, Bath, England BA1 1UP. Tel 01225 312191; www.citybathcoll.ac.uk

City of Bristol College Ashley Down Road, Bristol, England BS7 9BU. Tel 0117 312 5000; www.cityofbristol.ac.uk

City of Glasgow College (formed in 2010 from a merger between Glasgow Nautical College, Glasgow Metropolitan and College of Commerce) 60 North Hanover Street, Glasgow, Scotland G1 2BP. Tel 0141 566 6222; www.cityofglasgowcollege.ac.uk

City of Liverpool College Bankfield Road, Liverpool, England L13 0BQ. Tel 0151 252 3000; www.liv-coll.ac.uk

City of Sunderland College Bede Centre, Durham Road, Sunderland, England SR3 4AH. Tel 0191 511 6000; HE Admissions 0191 511 6260; www.sunderlandcollege.ac.uk

City of Westminster College Paddington Green Campus, London, England W2 1NB. Tel 020 7723 8826; www.cwc.ac.uk

City of Wolverhampton College Paget Road Campus, Paget Road, Wolverhampton, England WV6 0DU. Tel 01902 836000; www.wolvcoll.ac.uk

Cliff College Calver, Hope Valley, Derbyshire, England S32 3XG. Tel 01246 584202; www.cliffcollege.ac.uk

Clydebank College College Square, Queens' Quay, Clydebank, Scotland G81 1BF. Tel 0141 951 7400; www.clydebank.ac.uk

Coatbridge College Kildonan Street, Coatbridge, Scotland ML5 3LS. Tel 01236 436000; www.coatbridge.ac.uk

Coleg Llandrillo Cymru Llandudno Road, Rhos-on-Sea, Wales LL28 4HZ. Tel 01492 546666; www.llandrillo.ac.uk

Coleg Menai Ffriddoedd Road, Bangor, Gwynedd, Wales LL57 2TP. Tel 01248 370125; www.menai.ac.uk

Coleg Sir Gâr Graig Campus, Sandy Road, Pwll, Wales SA15 4DN. Tel 01554 748000; www.colegsirgar.ac.uk

College of Haringey, Enfield and North East London (formed in 2009 from a merger between Enfield College and the College of North East London) Enfield Centre, 73 Hertford Road, Enfield, England EN3 5HA. Tel 020 8442 3103; www.conel.ac.uk

College of North West London Willesden Centre, Dudden Hill Lane, London, England NW10 2XD. Tel 020 8208 5000; Course Information 020 8208 5050; www.cnwl.ac.uk

College Ystrad Mynach Twyn Road, Ystrad Mynach, Hengoed, Wales CF82 7XR. Tel 01443 816888; www.ystrad-mynach.ac.uk

Cornwall College Camborne Campus, Trevenson Road, Pool, Redruth, England TR15 3RD. Tel 01209 616161; www.cornwall.ac.uk

Craven College High Street, Skipton, England BD23 1JY. Tel 01756 708001; www.craven-college.ac.uk

Croydon College College Road, Croydon, England CR9 1DX. Tel 020 8760 5934; www.croydon.ac.uk

Cumbernauld College Town Centre, Cumbernauld, Glasgow, Scotland G67 1HU. Tel 01236 731811; www.cumbernauld.ac.uk

Darlington College Central Park, Haughton Road, Darlington, England DL1 1DR. Tel 01325 503030; www.darlington.ac.uk

Dearne Valley College Manvers Park, Wath-upon-Dearne, Rotherham, England S63 7EW. Tel 01709 513355; www.dearne-coll.ac.uk

Derby College Prince Charles Avenue, Mackworth, Derby, England DE22 4LR. Tel 0800 028 0289; Course Enquiries 01332 387473; www.derby-college.ac.uk

Derwentside College Consett Campus, Front Street, Consett, England DH8 5EE. Tel 01207 585900; www.derwentside.ac.uk

Duchy College Rosewarne Campus, Camborne, England TR14 0AB. Tel 01209 722100; www.duchy.ac.uk

Dudley College The Broadway, Dudley, England DY1 4AS. Tel 01384 363000; Course Enquiries 01384 363363; www.dudleycol.ac.uk

Dumfries and Galloway College College Gate, Bankend Road, Dumfries, Scotland DG1 4FD. Tel 01387 734059; www.dumgal.ac.uk

Dundee College Kingsway Campus, Old Glamis Road, Dundee, Scotland DD3 8LE. Tel 01382 834834; Student Services 01382 834844; www.dundeecollege.ac.uk

Ealing, Hammersmith and West London College The Green, London, England W5 5EW. Tel 0800 980 2175; www.wlc.ac.uk

East Berkshire College Langley Campus, Station Road, Langley, England SL3 8BY. Tel 0845 373 2500; www.eastberks.ac.uk

East Durham College Houghall Campus, Houghall, England DH1 3SG. Tel 0191 375 4700; www.east-durham.ac.uk

East Kent College Ramsgate Road, Broadstairs, England CT10 1PN. Tel 01843 605040; Admissions 01843 605049; www.eastkent.ac.uk

East Riding College Beverley Campus, Gallows Lane, Beverley, England HU17 7DT. Tel 0845 120 0037; www.eastridingcollege.ac.uk

East Surrey College Gatton Point, London Road, Redhill, England RH1 2JT. Tel 01737 788445; www.esc.ac.uk

Eastleigh College Chestnut Avenue, Eastleigh, England SO50 5FS. Tel 023 8091 1299; www.eastleigh.ac.uk

Easton and Otley College Easton, Norwich, England NR9 5DX. Tel 01603 731200; www.eastonotley.ac.uk

Edinburgh College Granton Campus, 350 West Granton Road, Edinburgh, Scotland EH5 1QE. Tel 0131 669 4400; www.edinburghcollege.ac.uk

Edinburgh's Telford College Now part of Edinburgh College. Granton Campus, 350 West Granton Road, Edinburgh, Scotland EH5 1QE. Tel 0131 669 4400; www.edinburghcollege.ac.uk

European Business School Admissions Department, Regent's College, Regent's Park, Inner Circle, London, England NW1 4NS. Tel 020 7487 7505; www.regents.ac.uk/about/schools/european-business-school-london

Exeter College Hele Road, Exeter, England EX4 4JS. Tel 01392 400500; www.exe-coll.ac.uk

Fareham College Bishopsfield Road, Fareham, England PO14 1NH. Tel 01329 815200; www.fareham.ac.uk

Farnborough College of Technology Boundary Road, Farnborough, England GU14 6SB. Tel 01252 407040; www.farn-ct.ac.uk

Fife College St Brycedale Campus, St Brycedale Avenue, Kirkcaldy, Scotland KY1 1EX. Tel 01592 223400; www.fife.ac.uk

Filton College Now part of South Gloucestershire and Stroud College. Filton Avenue, Filton, England BS34 7AT. Tel 0117 931 2121; www.filton.ac.uk

Forth Valley College Falkirk Campus, Grangemouth Road, Falkirk, Scotland FK2 9AD. Tel 0845 634 4444; www.forthvalley.ac.uk

Furness College Channelside, Barrow-in-Furness, England LA14 2PJ. Tel 01229 825017; www.furness.ac.uk

Gateshead College Baltic Campus, Baltic Business Quarter, Quarryfield Road, Gateshead, England NE8 3BE. Tel 0191 490 2246; www.gateshead.ac.uk

Glasgow Clyde College Mosspark Drive, Glasgow, Scotland G52 3AY. Tel 0141 272 3333; www.cardonald.ac.uk

Gloucestershire College Gloucester Campus, Llanthony Road, Gloucester, England GL2 5JQ. Tel 0845 155 2020; www.gloscol.ac.uk

Gower College Swansea (Coleg Abertawe; now part of Gower College Swansea) Tycoch Campus, Tycoch Road, Swansea, Wales SA2 9EB. Tel 01792 284000; www.gowercollegeswansea.ac.uk

Grantham College Stonebridge Road, Grantham, England NG31 9AP. Tel 01476 400200; Course Information 0800 052 1577; www.grantham.ac.uk

Great Yarmouth College Suffolk Road, Southtown, Great Yarmouth, England NR31 0ED. Tel 01493 655261; www.gyc.ac.uk

Greenwich School of Management Meridian House, Royal Hill, London, England SE10 8RD. Tel 020 8516 7800; http://gsm.org.uk

Guildford College Stoke Park Campus, Stoke Road, Guildford, England GU1 1EZ. Tel 01483 448500; www.guildford.ac.uk

Hackney Community College Shoreditch Campus, Falkirk Street, London, England N1 6HQ. Tel 020 7613 9123; www.tcch.ac.uk

Hadlow College Hadlow College, Hadlow, Tonbridge, England TN11 0AL. Tel 0500 551434; www.hadlow.ac.uk

Halesowen College Whittingham Road, Halesowen, England B63 3NA. Tel 0121 602 7777; www.halesowen.ac.uk

Harlow College Velizy Avenue, Harlow, England CM20 3EZ. Tel 01279 868000; www.harlow-college.ac.uk

Harrow College Harrow on the Hill Campus, Lowlands Road, Harrow, England HA1 3AQ. Tel 020 8909 6000; www.harrow.ac.uk

Hartlepool College of Further Education Stockton Street, Hartlepool, England TS24 7NT. Tel 01429 295000; www.hartlepoolfe.ac.uk

Havering College Ardleigh Green Road, Hornchurch, England RM11 2LL. Tel 01708 455011; Course Information 01708 462801; www.havering-college.ac.uk

Henley College Coventry Henley Road, Bell Green, Coventry, England CV2 1ED. Tel 024 7662 6300; www.henley-cov.ac.uk

Herefordshire and Ludlow College Folly Lane, Hereford, England HR1 1LS. Tel 0800 032 1986; www.hlcollege.ac.uk

Hertford Regional College Ware Centre, Scotts Road, Ware, England SG12 9JF. Tel 01992 411400; www.hrc.ac.uk

Highbury College Portsmouth Tudor Crescent, Portsmouth, England PO6 2SA. Tel 023 9238 3131; www.highbury.ac.uk

Highland Theological College (UHI partner college – see Section 1) High Street, Dingwall, Scotland IV15 9HA. Tel 01349 780000; www.htc.uhi.ac.uk

Hillcroft College South Bank, Surbiton, England KT6 6DF. Tel 020 8399 2688; www.hillcroft.ac.uk

Hopwood Hall College Rochdale Campus, St Mary's Gate, Rochdale, England OL12 6RY. Tel 01706 345346; www.hopwood.ac.uk

Hugh Baird College Balliol Road, Bootle, England L20 7EW. Tel 0151 353 4444; www.hughbaird.ac.uk

Hull College The Queen's Gardens Centre, Wilberforce Drive, Hull, England HU1 3DG. Tel 01482 598744; www.hull-college.ac.uk

Huntingdonshire Regional College California Road, Huntingdon, England PE29 1BL. Tel 01480 379100; www.huntingdon.ac.uk

Islamic College for Advanced Studies 133 High Road, London, England NW10 2SW. Tel 020 8451 9993; www.islamic-college.ac.uk

Isle of Wight College Medina Way, Newport, Isle of Wight, England PO30 5TA. Tel 01983 526631; www.iwcollege.ac.uk

James Watt College Finnart Street, Greenock, Scotland PA16 8HF. Tel 01475 724433; www.jameswatt.ac.uk

Jewel and Esk College (now part of Edinburgh College) Edinburgh Campus, 24 Milton Road East, Edinburgh, Scotland EH15 2PP. Tel 0131 334 7000; Information Services 0131 334 7163; www.jec.ac.uk

K College Brook Street, Tonbridge, England TN9 2PW. Tel 0845 207 8220; www.kcollege.ac.uk

Kaplan Holborn College 179–191 Borough High St, London, England SE1 1HR. Tel 020 3642 1999; www.holborncollege.ac.uk

Kendal College Milnthorpe Road, Kendal, England LA9 5AY. Tel 01539 814700; www.kendal.ac.uk

Kensington College of Business Wesley House, 4 Wild Court, London, England WC2B 4AU. Tel 020 7404 6330; www.kensingtoncoll.ac.uk

Kidderminster College Market Street, Kidderminster, England DY10 1AB. Tel 01562 512025; www.kidderminster.ac.uk

Kilmarnock College Holehouse Road, Kilmarnock, Scotland KA3 7AT. Tel 01563 523501; www.kilmarnock.ac.uk

Kingston College Kingston Hall Road, Kingston upon Thames, England KT1 2AQ. Tel 020 8546 2151; www.kingston-college.ac.uk

Kingston Maurward College Kingston Maurward, Dorchester, England DT2 8PY. Tel 01305 215000; Course Enquiries 01305 215215; www.kmc.ac.uk

Kirklees College (formerly Dewsbury College) Information Office, Waterfront Quarter, Manchester Road, Huddersfield, England HD1 3HH. Tel 01484 437000; Course Enquiries 01484 437070; www.kirkleescollege.ac.uk

Knowsley Community College Rupert Road, Roby, Kirkby, England L36 9TD. Tel 0845 155 1055; www.knowsleycollege.ac.uk

Lakes College, West Cumbria Hallwood Road, Lillyhall Business Park, Workington, England CA14 4JN. Tel 01946 839300; www.lcwc.ac.uk

Lambeth College 45 Clapham Common South Side, London, England SW4 9BL. Tel 020 7501 5010; Course Information 020 7501 5000; www.lambethcollege.ac.uk

Lancaster and Morecambe College Morecambe Road, Lancaster, England LA1 2TY. Tel 01524 66215; www.lmc.ac.uk

Langside College 50 Prospecthill Road, Glasgow, Scotland G42 9LB. Tel 0141 272 3636; www.langside.ac.uk

Lansdowne College 40–44 Bark Place, London, England W2 4AT. Tel 020 7616 4400; www.lansdownecollege.com

Leeds City College Thomas Danby Campus, Roundhay Road, Leeds, England LS7 3BG. Tel 0113 386 1996; Course Enquiries 0113 386 1997; www.leedscitycollege.ac.uk

Leeds College of Building North Street, Leeds, England LS2 7QT. Tel 0113 222 6000; www.lcb.ac.uk

Leicester College Freemen's Park Campus, Aylestone Road, Leicester, England LE2 7LW. Tel 0116 224 2240; www.leicestercollege.ac.uk

Leo Baeck College The Sternberg Centre, 80 East End Road, London, England N3 2SY. Tel 020 8349 5600; www.lbc.ac.uk

Lewisham College Lewisham Way, London, England SE4 1UT. Tel 020 8692 0353; Course Enquiries 0800 834545; www.lewisham.ac.uk

Lews Castle College (UHI partner college – see Section 1) Castle Grounds, Stornoway, Isle of Lewis, Scotland HS2 0XR. Tel 01851 770000; www.lews.uhi.ac.uk

Lincoln College Monks Road, Lincoln, England LN2 5HQ. Tel 01522 876000; www.lincolncollege.ac.uk

London College of Business and Computing Millennium Place, 206 Cambridge Heath Road, London, England E2 9NQ. Tel 020 8983 4193; www.lcbc.com

London School of Commerce Chaucer House, White Hart Yard, London, England SE1 1NX. Tel 020 7357 0077; www.lsclondon.co.uk

Loughborough College Radmoor Road, Loughborough, England LE11 3BT. Tel 01509 618375; www.loucoll.ac.uk

Macclesfield College Park Lane, Macclesfield, England SK11 8LF. Tel 01625 410002; www.macclesfield.ac.uk

Mid-Cheshire College Hartford Campus, Chester Road, Northwich, England CW8 1LJ. Tel 01606 74444; www.midchesh.ac.uk

Middlesbrough College Dock Street, Middlesbrough, England TS2 1AD. Tel 01642 333333; www.mbro.ac.uk

Mid-Kent College Medway Campus, Medway Road, Gillingham, England ME7 1FN. Tel 01634 402020; www.midkent.ac.uk

Milton Keynes College Chaffron Way Campus, Woughton Campus West, Leadenhall, Milton Keynes, England MK6 5LP. Tel 01908 684444; www.mkcollege.ac.uk

Moray College (UHI partner college – see Section 1) Moray Street, Elgin, Scotland IV30 1JJ. Tel 01343 576000; Course Enquiries 0845 272 3600; www.moray.uhi.ac.uk

Moulton College West Street, Moulton, England NN3 7RR. Tel 01604 491131; www.moulton.ac.uk

Nazarene Theological College Dene Road, Didsbury, Manchester, England M20 2GU. Tel 0161 445 3063; www.nazarene.ac.uk

Neath Port Talbot College Dwr-y-Felin Road, Neath, Wales SA10 7RF. Tel 01639 648000; www.nptcgroup.ac.uk

Nelson and Colne College Reedyford Site, Scotland Road, Nelson, England BB9 7YT. Tel 01282 440272; www.nelson.ac.uk

Nescot, North East Surrey College of Technology Reigate Road, Ewell, Epsom, England KT17 3DS. Tel 020 8394 3038; www.nescot.ac.uk

New College Durham Framwellgate Moor Campus, Durham, England DH1 5ES. Tel 0191 375 4000; www.newcollegedurham.ac.uk

New College Nottingham The Adams Building, Stoney Street, Nottingham, England NG1 1NG. Tel 01159 100100; www.ncn.ac.uk

New College Stamford Drift Road, Stamford, England PE9 1XA. Tel 01780 484300; www.stamford.ac.uk

New College Swindon New College Drive, Swindon, England SN3 1AH. Tel 01793 611470; www.newcollege.ac.uk

New College Telford King Street, Wellington, Telford, England TF1 1NY. Tel 01952 641892; www.nct.ac.uk

Newbury College Monks Lane, Newbury, England RG14 7TD. Tel 01635 845000; www.newbury-college.ac.uk

Newcastle College Rye Hill Campus, Scotswood Road, Newcastle-upon-Tyne, England NE4 7SA. Tel 0191 200 4000; www.ncl-coll.ac.uk

Newcastle-under-Lyme College Knutton Lane, Newcastle-under-Lyme, England ST5 2GB. Tel 01782 254254; www.nulc.ac.uk

Newham College of Further Education East Ham Campus, High Street South, London, England E6 6ER. Tel 020 8257 4446; www.newham.ac.uk

North Atlantic Fisheries College (UHI partner college – see Section 1) NAFC Marine Centre, Port Arthur, Scalloway, Scotland ZE1 0UN. Tel 01595 772000; www.nafc.ac.uk

North East Scotland College Gallowgate Centre, Gallowgate, Aberdeen, Scotland AB25 1BN. Tel 01224 612000; Information and Booking Centre 01224 612330; www.nescol.ac.uk

North East Worcestershire College Redditch Campus, Peakman Street, Redditch, England B98 8DW. Tel 01527 570020; www.ne-worcs.ac.uk

North Glasgow College 123 Flemington Street, Springburn, Glasgow, Scotland G21 4TD. Tel 0141 630 5000; www.northglasgowcollege.ac.uk

North Hertfordshire College Monkswood Way, Stevenage, England SG1 1LA. Tel 01462 424242; www.nhc.ac.uk

North Highland College (UHI partner college – see Section 1) Ormlie Road, Thurso, Scotland KW14 7EE. Tel 01847 889000; www.northhighland.ac.uk

North Lindsey College Kingsway, Scunthorpe, England DN17 1AJ. Tel 01724 281111; www.northlindsey.ac.uk

North Nottinghamshire College Carlton Road, Worksop, England S81 7HP. Tel 01909 504504; Student Services 01909 504500; www.nnotts-col.ac.uk

North Warwickshire and Hinckley College Nuneaton Campus, Hinckley Road, Nuneaton, England CV11 6BH. Tel 024 7624 3000; www.nwhc.ac.uk

North West Kent College Oakfield Lane, Dartford, England DA1 2JT. Tel 0800 074 1447; www.nwkcollege.ac.uk

Northampton College Booth Lane, Northampton, England NN3 3RF. Tel 0845 300 4401; www.northamptoncollege.ac.uk

Northbrook College, Sussex West Durrington Campus, Littlehampton Road, Worthing, England BN12 6NU. Tel 0845 155 6060; www.northbrook.ac.uk

Northern Regional College (formerly North East Institute of Further and Higher Education) Ballymena Campus, Trostan Avenue Building, Ballymena, Northern Ireland BT43 7BN. Tel 028 2563 6221; www.nrc.ac.uk

Northumberland College College Road, Ashington, England NE63 9RG. Tel 01670 841200; www.northumberland.ac.uk

Norton Radstock College South Hill Park, Radstock, England BA3 3RW. Tel 01761 433161; www.nortcoll.ac.uk

Oaklands College, St Albans Smallford Campus, Hatfield Road, St Albans, England AL4 0JA. Tel 01727 737000; www.oaklands.ac.uk

Oatridge College Ecclesmachan, Broxburn, Scotland EH52 6NH. Tel 01506 864800; www.oatridge.ac.uk

Orkney College (UHI partner college – see Section 1) East Road, Kirkwall, Scotland KW15 1LX. Tel 01856 569000; www.orkney.uhi.ac.uk

Otley College Otley, Ipswich, England IP6 9NE. Tel 01473 785543; www.otleycollege.ac.uk

Oxford and Cherwell Valley College Banbury Campus, Broughton Road, Banbury, Oxford, England OX16 9QA. Tel 01865 550550; www.ocvc.ac.uk

Pembrokeshire College (Coleg Sir Benfro) Merlins Bridge, Haverfordwest, Wales SA61 1SZ. Tel 01437 753000; Freephone 0800 977 6788; www.pembrokeshire.ac.uk

Perth College (UHI partner college – see Section 1) Crieff Road, Perth, Scotland PH1 2NX. Tel 0845 270 1177; www.perth.uhi.ac.uk

Peterborough Regional College Park Crescent, Peterborough, England PE1 4DZ. Tel 0845 872 8722; www.peterborough.ac.uk

Petroc Old Sticklepath Hill, Sticklepath, Barnstaple, England EX31 2BQ. Tel 01271 345291; www.petroc.ac.uk

Plumpton College Ditchling Road, Near Lewes, England BN7 3AE. Tel 01273 890454; www.plumpton.ac.uk

Portsmouth College Tangier Road, Copnor, Portsmouth, England PO3 6PZ. Tel 023 9266 7521; www.portsmouth-college.ac.uk

Preston College Fulwood Campus, St Vincent's Road, Preston, England PR2 8UR. Tel 01772 225000; www.preston.ac.uk

Redbridge College Little Heath, Barley Lane, Romford, England RM6 4XT. Tel 020 8548 7400; www.redbridge-college.ac.uk

Redcar and Cleveland College Corporation Road, Redcar, England TS10 1EZ. Tel 01642 473132; www.cleveland.ac.uk

Reid Kerr College Admission Unit, Renfrew Road, Paisley, Scotland PA3 4DR. Tel 0800 052 7343; www.reidkerr.ac.uk

Richmond-upon-Thames College Egerton Road, Twickenham, England TW2 7SJ. Tel 020 8607 8000; Courses Information Unit 020 8607 8306; www.rutc.ac.uk

Riverside College Halton Kingsway Campus, Kingsway, Widnes, England WA8 7QQ. Tel 0151 257 2800; www.riversidecollege.ac.uk

Rotherham College of Arts and Technology Town Centre Campus, Eastwood Lane, Rotherham, England S65 1EG. Tel 01709 722777; www.rotherham.ac.uk

Royal National College for the Blind College Road, Hereford, England HR1 1EB. Tel 01432 265725; www.rncb.ac.uk

Runshaw College Langdale Road, Leyland, England PR25 3DQ. Tel 01772 622677; www.runshaw.ac.uk

Ruskin College Ruskin Hall, Dunstan Road, Old Headington, Oxford, England OX3 9BZ. Tel 01865 759600; www.ruskin.ac.uk

Sabhal Mòr Ostaig (UHI partner college – see Section 1) ACC, Sleat, Scotland IV44 8RQ. Tel 01471 888000; www.smo.uhi.ac.uk

St Helens College Water Street, St Helens, England WA10 1PP. Tel 0800 996699; www.sthelens.ac.uk

Salford City College Worsley Campus, Walkden Road, Worsley, England M28 7QD. Tel 0161 631 5000; www.salfordcc.ac.uk

Sandwell College Central Campus, 1 Spon Lane, West Bromwich, England B70 6AW. Tel 0800 622006; www.sandwell.ac.uk

School of Audio Engineering Institute Head Office, Littlemore Park, Armstrong Road, Oxford, England OX4 4FY. Tel 020 7923 9159; uk.sae.edu

Scottish Association for Marine Science (UHI partner college – see Section 1) Scottish Marine Institute, Oban, Argyll, Scotland PA37 1QA. Tel 01631 559000; www.sams.ac.uk

Selby College Abbot's Road, Selby, England YO8 8AT. Tel 01757 211000; www.selby.ac.uk

Sheffield College Granville Road, Sheffield, England S2 2RL. Tel 0114 260 2600; www.sheffcol.ac.uk

Shetland College (UHI partner college – see Section 1) Gremista, Lerwick, Scotland ZE1 0PX. Tel 01595 771000; www.shetland.uhi.ac.uk

Shrewsbury College of Arts and Technology London Road, Shrewsbury, England SY2 6PR. Tel 01743 342342; www.shrewsbury.ac.uk

Shuttleworth College Old Warden Park, Biggleswade, England SG18 9DX. Tel 01767 626222; www.shuttleworth.ac.uk

Solihull College Blossomfield Campus, Blossomfield Road, Solihull, England B91 1SB. Tel 0121 678 7000; www.solihull.ac.uk

Somerset College Wellington Road, Taunton, England TA1 5AX. Tel 01823 366331; www.somerset.ac.uk

South and City College Birmingham Digbeth Campus, High Street Deritend, Digbeth, England B5 5SU. Tel 0800 111 6311; www.sccb.ac.uk

South Cheshire College Dane Bank Avenue, Crewe, England CW2 8AB. Tel 01270 654654; www.s-cheshire.ac.uk

South Devon College Vantage Point, Long Road, Paignton, England TQ4 7EJ. Tel 01803 540540; www.southdevon.ac.uk

South Downs College College Road, Waterlooville, England PO7 8AA. Tel 023 9279 7979; www.southdowns.ac.uk

South Essex College (formerly South East Essex College; merged in January 2010 with Thurrock and Basildon College) Nethermayne, Basildon, England SS16 5NN. Tel 0845 521 2345; www.southessex.ac.uk

South Gloucestershire and Stroud College Stratford Road, Stroud, England GL5 4AH. Tel 0800 056 7253; www.sgscol.ac.uk

South Lanarkshire College College Way, East Kilbride, Scotland G75 0NE. Tel 01355 807780; www.south-lanarkshire-college.ac.uk

South Leicestershire College South Wigston Campus, Blaby Road, South Wigston, England LE18 4PH. Tel 0116 264 3535; www.slcollege.ac.uk

South Staffordshire College Cannock Campus, Crown House, Beecroft Road, Cannock, England WS11 1JP. Tel 0300 456 2424; www.southstaffs.ac.uk

South Thames College Wandsworth High Street, London, England SW18 2PP. Tel 020 8918 7777; www.south-thames.ac.uk

South Tyneside College Westoe Campus, St George's Avenue, South Shields, England NE34 6ET. Tel 0191 427 3500; www.stc.ac.uk

Southampton City College St Mary Street, Southampton, England SO14 1AR. Tel 023 8048 4848; www.southampton-city.ac.uk

Southern Regional College (formerly Upper Bann Institute) Portadown Campus, 36–44 Lurgan Road, Portadown, Craigavon, Northern Ireland BT63 5BL. Tel 028 3839 7777; www.src.ac.uk

Southport College Mornington Road, Southport, England PR9 0TT. Tel 01704 500606; www.southport-college.ac.uk

Southwark College (now part of Lewisham College) Waterloo Centre, The Cut, London, England SE1 8LE. Tel 020 7815 1500; www.lewisham.ac.uk

Stafford College Earl Street, Stafford, England ST16 2QR. Tel 01785 223800; www.staffordcoll.ac.uk

Staffordshire University Regional Federation Partnerships Office, F200 Cadman Building, College Road, Stoke-on-Trent, England ST4 2DF. Tel 01782 353517; www.staffs.ac.uk

Stephenson College Thornborough Road, Coalville, England LE67 3TN. Tel 01530 836136; www.stephensoncoll.ac.uk

Stevenson College Edinburgh (now part of Edinburgh College) Sighthill, Bankhead Avenue, Edinburgh, Scotland EH11 4DE. Tel 0131 669 4400; www.stevenson.ac.uk

Stockport College Town Centre Campus, Wellington Road South, Stockport, England SK1 3UQ. Tel 0161 958 3100; www.stockport.ac.uk

Stockton Riverside College Harvard Avenue, Stockton-on-Tees, England TS17 6FB. Tel 01642 865400; www.stockton.ac.uk

Stoke-on-Trent College Cauldon Campus, Stoke Road, Shelton, Stoke-on-Trent, England ST4 2DG. Tel 01782 208208; www.stokecoll.ac.uk

Stourbridge College Hagley Road Centre, Hagley Road, Stourbridge, England DY8 1QU. Tel 01384 344344; www.stourbridge.ac.uk

Stow College 43 Shamrock Street, Glasgow, Scotland G4 9LD. Tel 0844 249 8585; www.stow.ac.uk

Stratford-upon-Avon College The Willows North, Alcester Road, Stratford-upon-Avon, England CV37 9QR. Tel 01789 266245; www.stratford.ac.uk

Strode College Church Road, Street, England BA16 0AB. Tel 01458 844400; www.strode-college.ac.uk

Strode's College High Street, Egham, England TW20 9DR. Tel 01784 437506; www.strodes.ac.uk

Sussex Coast College Hastings (formerly Hastings College of Art and Technology) Station Plaza Campus, Station Approach, Hastings, England TN34 1BA. Tel 01424 442222; www.sussexcoast.ac.uk

Sussex Downs College EVOC (Eastbourne Campus), Cross Levels Way, Eastbourne, England BN21 2UF. Tel 01323 637637; www.sussexdowns.ac.uk

Swindon College North Star Campus, North Star Avenue, Swindon, England SN2 1DY. Tel 0800 731 2250; www.swindon-college.ac.uk

Tameside College Beaufort Road, Ashton-under-Lyne, England OL6 6NX. Tel 0161 908 6600; www.tameside.ac.uk

Telford College of Arts and Technology Haybridge Road, Wellington, Telford, England TF1 2NP. Tel 01952 642200; www.tcat.ac.uk

The London College UCK Kensington Campus, Victoria Gardens, London, England W11 3PE. Tel 020 7243 4000; www.lcuck.ac.uk

The Manchester College (formerly Manchester College of Art and Technology and City College Manchester) Ashton Old Road, Openshaw, Manchester, England M11 2WH. Tel 0161 909 6655; www.themanchestercollege.ac.uk

The Oldham College Rochdale Road, Oldham, England OL9 6AA. Tel 0800 269480; www.oldham.ac.uk

Tottenham Hotspur Foundation Tottenham Hotspur Foundation, Bill Nicholson Way, 748 High Road, London, England N17 0AP. Tel 020 8365 5138; www.tottenhamhotspur.com/foundation

Totton College Water Lane, Totton, England SO40 3ZX. Tel 023 8087 4874; www.totton.ac.uk

Trafford College Talbot Road Campus, Talbot Road, Stretford, England M32 0XH. Tel 0161 886 7000; www.trafford.ac.uk

Tresham College of Further and Higher Education Kettering Campus, Windmill Avenue, Kettering, England NN15 6ER. Tel 0845 658 8990; www.tresham.ac.uk

Truro College College Road, Truro, England TR1 3XX. Tel 01872 267000; www.truro-penwith.ac.uk

Tyne Metropolitan College Battle Hill Drive, Wallsend, England NE28 9NL. Tel 0191 229 5000; www.tynemet.ac.uk

Uxbridge College Park Road, Uxbridge, England UB8 1NQ. Tel 01895 853333; www.uxbridge.ac.uk

Wakefield College Margaret Street, Wakefield, England WF1 2DH. Tel 01924 789111; www.wakefield.ac.uk

Walford and North Shropshire College Oswestry Campus, Shrewsbury Road, Oswestry, England SY11 4QB. Tel 01691 688000; www.wnsc.ac.uk

Walsall College Wisemore Campus, Littleton Street West, Walsall, England WS2 8ES. Tel 01922 657000; www.walsallcollege.ac.uk

Waltham Forest College Forest Road, Walthamstow, London, England E17 4JB. Tel 020 8501 8501; www.waltham.ac.uk

Warrington Collegiate Winwick Road, Warrington, England WA2 8QA. Tel 01925 494494; www.warrington.ac.uk

Warwickshire College Leamington Centre, Warwick New Road, Leamington Spa, England CV32 5JE. Tel 01926 318000; www.warwickshire.ac.uk

West Cheshire College Chester Campus, Eaton Road, Handbridge, Chester, England CH4 7ER. Tel 01244 656555; www.west-cheshire.ac.uk

West Herts College Watford Campus, Hempstead Road, Watford, England WD17 3EZ. Tel 01923 812000; www.westherts.ac.uk

West Highland College (formed from a merger between Lochaber and Skye and Wester Ross College; UHI partner college – see Section 1) Carmichael Way, Fort William, Scotland PH33 6FF. Tel 01379 874000; www.whc.uhi.ac.uk

West Lothian College Almondvale Crescent, Livingston, Scotland EH54 7EP. Tel 01506 418181; www.west-lothian.ac.uk

West Nottinghamshire College Derby Road, Mansfield, England NG18 5BH. Tel 0808 100 3626; www.wnc.ac.uk

West Suffolk College Out Risbygate, Bury St Edmunds, England IP33 3RL. Tel 01284 701301; www.west-suffolkcollege.ac.uk

West Thames College London Road, Isleworth, England TW7 4HS. Tel 020 8326 2000; www.west-thames.ac.uk

Westminster Kingsway College St James's Park Centre, Castle Lane, London, England SW1E 6DR. Tel 0870 060 9800; www.westking.ac.uk

Weston College Knightstone Campus, Weston College, Knightstone Road, Weston-super-Mare, England BS23 2AL. Tel 01934 411411; www.weston.ac.uk

Weymouth College Cranford Avenue, Weymouth, England DT4 7LQ. Tel 01305 761100; Course Applications 0870 060 9800/1; www.weymouth.ac.uk

Wigan and Leigh College Parsons Walk, Wigan, England WN1 1RU. Tel 01942 761600; www.wigan-leigh.ac.uk

Wiltshire College Chippenham Campus, Cocklebury Road, Chippenham, England SN15 3QD. Tel 01249 464644; www.wiltshire.ac.uk

Wirral Metropolitan College Conway Park Campus, Europa Boulevard, Conway Park, Birkenhead, England CH41 4NT. Tel 0151 551 7777; www.wmc.ac.uk

Worcester College of Technology Deansway, Worcester, England WR1 2JF. Tel 01905 725555; www.wortech.ac.uk

Yeovil College Mudford Road, Yeovil, England BA21 4DR. Tel 01935 423921; www.yeovil.ac.uk

York College Sim Balk Lane, York, England YO23 2BB. Tel 01904 770400; www.yorkcollege.ac.uk

Yorkshire Coast College Lady Edith's Drive, Scarborough, England YO12 5RN. Tel 01723 372105; www.yorkshirecoastcollege.ac.uk

APPENDIX 2
BOOKLIST AND USEFUL WEBSITES

BOOKS

A Guide to Uni Life, Lucy Tobin, Trotman Publishing
British Qualifications 2014, 44th edition, Kogan Page
British Vocational Qualifications, 13th edition, Kogan Page
Cut the Cost of Uni, , Trotman Publishing
Destinations of Leavers from Higher Education 2011/13, Higher Education Statistics Agency Services
  (available from HESA)
'Getting Into' course guides: Art & Design Courses, Business & Economics Courses, Dental School,
  Engineering Courses, Law, Medical School, Nursing & Midwifery, Oxford & Cambridge, Pharmacy and
  Pharmacology Courses, Physiotherapy Courses, Psychology Courses, Veterinary School, Trotman
  Publishing
HEAP 2015, 46th edition, Brian Heap, Trotman Publishing
How to Complete Your UCAS Application: 2015 Entry, Trotman Publishing
Insiders' Guide to Applying to University, 2nd edition, Karla Fitzhugh, Trotman Publishing
Studying Abroad 2015, Cerys Evans, Trotman Publishing
Studying and Learning at University, Alan Pritchard, Sage Study Skills Series
Studying in the UK, Cerys Evans, Trotman Publishing
The Times Good University Guide 2014, John O'Leary, Times Books
University Scholarships, Awards and Bursaries, 8th edition, Brian Heap, Trotman Publishing
Which Uni? Find the Best University for You, Karla Fitzhugh, Trotman Publishing
Working in Accountancy, Sherridan Hughes, Trotman Publishing
Working in Engineering, Tony Price, Trotman Publishing
Working in Law, Charlie Phillips, Trotman Publishing
Working in Science, Tracy Johnson, Trotman Publishing
Working in Teaching, Alan Newland, Trotman Publishing
Working in the City, Mike Poole, Trotman Publishing
Your Gap Year, 7th edition, Susan Griffith, Crimson Publishing

USEFUL WEBSITES

Don't forget that the internet can be an extremely useful resource. You can:

* search for job vacancies
* send your CV to employment agencies and employers
* find relevant careers information, including hints and tips on job hunting and CVs.

Try these websites:

www.jobsearch.co.uk Vacancy site where you can submit your CV
www.reed.co.uk A wide range of jobs sourced from Reed
www.peoplebank.com Job search and online CV writing site
www.totaljobs.com Search all types of jobs by location and type
www.alec.co.uk Advice on interview techniques, CV writing, how to approach employers and how to use
  the internet effectively
www.fish4.co.uk Search for jobs by location and type
www.fulbright.org.uk Information on American universities
www.prospects.ac.uk Information includes graduate employment, job search and graduate destinations
www.careerseurope.co.uk Information on careers in Europe
www.disabilityrightsuk.org Information for disabled students

www.heacademy.ac.uk Careers guidance and information about higher education courses, finance and university/college applications

www.nhscareers.nhs.uk National Health Service careers information

www.opendays.com Information on university and college open days

www.ucas.com The site for university applications

COURSE INDEX

Choosing Your University And Degree Course...And Completing Your UCAS Application

Why not contact Brian Heap at HEAPS (*Higher Education Advice and Planning Service***) for a telephone consultation for advice on such issues as:**

- **Choosing A-level subjects (which are the best and required subjects and for which degree courses)**
- **Degrees and Diploma courses (making the right choice from a list of thousands!)**
- **Completing your UCAS application (will the admissions tutor remember your personal statement?)**
- **Choosing the right university or college (the best ones for you and your courses)**

For details of services and consultation fees contact:

**The Higher Education Advice and Planning Service
Email heapservice@gmail.com**